# Lecture Notes in Computer Science 15172

Founding Editors

Gerhard Goos
Juris Hartmanis

AF148473

The series Lecture Notes in Computer Science (LNCS), including its subseries Lecture Notes in Artificial Intelligence (LNAI) and Lecture Notes in Bioinformatics (LNBI), has established itself as a medium for the publication of new developments in computer science and information technology research, teaching, and education.

LNCS enjoys close cooperation with the computer science R & D community, the series counts many renowned academics among its volume editors and paper authors, and collaborates with prestigious societies. Its mission is to serve this international community by providing an invaluable service, mainly focused on the publication of conference and workshop proceedings and postproceedings. LNCS commenced publication in 1973.

Alexis Quesada-Arencibia · Michael Affenzeller ·
Roberto Moreno-Díaz
Editors

# Computer Aided Systems Theory – EUROCAST 2024

19th International Conference
Las Palmas de Gran Canaria, Spain, February 25 – March 1, 2024
Revised Selected Papers, Part I

 Springer

*Editors*
Alexis Quesada-Arencibia ⓘ
Universidad de Las Palmas de Gran Canaria
Las Palmas de Gran Canaria, Spain

Michael Affenzeller ⓘ
FH OÖ Studienbetriebs GmbH
Hagenberg, Austria

Roberto Moreno-Díaz
Universidad de Las Palmas de Gran Canaria
Las Palmas de Gran Canaria, Spain

ISSN 0302-9743        ISSN 1611-3349 (electronic)
Lecture Notes in Computer Science
ISBN 978-3-031-82951-2        ISBN 978-3-031-82949-9 (eBook)
https://doi.org/10.1007/978-3-031-82949-9

This Springer imprint is published by the registered company Springer Nature Switzerland AG
The registered company address is: Gewerbestrasse 11, 6330 Cham, Switzerland

If disposing of this product, please recycle the paper.

# Preface

The EUROCAST conference is particularly unique among the European Scientific Technical Congresses because it is one of the few periodic meetings promoted and organized exclusively by university and socio-cultural institutions, without the tutelage, direction or funding of associations, professionals or companies. It is currently the oldest of those. It is celebrated every two years, initially alternating Las Palmas de G.C. and a university in continental Europe, and since 2001, always in Las Palmas de G.C.

The idea of the first EUROCAST was developed in 1988 by Franz Pichler of the University of Linz and Roberto Moreno at a meeting in Vienna promoted by the past Honorary President, the late Werner Schimanovich. The first meeting, EUROCAST 1989, took place in February of that year, at Las Palmas School of Industrial Engineers, promoted by the Faculty of Informatics of Las Palmas and the Institute of Systems of the University of Linz. The Opening Session took place in the town of Gáldar, on February 26th, 1989.

Science, and especially technology, have moved in an almost vertiginous way, driven by the need for the promotion of consumerism, which is associated with the change of values that has taken place in recent generations. And EUROCAST, within what we understand as a certain freedom, and with prudence, has been adapting the profile of its organization from a meeting of very specific specialists, to a practically multidisciplinary, flexible and changing conference, which in each event tries to attract experts and especially young researchers, facilitating the interaction between them, which is a generator of creativity.

The key to the success of EUROCAST for 35 years has been in the quality of the contributions of its participants. This has to be recognized in the first place. They have made possible, with the help of the Springer publications in Computer Science, the worldwide distribution of the most important effect of EUROCAST: bringing together for many years scientists and engineers of different ages, training, interests and from very different European and non-European institutions. And they could share their experiences in the design and analysis of systems using the most advanced mathematical methods to make efficient models and algorithms in computers. And this from the socio-economic, biological, medical technologies and sciences and information and communication engineering topics. All in a multidisciplinary atmosphere, which has facilitated the appearance and discussion of new and creative ideas and developments.

Selected papers from previous editions have been published as Springer Lecture Notes in Computer Science volumes 410, 585, 763, 1030, 1333, 1798, 2178, 2809, 3643, 4739, 5717, 6927, 6928, 8111, 8112, 9520, 10671, 10672, 12013, 12014 and 13789 and in several special issues of Cybernetics and Systems: An International Journal. EUROCAST and CAST meetings are consolidated, as shown by the number and quality of the contributions over the years.

In this open multidisciplinary spirit, the 2024 Conference was composed of three plenary lectures by distinguished international Professors and 14 major thematic workshops, which covered a broad spectrum of cutting-edge research in Systems Theory, Applications, Pioneers, and Landmarks, Theory and Applications of Metaheuristic Algorithms, Mechatronic Product Development, Model-Based System Design, Verification and Simulation, Applications of Signal Processing Technology, Applied Data Science and Engineering for Intelligent Transportation Systems and Smart Mobility, Computer and Systems-Based Methods and Electronic Tools in Clinical and Academic Medicine, Systems in Industrial Robotics, Automation and IoT, Systems Thinking: Applications in Technology, Science, and Management, Data Science in Medical and Bio-Informatics, Modeling, Simulation, and Optimization in Production and Logistics, "Green AI" and SW-Tools for Sustainable Energy and Materials Consumption, Stochastic Models, Statistical Methods, and Applied Systems Simulations.

In this conference, as in previous ones, most of the credit for the success lays in the quality of proposals of subjects for Workshops, their resonance and impact, their diffusion and their strict selection of the many intended contributions. From 150 proposals, 104 revised papers were selected to be included in these volumes. The reviews of papers and their selection was made by the agreement of at least two members of the Program Committee, listed in the following pages, by a double open peer review process.

The editors would like to express their thanks to all the contributors, many of whom have already been EUROCAST participants for years, particularly in the considerable interaction of young and senior researchers, as well as to the invited speakers, Manuel Maynar from the University of Las Palmas de Gran Canaria; Ryszard Klempous from Wrocław University of Technology; and Dirk Jacob from Kempten University of Applied Sciences. We would also like to thank the director of the Elder Museum of Science and Technology, José Gilberto Moreno, and the museum staff. Special thanks are due to the staff of Springer for their valuable support.

October 2024

Alexis Quesada-Arencibia
Michael Affenzeller
Roberto Moreno-Díaz

# Organization

## Workshops

### Systems Theory, Applications, Pioneers, and Landmarks

**Chairpersons**

F. Pichler, Linz, Austria
R. Moreno-Díaz, Las Palmas, Spain

### Theory and Applications of Metaheuristic Algorithms

**Chairpersons**

M. Affenzeller, Hagenberg, Austria
S. Wagner, Hagenberg, Austria
G. Raidl, Vienna, Austria

### Mechatronic Product Development

**Chairpersons**

M. Jungwirth, Wels, Austria
T. Schlechter, Wels, Austria

### Model-Based System Design, Verification and Simulation

**Chairpersons**

J. Nikodem, Wrocław, Poland
Ito, A., Chuo, Japan
Nikodem, M., Wrocław, Poland

### Applications of Signal Processing Technology

**Chairpersons**

Zagar, MULeoben, Austria
Lunglmayr, Linz, Austria

## Applied Data Science and Engineering for Intelligent Transportation Systems and Smart Mobility

### Chairpersons

J. Sanchez-Medina, Las Palmas, Spain
J. del Ser, Bilbao, Spain
H. B. Celikoglu, Istanbul, Turkey
R. Rossetti, Lisboa, Portugal
L. Acosta, La Laguna, Spain

## Computer and Systems Based Methods and Electronic Tools in Clinical and Academic Medicine

### Chairpersons

J. Rozenblit, Tucson, USA
M. Maynar, Las Palmas, Spain
R. Klempous, Wroclaw, Poland
L. Kovacs, Budapest, Hungary

## Systems in Industrial Robotics, Automation and IoT

### Chairpersons

D. Jacob, Kempten, Germany
R. Stetter, Munich, Germany
E. Markl, Vienna, Austria

## Systems Thinking: Applications in Technology, Science, and Management

### Chairpersons

M. Schwaninger, St. Gallen, Switzerland
S. Groesser, Bern, Switzerland

## Data Science in Medical and Bio-informatics

### Chairpersons

M. Giretzlehner, RISC Software, Hagenberg, Austria
M. Geiß, Software Competence Center, Hagenberg, Austria
S. Winkler, FH OÖ, Hagenberg, Austria

**Modeling, Simulation, and Optimization in Production and Logistics**

**Chairpersons**

S. Wagner, Hagenberg, Austria
F. Longo, Calabria, Italy
A. Padovano, Calabria, Italy

**"Green AI" and SW-Tools for Sustainable Energy and Materials Consumption**

**Chairpersons**

D. Jacob, Kempten, Germany
R. Stetter, Munich, Germany
E. Markl, Vienna, Austria

**Stochastic Models, Statistical Methods, and Applied Systems Simulations**

**Chairpersons**

E. Pirozzi, Napoli, Italy
V. Giorno, Salerno, Italy

**Systems Cybersecurity Technologies and Quantum Approaches Potentials**

**Chairpersons**

P. Caballero, La Laguna, Spain
A. Quesada-Arencibia, Las Palmas, Spain

# Invited Plenary Lectures

**Towards the Technologically Intelligent Hospital**

Manuel Maynar                     Universidad de Las Palmas de Gran Canaria

**Eurocast from the 1990s: Personal Perspective and Contributions**

Ryszard Klempous                  Wrocław University of Technology

# Programs for Motivation of Science and Technology Among Youngsters

### Makeathon Green Island

Dirk Jacob                          Kempten University of Applied Sciences

### Ciberlandia Canarias

Alexis Quesada-Arencibia            Universidad de Las Palmas de Gran Canaria

## Program Committee

| | |
|---|---|
| Acosta, L. | Univ. of La Laguna, Spain |
| Affenzeller, M. | Univ. of Applied Sciences, Upper Austria, Austria |
| Berk Celikoglu, H. | Istanbul Technical University, Turkey |
| Caballero, P. | Univ. of La Laguna, Spain |
| del Ser, J. | Univ. of Bilbao, Spain |
| Geiß, M. | SCCH, Austria |
| Giorno, V. | Univ. di Salerno, Italy |
| Giretzlehner, M. | RISC Soft, Austria |
| Groesser, S. | Univ. of Applied Sciences, Bern, Switzerland |
| Jacob, D. | Univ. of Applied Sciences, Kempten, Germany |
| Jungwirth, M. | Univ. of Applied Sciences, Wels, Austria |
| Klempous, R. | Wrocław University of Science and Technology, Poland |
| Kovacs, L. | Univ. of Obuda, Hungary |
| Longo, F. | Univ. of Calabria, Italy |
| Ito, A. | Univ. of Chuo, Japan |
| Lunglmayr, M. | JKU, Linz, Austria |
| Markl, E. | Univ. of Applied Sciences, Vienna, Austria |
| Maynar, M. | Univ. of Las Palmas de Gran Canaria, Spain |
| Moreno-Díaz, R. | Univ. of Las Palmas de Gran Canaria, Spain |
| Nikodem, M. | Wrocław University of Science and Technology, Poland |
| Nikodem, J. | Wrocław University of Science and Technology, Poland |
| Padovano, A. | Univ. of Calabria, Italy |
| Pichler, F. | JKU, Linz, Austria |
| Pirozzi, E. | Univ. di Napoli, Italy |

| Quesada-Arencibia, A. | Univ. of Las Palmas de Gran Canaria, Spain |
| Raidl, G. | TU Wien, Austria |
| Rossetti, R. | Univ. of Lisbon, Portugal |
| Rozenblit, J. | Univ. of Arizona, USA |
| Sanchez-Medina, J. | Univ. of Las Palmas de Gran Canaria, Spain |
| Schlechter, T. | Univ. of Applied Sciences, Wels, Austria |
| Schwaninger, M. | Univ. of St Gallen, Switzerland |
| Stetter, R. | Munich, Germany |
| Wagner, S. | Univ. of Applied Sciences, Upper Austria, Austria |
| Winkler, S. | FH OÖ, Hagenberg, Austria |
| Zagar, B. | Montan univ. Leoben, Austria |

## Program Committee Chairs

| R. Moreno Díaz | Las Palmas de Gran Canaria |
| M. Affenzeller | Hagenberg |
| A. Quesada-Arencibia | Las Palmas de Gran Canaria |

## Conference Chairs

### Founder and Honorary

F. Pichler, Linz

### General

R. Moreno Díaz
Las Palmas de G.C.

### Program

M. Affenzeller, Hagenberg

### Logistics

A. Quesada-Arencibia, Las Palmas de G.C.

## Conference Web

https://eurocast2024.fulp.ulpgc.es.

## Supporter Institutions

Instituto Universitario de Ciencias y Tecnologías Cibernéticas
Universidad de Las Palmas de Gran Canaria

Johannes Kepler University Linz

University of Applied Sciences Upper Austria

Museo Elder de la Ciencia y la Tecnología

Fundación Universitaria de Las Palmas

# Contents – Part I

**Mechatronic Product Development**

**Model-Based System Design, Verification and Simulation**

# Contents – Part II

## Systems in Industrial Robotics, Automation and IoT

## Systems Thinking: Applications in Technology, Science, and Management

# Contents – Part III

**"Green AI" and SW-Tools for Sustainable Energy and Materials
Consumption**

**Stochastic Models, Statistical Methods, and Applied Systems Simulations**

**Systems Cybersecurity Technologies and Quantum Approaches Potentials**

# Invited Lectures

# Smart Green Island Makeathon

Dirk Jacob$^{(\boxtimes)}$ 🆔

University of Applied Sciences Kempten, Bahnhofstraße 61, 87435 Kempten, Germany
`dirk.jacob@hs-kempten.de`

**Abstract.** The Smart Green Island Makeathon has been organised on Gran Canaria since 2016. At the event, student teams carry out interdisciplinary projects developed using agile methods. The focus of the projects' tasks is on sustainability. This article presents the history, background, and the current Smart Green Island Makeathon 2024 in particular.

**Keywords:** Innovation · Agile Development · Sustainability

## 1 Definition Makeathon

A makeathon is an intensive innovation competition in which participants work in teams on specific projects within a limited period of time (usually several days). The makeathon was derived from similar events that have become established in the field of software development, the Hackathons.

### 1.1 Hackathons and Agile Development Methods

A hackathon usually focuses on the development of software solutions. The participants, often programmers and designers, work together to create functional software prototypes within a short period of time. The aim is to develop innovative software solutions that solve specific problems or enable new applications. Agile development methods first proposed in the manifesto of agile software development [1], which have become established in the development of complex software development projects, are used here. The values defined in the manifesto emphasize flexibility, customer proximity and continuous improvement. Agile principles include the delivery of working software at short, regular intervals, the promotion of sustainable development and constant attention to technical excellence and good design. SCRUM is often used as a framework for the implementation of agile software development projects [2]. Here, the roles of the participants in the framework are defined as well as events that structure and support agile development in line with the values of the manifesto.

While agile development methods were introduced comparatively quickly in software development and are now state of the art, the development of mechanical or electronic components and systems often still relies on traditional sequential development methods. On the one hand, this means that developments take a long time, and errors

© The Author(s), under exclusive license to Springer Nature Switzerland AG 2025
A. Quesada-Arencibia et al. (Eds.): EUROCAST 2024, LNCS 15172, pp. 3–11, 2025.
https://doi.org/10.1007/978-3-031-82949-9_1

cannot be recognized and eliminated through a continuous improvement process during development. Instead, many errors only occur at the end of development, when the individual components are brought together, and then have to be eliminated in a lengthy process. For this reason, the introduction of agile development methods is increasingly being used in the development of complex mechatronic systems, which are based on mechanics, electronics and software complementing each other and maximizing efficiency and functionality through the interplay of all components.

## 1.2 Makeathons

Organizers of makeathons have set themselves the goal of supporting this development. The term"makeathon" is derived from the words"make" and"marathon". In contrast to hackathons, which focus on the development of software, a makeathon concentrates more on hardware and combined hardware and software projects. In addition to software developers, engineers, designers, and other professionals often take part in order to create physical prototypes in conjunction with the necessary software. The projects often involve the development of devices, machines or systems that provide practical and tangible solutions.

A typical makeathon consists of several phases: brainstorming, team building, the development phase, and the final presentation. During the brainstorming phase, the participants brainstorm and choose a project that they would like to develop. In the development phase, the teams work intensively on their projects. This structure encourages creativity, collaboration, and rapid progress.

The event offers a comprehensive infrastructure that includes workspaces, tools, materials, and technical support. Mentors and experts from industry and academia are on hand to provide technical advice and feedback to the teams.

Where possible, workspaces are designed to support creative and collaborative work. They are equipped with modern technologies and tools that facilitate the development process. These include 3D printers, electronic tools, computers and software for design and simulation. In addition, classic workshop equipment with drills, saws etc. as well as wood, aluminum profiles or profile construction kits, so-called makerbeams, are also available to enable the quick construction of simple superstructures and mockups.

Mentors and experts play an important role by providing the teams with valuable insights and advice. These experts often come from areas relevant to the teams' projects and can address specific technical and market-related challenges. Parallel to the Makeathon, small workshops are often offered for individual technologies, such as image processing, which participants can use to further develop their skills at the Makeathon.

## 2   Development of the Smart Green Island Makeathon

### 2.1   Forerunner of the Smart Green Island Makeathon

Dr Rainer Stetter, Managing Director of ITQ GmbH, has long been involved in the training and further education of young people to promote young people's enthusiasm for technology, thereby counteracting the shortage of skilled workers in the industry, and to promote digitalization, particularly in more traditional sectors such as special machine construction.

With this aim in mind, the first smaller projects were carried out together with the Technical University of Munich. For example, an accurate dartboard was developed with students. The trajectory of a dart thrown by a player is recorded using machine vision. The further trajectory can be calculated in advance from the captured trajectory and thus the point of impact at the end of the flight path can be calculated. The dartboard is mounted on an X-Y carriage based on linear direct drives and can therefore be moved in such a way that the dart always hits the center (Fig. 1).

Based on the experience gained from student projects, the first makeathons were then organized with a larger number of participants at the Automatica 2016 and Laser 2017 trade fairs, for example. The events were also organized with a competitive character, so that at the end a jury decided on the best completed project. The best presentations were also honored to sensitize the participants to the fact that the presentation and marketing of ideas and projects are also an important part of an overall project.

**Fig. 1.** Student project for an accurate dartboard (Source: itq GmbH)

## 2.2  History of the Smart Green Island Makeathon

The first Smart Green Island Makeathon was held on Gran Canaria in autumn 2016 to bring the focus on sustainability and climate protection even more to the fore. From the perspective of initiator Dr Stetter, Gran Canaria is the ideal environment for Makeathons with a focus on sustainability. The Spanish volcanic island not far from the African mainland is a "perfect real-life laboratory" due to its numerous climate zones. Sun, geothermal energy, the tidal power of the sea and mountains for pumped storage power plants offer the best conditions for implementing smart energy concepts. In the long term, for example, he has projects for hydrogen production using solar energy in mind. In 2016, however, the use of renewable energy sources to supply the island was in the single-digit percentage range. The majority of the energy was provided by oil-fired power plants.

Accordingly, the 2016 Makeathon was held under the title "How can digital technology and connected devices help to build a smart and green island?". Under this title, projects in the areas of smart home, energy generation, intelligent water usage, efficient transport and connected logistics were to be developed. Around 40 participants took part in the first edition of the Makeathon and developed in 4 days their first projects.

Since 2017, the Smart Green Island Makeathon has been held regularly in spring for four days. In years when the EUROCAST conference is taking place it is synchronized with it. As can be seen in Fig. 2, the number of participants increased massively between 2016 and 2019, rising from 40 to just over 400 participants. Establishing contact with motivated participants from the university environment to attract specialists is an important motivational tool for sponsors, not only for financing the event, but also for participation on site. This means that not only technical specialists from the companies take part to mentor the participants, but also specialists from the human resources sector.

In 2020, the first year of the coronavirus crisis, the makeathon was timed so that the first travel warnings were issued in the days leading up to the makeathon, causing many companies and participants to cancel their participation at short notice. However, as many participants had already travelled to the event, the makeathon was still held with limited possibilities, at least for those participants who were already present.

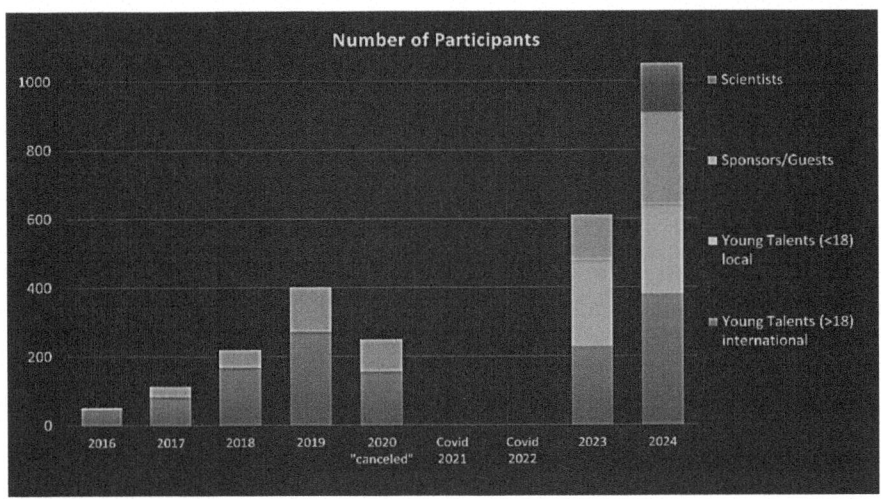

**Fig. 2.** Development of the number of participants in the Smart Green Island Makeathon (source: itq GmbH)

With the resumption of the event after the coronavirus crisis in 2023, the concept of the Smart Green Island Makeathon was expanded. While until 2020 the focus was on international talents over the age of 18 as participants, events for young people under the age of 18 who live in Gran Canaria were introduced in parallel to this classic makeathon. These so-called"Educational Workshops" are intended to arouse and deepen interest in technology with age-group-specific topics such as the"Brushrob" for the 6–10 age group, LEGO Mindstorms robots for 10–16-year-olds and robotics and 3D printing workshops for 16–18 year old participants in order to generate new skilled workers here as well.

# 3  Smart Green Island Makeathon 2024

With more than 1000 participants, the Smart Green Island Makeathon in 2024 represents a new milestone. In order to deepen the network between experts from the international participating universities and the Gran Canaria-based Universidad de Las Palmas de Gran Canaria (ULPGC), workshops on special topics such as mobile robotics, industrial image processing, etc. were offered at the ULPGC for students and interested lecturers at a scientific level.

## 3.1  Classic Makeathon

A total of 587 participants from 47 countries took part in the classic Makeathon 2024 (Fig. 3). The 379 Young Talents were sent by 70 universities to gain new experience. The interdisciplinary nature of the event is illustrated by the fact that these participants were enrolled in 48 different degree programs, ranging from traditional technical courses such as mechanical engineering, electrical engineering and mechatronics to computer science, business administration and project management. A total of 35 teams of various sizes were formed to work on projects in the following subject areas [3].

**Fig. 3.**  Participants in the Smart Green Island Makeathon 2024 (Source: itq GmbH)

**Smart Farming:** Smart Farming applications are becoming increasingly important due to the growing demand for sustainable agriculture practices. These applications can monitor soil moisture levels, nutrient content to form decisions around irrigation, fertilization, and planting. 13 Teams worked on ideas to make farming more energy and labor efficient.

**Smart Warehousing & Automation:** Smart Warehousing focuses on enhancing logistics efficiency and accelerate order processing by streamlining the picking and packing process. 5 Teams took on the task to develop robots capable of safely and accurately picking and placing products from warehouse shelves. Furthermore 1 Team focused on the most energy-efficient trajectory.

**Smart Production:** Smart Production is essential for efficient and sustainable development of an enhancement of products. During the SMART GREEN ISLAND MAKEATHON 4 Teams worked on challenges to make production processes more efficient and optimize the products in the way of sustainability and digitalization.

**Smart Recycling & Circular Manufacturing:** Recycling is crucial for maintaining a healthy and sustainable environment. At the SMART GREEN ISLAND MAKEATHON 3 Teams formed about the topics of Smart Recycling & Circular Manufacturing. The students had various ideas to clean and protect the environment from Garbage using robots as well as to recycle batteries.

**Smart Green Energy:** Hydrogen and renewable energies are no buzzwords anymore, but key to a sustainable and ecofriendly future. At the SMART GREEN ISLAND MAKEATHON 4 Teams focused on sustainable resources and energies and developed applications for Hydrogen use and detection and learned about renewable wind and solar energy, as well as water collection from dew.

**Smart Building:** With the topic Smart Building 3 Teams worked on improving energetic efficiency in buildings. One group focused on the environment of a classroom, whilst the other groups worked on improvements in workspaces/offices and buildings in general. They used multiple sensors to scan different parameters like luminosity, temperature, and humidity.

**Smart Green Mobility:** By investing in Smart Mobility several aspects of transportation can be improved. This year 2 Teams took on the challenge to electrify an old tractor by harnessing the power of an electric motor, batteries, and a photovoltaic panel. Also, they implemented a Range Extender. The projects seek to reduce fossil fuels to mitigate environmental impact.

### 3.2 Example Project from the Smart Recycling & Circular Manufacturing Focus Area

B&R Automation had set an extensive challenge in the field of battery recycling. The task was to check used battery cells to see whether they were still functional and then either recycle them or make them available for further use.

This project was divided into several sub-projects in order to break down various aspects into manageable tasks. The process of battery testing and allocation was fully automated with the help of 2 robots, supplementary conveyor technology and a testing station as well as a discharging and charging station (Fig. 4). The robots and conveyor technology were used to handle the batteries. In the test station, image processing was used to recognize which batteries were involved and at the same time an initial function test was carried out by contacting the cells.

The batteries were then discharged in a separate station and the energy extracted from the batteries was fed into an electrolyser, which produced hydrogen and oxygen from the energy (Fig. 5 right picture). From the discharge curves, the condition of the cells could once again be recorded in detail and thus classified. Cells that could be reused were recharged in the charging station, in this case with energy from a fuel cell, which

**Fig. 4.** Handling area with test cell on the front left, display of test results on the front right and automated handling of the battery cells in the centre

used the hydrogen produced during discharging to generate the required electricity, and with electricity from a wind turbine developed in parallel. The cells that were no longer functional were sent for material recycling, but this was not part of the project. In addition, a complete digital twin was created for the robots, the conveyor technology and the test cells, with which the processes in the plant could be visualized and, in the long term, programmed (Fig. 5 left picture).

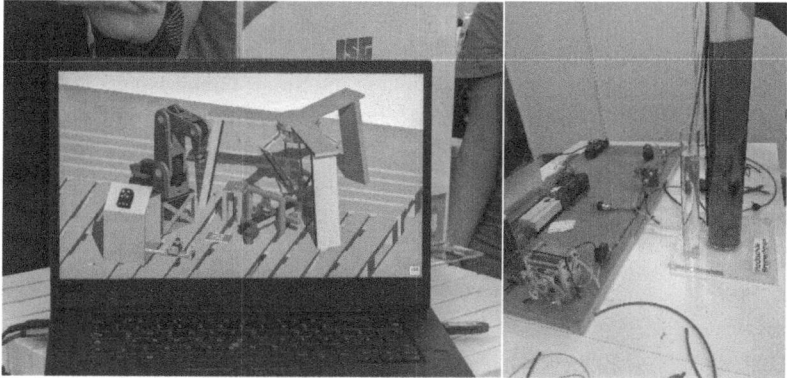

**Fig. 5.** Digital twin of the handling area (left) and structure of the electrolyser, the hydrogen storage unit and the fuel cell (right)

### 3.3  Challenges in Organizing the Makeathon

The challenges of organizing a makeathon, especially one on the scale of the Smart Green Island Makathon, are manifold. The biggest challenge is the financing of such an event. The personnel costs for the people who organize and support the makeathon represent a major cost block. In addition, rental costs for the event rooms have to be financed and the technical equipment of the makerspace, from 3D printers and the necessary electronic components to the workshop with the corresponding materials, has to be provided. Another major cost block is catering for the participants. These costs are borne by sponsors, i.e. companies and organizations that have to be found in the run-up to the makeathon and convinced that the investment makes sense.

In the run-up to the makeathon, it is necessary to coordinate the tasks of the companies and clarify whether special hardware is required on site. This is particularly important for the makeathon on Gran Canaria, as transport times and costs as well as the status of the Canary Islands as a special customs area must be considered. Once the challenges have been defined by the companies, it can be helpful to compare them with participating groups in advance. This can determine which additional special components still need to be procured so that the task can be completed with a high chance of success.

During the makeathon, the most important and critical phase is the team's discovery phase for the individual tasks. This is where the different participants have to find each other for the individual tasks. As soon as the teams have formed, the idea phase takes place, in which the assessment of the generated ideas with regard to feasibility is another critical point. When realizing the idea, the distribution of tasks and the clear definition of interfaces represent a challenge for the teams. The challenges that arise within a group are one of the most important points that are communicated to the participants through the collaboration. These challenges are also typical for later projects in companies. Participation in the Makeathon thus raises everyone's awareness of the critical points in the realization of interdisciplinary projects, but also highlights the potential of such projects.

### 3.4  Educational Technology Workshops

In addition to the classic Makeathon and the workshops at the university, 25 workshops were organised for children and young people at the Smart Green Island Makeathon for a total of 320 participants. The topics were Robot & 3D Printing, including collaborative robots, LEGO Mindstorms robots, Brush Robots, Hydrogen and Smart Green Energy and Smart Robotics & Handling. The workshops provided participants with age-appropriate and low-threshold access to current technology topics in order to promote enthusiasm for technology as early as possible. Figure 6 shows impressions from the various workshops.

**Fig. 6.** Impressions from the Educational Technology Workshop (Source: itq GmbH)

## 4  Summary

The Smart Green Island Makeathon is a model project for promoting enthusiasm among children, young people and students. In addition to the Educational Technology Workshops, the classic Makeathon is particularly noteworthy. Here, innovative projects focusing on sustainability are developed in interdisciplinary and international teams over 4 days. The experience gained by the participants strengthens their position on the labor market and leads to better trained specialists who are able to carry out complex and interdisciplinary projects. Only by strengthening the next generation in the field of digitalization and technology will companies be able to remain competitive on the global market in the coming years.

## References

1. Beck, K., Beedle, M., van Bennekum, A., Cockburn, A., et al.: Manifesto for Agile Software Development. 13 02 2001. [Online]. Available: https://agilemanifesto.org. [Accessed 30 05 2024]
2. Schwaber, K., Sutherland, J.: The SCRUM Guide, 11 2020. [Online]. Available: https://scrumguides.org. [Accessed 30 05 2024]
3. itq GmbH: Smart Green Island Makeathon 2024 - Team Overview, 03 2024. [Online]. Available: https://www.itq.de/wp-content/uploads/2024/04/ITQ-SMART-GREEN-ISLAND-MAKEATHON-2024-Team-Overview.pdf. [Accessed 30 05 2024]

# Systems Theory, Applications, Pioneers, and Landmarks

# The Application of Named Entity Recognition in Military Intelligence

Christian Nitzl[1], Achim Cyran[1], Sascha Krstanovic[2],
and Uwe M. Borghoff[1,3(✉)]

[1] Center for Intelligence and Security Studies (CISS), Neubiberg, Germany
[2] Aleph Alpha, Heidelberg, Germany
[3] Institute for Software Technology, University of the Bundeswehr Munich,
Neubiberg, Germany
{uwe.borghoff,ciss}@unibw.de

**Abstract.** Named Entity Recognition (NER) can be used to identify times, locations, organizations and persons in texts. In this study, the potential added value of NER in the military analysis process is tested through an experiment.

The military analysis process is a highly sensitive area of work that requires a high degree of maturity of NER. As part of the experimental test, a demonstrator deepCOM was developed. The results of the experiment show, on the one hand, that there is a clear added value of artificial intelligence in military information processing. On the other hand, the specificity of NER shows that the added value can be further increased by more precise labeling.

**Keywords:** Named Entity Recognition · Experiment · Digitization · Military Intelligence

## 1 Introduction

Digitization offers a wide range of possibilities and opportunities. This is especially true in the sensitive area of national and allied defense. Military intelligence plays a pioneering role in digitization and intelligence studies [14].[1]

Developments in artificial intelligence (AI) and the associated automated processing of information are having an enormous impact on the field of intelligence collection and analysis. The primary mission of military intelligence is to ensure the analysis and reporting of militarily relevant developments abroad. Due to the increasing volume of information, analysis software with integrated AI components is required to ensure the operator's analysis capabilities. Mature analysis software provides a real-time picture of the current situation and is the prerequisite for a functioning crisis early warning system [2].

The wide range of potential applications of AI for military intelligence is undeniable, although a high degree of ethical responsibility in the application of

---

[1] For a European perspective, see also [4, 7].

A. Quesada-Arencibia et al. (Eds.): EUROCAST 2024, LNCS 15172, pp. 15–22, 2025.
https://doi.org/10.1007/978-3-031-82949-9_2

AI in a military context is self-evident. In the context of this paper, a customized AI demonstrator has been developed to serve as a secure testbed and experimental environment for various AI components. The capabilities of this tool, called deepCOM, are outlined below. The company Aleph Alpha developed the demonstrator for this application. The goal of deepCOM is to demonstrate possible perspectives and potentials for the future use of AI in military intelligence.

The deepCOM demonstrator provides a military analyst with interactive access to a database of texts and images via a browser interface. The core functionality of the system is a semantic search. This allows the user to ask direct questions that are answered by the system, citing the sources used [8]. In addition, deepCOM allows the automatic summarization of each report in the database, enabling the analyst to identify potentially relevant sources through a summary of a few sentences.

A NER implemented in the system automatically tags all reports: If present in the text, tags are derived from mentions of times, locations, organizations and persons, which are color-coded for the user both when identifying relevant sources and when reading [9,15]. An implementation of Contrastive Language-Image Pretraining (CLIP) allows the same prompt to also search for images that occur within sources by having the operator describe in their own words what is seen in the graphic or photograph [13]. Finally, text corpora in deepCOM can be explored using an interactive graph to show relevant actors and their relationship to each other.

The following section focuses on the NER. On the one hand, a detailed presentation of all the functions tested in the demonstrator would go beyond the scope of this paper. On the other hand, the NER is one of the key AI functions that promises a high potential added value for military intelligence. However, it should be noted at this point that it is also an often vulnerable function. The use of novel technologies is hardly desirable if their use does not result in added value for the analyst or decision maker. Therefore, weak features and the possible added value from the user's perspective must be demonstrated experimentally. Experimental studies also serve to eliminate as many correctable errors as possible before a possible broad application.

## 2     The deepCOM Demonstrator from Aleph Alpha

The deepCOM demonstrator is a software tool with integrated AI capabilities designed to support military analysts, particularly in intelligence analysis. deepCOM can be accessed via a browser, so no local installation on a computer is required. However, the demonstrator could also be made available on a local computer network without an Internet connection, which is a prerequisite for use in military intelligence.

The basic structure of the deepCOM demonstrator emulates an Internet browser. It allows the analyst to mark individual texts as favorites, which can be collected in a separate tab and sorted by drag-and-drop. If required, a search can also be limited to these favorites, allowing a targeted search by selecting specific texts. All open tabs, favorites and last searches are saved in deepCOM, so that the user can continue with the previous processing status after logging in again. Overall, the user interface is designed to be as intuitive as possible to minimize the time needed to familiarize the user with the system and to avoid distraction by unnecessary features. Although the German Federal Armed Forces, and especially the Military Intelligence, are increasingly working in English due to their integration into international structures such as NATO, the UN or the EU, the creation of their own products at national level takes place exclusively in German. It is therefore necessary for deepCOM to be able to work with more than just English texts.

## 3    The Use of NER in Military Intelligence

This section first explains the Processing phase, based on the NATO Allied Joint Doctrine for Intelligence Procedures [1]. It serves to identify the potential added value of NER in the military analysis process. The goal of the Processing phase is to meet the information needs of commanders and to recommend possible courses of action. An overview of the sub-steps of the Processing phase of the NATO Allied Joint Doctrine is shown in Fig. 1.

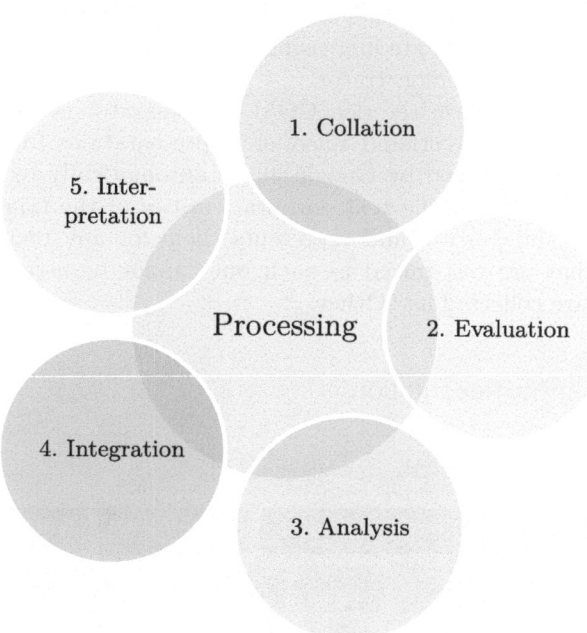

**Fig. 1.** Processing Phase according to the NATO Allied Joint Doctrine for Intelligence Procedures.

The first sub-step, Collation, is the grouping of thematically related information and existing finished products. This is done, for example, by tagging with metadata and then merging using timestamps or geographic identifiers. This is followed by the Evaluation sub-step, which aims to assess the trustworthiness of the information and its reliability with respect to the source from which it originated. In the subsequent Analysis sub-step, the information that may be relevant for subsequent interpretation is extracted from all the information collected. In this sub-step, facts are searched for and related to each other. In the Integration sub-step, the information analyzed in the Analysis sub-step is further selected and combined to identify patterns and relationships. The final sub-step, Interpretation, places this information in a larger context by evaluating it against the current state of knowledge. This evaluation results in an intelligence assessment, which may include recommendations for action by the military leader or a prediction.

NER is the extraction of entities found in an unstructured text and their classification into predefined categories [11,15]. Early research in text categorization focused on using a limited number of keywords extracted from a given document to classify the document into predefined categories [16]. Bohne et al. [6] use the Helmholtz principle [3] for their keyword extraction algorithm. Simply put, this principle states that keywords occur as large deviations from random words in the text. In addition to such simple methods of keyword extraction as a basis for exploratory categorization, either automatically or with the help of expert knowledge, AI-based methods are increasingly being used today [5]. This is also the case in the deepCOM demonstrator.

The NER implemented in the deepCOM demonstrator is based on a German retraining of the Bidirectional Encoder Representations from Transformers model originally published by Google [9]. It automatically recognizes, even without optimization to specific text corpora, entities of the types time, location, organization and person, and represents them for any text as shown in Fig. 2. Entities that are recognized as such but cannot be assigned to any of these categories are collected as "Other".

**Fig. 2.** Identification of Time, Location, Organization and Person by NER.

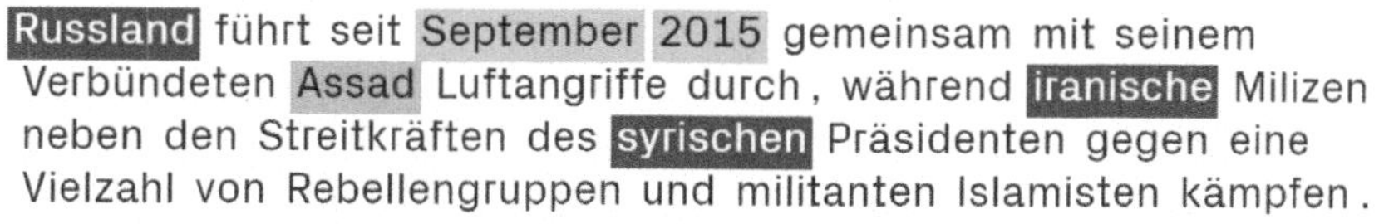

Russland führt seit September 2015 gemeinsam mit seinem Verbündeten Assad Luftangriffe durch, während iranische Milizen neben den Streitkräften des syrischen Präsidenten gegen eine Vielzahl von Rebellengruppen und militanten Islamisten kämpfen.

**Fig. 3.** Color-Coding of Recognized Entities.

Since entities in texts often occur in inflected form, lemmatization is also necessary to convert them to their stem form and thus make them comparable. This works correctly for the most part, although some rare entities may be placed in the wrong categories or incorrectly converted to a non-inflected stem form (in Fig. 2: "an Dienstag", "Islamischer [Staat]"). These errors are also due to the fact that both source texts and automated translations are not always grammatically correct. For the text shown in Fig. 2, additional entities were extracted by NER, which are not shown for the sake of clarity. Their number can be determined by a cut-off value, where a higher value results in more, but increasingly incorrectly recognized or classified entities.

On the one hand, NER helps the analyst to get a first impression of the content without having to read the entire full text. This allows the analyst to decide more quickly whether a text is relevant for analysis. Even when reading the full text, the color-coding shown in Fig. 3 speeds up the search for relevant information. It is clear that NER has now reached a stage of development that makes it useful for applications in military intelligence, where many source texts are sometimes unlabeled or manually labeled, which is time-consuming.

Finally, the entities automatically extracted as locations can be displayed on a map in deepCOM. A section of such a map can be seen in Fig. 4.

This allows the analyst to see the location of incidents at a glance and interactively integrate them into a situational picture. A heat map can also be used to quickly identify geographic clusters of incidents.

# 4    Experimental Testing of NER in Military Intelligence

An experiment was conducted to test whether NER adds value to military analysis. The toxic gas attack in Chan Shaykhun in northwestern Syria served as the analysis scenario. According to current knowledge, at least 86 people were killed and several hundred injured by Sarin gas on April 4, 2017. The release of the toxic gas is undisputed, but accounts of how it happened vary widely: According to U.S., British, French, and German reports, the toxic gas was released by an airstrike carried out by the Syrian air force of the Assad government. The analysis scenario was supported by 50 news texts provided to deepCOM. These included articles from both local and international news websites.

The analysis task began four days after the toxic gas attack in Chan Shaykhun, on April 4, 2017: A military leader needed detailed information on the toxic gas attack in Syria for decision-making purposes and wanted to be briefed

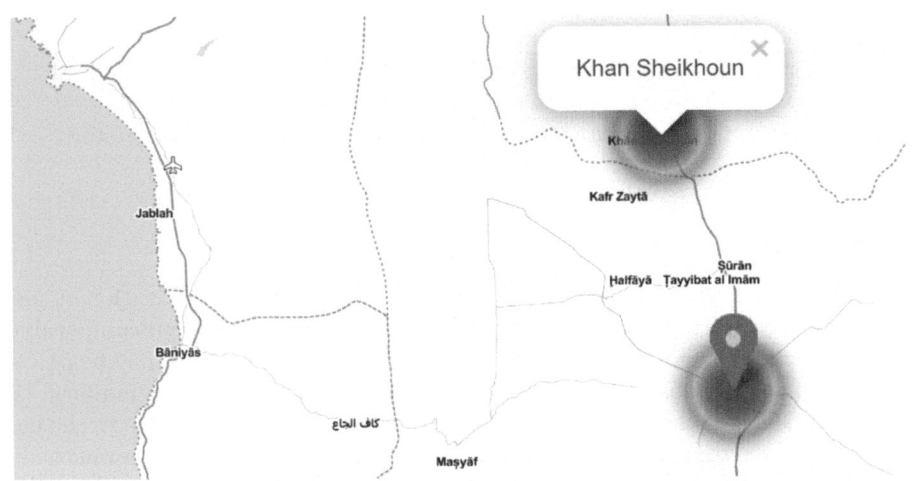

**Fig. 4.** Geographical Representation of Identified Locations on a Map.

in writing on developments to date. 30 analyst trainees worked on the analysis task. Their average age was 26.6 years. The analysis consisted of 21 questions about the poison gas attack. Participants were randomly assigned to either the experimental or control group. Both worked with the same deepCOM browser interface during the experiment, except that the AI functions were disabled in the control group. The predefined completion time for the analysis task was 25 min.

The responses of experienced military analysts who completed the analysis task under the conditions of the control group, but without time constraints, served as a benchmark. The experts were on average 41.1 years old and had 21.5 years of professional experience. They took an average of 3:49 h to complete the analysis task. The experts' responses served as ground truth to evaluate the analysis performance of the experimental and control groups.

Due to space limitations, the results of the experiment conducted are only briefly outlined. The 21 responses of the participants in the analysis task were scored for the experimental and control groups and the average score was calculated. This score was then compared to the expert judgment, the ground truth. The results of the statistical comparison show that the total score of the experimental group was significantly higher than that of the control group, with a p-value of 0.007. This means that the experimental group scored higher than the control group. Therefore, it can be affirmed that the AI functions provide added value in the military analysis process.

It should be noted that the present results do not only refer to the NER function implemented in deepCOM, but also to the other AI functions implemented in deepCOM, the automatic text summary and the AI search. A post-hoc survey of the participants can be used to identify the specific benefits and contribution of NER. In general, the participants rated the usability of deepCOM with more than 80, i.e. as very helpful [12]. It should also be noted that compared to the other implemented AI capabilities, NER was rated as average and thus lower than the other mentioned capabilities in terms of its usefulness for military intelligence analysis.

There are three reasons for the average rating of NER: First, the participants could not see any additional benefit of NER beyond the automatic summarization that was also implemented. Both AI functions were implemented in deepCOM with the aim of identifying suitable source texts more quickly. In a head-to-head comparison, the participants tended to prefer the automatic summarization for this purpose. It can therefore be assumed that the NER is not unsuitable for use in intelligence analysis, but that there was a crowding out effect due to the automatic text summary. In addition, the subjects mentioned the misclassifications that sometimes occurred in the average scoring of the NER. Three participants stated that at the beginning of the test they were willing to use NER to identify relevant source texts, but that during the course of the test they refrained from doing so because persons were sometimes misclassified as locations. Finally, several participants in the experimental group reported that some sub-functions of NER, such as color-coding in the text or displaying it on a world map, were considered useful during the briefing on deepCOM, but were later neglected due to time constraints.

## 5    Conclusion

The applications of Named Entity Recognition (NER) extend far beyond military intelligence analysis. Other potential applications include corporate security, the analysis of newspaper articles about companies or products, and supply chain monitoring. The added value of NER has been experimentally proven. However, there is still room to optimize NER for large-scale applications, especially in the sensitive area of military intelligence analysis. Entities are correctly recognized and extracted as such, but the classification into different groups (person, location, etc.) is too often error-prone. Lemmatization also fails in some cases. These problems could be solved by retraining: The NER used in the experiment was not trained for a specific application, but for German texts in general. However, it could be adapted for the entities that occur exclusively in military source texts (e.g. weapon designations, names of military leaders). Another possibility for improvement would be the automated creation of domain-specific dictionaries [10]. A high degree of maturity is a prerequisite for NER to provide added value to the daily work of the end user.

## References

1. AJP-2.1: Allied joint doctrine for intelligence procedures – NATO Standardization Office (2016)
2. Albrecht, K., Nitzl, C., Borghoff, U.M.: Transdisciplinary software development for early crisis detection. In: EUROCAST. LNCS, vol. 13789, pp. 3–10. Springer, Cham (2022)

3. Balinsky, A.A., Balinsky, H.Y., Simske, S.J.: On Helmholtz's principle for documents processing. In: Proceedings of 10th ACM Symposium on Document Engineering, pp. 283–286 (2010)
4. Berger, L., Borghoff, U.M., Conrad, G., Pickl, S.: Intelligence education made in Europe. CoRR abs/2404.12125 (2024). https://doi.org/10.48550/arXiv.2404.12125
5. Bharadwaj, A., Ramanna, S.: Fuzzy rough set-based unstructured text categorization. In: Advances in Artificial Intelligence. LNCS, vol. 10233, pp. 335–340. Springer, Cham (2017)
6. Bohne, T., Rönnau, S., Borghoff, U.M.: Efficient keyword extraction for meaningful document perception. In: Proceedings of 11th ACM Symposium on Document Engineering, pp. 185–194 (2011)
7. Borghoff, U.M., Berger, L., Fischer, F.: The intelligence college in Europe (ICE): an effort to create a European intelligence community. CoRR abs/2312.17107 (2023). https://doi.org/10.48550/arXiv.2312.17107
8. Deb, M., et al.: Atman: understanding transformer predictions through memory efficient attention manipulation. CoRR abs/2301.08110 (2023). https://doi.org/10.48550/arXiv.2301.08110
9. Devlin, J., et al.: BERT: pre-training of deep bidirectional transformers for language understanding. CoRR abs/1810.04805 (2018). https://doi.org/10.48550/arXiv.1810.04805
10. Häffner, S., et al.: Introducing an interpretable deep learning approach to domain-specific dictionary creation: a use case for conflict prediction. Polit. Anal. 1–19 (2023)
11. Lample, G., Ballesteros, M., Subramanian, S., Kawakami, K., Dyer, C.: Neural architectures for named entity recognition. CoRR abs/1603.01360 (2016). https://doi.org/10.48550/arXiv.1603.01360
12. Lewis, J.R.: The system usability scale: past, present, and future. International J. Hum.-Comput. Interact. 34(7), 577–590 (2018)
13. Radford, A., et al.: Learning transferable visual models from natural language supervision. In: International Conference on Machine Learning, pp. 8748–8763 (2021)
14. Scheffler, A.C., Jeraj, B., Borghoff, U.M.: The rise of intelligence studies: a model for Germany? Connect. Q. J. 15(1), 79–106 (2016)
15. Yadav, V., Bethard, S.: A survey on recent advances in named entity recognition from deep learning models. CoRR abs/1910.11470 (2019). https://doi.org/10.48550/arXiv.1910.11470
16. Zhu, D., Wong, K.W.: An evaluation study on text categorization using automatically generated labeled dataset. Neurocomputing 249, 321–336 (2017)

# A System-Theoretical Multi-agent Approach to Human-Computer Interaction

Uwe M. Borghoff[1(✉)], Paolo Bottoni[2], and Remo Pareschi[3]

[1] Computer Science, University of the Bundeswehr Munich, Neubiberg, Germany
uwe.borghoff@unibw.de
[2] Computer Science, Sapienza University of Rome, Rome, Italy
[3] Stake Lab, Universitá degli Studi del Molise, Campobasso, Italy

**Abstract.** We explore a novel perspective on Human-Computer Interaction (HCI), conceptualizing it as a dynamic interplay among a diverse set of human and computational agents within a networked system. The essence of our model lies in the understanding that HCI is not just about the human-computer interface, but is fundamentally about coordination and communication within a network of heterogeneous agents. These agents, each with different capabilities, roles, and goals, engage in a continuous process of interaction governed by well-defined protocols and procedures to achieve collective goals, from which potentially unforeseen behaviors may emerge.

**Keywords:** network of agents · communication space · satellite and swarm robots · large action models (LAMs) · use cases

## 1 Introduction

The evolution of Human-Computer Interaction (HCI) systems is increasingly influenced by the integration of multi-agent dynamics, where human and artificial agents collaborate within a complex networked ecosystem. Our approach draws inspiration from models of living systems and systems theory, emphasizing the autonomous yet interdependent nature of diverse interacting agents [2].

Central to our framework is the nuanced distinction between human and computational agents. Human agents, embedded in network nodes, play a pivotal role in shaping interaction outcomes and applying those interactions to different activities. Computational agents, distributed across the network, perform activities ranging from reactive responses to proactive initiatives, adhering to well-defined protocols such as computation [1], distributed problem solving [3], and intention recognition [5,6].

This dichotomy marks the multifaceted nature of HCI, where the computational efficiency of software agents complements human intuition and judgment. Our model posits that interactive computational systems resemble populations of heterogeneous agents, with human users guiding their interactions and evolution. This conceptualization aligns with systems as open entities where multiple concurrent processes interact and constrain each other, preserving the system's identity until a terminal point akin to the concept of "death" in living systems.

## 2    Agent Communication and Coordination

Agent interactions, particularly how they communicate and coordinate, are critical to the robustness and adaptability of HCI systems. Each agent in the system interacts with a limited number of peers at any given time based on spatial, temporal, and channel constraints. These dynamics create what we call "communication spaces" that are critical to the efficient operation of the system. The following pseudo-code illustrates the construction of communication spaces through which agents adapt their interactions based on their current state:

```
Create(agent) {
/* Determine communication spaces for active modality */
      foreach typeOfMessage the agent can issue {
            let rec[typeOfMessage] be the set of agents that can
            receive typeOfMessage
      }
/* Determine communication spaces for passive modality */
      foreach typeOfMessage the agent can receive {
            let snd[typeOfMessage] be the set of agents that can
            issue typeOfMessage
      }
/* Establish active and passive links */
      foreach group in rec do snd {
            FormGroup(group,agent)
      }
}
```

A group agent is a software component or entity designed to facilitate, for example, distributed problem solving among a group of users within a networked system or application. These agents are particularly valuable in collaborative systems where multiple users work together to solve complex problems or tasks. Figure 1 shows our modeling of a group agent.

A group-agent has to guarantee that any message from a member of the group can be read by all other members, and to regulate composition modification through a protocol which respects the localization constraints, as specified by the following pseudo-code.

```
register(component) {
      let m be the type of messages issued or received by component
      if g-group.ID[msg] = m then {
            if component.ST = On
            then Add(component.g-group.CMP[active])
```

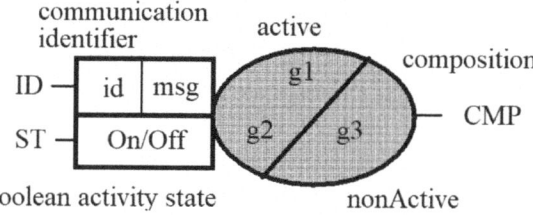

Fig. 1. A schematization of the basic structure of a group agent.

**else Add(component.g-group.CMP[nonActive])**
     }
}

Figure 2 shows a layered architecture similar to the MVC (model-view-controller) paradigm, where executive agents implement the actual computations, observers realize a bridge between the computations, and surface agents are responsible for maintaining the presentation of the overall state to the users.

Note that in this architecture, the actions performed by the executive agents, and not just their results, can be subject to observation.

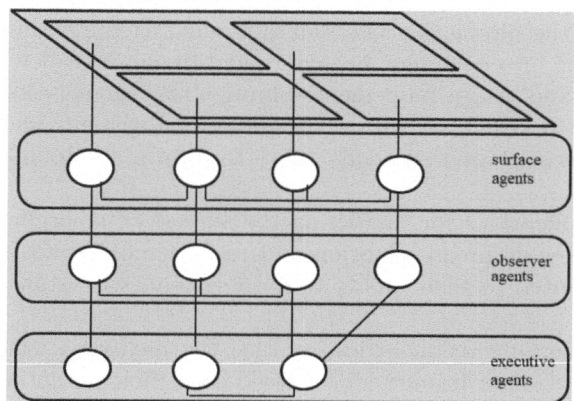

Three typologies of agents, organized in layers, have been defined:
1. *executive agents* - managing the application;
2. *observer agents* - managing the formatting of data for presentation and decoding user interactive commands and data entry;
3. *surface agents* (or *mediators*) - managing the materialization of the formatted data and the presentation layout and providing support to capture user interactions.

Fig. 2. A layered architecture for HCI.

Figure 3 shows how the layered architecture induces a collection of communication spaces. Of particular note is that the surface space can be further structured into event spaces, identifying collections of agents that react concurrently to the same event.

Vertical structuring is also shown, relating surface agents and executive agents through an observation space.

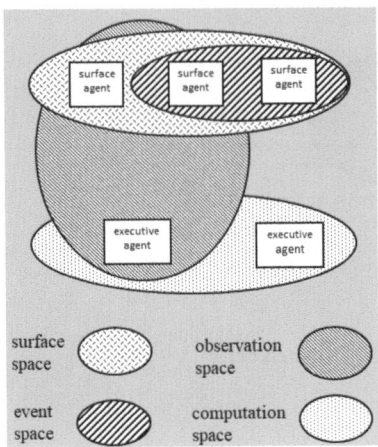

An **event space** relates a set of surface agents. Agents in an event space respond to an event concurrently.

An **observation space** relates agents across layers. It allows bi-directional interaction between users and objects. Recall that communication is considered abstractly as diffusion of projections of agent states.

A **computation space** relates agents within the same layer. These agents can cooperate to respond to a user action. A computation space has a twofold characterization: a) it supports multi-casting of changes in an agent state component in the same way as in an observation space; b) it can be explored by an agent, in a way mediated by group-agents, to identify agents with given characteristics in a space.

A **surface space** relates a set of simultaneously active surface agents. Only one surface space is active at a time and defines which components of the surface layer manage the current appearance of the surface and with which the user can interact.

**Fig. 3.** A schematization of communication spaces in the proposed architecture.

# 3   Applicability of the Model for System Design and Evaluation

The application of this model is particularly relevant in the area of system design and evaluation. By simulating the interaction between individual agents within the system, we can gain insight into emergent behaviors and dynamics, allowing for better decision-making and design refinement. Through this agent-based approach, we can model both existing and future computational systems and evaluate their potential for success based on their ability to form a stable and persistent identity over time.

This also has practical implications for predicting the success of emerging technologies. For example, the widespread adoption and resilience of browsers and smartphones can be attributed to their ability to form systems with stable identities.

Applying this model to emerging technologies, such as the metaverse and generative AI platforms [7], provides a framework for evaluating their potential to create similarly resilient systems.

In addition, the inclusion of quantitative metrics and methodologies could lead to a systematic approach to optimizing agent interactions. Methodologies such as genetic algorithms and network optimization algorithms appear to be appropriate to the nature of the system, which is reminiscent of biological ecosystems and can be modeled by complex networks. This not only enhances the efficiency and effectiveness of HCI systems, but also ensures their adaptability and sustainability over time.

In conclusion, our model provides a comprehensive framework for understanding and designing HCI systems, emphasizing the synergistic and evolving nature of human-computer interactions within a network of diverse agents.

# 4     Use Case 1: Multi-agent Interaction with Satellite and Swarm Robots

Figure 4 illustrates an experiment with a semi-centralized coordinated swarm of robots, using both "rigid" optimization algorithms and "flexible" intervention through a large language model (LLM). This setup encapsulates a true multi-agent HCI interaction, integrating human operators, conversational AI, a satellite control unit, and swarm robots.

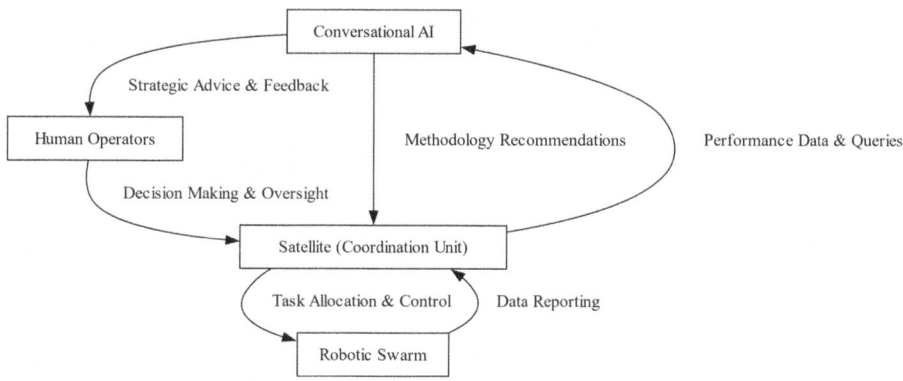

**Fig. 4.** Interaction of human operators, conversational AI, satellite, and a robotic swarm.

This use case extends the application of a semi-centralized control strategy, originally enhanced with blockchain technology for security and transparency (see [4]). In this extended scenario, the LLM acts as a dynamic advisor, using real-time data to recommend adjustments to the optimization algorithms that govern the swarm's behavior, thereby increasing efficiency and adaptability in response to environmental changes. Human operators play a critical role by monitoring system operations, making strategic decisions, and manually adjusting parameters based on the LLM's recommendations. This integration ensures a flexible, responsive, and human-centered interaction framework that goes beyond the original scope of the cited work. The overall information and decision-making flow, described in detail in the following sections, is shown in Fig. 5.

## 4.1     System Overview

The system consists of a satellite control unit, a swarm of robotic agents, an LLM, and human operators. The satellite provides centralized coordination and processes the data collected by the swarm. Meanwhile, the LLM offers strategic advice on algorithm selection and parameter tuning. Human operators monitor these interactions and intervene when necessary to guide the system through complex decision-making processes or when unique human insights are required.

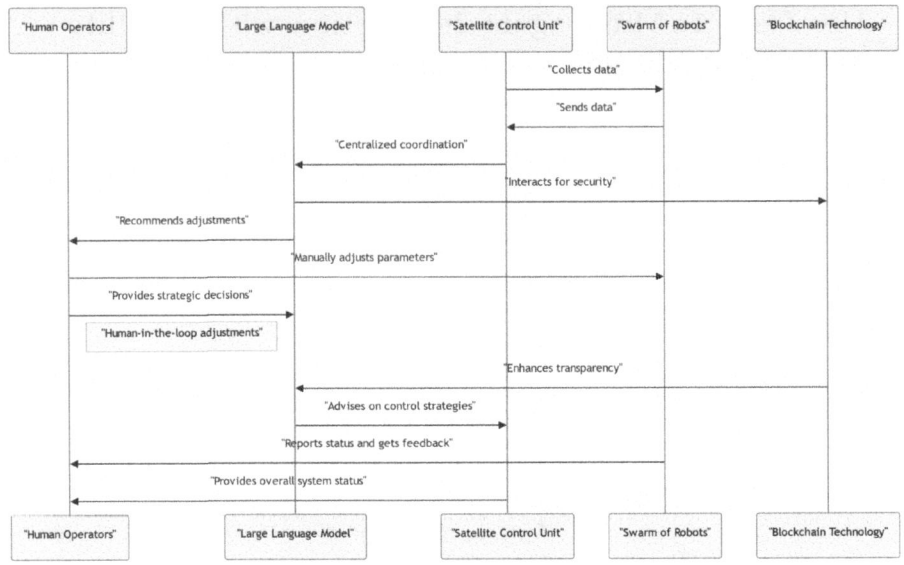

**Fig. 5.** Information and decision flows in the semi-centralized control strategy.

## 4.2    Integration with LLM and Human Operators

The LLM interacts with the blockchain and control algorithms to provide a flexible intelligence layer. It analyzes patterns and predicts potential issues, allowing the system to actively adjust its strategies based on both human judgment and algorithmic recommendations. Through this dual-input system, the system remains robust and adaptive to effectively handle complex, dynamic tasks.

## 4.3    Practical Applications

Key applications include path optimization and adaptive problem solving, where the LLM's input, combined with human oversight, improves system performance. For example, in path planning, the LLM can suggest changes to curve parameters based on detected obstacles or changes in terrain. Human operators then review these suggestions and make final decisions that dynamically optimize route efficiency, which is essential for human-in-the-loop methodologies.

## 4.4    Human-Agent Collaboration

In fact, human operators are not just supervisors, but active participants in the decision-making loop. They interact directly with system output, fine-tuning responses and strategies, exemplifying the synergy between human expertise and machine-generated intelligence. This collaboration not only protects against the risks of automation, but actively leverages the unique strengths of humans and machines. It unlocks new opportunities for innovation in advanced robotic systems, enhancing human capabilities and pushing the boundaries of what technology can achieve in partnership with human insight.

## 5    Use Case 2: Large Action Models (LAMs) Through Feedback Loops on HCI Interactions

Figure 6 shows the framework of RABBIT TECH's Large Action Model (LAM)[1], which integrates advanced computational agents to effectively model and predict human actions on computer applications. This model is a prime example of a multi-agent system in which both human and artificial agents dynamically interact to enhance the HCI experience.

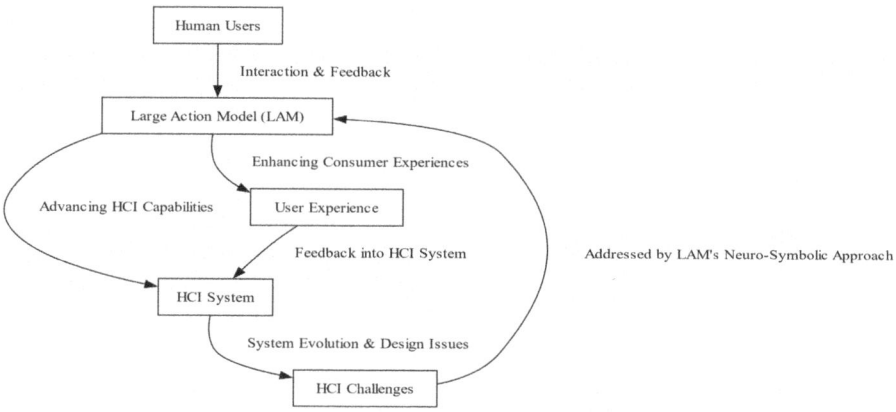

**Fig. 6.** Agent interactions for improved agent interactions.

This use case explores the transformative impact of LAM in creating a new paradigm for human-computer interaction. LAM acts as a multi-agent system that continuously learns from user input and refines its predictive capabilities to improve the interaction framework. It embodies a sophisticated feedback loop system in which ongoing user interaction data refines the AI's understanding, thus progressively improving the HCI system.

### 5.1    System Overview

The LAM framework at RABBIT API is built around several core components: the LAM node, human users, the HCI system, and the challenges that this integration addresses. The LAM node serves as the central computational agent, using neuro-symbolic programming to contextually interpret and respond to user commands and behaviors, demonstrating the essence of a multi-agent system, as shown in Fig. 7.

---

[1] https://www.rabbit.tech/research.

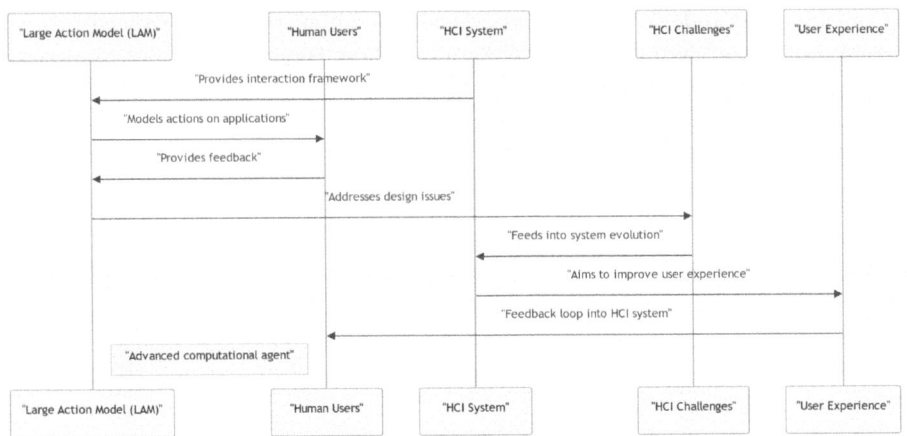

**Fig. 7.** Illustration of the feedback loop underlying the RABBIT LAM.

## 5.2   Neuro-symbolic Integration

LAM performs complex tasks across multiple applications with high accuracy and minimal latency by leveraging neural network capabilities for pattern recognition and symbolic AI for rule-based processing. This neuro-symbolic approach allows LAM to effectively understand and execute user intent, making it a key component of multi-agent interaction within HCI.

## 5.3   Human-Agent Interaction

Human users interact with LAM through a natural language-based user interface that processes spoken or typed commands to perform actions on applications. This interaction is supported by a feedback system where LAM learns from each interaction and adapts its models to better match user preferences and improve the overall experience. The multi-agent dynamics of this system underscore its flexibility and responsiveness to change.

## 5.4   Practical Applications and Challenges

LAM goes beyond simple command execution to include proactive task management and problem solving within software environments. It anticipates user needs and provides solutions, significantly improving productivity and user satisfaction. Key challenges include ensuring that AI decisions are transparent and aligned with user expectations, maintaining privacy, and managing the complexity of real-time data processing.

## 5.5   Key Takeaways

The feedback loops in LAM are critical to its evolution. They include not only adapting to user behavior, but also incorporating user feedback to refine its understanding of human intent. This dynamic adaptation helps LAM closely match the practical needs and complexities of modern HCI environments. Integrating LAM into HCI systems promises more intuitive and interactive environments where computers seamlessly understand and anticipate user needs. These capabilities demonstrate the powerful potential of multi-agent systems to transform human-computer interactions.

## 6    Conclusion

We have outlined a framework that systematically considers how human and artificial agents interact within a networked ecosystem. By articulating HCI not just as human-computer interactions, but as dynamic interactions among different agents within a flexible, multi-agent system, we have highlighted the potential for interactions that are both more complex and more effective.

The application of our multi-agent model to two different use cases—satellite and swarm robotics, and Large Action Models (LAMs)—has not only validated our theoretical constructs, but also underscored the practical implications of such interactions.

In the first use case, we observed how a semi-centralized system, enabled by a large language model, could improve decision-making processes and adaptability through real-time data-driven adjustments. This setup not only ensures efficiency, but also preserves human oversight, which is critical for managing complex, dynamic environments.

The second use case involving LAMs further highlighted the potential of integrating advanced computational agents to predict and shape human-computer interactions. Using neuro-symbolic programming, the LAM framework demonstrated its ability to refine its operations based on continuous feedback from human interactions, promoting an adaptive and responsive HCI system.

We have thus established a foundational framework for the design and analysis of HCI systems that views these interactions as a complex interplay among multiple agents. This approach allows us to better understand and harness the collective capabilities of different agents, thereby enhancing the adaptability and resilience of the system. Importantly, this perspective aligns with emerging technology paradigms that foster a deep understanding and integration of human agents. Indeed, our contribution can be seen as a systemic evolution in design approaches, emphasizing the front-end to enhance usability and effectiveness. This contrasts with, but complements, systemic approaches that prioritize the back-end for security and robustness, as illustrated in [8]. Together, these perspectives synergistically improve the overall architecture of HCI systems.

Ultimately, our study enriches the understanding of HCI as a dynamic and evolving field characterized by the complex yet symbiotic relationships between humans and machines. As we delve deeper into these interactions, the possibility of transforming human-computer interactions into more seamless and effective experiences becomes increasingly tangible. This promises a future in which the human and artificial dimensions are not merely aligned, but fully integrated in a balanced and complementary manner. Such integration could pave the way for a new era of collective and hybrid intelligence—where humans and machines work closely together—potentially the most significant and immediate outcome of current rapid technological advances.

# References

1. Aspnes, J., Ruppert, E.: An introduction to population protocols. In: Garbinato, B., Miranda, H., Rodrigues, L.E.T. (eds.) Middleware for Network Eccentric and Mobile Applications, pp. 97–120. Springer, Cham (2009). https://doi.org/10.1007/978-3-540-89707-1_5
2. Borghoff, U.M., Bottoni, P., Mussio, P., Pareschi, R.: Multi-agent coordination in living systems. In: BIES '95, Tokyo, Japan, pp. 93–100 (1995)
3. Borghoff, U.M., Pareschi, R., Fontana, F.A., Formato, F.: Constraint-based protocols for distributed problem solving. Sci. Comput. Program. **30**(1–2), 201–225 (1998). https://doi.org/10.1016/S0167-6423(97)00011-7
4. Carovilla, A., Pareschi, R., Salzano, F.: Integrating blockchain for enhanced coordination and security in semi-centralized robotic swarms. In: Proceedings of IEEE International Workshop on Technologies for Defense and Security (TechDefense), pp. 95–99 (2023)
5. de Greef, T., van Dongen, K., Grootjen, M., Lindenberg, J.: Augmenting cognition: reviewing the symbiotic relation between man and machine. In: Schmorrow, D., Reeves, L. (eds.) FAC 2007. LNCS, vol. 4565, pp. 439–448. Springer, Cham (2007). https://doi.org/10.1007/978-3-540-73216-7_51
6. Inga, J., et al.: Human-machine symbiosis: a multivariate perspective for physically coupled human-machine systems. Int. J. Hum. Comput. Stud. **170** (2023). https://doi.org/10.1016/J.IJHCS.2022.102926
7. Min, B., et al.: Recent advances in natural language processing via large pre-trained language models: a survey. ACM Comput. Surv. **56**(2), 30:1–30:40 (2024). https://doi.org/10.1145/3605943
8. Salzano, F., Pareschi, R., Marchesi, L., Tonelli, R.: Blockchain-based information ecosystems. In: Mori, P., Visconti, I., Bistarelli, S. (eds.) Proceedings of the Fifth Distributed Ledger Technology Workshop (DLT 2023), Bologna, Italy, 25–26 May 2023. CEUR Workshop Proceedings, vol. 3460. CEUR-WS.org (2023)

# Data Transformation: Limitless Strategies in Energy Consumption

Margaret Miró-Julià[1]([✉])([iD]), Monica J. Ruiz-Miró[1,2], Ricardo Alberich[1]([iD]), Francisco Cordero Piñero[2], and Nelson Alirio Cruz[1]([iD])

[1] Departament de Ciències Matemàtiques i Informàtica, Universitat de les Illes Balears, 07122 Palma, Spain
{margaret.miro,monica.ruiz,r.alberich,nelson-aliro.cruz}@uib.es
[2] Energy Solutions & Technologies, BALANTIA, 07012 Palma, Spain
{mruiz,fcordero}@balantia.com
http://www.uib.es

**Abstract.** By combining Artificial Intelligence and Data Mining, complex domain problems can be analyzed. The knowledge of energy consumers' profile has been an important tool when making decisions in the energy sectors. The aim of this paper is to explain and evaluate the use of different Data Mining techniques and learn which strategies are more adequate to analyze consumer profiles. By using smart meters, raw data can be easily collected and stored in a database. Extensive volumes of data is generated and optimal efficiency in data management is crucial. Such data have a time-series notion typically consisting of consumers' energy usage measurements over a time interval together with a detailed level of consumer profile data. Data preprocessing is vital for reliable insights and an appropriate choice of data transformation provides better outcomes in model construction.

In this paper, anonymized electricity power consumption data will be analyzed. Data preprocessing using weekly time intervals is proposed together with an analytical model that consolidates observations of weekly time series by consumer. Following the generation of consumers' weekly energy usage, a set of typical weeks will be found and compositional data analysis will be applied. The performance of the proposed model will be evaluated and the results will be discussed.

**Keywords:** Power consumption · Time series clustering · Compositional data analysis

## 1 Introduction to the Energy Consumption Problem

Artificial Intelligence and Data Mining techniques can be properly combined to analyze complexity in specific domain problems and provide understanding of the phenomena. In real-world applications of Artificial Intelligence, considerable human effort is used in designing the representation of any domain-specific problem in such a way that generalised algorithms can be used to deliver decision-support solutions to human decision makers [1]. On the other hand, Data Mining

A. Quesada-Arencibia et al. (Eds.): EUROCAST 2024, LNCS 15172, pp. 33–41, 2025.
https://doi.org/10.1007/978-3-031-82949-9_4

addresses the treatment of large amounts of data [2], aiming to discover interesting, unexpected, or valuable structures within it.

Energy is a crucial feature in modern life, and advancements in technology have led to the development of smart meters that generate a significant amount of data on power consumption (electricity, gas, water, ...). The knowledge of energy consumers' profile has been an important tool when making decisions in the energy sectors. The aim of this paper is to explain and evaluate the use of different Data Mining techniques and learn which strategies are more adequate to analyze customer profiles. Efficient management of energy resources is an important aspect that must be thoughtfully considered. Responsible, efficient and environmentally aware energy consumption behavior is a necessity in present-day life. Utility companies are constantly working towards determining the best ways to reduce cost and improve profitability by introducing programs that best fit the consumers' energy consumption profiles. Furthermore, this type of analysis results in a better energy generation forecast favoring efficiency, sustainability, emissions reduction, flexibility and demand respond.

With advancements in sensor technology, smart meters enable the easy collection and storage of raw data in databases. This data, characterized by extensive volumes, high velocity, and veracity attributes, typically comprises time-series measurements of customers' energy usage alongside detailed consumer profile data [3]. Mining and extracting patterns from this data can facilitate effective energy management. However, as the energy usage database grows over time, maintaining and updating mining results becomes inefficient. Algorithms capable of incremental maintenance are necessary, along with preprocessing techniques that prepare the database for further analysis.

Energy consumption patterns vary among consumers, influenced by factors such as geographical area, weather conditions, day of the week, consumer behavior, and customer characteristics. Models approximating energy usage must accommodate various criteria, utilizing Data Mining techniques such as exploratory data analysis, data visualization, frequent pattern mining, classification, clustering, and anomaly detection. Data preprocessing is crucial for reliable results, ensuring data quality and consistency throughout the Knowledge Discovery Process. Selecting the most suitable data source and transformation methods will enhance model construction and lead to better patterns [4]. In this paper, data preprocessing using weekly time intervals is proposed.

## 1.1  The Data

In this paper, we will examine anonymized power data obtained from an electric utility company. Raw data consists in hourly energy consumption for over $35,000$ customers. The sequential data set hides a customer profile of energy usage on a daily, weekly or seasonal basis. The power data corresponds to around $280$ million observations loaded each day.

Customers' hourly consumption information is transformed into weekly intervals (each interval is a vector of size $7 \times 24 = 168$). For each client will have a maximum of 52 complete weekly intervals. Since we have $35,139$ different customers, the data preprocessing results in a data frame of 168 sorted columns and a maximum of $1,827,228$ rows ($35,139 \times 52$). Unobserved or missing data are imputed to the mean of the nearest previous and following observed time period. It is important to remark that these weeks can span different years, going from 2021 to 2023. Each client may have a varying number of observations resulting in slightly shorter time periods. Additionally, only full weeks (from Monday to Sunday) are included in the analysis.

All calculations are performed on a standard computer with 36 GB of RAM and an Intel i7 processor. R and RStudio have been chosen for data analysis and results reporting.

## 1.2   Classical Data Analysis

Since weekly power usage is considered, we start by choosing customers with complete weekly data after pre-scaling. Figure 1 shows consumer's weekly behavior. A uniform pattern is observed throughout the year. Additionally, it is observed, that almost all customers appear in more than 49 weeks. Therefore, yearly power usage analysis by groupings of weeks seems reasonable.

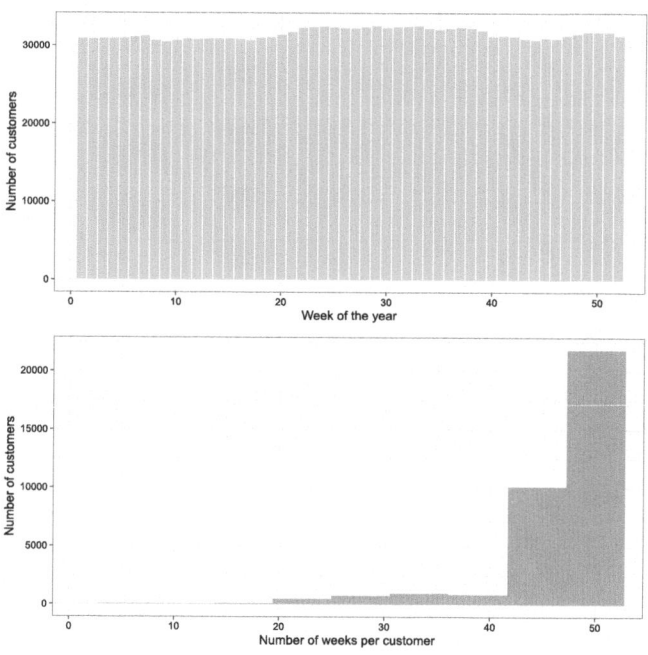

**Fig. 1.** Weekly power usage observations.

The first step is to find, from a power usage point of view, groups of "similar" weeks using cluster analysis. By clustering the data, different types of weekly energy consumption patterns are found. Due to the large amount of data contemplated, the use of the $k$-means algorithm is not feasible. In order to reduce calculation time $k$-means mini-batch (MiniBatchKMeans), a variant of the $k$-means algorithm that uses mini-batches, is considered. The use of mini-batches (equivalent to a small training set) reduces dramatically the amount of computation time required to converge to a local solution. Unlike other algorithms that reduce the $k$-means convergence time, the $k$-means mini-batch produces results that are generally only slightly worse than the standard algorithm [5].

One of the limitations of the $k$-means algorithm is how to choose the value of $k$ (number of clusters). For values from $k = 2$ to $k = 40$ cluster analysis was performed, the clusters obtained were tested and the torsion index $f_K$ presented in [6] was calculated. The results obtained suggest the use of $k = 6$.

For $k = 6$, six clusters $C_1, C_2, C_3, C_4, C_5, C_6$ are found. This is equivalent to saying that there are six typical weeks of power usage. These consumption behaviors are shown in Figs. 2 and 3. Figure 2 shows the average weekly consumption for clusters $C_1$, $C_2$ and $C_3$ while the other three clusters with the highest power usage are shown in Fig. 3. The line corresponds to the median, whereas the first and third quartiles for each cluster are also shown as colored bands. All clusters present a repeated pattern throughout the week. Patterns in clusters $C_1$, $C_2$ and $C_3$ are similar in shape but with different scale factors. Patterns in clusters $C_4$, $C_5$ and $C_6$ are completely distinct.

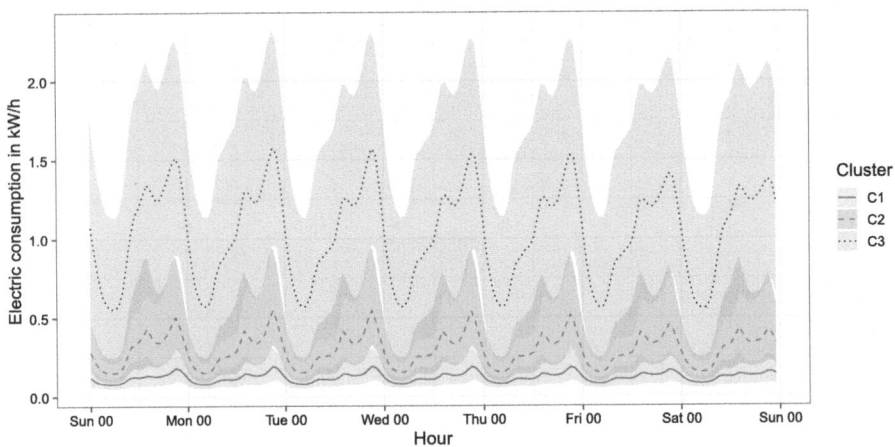

**Fig. 2.** Weekly electricity consumption per cluster.

Table 1 summarizes the weekly energy consumption measures for each cluster. From the summary, it is observed that clusters $C_1$, $C_2$ and $C_3$ are the largest with most common average consumption, and clusters $C_4$, $C_5$ and $C_6$ are the smallest clusters that correspond to the greatest power consumption customers and have the largest dispersion.

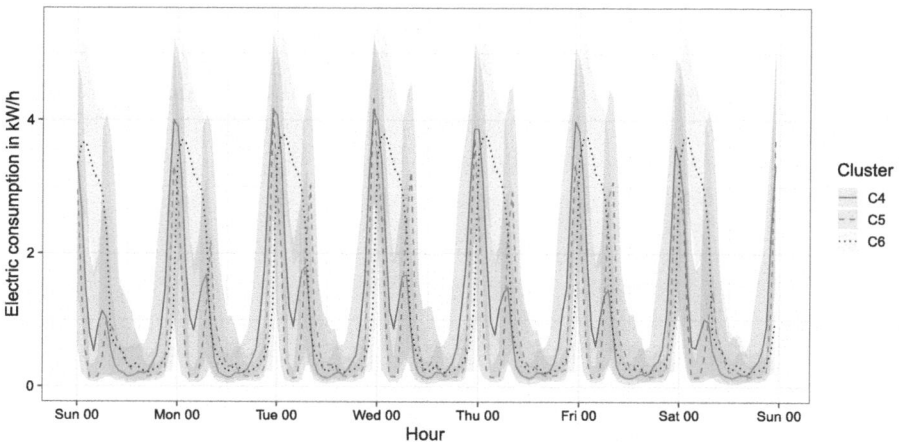

**Fig. 3.** Weekly electricity consumption per cluster.

**Table 1.** Statistical summary of total weekly consumption by cluster.

| Cluster | N | Min | Q1 | Median | Mean | Q3 | Max |
|---|---|---|---|---|---|---|---|
| $C_1$ | 897553 | 0.0490 | 0.0805 | 0.1171 | 0.1670 | 0.1856 | 1.0682 |
| $C_2$ | 652771 | 0.0907 | 0.1676 | 0.2873 | 0.4378 | 0.5598 | 2.1633 |
| $C_3$ | 54394 | 0.2272 | 0.5520 | 1.0237 | 1.2569 | 1.7843 | 3.9733 |
| $C_4$ | 613 | 0.0570 | 0.2231 | 0.7792 | 1.4595 | 2.2005 | 6.1907 |
| $C_5$ | 144 | 0.0555 | 0.1424 | 0.4680 | 1.5973 | 1.7039 | 24.0570 |
| $C_6$ | 3589 | 0.0856 | 0.3138 | 0.9078 | 1.6718 | 2.7006 | 6.0880 |

## 2 Compositional Data Analysis

In statistics, Compositional Data Analysis (CoDa) [7] are vectors whose components are strictly positive and they often represent proportions, percentages, concentrations, or frequencies of some whole and are therefore constrained. Their applications can be found in many domains such as chemical researches, econometric and survey data analyses, and food industry. The sample space of CoDa is the simplex:

$$S^d = \left\{ (x_1, \ldots, x_d) \in \mathbb{R}^d : x_i > 0, \text{ for } i = 1, \ldots, d, \text{ and } x_1 + \cdots + x_d = 1 \right\}.$$

Since the sum of consumers is always constant, compositional data analysis can be applied. The important aspect in compositional data is not the specific value of each component, but the relative ratio of each component. For each of the typical six weekly patterns, a compositional analysis of the consumer's distribution is carried out. The starting point are the customer's absolute frequencies in each of the six clusters $C_1, C_2, C_3, C_4, C_5, C_6$. Remember that these clusters group similar weekly power usages. These absolute frequencies are transformed into relative frequencies, that is, the proportion of each group in the total number of consumers in each week. In compositional space, each observation is a six element vector $(\nu_1, \nu_2, \ldots, \nu_6)$, where $\nu_i$ is proportional to the number of weeks with power usage of type $C_i$. The percentages are shown in Figs. 4 and 5. Figure 4 shows the behavior of the largest clusters, whereas the behavior of the smallest ones is shown in Fig. 5.

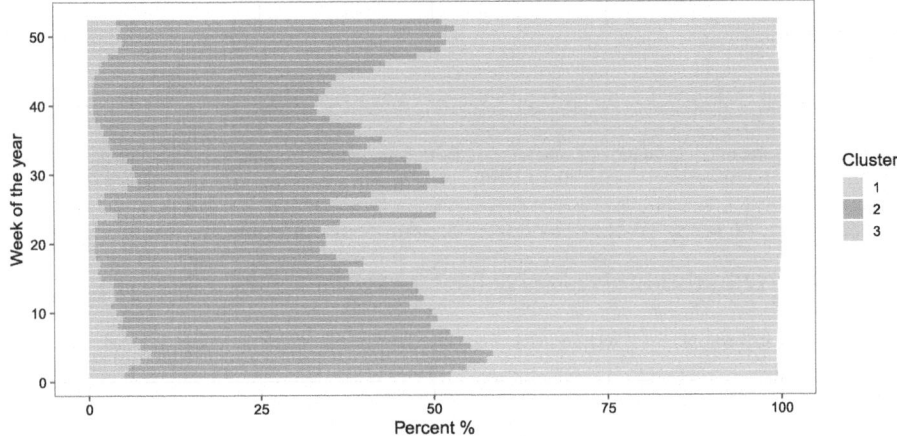

**Fig. 4.** Percent of consumers by cluster per week.

In order to proceed with the compositional analysis, zeros must be imputed. The value chosen is not relevant since it does not modify the results of the analysis. The Bayesian imputation provided by the R package zCompositions [8] has been used. All zero values of the absolute frequencies have been imputed with the cmultRepl function.

The next step is the centered log ratio (clr) transformation of the vector formed by positive relative frequencies. Given the vector $\mathbf{x} = (x_1, \ldots, x_d) \in S^d$, the centered log ratio transformation is:

$$x_{clr} = \left( \log \left( \frac{x_1}{g(\mathbf{x})} \right), \ldots, \log \left( \frac{x_d}{g(\mathbf{x})} \right) \right).$$

where $g(\mathbf{x}) = \sqrt[d]{\prod_{i=1}^{d} xi}$ is the geometric mean of $\mathbf{x}$.

Since $\sum x_i = 1$ (constraint), the centered log ratio transformation is a bijection between the simplex and the real space of dimension $d - 1$.

All centered log ratio transformations of the frequency data together with imputed zeros are calculated using the coordinates function of the R package coda.base [9]. The Euclidean distance between the clr coordinates of two compositional data is known as the Aitchison distance. This distance can be

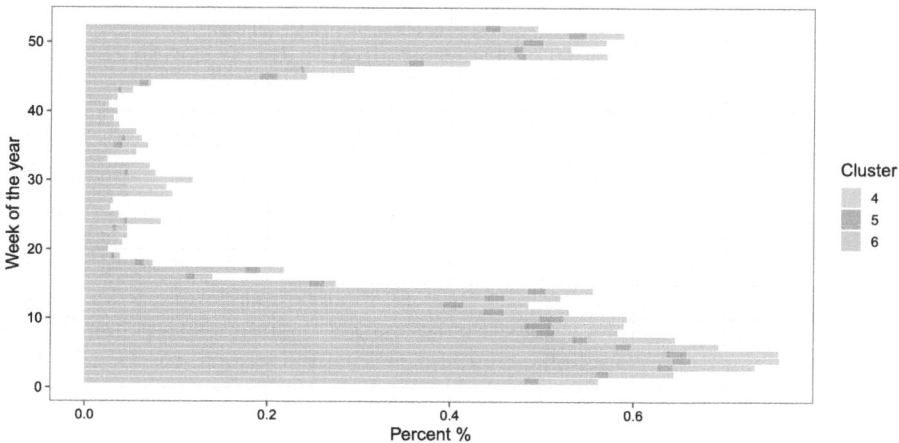

**Fig. 5.** Percent of consumers by cluster per week.

used to cluster compositional data. Hierarchical clustering using Ward's method and Aitchison distance is performed. The number of clusters $n$ is determined by inspection of the resulting dendrogram.

**Table 2.** Customer cluster distribution by types of weekly consumption.

| Customer Cluster | C1 | C2 | C3 | C4 | C5 | C6 |
|---|---|---|---|---|---|---|
| G1 | 381063 | 3347 | 12 | 0 | 1 | 0 |
| G2 | 193046 | 64380 | 0 | 2 | 2 | 0 |
| G3 | 122546 | 166749 | 0 | 1 | 0 | 0 |
| G4 | 49155 | 43728 | 8893 | 102 | 38 | 0 |
| G5 | 381 | 63651 | 28312 | 94 | 12 | 0 |
| G6 | 5024 | 5928 | 2499 | 316 | 45 | 3589 |
| G7 | 120028 | 12581 | 0 | 0 | 0 | 0 |
| G8 | 15851 | 131133 | 335 | 5 | 16 | 0 |
| G9 | 9664 | 55266 | 13471 | 90 | 29 | 0 |
| G10 | 795 | 106008 | 872 | 3 | 1 | 0 |

Table 2, shows the results for $n = 10$ compositional data clusters. Individual customers are segmented into 10 groups $G_1, G_2, G_3, G_4, G_5, G_6, G_7, G_8, G_9, G_{10}$ described by the 6 different types of consumption $C_1, C_2, C_3, C_4, C_5, C_6$. For each customer cluster $G_i$, the distribution of the typical weeks has been obtained. Clearly, there are significant differences in the customer clusters due to the different typical weeks (energy usage patterns).

The partitioning of the compositional data into 10 customer clusters reveal notable differences in the weekly distribution among the clusters. All customers with $C_6$ usage pattern belong to customer group $G_6$. The majority of energy users with typical week $C_4$, belong to customer groups $G_4$, $G_5$, $G_6$ or $G_9$. Customer group $G_7$ has energy usage pattern $C_1$ (with probability 0.905).

## 3   Conclusion and Future Work

Patterns corresponding to consumers' energy usage can be mined and extracted to facilitate effective energy management. Furthermore, in order to deal with big data, it is convenient to prepare and process the original database for further analysis. We consider different data transformation techniques that help reduce the volume of data points and offer more interesting patterns in the energy data.

Firstly, energy consumption is presented using weekly intervals and six groups of "similar" weeks are found using cluster analysis. Clusters $C_1$, $C_2$ and $C_3$ are the largest ones and they present similar behavior patterns with different scales. An almost identical daily power consumption shape is repeated throughout the week. Clusters $C_4$, $C_5$ and $C_6$ are the smallest ones and correspond to the highest values for electricity consumption. The dispersion in the data suggests the presence of outliers. The daily power consumption shape is repeated throughout the week for each cluster, but the three patterns are completely different. Future study, focused on the relationship between clusters and other available variables such as location, dwelling size, ... is required.

Also, compositional data analysis based on the relative values of components within a larger whole is applied. Compositional data are quantitative descriptions of the parts of some whole, conveying relative information. Compositional data is clustered in such a way that groups of consumers are described by frequencies of the six types of weekly power usage and viceversa. As future work, it is interesting to study the effect of other covariates, such as climate or type of housing in the description of consumer groups. Another aspect to consider would be to investigate whether known ranges of variables (such as, contracted power) would reduce the number of outliers and affect the behavior patterns found, and which variables do so the most.

**Acknowledgments.** This work has been partially funded by Grant PID2021-126114NB-C44 funded by MCIN/AEI/ 10.13039/501100011033 and by "ERDF A way of making Europe".

**Disclosure of Interests.** Authors have no known competing interests to declare that are relevant to the content of this article.

## References

1. Russell, S., Norvig, P.: Artificial Intelligence: A Modern Approach, 4h edn. Pearson, London (2020)
2. Cios, K.J., Pedrycz, W., Swiniarski, R.W., Kurgan, L.A.: Data Mining. A Knowledge Discovery Approach. Springer, New York (2007)

3. Chen, Y.C., Hung, H.C., Chiang, B.Y., Peng, S.Y., Chen, P.J.: Incrementally mining usage correlations among appliances in smart homes. In: Proceedings of the 2015 18th International Conference on Network-Based Information Systems (NBiS), Taipei, Taiwan, pp. 273–279 (2015)
4. Pitt, B.: Applications of data mining techniques to electric load profiling, Ph.D. thesis, University of Manchester, UK (2000)
5. Chavan, M., Patil, A., Dalvi, L., Patil, A.: Mini batch k-means clustering on large dataset. Int. J. Sci. Eng. Technol. Res $4$(07), 1356–1358 (2015)
6. Pham, D.T., Dimov, S., Nguyen, C.D.: Selection of K in K-means clustering. Proc. Inst. Mech. Eng. Part C J. Mech. Eng. Sci. **219**(1), 103–119 (2005). https://doi.org/10.1243/095440605X8298
7. Aitchinson, J.: The statistical analysis of compositional data. J. Roy. Stat. Soc. Ser. B (Methodo/.) **44**(2), 139–177 (1982). https://doi.org/10.1111/j.2517-6161.1982.tb01195.x
8. Palarea-Albaladejo, J., Martín-Fernández, J.A.: zCompositions - R package for multivariate imputation of left-censored data under a compositional approach. J. Chemometrics Intell. Lab. Syst. **143**, 85–96 (2015). https://doi.org/10.1016/j.chemolab.2015.02.019
9. Comas-Cufí, M. :coda.base: A Basic Set of Functions for Compositional Data Analysis (2023). https://mcomas.net/coda.base/, https://github.com/mcomas/coda.base

# Theory and Applications
# of Metaheuristic Algorithms

# VFLBench: A Practical Benchmark for Vertical Federated Learning in Smart Manufacturing

Du Nguyen Duy[1]([✉]) [iD], Ramin Nikzad-Langerodi[1] [iD],
and Michael Affenzeller[2] [iD]

[1] Software Competence Center Hagenberg, Hagenberg, Austria
{du.nguyen.duy,ramin.nikzad-langerodi}@scch.at
[2] University of Applied Sciences Upper Austria, Wels, Austria
michael.affenzeller@fh-ooe.at

**Abstract.** Modern manufacturing value chains require strategic coordination of processes across organizational boundaries to optimize profits while promoting sustainability. However, the adoption of integrated process modeling approaches across value chains faces challenges due to privacy concerns surrounding cross-organizational data sharing. Vertical Federated Learning (VFL) surfaces as a prospective resolution to this predicament, facilitating the joint training of models while preserving the privacy of individual data. Nevertheless, the absence of standardized benchmarks and datasets has so far hindered the progression of research and practical deployment of VFL. In an effort to mitigate this hindrance, we introduce VFLBench, a practical benchmark for VFL focused on smart manufacturing. This benchmark includes a collection of datasets with natural partitions and provides a comprehensive evaluation of state-of-the-art VFL algorithms. Through the establishment of a structured framework for comparative analysis, we aim to stimulate both the research and application of VFL solutions in practical scenarios, particularly within the manufacturing sector.

**Keywords:** Vertical federated learning · Smart manufacturing · Benchmarking

## 1 Introduction

The modern manufacturing value chain is frequently comprised of multiple stages, each operated by distinct companies. Due to the intricate interactions between these stages, the Key Performance Indicators (KPIs) for any given stage might be influenced by the activities of previous stages managed by different corporations [1]. Consequently, effective quality control mandates a holistic view of the entire value chain. This broad perspective can be accomplished by transcending corporate boundaries and leveraging data available across the entire chain.

ⓒ The Author(s), under exclusive license to Springer Nature Switzerland AG 2025
A. Quesada-Arencibia et al. (Eds.): EUROCAST 2024, LNCS 15172, pp. 45–52, 2025.
https://doi.org/10.1007/978-3-031-82949-9_5

Nonetheless, increasing concerns regarding data security and privacy pose significant challenges to inter-company data sharing, rendering it increasingly difficult, if not outright impossible.

In this context, Federated Learning (FL) [2] has recently surfaced as an innovative approach to address these concerns, as it allows data providers to build models while maintaining the confidentiality of sensitive data. Depending on how data is distributed among the clients, FL can be broadly categorized into Horizontal Federated Learning (HFL) and Vertical Federated Learning (VFL) [3] (see Fig. 1). HFL involves scenarios where private datasets possess identical feature spaces but differ in the sample space. This partitioning of data is a common approach, particularly in the cross-device setting, where various users aim to enhance their model performance for the same task. On the other hand, VFL refers explicitly to scenarios where private datasets share the same sample space but differ in the feature space. This setup is typically seen in cooperation among different enterprises across a value chain. In such instances, even though local datasets can be linked using product or batch IDs, local features are often different as each company operates distinct sub-processes.

Despite its potential to foster collaboration among industrial partners, the integration of VFL within the manufacturing sector is still in its infancy [4]. However, this is not out of the ordinary as VFL, in general, has been understudied [3]. A significant challenge hindering the development and application of VFL is the lack of suitable datasets and benchmarks for experimental evaluation [3]. While there are existing benchmarks for federated settings, they are predominantly designed for HFL, leaving a gap in resources for VFL studies. This scarcity necessitates researchers to rely on unexplained random or manual feature splitting, which is often impractical and not reproducible [3].

In this study, we put forward VFLBench, an evaluation of advanced VFL algorithms on a suite of federated datasets with natural splits curated from manufacturing sources. By addressing the shortage of standard datasets and benchmarks, we aim to propel research towards fully leveraging the potential of VFL, especially in practical applications within the manufacturing sector.

## 2   Related Work

The rapid growth of FL necessitates effective benchmarking strategies to evaluate and contrast the efficiency of numerous algorithms and systems. Toward this end, the existing FL benchmarking landscape is being constantly enriched with new methods, tools, and datasets. This landscape typically involves using public datasets and simulating distinctive scenarios ranging from varied data distributions to diverse network conditions. In addition, benchmarks scrutinize evaluation metrics, including model accuracy, computational resources, communication efficiency, and fairness among participating data holders.

Nevertheless, the majority of the current frameworks, including contributions such as FLWB [6], FedScale [7], FedEval [8], and NIID-Bench [9], primarily serves the horizontal setting, whereas the vertical scheme is significantly underexplored. Due to the lack of standard benchmarks, most VFL papers simulate vertically federated datasets by artificially or heuristically partitioning public datasets into subsets assigned to hypothetical data holders. For instance, FedML [10], and LEAF [11] generate vertical datasets by randomly distributing an equal number of features to hypothetical parties. Other research [5,12] adopts a simplistic method, manually dividing features without providing a credible rationale. However, such arbitrary divisions can result in performance variability, potentially biasing comparisons. Thus, there is a strong need for practical datasets with natural boundaries that allow researchers to simulate vertical settings more accurately and systematically [3].

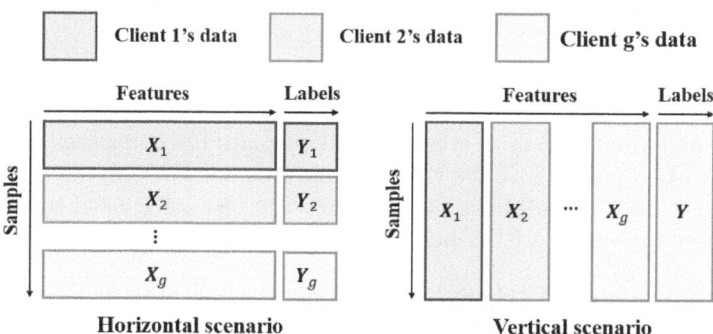

**Fig. 1.** Two common types of FL. $X_i$ and $Y_i$ represent the local features and local labels of Client-$i$, respectively. In VFL, only the last client owns the labels.

The current pool of actual VFL datasets include those in the OARF benchmark (movies, games, songs) [13], NUS-WIDE (images) [14], and Vehicle (vehicle sensors) [15]. However, these datasets do not adequately reflect the diverse challenges encountered in real-world scenarios, particularly in manufacturing applications. In industrial manufacturing, some vertical datasets derived from real data with natural partitions have been utilized in [16]. Nevertheless, the main focus of the study has been to compare the performance of their proposed methods against centralized counterparts rather than conducting a comparative analysis of state-of-the-art VFL algorithms. To the best of our knowledge, no extensive benchmark with natural splits is available for VFL.

## 3  VFLBench

### 3.1  Overall Structure

As illustrated in Fig. 2, the benchmark is composed of three primary modules: (1) a collection of vertical federated datasets, (2) a set of standard VFL techniques, and (3) an array of unified evaluation metrics. This modular structure, inspired by LEAF [11], enables smooth integration of these components into different experimental workflows. Further details regarding each module will be provided in subsequent subsections.

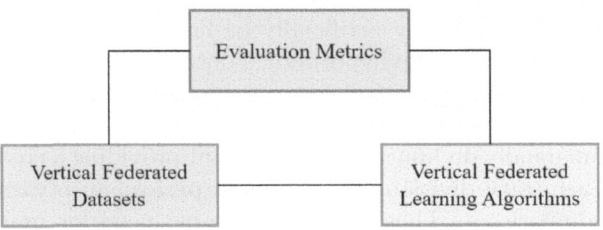

**Fig. 2.** The main modules of VFLBench.

## 3.2 Vertical Federated Datasets

VFLBench emphasizes datasets with inherent boundaries suitable for splitting and assigning features to hypothetical data holders. All datasets have been pre-processed and prepared in a standardized format. Each dataset is randomly divided into two parts: 80% for the training set and 20% for the test set. The training set is used to build the model, while the test set is used to evaluate its performance. Presently, VFLBench includes the following datasets:

- **Hydraulic system I (HySyS I)**: This dataset was obtained experimentally using a hydraulic test rig [17], which consists of two circuits interconnected via an oil tank. The system operates by cyclically repeating constant load cycles, during which various process values are measured. The aim is to develop a regression model for predicting valve conditions. In order to replicate a vertical setup, the features are divided into two blocks based on the rig's configuration [17], with each block assigned to a different data holder. Following the data split, feature reduction was applied separately to each data holder's private data to reduce the number of features.
- **Hydraulic system II (HySyS II)**: Derived from the same source as HySyS I, this dataset has the same feature split. However, the task is different: to predict the stable flag, which is binary.
- **Steel fatigue strength (SFS)**: This dataset includes various experimental conditions during steel preparation, such as chemical composition, upstream processing details, and heat treatment [18]. The target variable is fatigue strength. Features are vertically divided into two blocks and allocated to two hypothetical data holders: the first block contains chemical composition and upstream details, while the second block includes heat treatment information.
- **Simulated multistage process (SMP)**: This synthetic dataset is generated using a multistage process simulator [16]. It emulates a three-stage process, assuming that three distinct manufacturing companies control and possess data from each specific stage. The primary goal of the data federation is to construct a predictive model for the output quality of the final stage.

Of the curated datasets, HySys I and SMP were utilized in [16] to compare the performance of Privacy-preserving Partial Least Squares with its centralized version. However, these datasets have not yet been employed to benchmark

VFL algorithms. Currently, VFLBench only consists of manufacturing datasets. However, suitable datasets from other domains will be considered in the future.

### 3.3 Vertical Federated Learning Algorithms

This module is a growing repository of VFL techniques. Currently, it consists of the following methods:

- **Privacy-preserving Partial Least Squares (P3LS)** [16]. A federated version of Partial Least Squares (PLS), which is a technique commonly used for monitoring and controlling manufacturing processes. P3LS involves a PLS algorithm based on singular value decomposition (SVD) and incorporates removable, randomly generated masks provided by a trusted authority to protect each data holder's private information.
- **Privacy-preserving Symbolic Regression (PPSR)** [5]. A privacy-preserving variant of Symbolic Regression (SR). PPSR employs Secure Multiparty Computation to allow parties to collaboratively build SR models in a vertical scenario without disclosing private data.
- **Secureboost** [19]. A federated learning algorithm that extends the gradient boosting framework, specifically XGBoost, to enable collaborative model training across multiple parties without sharing raw data. It ensures data confidentiality by performing secure aggregation of local computations utilizing Homomorphic Encryption, thereby preventing sensitive information leakage.
- **Split Neural Network (SplitNN)** [20]. Split learning involves dividing the network structure so that each party retains only a portion of it. These smaller structures combine to form a complete network model. During training, parties perform forward or backward calculations on their local structures and transfer the results to the next party. This way, it allows multiple data holders to contribute to the training of a joint model until it converges. During this process, Differential Privacy technology might be employed to enhance privacy protection.

### 3.4 Evaluation Metrics

VFLBench establishes an initial set of metrics chosen specifically for assessing the predictive performance of the VFL algorithms.

- Regression tasks: $R^2$ score and root mean squared error (RMSE).
- Classification tasks: Accuracy and F1 score.

In the future, to provide a comprehensive assessment of VFL algorithms, we will consider other critical aspects such as communication, computation complexity, incentive mechanisms, and robustness against attacks.

# 4   Experiment

## 4.1   Experimental Settings

We tested all algorithms in simulation mode on a single workstation. Given the algorithm's inherent randomness, PPSR and SplitNN results can fluctuate between runs. Therefore, we conducted 20 independent runs with the same train/test split for each algorithm, calculating the average metrics and interquartile ranges. For each method, the same default hyperparameter settings were used for all datasets. Detailed environments and hyperparameter settings can be found in the benchmark repository[1].

## 4.2   Experimental Results

Table 1 and Table 2 summarize the performance of the selected algorithms on regression and the classification tasks, respectively. The results indicate that different modeling approaches vary in suitability for different federated datasets. P3LS and SplitNN consistently performed well across all datasets for both classification and regression tasks. SecureBoost excelled on the SFS and HysSys II datasets but did not perform as well on the SMP dataset compared to P3LS and SplitNN. The performance of PPSR was not comparable to the others, especially in HySys I. However, part of the reason is PPSR's fixed computation budget due to its long training time.

**Table 1.** Performance report of regression tasks.

| Dataset | Method | $R^2$ | | | RMSE | | |
|---|---|---|---|---|---|---|---|
| | | $Q_1$ | Avg | $Q_3$ | $Q_1$ | Avg | $Q_3$ |
| HySys I | P3LS | 0.995 | 0.995 | 0.995 | 0.744 | 0.744 | 0.744 |
| | PPSR | 0.934 | 0.946 | 0.950 | 2.314 | 2.409 | 2.671 |
| | Secureboost | 0.953 | 0.953 | 0.953 | 2.248 | 2.248 | 2.248 |
| | SplitNN | 0.982 | 0.986 | 0.988 | 1.131 | 1.238 | 1.411 |
| SFS | P3LS | 0.955 | 0.955 | 0.955 | 42.058 | 42.058 | 42.058 |
| | PPSR | 0.931 | 0.952 | 0.958 | 40.533 | 43.400 | 52.154 |
| | Secureboost | 0.980 | 0.980 | 0.980 | 28.021 | 28.021 | 28.021 |
| | SplitNN | 0.953 | 0.954 | 0.957 | 41.197 | 42.625 | 43.229 |
| SMP | P3LS | 0.981 | 0.981 | 0.981 | 0.014 | 0.014 | 0.014 |
| | PPSR | 0.934 | 0.938 | 0.943 | 0.025 | 0.026 | 0.026 |
| | Secureboost | 0.848 | 0.848 | 0.848 | 0.040 | 0.040 | 0.040 |
| | SplitNN | 0.932 | 0.956 | 0.969 | 0.018 | 0.022 | 0.027 |

---

[1] https://github.com/software-competence-center-hagenberg/vflbench.

**Table 2.** Performance report of classification tasks.

| Dataset | Method | Accuracy | | | F1 score | | |
|---|---|---|---|---|---|---|---|
| | | $Q_1$ | Avg | $Q_3$ | $Q_1$ | Avg | $Q_3$ |
| HySys II | P3LS | 0.937 | 0.937 | 0.937 | 0.917 | 0.917 | 0.917 |
| | PPSR | 0.931 | 0.943 | 0.951 | 0.904 | 0.922 | 0.933 |
| | Secureboost | 0.964 | 0.964 | 0.964 | 0.950 | 0.950 | 0.950 |
| | SplitNN | 0.939 | 0.939 | 0.941 | 0.916 | 0.916 | 0.919 |

## 5    Summary

In the present work, we introduce VFLBench, a practical benchmark for vertical federated learning. The primary objective of VFLBench is to provide researchers with naturally-split federated datasets and tools to systematically assess the efficacy of VFL algorithms. Although VFLBench currently has a limited selection of curated datasets, strategies, and evaluation metrics, our long-term vision involves enriching it with newly developed algorithms and datasets from diverse domains, with input from the federated learning community. The instructions on how to use and contribute to VFLBench are provided in the benchmark repository[1]. Moreover, we aim to incorporate other crucial factors to offer a more comprehensive assessment of the technology's capabilities.

**Acknowledgements.** The research reported in this paper has been partly funded by the Federal Ministry for Climate Action, Environment, Energy, Mobility, Innovation and Technology (BMK), the Federal Ministry for Digital and Economic Affairs (BMDW), and the State of Upper Austria in the frame of SCCH, a center in the COMET - Competence Centers for Excellent Technologies Program managed by the Austrian Research Promotion Agency FFG and the FFG project circPlast-mr (Grant No. 889843).

## References

1. Shi, J., Zhou, S.: Quality control and improvement for multistage systems: a survey. IIE Trans. **41**, 744–753 (2009)
2. McMahan, B., Moore, E., Ramage, D., Hampson, S., Arcas, B.: Communication-efficient learning of deep networks from decentralized data. Artif. Intell. Stat. 1273–1282 (2017)
3. Cai, D., et al.: Accelerating vertical federated learning. IEEE Trans. Big Data, 1–10 (2024). http://dx.doi.org/10.1109/TBDATA.2022.3192898
4. Li, Q., et al.: A survey on federated learning systems: vision, hype and reality for data privacy and protection. IEEE Trans. Knowl. Data Eng. (2021)
5. Nguyen Duy, D., Affenzeller, M., Nikzad-Langerodi, R.: Towards vertical privacy-preserving symbolic regression via secure multiparty computation. Proceedings of the Companion Conference on Genetic and Evolutionary Computation, pp. 2420–2428 (2023)

6. Casalicchio, E., Esposito, S., Al-Saedi, A.: FLWB: a workbench platform for performance evaluation of federated learning algorithms. In: 2023 IEEE International Workshop on Technologies for Defense and Security (TechDefense), pp. 401–405 (2023)
7. Lai, F., et al.: Fedscale: benchmarking model and system performance of federated learning at scale. In: International Conference on Machine Learning, pp. 11814–11827 (2022)
8. Chai, D., Wang, L., Chen, K., Yang, Q.: Fedeval: a benchmark system with a comprehensive evaluation model for federated learning. arXiv Preprint arXiv:2011.09655 (2020)
9. Li, Q., Diao, Y., Chen, Q., He, B.: Federated learning on non-IID data silos: an experimental study. In: 2022 IEEE 38th International Conference on Data Engineering (ICDE), pp. 965–978 (2022)
10. He, C., et al.: FedML: a research library and benchmark for federated machine learning. arXiv Preprint arXiv:2007.13518 (2020)
11. Caldas, S., et al.: Leaf: a benchmark for federated settings. arXiv Preprint arXiv:1812.01097 (2018)
12. Hu, Y., Niu, D., Yang, J., Zhou, S.: FDML: a collaborative machine learning framework for distributed features. In: Proceedings Of The 25th ACM SIGKDD International Conference On Knowledge Discovery and Data Mining, pp. 2232–2240 (2019)
13. Hu, S., Li, Y., Liu, X., Li, Q., Wu, Z., He, B.: The OARF benchmark suite: characterization and implications for federated learning systems. ACM Trans. Intell. Syst. Technol. (TIST) 13, 1–32 (2022)
14. Chua, T., Tang, J., Hong, R., Li, H., Luo, Z., Zheng, Y.: Nus-wide: a real-world web image database from national university of Singapore. In: Proceedings of the ACM International Conference on Image and Video Retrieval, pp. 1–9 (2009)
15. Duarte, M., Hu, Y.: Vehicle classification in distributed sensor networks. J. Parallel Distrib. Comput. 64, 826–838 (2004)
16. Nguyen Duy, D., Nikzad-Langerodi, R.: P3LS: partial least squares under privacy preservation. J. Process. Control 138, 103229 (2024). https://www.sciencedirect.com/science/article/pii/S0959152424000696
17. Helwig, N., Pignanelli, E., Schütze, A.: Condition monitoring of a complex hydraulic system using multivariate statistics. In: 2015 IEEE International Instrumentation and Measurement Technology Conference (I2MTC) Proceedings, pp. 210–215 (2015)
18. Agrawal, A., Deshpande, P., Cecen, A., Basavarsu, G., Choudhary, A., Kalidindi, S.: Exploration of data science techniques to predict fatigue strength of steel from composition and processing parameters. Integr. Mater. Manuf. Innov. 3, 90–108 (2014)
19. Cheng, K., et al.: SecureBoost: a lossless federated learning framework. IEEE Intell. Syst. 36, 87–98 (2021)
20. Vepakomma, P., Gupta, O., Swedish, T., Raskar, R.: Split learning for health: distributed deep learning without sharing raw patient data. arXiv Preprint arXiv:1812.00564 (2018)

# A Hybrid Cooperative Approach for Symbolic Regression

Bahareh Etaati[1,2]([✉]), Stefan Wagner[1], and Michael Affenzeller[1,2]

[1] Heuristic and Evolutionary Algorithm Laboratory, University of Applied Sciences Upper Austria, Softwarepark 11, 4232 Hagenberg, Austria
bahareh.etaati@fh-hagenberg.at,
{stefan.wagner,michael.affenzeller}@fh-ooe.at
[2] Institute for Computational Perception, Johannes Kepler University, 4040 Linz, Austria

**Abstract.** In multi-objective symbolic regression, the objective is to improve the model's accuracy while minimizing its complexity. It results in a Pareto front, including a fair compromise between accuracy and complexity. In this study, we propose a hybrid cooperative genetic programming approach containing the hybridization of NSGA-II and an adaptive weighted multi-population GA, which cooperatively optimize both models' accuracy and tree length. In the weighted multi-population GA, the weights are assigned adaptively. We also propose a new version of offspring selection to suit the needs of multi-objective symbolic regression. The two algorithms communicate solutions with each other in specific intervals. The proposed algorithm is tested on the Feynman benchmark datasets, and the results are comparable to the NSGA-II in terms of accuracy and models' tree length.

**Keywords:** Symbolic Regression · Multi-objective Optimization · NSGA-II · Genetic Programming

## 1 Introduction

Symbolic regression is a machine learning technique to discover the underlying complex relationships between variables as mathematical formulas. Unlike traditional regression methods, symbolic regression requires no a-priori knowledge about model structure, as the algorithm searches automatically for model structure and its coefficients. Another advantage of symbolic regression is that mathematical expressions are meaningful, interpretable, and understandable [1]. Nevertheless, the complexity of symbolic regression models can reduce their interpretability due to the bloat phenomenon and the appearance of introns [2]. Additionally, overly complex formulas, especially those that capture noise or outliers in the training data, usually lead to overfitting and thus may have

The project is funded by the FWF DFH 23 doc.funds.connect Human Centered Artificial Intelligence.

poorer prediction performance on unseen data. Hence, simpler formulas with similar training accuracy tend to be preferred to complex ones [3]. With this in mind, many researchers have considered model accuracy and complexity simultaneously when solving symbolic regression problems. Some studies formulized the symbolic regression problem as a multi-objective problem, with tree length or complexity as another objective besides model accuracy [3,4].

The most widely used learning algorithm for symbolic regression problems is tree-based genetic programming, which continuously evolves a population of expression trees as candidate solutions by applying genetic operators such as selection, crossover, mutation, and replacement. In recent years, various studies have been conducted to prevent genetic programming from producing overly complex expression trees [2,5].

Non-dominated sorting genetic algorithm (NSGA-II) [6] is one of the most popular elitist algorithms for multi-objective optimization. Recently, NSGA-II has been successfully used to solve bi-objective symbolic regression problems [3,4]. The algorithm ensures elitism by merging the parent population with the generated offspring and integrating the non-dominated sorting and crowding distance into the selection process to obtain the new population and a more uniformly distributed Pareto front.

One widely used method besides Pareto optimality is the decomposition-based multi-objective evolutionary algorithm (MOEA/D), which divides a multi-objective problem into several single-objective problems and collaboratively solves them [7]. Three commonly used decomposition strategies for MOEA/D are the weighted sum, the Tchebycheff decomposition method (TCH), and penalty-based boundary intersection (PBI) [8]. In this paper, we employ the Tchebycheff method.

In our work, we propose a hybrid cooperative genetic programming approach for the symbolic regression problem. The proposed algorithm is a hybridization of a new MOEA/D and an NSGA-II. The objective is that the two algorithms support each other cooperatively by communicating the most promising solutions to create a smoother and well-distributed Pareto front on the NSGA-II side. In the migration phase, the individuals from weighted sum GA are added to the NSGA-II population to cover the less-crowded areas of the Pareto front. On the other hand, the candidate solutions from NSGA-II can contribute to the multi-population weighted GA to guide the search in different locations within the objective space. Additionally, a new version of offspring selection is proposed to consider both models' accuracy and expression tree length, suiting the needs of the multi-objective symbolic regression. For this purpose, having a synchronization strategy to create an appropriate balance between exploration and exploitation is critical. An appropriate synchronization strategy can lead to a better convergence speed and diversity on both sides. With this in mind, the main research contributions are as follows:

1. Proposing a hybrid multi-objective algorithm for a multi-objective symbolic regression problem, optimizing the model accuracy and expression tree length at the same time.

2. Making a proper balance between exploration and exploitation using the powerful characteristics of NSGA-II and multi-population weighted GA.

## 2 Multi-objective Symbolic Regression Problem

In symbolic regression $(SR)$, mathematical expressions model the relationship between multiple independent inputs and one dependent output. These equations can be interpreted, verified, and integrated into the other programs [1]. Nevertheless, this interpretability may be reduced by very complex and large models, bloating, introns, and many variables. Additionally, complex models are more likely to be overfit on training data, resulting in poor prediction on test data. With this in mind, simpler models are generally preferred in symbolic regression.

So far, multiple approaches have been proposed to decrease the size of GP individual trees to prevent them from growing larger (bloat phenomenon). One method is restricting the size and depth of symbolic expression trees in GP, as described in [9]. This approach can produce accurate and less complex models as the tree length must not exceed the specific size. Alternative techniques for managing tree size include imposing dynamic size limits [10], applying parsimony pressure methods [11], or regulating the distribution of tree sizes [12]. The former methods do not consider symbolic expression trees' semantic information and only hinder individual trees from expanding further. In [13], authors suggested a new complexity criterion that took semantic information of individual trees into account. In this paper, the order of non-linearity of symbolic models was computed based on Chebyshev polynomial approximation genotypically, enhancing the overall smoothness of model outputs. In another work [14], three measures were proposed to calculate bloat, overfitting, and functional complexity, respectively. The functional complexity was based on the response curvature, which indicates the geometric deviation of the model from a flat. The proposed measure was not used as an objective criterion, but reported for the current best individual during the evolution to represent its relationship with bloat and overfitting. Based on the two above-mentioned complexity measures, in [3,15], authors suggested a recursive complexity measure that calculated the complexity from child nodes to the root iteratively.

In multi-objective symbolic regression, the objectives are the models' prediction accuracy and the expression tree complexity [16]. In [13], a new algorithm called ParetoGP was proposed, which considered an archive to store the Pareto front beside the population. ParetoGP chose solutions from the Pareto front for breeding and then updated the Pareto front, where the objectives were the Pearson $R^2$ error and model complexity. In [3,15], the non-dominated sorting genetic algorithm (NSGA-II) [6] was used to optimize model accuracy and complexity simultaneously. NSGA-II and MOEA/D used in [4] to optimize tree size and model accuracy for shape-constrained symbolic regression. In this approach, the authors used prior knowledge to estimate the model shape to obtain smoother expression trees. In their other work [17], the authors proposed two novel algorithms for shape-constrained symbolic regression to enhance model generalization. The first algorithm eliminated infeasible solutions (the solutions that violated shape constraints) in the selection process, while the other algorithm considered two populations to separate feasible and infeasible solutions.

In this paper, the accuracy is normalized mean square error ($NMSE$), calculated as mean squared error ($MSE$) divided by the variance of actual target values. Additionally, complexity is considered to be the expression tree length.

# 3  Methodology

Firstly proposed by Zhang and Li in 2007 [18], MOEA/Ds has attracted many researchers in a wide range of application areas [19]. These areas include scheduling problems [20], wireless sensor networks [21], and combinatorial optimization [22], to name but a few.

However, MOEA/Ds suffer from diversity issues [7]. To solve this problem, some researchers combined this algorithm with other multi-objective algorithms to better balance diversity and convergence within the non-dominated solutions [23,24]. More recently, in [25], the authors suggested a bi-criterion evolution of MOEA/D and a Pareto-based algorithm, where the two algorithms evolve and exchange information cooperatively.

Similarly, in this section, we propose a hybrid cooperative multi-objective algorithm for symbolic regression. This hybrid algorithm is a combination of a non-dominated sorting genetic algorithm (NSGA-II) and a multi-objective evolutionary algorithm based on decomposition (MOEA/D). The two algorithms communicate with each other. NSGA-II has already been used to optimize multi-objective symbolic regression. This uses non-domination ranking and crowding distance for selection to make a uniformly distributed Pareto front. To obtain more information about NSGA-II, please refer to [6]. Furthermore, the proposed algorithm framework consists of several parts described in more detail in the subsections below.

## 3.1  Hybrid Cooperative Approach Framework

Figure 1 shows the proposed algorithm framework. The figure's design is inspired by [25]. As you can see, the proposed algorithm is a hybridization of NSGA-II and MOEA/D in which the two algorithms communicate with each other. It is worth mentioning that the communication happens considering both generation intervals and hypervolume indicator of NSGA-II Pareto front. At first, NSGA-II starts to run for a number of generations, generation interval ($gen\_interval$) of 20, while the hypervolume indicator is calculated in each iteration. If the generation interval is larger than $gen\_interval$, and the hypervolume indicator improves, then the NSGA-II execution is paused, and MOEA/D starts to run. At every $gen\_interval$ generations, the best individuals from each sub-population in MOEA/D are stored in *Elites* archive. Then, it checks if MOEA/D improves the hypervolume indicator of NSGA-II Pareto front. If so, the algorithm migrates contributed elites from MOEA/D to NSGA-II, pauses MOEA/D, and resumes NSGA-II. Otherwise, if MOEA/D elites could not contribute to the hypervolume indicator of NSGA-II, the algorithm migrates some non-dominated solutions from NSGA-II to MOEA/D to improve the diversity of MOEA/D in its various sub-populations. Furthermore, the proposed MOEA/D includes a novel offspring selection strategy and a weighting adaptation method to guide the search into various locations within the Pareto front. The proposed offspring selection strategy, weighting adaptation, and communication ways between MOEA/D and NSGA-II are described in the subsections below.

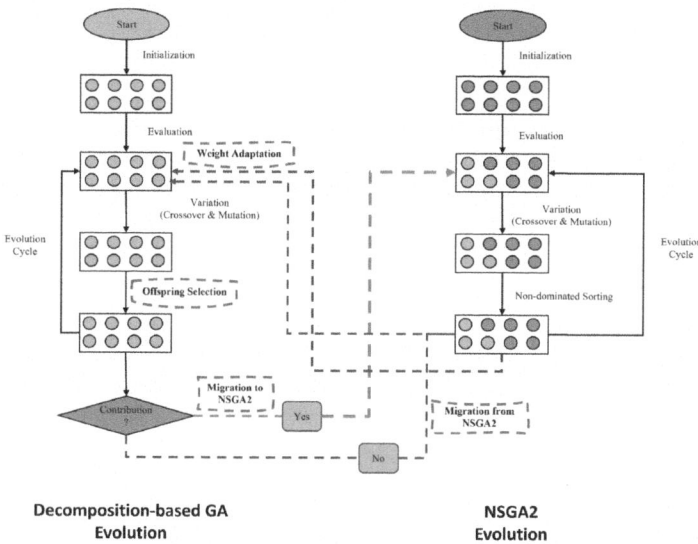

**Fig. 1.** Proposed algorithm framework

## 3.2   Proposed MOEA/D

In this section, we propose a new multi-objective evolutionary algorithm based on decomposition. This algorithm uses a novel version of offspring selection proposed in [26] adapted for the needs of multi-objective symbolic regression. In this subsection, we first describe the adaptive $\epsilon$-lexicase selection algorithm from which the proposed offspring selection is inspired, and then, we will explain the proposed offspring selection in more detail.

## 3.3   Communication

In this subsection, we describe the ways the two algorithms exchange information between each other. Additionally, we explain how the non-dominated solutions from NSGA-II contribute to adapting weights in the MOEA/D side.

### 3.3.1   Communication from MOEA/D to NSGA-II

While MOEA/D execution, in every generation interval *gen_interval*, the elites gathered from each subpopulation are added to NSGA-II population. Then, non-domination ranking and crowding distance sorting are applied to the whole population. In this case, the algorithm checks if any elite dominates any of the non-dominated solutions in NSGA-II or if MOEA/D elites could improve the hypervolume indicator of NSGA-II. If so, the MOEA/D is paused, and NSGA-II is resumed to execute. If not, the communication from NSGA-II to MOEA/D is applied to boost diversity within the MOEA/D's subpopulations.

### 3.3.2   Communication from NSGA-II to MOEA/D

As mentioned above, if the MOEA/D's contribution to the NSGA-II is zero, the algorithm migrates non-dominated solutions from NSGA-II to the subpopulations in MOEA/D. In this communication, at first, the Euclidean distance between each non-dominated solution and each elite within the objective space is calculated. Then, each non-dominated solution is migrated to the closest elite's subpopulation. This procedure is shown in Fig. 2. As Fig. 2 shows, the non-dominated solution from Pareto front is migrated to the third subpopulation in MOEA/D as the closest elite to the non-dominated solution is the third one.

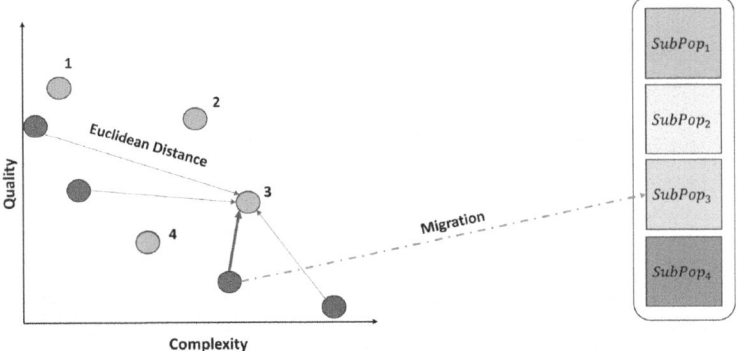

**Fig. 2.** Migration from NSGA-II to MOEA/D

### 3.3.3   MOEA/D's Weight Adaptation

The performance of MOEA/D depends on the distribution of weight vectors. Thus, it is significant that the weight vectors cover the promising areas within the Pareto front. Before going through this weight adaptation process, we first describe the decomposition strategy and weight initialization in MOEA/D as follows:

*Decomposition Strategy.* There are three decomposition strategies that are widely used in MOEA/D, including weighted sum (WS), the Tchebycheff decomposition method (TCH), and penalty boundary intersection (PBI) [27]. This paper uses the Tchebycheff decomposition strategy to evolve the population as follows:

$$TCH(x, w, z^*) = max_{1 \leq j \leq m} \, w_j |f_j(x) - z_j^*| \tag{1}$$
$$\textbf{subject to } x \in \Omega$$

where the weight vector $w = (w_1, w_2, ..., w_m)^T$, $\sum_i^m w_i = 1$, and $w_i \geq 0$, subject to $i \in \{1, 2, ..., m\}$. Additionally, $z^* = (z_1^*, z_2^*, ..., z_m^*)^T$ is the ideal point, the optimal values of each objective on the true Pareto front.

*Weight Initialization.* This work utilizes Das and Dennis technique [28] for weight initialization. This technique generates a set of uniformly distributed reference points from which the uniformly distributed reference vectors are constructed.

*Weight Adaptation.* In the proposed algorithm, we use non-dominated solutions for directing the search towards less crowded areas within the objective space. To begin, the sparsity level of each non-dominated solution in NSGA-II regarding the MOEA/D's elites is calculated. The sparsity level is calculated by the formula suggested in [29] as follows:

$$SL(x^j, pop) = \Pi_{i=1}^m L_2^{NN_i^j} \tag{2}$$

where $L_2^{NN_i^j}$ is the Euclidean distance from $j$th non-dominated solution in NSGA-II to each MOEA/D's elite. Then, the solution with the largest sparsity is chosen, and its nearest weight vector is directed toward the non-dominated solution. The new weight vector is computed based on the formula suggested by [8] as follows:

$$w^{sp} = \left( \frac{\frac{1}{f_1^{sp} - z_1^*}}{\sum_{k=1}^m \frac{1}{f_k^{sp} - z_k *}}, \frac{\frac{1}{f_2^{sp} - z_2^*}}{\sum_{k=1}^m \frac{1}{f_k^{sp} - z_k *}}, ..., \frac{\frac{1}{f_m^{sp} - z_m^*}}{\sum_{k=1}^m \frac{1}{f_k^{sp} - z_k *}} \right) \tag{3}$$

where $F(x^{sp}) = (f_1^{sp}, f_2^{sp}, ..., f_m^{sp})^T$ and $z^*$ is the current ideal point (Fig. 3).

## 4 Experimental Evaluation

### 4.1 Experimental Setting

Table 1 shows the parameter setting for the proposed algorithm, including the parameter setting for both NSGA-II and MOEA/D. The performance of the proposed algorithm is compared to that of NSGA-II. Thus, in the second column of

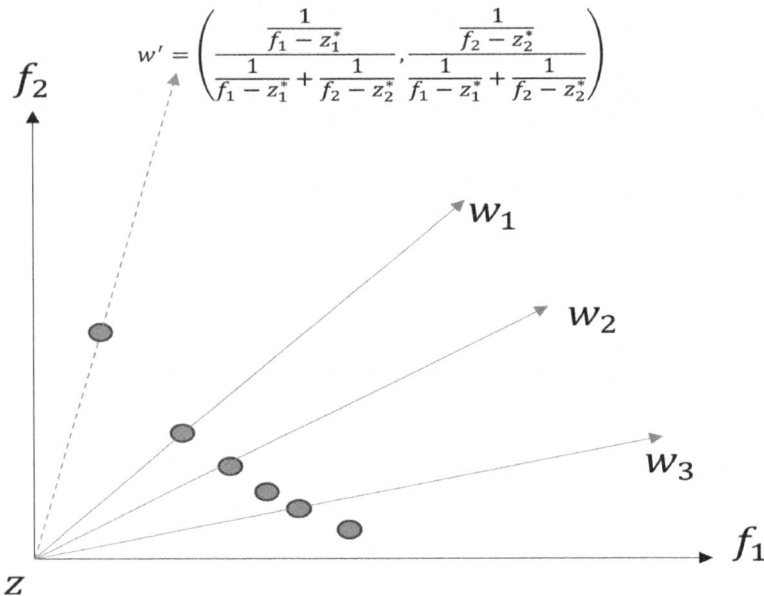

**Fig. 3.** Weight adaptation towards the sparsest non-dominated solution

Table 1, the first and second values show the NSGA-II's setting for the proposed algorithm and NSGA-II, respectively.

In this study, we applied the proposed algorithm to Feynman dataset benchmark problems proposed in [30]. This benchmark set contains 120 equations selected from seminal Feynman lectures on Physics and is introduced in two small and large sets with and without noise. The benchmark instances employed in this paper are 1.6.20b and 1.8.14 with noise levels of $\{0.1, 0.25, 0.5, 0.75\}$.

### 4.2    Experimental Results and Analysis

#### 4.2.1    Effects of Number of Segments versus Hypervolume Indicator

Figure 4 illustrates the hypervolume indicator's mean for various segments with different noise levels. The experiment shows that the smaller number of segments performs better when $0.1 \leq noise \leq 0.5$. In this case, when the number of segments gets larger, it can waste a lot of fitness evaluations to explore different areas within the search space. At the same time, the convergence speed as a result of poor exploitation within each region reduces. However, when the noise level increases ($noise \geq 0.75$), the larger number of segments tends to perform better as the algorithm needs stronger exploration to look for promising areas. Overall, a trade-off between diversity and convergence is achieved by $Seg\_No \in [10, 20]$.

**Table 1.** Parameter setting of the proposed algorithm

| Parameter | NSGA-II | MOEA/D |
|---|---|---|
| Population Size | 500, 1000 | 500 |
| Function Set | add, sub, mul, div, pow, square, root | add, sub, mul, div, pow, square, root |
| Fitness Function | NMSE, HV, Tree Length | NMSE, HV, Tree Length |
| Selection Method | Crowded tournament selection | Tournament selection (group size of 2) |
| Crossover Rate | 100% | 100% |
| Mutation Rate | 25% | 25% |
| Maximum Tree Depth | 20 | 20 |
| Maximum Tree Length | 25 | 25 |
| Maximum Evaluation No. | 500,000, 1,000,000 | 500,000 |
| No. of Runs | 30 | 30 |

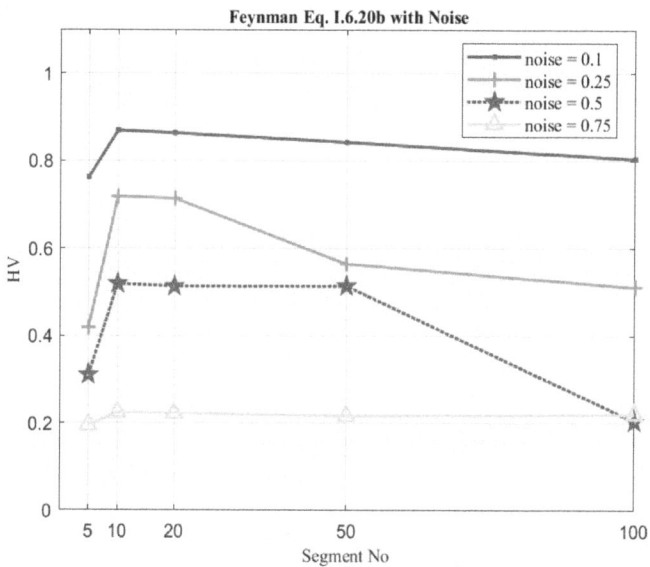

**Fig. 4.** Illustration of mean of hypervolume indicator for different segment numbers with different levels of noise.

### 4.2.2 Effects of Number of Segments versus Fitness

Figure 5 shows the impacts of the average of best fitness values for various numbers of segments. As we can see, the smaller number of segments achieves better results for the lower rate of noise ($0.1 \leq noise \leq 0.5$). The reason is that the larger number of segments ($Seg\_No \geq 50$) may waste quite a few fitness evaluations, which otherwise can track the global optimum. Nevertheless, too small values for segment numbers ($Seg\_No \leq 5$) are also inefficient, as the algorithm loses its capability of doing global search and maintaining diversity. However, when the rate of noise gets higher ($noise \geq 0.75$), similar to Fig. 4, the larger number of segments is more efficient as it boosts the global search abilities of the algorithm.

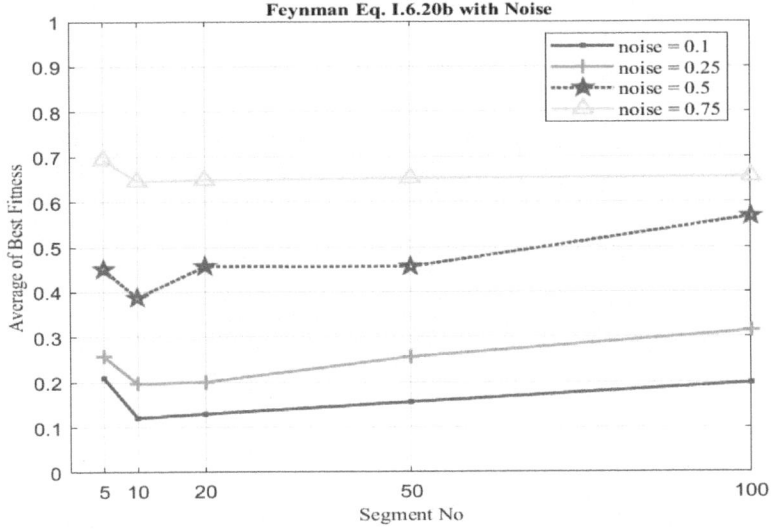

**Fig. 5.** Illustration of the mean of best fitness for different segment numbers with different levels of noise.

### 4.2.3  Comparison Between the Proposed Algorithm and NSGA-II

Figure 6 represents the performance of the proposed algorithm versus NSGA-II on the Feynman 1.6.20*b* benchmark problem with various noise levels in terms of the average of the hypervolume indicator. As we can see, the proposed algorithm outperforms NSGA-II through all noise levels. The proposed algorithm obtains the best and worst results when $noise = 0.1$ and $noise = 0.75$, respectively. Similarly, in Fig. 7, the proposed algorithm outdoes NSGA-II in terms of the average of best fitness. As we can see, the difference in the performance of the two algorithms decreases significantly as the level of noise increases ($noise = 0.75$).

Figure 8 illustrates the comparison between the two algorithms' performance in terms of hypervolume indicator on the Feynman 1.8.14 dataset with various levels of noise. The proposed algorithm outshines NSGA-II on various levels of noise. As we can see, the difference between the performance of the two algorithms is not too much as the noise rate increases ($noise = 0.75$). Likewise, in Fig. 9, the proposed algorithm obtains better fitness values compared to those of NSGA-II.

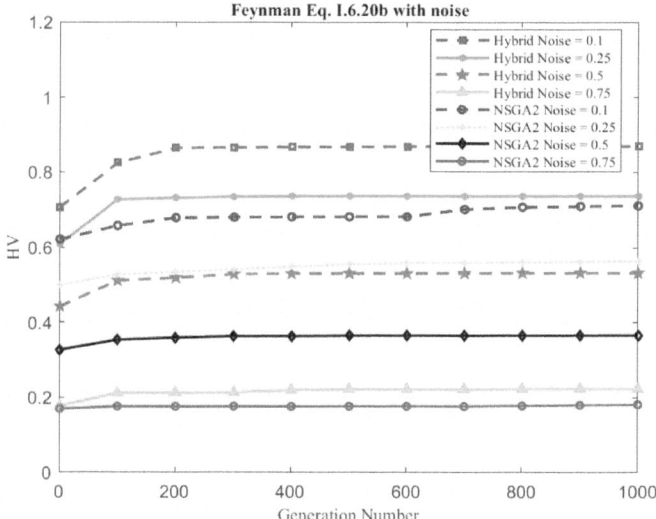

**Fig. 6.** Illustration of the mean of hypervolume indicator for the proposed algorithm and NSGA2 with different levels of noise.

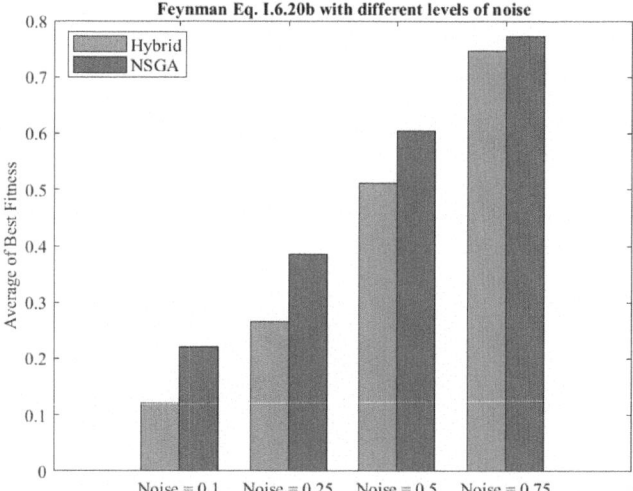

**Fig. 7.** Illustration of the mean of best fitness value for the proposed algorithm and NSGA2 with different levels of noise.

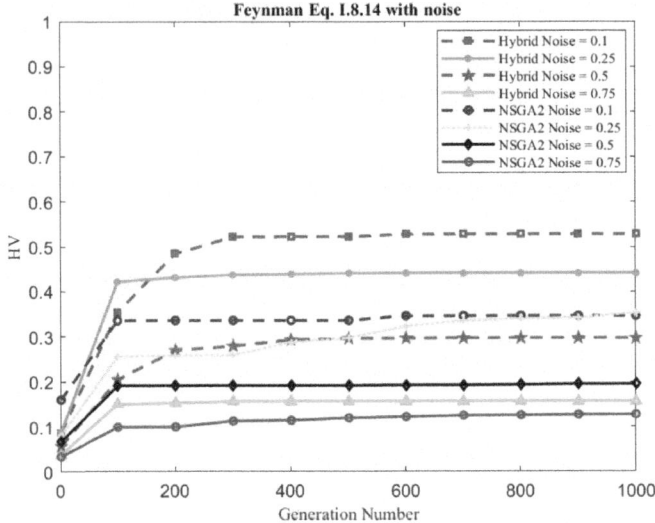

**Fig. 8.** Illustration of the mean of hypervolume indicator for the proposed algorithm and NSGA2 with different levels of noise.

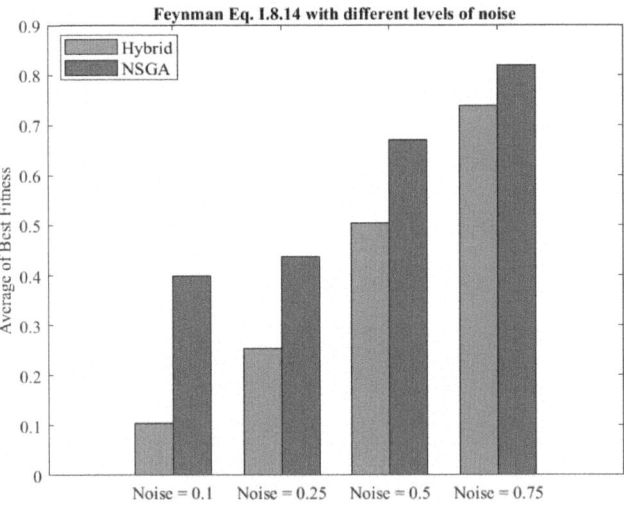

**Fig. 9.** Illustration of the mean of best fitness value for the proposed algorithm and NSGA2 with different levels of noise.

## 5    Conclusion

In multi-objective symbolic regression, the objective is to enhance the model's accuracy while minimizing the model's complexity. In this work, we proposed a hybrid cooperative multi-objective algorithm, which is a hybridization of MOEA/D and NSGA-II. We employed a weight adaptation strategy for MOEA/D using non-dominated solutions from NSGA-II. Besides, the two algorithms communicate the most promising individuals to each other at specific intervals considering the hypervolume indicator of the Pareto front.

We applied the proposed algorithm to two Feynman benchmark problems, which are physics-based benchmark problems containing various levels of noise. Different experiments were conducted to compare the proposed algorithm's performance with that of NSGA-II. The results show that the proposed algorithm outperforms NSGA-II in terms of convergence speed and diversity.

We plan to use our hybrid approach to solve more complex symbolic regression problems involving multiple objectives, such as handling constraint violations, shape constraints, and recursive complexity [15]. We also aim to improve the flexibility of our approach by dynamically adjusting the number of weight vectors and subpopulations as needed. Furthermore, the hybrid approach offers a flexible framework where any two algorithms can communicate. As part of our future work, we plan to incorporate NSGA-III alongside the decomposition-based GA to enhance the performance when dealing with many objectives.

# References

1. Affenzeller, M., Winkler, S.M., Kronberger, G., Kommenda, M., Burlacu, B., Wagner, S.: Gaining deeper insights in symbolic regression. Genetic Program. Theory Pract. XI, pp. 175–190 (2014)
2. Haeri, M.A., Ebadzadeh, M.M., Folino, G.: Statistical genetic programming for symbolic regression. Appl. Soft Comput. **60**, 447–469 (2017)
3. Kommenda, M., Kronberger, G., Affenzeller, M., Winkler, S.M., Burlacu, B.: Evolving simple symbolic regression models by multi-objective genetic programming. Genetic Program. Theory Pract. **XIII**, 1–19 (2016)
4. Haider, C., de França, F.O., Burlacu, B., Kronberger, G.: Using shape constraints for improving symbolic regression models. arXiv preprint arXiv:2107.09458 (2021)
5. Liang, J., Xue, Yu.: Bloat-aware GP-based methods with bloat quantification. Appl. Intell. **52**(4), 4211–4225 (2022)
6. Deb, K., Agrawal, S., Pratap, A., Meyarivan, T.: A fast elitist non-dominated sorting genetic algorithm for multi-objective optimization: NSGA-II. In: Parallel Problem Solving from Nature PPSN VI: 6th International Conference Paris, France, 18–20 September 2000, Proceedings 6, pp. 849–858. Springer, Cham (2000)
7. Li, H., Deng, J., Zhang, Q., Sun, J.: Adaptive epsilon dominance in decomposition-based multiobjective evolutionary algorithm. Swarm Evol. Comput. **45**, 52–67 (2019)
8. Qinghua, G., Li, K., Wang, D., Liu, D.: A MOEA/D with adaptive weight subspace for regular and irregular multi-objective optimization problems. Inf. Sci. **661**, 120143 (2024)
9. O'Neill, M., Poli, R., Langdon, W.B., McPhee, N.F.: A field guide to genetic programming: Lulu.com, 250 p. (2008). ISBN 978-1-4092-0073-4 (2009)
10. Silva, S., Costa, E.: Dynamic limits for bloat control in genetic programming and a review of past and current bloat theories. Genet. Program Evol. Mach. **10**, 141–179 (2009)

11. Poli, R.: Covariant Tarpeian method for bloat control in genetic programming. In: Genetic Programming Theory and Practice VIII, pp. 71–89 (2011)
12. Dignum, S., Poli, R.: Operator equalisation and bloat free GP. In: Genetic Programming: 11th European Conference, EuroGP 2008, Naples, Italy, 26–28 March 2008. Proceedings 11, pp. 110–121. Springer, Heidelberg (2008)
13. Vladislavleva, E.J., Smits, G.F., Den Hertog, D.: Order of nonlinearity as a complexity measure for models generated by symbolic regression via pareto genetic programming. IEEE Trans. Evol. Comput. **13**(2), 333–349 (2008)
14. Vanneschi, L., Castelli, M., Silva, S.: Measuring bloat, overfitting and functional complexity in genetic programming. In: Proceedings of the 12th Annual Conference on Genetic and Evolutionary Computation, pp. 877–884 (2010)
15. Kommenda, M., Beham, A., Affenzeller, M., Kronberger, G.: Complexity measures for multi-objective symbolic regression. In: Computer Aided Systems Theory–EUROCAST 2015: 15th International Conference, Las Palmas de Gran Canaria, Spain, 8–13 February 2015, Revised Selected Papers 15, pp. 409–416. Springer, Heidelberg (2015)
16. Smits, G.F., Kotanchek, M.: Pareto-front exploitation in symbolic regression. In: Genetic Programming Theory and Practice II, pp. 283–299 (2005)
17. Kronberger, G., de França, F.O., Burlacu, B., Haider, C., Kommenda, M.: Shape-constrained symbolic regression-improving extrapolation with prior knowledge. Evol. Comput. **30**(1), 75–98 (2022)
18. Zhang, Q., Li, H.: MOEA/D: a multiobjective evolutionary algorithm based on decomposition. IEEE Trans. Evol. Comput. **11**(6), 712–731 (2007)
19. Qian, X., Zhanqi, X., Ma, T.: A survey of multiobjective evolutionary algorithms based on decomposition: variants, challenges and future directions. IEEE Access **8**, 41588–41614 (2020)
20. Wang, L., Peng, Z., et al.: Solving energy-efficient distributed job shop scheduling via multi-objective evolutionary algorithm with decomposition. Swarm Evol. Comput. **58**, 100745 (2020)
21. Özdemir, S., Attea, B., Khalil, Ö.A.: Multi-objective evolutionary algorithm based on decomposition for energy efficient coverage in wireless sensor networks. Wirel. Pers. Commun. **71**, 195–215 (2013)
22. Cai, X., Li, Y., Fan, Z., Zhang, Q.: An external archive guided multiobjective evolutionary algorithm based on decomposition for combinatorial optimization. IEEE Trans. Evol. Comput. **19**(4), 508–523 (2014)
23. Al Moubayed, N., Petrovski, A., McCall, J.: D2MOPSO: MOPSO based on decomposition and dominance with archiving using crowding distance in objective and solution spaces. Evol. Comput. **22**(1), 47–77 (2014)
24. Deb, K., Jain, H.: An evolutionary many-objective optimization algorithm using reference-point-based nondominated sorting approach, part i: solving problems with box constraints. IEEE Trans. Evol. Comput. **18**(4), 577–601 (2013)
25. Li, M., Yang, S., Liu, X.: Pareto or non-pareto: bi-criterion evolution in multiobjective optimization. IEEE Trans. Evol. Comput. **20**(5), 645–665 (2015)
26. Affenzeller, M., Wagner, S.: Offspring selection: a new self-adaptive selection scheme for genetic algorithms. In: Adaptive and Natural Computing Algorithms: Proceedings of the International Conference in Coimbra, Portugal, 2005, pp. 218–221. Springer, Cham (2005)
27. Wu, M., Kwong, S., Jia, Y., Li, K., Zhang, Q.: Adaptive weights generation for decomposition-based multi-objective optimization using gaussian process regression. In: Proceedings of the Genetic and Evolutionary Computation Conference, pp. 641–648 (2017)

28. Das, I., Dennis, J.E.: Normal-boundary intersection: a new method for generating the pareto surface in nonlinear multicriteria optimization problems. SIAM J. Optim. **8**(3), 631–657 (1998)
29. Kukkonen, S., Deb, K.: A fast and effective method for pruning of non-dominated solutions in many-objective problems. In: International Conference on Parallel Problem Solving from Nature, pp. 553–562. Springer, Cham (2006)
30. Udrescu, S.-M., Tegmark, M.: AI Feynman: a physics-inspired method for symbolic regression. Sci. Adv. **6**(16), eaay2631 (2020)

# Comparing Constraint Evaluation Methods for Shape-Constrained Regression

Christian Haider[1]([✉])(iD), Florian Bachinger[1,2](iD), Florian Holzinger[1],
and Fabrício Olivetti de França[3](iD)

[1] Heuristic and Evolutionary Algorithms Laboratory, University of Applied Sciences
Upper, Hagenberg, Austria
`christian.haider@fh-hagenberg.at`
[2] Institute for Application-oriented Knowledge Processing (FAW), Johannes Kepler
University, Linz, Austria
[3] Center for Mathematics, Computing and Cognition, Federal University of ABC,
Santo André, Brazil

**Abstract.** Shape-constrained regression is an important desideratum of data-based modeling when you want to enforce your model to possess an expected behavior despite the intrinsic noise of the collected data. Conventional data-based modeling approaches are solely reliant on empirical data, and thus, often fail to incorporate the essential physical constraints inherent to the underlying systems. This leads to a lack of trust in the model and a reduction of explanatory power. Recognizing these limitations of traditional data-based methodologies, the integration of shape constraints, derived from domain expertise or fundamental physical principles, emerges as a promising extension to enhance the quality of models. In this paper, we distinguish between single-objective and multi-objective approaches, as well as soft and hard constraint methods to evaluate the constraint violations of models. In the context of this research, the primary focus is on single-objective approaches that incorporate an expanded scope of features and dynamics for constraint handling. Instead of strictly enforcing hard constraints and discarding solutions solely based on constraint violation, the paper presents a dynamic method for calculating constraint violation and prediction error. The presented approach involves an incremental increase in the weighting of constraint violation during the modeling process, achieving an initial, wide-ranging exploration of the solution space followed by a comprehensive investigation of potential models through an in-depth search. Furthermore, we want to explore the critical issue of premature stagnation, a phenomenon wherein the search for a conformant model, plateaus before reaching an acceptable local optima solution. This paper tries to address this challenge through different strategies to maintain a certain diversity of solutions.

**Keywords:** Shape-constrained Regression · Symbolic Regression · Dynamic Constraint Measurement · Genetic Programming

# 1    Introduction

Interpretable and trustworthy machine learning (ML) is becoming an increasingly important factor in the field of artificial intelligence, as models are more often deployed in high-stakes social sectors such as medicine and finance [10]. Usually ML algorithms are solely trained on data and only focus on achieving well-predicting models without paying attention to whether these models also reflect the underlying reality. Such models are referred to as black-box models and often exhibit a complex internal structure that hampers interpretation and leads to a lack of trust [13].

However, as the demand for trustworthy models grows, it is crucial to ensure that these data-based models conform to some specific properties, such as physical constraints, of the system they represent. This adherence is essential for the successful deployment of the model [11]. These properties can be derived from different sources, such as physical principles, prior knowledge from previous experiments, or domain expert knowledge. This additional prior knowledge can be incorporated into the modeling process to create more accurate representations of the real-world system. One way to integrate these properties is by enforcing the desired form of the final function, thus this method is referred to as shape-constrained regression [3,4,8].

Symbolic Regression (SR) is one algorithm that lends itself well for integration of prior knowledge in the form of shape constraints [7,9]. SR is an ML approach that aims to find simple mathematical expressions that explain the interaction in training data. These simple expressions enhance the interpretability of the discovered models. The main characteristic of SR is its ability to determine both the functional form as well as the optimized parameters. This differs from other regression methods, where the functional form is already provided and only the parameters are optimized.

In [8] the authors introduce shape-constrained symbolic regression (SCSR), a method that aims to find well-fitting models that adhere to specified constraints. Their findings show that the proposed approach can achieve results comparable to other genetic programming (GP) methods, while also satisfying the desired behavior.

Similar work is done in the field of polynomial regression. In [5] the author describes a multi-variant shape-constrained polynomial regression method, that is based on semidefinite programming. Another closely related work is presented by Bladek and Krawiec [1]. They use a counter-example GP approach to incorporate prior knowledge via constraints in SR. In the field of NN, similar work is done, as highlighted by the authors in [2] who demonstrate the capability of an advanced physics-informed neural network (PINN) that includes prior knowledge.

The motivation for this research is to advance shape-constrained symbolic regression by delving into various constraint evaluation methods. Specifically, we aim to propose a combined evaluation approach that optimizes the prediction error while penalizing the constraint violation with a dynamic penalty coefficient. By looking into the detailed mechanics of this combined evaluation method, we aspire to get a deeper understanding of the interplay between shape constraints and modeling accuracy.

## 2  Methodology

The proposed constraint evaluation method, referred to as the single-objective combined approach, aims to contribute to the domain of shape-constrained regression modeling. Therein, we implemented a single-objective function designed to yield soft constraints, combining shape constraint evaluation as a penalty function with a measurement of prediction error such as the normalized mean squared error (NMSE). The key aspect of the presented method is the dynamic constraint weighting adaption throughout the runtime of the algorithm. This strategic approach involves a variation in constraint weights, enabling an extensive exploration of the search space in the first step. Subsequently, the algorithm transitions into a deeper and more focused investigation of potential solution candidates. Using this dynamic adaption allows us to counter the limitation of exploring the complete search space by using constraints at the beginning and allowing the algorithm to freely find good solutions, without hindering it too much. To make this transition smooth we developed and tested different methods for incrementing the weights during the evaluation process. These methods include a linearly increasing function, an exponentially increasing function, and an adaptive weighting function that adjusts weights based on the generations. Each function offers a unique perspective on the interplay between shape constraints and prediction accuracy as depicted in Fig. 1.

In our constraint evaluation setup, we explored different methods for calculating constraint violations. The first approach uses interval arithmetic (IA), a method that allows us to handle uncertainties and provide rigorous bounds on constraint violations [6]. As a second approach, we investigate a sampling approach, aiming for a more granular examination of the solution space. We utilized the sampling approach to estimate the expression using a finite number of samples and determined the minimum and maximum values from the sample. This approach is easier to implement but only finds the correct value if the global minima or maxima are present in the samples.

## 3  Experimental Setup

For the experimental setup, we used the well-known equations from the Feynman Symbolic Regression Database [12], containing expressions from physics textbooks. The database contains more than 100 instances, and we took a subset of the available expressions (see Table 1) based on the reported difficulty in [12]. For each of the selected instances, we extracted the corresponding monotonicity constraints by sampling the ground truth expression. To generate the dataset, we sampled 500 points uniformly at random from the given expression. We then split the data by calculating the convex hull and selecting the outer points from the hull for the test set until we reached the desired amount of 100

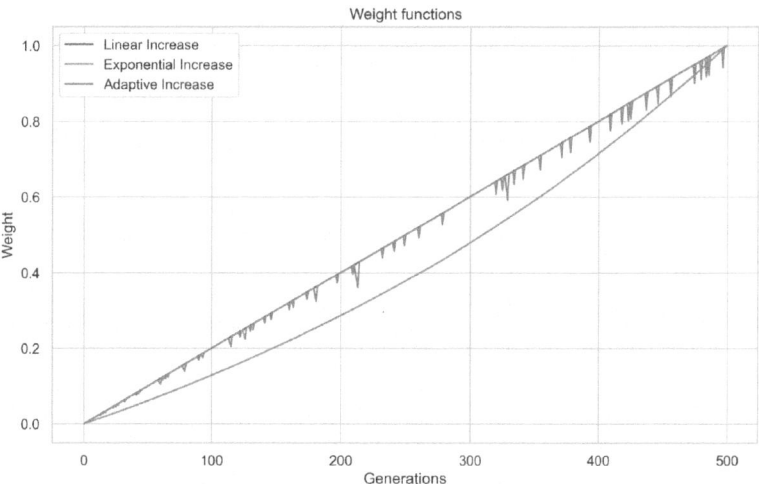

**Fig. 1.** Different weight functions over the number of generations.

data points. These data points are chosen to test the extrapolation capabilities of the proposed method. From the remaining data points within the convex hull, we sampled 100 data points for the training set and 100 for the validation set. Additionally, we generated a second set using the same generation process but added normally distributed noise to the data. The noise is calculated using

$$y' = y + N(0, \sqrt{P_{noise} * \sigma_y}), \tag{1}$$

where $P_{noise}$ specifies the noise level in percent. The noise was only added to the training data.

In this paper, we used four different algorithms for comparison. First, a tree-based single-objective GP, that ignores all constraints completely and serves as a baseline for the prediction error. Secondly, GP using hard constraints (GPSC) [8], is an extension of the standard GP, that allows to specify constraints. The algorithm will check for each constraint and if any constraint is violated the prediction error will be set to the worst possible value. Third, the multi-objective NSGA-II minimizes the prediction error and the sum of constraint violations in two separate objectives [4]. Due to the possibility of splitting the objectives, we use a soft-constraint approach here. Fourth, the proposed combined single-objective approach, that uses one objective function for calculating the prediction error and soft constraints.

We applied the same parameters across all algorithms: a population size of 1000, 500 generations for 500k evaluations, tournament selection with a group size of 5, a 20% mutation rate, a maximum tree size of 25 nodes, and 100% subtree crossover. The primary objective was minimizing prediction error, with minimizing constraint violations as the secondary objective.

**Table 1.** Selected instances from the Symbolic Regression Feynman Database.

| Instance | Expression |
|----------|-----------|
| I.6.20 | $\exp\left(\frac{-\left(\frac{\theta}{\sigma}\right)^2}{2}\right)\frac{1}{\sqrt{2\pi\sigma}}$ |
| I.9.18 | $\frac{G\,m1\,m2}{(x2-x1)^2+(y2-y1)^2+(z2-z1)^2}$ |
| I.15.3x | $\frac{x-ut}{\sqrt{1-u^2/c^2}}$ |
| I.32.17 | $\frac{1}{2}\epsilon c\,Ef^2\,\frac{8\pi r^2}{3}\,\frac{\omega^4}{\left(\omega^2-\omega_0{}^2\right)^2}$ |
| I.48.20 | $\frac{m\,c^2}{\sqrt{1-\frac{v^2}{c^2}}}$ |
| II.11.27 | $\frac{na}{1-na/3}\in E_f$ |
| II.11.28 | $1+\frac{na}{1-(na/3)}$ |
| III.9.52 | $\frac{p_d Eft}{h}\sin\left(\frac{(\omega-\omega_0)t}{2}\right)^2$ |
| III.10.19 | $mom\,\sqrt{Bx^2+By^2+Bz^2}$ |

## 4    Results

In Table 2 and Table 3 we can observe the prediction error over 30 independent runs on the test set for the dataset without and with additional noise respectively. We report the NMSE in percent. The leftmost column shows the problem instance number for the Feynman dataset. On the left side of the table, we can see the baseline prediction using GP without any additional information. On the right side, 4 different algorithms using shape constraints are compared to each other. The following algorithms are compared - shape-constrained symbolic regression (GPSC), non-dominated sorting genetic algorithm II (NSGA-II), single-objective dynamic constraint evaluation using sampling evaluation (CombOpt) and single objective dynamic constraint evaluation using IA for constraint evaluation (CombPes).

We can observe that the multi-objective algorithm (NSGA-II) and the two combined single-objective algorithms (CombOpt and CombPes) perform best on both datasets. On the dataset with higher noise, the difference is even larger and we can observe that the combined approach performs better. Further, we can observe that the optimistic approach works better on instances with fewer input variables (2–4) and the pessimistic approach works better on instances with more instances. This indicates that evaluation using sampling on high-dimensional problems get more difficult. We can observe that the CombOpt approach almost always ranks first or second when comparing the test values.

In Fig. 2, we can see the average percentage of constraint violations over all 30 runs and all instances. We can observe that, using GP without any additional information, most likely results in models that do not conform to the expected properties. Further, we see that GPSC performs best due to the hard-constraint evaluation. NSGA-II performs pretty well using the multi-objective approach separating the objectives into a data fitting and a constraint violation compo-

**Table 2.** Median NMSE values for extrapolation datasets with no noise added.

|          |           | w/o. info | w. info |          |          |          |
|          |           | *GP*      | *GPSC*  | *NSGA-II* | *CombOpt* | *CombPes* |
|----------|-----------|-----------|---------|-----------|-----------|-----------|
| no noise | I.6.20    | 1.30      | 7.20    | 3.49      | **3.05**  | 3.48      |
|          | I.9.18    | 0.91      | 17.78   | **1.68**  | 8.30      | 3.16      |
|          | I.15.3x   | 0.18      | **0.27**| **0.27**  | 0.30      | 0.30      |
|          | I.32.17   | 0.13      | **0.74**| 1.62      | 0.97      | 1.17      |
|          | I.48.20   | 0.00      | **0.00**| **0.00**  | **0.00**  | **0.00**  |
|          | II.11.27  | 0.00      | **0.00**| **0.00**  | **0.00**  | **0.00**  |
|          | II.11.28  | 0.00      | **0.00**| **0.00**  | **0.00**  | **0.00**  |
|          | III.9.52  | 7.34      | 44.67   | 50.40     | 44.32     | **36.38** |
|          | III.10.19 | 0.38      | 0.71    | 0.76      | **0.47**  | 0.68      |

**Table 3.** Median NMSE values for extrapolation datasets with 30% additional noise.

|           |           | w/o. info | w. info |           |           |           |
|           |           | GP        | GPSC    | NSGA-II   | CombOpt   | CombPes   |
|-----------|-----------|-----------|---------|-----------|-----------|-----------|
| noise 30% | I.6.20    | 8.95      | 10.42   | **10.03** | 11.32     | **10.03** |
|           | I.9.18    | 29.23     | 17.95   | **5.95**  | 10.78     | 7.51      |
|           | I.15.3x   | 5.64      | 4.39    | **2.88**  | 7.21      | 5.41      |
|           | I.32.17   | 5.45      | 7.91    | 8.47      | **6.83**  | 7.44      |
|           | I.48.20   | 2.97      | **0.81**| **0.81**  | 1.02      | 0.86      |
|           | II.11.27  | 1.94      | 2.10    | 2.19      | 2.21      | **2.09**  |
|           | II.11.28  | 2.22      | 0.46    | 0.37      | 0.42      | **0.35**  |
|           | III.9.52  | 13.25     | 51.96   | 54.98     | 54.94     | **54.03** |
|           | III.10.19 | 6.12      | 4.97    | 4.88      | **4.72**  | 5.02      |

nent. The proposed combined single-objective approach performs slightly worse than the multi-objective approach but still generates many conformant models.

We also investigated the mean runtime over all independent runs for each algorithm. The overall best runtime had SCSR with 329.65 s, followed by the proposed combined approach with 391.72 s and the multi-objective NSGA-II approach with 470.00 s. The results show that using soft constraints has a higher runtime than using hard constraints. We can also see that using a single-objective approach using soft constraints as proposed in the paper will outperform the multi-objective algorithm by roughly 20% in runtime.

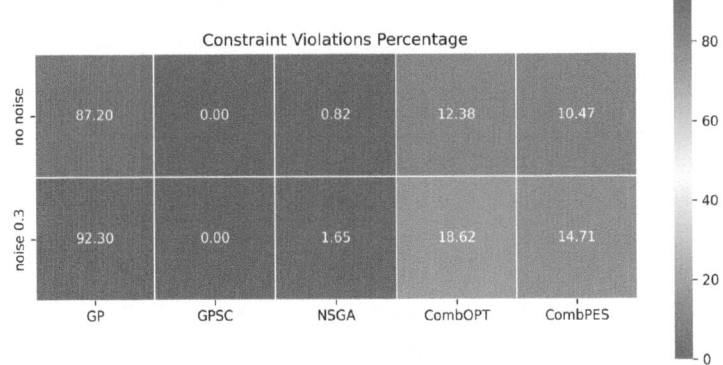

**Fig. 2.** Average constraint violations over 30 independent runs for all instances and algorithms.

## 5   Summary

In this paper, we proposed a new method for shape constraint evaluation. The approach combines a dynamic constraint evaluation with an error prediction such as NMSE. The combination of these two objectives allows us to use single-objective algorithms. We implemented and tested different methods for the dynamic weight adaption for this methodology. This dynamic approach allows us to perform a broad first search followed by a depth search on later generations. This enables us to first find a large variety of well-fitting models and then limit the selection to models that conform to the expected behavior.

The proposed approach was implemented in the heuristic and evolutionary algorithm framework (HeuristicLab) and tested on a selected set of instances from the AI Feynman symbolic regression database. These equations are taken from physics textbooks, which allows us to extract monotonicity constraints by sampling the real expression.

The proposed approach was tested in conjunction with 3 different algorithms, where GP without any information served as a baseline for the prediction error, GP with hard constraints served as a baseline for shape-constrained regression single-objective approach and NSGA-II served as a baseline for a multi-objective evaluation of shape constraints. We tested the approach on 2 different settings once without and once with 30% of noise. We discovered that the new combined approach was able to compete and even slightly outperform the multi-objective approach in terms of prediction error. Whereas, the multi-objective approach was better when it comes to constraint satisfaction. The hard-constrained GP approach was worse at finding models with low prediction errors but allowed us to only find valid models. For the no-noise instances, GP without any information showed the best prediction errors but violated almost all known constraints. On the noisy set, GP was not superior in finding well-fitting models anymore.

Overall, the most stable approach in terms of model quality and constraint satisfaction is still the multi-objective approach. However, we showed that the combined approach can be used to test different algorithms and has a better runtime performance. Further, we showed that hard constraints work only on easier instances and fall off when dealing with noisy datasets.

**Acknowledgement.** This work was carried out within the Dissertationsprogramm der Fachhochschule OÖ *#50549324 Integration von Domänenwissen in Symbolische Regression (IDSR)*, funded by the Austrian Research Promotion Agency FFG.

F.O.F. is supported by Conselho Nacional de Desenvolvimento Científico e Tecnológico (CNPq) through the grant 301596/2022-0.

Part of this work was done within the project "Secure Prescriptive Analytics", which is funded by the state of Upper Austria as part of the program "#upperVISION2030".

# References

1. Błądek, I., Krawiec, K.: Solving symbolic regression problems with formal constraints. In: Proceedings of the Genetic and Evolutionary Computation Conference, pp. 977–984. GECCO '19, Association for Computing Machinery, New York, NY, USA (2019). https://doi.org/10.1145/3321707.3321743
2. Cuomo, S., Di Cola, V.S., Giampaolo, F., Rozza, G., Raissi, M., Piccialli, F.: Scientific machine learning through physics-informed neural networks: where we are and what's next. J. Sci. Comput. **92**(3), 88 (2022)
3. Gupta, M., Louidor, E., Mangylov, O., Morioka, N., Narayan, T., Zhao, S.: Multidimensional shape constraints. In: International Conference on Machine Learning, pp. 3918–3928. PMLR (2020)
4. Haider, C., de Franca, F., Burlacu, B., Kronberger, G.: Shape-constrained multiobjective genetic programming for symbolic regression. Appl. Soft Comput. **132**, 109855 (2023)
5. Hall, G.: Optimization over Nonnegative and Convex Polynomials With and Without Semidefinite Programming. Phd thesis, Princeton University (2018)
6. Hickey, T., Ju, Q., Van Emden, M.H.: Interval arithmetic: from principles to implementation. J. ACM **48**(5), 1038–1068 (2001). https://doi.org/10.1145/502102.502106
7. Koza, J.R., Poli, R.: Genetic programming. In: Search Methodologies, pp. 127–164. Springer (2005)
8. Kronberger, G., de Franca, F.O., Burlacu, B., Haider, C., Kommenda, M.: Shape-constrained symbolic regression-improving extrapolation with prior knowledge. Evol. Comput. **30**(1), 75–98 (2022). https://doi.org/10.1162/evco_a_00294
9. Poli, R., Langdon, W.B., McPhee, N.F., Koza, J.R.: A field guide to genetic programming. Lulu. com (2008)
10. Rudin, C.: Stop explaining black box machine learning models for high stakes decisions and use interpretable models instead. Nat. Mach. Intell. **1**(5), 206–215 (2019)

11. Rudin, C., Chen, C., Chen, Z., Huang, H., Semenova, L., Zhong, C.: Interpretable machine learning: fundamental principles and 10 grand challenges. Stat. Surv. **16**, 1–85 (2022)
12. Udrescu, S.M., Tegmark, M.: AI Feynman: a physics-inspired method for symbolic regression. Sci. Adv. **6**(16), eaay2631 (2020). https://doi.org/10.1126/sciadv.aay2631
13. Willard, J., Jia, X., Xu, S., Steinbach, M., Kumar, V.: Integrating physics-based modeling with machine learning: A survey. arXiv preprint arXiv:2003.04919 **1**(1), 1–34 (2020)

# Re-evaluation in Dynamic Tree-Search with Backtracking from Known Solutions

Philipp Fleck[1,2]([✉]) [iD], Philipp Neuhauser[1,2] [iD], Sebastian Leitner[1,2] [iD],
and Stefan Wagner[1,2] [iD]

[1] Heuristic and Evolutionary Algorithms Laboratory, University of Applied Sciences
Upper Austria, Wels, Austria
philipp.fleck@fh-hagenberg.at
[2] Josef Ressel Center for Adaptive Optimization in Dynamic Environments,
University of Applied Sciences Upper Austria, Wels, Austria

**Abstract.** In dynamic environments, solutions may become invalid during or after the execution of an optimization algorithm due to changing circumstances, requiring the adaptation or creation of new solutions. This paper uses the hot-storage area of a steel processing plant as a dynamic environment, where the optimization task involves creating lot-assignments of steel slabs for efficient transportation. The lot-assignment problem is represented as a search tree, where slabs are gradually assigned to new or existing lots as the tree is traversed. Unforeseen events in the dynamic hot-storage area can render existing lot-assignments invalid or make them less effective. Instead of completely re-running a tree-search algorithm in response to such dynamic events, we propose a backtracking strategy that uses information from outdated solutions. This strategy involves constructing a backtracking chain to check the validity of the lot-assignments used to construct the outdated solution and to identifying potential restart points for partial search spaces. Through experiments, we show the performance and reliability of various tree-search algorithms under different runtime budgets, with and without backtracking-based restart strategies. Our results strongly suggest that using information from a previous solution significantly enhances algorithm performance to identify valid solutions compared to a complete rerun. Additionally, using backtracking within the same runtime budget as a complete rerun can also improve solution quality.

**Keywords:** Dynamic Optimization · Tree-Search · Lot-Assignment

## 1 Motivation

Dynamic optimization problems [4] in industrial applications present numerous challenges because solution candidates may become obsolete due to changes in the environment. Additionally, different circumstances require different optimization strategies, which can also change dynamically. In this paper, we use as

A. Quesada-Arencibia et al. (Eds.): EUROCAST 2024, LNCS 15172, pp. 77–89, 2025.
https://doi.org/10.1007/978-3-031-82949-9_8

an example a lot-assignment problem from the steel industry [2], where the goal is to efficiently group steel slabs into lots for joint transportation.

Figure 1 shows a sample section of the *hot-storage area*, where steel slabs are continuously produced in casters (the incoming area) and must exit the hot-storage via handovers (the outgoing area). The slabs come out of the casters one at the time and can then be stacked on buffer stacks (sorting area) or directly put onto handover stacks. In a real scenario, the hot-storage consist of six casters, approx. 20 handover stacks (serviced by different types of vehicles) and almost a 100 buffer stacks.

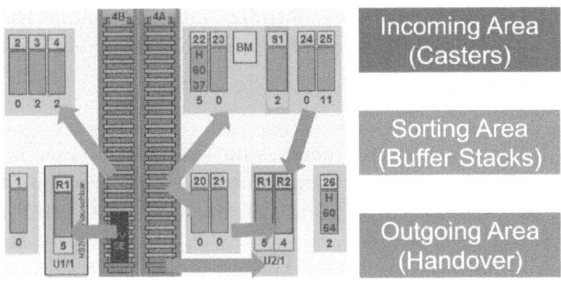

**Fig. 1.** A schematic view of the hot-storage with casters, handovers and buffer stacks.

To move slabs in the hot-storage, a stacking algorithm creates movement requests for a crane, which are then executed by human crane operators [7]. Because slabs are transported from the hot storage in batches, we perform a *lot-assignment* before stacking that groups slabs that should be transported together. For example, if several slabs are going to be processed in the rolling mill within a similar time frame, transporting them together in a lot greatly increases vehicle utilization and reduces the need for additional restacking at the rolling mill, especially if the lot is already properly sorted upon delivery. Similarly, when slabs are transported to the slab yard for storage, slabs with similar characteristics that are likely to be used together in the future should also be grouped into a lot.

Building suitable lots can be challenging because grouping and stacking are subject to various *constraints* such as weight and length restrictions, or various other limitations and optimization goals. Since the casters in the hot-storage continuously producing slabs, the lot-assignment problem is also a *dynamic problem*. Therefore, any algorithm optimizing lot-assignments must either be able to incorporate dynamic changes during the algorithm's execution, or must be fast enough top re-execute when dynamic changes occur. Additionally, to produce stable movement requests for crane operators, the algorithm should aim to produce robust results so that planned movement requests do not change drastically when a small unplanned change appears. For example, a slab may arrive at the caster defective and require additional, unplanned handling. Therefore, this slab needs to be transported to a different location for this treatment, while the lot for which this slab was planned now has a vacant slot that can be filled up with another suitable slab.

Currently, the lot-assignment problem is encoded as a search tree [6,9], where efficient tree-search algorithms can be used to efficiently traverse the tree and identify good lot-assignments. A single node in the tree contains a list of unassigned slabs, that have not yet allocated to a lot, and a list of slabs that have already been partitioned into lots, as shown in Fig. 2. Each child node represents a choice for assigning of one of the unassigned slabs to an existing lot, or to a new lot. Any node that still has some unassigned slabs is a partial solution, while the leaf nodes with no more unassigned slabs are final solutions of the lot-assignment problem.

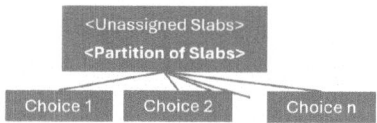

**Fig. 2.** A tree node representing a (partial) solution, containing unassigned lots and already partitioned slabs.

An example of a tree that builds lots for four slabs called A, B, C and D is shown in Fig. 3. It starts at the root node, with all four slabs unassigned, where no lots have been formed yet. At the first layer, we have four different options to create a new single-slab lot with any of the four slabs. At the second layer, in the case where we created a single-slab lot A, we now have the options of either adding any of the remaining slabs B, C or D to the existing lot with A, or creating a new, second single-slab-lot with any of the remaining slabs. This process continues until all the slabs are assigned to lots, creating leaf-nodes with no unassigned slots.

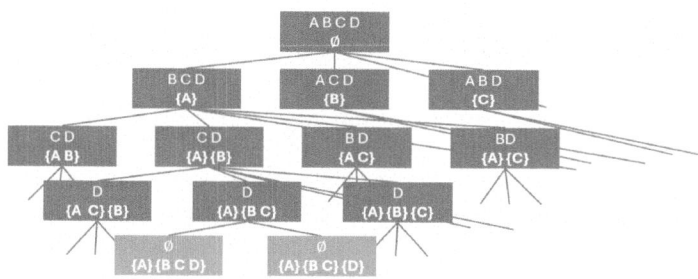

**Fig. 3.** An incomplete example of the search-tree for partitioning slabs into lots.

A solution (final or partial) can be used as input to the stacking algorithm to create the movement request. By simulating the movement requests, we can also obtain the *makespan* for a solution, which measures the time it takes to process all movement requests, including waiting times for future slabs to be cast and waiting times for the arrivals of transport vehicles. This simulated makespan can then be used to evaluate the quality of a solution.

In this simplified overview, we have omitted some details that differ from the hot-storage in the real world. For example, in addition to partitioning the slabs, each lot is assigned to a handover location where the lot is placed on for transport. There are also additional sequencing requirements that dictate the importance of considering the order of the slabs within each lot. We also need to handle previous lot-assignments from older algorithm runs to provide robust solutions to crane operators where we do not change movement requests that have already been sent. Nevertheless, this simplified version already shows the complexity and size of the search space of the lot-assignment problem. To estimate the size of the search space, we can use the Bell-number [8] to obtain the number of possible partitions of a set (of slabs). While for the example with four slabs we have only 15 different partitions (only leaf nodes, not counting partial solutions), a set of 10 slabs already has over 100000 different partitions, and 50 slabs, which is a reasonable amount in a real-world case, has about $10^{47}$ different partitions.

Since the total tree size of the lot-assignment problem can be quite large, efficient traversal of the tree is important for any tree-search algorithm. Therefore, the tree-search algorithm relies on the premise that the children of a tree node are ordered such a way that those that appear first are more likely to lead to better solutions. This order is given by various rules from domain experts, along with a set of constraints that must be satisfied to form a valid lot.

While it is possible to rerun the entire algorithm when the dynamic environment changes, this is not the most optimal approach, despite the efficiency of tree-search algorithms. In the remainder of the paper, our focus shifts to the dynamic aspects of the lot-assignment problem, with the goal of enhancing the tree-search algorithms to improve performance. Our strategy is to use existing solutions from previous runs to avoid a complete rerun of the algorithm.

## 2   Problem Description

The original lot-assignment problem is already defined based on a dynamic environment, the hot-storage area. Slabs are continuously cast with some unpredictability in the exact properties of the slab, which can sometimes lead to additional, unplanned processing steps of slabs. Vehicles and other aspects are also influenced by various uncertainties. In this paper, we add two additional factors to the optimization, which do not come from the uncertainty of the environment, but from the changing optimization strategies of a human operator on various goals of the hot-storage. For example, constraints may become more relaxed when the hot-storage is in danger of overflowing, or optimization objectives may shift to accommodate a target hot-storage fill level.

To influence optimization strategies, the operator now has control over

– the *search heuristics* defining which lots are more likely to produce better solutions and
– the *constraints* defining which lots are valid.

Changing the search heuristics alters the order of child nodes for a given tree node, and thus adjusts the guidance for the tree-search toward preferred lot-assignments. Changing constraints can alter the validity of lot assignments. For example, relaxing a weight constraint can make previously invalid lots valid under the new conditions. Similarly, previously valid solutions may become invalid after a rule change.

Figure 4 shows an example of changing heuristics and constraints. The nodes contain the quality (maximizing), with the quality increasing only towards the leaf nodes. It's important to note that while the objective value tends to be higher for the first child nodes of a parent, this is not a strict rule, as the heuristic only guides the search. Better solutions may be found through non-greedy approaches. Also, invalid nodes are still shown in this representation, even though they would not be encountered by the tree-search algorithm during traversal.

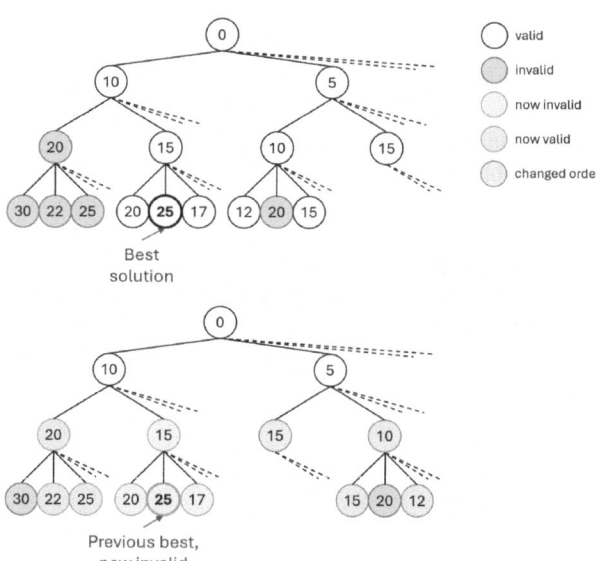

**Fig. 4.** Top: The original search space with the best solution found with objective 25. Bottom: After the validity and order of some child nodes changed, the previous best solution is now invalid.

In the example in Fig. 4, the validity of certain nodes change, and the previous best solution is now invalid, requiring a rerun of the tree-search. While a simple rerun of an algorithm is possible, it would waste the information generated by the previous run that identified the old best solution. For example, if we recognize that the right subtree, starting with a node of objective 5, is less promising than the one starting with 10, it is more efficient to concentrate on exploring the left subtree with higher quality than to rerun the algorithm entirely.

## 3   Method

As discussed in the previous section, completely rerunning the tree-search after nodes validities change wastes information from previous runs. In this paper, our approach to quickly identifying an alternative solution is a simple *backtracking* approach. Since a solution (a leaf node) is essentially defined by the path through the tree search space, backtracking can be performed by going back to the parent nodes up to the root node. During backtracking, the validity of nodes can be re-checked, building a *backtracking chain* of nodes with given validity information after the dynamic change.

Moving up a search node to its parent can be done very fast. In a naive approach, the parent solution can be cached during the search, which can lead to high memory consumption for large search trees. Instead, nodes can have explicit "apply" and "undo" operations, which mutate a node to become a child node or the parent node [1]. In the case of the lot-assignment problem, this can be accomplished by building a stack of assigned slabs during the apply operation, and then removing slabs from the lot-assignments and reintegrating them into the pool of unassigned slabs during an undo operation.

After obtaining the backtracking chain, the next step is to assess the validity of the nodes within the chain and select a node along the chain that could serve as restarting point. Of course, to get a valid solution in the end, a restarting node must also be valid, along with all of its parents up to the root. If one of the parents in the chain were invalid, the whole subtree in the search space would actually be invalid. Therefore, the simplest way of selecting a viable restarting node is to select the node closest to the old solution that has continuous validity up the parents to the root node, as shown in Fig. 5.

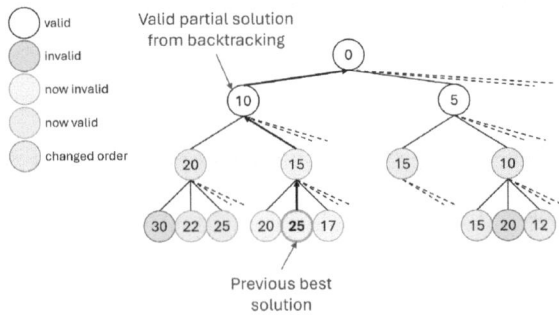

**Fig. 5.** Backtracking from now invalid solutions to the closest valid node.

In the example shown, backtracking is started from the previous node with quality 25 to the root node. The best valid node is selected with quality 10, since it is closest to the previous solution and is still valid. After a suitable restart node is found after backtracking, we can use this node to restart the tree-search from this node, as shown in Fig. 6. After the restart, a new solution is found, again with quality 25.

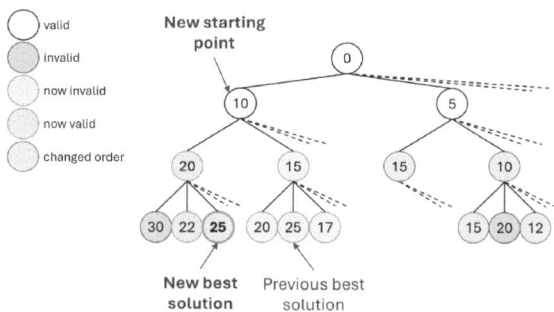

**Fig. 6.** Tree-search with restart after backtracking to find a new valid solution.

If we compare the *restart* of the algorithm with a starting point given by the backtracking with a complete *rerun* of the algorithm, we can see that the whole search area given by the subtree with quality 5 is completely omitted by the search since we found a valid starting point closer to the previous best solution. In the rest of this paper, we will continue to use the term "restart" when we mean restarting from a given solution from the backtracking, and we will use the term "rerun" when we mean a complete new execution of the tree-search algorithm from the root node.

This simple backtracking strategy does not guarantee that the best solution will be found after backtracking. For example, consider a slightly different scenario in Fig. 7, where relative to the previous best solution, going up two parents, the first child (20) is now valid after the change. After backtracking, this means that the node with quality 15 is the new starting point, which would immediately return the child node with objective 20 as the best solution, not knowing that another subtree that is now valid would contain a better solution with quality 25.

To counteract the potential trap in a small search space with only local optima, we can break out by further "climbing up" towards the next valid solution in the backtracking chain. For example, after a restarted algorithm finishes, we can also use the parent node of the starting point and restart the algorithm again, now with a larger search space. To avoid wasting computational resources, it is also important to keep track of already evaluated subtrees, so that an additional restart from a different starting point does not search the same subtree again. In this way, multiple restarts along the backtracking chain can be done

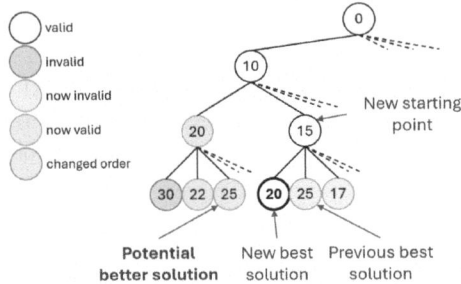

**Fig. 7.** Backtracking to the closest valid solution as a new starting point may overlook other viable solutions in the search tree with better objectives.

until a total number of evaluations is reached, similar to any termination criterion a normal tree-search would have.

## 4    Experiments

To compare the effectiveness and potential runtime savings of using backtracking to obtain restart points for the tree-search, we compare the following strategies:

- *Complete rerun* means that no backtracking is used and a new tree search algorithm is started at the root node.
- *Single restart* means that backtracking is used to find the closest valid node to the previous solution.
- *Multiple restarts* means that multiple restarts are performed along the backtracking chain, starting with the closest valid solution to the previous one and going up to the root node, until a certain runtime budget is exceeded.

To analyze the results, we measure the solution *quality* and the *number of node expansions* as a measure of algorithm performance and computational effort. The quality of a solution is measured by simulating the crane movements resulting from the given lot-assignments and then running the stacking algorithm to obtain the total makespan, where a lower makespan is preferable. The number of node expansions serves as a measure of how efficiently the tree-search algorithm traversed the search space, with fewer expansions being preferred.

### 4.1    Parameters

To compare different tree-search algorithms, we use the following 5 algorithms:

- *Depth-first search* is used as a baseline, which always selects the first choice.
- *Beam search* is a breath-first search, where only a fixed number of nodes per layer are kept to progress the search [3]. We use a beam-with of 100 nodes.
- *Monotonic beam search* modifies the beam search to ensure that the quality does not deteriorate with higher beam-width [5].

- *Rake search* uses a look-ahead strategy to decide which node to traverse next. A breadth-first search selects a number of nodes (the rake-width), then initiates depth-first searches for all selected nodes until leaf nodes are reached. The rake-width is set to 100 for this experiment.
- The *pilot method* [10] also uses a look-ahead strategy. Again, depth-first searches are initiated until leaf are encountered, but all child nodes of the current nodes are used as starting points.

As for variations of the actual problem, we have 150 different scenarios for the hot-storage lot-assignment optimization problem, with different states of the hot-storage (current number and location of slabs, different slab casting forecasts, different vehicle availabilities, etc.). We also use different maximum number of nodes expansion as termination of 1000, 10000 and 100000 to assert the viability of backtracking for low, medium and high computational budgets. Note that although a runtime budget is given at with fixed number of node expansions, some of the algorithms may take longer than this maximum. This is most pronounced for algorithms with look-ahead strategies (rake search and pilot method), as look-aheads are waited for before the runtime budget is checked, and therefore these algorithms will often exceed the runtime budget. Each combination of scenario, algorithm and maximum nodes is repeated five times, despite the deterministic nature of the algorithms, because their parallel implementations introduce a degree of nondeterminism.

## 4.2   Results

First, we look at the overall performance of the algorithm runs for the complete reruns, single restarts and multiple restarts variants separately in Fig. 8, Fig. 9 and Fig. 10 respectively. The charts show the success rate as a bar chart, i.e. if a valid solution was found over the 5 repetitions and 150 different scenarios, the quality of the returned solution shown as a violin chart and the nodes visited also as a violin chart.

For the complete reruns, shown in Fig. 8, it can immediately be seen that the success rate of both beam search variants is very low for a runtime budget of maximum 10000 node expansions, meaning that the budget is too low (and/or beam-with too large) for these algorithms to find a valid leaf node before the runtime budget is exceeded. In terms of quality, all algorithms produced comparable results, with rake search and pilot method usually identifying slightly better solutions. In terms of using and respecting the runtime budget, depth-first search always used the exact number of node expansions allowed, while rake search tended to overshoot the budget for lower maximum number of nodes. For higher maximum number of nodes, the pilot method usually does not even fully utilize the allowed number of node expansions and terminates earlier while still yielding good results, making it the most efficient of the presented algorithms.

When performing a single restart, as shown in Fig. 9, we see that the overall success rate is very low, indicating that although a valid partial solution was found during backtracking, the corresponding subtree in the search space did not

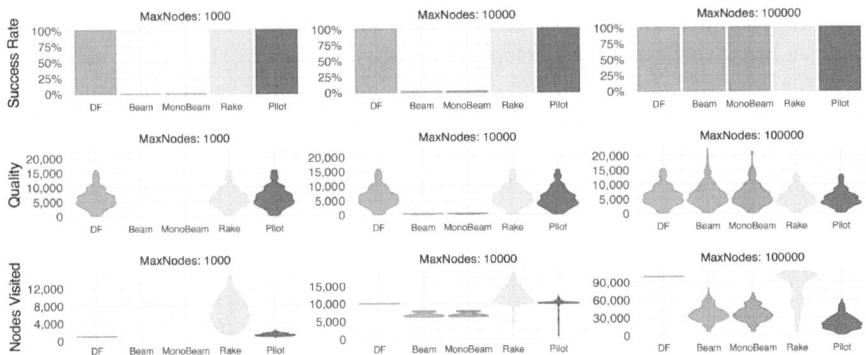

**Fig. 8.** Overview of the algorithm results after complete reruns (from the root node).

contain a valid leaf node or it was hard to find, so the algorithm failed in more than half of the cases. The qualities of the found solutions are comparable to a complete rerun, again with rake search and pilot method often identifying slightly better solutions. The number of visited nodes are usually very low, meaning that valid solutions were often found very close to the previous solution, or even the previous solution itself was still valid. The low number of visited nodes may also caused the low success rate, indicating that the backtracking resulted in a restarting node very close to the original solution, meaning that the resulting search space is very limited.

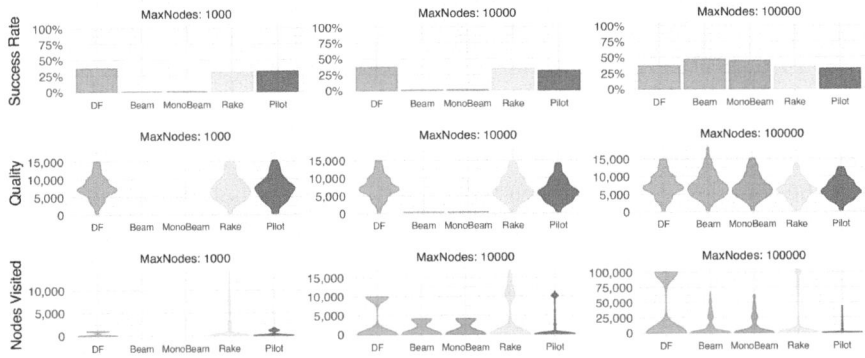

**Fig. 9.** Overview of the algorithm runs with a single restart from the closest node to the previous solution.

When performing multiple restarts, as shown in Fig. 10, we can observe a significantly higher success rate and a better utilization of the runtime budget. The result also shows that depth-first, rake search and pilot method were able to find valid solutions with good quality even with a small number of maximum nodes. This strongly suggests that backtracking with multiple restarts and a tight runtime budget is viable for quickly identifying new valid solutions. Regarding the used runtime budget, we also see that with multiple restarts all algorithms tend to better utilize the available runtime budget and thus explore more of the search space than their original counterpart with a complete rerun.

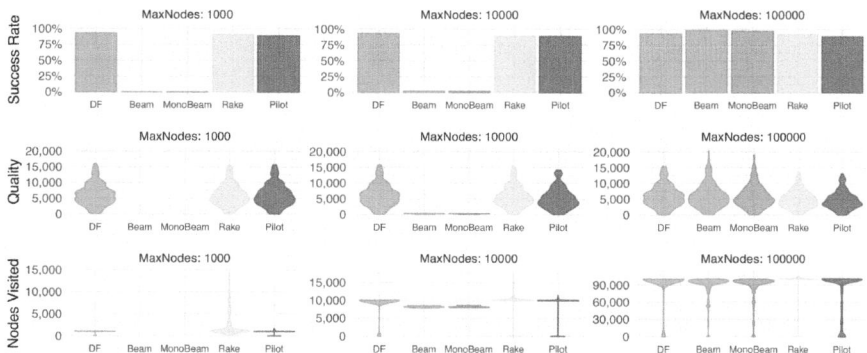

**Fig. 10.** Overview of algorithms runs with multiple restarts along the backtracking chain.

In the following, we look at the quality improvements and reductions in visited nodes of the single restart and multiple restarts strategies compared to complete reruns. Since the overall goal of backtracking and restarting is to be able to quickly find a valid solution after a rule change has invalidated the previous solution, we hope to show that backtracking with restarts provides runtime benefits with similar qualities, or that it provides quality benefits when the same runtime budget is used along with the reuse of information that backtracking provides.

Figure 11 again shows the success rates of single and multiple restarts after backtracking, but also shows the quality improvements over the complete rerun (higher is better) and the reductions in visited nodes (higher is better).

In a scenario with limited time budget (1000 max nodes), both the rake search and the pilot method produce comparable results, often leading to either better results or no improvement over a complete rerun. Cases of worse solutions than a complete rerun are rare. Meanwhile, these results are achieved with a significant reduction in visited nodes, suggesting that with a low budget, an informed restart via backtracking helps to quickly identify valid solutions. Depth-first search predominantly yields similar quality results compared to complete restarts.

In the medium time budget scenario (10000 max nodes), both the rake search and the pilot method show significant improvements in result quality for both restarting strategies. However, the reduction in visited nodes is more pronounced for the single restart strategy, at the cost of a lower success rate.

At higher runtime budgets (100000 max nodes), lower success rates for single restarts are also observed. However, in this scenario, the quality tends to improve

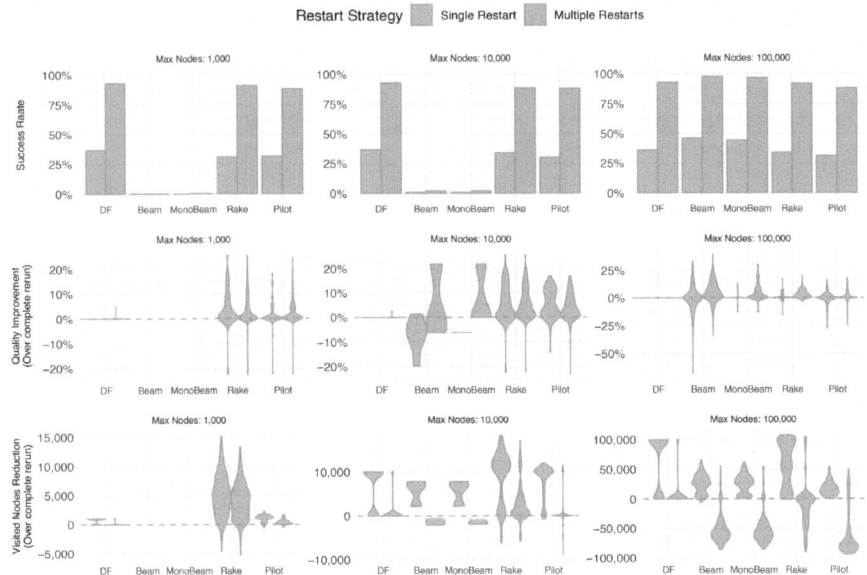

**Fig. 11.** Comparing the quality improvements and reductions in node evaluations of restart strategies compared to complete algorithm reruns.

further, but with runtime savings for single restarts and a significant increase in runtime for multiple restarts.

## 5  Summary and Conclusion

In this paper, we presented the lot-assignment problem as a use case for performing backtracking and intelligent restarts of tree-search algorithms after a rule-set change causes solutions to become invalid. We motivated the need for an alternative to a complete rerun of the tree-search algorithm, which would waste valuable information from previous runs by losing information about promising areas in the search space where the last solution came from. Therefore, we introduced a backtracking strategy that retraces the trajectory of a solution within the search space to determine viable restart points for the algorithm, limiting the search regions to promising areas. The experiments conducted in this paper were designed to show the quality improvement and/or reductions in node expansions when using single or multiple restart strategies compared to a complete rerun. We evaluated five different tree-search algorithms on a variety of problem instances with different runtime budget settings.

The results show that rake search and the pilot method work very well with backtracking, as they were able to quickly find an alternative valid solution with similar or better quality with very limited runtime budgets. By allowing higher runtime budgets, the qualities can be further improved. Performing single or multiple restarts mainly effect the success rates (approx. 35% for single restarts and approx. 95% for multiple restarts) and the runtime improvements (decreasing for single restarts and increasing for multiple restarts). As for the algorithms used, rake search and the pilot method worked very well, with the pilot method usually having better runtime performance, while the beam search variants performed quite poorly in limited runtime scenarios. Depth-first search also managed to identify valid solutions quickly, but without any quality benefits.

The selection mechanism of restart points from the backtracking chain used in this paper was very simple, since we only considered at the validity and the distance to the original solutions. However, one could also consider the quality of partial solutions or bounding information to better select starting points for a restart attempt. Also, we had fixed settings for the tree-search algorithm, regardless of the available runtime budgets. By better tuning the algorithm parameters for a backtracking restart, additional performance benefits could be achieved. In conclusion, the simple strategies presented in this paper worked very well, but there is still potential in applying intelligent restarts in dynamic tree-search scenarios.

**Acknowledgments.** The financial support from the Austrian Federal Ministry for Digital and Economic Affairs and the National Foundation for Research, Technology and Development and the Christian Doppler Research Association is gratefully acknowledged.

**Disclosure of Interests.** The authors have no competing interests to declare that are relevant to the content of this article.

# References

1. Beham, A., Leitner, S.: TreesearchLib. https://github.com/heal-research/TreesearchLib. Accessed 29 May 2024
2. Beham, A., Raggl, S., Hauder, V.A., Karder, J., Wagner, S., Affenzeller, M.: Performance, quality, and control in steel logistics 4.0. Procedia Manufacturing **42**, 429–433 (2020)
3. Bisiani, R.: Encyclopedia of artificial intelligence, chapter beam search (1987)
4. Cruz, C., González, J.R., Pelta, D.A.: Optimization in dynamic environments: a survey on problems, methods and measures. Soft. Comput. **15**, 1427–1448 (2011)
5. Lemons, S., López, C.L., Holte, R.C., Ruml, W.: Beam search: faster and monotonic. In: Proceedings of the International Conference on Automated Planning and Scheduling. vol. 32, pp. 222–230 (2022)
6. Pearl, J.: Heuristics: intelligent search strategies for computer problem solving. Addison-Wesley Longman Publishing Co., Inc (1984)
7. Raggl, S., Beham, A., Tricoire, F., Affenzeller, M.: Solving a real world steel stacking problem. Int. J. Serv. Comput. Oriented Manufact. **3**(2–3), 94–108 (2018)
8. Riordan, J.: An introduction to combinatorial analysis (2014)
9. Russell, S.J., Norvig, P.: Artificial intelligence: a modern approach. Pearson (2016)
10. Voß, S., Fink, A., Duin, C.: Looking ahead with the pilot method. Ann. Oper. Res. **136**, 285–302 (2005)

# Application of Adapt-CMSA to the Electric Vehicle Routing Problem with Simultaneous Pickup and Deliveries

Mehmet Anıl Akbay[1](✉)(iD), Christian Blum[1](iD), and Can Berk Kalayci[2](iD)

[1] Artificial Intelligence Research Institute (IIIA-CSIC), Campus UAB,
Bellaterra, Spain
makbay@iiia.csic.es, christian.blum@csic.es
[2] Department of Industrial Engineering, Pamukkale University, Denizli, Turkey
cbkalayci@pau.edu.tr

**Abstract.** The Vehicle Routing Problem (VRP) has long been a cornerstone in combinatorial optimization, aiming to optimize the fleet of vehicles delivering goods in a transportation network. With the global shift towards sustainability, Electric Vehicles (EVs) have emerged as a green logistics alternative, leading to the Electric Vehicle Routing Problem with Simultaneous Pickup and Delivery (EVRP-SPD). This problem variant introduces the complexities of EV constraints, such as battery limitations and recharging necessities, coupled with handling delivery and pickup demands simultaneously during a single customer visit. This paper presents the application of the recent hybrid metaheuristic Construct, Merge, Solve & Adapt (CMSA) to the EVRP-SPD. Our self-adaptive version of CMSA, combined with a set covering-based mathematical formulation, offers a promising approach to efficiently tackle larger instances of the problem, aiming to provide high-quality solutions.

**Keywords:** electric vehicle routing · simultaneous pickup and delivery · construct · merge · solve & adapt · set covering

## 1 Introduction

The Vehicle Routing Problem (VRP) stands as one of the most studied combinatorial optimization problems, with its roots dating back to the 1950s [5]. The primary objective of the VRP is to determine the most efficient routes for a fleet of vehicles to deliver goods to a group of customers. As the global emphasis on sustainability and environmental conservation has grown, the logistics sector has begun to adapt and transform its operations to align with this trend. Introducing Electric Vehicles (EVs) into the logistics landscape has been a significant step in this direction, offering a more environmentally friendly alternative to traditional combustion engine vehicles.

In this line, the Electric Vehicle Routing Problem with Simultaneous Pickup and Delivery (EVRP-SPD) was proposed as a complex variant of the traditional

© The Author(s), under exclusive license to Springer Nature Switzerland AG 2025
A. Quesada-Arencibia et al. (Eds.): EUROCAST 2024, LNCS 15172, pp. 90–106, 2025.
https://doi.org/10.1007/978-3-031-82949-9_9

VRP, accounting for the unique constraints of EVs, such as a limited battery capacity and the need for recharging. Furthermore, the simultaneous pickup and delivery aspect requires that each customer's demand for both delivery and pickup be satisfied at the same time, adding another layer of complexity to the problem. Note that simultaneous pickup and delivery operations can lead to significant cost savings and operational efficiencies, particularly in managing vehicle capacity. However, these operations also require more intricate planning and optimization. However, there exists a gap in the literature when it comes to efficient solution methodologies for this problem, especially when large-scale instances are concerned. Traditional optimization methods often struggle with the problem's complexity.

**Our Contribution.** Our first contribution is the formulation of the EVRP-SPD as a mixed integer linear programming (MILP) model, which can then be solved by employing integer linear programming (ILP) solvers like CPLEX or Gurobi. However, our computational experiments revealed that the complexity of the problem makes it challenging for solvers like CPLEX 20.1 to achieve optimal solutions for even small-sized instances. Therefore, we developed a self-adaptive variant (Adapt-CMSA) of the Construct, Merge, Solve & Adapt (CMSA) algorithm [2], which is a hybrid metaheuristic that has been applied to a range of different combinatorial optimization problems in recent years; see, for example, [7,10]. At its core, this algorithm iteratively solves sub-instances of the main problem instance obtained by merging heuristically generated solutions. This approach solves sub-instances by a set covering-based mathematical formulation, enabling efficient handling of larger sub-instances. The performance of the proposed algorithm is tested against probabilistic runs of two construction heuristics—the Clark&Wright Savings algorithm and a sequential insertion algorithm—and 12 different variants of variable neighborhood search (VNS) algorithms from [23]. Computational results reveal that Adapt-CMSA significantly outperforms the competitors.

**Related Literature.** VRPs have been a focal point of research since the foundational work of [5]. Over the years, numerous extensions of the original problem were introduced to cater to real-world constraints. Comprehensive overviews are provided in [11,22] and a classification in [18]. Metaheuristic-based solutions for such problems are extensively reviewed by [8].

The rise of environmental concerns has shifted the research focus towards Green Vehicle Routing Problems (GVRPs), particularly those involving electric vehicles (EVRPs). Comprehensive reviews on this topic are provided by [1,16]. The seminal work of Conrad et al. [4] laid the foundation for optimizing routes for rechargeable vehicles. Subsequent studies, such as those by [9] and [21], introduced variations and solution methodologies, considering constraints like time windows and vehicle capacities.

Recent research has addressed EVRPs from various aspects. For instance, [12] analyzed the effects of partial battery recharging, while [17] emphasized the non-linear charging time of batteries. The energy consumption of EVs, influenced by many factors, has been challenging. [19] addressed this by considering energy consumption uncertainty. Other notable contributions include the works of [13], which used a non-approximated charging function, and [14], which estimated energy consumption considering various factors. More recent studies, such as [6] and [20], have proposed both exact and heuristic algorithms, with the latter introducing a multi-depot GVRP.

## 2   Problem Description

The EVRP-SPD involves a set of $N$ customers indexed by $V = \{1, \ldots, N\}$, and a set of charging stations $F$. A charging station can be visited multiple times. Therefore, we defined a set of dummy charging stations, $F'$. Indexes 0 and $N+1$ are used for the same depot, representing the starting and ending locations. The set $V' = V \cup F'$ contains all customers and dummy charging stations, with the sub-indexes 0, $N+1$, or both, indicating the inclusion of the respective instances of the depot. Based on these sets and notations, the EVRP-SPD can be defined on a complete, directed graph $G(V'_{0,N+1}, A)$. $A = \{(i,j)|i,j \in V'_{0,N+1}, i \neq j\}$ is the set of arcs where each arc has a distance $d_{ij}$ and travel time $t_{ij}$. The constant $h$ represents the energy consumed per unit distance traveled by an EV. A fleet of EVs with identical loading capacity $C$ and battery capacity $Q$ are initially positioned at the depot. When an EV visits a customer, it must simultaneously satisfy its delivery demand $q_i > 0$ and pickup demand $p_i > 0$. Furthermore, when the EV stops at a charging station, its battery is charged with a constant charging rate of $g > 0$. In the MILP model formulation for the problem, we use the following decision variables:

- Binary variable $x_{ij}$: indicates whether or not arc $(i,j)$ forms part of a vehicle route.
- $\tau_i$: service start time for each each node $i \in V'_{0,N+1}$ visited by the EV.
- $y_i$ and $Y_i$: these variables keep track of the battery's state of charge upon arrival and departure at each node $i \in V'_{0,N+1}$, respectively.
- $u_{ij}$ and $v_{ij}$: Represent remaining cargo for delivery and cargo already picked up from prior customers, respectively.

The MILP model is formalized as follows.

$$\textbf{Min} \quad \sum_{i \in V'_0, j \in V'_{N+1}} d_{ij} x_{ij} \tag{1}$$

**s.t.**

$$\sum_{j \in V'_{N+1}, i \neq j} x_{ij} = 1 \qquad \forall i \in V \quad (2)$$

$$\sum_{j \in V'_{N+1}, i \neq j} x_{ij} \leq 1 \qquad \forall i \in F' \quad (3)$$

$$\sum_{i \in V'_0, i \neq j} x_{ij} - \sum_{i \in V'_{N+1}, i \neq j} x_{ji} = 0 \qquad \forall j \in V' \quad (4)$$

$$\tau_i + (t_{ij} + s_i)x_{ij} - l_0(1 - x_{ij}) \leq \tau_j \qquad \forall i \in V_0, j \in V'_{N+1}, i \neq j \quad (5)$$

$$\tau_i + t_{ij}x_{ij} + g(Q - y_i) - (l_0 + gQ)(1 - x_{ij}) \leq \tau_j \quad \forall i \in F', \forall j \in V'_{N+1}, i \neq j \quad (6)$$

$$0 \leq u_{0j} \leq C \qquad \forall j \in V'_{N+1} \quad (7)$$

$$v_{0j} = 0 \qquad \forall j \in V'_{N+1} \quad (8)$$

$$\sum_{i \in V'_0, i \neq j} u_{ij} - \sum_{i \in V'_{N+1}, i \neq j} u_{ji} = q_j \qquad \forall j \in V' \quad (9)$$

$$\sum_{i \in V'_{N+1}, i \neq j} v_{ji} - \sum_{i \in V'_0, i \neq j} v_{ij} = p_j \qquad \forall j \in V' \quad (10)$$

$$u_{ij} + v_{ij} \leq Cx_{ij} \qquad \forall i \in V'_0, j \in V'_{N+1}, i \neq j \quad (11)$$

$$0 \leq y_j \leq y_i - (hd_{ij})x_{ij} + Q(1 - x_{ij}) \qquad \forall i \in V, \forall j \in V'_{N+1}, i \neq j \quad (12)$$

$$0 \leq y_j \leq Q - (hd_{ij})x_{ij} + Q(1 - x_{ij}) \qquad \forall i \in F'_0, \forall j \in V'_{N+1}, i \neq j \quad (13)$$

$$x_{ij} \in 0, 1 \qquad \forall i \in V'_0, j \in V'_{N+1}, i \neq j \quad (14)$$

The objective function (Eq. 1) minimizes the total distance traveled. Constraints (2) and (3) control the connectivity of customers and charging stations, while constraints (4) are flow balance constraints. Constraints (5) and (6) calculate arrival and departure times considering service and battery charging times. Note that constraint (6) enforces vehicles to be charged up to the full battery level when they visit a charging station rather than allowing partial recharging. Constraints (7)–(11) guarantee that the delivery and pickup demands of customers are satisfied simultaneously. Finally, constraints (12)–(13) calculate the battery states.

## 3   Adapt-CMSA for the EVRP-SPD

In this section, we will describe the Adapt-CMSA algorithm we designed for the application to the EVRP-SPD. However, before describing the algorithm, we first explain the solution representation. Any solution $S$ produced by the algorithm consists of a set of feasible tours where a tour is defined as the trip of one single vehicle returning to the depot from which it originally departed. Consider the following example. The vector **I** comprises all the node indexes for a small problem instance involving three charging stations and five customers. Nodes indexed with 0 and 6 denote the depot.

$$\mathbf{I} = (\ \underbrace{0,}_{\text{depot}}\ \ \underbrace{1, 2, 3, 4, 5,}_{\text{customers}}\ \ \underbrace{6,}_{\text{depot}}\ \ \underbrace{7, 8, 9}_{\text{charging stations}}\ )$$

Considering the example above, a possible solution $S$ comprises two tours $T_1$ and $T_2$, where $T_1 \ =< 0\ \rightarrow\ 9\ \rightarrow\ 1\ \rightarrow\ 4\ \rightarrow\ 6 >$ and $T_2 =< 0\ \rightarrow\ 2\ \rightarrow\ 8\ \rightarrow\ 3\ \rightarrow\ 7\ \rightarrow\ 5\ \rightarrow\ 6 >$ is represented in Adapt-CMSA as follows:

$$S = \begin{cases} T_1 =< 0\ \rightarrow\ 9\ \rightarrow\ 1\ \rightarrow\ 4\ \rightarrow\ 6 > \\ T_2 =< 0\ \rightarrow\ 2\ \rightarrow\ 8\ \rightarrow\ 3\ \rightarrow\ 7\ \rightarrow\ 5\ \rightarrow\ 6 > \end{cases}$$

### 3.1   Set Covering Based Model

Besides assignment-type ILP models such as the one presented in Sect. 2, the EVRP-SPD can also be modeled in terms of a set-covering-based ILP in the following way. Let $\mathcal{T}$ be the set of all possible (and feasible) tours. Each tour $T_r \in \mathcal{T}$ is evaluated by the total distance traveled $d_r$, that is, the sum of the distances of all arcs on the tour. Finally, let $\mathcal{T}_i \subset \mathcal{T}$ be the set of tours that serve customer $i \in V$. With these definitions, the set-covering-based ILP model for the EVRP-SPD can be stated as follows.

$$\min \sum_{T_r \in \mathcal{T}} d_r x_r + M \sum_{T_r \in \mathcal{T}} x_r \tag{15}$$

$$\text{s.t.} \sum_{T_r \in \mathcal{T}_i} x_r \geq 1 \qquad\qquad \forall\, i \in V \tag{16}$$

$$x_r \in \{0, 1\} \qquad\qquad \forall\, T_r \in \mathcal{T} \tag{17}$$

The objective function minimizes the total travel and vehicle costs and constraints (16) ensure that each customer is visited at least once. Note that multiple occurrences of a customer are easily fixed by deleting all occurrences but one.

### 3.2   The Adapt-CMSA Algorithm

The pseudo-code presented in Algorithm 1 describes the general algorithmic framework of Adapt-CMSA for the EVRP-SPD. First, the function Generate-GreedySolution() is used to generate a feasible solution to initialize the best-so-far solution $S^{\text{bsf}}$. More precisely, this function applies an insertion heuristic, which is further explained in Sect. 3.3. Parameters $\alpha_{\text{bsf}}$, $n_a$, and $lsize$ are then set to their default values in lines 4 and 5. Below, we will break down how the algorithm handles these variables.

The algorithm creates a sub-instance $C'$ of the original problem instance in each iteration. Similar to the solution representation, a sub-instance is a set

---

**Algorithm 1.** Pseudo-code of Adapt-CMSA for the EVRP-SPD

---

1: **input 1:** values for CMSA parameters $t_{\mathrm{prop}}$, $t_{\mathrm{ILP}}$
2: **input 2:** values for solution construction parameters $\alpha^{\mathrm{LB}}$, $\alpha^{\mathrm{UB}}$, $\alpha_{\mathrm{red}}$
3: $S^{\mathrm{bsf}} :=$ GenerateGreedySolution()
4: $\alpha_{\mathrm{bsf}} := \alpha^{\mathrm{UB}}$
5: Initialize($n_{\mathrm{a}}, l_{\mathrm{size}}$)
6: **while** CPU time limit not reached **do**
7:    $C' := S^{\mathrm{bsf}}$
8:    **for** $i := 1, \ldots, n_{\mathrm{a}}$ **do**
9:       $S :=$ ProbabilisticSolutionConstruction($S^{\mathrm{bsf}}$, $\alpha_{\mathrm{bsf}}$, $l_{size}$)
10:       LocalSearch1($S$)
11:       **for all** tours $T \in S$ **and** $T \notin C'$ **do** $C' := C' \cup \{T\}$ **end for**
12:    **end for**
13:    $(S^{\mathrm{cplex}}, t_{\mathrm{solve}}) :=$ SolveSubinstance($C'$, $t_{\mathrm{ILP}}$) {This function returns two objects: (1) the obtained solution ($S^{\mathrm{cplex}}$), (2) the required computation time ($t_{\mathrm{solve}}$)}
14:    LocalSearch2($S^{\mathrm{cplex}}$)
15:    **if** $t_{\mathrm{solve}} < t_{\mathrm{prop}} \cdot t_{\mathrm{ILP}}$ and $\alpha_{\mathrm{bsf}} > \alpha^{\mathrm{LB}}$ **then** $\alpha_{\mathrm{bsf}} := \alpha_{\mathrm{bsf}} - \alpha_{\mathrm{red}}$ **end if**
16:    **if** $f(S^{\mathrm{cplex}}) < f(S^{\mathrm{bsf}})$ **then**
17:       $S^{\mathrm{bsf}} := S^{\mathrm{cplex}}$
18:       Initialize($n_{\mathrm{a}}, l_{\mathrm{size}}$)
19:    **else**
20:       **if** $f(S^{\mathrm{cplex}}) > f(S^{\mathrm{bsf}})$ **then**
21:          **if** $n_a = n^{\mathrm{init}}$ **then** $\alpha_{\mathrm{bsf}} := \min\{\alpha_{\mathrm{bsf}} + \frac{\alpha_{\mathrm{red}}}{10}, \alpha^{\mathrm{UB}}\}$ **else** Initialize($n_{\mathrm{a}}, l_{\mathrm{size}}$) **end if**
22:       **else**
23:          Increment($n_{\mathrm{a}}, l_{\mathrm{size}}$)
24:       **end if**
25:    **end if**
26: **end while**
27: **output:** $S^{\mathrm{bsf}}$

---

of tours. At the start of each iteration, $C'$ is initialized with the tours found in the best-so-far solution ($S^{\mathrm{bsf}}$). Then, a probabilistic solution construction process shown in lines 8–12 probabilistically generates $n_a$ solutions using function ProbabilisticSolutionConstruction($S^{\mathrm{bsf}}$, $\alpha_{\mathrm{bsf}}$, $l_{size}$). This function takes as input two additional parameters apart from $S^{\mathrm{bsf}}$: (1) $\alpha_{\mathrm{bsf}}$ ($0 \leq \alpha_{\mathrm{bsf}} < 1$), which biases the creation of new solutions towards the best-so-far solution, and (2) $l_{size}$, which determines the number of options considered at each solution construction step. Note that higher values of $\alpha_{\mathrm{bsf}}$ lead to an increase of similarity between the constructed solutions and $S^{\mathrm{bsf}}$. On the contrary, a higher value of $l_{size}$ results in constructing more diverse solutions and, consequently, contributes to forming a larger sub-instance.

After constructing a solution $S$ by calling the above-mentioned function in line 9 of Algorithm 1, each tour of $S$ undergoes a local search process, as indicated in line 10. This local search procedure applies well-known intra-route operators such as *relocation*, *swap*, and *two_opt* in sequential order. Moreover, the best-improvement strategy is adopted in the context of the applied operators. The so-called *relocation* operator sequentially extracts each node from its existing position within a route and repositions it at an alternative location inside the same route. On the other hand, the *swap* operator works by interchanging the positions of a pair of selected nodes belonging to the same route. Lastly, the *two_opt* neighborhood explores every feasible combination of choosing two non-adjacent nodes in the same route and then reverses the arrangement of the nodes situated between the chosen pair of nodes.

Upon applying local search, the so-called *merge step* is executed in line 11 by adding all tours from $S$ to the sub-instance $C'$. After probabilistically constructing $n_a$ solutions and forming the sub-instance $C'$, the sub-instance is solved by utilizing the set-covering-based ILP model with a CPU time limit of $t_{\text{ILP}}$ seconds with CPLEX in function SolveSubinstance($C'$, $t_{\text{ILP}}$). Note that—due to the employed CPU time limit for each application of CPLEX—the output of function SolveSubinstance($C'$, $t_{\text{ILP}}$), denoted as $S^{\text{cplex}}$, is not necessarily an optimal solution to the sub-instance. In any case, $S^{\text{cplex}}$ is subject to applying a local search method different from the one described before. In particular, this local search procedure utilizes inter-tour neighborhoods such as *exchange (1,1)* and *shift (1,0)*. The *exchange (1,1)* neighborhood investigates all potential two-customer swaps not part of the same tour, whereas the *shift (1,0)* neighborhood examines every option for removing a customer from its existing tour and placing it at any possible location in other tours. As is done within LocalSearch1($S$), operators used by LocalSearch2($S$) employ the best-improvement search strategy.

The self-adaptive nature of CMSA can be found in the dynamical adjustment of the values of parameters $\alpha_{\text{bsf}}$, $n_a$, and $l_{\text{size}}$. The value of the dynamic parameter $\alpha_{\text{bsf}}$ is bounded by $\alpha^{\text{LB}}$ and $\alpha^{\text{UB}}$. Both $\alpha^{\text{LB}}$ and $\alpha^{\text{UB}}$ are input parameters of the algorithm. Moreover, if needed, the value of a step size parameter $\alpha_{\text{red}}$ is employed for systematically reducing $\alpha_{\text{bsf}}$'s value. Initially, the value of $\alpha_{\text{bsf}}$ is set to the highest possible value, $\alpha^{\text{UB}}$, as shown in line 4.[1] If the resulting ILP is solved within a computation time $t_{\text{solve}}$ that is below a proportion $t_{\text{prop}}$ of the maximum possible computation time $t_{\text{ILP}}$—that is, if $t_{\text{solve}} \leq t_{\text{prop}} \cdot t_{\text{ILP}}$—$\alpha_{\text{bsf}}$'s value is reduced by $\alpha_{\text{red}}$, as seen in line 15. The reasoning behind this step is as follows. If the resulting ILP can be easily solved to optimality for the respective sub-instance, the search space is too small, owing to a relatively low number of free variables. To increase the number of free variables in the ILP, solutions produced in ProbabilisticSolutionConstruction($S^{\text{bsf}}$, $\alpha_{\text{bsf}}$, $l_{\text{size}}$) should differ more from $S^{\text{bsf}}$, which is achievable by lowering the value of $\alpha_{\text{bsf}}$.

Adjusting parameters $n_a$ and $l_{\text{size}}$ follows a similar scheme as the one described above. Their initial values are set as follows: $n_a := n^{\text{init}}$ and $l_{\text{size}} = l_{\text{size}}^{\text{init}}$, which is done in the Initialize($n_a$, $l_{\text{size}}$) function. This function can be called under three distinct circumstances: (1) at the beginning of the algorithm (line 5), (2) when solution $S^{\text{cplex}}$ is strictly better than $S^{\text{bsf}}$ (line 18), and (3) when solution $S^{\text{cplex}}$ is strictly worse than $S^{\text{bsf}}$ while $n_a$ concurrently exceeds $n^{\text{init}}$ (line 21). On the other hand, when $S^{\text{cplex}}$ and the $S^{\text{bsf}}$ have the same objective function

---

[1] Remember that solutions constructed with a high value of $\alpha_{\text{bsf}}$ will be rather similar to the best-so-far solution $S^{\text{bsf}}$.

value, the algorithm can create larger sub-instances, leading to an increase in the values of the three parameters in $\mathsf{Increment}(n_\mathrm{a}, l_\mathrm{size})$ function. Specifically, $n_\mathrm{a}$ is increased by $n^\mathrm{inc}$, and $l_\mathrm{size}$ is increased by $l^\mathrm{inc}_\mathrm{size}$.

### 3.3  Solution Construction

Whenever the function $\mathsf{ProbabilisticSolutionConstruction}(S^\mathrm{bsf}, \alpha_\mathrm{bsf}, l_{size})$ is called, it randomly selects one of two heuristics to generate a feasible solution: (1) a version of the Clarke & Wright (C&W) savings algorithm [3], or (2) a variant of the insertion algorithm. The following sections describe both algorithms in detail.

**Probabilistic C&W Savings Algorithm.** Initially, a set of routes $R = \{(0 \;\rightarrow\; i \;\rightarrow\; (N+1)) \mid i \in V\}$ is created, where each route begins at the depot, visits a single customer, and then returns to the depot. Subsequently, a savings list $L$ is generated for each pair of nodes $(i, j) \in V'$ satisfying the following conditions: (1) $i$ and $j$ are part of two different tours, and (2) both $i$ and $j$ must be adjacent to the depot in the tour of which they form part. Each entry in the list is associated with a savings value calculated using the following equation:

$$\sigma_{ij} := d_{0i} + d_{0j} - \lambda d_{ij} + \mu|d_{0i} - d_{0j}| \tag{18}$$

This formulation employs the *route shape* ($\lambda$) and *asymmetry scaling* ($\mu$) parameters. The former prioritizes the selection of nodes based on their mutual distance, while the latter scales the asymmetry between the selected nodes considering their distances to the depot. Section 4 describes the employed tuning procedure to determine well-working values of these parameters.

In contrast to the original C&W Savings algorithm, which constructs solutions solely based on the savings values of node pairs $(i, j)$, our variant also considers whether the arc $a_{ij}$ is part of the best-so-far solution. So, apart from the savings values, each entry $(i, j) \in L$ is associated with an additional value, $q_{ij}$ which is calculated as follows:

$$q_{ij} := \begin{cases} (\sigma_{ij} + 1) \cdot \alpha_\mathrm{bsf} & \text{if } c_{ij} \in S^\mathrm{bsf} \\ (\sigma_{ij} + 1) \cdot (1 - \alpha_\mathrm{bsf}) & \text{otherwise} \end{cases} \tag{19}$$

Note that the entries in the savings list $L$ are kept sorted in descending order based on their $q_{ij}$. After creating the initial tours and the savings list $L$, the algorithm executes the following steps until no more entry remains in $L$:

1. An entry $(i, j)$ is chosen from $L$. Another key distinction between the original C&W Savings algorithm and our implementation lies in the selection procedure. While the original algorithm selects the topmost candidate in $L$, our variant employs a probabilistic selection approach. To facilitate this, we first

create a reduced list $L_r$ containing the first $l_{size}$ elements of $L$. Subsequently, an entry is selected from $L_r$ with respect to the following probabilities:

$$\mathbf{p}(ij) := \frac{q_{ij}}{\sum_{(i',j') \in L_r} q_{i'j'}} \quad \forall\ (i,j)\ \in L_r \tag{20}$$

Note that the higher the value of $\alpha_{bsf}$, where $0 \leq \alpha^{LB} \leq \alpha_{bsf} \leq \alpha^{UB} \leq 1$, the higher the probability of selecting arcs that are part of the best-so-far solution $S^{bsf}$.

2. Then, the chosen tours corresponding to nodes $i$ and $j$ are merged. The merging process is determined by one of the four possible cases shown in Table 1, depending on the positions of nodes $i$ and $j$ in the tour. It may be required to reverse one or both of the tours selected to ensure a direct connection from $i$ to $j$. In such a case, the reversed form of tour $T_1$ is represented by $\mathsf{rev}(T_1)$.

**Table 1.** Merging cases for tours corresponding to nodes $i$ and $j$

| Case | Tours | Merging Procedure | Result |
|---|---|---|---|
| 1 | $T_1 : \{0 \to i \to \dots \to N+1\}$ | Reverse $T_1$, $\mathsf{rev}(T_1)$ | $T_m : \{0 \to \dots \to i \to j \dots \to N+1\}$ |
|   | $T_2: \{0 \to j \to \dots \to N+1\}$ | Concatenate with $T_2$ | |
| 2 | $T_1 : \{0 \to i \to \dots \to N+1\}$ | Reverse both $T_1$ and $T_2$ | $T_m : \{0 \to \dots \to i \to j \to \dots \to N+1\}$ |
|   | $T_2: \{0 \to \dots \to j \to N+1\}$ | $\mathsf{rev}(T_1)$, $\mathsf{rev}(T_2)$ | |
| 3 | $T_1 : \{0 \to \dots \to i \to N+1\}$ | Concatenate $T_1$ and $T_2$ | $T_m : \{0 \to \dots \to i \to j \to \dots \to N+1\}$ |
|   | $T_2: \{0 \to j \to \dots \to N+1\}$ | | |
| 4 | $T_1 : \{0 \to \dots \to i \to N+1\}$ | Reverse $T_2$, $\mathsf{rev}(T_2)$ | $T_m : \{0 \to \dots \to i \to j \to \dots \to N+1\}$ |
|   | $T_2: \{0 \to \dots \to j \to N+1\}$ | Concatenate with $T_1$ | |

3. Following the merging process, the feasibility of the merged tour $T_m$ is checked in terms of vehicle loading and battery capacities. Routes that violate vehicle capacity are discarded, and the respective entry is removed from the savings list. On the other hand, battery-infeasible tours are attempted to be repaired by inserting a charging station into the tour. This procedure initially identifies the first node in the tour to which the EV arrives with a depleted battery. Then, the charging station, which minimizes the increase in overall tour distance, is inserted between this node and its predecessor. If the tour remains infeasible, then the same procedure is repeated for the previous arcs. Suppose infeasibility persists after multiple charging station insertions. In that case, the merged tour is discarded, its associated nodes are removed from the savings list, and the next node pair is selected using the probabilistic selection procedure.

4. Finally, the savings list $L$ is updated as described above.

**Probabilistic Insertion Algorithm.** The second heuristic used to construct solutions sequentially inserts customers into existing tours until all are visited. The process starts with inserting the farthest customer to the depot to establish the initial tour. Subsequently, we create a cost list outlining all possible insertion points for each unvisited customer, along with the corresponding costs. To determine the insertion cost at a particular point, we use the following equation, which particularly calculates the cost of inserting customer $i$ between nodes $j$ and $k$

$$c(j, i, k) = d_{ji} + d_{ik} - d_{jk} \tag{21}$$

Then, $q_{jik}$ is calculated for each entry $(j, i, k) \in L$ as follows:

$$q_{jik} := \begin{cases} (c(j, i, k) + 1) \cdot (1 - \alpha_{\mathrm{bsf}})(1 - \alpha_{\mathrm{bsf}}) & \text{if } c_{ji} \in S^{\mathrm{bsf}} \text{ and } c_{ik} \in S^{\mathrm{bsf}} \\ (c(j, i, k) + 1) \cdot (\alpha_{\mathrm{bsf}})^2 & \text{if } c_{ji} \notin S^{\mathrm{bsf}} \text{ and } c_{ik} \notin S^{\mathrm{bsf}} \\ (c(j, i, k) + 1) \cdot \alpha_{\mathrm{bsf}}(1 - \alpha_{\mathrm{bsf}}) & \text{otherwise} \end{cases} \tag{22}$$

Afterward, selecting an entry $(j, i, k)$ from the generated list follows the probabilistic selection procedure described in the C&W savings algorithm. If the capacity of the vehicle permits, the customer is added to the corresponding location in the tour. In addition, if the insertion results in battery infeasibility, the tour is attempted to be repaired using the charging station insertion process described in the C&W savings algorithm. In situations where the insertion of a customer results in infeasibility in load capacity or battery capacity (even after charging station insertion), a new tour is initiated, which includes only the respective customer.

## 4  Experimental Evaluation

To evaluate the performance of Adapt-CMSA, in the context of small problem instances it was compared to 'CPLEX1' (application of CPLEX to the three-index ILP model from [23]), to 'CPLEX2' (application of CPLEX to the two-index MILP model presented in this paper), and to the VNS algorithm from [23]. Note that in this latter paper, 12 different VNS variants for solving the EVRP-SPD were designed. In our result tables we will, for each problem instance, report on the results of the best of these 12 variants. For large problem instances, we replaced the two CPLEX variants with probabilistic versions of the C&W Savings algorithm (pC&W) and the sequential insertion algorithm (pIns).

All experiments were performed on a cluster of machines with Intel® Xeon® 5670 CPUs with 12 cores of 2.933 GHz and a minimum of 32 GB RAM. CPLEX version 20.1 was used in one-threaded mode within Adapt-CMSA for solving the respective sub-instances and in standalone mode for solving the MILP models representing the complete problem instances.

**Benchmark Instances.** We utilized the same problem instances as those used for the experimental evaluation of VNS variants for the EVRP-SPD problem in [23]. This benchmark set is based on the EVRP-TW problem instances originally introduced by [21]. This set contains small instances with 5, 10, and 15 customers and large instances with 100 customers and 21 charging stations. The instances are categorized based on the spatial distribution of customer locations: prefixes "c", "r", and "rc" denote clustered, randomly distributed, and a hybrid of the two distributions, respectively.

**Parameter Tuning for Adapt-CMSA.** To determine the optimal parameter values for our algorithms, we employed the scientific tuning software irace [15]. The tuning process was executed using six instances, namely r107, r205, rc101, rc104, rc105, and rc205. The budget of irace was set to 2500 algorithm runs, where each algorithm run was stopped after a maximum computation time of 900 CPU seconds. The precision of irace was set to two decimal places for numerical parameters. Table 2 presents the parameters, their respective domains, and the optimal values as determined by irace. Note that the $l_{size}$ and $\alpha_{bsf}$ parameters of pC&W and pIns were fixed to their upper bounds tuned by irace.

**Table 2.** Parameters, their domains, and the chosen values as determined by irace.

| Parameter | Domain | Adapt-CMSA | pC&W | pIns |
|---|---|---|---|---|
| $\lambda$ | $[1, 2]$ | 1.38 | 1.98 | – |
| $\mu$ | $[0, 1]$ | 0.58 | 0.75 | – |
| $l_{size}^{init}$ | $\{3, 5, 10, 15, 20, 50, 100, 200\}$ | 10 | 3 | 15 |
| $l_{size}^{inc}$ | $\{3, 5, 10, 15, 20, 50, 100, 200\}$ | 20 | – | – |
| $n^{init}$ | $\{1, 3, 5, 10, 50, 100, 200, 300, 500\}$ | 10 | – | – |
| $n^{inc}$ | $\{1, 3, 5, 10, 50, 100, 200, 300, 400\}$ | 50 | – | – |
| $t_{ILP}$ | $\{5, 7, 10, 15, 20, 25, 30, 35, 40\}$ | 20 | – | – |
| $\alpha^{LB}$ | $[0.6, 0.99]$ | 0.75 | – | – |
| $\alpha^{UB}$ | $[0.6, 0.99]$ | 0.86 | 0.97 | 0.73 |
| $\alpha_{red}$ | $[0.01, 0.1]$ | 0.07 | – | – |
| $t_{prop}$ | $[0.1, 0.8]$ | 0.23 | – | – |

## 4.1   Computational Results

Tables 3, 4 and 5 show the results for small problem instances with 5, 10 and 15 customers. Note that Adapt-CMSA was applied six times—with a computation time limit of 2400 CPU seconds—to each problem instance for consistency with [23]. The CPLEX variants were given 2 CPU hours for each problem instance. Results for large problem instances are presented in Table 6, where we compare Adapt-CMSA with Reduced VNS and General VNS from [23], in addition to pC&W and pIns. These two VNS variants were reported to provide the best performance for large-sized problem instances in the respective publication. Note also that the VNS results given in these tables are directly taken from the respective publication.

The tables displaying the results are organized as follows. In the first column, the names of the problem instances are listed. The 'best' columns indicate the objective function values of the best solutions obtained from six independent runs. Additionally, columns with the heading 'avg.' show the average objective function values of the best solutions from the six runs. These objective function values correspond to the total distance traveled by the vehicles used in the respective solutions. The remaining columns with the heading 'time' display the computation time (measured in seconds) of CPLEX, as well as the average computation times of the remaining algorithms to obtain the best solution of each run

**Table 3.** Comparison for small-sized EVRP-SDP instances with 5 customers.

| Instance | CPLEX1 | | | CPLEX2 | | | VNS | | Adapt-CMSA | | |
|---|---|---|---|---|---|---|---|---|---|---|---|
| name | best | time | gap(%) | best | time | gap(%) | best | time | best | avg. | time |
| c101C5 | 208.90 | 1.35 | 0 | 208.90 | 0.30 | 0 | 208.90 | 0.02 | 208.90 | 208.90 | 0.0003 |
| c103C5 | 154.50 | 1.20 | 0 | 154.50 | 0.21 | 0 | 154.50 | 0.11 | 154.50 | 154.50 | 0.0002 |
| c206C5 | 201.55 | 1.92 | 0 | 201.55 | 0.27 | 0 | 201.55 | 0.02 | 201.55 | 201.55 | 0.0004 |
| c208C5 | 158.48 | 1.34 | 0 | 158.48 | 0.15 | 0 | 158.48 | 0.05 | 158.48 | 158.48 | 0.0004 |
| r104C5 | 136.69 | 1.75 | 0 | 136.69 | 0.14 | 0 | 136.69 | 0.00 | 136.69 | 136.69 | 0.0008 |
| r105C5 | 139.48 | 1.23 | 0 | 139.48 | 0.10 | 0 | 139.48 | 0.00 | 139.48 | 139.48 | 0.0003 |
| r202C5 | 128.78 | 1.29 | 0 | 128.78 | 0.10 | 0 | 128.78 | 0.23 | 128.78 | 128.78 | 0.0003 |
| r203C5 | 179.06 | 1.37 | 0 | 179.06 | 0.10 | 0 | 179.06 | 0.03 | 179.06 | 179.06 | 0.0003 |
| rc105C5 | 208.43 | 1.89 | 0 | 208.43 | 1.70 | 0 | 208.43 | 0.13 | 208.43 | 208.43 | 0.001 |
| rc108C5 | 211.53 | 1.36 | 0 | 211.53 | 0.10 | 0 | 211.53 | 0.16 | 211.53 | 211.53 | 0.0006 |
| rc204C5 | 176.39 | 2.54 | 0 | 176.39 | 0.33 | 0 | 176.39 | 0.20 | 176.39 | 176.39 | 0.0377 |
| rc208C5 | 167.98 | 2.29 | 0 | 167.98 | 0.11 | 0 | 167.98 | 0.02 | 167.98 | 167.98 | 0.0003 |
| average | 172.65 | 1.63 | | 172.65 | 0.30 | | 172.65 | 0.08 | 172.65 | 172.65 | **0.0036** |

The following can be noted. CPLEX optimally solved every small problem instance (with 5, 10, and 15 customers) in terms of both the MILP model from [23] and the one presented in this paper. However, CPLEX2 showed this performance with considerably less computation time than CPLEX1. More specifically, CPLEX1 and CPLEX2 found their best solutions on average in 87.94 and 16.65 s, respectively. It can be deduced that our formulation is more efficient than the one employed by CPLEX1. However, a definite conclusion can only be reached by solving both models under the same computational conditions. Concerning the heuristic approaches, VNS and Adapt-CMSA were able to find all the optimal solutions provided by CPLEX. However, Adapt-CMSA presented

**Table 4.** Comparison for small-sized EVRP-SDP instances with 10 customers.

| Instance | CPLEX1 | | | CPLEX2 | | | VNS | | Adapt-CMSA | | |
|---|---|---|---|---|---|---|---|---|---|---|---|
| name | best | time | gap(%) | best | time | gap(%) | best | time | best | avg. | time |
| c101C10 | 260.01 | 4.85 | 0 | 260.01 | 12.46 | 0 | 260.01 | 3.13 | 260.01 | 260.01 | 0.0057 |
| c104C10 | 239.13 | 3.39 | 0 | 239.13 | 0.56 | 0 | 239.13 | 1.53 | 239.13 | 239.13 | 0.0032 |
| c202C10 | 214.96 | 4.12 | 0 | 214.96 | 2.12 | 0 | 214.96 | 3.05 | 214.96 | 214.96 | 0.0038 |
| c205C10 | 224.78 | 4.45 | 0 | 224.78 | 2.10 | 0 | 224.78 | 0.36 | 224.78 | 224.78 | 0.9274 |
| r102C10 | 220.97 | 19.01 | 0 | 220.97 | 5.10 | 0 | 220.97 | 0.72 | 220.97 | 220.97 | 14.4919 |
| r103C10 | 160.41 | 10.35 | 0 | 160.41 | 5.24 | 0 | 160.41 | 2.55 | 160.41 | 160.41 | 0.0012 |
| r201C10 | 183.11 | 2.36 | 0 | 183.11 | 5.20 | 0 | 183.11 | 2.30 | 183.11 | 183.11 | 0.0049 |
| r203C10 | 214.90 | 5.43 | 0 | 214.90 | 1.62 | 0 | 214.90 | 1.86 | 214.90 | 214.90 | 0.0044 |
| rc102C10 | 346.70 | 4.03 | 0 | 346.70 | 2.11 | 0 | 346.70 | 1.65 | 346.70 | 346.70 | 0.0063 |
| rc108C10 | 317.96 | 6.00 | 0 | 317.96 | 7.11 | 0 | 317.96 | 3.30 | 317.96 | 317.96 | 0.0029 |
| rc201C10 | 246.99 | 5.26 | 0 | 246.99 | 10.61 | 0 | 246.99 | 9.78 | 246.99 | 246.99 | 0.0029 |
| rc205C10 | 306.82 | 4.14 | 0 | 306.82 | 1.47 | 0 | 306.82 | 0.79 | 306.82 | 306.82 | 0.0039 |
| average | 244.73 | 6.12 | | 244.73 | 4.64 | | 244.73 | 2.59 | 244.73 | 244.73 | **1.29** |

**Table 5.** Comparison for small-sized EVRP-SDP instances with 15 customers.

| Instance | CPLEX1 | | | CPLEX2 | | | VNS | | Adapt-CMSA | | |
|---|---|---|---|---|---|---|---|---|---|---|---|
| name | best | time | gap(%) | best | time | gap(%) | best | time | best | avg. | time |
| c103C15 | 255.68 | 30.81 | 0 | 255.68 | 14.88 | 0 | 255.68 | 20.29 | 255.68 | 255.68 | 67.0909 |
| c106C15 | 223.84 | 142.65 | 0 | 223.84 | 15.62 | 0 | 223.84 | 6.36 | 223.84 | 223.84 | 0.0214 |
| c202C15 | 314.62 | 373.20 | 0 | 314.62 | 35.95 | 0 | 314.62 | 40.32 | 314.62 | 314.62 | 0.0345 |
| c208C15 | 262.50 | 244.40 | 0 | 262.50 | 22.41 | 0 | 262.50 | 2.84 | 262.50 | 262.50 | 70.4837 |
| r102C15 | 258.59 | 681.12 | 0 | 258.59 | 110.70 | 0 | 258.59 | 23.27 | 258.59 | 258.59 | 0.0846 |
| r105C15 | 231.96 | 119.88 | 0 | 231.96 | 15.31 | 0 | 231.96 | 10.78 | 231.96 | 231.96 | 8.3377 |
| r202C15 | 275.04 | 64.31 | 0 | 275.04 | 177.24 | 0 | 275.04 | 13.64 | 275.04 | 275.04 | 0.021 |
| r209C15 | 239.70 | 49.60 | 0 | 239.70 | 6.15 | 0 | 239.70 | 9.22 | 239.70 | 239.70 | 3.8396 |
| rc103C15 | 291.07 | 52.73 | 0 | 291.07 | 11.31 | 0 | 291.07 | 9.73 | 291.07 | 291.07 | 0.0462 |
| rc108C15 | 330.01 | 1197.23 | 0 | 330.01 | 50.98 | 0 | 330.01 | 5.76 | 330.01 | 330.01 | 0.0137 |
| rc202C15 | 295.60 | 87.00 | 0 | 295.60 | 22.05 | 0 | 295.60 | 50.44 | 295.60 | 295.60 | 0.0302 |
| rc204C15 | 285.13 | 29.20 | 0 | 285.13 | 57.57 | 0 | 285.13 | 14.64 | 285.13 | 285.13 | 0.3149 |
| average | 271.98 | 256.01 | | 271.98 | 45.01 | | 271.98 | 17.27 | 271.98 | 271.98 | **12.53** |

this performance requiring less computation time than VNS. More specifically, VNS could derive its best solutions on average in 6.65 s, while Adapt-CMSA could do so in just 4.61 s.

Regarding the large-sized EVRP-SDP instances, Adapt-CMSA significantly outperforms the best VNS variants and the two probabilistic construction heuristics regarding best and average results. Adapt-CMSA showed this performance using considerably less computation time than both VNS variants.

**Table 6.** Comparison for large-sized EVRP-SDP instances with 100 customers

| Instance | CWSavings | | | pIns | | | Reduced VNS - Cyclic | | | General VNS - Cyclic | | | Adapt-CMSA | | |
|---|---|---|---|---|---|---|---|---|---|---|---|---|---|---|---|
| name | best | avg. | time | best | avg. | time | best | avg. | time | best | avg. | time | best | avg. | time |
| c101 | 789.22 | 832.50 | 198.1 | 896.04 | 919.92 | 992.3 | 734.89 | 775.05 | 2185.0 | 718.96 | 753.76 | 2402.7 | **693.50** | **695.25** | 1079.2 |
| c201 | 634.06 | 645.53 | 945.3 | 732.98 | 762.26 | 1300.4 | 567.14 | 606.36 | 2067.0 | **563.09** | 598.29 | 2244.5 | 576.52 | **578.86** | 1142.2 |
| c204 | 633.03 | 657.93 | 582.1 | 723.69 | 766.51 | 1354.4 | 585.63 | 613.19 | 2405.0 | 579.59 | 609.54 | 2356.90 | **576.52** | **577.45** | 1613.7 |
| c206 | 624.93 | 650.85 | 395.0 | 759.95 | 779.06 | 378.3 | **569.20** | 606.71 | 2288.0 | 597.46 | 619.09 | 2155.3 | 576.52 | 579.95 | 1259.3 |
| c207 | 626.26 | 656.40 | 265.2 | 758.76 | 777.13 | 1226.0 | 567.76 | 606.47 | 2513.0 | 599.72 | 620.50 | 1793.2 | 576.79 | **584.72** | 1588.2 |
| r101 | 888.09 | 925.34 | 779.7 | 981.79 | 1007.60 | 1299.3 | 823.51 | 884.72 | 2305.0 | 843.74 | 866.86 | 2395.3 | **762.73** | **770.90** | 831.8 |
| r104 | 849.58 | 880.66 | 533.0 | 976.85 | 1004.05 | 1147.2 | 880.77 | 923.77 | 1222.0 | 888.24 | 918.66 | 2334.8 | **758.26** | **773.21** | 679.3 |
| r106 | 897.19 | 935.43 | 143.2 | 998.29 | 1017.07 | 1047.2 | 864.58 | 899.18 | 1812.0 | 886.88 | 915.67 | 2290.6 | **766.06** | **775.98** | 773.5 |
| r107 | 864.50 | 890.46 | 162.6 | 983.06 | 1005.41 | 1195.7 | 856.46 | 907.39 | 2347.0 | 864.49 | 927.58 | 2363.4 | **755.29** | **771.88** | 1059.3 |
| r108 | 893.37 | 913.11 | 339.2 | 983.43 | 1015.05 | 1231.7 | 842.01 | 887.50 | 2291.0 | 857.77 | 885.94 | 2188.1 | **760.38** | **771.47** | 860.7 |
| r109 | 871.70 | 909.80 | 105.7 | 981.63 | 1012.31 | 902.2 | 865.47 | 895.36 | 2272.0 | 854.32 | 901.75 | 1848.1 | **752.02** | **764.97** | 1350.0 |
| r110 | 864.68 | 893.28 | 457.3 | 983.70 | 1004.74 | 1245.2 | 880.77 | 922.45 | 1235.0 | 857.25 | 911.79 | 1834.6 | **759.76** | **771.24** | 864.6 |
| r111 | 899.24 | 914.39 | 335.8 | 976.61 | 1017.97 | 1362.2 | 879.50 | 904.20 | 1596.0 | 862.00 | 905.00 | 2333.7 | **761.32** | **775.02** | 724.5 |
| r112 | 882.58 | 905.55 | 703.4 | 1015.8 | 1027.25 | 930.4 | 876.19 | 903.22 | 1637.0 | 854.32 | 892.78 | 1924.6 | **761.28** | **776.42** | 729.5 |
| r201 | 677.77 | 695.29 | 22.4 | 720.20 | 738.08 | 1456.7 | 690.73 | 719.61 | 2133.0 | 713.90 | 736.72 | 1687.4 | **650.73** | **653.18** | 1108.0 |
| r202 | 674.34 | 693.05 | 248.9 | 698.62 | 725.50 | 1182.2 | 690.38 | 707.28 | 2247.0 | 711.74 | 740.64 | 1791.3 | **643.27** | **650.63** | 1055.5 |
| r203 | 689.06 | 697.99 | 528.6 | 724.15 | 735.98 | 1512.5 | 708.41 | 719.08 | 1964.0 | 713.90 | 740.60 | 2239.7 | **646.45** | **652.14** | 891.7 |
| r204 | 675.58 | 689.32 | 442.3 | 718.17 | 733.94 | 1630.6 | 698.59 | 707.81 | 1477.0 | 708.64 | 730.32 | 2282.2 | **643.85** | **649.09** | 990.9 |
| r205 | 676.60 | 689.13 | 171.9 | 730.74 | 742.50 | 984.3 | 690.35 | 711.13 | 2425.0 | 704.02 | 730.47 | 2378.9 | **645.79** | **651.43** | 818.7 |
| r206 | 673.42 | 686.30 | 246.1 | 720.63 | 732.98 | 1162.3 | 694.54 | 717.43 | 2099.0 | 692.95 | 723.98 | 2205.3 | **650.64** | **653.66** | 813.3 |
| r207 | 667.24 | 688.48 | 192.9 | 709.49 | 732.31 | 1479.7 | 701.66 | 710.63 | 1020.0 | 701.42 | 722.25 | 2265.3 | **643.26** | **648.80** | 1159.5 |
| r208 | 677.65 | 692.82 | 402.1 | 728.53 | 738.61 | 1516.4 | 687.23 | 706.42 | 2283.0 | 714.12 | 742.15 | 2210.4 | **644.39** | **649.03** | 696.9 |
| r209 | 673.61 | 688.26 | 237.9 | 733.47 | 744.76 | 1644.0 | 696.17 | 718.88 | 2141.0 | 692.95 | 725.09 | 2178.9 | **647.80** | **654.40** | 1121.4 |
| r210 | 683.18 | 696.69 | 264.0 | 731.10 | 752.20 | 1175.4 | 708.41 | 720.19 | 1991.0 | 713.90 | 739.96 | 2166.8 | **645.93** | **653.84** | 1167.7 |
| r211 | 681.80 | 699.36 | 840.2 | 719.61 | 736.22 | 1409.27 | 701.66 | 710.63 | 1031.0 | 700.53 | 720.87 | 2208.0 | **644.02** | **649.45** | 1160.2 |
| rc101 | 1029.02 | 1064.90 | 359.1 | 1107.96 | 1133.05 | 1360.44 | 887.66 | 935.90 | 2404.0 | 885.96 | 920.75 | 1812.1 | **832.30** | **843.94** | 724.2 |
| rc201 | 691.09 | 711.46 | 176.1 | 748.59 | 759.89 | 1924.72 | 682.65 | 726.47 | 1767.0 | 698.37 | 722.56 | 1658.4 | **651.88** | **655.83** | 931.6 |
| rc202 | 695.83 | 716.11 | 479.4 | 746.80 | 759.04 | 1416.76 | 703.03 | 712.23 | 2187.0 | 710.30 | 726.25 | 2100.2 | **649.68** | **653.99** | 1045.0 |
| rc203 | 694.54 | 705.22 | 424.1 | 745.79 | 767.26 | 899.90 | 685.09 | 728.94 | 2305.0 | 698.37 | 730.03 | 2358.5 | **651.68** | **656.76** | 991.6 |
| rc204 | 710.25 | 729.71 | 1236.9 | 736.77 | 761.07 | 1350.92 | 723.14 | 734.23 | 2341.0 | 731.65 | 762.60 | 2168.8 | **649.42** | **655.57** | 773.8 |
| rc205 | 694.48 | 707.11 | 309.8 | 742.66 | 766.21 | 1481.88 | 715.51 | 739.29 | 1828.0 | 721.60 | 753.78 | 2437.4 | **649.68** | **656.75** | 1249.4 |
| rc206 | 712.95 | 721.54 | 82.7 | 733.43 | 761.05 | 1188.83 | 691.17 | 718.47 | 2402.0 | 735.66 | 767.70 | 1682.5 | **646.39** | **654.16** | 587.1 |
| rc207 | 691.15 | 709.10 | 336.0 | 751.20 | 767.01 | 817.72 | 685.09 | 727.85 | 2309.0 | 707.51 | 732.01 | 2024.8 | **652.64** | **656.07** | 1384.8 |
| rc208 | 683.28 | 711.04 | 529.1 | 742.29 | 769.75 | 940.02 | 721.41 | 752.14 | 2100.0 | 743.13 | 774.94 | 2438.8 | **652.08** | **656.02** | 957.7 |
| average | 743.27 | 764.83 | 396.4 | 815.96 | 837.46 | 1239.6 | 734.02 | 763.53 | 2018.5 | 742.01 | 772.67 | 2140.0 | **675.85** | **683.00** | 1011.4 |

Figure 1 visually supports this observation, presenting two heatmaps that compare the performance of algorithms across multiple instances. Each cell in these heatmaps denotes the proportion of instances where the corresponding row's algorithm outperforms the column's algorithm. For ease of reference, algorithms are numerically labeled—such as [1], [2], etc.—to represent their lengthy names. The heatmap labeled "Best Results" displays the proportion of instances for which the row algorithm yielded superiority in the best results produced among six runs compared to the column algorithm. Similarly, the "Average Results" heatmap provides the proportion of instances for which the row algorithm's mean performance was more commendable than that of the column

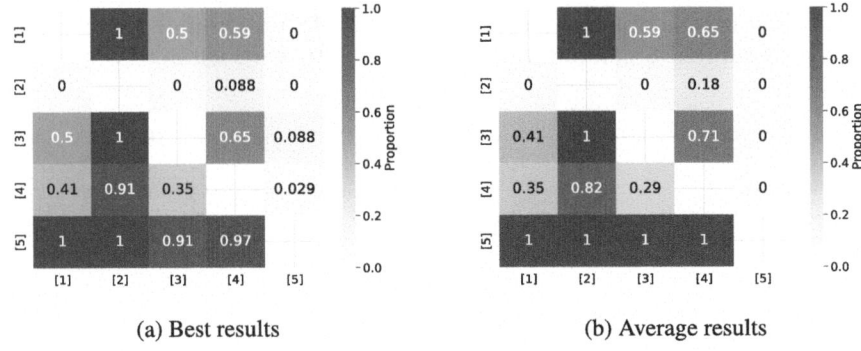

(a) Best results                    (b) Average results

**Fig. 1.** Heatmaps for a pairwise algorithm comparison. (a) Best solution quality. (b) Average solution quality. Each cell indicates the proportion of instances for which the row algorithm outperforms the respective column's algorithm. Algorithms are labeled as follows: [1]: pC&W; [2]: pIns; [3]: Reduced VNS-Cyclic; [4]: General VNS-Cyclic; [5]: Adapt-CMSA.

algorithm. Darker shades in the heatmaps emphasize a higher proportion, signifying the row algorithm's frequent dominance over the column algorithm, while lighter shades indicate the contrary.

## 5 Conclusion and Outlook

In this study, we tackled the Electric Vehicle Routing Problem with Simultaneous Pickup and Delivery (EVRP-SPD), a complex extension of the traditional VRP due to challenges related to EVs. We began by setting up the EVRP-SPD as a MILP model, highlighting the problem's complexity. To address this, we applied the self-adaptive variant of the recent hybrid metaheuristic Construct, Merge, Solve&Adapt, especially for solving large-scale problem instances. This approach first creates a sub-instance of the original problem instance by applying two constructive heuristics, the C&W Savings algorithm and sequential insertion algorithm probabilistically, and then solves a set-covering-based model of the problem using an exact solver for the constructed sub-instance. Our tests showed that Adapt-CMSA performed well across different instance sizes. It outperformed existing VNS variants from the literature as well as probabilistic versions of our construction heuristics.

Looking ahead, we plan to improve Adapt-CMSA by adding additional solution construction methods. Moreover, we intend to improve the MILP models. We also aim to test the algorithm on a broader range of instances to ensure it is robust and adaptable. Developing even more realistic EVRP variants could be seen as another future research line.

**Acknowledgments.** This paper was supported by grants TED2021-129319B-I00 and PID2019-104156GB-I00 funded by MCIN/AEI/10.13039/501100011033. Moreover,

M.A. Akbay and C.B. Kalayci received support from the Technological Research Council of Turkey (TUBITAK) under grant number 119M236. The corresponding author was funded by the Ministry of National Education, Turkey (Scholarship Prog.: YLYS-2019).

# References

1. Asghari, M., Mirzapour Al-e-hashem, S.M.J.: Green vehicle routing problem: a state-of-the-art review. Int. J. Prod. Econ. **231**, 107899 (2021)
2. Blum, C., Pinacho Davidson, P., López-Ibáñez, M., Lozano, J.A.: Construct, merge, solve & adapt: a new general algorithm for combinatorial optimization. Comput. Oper. Res. **68**, 75–88 (2016)
3. Clarke, G., Wright, J.W.: Scheduling of vehicles from a central depot to a number of delivery points. Oper. Res. **12**(4), 568–581 (1964)
4. Conrad, R.G., Figliozzi, M.A.: The recharging vehicle routing problem. In: Proceedings of the 2011 Industrial Engineering Research Conference, p. 8. IISE, Norcross (2011)
5. Dantzig, G.B., Ramser, J.H.: The truck dispatching problem. Manag. Sci. **6**(1), 80–91 (1959)
6. Duman, E.N., Taş, D., Çatay, B.: Branch-and-price-and-cut methods for the electric vehicle routing problem with time windows. Int. J. Prod. Res. **60**(17), 5332–5353 (2022)
7. Dupin, N., Talbi, E.G.: Matheuristics to optimize refueling and maintenance planning of nuclear power plants. J. Heurist. **27**(1), 63–105 (2021)
8. Elshaer, R., Awad, H.: A taxonomic review of metaheuristic algorithms for solving the vehicle routing problem and its variants. Comput. Ind. Eng. **140**, 106242 (2020)
9. Erdoğan, S., Miller-Hooks, E.: A green vehicle routing problem. Transport. Res. Part E: Logistics Transport. Rev. **48**(1), 100–114 (2012)
10. Ferrer, J., Chicano, F., Ortega-Toro, J.A.: CMSA algorithm for solving the prioritized pairwise test data generation problem in software product lines. J. Heurist. **27**(1), 229–249 (2021)
11. Golden, B.L., Raghavan, S., Wasil, E.A.: The Vehicle Routing Problem: Latest Advances and New Challenges, vol. 43. Springer Science & Business Media, Heidelberg (2008)
12. Keskin, M., Çatay, B.: Partial recharge strategies for the electric vehicle routing problem with time windows. Transport. Res. Part C: Emerg. Technol. **65**, 111–127 (2016)
13. Lee, C.: An exact algorithm for the electric-vehicle routing problem with nonlinear charging time. J. Oper. Res. Soc. **72**(7), 1461–1485 (2021)
14. Li, J., Wang, F., He, Y.: Electric vehicle routing problem with battery swapping considering energy consumption and carbon emissions. Sustainability **12**(24), 10537 (2020)
15. López-Ibáñez, M., et al.: The irace package: iterated racing for automatic algorithm configuration. Oper. Res. Perspect. **3**, 43–58 (2016)
16. Moghdani, R., Salimifard, K., Demir, E., Benyettou, A.: The green vehicle routing problem: a systematic literature review. J. Clean. Prod. **279**, 123691 (2021)
17. Montoya, A., Guéret, C., Mendoza, J.E., Villegas, J.G.: The electric vehicle routing problem with nonlinear charging function. Transport. Res. Part B: Methodol. **103**, 87–110 (2017)

18. Montoya-Torres, J.R., Franco, J.L., Isaza, S.N., Jiménez, H.F., Herazo-Padilla, N.: A literature review on the vehicle routing problem with multiple depots. Comput. Ind. Eng. **79**, 115–129 (2015)
19. Pelletier, S., Jabali, O., Laporte, G.: The electric vehicle routing problem with energy consumption uncertainty. Transport. Res. Part B: Methodol. **126**, 225–255 (2019)
20. Sadati, M.E.H., Çatay, B.: A hybrid variable neighborhood search approach for the multi-depot green vehicle routing problem. Transport. Res. Part E: Logist. Transport. Rev. **149**, 102293 (2021)
21. Schneider, M., Stenger, A., Goeke, D.: The electric vehicle-routing problem with time windows and recharging stations. Transp. Sci. **48**(4), 500–520 (2014)
22. Toth, P., Vigo, D.: Vehicle Routing: Problems, Methods, and Applications. SIAM, Philadelphia (2014)
23. Yilmaz, Y., Kalayci, C.B.: Variable neighborhood search algorithms to solve the electric vehicle routing problem with simultaneous pickup and delivery. Mathematics **10**(17), 3108 (2022)

# Optimising Public Transport Through the Integration of Micro and Macro-level Simulations

Kate Han[1](✉)  , Lee A. Christie[2]  , Alexandru-Ciprian Zăvoianu[2]  ,
and John A. W. McCall[2]  

[1] Salford Business School, University of Salford, Manchester, UK
k.han3@salford.ac.uk
[2] National Subsea Centre, Robert Gordon University, Aberdeen, Scotland, UK
{l.a.christie,c.zavoianu,j.mccall}@rgu.ac.uk

**Abstract.** The European Commission and the UK aim for net zero emissions in transportation by 2050. This work explores the potential of connected and autonomous vehicles (CAVs) to support this goal by enhancing public transport (PT) via strategic deployment within optimised services. Macro-level mobility simulations integrating open data are coupled with meta-heuristic solvers to offer insight into optimal CAV route design while micro-level mobility simulations are used to increase the realism of generated solutions by providing insights on realistic travel speed variability in rush hour traffic across the considered study area. Results obtained with different solvers and two methods of transferring micro-level simulation insights to the macro-level service planning strategy indicate the potential for 3.0% to 38% average area-wide commuting time improvement when an optimised CAV service is added into the existing PT system.

**Keywords:** multi-modal public transport · micro-level mobility simulations · macro-level mobility simulations · meta-heuristic optimisation · reachability isochrones

## 1 Introduction and Motivation

In the realm of road traffic simulation research, a significant challenge lies in seamlessly integrating complex traffic networks that underpin modern multi-modal travel patterns. The goal is to develop simulated networks that are computationally efficient and support robust connectivity parameterisation as they accommodate various travel modes. While tailoring the overall simulation design to specific research objectives is a frequent requirement, a commonly employed general strategy involves constructing layer-based networks as these facilitate the implementation of spatial-temporal structures that mimic the real-world traffic dynamics required by numerous types of analyses.

Workshop: Theory and Applications of Metaheuristic Algorithms

Over the past decades, interest in traffic simulation has grown increasingly interdisciplinary, with research endeavors spanning a wide spectrum-from green city planning aimed at alleviating traffic congestion [5] to initiatives focused on enhancing travel efficiency and urban living standards [17]. Moreover, these interdisciplinary projects increasingly leverage data-driven technologies and artificial intelligence techniques.

Transportation research plays a crucial role in developing safe and efficient travel systems. Cross-level simulation has emerged as a significant tool in this field, offering comprehensive insights into various transportation aspects, including, but not limited to driver behavior [1], traffic patterns [15], and vehicular interactions [14].

The present research builds on our previous public transport simulation and optimisation work [8,9] by complementing our macro-level multi-modal modeling approach with insights from micro-level traffic simulations carried out with insights from the Simulation of Urban Mobility (SUMO) package [16] developed by the Institute of Transportation Systems at the German Aerospace Center (Deutsches Zentrum für Luft- und Raumfahrt – DLR). In particular, through this collaboration with the West Yorkshire Combined Authority (WYCA) and DLR, we aimed to demonstrate how the presently proposed innovative multilevel analysis can help identify optimal Connected Autonomous Vehicle (CAV) services that ultimately encourage the use of the public transport (PT) system.

Subsequent sections of this paper will give an overview of the proposed micro- and macro-level transport network modelling approach, the particularities of the real-world scenario we have used as a case study, and the results of the numerical optimisation experiments we have carried out to discover CAV services that can improve area-wide commuting even when considering rush hour traffic delays.

## 2   Proposed Approach

As we aim to integrate macro-level and micro-level simulations to provide enhanced highly reactive, data-informed decision-making capabilities for the WYCA, this section first introduces the real-world case study scenario we target. Following this, we describe the key characteristics of both simulation levels that underpin our numerical optimisation experiments.

### 2.1   Real-World A65 Scenario

To demonstrate the benefits of coupling both macro- and micro-level simulations prior to optimising PT services, we consider a real-world mobility scenario defined by WYCA, referred to as the A65 scenario. This scenario focuses on a region/corridor surrounding the A65, a major urban high-speed road (30–40 mph limit) in the North-West of Leeds (UK) that ensures connectivity towards the Leeds Central area.

The A65 scenario aims to analyse the influence on expected optimal PT planning outcomes of congestion caused by traffic flowing from residential areas via a busy main road. To evaluate the impact of traffic on actual vehicle speeds, a SUMO simulation was conducted by DLR [20]. The approach involved the definition of seven speed detector points along a 4.7 mi stretch of the A65 road (see Fig. 1a). The SUMO model simulates average traffic volumes towards the city center during a typical workday morning (6:00 AM – 10:00 AM), including the peak rush hour of 7:00 AM – 8:30 AM. Figure 1b presents a snapshot of the entire road network in the SUMO simulation area with vehicles heading towards the city center being color-coded by their instant speed.

Based on the placement of the speed detector points in relation to the case study area, we have divided the A65 scenario into eight polygon-segmented sub-areas that will be used to transfer SUMO-simulated speed effects to the macro-level simulation. In Fig. 2a we present this sub-area partitioning of the A65 scenario and in Fig. 2b we plot the full road network considered by both the micro- and macro- level simulations.

## 2.2    Macro-level Simulation

Over the years, several researchers have proposed graph-based and data-driven techniques for simulating the accessibility and reachability provided by multi-modal transport systems at a macro level [6,11,12]. In this study, as we wished to investigate how to optimally deploy CAVs to enhance the rush hour accessibility provided by the Leeds PT network, we have tailored our bespoke lightweight macro-level simulation [7] to the requirements of the A65 scenario. The advantages of our approach are that it is very computationally efficient (and thus suitable for integration with a wide range of optimisation algorithms) and can be used to compute both inbound and outbound isochrones.

Our simulation approach relies on using graph traversal algorithms to explore an abstract multi-modal PT network grounded in open-source datasets: OSM [4] for road data and GTFS [2] for PT timetable data. When constructing the abstract PT network (see Fig. 3), artificial edges are added to represent the movement between OSM-based vertices and GTFS-based vertices. This is necessary because the GPS coordinates in the two datasets do not align exactly. For each GTFS-based vertex, the nearest OSM-based vertex is identified and the Haversine distance is used to calculate the cost associated with travelling along the newly introduced edge.

## 2.3    Micro-level Simulation Using SUMO

SUMO [13,16] is an open-source traffic simulation package which allows researchers and practitioners to model and analyse transportation systems at various levels of detail. Developed as a versatile tool for traffic analysis and planning, SUMO offers capabilities for simulating individual vehicles, PT services, and traffic control strategies. Its flexibility and extensibility make it a valuable and widely-used resource for studying traffic flow, congestion patterns, and the impacts of transportation interventions on urban mobility.

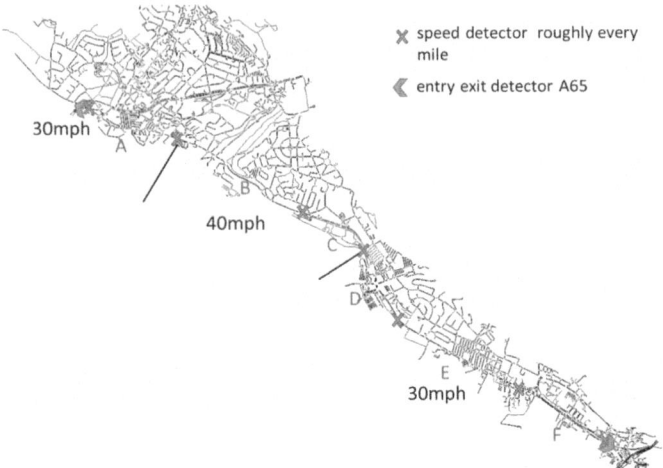

(a) The positioning of the seven A65 speed detectors within the SUMO model divides the main road in six segments (marked A to F).

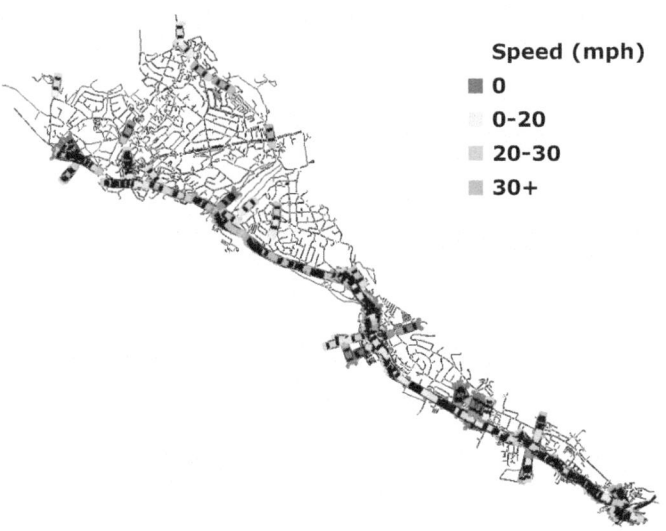

(b) SUMO baseline simulation result.

**Fig. 1.** The A65 scenario as modelled in SUMO [20].

In contrast to our previous approaches, this study refines macro-level modelling assumptions by replacing the static and somewhat optimistic speed estimates (i.e., min of road speed limit or 35 mph) used for the simulation and evaluation of CAV movements with time and location dependent variable speeds that are informed by the results of the micro-level SUMO simulation. Thus, in

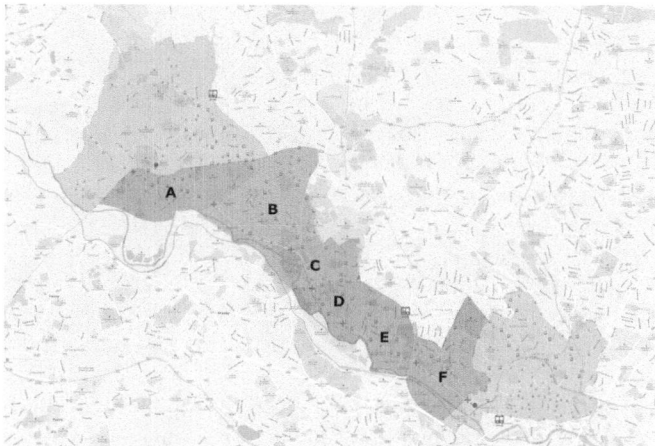

(a) SUMO-based sub-area segmentation of the A65 scenario. The six central sub-areas correspond to the six A65 segments in Figure 1a.

(b) Full road network covered by the A65 scenario.

**Fig. 2.** Key simulation features of the A65 scenario: sub-area segmentation and full road network.

Table 1 we provide an overview of the average SUMO-simulated speeds across the six A65 road segments illustrated in Fig. 1a during a 30-minute rush hour interval. It is noteworthy that the reduction in average speed when comparing with the nominal speed limit for each A65 segment ranges from ≈ 56% (D and E) to 26% (F).

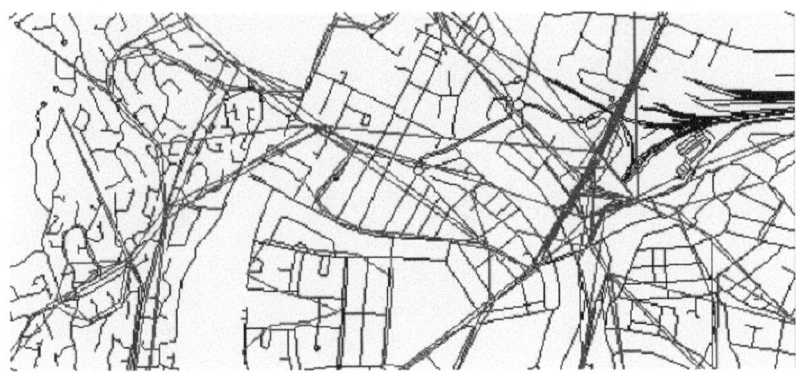

**Fig. 3.** Example of the abstract network for a given geographic area. Black lines denote the road and walkway network, blue lines indicate PT links and red segments mark the artificial edges needed to ensure graph connectivity. (Color figure online)

**Table 1.** Average SUMO estimated speed in each of the six A65 segments in the interval 8:00 AM to 8:30 AM [20].

| Distance (miles) | Speed Limit (mph) | Segment ID | Average SUMO Speed(mph) |
|---|---|---|---|
| 0.7 | 30 | A | 24.7 |
| 1.1 | 40 | B | 29.3 |
| 0.5 | 40 | C | 23.1 |
| 0.6 | 30 | D | 13.2 |
| 1.0 | 30 | E | 13.1 |
| 0.8 | 30 | F | 22.2 |
| 4.7 | 33.4 | All | 21.2 |

# 3    Integrated Simulation and Fitness Evaluation

## 3.1    Integrated Simulation

To best leverage the SUMO micro-simulated realistic speeds when exploring optimal CAV services along the A65 route, we propose two approaches that ensure our macro-level simulation retains its computational efficiency.

**Capped Speed.** In this approach, we cap the speed limit (i.e., max speed) on all roads within each A-F polygonal sub-area to the average SUMO-based speed of the corresponding A65 road segment. Given that the A65 road is the only main road and the default speed limit on secondary roads is lower by default (i.e., 20–30 mph), this approach is intuitive, but the subplot in Fig. 4a indicates that its result is a somewhat homogeneous speed limitation for CAVs of $\approx 14 mph$ (23 km/h) for a large part of the road network within the case study area. The only exceptions are the A65 main road itself and certain road stretches in the

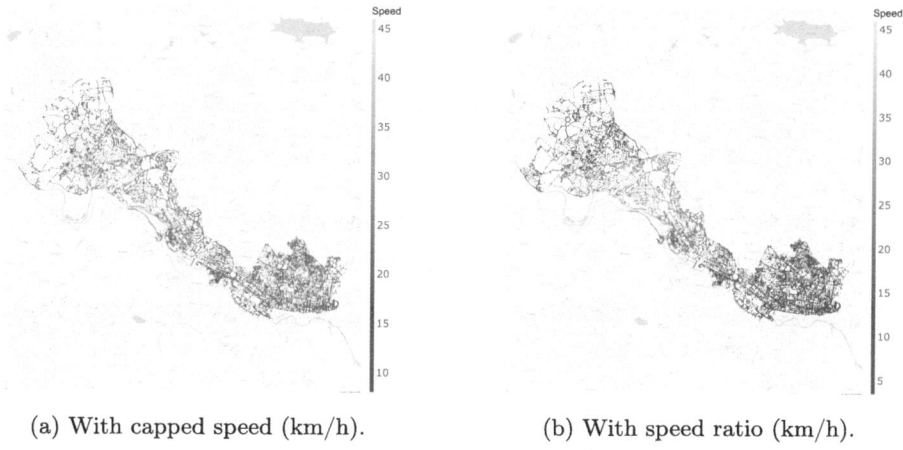

(a) With capped speed (km/h).          (b) With speed ratio (km/h).

**Fig. 4.** Effects of applying the two proposed methods of speed limitation on the A65 scenario road network.

Nort-West and South-East (i.e., Leeds Central) sub-areas that are by definition not affected by the caps as they are outwith the A65 SUMO speed simulation zone. It is also noteworthy that under the capped speed limitation, speed limits for CAVs travelling on roads outside the A65 scenario area remain unchanged.

**Speed Limit Ratio.** Wishing to address the somewhat lax restrictions imposed by the capped speed approach, we also implemented a second limitation method based on speed ratios. This approach modifies speed limits on all roads within each A-F polygonal sub-area proportionally to the observed ratio between the nominal speed limit of the corresponding A65 segment and the SUMO-based averaged speed across that segment. As illustrated in Fig. 4a, the speed limit ratio approach provides a more nuanced adjustment in which the max speed of secondary roads is more heavily influenced by the reduction of average speed on the A65 segment they feed into as a means of highlighting that variations in traffic conditions tend to diffuse across the residential areas during rush hour. The speed limit ratio for the two scenario areas without corresponding A65 segments is set at the maximal value observed across the two A65 segments with a 40 mph base speed limit (B and C). As we wished to further limit CAV routing to the study area (in contrast to the capped speed approach), we set an artificially low speed limit ratio for all road segments outside the A65 scenario.

By considering both speed limitation approaches, we aimed to enhance the accuracy and reliability of CAV service simulations. The capped speed method ensures that CAVs operate within generous, but safe and realistic speed limits, while the ratio speed approach allows for stricter, but more flexible and context-sensitive speed adjustments. Together, these methods support a well rounded strategy for optimizing CAV services along the A65 route using valuable key insights from realistic micro-level mobility simulations.

## 3.2    CAV Service Definition

In this work, the CAV service configuration uses the settings from our previous studies [7,8] that were based on feedback from WYCA domain experts:

1. The CAV service is bi-directional and circular. Starting from Horsforth Station, it traverses the list of selected PT stops in both clockwise and counter-clockwise directions, returning to Horsforth after visiting the last stop.
2. The frequency $R$ of the CAV service is 10 min, with a waiting time of 30 s at each PT stop.
3. The average travel speed of the CAVs is the maximum of 20 mph (32 km/h) or the road speed limit.
4. The average walking speed (to and from PT stops) is 3.10 mph (5 km/h).

The speed restrictions imposed by the two aforementioned approaches for integrating SUMO-based observations are summarised in Table 2. It is noteworthy that both methods yield max speeds under the default 20mph default CAV service speed, although the plots in Fig. 4 indicate that the speed limit ratio is expected to have a larger impact on CAV service performance.

**Table 2.** CAV service speed limits in the 08:00 AM to 08:30 AM interval.

| Segment | Capped Speed (mph) | Speed Limit Ratio (%) |
|---|---|---|
| A | 24.7 | 0.62 |
| B | 29.3 | 0.73 |
| C | 23.1 | 0.58 |
| D | 13.2 | 0.44 |
| E | 13.1 | 0.44 |
| F | 22.2 | 0.74 |
| Rest of scenario | N/A | 0.73 |
| Outside scenario | N/A | 0.03 |

## 3.3    Fitness Evaluation

Our PT optimisation research endeavors to date have aimed to evaluate and maximise the potential mobility improvements that can be achieved by introducing CAV services. In the present work, the goal is to identify an optimal CAV service (PT stops and routing) that reduces the average commute time towards the Leeds Central Area from across the entire case study area. *Leeds Central Railway Station*, one of the busiest transfer points for entering and leaving the central area, has been selected as the commute destination point due to its significance in the local and regional transport network.

In the A65 scenario, *Horsforth Train Station* has been chosen as both the start and end point for the newly introduced CAV service. This choice is justified given the overall goal of increasing public transport usage by the fact that Horsforth Train Station already links various public transport modes (i.e., is a PT hub).

To calculate the average commute time $f(x)$ for a candidate CAV service $x$ we use a grid $G$ of equidistant sample points covering the entire study are with a spacing of 50 m. For any grid point $g$, we compute $t_g(x)$ – the shortest multimodal travel time to Leeds Central Railway Station. This uses the baseline (i.e., existing) public transport system, walking, and the CAV service encoded in $x$ and is calculated by obtaining an inbound isochrone centered on the destination. This process uses the lightweight macro-level simulation strategy outlined in Sect. 2.2.

In addition to the inclusion of Horsforth Train Station, a key suggestion by WYCA domain experts is that the generated CAV service should require at most 8 vehicles due to real-world implementation and operational costs. The number of vehicles $n(x)$ required to realise a CAV service is modelled as a constraint calculated from the encoded service $x$. To avoid excessively restricting the search space and thus potentially limit the novelty of discovered solutions, we have chosen to use a soft constraint. Therefore, a parameter of $p \in [0, 1]$ representing the severity of the penalty is applied to the average area commute time for each extra CAV required to service a given route.

The final fitness function to be minimized is given by Eq. 1:

$$f(x) = \left( \frac{1}{|G|} \sum_{g \in G} t_g(x) \right) \cdot (1 + p \cdot \max(n(x) - 8, 0)) \tag{1}$$

### 3.4 Solution Encoding and Optimisation Algorithms

In this work, we explore two distinct encodings to represent the CAV services. These encodings, binary and continuous, were chosen to examine how different representations can impact the efficiency and overall effectiveness of widely applied optimisation algorithms in determining optimal CAV routes.

For both speed limitation methods, each optimisation algorithm we experimented with was run 30 times to ensure the statistical reliability of results. Each independent optimisation run involved 100, 000 fitness evaluations.

**The Binary Encoding** defines the CAV services as a bit string with length equal to the number of potential stops. Each 1 indicates that the stop is included and 0 indicates that the stop is excluded. For this encoding, we applied a standard genetic algorithm (GA) [10] and population-based incremental learning (PBIL) [3]. These two algorithms were selected based on promising experimental results from our previous work [7] where the GA in particular demonstrated superior outcomes for binary encoding, making it a strong default solver for tackling problems in this domain.

**The Continuous Encoding** uses a vector of real numbers ranging from 0 to 1, with the length corresponding to the number of potential stops. Particle swarm optimization (PSO) [19] demonstrated promising outcomes for the continuous encoding in our previous experiments [9]. Additionally, we have also applied differential evolution (DE) [18] on this encoding given the popularity and versatility associated with this optimisation strategy.

## 4    Results

To facilitate result comparison, we first present the baseline plot of the A65 scenario area in Fig. 5. The baseline fitness is associated with an area-wide average commute time of 1570.6 s. We used a grid map sampling method for this evaluation (as discussed in Sect. 3.3). The color scale in this plot is used in subsequent experiment result plots as well.

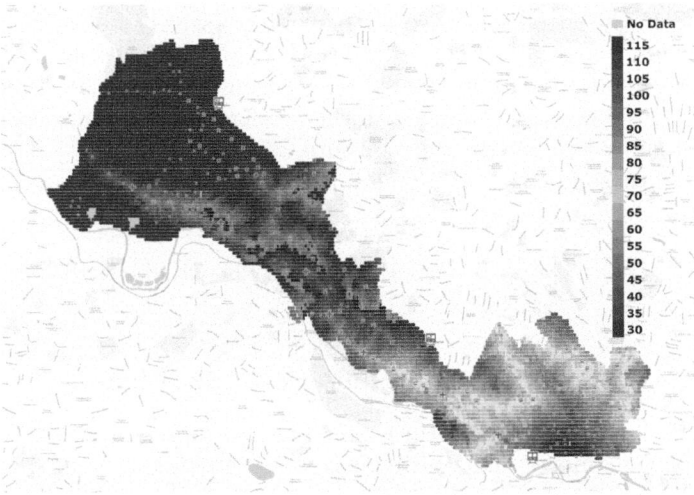

**Fig. 5.** Baseline traffic conditions for the scenario area. Color scale indicates travel time in minutes. Grey areas indicate a commute time longer than 120 min (Color figure online).

In the baseline plot from Fig. 5, green areas indicate good commuting conditions, where the average travel time is within an hour. Red areas show poor commuting conditions, with travel times up to two hours, while grey areas indicate virtual inaccessibility via PT (i.e., average commutes longer than two hours).

### 4.1    Capped Speed

In Table 3, we present the results of each meta-heuristic solver across the 30 independent optimisation runs when applying the capped speed method.

**Table 3.** Capped speed optimisation results

| Solver | Limit | Num. CAV | Fitness | | Penalty Fitness | |
|--------|-------|----------|---------|------|---------|------|
| | | | Average | Best | Average | Best |
| DE | capped | 8 | 1048.0 | 1028.4 | 1048.0 | 1028.4 |
| PBIL | capped | 22 | 1506.6 | 1432.9 | 3202.0 | 2973.0 |
| GA | capped | 6 | **997.4** | **974.5** | **997.4** | **974.5** |
| PSO | capped | 16 | 1059.9 | 997.6 | 1059.9 | 997.6 |

The GA identified the most promising CAV service using only 6 CAVs, fewer than the upper bound suggested by WYCA experts. The best CAV service identified under the capped speed limitation achieved an average fitness time of 974.5 s, representing a 38.0% improvement over the baseline fitness. The associated plots of this service from Fig. 6 indicate that it only uses the relatively fast A65 segments (A-C) whilst using uncapped roads outside the study area to ensure the destination is reached as fast as possible.

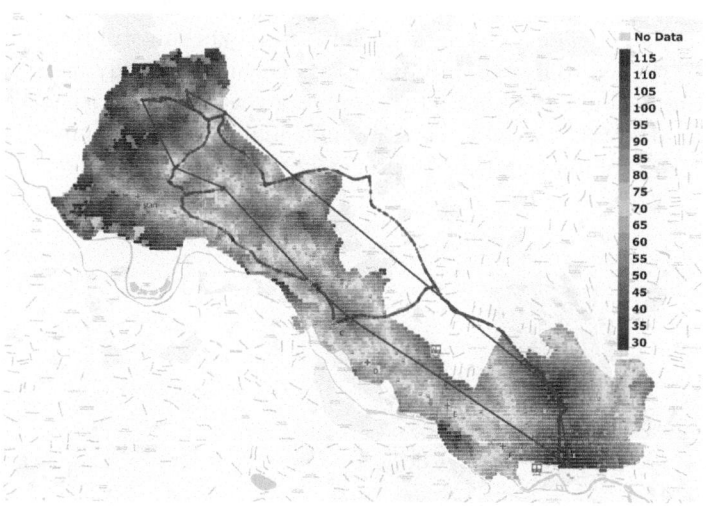

**Fig. 6.** Best result under the capped speed limitation.

## 4.2 Speed Limit Ratio

Table 4 shows the results of each meta-heuristic solver across the 30 independent optimisation runs when applying the more restrictive speed limit ratio method.

Among all algorithms, PSO identified the best fitness, however, this exceeds the desired limit of 8 CAVS. The GA identified the optimal CAV service using at

**Table 4.** Speed limit ratio optimisation results

| | Limit | Num. CAV | Fitness | | Penalty Fitness | |
|---|---|---|---|---|---|---|
| | | | Average | Best | Average | Best |
| DE | ratio | 8 | 1537.1 | 1530.1 | 1537.1 | 1530.1 |
| PBIL | ratio | 54 | 1564.5 | 1553.6 | 8500.4 | 7189.7 |
| GA | ratio | 8 | 1526.7 | 1522.1 | **1526.7** | **1522.1** |
| PSO | ratio | 16 | **1509.1** | **1428.4** | 2387.6 | 1538.3 |

most 8 CAVs, in alignment with the requirements of WYCA experts. The best CAV service in the speed limit ratio optimisation (enforcing the 8 CAV limit) achieved an average fitness time of 1522.1 s, which is only a 3.1% improvement over the baseline fitness. By comparing the plots in Figs. 7 and 8 we can infer that the lower speeds induced by the speed limit ratio method coupled with the mandatory Horsforth Train Station inclusion and high-frequency constraints severely limit the spatial reachability of an 8-CAV service. As this also likely hinders connectivity with the existing PT network, the overall PT commute time improvement is marginal. However, by relaxing the max CAV constraint to 12 and especially 14 vehicles, significant improvements can still be achieved even when forcing service routes to only use roads within the study area. The result plotted in Fig. 8b indicates that when applying the more restrictive speed limit ratio method, the full usage of the A65 main main road is required in order to deliver maximal commuting time improvements.

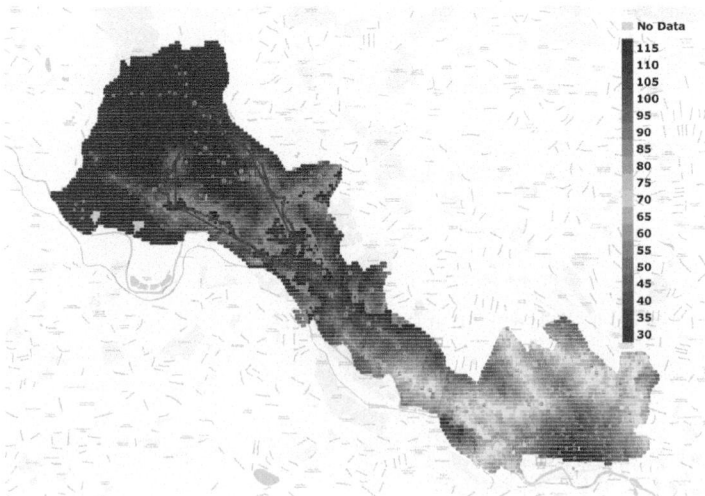

**Fig. 7.** Best result under the speed limit ratio limitation (max 8 CAVs).

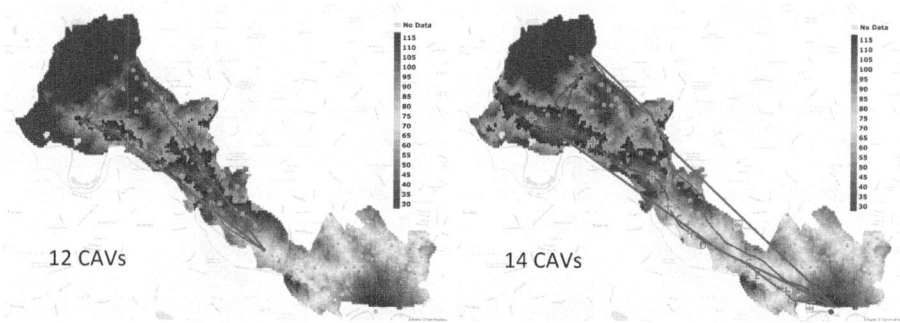

(a) Best result using max 12 CAVs and the speed limit ratio limitation: 4.5% improvement.

(b) Best result using max 12 CAVs and the speed limit ratio limitation: 12.5% improvement.

**Fig. 8.** Speed limit ratio results with a higher max CAVs limit.

## 5    Conclusion

In this work, we showcased how integrating macro- and micro-level simulations can address city transport challenges, using the real-world A65 scenario proposed by WYCA domain experts to illustrate our approach. By combining high-level PT planning with detailed vehicle behavior modeling during rush hour intervals, we gained a fuller, more realistic picture of the overall capabilities of the modelled transportation system. This dual-layer method offers insights that neither simulation type can provide on its own.

The efficient integration of micro- and macro- simulations brings several advantages. It allows for a more comprehensive analysis, merging broad traffic trends with detailed vehicle interactions to better understand transport dynamics. Moreover, the proposed approach enables predictive scenario modeling, which can improve PT efficiency and road usage through better resource allocation and planning.

There are several opportunities to explore across future work streams: new methods for integrating micro- and macro-level simulations to further enhance transportation models, applications to more complex, real-world problems, support for additional data sources. Furthermore, the application of our simulation-optimisation approach within other research fields like urban planning, environmental science, and economics can help crystallise a more holistic understanding of transportation impacts, leading to more sustainable and effective solutions.

**Acknowledgements.** The authors would like to acknowledge the support and constructive feedback provided by both West Yorkshire Combined Authority transport policy officers and experts at the Institute of Transportation Systems at the German Aerospace Center (Deutsches Zentrum für Luft- und Raumfahrt - DLR).

This research was supported as part of Automated Road Transport Forum (ART-Forum) Interreg project supported by the North Sea Programme of the European Regional Development Fund of the European Union.

# References

1. Ali, Y., Sharma, A., Haque, M.M., Zheng, Z., Saifuzzaman, M.: The impact of the connected environment on driving behavior and safety: a driving simulator study. Accid. Anal. Prev. **144**, 105643 (2020)
2. Antrim, A., Barbeau, S.J., et al.: The many uses of GTFS data–opening the door to transit and multimodal applications. Location-Aware Information Systems Laboratory at the University of South Florida **4** (2013)
3. Baluja, S.: Population-based incremental learning. a method for integrating genetic search based function optimization and competitive learning. Tech. rep., Carnegie-Mellon Univ Pittsburgh Pa Dept Of Computer Science (1994)
4. Bennett, J.: OpenStreetMap. Packt Publishing Ltd (2010)
5. Bibri, S.E.: Data-driven smart sustainable cities of the future: an evidence synthesis approach to a comprehensive state-of-the-art literature review. Sustain. Futures **3**, 100047 (2021)
6. Chondrogiannis, T., Nascimento, M.A., Bouros, P.: Relative reachability analysis as a tool for urban mobility planning: Position paper. In: Proceedings of the 12th ACM SIGSPATIAL International Workshop on Computational Transportation Science, pp. 1–4 (2019)
7. Han, K., Christie, L.A., Zǎvoianu, A.C., McCall, J.: Optimising the introduction of connected and autonomous vehicles in a public transport system using macro-level mobility simulations and evolutionary algorithms. In: Proceedings of the Genetic and Evolutionary Computation Conference Companion, pp. 315–316 (2021)
8. Han, K., Christie, L.A., Zǎvoianu, A.C., McCall, J.: On discovering optimal trade-offs when introducing new routes in existing multi-modal public transport systems. In: International Conference on Computer Aided Systems Theory, pp. 104–111. Springer (2022)
9. Han, K., Christie, L.A., Zǎvoianu, A.C., McCall, J.A.: Exploring representations for optimizing connected autonomous vehicle routes in multi-modal transport networks using evolutionary algorithms. IEEE Transactions on Intelligent Transportation Systems (2024)
10. Holland, J.H.: Genetic algorithms. Sci. Am. **267**(1), 66–73 (1992)
11. Innerebner, M., Böhlen, M., Gamper, J.: ISOGA: a system for geographical reachability analysis. In: International Symposium on Web and Wireless Geographical Information Systems, pp. 180–189. Springer (2013)
12. Kirchler, D.: Efficient routing on multi-modal transportation networks. Ph.D. thesis, Ecole Polytechnique X (2013)
13. Krajzewicz, D., Hertkorn, G., Rössel, C., Wagner, P.: An example of microscopic car models validation using the open source traffic simulation sumo. In: Proceedings of Simulation in Industry, 14th European Simulation Symposium, pp. 318–322 (2002)
14. Li, N., Yao, Y., Kolmanovsky, I., Atkins, E., Girard, A.R.: Game-theoretic modeling of multi-vehicle interactions at uncontrolled intersections. IEEE Trans. Intell. Transp. Syst. **23**(2), 1428–1442 (2020)
15. Liu, Z., Jia, H., Wang, Y.: Urban expressway parallel pattern recognition based on intelligent IoT data processing for smart city. Comput. Commun. **155**, 40–47 (2020)
16. Lopez, P.A., et al.: Microscopic traffic simulation using sumo. In: 2018 21st International Conference on Intelligent Transportation Systems (ITSC), pp. 2575–2582. IEEE (2018)

17. Mouratidis, K.: Urban planning and quality of life: a review of pathways linking the built environment to subjective well-being. Cities **115**, 103229 (2021)
18. Price, K., Storn, R.M., Lampinen, J.A.: Differential evolution: a practical approach to global optimization. Springer Science & Business Media (2006)
19. Shi, Y.: Particle swarm optimization. IEEE Connections **2**(1), 8–13 (2004)
20. of Transportation Systems DLR, I.: Report_dlr_leeds_a65_220809_draft. Technical Report 42, Deutsches Zentrum für Luft- und Raumfahrt (DLR) (2022). unpublished

# Automated Inference of Domain Knowledge in Scientific Machine Learning

Florian Bachinger[1,2]($\boxtimes$)(ID), Christian Haider[1](ID), Jan Zenisek[1,3](ID),
Fabrício Olivetti de França[4](ID), and Michael Affenzeller[1,3](ID)

[1] Heuristic and Evolutionary Algorithms Laboratory,
University of Applied Sciences Upper Austria, Hagenberg, Austria
`florian.bachinger@fh-hagenberg.at`
[2] Institute for Application-oriented Knowledge Processing (FAW),
Johannes Kepler University, Linz, Austria
[3] Institute for Symbolic Artificial Intelligence, Johannes Kepler University,
Linz, Austria
[4] Center for Mathematics, Computing and Cognition, Federal University of ABC,
Santo André, Brazil

**Abstract.** The integration of prior knowledge into the training of machine learning (ML) models can improve their inter- and extrapolation capabilities and increases the trust of domain experts in model predictions. Shape-constrained regression is one category of ML algorithms capable of integrating knowledge about the shape of the model. Such knowledge is represented by boundary information of partial derivatives of different orders.

However, the translation or formulation of (intrinsic) domain expert knowledge into such constraints is challenging and requires experience. Sometimes, this knowledge may even be unavailable for certain domains. We propose an approach that can automatically infer such knowledge from observational data. We envision this approach as an additional tool in the data analysis toolbox that provides suggestions, which can be incorporated into the training of prediction models.

In this work, we describe our approach for automated knowledge inference from data. Additionally, we show the applicability of our approach by testing it on synthetic data generated from a set of physics equations.

**Keywords:** Knowledge Inference · Shape-Constrained Regression

## 1 Introduction

In applications of machine learning (ML) we see the ever-increasing need for interpretable and domain-informed prediction models that increase trust in their predictions. One research direction tries to explain already trained models after the fact [8], while another tries to introduce domain knowledge during ML training to ensure that the resulting models adhere to expected behavior.

A. Quesada-Arencibia et al. (Eds.): EUROCAST 2024, LNCS 15172, pp. 122–130, 2025.
https://doi.org/10.1007/978-3-031-82949-9_11

One category of ML algorithms, capable of domain knowledge integration, are algorithms of shape-constrained regression (SCR) [5]. Therein, interval bounds are introduced onto the image of the function or onto any of its partial derivatives to enforce the shape of the prediction function.

Possible examples for shape-constraints are: a function is known to be solely positive valued $f(X) \geq 0$ (e.g., the power production of a photovoltaic (PV) system), or a function is monotonic non-decreasing over a certain input $\frac{\partial}{\partial x_i} f(X) \geq 0$ (e.g., increasing solar radiation, in turn, increases PV power production). Shape-constraints are especially useful when training data is available in limited amount, or when certain extrapolation behavior should be enforced.

**Motivation:** Shape-constraints allow us to define and enforce behavior of prediction models, thereby, improving the quality of ML models and increasing trust in their predictions. They have been shown to improve motion control models of robots [7], models of economic functions [1], or have been successfully applied to detect erroneous data [2,3].

Currently, however, we rely on domain experts or first principles to gain the prior knowledge for domain-informed ML, and rely on data scientists to translate this knowledge into constraints. Yet, domain experts might be unaware of the existence of such knowledge in their respective fields. Or, in areas such as material sciences, require empirical research and subsequent analysis of recorded sensor data to gather this knowledge.

**Vision:** We present an approach that is able to automatically infer knowledge from data. We envision the application of our approach as an additional tool in the data preparation phase of ML. Data scientists apply our approach on new data to retrieve suitable constraints. This knowledge can improve the business- and data-understanding (cf. CRISP-DM) of data scientists and practitioners, or, can be integrated into model training, if a suitable ML algorithm is selected. Thereby, our approach will contribute towards improving ML results, can guide the ML algorithm's search, and can improve resulting prediction performance.

**Approach:** If certain properties, such as positivity or monotonicity, are true for the whole domain of the provided data, they are also true for any given subset. Thus, we split the available data spatially into two sets, one spatially inner dataset where we find knowledge and one extrapolation set where we test our hypothesis about suitable knowledge algorithmically.

The assumption being, that the application of correct knowledge will exhibit the best extrapolation performance, as prediction models, that are trained with correct knowledge, are being guided in the correct manner. We rank the models, by the validation error, to obtain the most likely ground truth.

**Structure:** This paper is structured as follows, Sect. 2 provides a background on shape-constrained regression and introduces the benchmark used to evaluate our approach. In Sect. 3 we present our approach, the experimental setup, and our method to evaluate our results. Finally, Sect. 4 presents and discusses the results, followed by our conclusion and discussion of future work in Sect. 5.

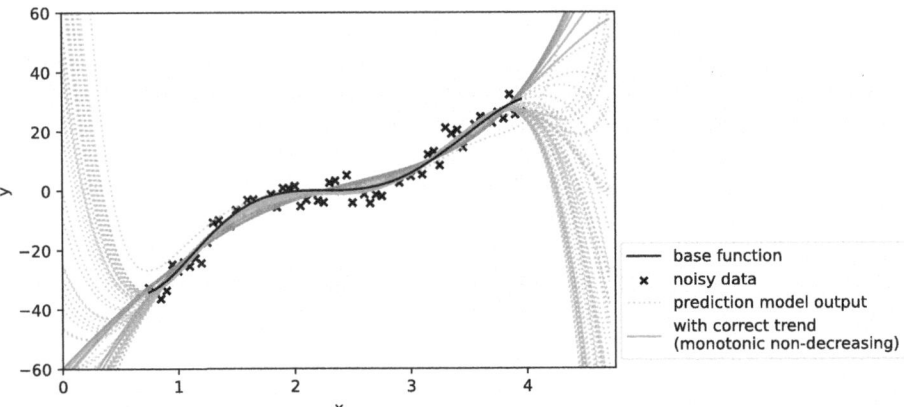

**Fig. 1.** An example to highlight the benefits of shape-constrained regression. A base function is defined for $x \in [1,4]$, and is used to sample data points. For the training data, we add normal distributed random noise. In the extrapolation range $x \in [0,1] \cup [4,5]$, only some models exhibit the desired monotonic non-decreasing behavior. Unconstrained prediction models are uninformed, and often show widely varied extrapolation behavior.

## 2    Background

This section provides an introduction to shape-constrained regression (SCR), a class of algorithms capable of integrating prior knowledge in the form of shape constraints. It also details the mathematical notation of shape constraints.

Additionally, we describe the benchmark suite used to generate the training data. From this suite, we select one instance to explain the type of knowledge represented by shape constraints.

### 2.1    Shape Constraints and Shape-Constrained Regression (SCR)

Shape-constrained regression (SCR) algorithms allow the enforcement of shape-properties on the image of a function or any of its partial derivatives. Shape constraints can be represented by a mathematical notation, such as $\forall_x\, x \in [a,b] \Rightarrow \frac{\partial f}{\partial x} > 0$. In this example, we declare the function to be monotonic increasing over x, but only for the input domain $x \in [a,b]$. Outside this domain, the function is unrestricted, and is only guided by training data, if available.

The logical conjunction $\wedge$ combines multiple constraints. Each can be defined for individual input domains. Therefore, constraints serve as an expressive language to convey prior (domain expert) knowledge.

The benefit of prior knowledge integration for ML is illustrated in Fig. 1, where we trained unconstrained models on noisy data. We purposefully highlight the often erratic, unguided behavior of ML models in areas, where no training data is available. By chance, some trained, unconstrained models extrapolate in the correct perceived trend of monotonic non-decreasing. Whereas, SCR algorithms can enforce this behavior and are guaranteed to return only models that adhere to the provided prior knowledge.

Shape constraints are available in a number of regression algorithms such as gradient boosted trees (XGBoost) [4], shape-constrained polynomial regression (SCPR) [5], or shape-constrained symbolic regression (SCSR) [6]. For the purpose of our work, SCPR was selected as it allows for more expressive constraints compared to XGBoost and is fast to execute (cf. [3] for a more detailed comparison).

## 2.2  AI Feynman Benchmark Set

In order to investigate the viability of our knowledge inference approach, we require datasets for which the knowledge is known beforehand. Based on this, we can compare the algorithm suggestions with the baseline of known constraints.

The AI Feynman [9] symbolic regression database serves as the benchmark suite for our paper. It contains a list of 120 numbered expressions (e.g., instance number I.13.12) from various engineering and physics related domains that were part of Richard Feynman's most popular lectures.

To obtain the baseline of known constraints for each expression, we begin by sampling a large, uniform random set of input data for the expression. This can be done, as each expression defines a list of inputs and their respective input domains. By evaluating the expression and its partial derivatives on the input data, we can determine the baseline of known constraints by analyzing the noiseless function output or the gradients, by evaluating the partial derivatives on the data (cf. [2] Appendix C for a more detailed description of this procedure).

## 2.3  The Type of Inferred Knowledge

Our approach is able to extract knowledge in the form of monotonic relationships represented in observational data, without any knowledge about the underlying truth (i.e., the expression itself). Instance I.13.12 serves as illustrative example:

$$W = GmM \cdot \left[ \frac{1}{r1} - \frac{1}{r2} \right],  \tag{1}$$

describes the potential energy of a small falling object m that is under the influence of the gravitational mass of a larger object M (cf. Fig. 2).

Obviously, a further larger radius r1 increases the travelled distance, and thus increases the potential energy of the fall. Whilst a larger radius r2 shortens the travelled distance, and lessens the potential energy. The constraints

$$\{ \frac{\partial W}{\partial r_1} \geq 0, \frac{\partial W}{\partial r_2} \leq 0 \},  \tag{2}$$

describe these facts in mathematical notation.

Our approach can infer such knowledge from observational data alone. It can, therefore, provide insights about the interactions between individual observations and their respective target automatically.

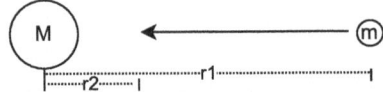

**Fig. 2.** An object of small mass m starts at distance r1 and falls towards the object M at distance r2, whilst being affected by M's gravity.

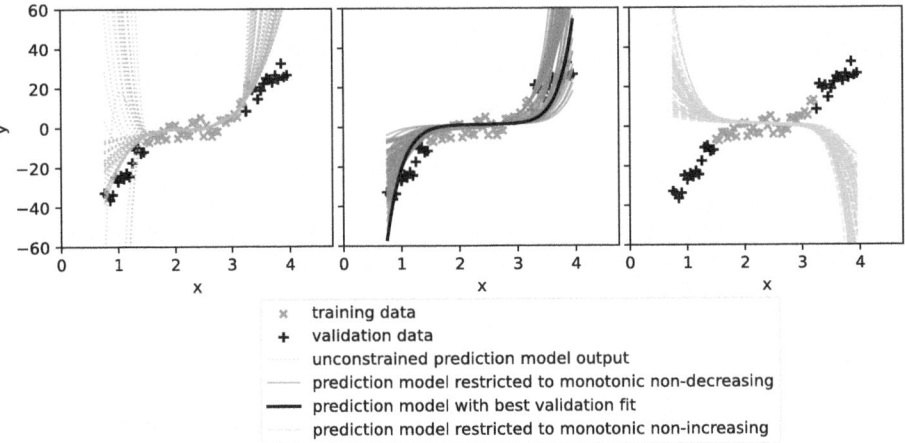

**Fig. 3.** An illustration of our approach based on a simple, univariate problem. The data is spatially split into an *inner* training- and an *outer* validation-set. ML models are trained for each possible combination of constraint. The prediction model with the best extrapolation behavior (bold black, monotonic non-decreasing) informs the most likely knowledge present in the data.

## 3  Automated Knowledge Inference

This section details our knowledge inference approach. We begin by exploring our approach based on a simple illustrative example. Then, we detail the setup of our experiments, with which we show the viability of our approach. Lastly, we explain how we calculate our metrics and present our final results.

### 3.1  General Idea

Our knowledge inference approach follows the idea that, if a certain trend is true for the whole dataset, it is also true for any section of the data. Thus, we can split the available data spatially into two sets. The *inner* data is used to form a hypothesis about the knowledge represented in the data, whereas the *outer* section is used to verify the hypotheses.

Figure 3 presents a visual example for a simple univariate problem. The input $x$ could have (1) none, or no consistent relationship, (2) a monotonic non-decreasing relationship, or (3) a monotonic non-increasing relationship with $y$. To test each of these possibilities, we train ML prediction models with each of the three constraint options on the training data. However, these constraints are enforced not only for the *inner* training data domain of $x \in [1.5, 3.5]$, but are instead enforced for the full domain $x \in [1, 4]$, of the originally provided data.

After this step, we evaluate each prediction model on the validation set. The assumption being, that a model with the correct constraint combination will exhibit the best extrapolation performance, i.e., the lowest validation error.

Complexity arises by the fact, that, the number of constraint combinations rises exponentially with the number of inputs. For example, instance I.13.4, as listed in Table 1, has 4 inputs $m, u, v, w$, which results in 81 possible constraint combinations, compared to the 9 for instance I.6.2.

### 3.2  Experimental Setup

To obtain a ground truth of known constraints, we calculated the constraints for each AI Feynman expression and hosted our results on our GitHub repository[1]. The benchmark suite contains 120 instances, from which we excluded any with more than 6 inputs, as their computational complexity is too high.

For each instance, we sample 200 uniform random data points for the defined input domain. We evaluate the expression on this data to obtain the target $y$. Onto $y$, we add a normal distributed random error

$$y_{\text{noisy}} = y + N \left( 0, \sigma_y \sqrt{\frac{\alpha}{1 - \alpha}} \right), \tag{3}$$

to obtain a noisy target feature. This is done, in order to simulate real-world sensor noise. In our experiments, we use a noise-level of $\alpha = 10\%$. After this step, we apply a $80\%/20\%$ training-/validation-split by sequentially moving the convex hull of the inputs and their associated target to the validation set.

Now, we have obtained 114 datasets for which we infer knowledge. For each dataset, we iterate over all possible constraint combinations. Table 2, for example, shows the 9 possible constraint combinations of instance I.6.2. Each constraint combination is applied in one SCPR run, to obtain a constrained prediction model. However, the constraints are enforced not only for the input domain of the test data, but for the full domain including the validation range. Each resulting model is evaluated on the validation data and ranked by ascending validation root mean squared error (RMSE). Again, Table 2 serves as an example, showing the result for each of the 9 possible constraint combinations.

## 4  Discussion of Results

We evaluate our approach based on two metrics. In the first metric, we report, if our approach suggested the correct combination of constraints as the topmost

---

[1] https://github.com/florianBachinger/FeynmanEquations-Python.

**Table 1.** Two exemplary instances as included in the AI Feynman benchmark suite. The number of variables determines the number of possible constraint combination, of which, only one combination is correct and is reported in the last column. Table 2, e.g., lists all possible constraint combinations of equation I.6.2.

| Instance | Expression | Variables | Combinations | Correct Combination |
|----------|-----------|-----------|--------------|---------------------|
| I.6.2 | $\frac{\sqrt{2}e^{-\frac{\theta^2}{2\sigma^2}}}{2\sqrt{\pi}\sigma}$ | 2 | 9 | $\{\frac{\partial f}{\partial \theta} \leq 0\}$ |
| I.13.4 | $\frac{m\left(u^2+v^2+w^2\right)}{2}$ | 4 | 81 | $\{\frac{\partial f}{\partial m} \geq 0, \frac{\partial f}{\partial v} \geq 0, \frac{\partial f}{\partial u} \geq 0, \frac{\partial f}{\partial w} \geq 0\}$ |

**Table 2.** Instance I.6.2 yields a total of 9 possible constraint combinations. The third column reports the RMSE on the validation set in ascending order. The last two columns report if the suggested constraints are at least correct but maybe complete, or if they fully match the known ground truth.

| Instance | Tested Combination | RMSE | Correct Subset | Full Match |
|----------|-------------------|------|----------------|------------|
| I.6.2 | $\{\frac{\partial f}{\partial \theta} \leq 0\}$ | 0.0154 | ☑ | ☑ |
| I.6.2 | $\{\}$ | 0.0158 | ☑ | ☐ |
| I.6.2 | $\{\frac{\partial f}{\partial \sigma} \leq 0, \frac{\partial f}{\partial \theta} \leq 0\}$ | 0.0285 | ☐ | ☐ |
| I.6.2 | $\{\frac{\partial f}{\partial \sigma} \leq 0\}$ | 0.0290 | ☐ | ☐ |
| I.6.2 | $\{\frac{\partial f}{\partial \sigma} \geq 0\}$ | 0.0361 | ☐ | ☐ |
| I.6.2 | $\{\frac{\partial f}{\partial \sigma} \geq 0, \frac{\partial f}{\partial \theta} \leq 0\}$ | 0.0362 | ☐ | ☐ |
| I.6.2 | $\{\frac{\partial f}{\partial \sigma} \leq 0, \frac{\partial f}{\partial \theta} \geq 0\}$ | 0.0630 | ☐ | ☐ |
| I.6.2 | $\{\frac{\partial f}{\partial \sigma} \geq 0, \frac{\partial f}{\partial \theta} \geq 0\}$ | 0.0714 | ☐ | ☐ |
| I.6.2 | $\{\frac{\partial f}{\partial \theta} \geq 0\}$ | 0.0861 | ☐ | ☐ |

results, i.e., the lowest validation RMSE. Instance I.6.2, as reported in Table 2, serves as one such example. This topmost *rank* of one was achieved for 21 of 114 instances. These 21 instances have, on average, 3.04 input variables, and an average of 2.04 known constraints. In total, the 114 selected benchmark instances have, on average, 3.73 input variables, and 2.83 known constraints. Over all 114 instances, we achieved an average rank of 16.07.

Another metric is motivated by instances such as I.13.4, as listed in Table 1, where numerous constraints are available. Every single one of them is true on their own, but only the exact combination is evaluated in the previous ranked metric. Therefore, we additionally calculated the *depth of the true set*, wherein we counted how many of the topmost entries, by ascending RMSE order, report a true but possibly incomplete constraint information. This streak is interrupted by the first erroneous suggestion. In total, for 78 of 114 instances, our approach presents the user with a true topmost suggestion. For 70 out of 114, the top two suggestions are true, and for 65 of 114 a minimum streak of 4 true top suggestions is achieved, to list some. In total, we achieved an average streak of 7.28.

# 5   Conclusion and Outlook

We present an approach that is able to infer knowledge, in the form of monotonic interactions, from observational data. We evaluated our approach on a large benchmark suite that represents common problems from the domains of physics and engineering. Our approach serves as a meaningful extension to the existing tooling landscape of the data science pipeline, as it increases the business- and data-understanding and provides the knowledge to improve predictive models.

Currently, however, we apply a brute force approach by investigating every possible combination of knowledge to determine the ground truth. In the future, we aim to improve in this area by, e.g., investigating single features, in a first step, to reduce the number of tested combinations. Additionally, we think that metrics from the research area of knowledge retrieval might improve future comparability with other approaches, and between our own future results.

**Acknowledgement.** The presented work was done within the project "Secure Prescriptive Analytics", which is funded by the state of Upper Austria as part of the program "#upperVISION2030". F.O.F. is supported by Conselho Nacional de Desenvolvimento Científico e Tecnológico (CNPq) through the grant 301596/2022-0. C. H. was supported within the Dissertationsprogramm der Fachhochschule OÖ #50549324 Integration von Domänenwissen in Symbolische Regression (IDSR), funded by the Austrian Research Promotion Agency FFG.

# References

1. Aït-Sahalia, Y., Duarte, J.: Nonparametric option pricing under shape restrictions. J. Econ. **116**(1–2), 9–47 (2003)
2. Bachinger, F., Ehrlinger, L., Kronberger, G., Wöss, W.: Data validation utilizing expert knowledge and shape constraints. J. Data Info. Qual. **16**(2), 1–27 (2024). https://doi.org/10.1145/3661826
3. Bachinger, F., Kronberger, G.: Comparing shape-constrained regression algorithms for data validation. In: Moreno-Díaz, R., Pichler, F., Quesada-Arencibia, A. (eds.) Computer Aided Systems Theory - EUROCAST 2022, pp. 147–154. Springer Nature Switzerland, Cham (2022). https://doi.org/10.1007/978-3-031-25312-6_17
4. Chen, T., Guestrin, C.: XGBoost: a scalable tree boosting system. In: Proceedings of the 22nd ACM SIGKDD International Conference on Knowledge Discovery and Data Mining, pp. 785–794. KDD 2016, Association for Computing Machinery, New York, NY, USA (2016)
5. Curmei, M., Hall, G.: Shape-constrained regression using sum of squares polynomials. Oper. Res. https://doi.org/10.1287/opre.2021.0383
6. Kronberger, G., de Franca, F.O., Burlacu, B., Haider, C., Kommenda, M.: Shape-Constrained symbolic regression-improving extrapolation with prior knowledge. Evol. Comput. **30**(1), 75–98 (2022)
7. Majumdar, A., Hall, G., Ahmadi, A.A.: Recent scalability improvements for semidefinite programming with applications in machine learning, control, and robotics. Ann. Rev. Control Robot. Auton. Syst. **3**, 331–360 (2020)

8. Rudin, C.: Stop explaining black box machine learning models for high stakes decisions and use interpretable models instead. Nat. Mach. Intell. **1**(5), 206–215 (2019)
9. Udrescu, S.M., Tegmark, M.: AI Feynman: A physics-inspired method for symbolic
   regression. Sci. Adv. **6**(16), eaay2631 (2020)

# Automated Guided Vehicles in Yard Logistics: A Time-Dependent Approach

Ulrike Ritzinger$^{(\boxtimes)}$ ⓘ, Bin Hu ⓘ, and Martin Reinthaler ⓘ

AIT Austrian Institute of Technology, Center for Energy, Integrated Energy Systems, Giefinggasse 4, 1210 Vienna, Austria
{ulrike.ritzinger,bin.hu,martin.reinthaler}@ait.ac.at

**Abstract.** Connected and automated vehicles will soon disrupt the logistics and freight transport system. While AI advancements offer potential solutions, challenges like high development costs, safety requirements, and legal issues persist. This paper presents an optimization algorithm for scheduling automated guided vehicles (AGV) in yard logistics. In the problem setting, a fleet of AGVs needs to fulfill orders in an industry compound. The problem is modeled as a time-dependent pickup and delivery problem with time windows and solved with a large neighborhood search approach with destroy and repair neighborhoods and integrated conflict detection.

Computational experiments show that the algorithm is able to handle instances with up to 100 orders over 8 h and a fleet of up to four AGVs. Furthermore, they show the potential and scalability of integrating an optimization algorithm with an effective fleet management system in such a logistics system.

**Keywords:** Automated guided vehicles · Yard logistics · Time-dependent travel times · Large Neighborhood Search

## 1 Introduction

Connected and automated vehicles significantly impact the global automotive industry, particularly the logistics and freight transport sector. The rise of autonomous driving technology is reshaping mobility paradigms, prompting established players and startups alike to adapt. While advancements in AI show promise in managing the complexities of autonomous driving, the challenges, such as high development costs, safety requirements, and legal questions, remain significant. Compared to public roads, operation in controlled environments such as yards lowers the risk factors. Still, yard logistics addresses issues such as a shortage of qualified drivers, high accident rates, and underutilized freight capacity.

In the project AWARD (All Weather Autonomous Real Logistics Operations and Demonstrations), a framework has been developed to support adopting autonomous technology in freight transport in real-life logistics scenarios [3].

A. Quesada-Arencibia et al. (Eds.): EUROCAST 2024, LNCS 15172, pp. 131–139, 2025.
https://doi.org/10.1007/978-3-031-82949-9_12

The goal is to create an automated guided vehicles (AGV) system with multiple sensors and a teleoperation system for 24/7 availability. AGV has been a popular research topic due to the advancements in CCAM technology and the demand for automation in freight logistics. A recent review by Rashidi et al. [8] provides insights into AGV applications, problem modeling, and algorithms used in real-world logistics and manufacturing systems. A more specialized work on AGV for pickup and delivery is presented in [5], where the authors use a time-space network to solve the conflict-free routing problem.

In the AWARD project, AGVs operate in real-world pilot demonstrations for validation. A crucial aspect is the dedication to outdoor logistics. Compared to indoor warehouse logistics where AGVs are already deployed in practice [2], the outdoor use cases in AWARD face much more complex challenges. The use cases address vehicle tasks in different settings, from industrial sites to public roadways, as well as scenarios with different automated vehicles and users. The AWARD project aims to demonstrate that automated vehicles work in all-weather conditions and address challenges related to deploying these vehicles in real logistics operations through several strategic use cases that meet market needs, from the factory to logistics hubs to airports.

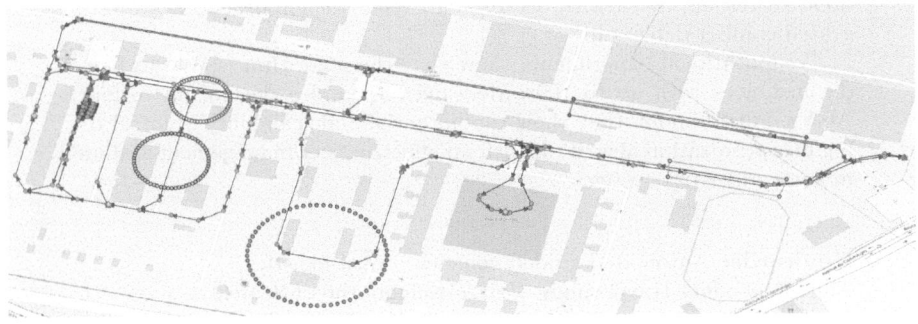

**Fig. 1.** It shows the real-world road network in Toulouse consisting of 173 nodes, 252 directed arcs, and five situations causing a change in the AGV's speed due to road restrictions or weather situations.

The fleet management system (FMS) is a central component for optimizing logistics processes integrating various information sources (e.g., vehicles, logistics systems, and roadside infrastructure). The system is designed to dispatch the most suitable vehicle for a logistics order based on the current conditions. For every vehicle, it generates and monitors the schedule with respect to the status of tasks, dynamic weather changes, and any unforeseen changes in the road network. Also, for a working fleet system, the schedule has to guarantee that the vehicles will never enter deadlock situations, i.e., it is conflict-free. To demonstrate the scalability of the FMS and its integrated optimization algorithm, we generate different test lab scenarios in an industrial compound in Toulouse, see

Fig. 1. The goal is to show that the implemented algorithms perform well for transportation requests in the outdoor logistic yard.

In this paper, we focus on the fleet navigation algorithm of the FMS, which assigns the orders and routes to the AGVs in the transport network. Orders are in the form that goods must be picked up and delivered at certain times. Orders can occur during the day, and road connections may change depending on weather conditions. Hence, algorithmically, this is a time-dependent pickup and delivery problem (PDP) [9] on a directed graph, where nodes represent junctions and arcs represent road segments. The optimization algorithm applied in this paper consists of three main components: building a graph of the road network, a time-dependent routing algorithm, and a large neighborhood search [7] for optimizing vehicle routes.

## 2    Problem Description

This work considers a road network with time-dependent travel times caused by weather situations and network restrictions. Thus, the given road network is a directed graph $G = (V, A)$, which consists of a set of vertices $V = \{0, \dots, n\}$ representing intersections and waypoints and a set of arcs $A$, representing the road segments between a pair of vertices $i, j \in V$. Each arc $(i, j) \in A$ is associated with a distance $d_{ij}$, a time-dependent speed function $v_{ij} : t- \to R^+$, and a time-dependent cost function $c_{ij} : t \to R^+$, which corresponds to the travel time.

The varying speeds and travel times result from different weather conditions and network restrictions, modeled as so-called *situations*. A situation can either arise according to the weather forecast (e.g., heavy rain in the afternoon) or be generated by an operator (e.g., restricted area). We have a set of situations $S$, where each situation $s \in S$ is defined by a polygon $\mathcal{N}_s$ including a subset of affected arcs $A_{\mathcal{N}_s} \subseteq A$, a period with a start and end time $p_s = [a_{p_s}, b_{p_s}]$ defining the temporal validity of $s$, and a corresponding speed $v_s \to v_{ij}(p_s)$ for all $(i, j) \in A_{\mathcal{N}_s} : v_{ij}(t)$ for all departure times $t \in [a_{p_s}, b_{p_s}]$. Each arc has at least one period with speed assigned, but respectively more if it is affected by one or more situations, resulting in a list of periods $\mathcal{P}_{ij}$ and a list of its corresponding speeds $\mathcal{D}_{ij}$ for each arc $(i, j) \in A$. Usually, other works (e.g., [1,6]) divide the planning horizon into periods set to be the same for all arcs. In this work, it is crucial to allow different periods and speeds because of different conditions, like weather (e.g., rain does not affect all segments equally: ramp vs. road), road frictions, and restricted areas. However, it is guaranteed that different situations do not occur simultaneously (i.e., only one speed is valid at a given moment). One specific scenario involves situations where entry into certain areas, such as closed road segments, is prohibited for the specified period.

Since goods must be transported from one location (pickup) to another (delivery) at a given time, we model the problem as a time-dependent pickup and delivery problem with time windows (TD-PDPTW). We have a set of orders $O$ generated by an operator or a logistics system that must be fulfilled. Each order $o \in O$ consists of a pickup and delivery node pair $\{p_o, d_o\}$ with $p_o, d_o \in V$

and a positive demand $q_o$ at the pickup node, and a negative demand $-q_o$ at the delivery node. Furthermore, a service time $s_{p_o}$ for the pickup and a service time $s_{d_o}$ for the delivery are given. Each order has a crucial time window $tw_o = [a_o, b_o]$ assigned at the pickup or delivery, and the other time window is set on the planning horizon. Time windows are modeled as mixed soft time windows, meaning the service should start within the given time window. Starting the service before $a_i$ is not allowed and results in (not penalized) waiting time, but starting the service after $b_i$ will be penalized in the objective function. Furthermore, a threshold is set to avoid significant delays beyond which fulfilling an order is not feasible. Additionally, a set of vehicles $K$ is given, where each vehicle $k$ has a defined parking position $z_k \in V$ and a defined maximum capacity $C_k$. Due to the given road network, a capacity for each node $c_i, i \in V$ is given, which limits the capacity of vehicles that can accommodate at node $i$ simultaneously. Note that there is no limit for the road segments set because they are double-tracked.

The TD-PDPTW formulated in this work aims to construct a conflict-free schedule for the vehicles to fulfill transportation orders by respecting capacity constraints, time window constraints, and time-dependent travel times. We consider a lexicographic objective, with the primary objective of serving as many requests as possible. The second objective is minimizing the total delay in serving orders, and the third is minimizing the total travel time.

## 3    Solution Approach

Here, we present all our solution approaches to generate conflict-free routes for the given real-world TD-PDPTW efficiently. Sections 3.1 and 3.2 examine the time-dependent setting, and Sect. 3.3 presents the meta-heuristic approach we implemented to generate efficient schedules for the vehicles.

### 3.1    Time-Dependent Shortest Paths

The first step is to adapt the directed graph according to the given situations $S$. For each situation $s \in S$, the arc set $A_{\mathcal{P}_s}$ is determined. It comprises all arcs within its polygon $\mathcal{P}_s$. Arcs that intersect $\mathcal{P}_s$ are split such that the original arc is removed, and a new vertex $i'$ at the intersection is added to $V$ with the corresponding arcs $(i, i')$ and $(i', j)$. Then, the speed $v_s$ is set for the given period $p_s$ for all arcs $(i, j) \in A_{\mathcal{P}_s}$.

A time-dependent variant of the Dijkstra algorithm is applied to get the path (i.e., sequence of consecutive arcs) with the minimum costs $c_{ij}$ (i.e., travel time) between a source node $i$ and a destination node $j$ with $i, j \in V$ at departure time $t$. At each iteration, the travel cost from the current node ($s$ at the beginning) to each non-permanently labeled successor is calculated by a weighting function, an extension of the procedure in [4]. Therefore, it uses the speed associated with that arc and period. Algorithm 1 depicts the weighting function. Note that

**Algorithm 1:** Travel costs to a successor of a node.

---

**Input:** arc $(i, j)$, arrival time $t$, period $p = 0$
**Output:** travel costs $c_{ij}$
**while** $t \geq a_p$ **do**
  | $p = p + 1$     // find period for $t$
**end**
$c' = b_p - t$     // remaining time in period $p$
$d' = c_{ij} = 0$     // covered distance $d'$ and its costs $c_{ij}$
$d = c' \cdot v_{ij}(p)$     // distance $d$ : if $v_{ij}(p)$ is road closed $\rightarrow d = 0$
**while** $d \leq d_{ij}$ **do**
  | $c_{ij} = c_{ij} + c'$
  | $p = p + 1$
  | $d' = d$     // if $v_{ij}(p)$ is road closed $\rightarrow d' = 0$
  | $c' = b_p - a_p$
  | $d = d' + (c' \cdots v_{ij}(p))$
**end**
**return** $c_{ij} + ((d_{ij} - d')/v_{ij}(p))$

---

it considers the special case when road segments are closed. In that case, no distance is covered while waiting.

To integrate the shortest path calculation later efficiently in the meta-heuristic, we implemented a *forward* and a *backward* variant, where forward means calculating the travel cost $c_{ij}$ for departure time $t$ at source node $i$, whereas backward means calculating $c_{ij}$ for the arrival time $t$ at destination $j$. Furthermore, we implemented a method to efficiently calculate and store the paths with minimum costs between order nodes in a matrix. Thus, we store intervals of departure times where their resulting minimum cost path is the same instead of creating an entry for every departure time. This is relevant because the given real-world application has a high time resolution (milliseconds).

### 3.2   Time Window Calculator with Time-Dependent Travel Times

To efficiently calculate a route's feasibility and duration, waiting times, and delays, we extend the sequence-based time window calculator presented in [10]. The extension is necessary to handle time-dependent travel times. Because a route's duration depends on its departure time, more sequence data must be stored than the earliest and latest departure times at the first node and their resulting duration and delays. In fact, duration and delays must be stored separately for the earliest and latest departures. Whenever the departure times change in the first node, the data for the sequence must be updated, and the travel times must be checked to see if there are any changes. If so, the data must be updated using a backward calculation. Note that, in the worst case, updates must be performed up to the beginning of the sequence.

### 3.3   Large Neighborhood Search

To optimize the schedules for the vehicles according to the given objective function, we implemented a Large Neighborhood Search (LNS) proposed in [7]. The concept of the LNS is to destroy larger parts of the solution (e.g., removing requests) and then repair the solution (e.g., reinsertion of requests). We implemented two destroy operators (worst and random removal) and three repair operators (greedy, random greedy, and regret repair). In each iteration, a temporary copy of the incumbent solution is created, where 30% of the requests are removed by randomly selecting one of the destroy operators and then inserted by a randomly selected repair operator into the temporary solution. The stopping criterion is the total number of iterations or the number of iterations without any improvement.

For evaluating the temporary solution, a feasibility check (order of pickup and delivery, capacity and time window constraints) and computation of the objective value (not inserted requests, delays, and travel times) are performed at each insertion step. Furthermore, since conflict-free schedules must be generated according to the capacity restriction at nodes limiting the number of vehicles simultaneously staying at a node, we applied a conflict detection evaluation at the end of each repair phase. A conflict arises if one vehicle blocks another at a node because it has to pass the node where another vehicle stays or because some action is scheduled simultaneously at the same node. Therefore, we calculate all times (serving a customer and dwell times) at any node and examine whether overlaps exceed a node's capacity. If this is the case, the temporary solution is infeasible and will not be accepted. Otherwise, if the temporary solution is feasible and better than the incumbent solution, the LNS proceeds with the temporary solution as the new incumbent solution. The LNS terminates after 1000 iterations or if there is no improvement over 50 iterations and returns the overall best incumbent solution identified during the runtime.

## 4    Computational Experiments

We tested the algorithms (implemented in Java) on a set of instances based on a real road network consisting of 173 nodes and 252 directed arcs (see Fig. 1). We have instances with 20, 40, 60, 80, or 100 requests with a given time to serve within a planning horizon of 8 h. Since yard logistics requires precise and punctual service, no delays should be accepted. Therefore, we have a set of instances with a time window length of 0. However, due to evaluating the potential of such a system, we also created instances where a delay of 5 min is allowed (but penalized in the objective). Additionally, instances consist of up to 4 vehicles and 5, 10, and 20 situations (varying geographically and temporally).

Due to complexity, only one vehicle was scheduled in the project's use cases demonstration. Our goal was to test and demonstrate the scalability of such a system and provide further insights into an efficient and reasonable setup. Another goal was to integrate the algorithms handling time-dependent travel times efficiently into the optimization algorithm.

First, we investigated the impact of the time window length on solution quality. As mentioned, such a logistics service requires precise order fulfillment. Therefore, we tested several time window lengths of 0, 5, 10, and 20 min. Unsurprisingly, the number of missing orders reduces when the time window length is increased. However, the investigation shows that allowing a 5-minute delay greatly benefits the quality of the solution. In that case, the average number of missing orders is 3.6 compared to 11.8 when no delays are allowed. Although missing orders can be reduced to 0.9 with a time window of 20, the average delay for each order increases to 60.9 seconds compared to 22.6. Furthermore, investigating 5, 10, or 20 situations does not significantly affect the solution quality. Only the total travel time and average delay increase slightly.

**Table 1.** Average results about the problem's scalability and the vehicles' utilization.

| requests | vehicles | missed | delay | travel time | dwell time | service time | conflicts |
|---|---|---|---|---|---|---|---|
| [#] | [#] | [#] | [s] | [%] | [%] | [%] | [%] |
| 20 | 1 | 0.00 | 17.00 | 17.05 | 76.61 | 6.33 | 0.00 |
| | 2 | 0.00 | 1.01 | 9.35 | 86.90 | 3.76 | 15.07 |
| | 3 | 0.00 | 0.00 | 6.42 | 90.85 | 2.74 | 17.84 |
| | 4 | 0.00 | 0.00 | 6.13 | 91.21 | 2.67 | 18.21 |
| 40 | 1 | 1.33 | 30.13 | 23.15 | 64.66 | 12.19 | 0.00 |
| | 2 | 0.03 | 3.48 | 12.37 | 81.06 | 6.57 | 13.41 |
| | 3 | 0.03 | 1.54 | 9.39 | 85.52 | 5.09 | 17.69 |
| | 4 | 0.03 | 0.87 | 7.88 | 87.77 | 4.35 | 22.41 |
| 60 | 1 | 6.00 | 46.66 | 38.08 | 44.27 | 17.65 | 0.00 |
| | 2 | 0.03 | 15.77 | 22.00 | 67.46 | 10.54 | 9.72 |
| | 3 | 0.41 | 11.48 | 15.67 | 76.66 | 7.67 | 15.61 |
| | 4 | 0.95 | 9.66 | 14.07 | 79.06 | 6.87 | 19.66 |
| 80 | 1 | 15.85 | 77.66 | 39.05 | 40.70 | 20.25 | 0.00 |
| | 2 | 2.72 | 39.17 | 24.91 | 62.72 | 12.37 | 15.68 |
| | 3 | 4.31 | 26.73 | 17.84 | 73.29 | 8.87 | 21.53 |
| | 4 | 3.62 | 21.52 | 14.25 | 78.61 | 7.14 | 26.29 |
| 100 | 1 | 21.00 | 65.00 | 47.41 | 28.09 | 24.50 | 0.00 |
| | 2 | 5.38 | 35.71 | 31.07 | 54.02 | 14.90 | 12.27 |
| | 3 | 4.59 | 26.10 | 22.49 | 66.77 | 10.74 | 17.23 |
| | 4 | 6.26 | 22.08 | 17.96 | 73.54 | 8.50 | 21.03 |

Second, test results on the problem's scalability and the vehicle's performance are shown in Table 1. The columns show the number of total requests, vehicles in operation, the number of unfulfilled orders, the average delay per order, the average percentage of travel time, dwell time, and service time, and the percentage of detected conflicts during the LNS. It shows a trade-off between the solution quality (missed orders, delays) and the utilization of the vehicles depending on the number of vehicles. Thus, the delays per request decrease when more vehicles are applied, but the dwell times increase. The biggest improvement with respect to fulfilled orders and delays can be achieved by using two vehicles compared to one. Another interesting finding is that the number of missing orders slightly increases for almost all instance sets when more than two vehicles are applied. This is because the number of conflicts increases when more vehicles are on the road (see last column), and some orders can not be fulfilled because of another blocking vehicle.

Finally, we measured the run times for the time-dependent routing when using the matrix to store the route data for intervals of departure times compared to a simple method, where every instant of a departure time is cached. The results show that applying the matrix improves the run times by a factor of four. However, it has to be mentioned that the routing run time is very small compared to the total run time of the LNS (about 1% for the caching method and 0.25% for the matrix).

## 5   Conclusion

This paper introduced the AWARD project, which uses automated guided vehicles (AGV) in yard logistics. Our work focused on optimizing the algorithm within the fleet management system for scheduling and routing the AGVs. The problem is modeled as a time-dependent pickup and delivery problem with time windows and solved with a large neighborhood search metaheuristic approach. The test instance is based on an industry compound in Toulouse, where up to 100 pickup and delivery requests are handled by up to four vehicles. Experimental results show that with an increasing number of requests, more vehicles are required to avoid unfulfilled orders. However, if too many vehicles are deployed, the idle time increases. Even worse, the vehicles start blocking each other, which might decrease the number of fulfilled orders. Hence, the main takeaway is that the fleet size should be appropriate for the number of expected requests and the size of the operation area. Future work focuses on runtime improvements to integrate the optimization algorithms even better in real-world applications.

**Acknowledgments.** This work received funding from the European Union's Horizon 2020 research and innovation program under Grant Agreement No 101006817 (AWARD). We thank Applied Autonomy AS, which provided the road network and instance data to test the algorithms.

## References

1. Dabia, S., Ropke, S., van Woensel, T., Kok, T.D.: Branch and price for the time-dependent vehicle routing problem with time windows. Transp. Sci. **47**(3), 380–396 (2013)
2. Elias, H.: Why AGV robots are taking over our warehouse floors (2020). https://techhq.com/tag/automation/
3. Guth, I.: Award deliverable 2.1 - system scope (2022). https://award-h2020.eu/
4. Ichoua, S., Gendreau, M., Potvin, J.Y.: Vehicle dispatching with time-dependent travel times. Eur. J. Oper. Res. **144**(2), 379–396 (2003)

5. Nishida, K., Nishi, T.: Dynamic optimization of conflict-free routing of automated guided vehicles for just-in-time delivery. IEEE Transactions on Automation Science and Engineering (2022)
6. Pan, B., Zhang, Z., Lim, A.: A hybrid algorithm for time-dependent vehicle routing problem with time windows. Comput. Oper. Res. **128**, 105193 (2021)
7. Pisinger, D., Ropke, S.: Large Neighborhood Search, pp. 99–127. Springer International Publishing, Cham (2019)
8. Rashidi, H., Matinfar, F., Parand, F.: Automated guided vehicles-a review on applications, problem modeling and solutions. Int. J. Transp. Eng. **8**(3), 261–278 (2021)
9. Sun, P., Veelenturf, L.P., Hewitt, M., Van Woensel, T.: The time-dependent pickup and delivery problem with time windows. Transp. Res. Part B: Methodol. **116**, 1–24 (2018)
10. Vidal, T., Crainic, T.G., Gendreau, M., Prins, C.: A hybrid genetic algorithm with adaptive diversity management for a large class of vehicle routing problems with time-windows. Comput. Oper. Res. **40**(1), 475–489 (2013)

# Diversity Management in Evolutionary Dynamic Optimization

Bernhard Werth[1,2](✉) (iD), Johannes Karder[1,2] (iD), Stefan Wagner[1] (iD),
and Michael Affenzeller[1,2] (iD)

[1] Josef Ressel Center for Adaptive Optimization in Dynamic Environments, Heuristic and Evolutionary Algorithms Laboratory, University of Applied Sciences Upper Austria, 4232 Hagenberg, Austria
bernhard.werth@fh-hagenberg.at
[2] Institute for Symbolic Artificial Intelligence, Johannes Kepler University, 4040 Linz, Austria

**Abstract.** The retention of diversity of genetic information is an important aspect of many population-based evolutionary optimizers. With the increasing relevance of dynamic optimization, where live data is streamed directly into a running optimization system, this algorithmic facet gains new importance. This study compares five different strategies for handling diversity in genetic algorithms in a dynamic open-ended optimization scenario. Using the traveling salesman problem as a benchmark, the algorithmic variations are compared and analyzed with respect to their performance and retained diversity. Results indicate that convergence patterns behave differently from static optimization and several algorithm features that are well understood for static optimization may have unintended consequences in dynamic scenarios.

**Keywords:** evolutionary algorithms · dynamic optimization · genetic algorithms

## 1 Introduction and Related Work

In recent years, dynamic optimization gained significant relevance in for example fields like Internet of Things or Industry 4.0. Dynamic optimization problems arise in fields like production planning [11], routing, scheduling [2], data analysis and forecasting [7].

Even though dynamic optimization is of high relevance, the majority of literature focuses on static problems. A prominent concept discussed in studies that deal with dynamic optimization problems is the usage of evolutionary algorithms. Dynamic optimization problems are characterized by time-dependent objective functions, meaning that decision variables which are considered optimal at one point in the optimization process might not be suitable at a later stage.

A highly relevant aspect of any dynamic evolutionary algorithm is the careful curation of the genetic diversity in the algorithm's population. Diversity in this

A. Quesada-Arencibia et al. (Eds.): EUROCAST 2024, LNCS 15172, pp. 140–147, 2025.
https://doi.org/10.1007/978-3-031-82949-9_13

context describes the amount and uniqueness of the genetic information present in the population. In static optimization it is slowly decreased via selection mechanisms until it converges at some point and all solutions in the population are fairly similar to each other. This similarity can arise in terms of both decision variables and objective values. In contrast to static optimization, a certain measure of diversity must be retained or periodically renewed in dynamic optimization, as an already converged population may struggle to re-crate essential building blocks or adapt quickly enough as it encounters a strong change.

In this paper we introduce and compare different mechanisms of managing diversity in *genetic algorithms* (GAs). As a test problem these mechanisms are operating on the dynamic traveling salesman problem (TSP).

- No specific management: In principle, mutation and crossover operations can introduce new diversity, but may severely impact anytime performance by destroying important building blocks as it is being constructed.
- Problem-triggered restarts: Recent research [1] reiterates that for certain scenarios restarting a genetic algorithm whenever a change is detected is preferable to complex schemes of memory or diversity management. For clarity, we will refer to this algorithm variant as *restarting genetic algorithm* (RGA)
- Population-triggered restarts: A simple way to govern algorithm restarts is measuring the likelihood for a child to outperform its parents. Variations of this approach that use dynamic population sizes were already applied to several dynamic scenarios [5]. The specific variant chosen for the following experiments is the *open-ended relevant alleles preserving genetic algorithm* (OERAPGA)
- Immigration schemes: These *random immigrants genetic algorithms* [9] (RIGA) continuously integrate either new solution candidates or memorized ones from previous epochs via immigration into the population, thereby trading the need for restarts for a constant influx of genetic material.
- Layered population structures: The *age-layered population structure* [4] (ALPS) respects the fact that newly generated solutions often have little chance of out-competing older members of the population while still potentially containing important building blocks. The population is therefore separated into layers of different age as to limit competition. The youngest layer is periodically reseeded and successful genetic information migrates slowly through the layers, negating the need for discrete restarts.

Performing this analysis on the dynamic TSP [8] provides the advantages of a well-known and well-defined problem, an intuitive encoding where building blocks are represented as sub-tours and the possibility of obtaining the current best solution via exact solvers with negligible computational effort. It allows for an analysis of the age of different optimal building blocks and measuring the correlation of genetic diversity with momentary and overall algorithmic performance. By better understanding the mechanics of diversity retention and loss, we expect to lay the groundwork for more fine-grained and adaptive diversity control mechanisms.

## 2  Benchmark Problem

For a meaningful analysis of algorithmic behavior, care must be taken that the particularities and properties of the problem do not overshadow the effects arising from the algorithm. It is therefore advisable to use a well-known and well-studied benchmark problem. In this work the Traveling Salesman Problem was chosen. The goal of a metric TSP is as follows: Given a set of city-coordinates, a tour has to be constructed that visits each city exactly once and then returns to the starting point, minimizing total distance moved. Mathematically, this is equivalent to finding the shortest Hamiltonian cycle in a graph. The first useful advantage of the TSP is the existence of powerful specialized exact solvers like Concorde[1], that make the optimal solution of most TSP instances accessible in reasonable time. The second benefit is that well-understood test instances are readily available (at least for static optimization). In this work the instances of the well-known TSPLIB[2] are taken as a starting post to generate dynamic TSP instances.

A number of different solution encodings have been proposed for this problem, but for simplicity and the above-mentioned reason of not introducing problem characteristics that might skew the diversity analysis, a simple permutation vector of cities is chosen. An allele is therefore easily defined as the city $c$ appearing in the position $i$ of the permutation after correcting for the rotational and directional invariance of the TSP tour.

The generation of a dynamic version of a static TSP instance is performed by only considering a subset of cities to be *active* and therefore included in the tour. The time interval during which the algorithm can optimize without the problem changing is usually referred to as an *epoch* and is for comparability reasons usually counted as a fixed number of evaluations rather than wall clock time. At the end of an epoch, a number of cities deactivate while a some of the currently inactive ones become active. Since most features for calculating diversity could be sensitive to changes in the length of the encoding, the numbers of deactivating and activating cities are kept equal in this work. Finally, a decision has to be made where to insert the newly activated cities in the permutation initially. For several optimization problems like dynamic scheduling, it is sensible to append new tasks to the end of the schedule, but here the uniform random nature of the activation/deactivation step does not imply that all new cities should be on a contiguous sub-tour, instead the newly activated cities simply take the places of the deactivated ones.

## 3  Experiment and Results

For the following results the five algorithm variations presented in Sect. 1 were applied to three static instances from TSPLIB, each dynamizised with four different epoch lengths, to simulate faster and slower evolving optimization problems. Table 1 lists all relevant parameters for a reconstruction of the experiment.

---

[1] https://www.math.uwaterloo.ca/tsp/concorde.html (last accessed May 2024).

[2] http://comopt.ifi.uni-heidelberg.de/software/TSPLIB95/ (last accessed May 2024).

**Table 1.** Algorithm and Problem configurations

| Parameter | Value |
|---|---|
| Population Size | 200 |
| Elites | 1 |
| Selector | Tournament(group size 4) |
| Selector (OERAPGA) | Random |
| Crossover | Edge Recombination [10], Maximal Preservative [6], Order [3] |
| Mutator | Inversion |
| Mutation Probability | 0.15 |
| Effort (OERAPGA) | 200 |
| Comparison Factor (OERAPGA) | 0.0 |
| Age Gap (ALPS) | 10 |
| Maximum Layers (ALPS) | 10 |
| Immigration Strength (RIGA) | 10% |
| Problem Instances | Berlin52, Kroa100, Ch150 |
| Swap Strength | 50% |
| Activation Strength | 80% |
| Epoch Length | 500, 1000, 1500, 2000 * cities |
| Update Policy | Between Evaluations |

Figure 1 overlays the *Solution Similarity* averaged over the whole population, the number of *Unique Alleles* as the two most expressive measures of genetic diversity and the *Current Best Quality* achieved by the algorithm. The x-axis in each plot denotes how far the time within an epoch has progressed while each epoch is represented by a single line, with brighter lines indicating later epochs. The columns of individual subplots are ordered by the different algorithms. A number of observations can be made:

– The first epochs where the algorithm needs to operate without any memory are noticeably different from later epochs. This difference is most strongly recognizable in the GA and RIGA cases where solution similarity, unique allele count and quality differ from the "standard behavior" especially in the earlier stages of the first epoch. Intuitively, this difference is absent for the RGA, since the population gets reseeded at the start of the epoch. The only form of memory for RGA is the elite solution from the last epoch, which is usually better than the best quality of the initial random sample, explaining the smaller, but still significant difference in initial quality between the first and later epochs.
– In the later stages of an epoch, RIGA usually retains slightly higher levels of genetic diversity than GA, RGA and OERAPGA, which reflects the effect of continuous influx of immigrants solutions.

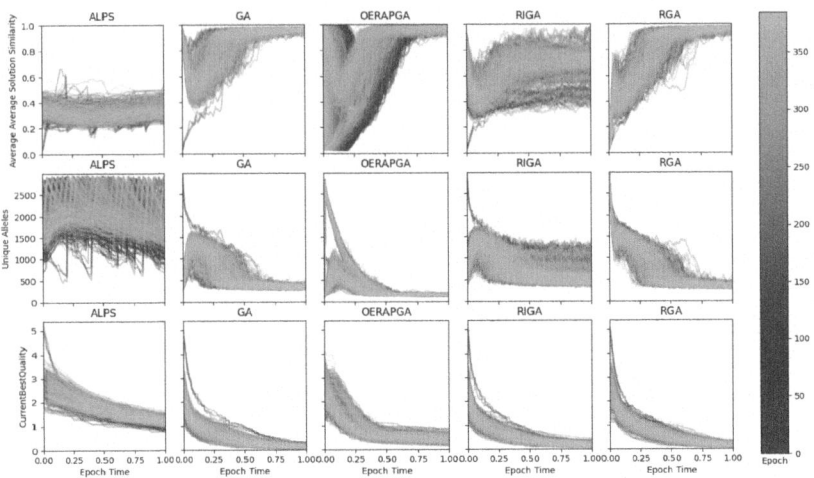

**Fig. 1.** Diversity Features

- All algorithms, irrespective of their memory scheme display a "response" to the epoch change, which is expressed in an increase of unique alleles and a (except for ALPS) decrease in the solution similarity. Notably, the measured diversity features are similar between all algorithms with a fixed population size (GA, RIGA and RGA) indicating all variations of the genetic algorithm reach similar states regardless of the diversity in the population at the start of the epoch. One notable exception to this pattern is the solution similarity of ALPS, where only a very slight decrease in similarity a bit later then the usual response is visible. A possible explanation for this pattern is, that the reseeding behavior of ALPS keeps the diversity in the total population inherently above the response levels.
- The number of unique alleles for ALPS shows two very distinct saw-tooth patterns. In the earlier generations the number of unique alleles decreases until it sharply rises in short intervals. This pattern can be ascribed to the initial convergence of ALPS and the subsequent creation of new layers until the maximum number of layers (10) is reached. Note that these saw-teeth are mirrored in the solution similarity. The second pattern is a number of sharp increases in the number of unique alleles with subsequent slow decreases. These increases in diversity are products of the reseeding mechanism of the lowest layer in ALPS and are independent of the actual problem or algorithm state but are governed by ALPS *age gap* parameter. Most unique alleles are located only in this lowest layer, and the unique alleles feature is much more sensitive to localized increases in diversity than the average solution similarity, which explains why only one measure reflects this behavior.
- The OERAPGA shows a distinct bi-section pattern in all measures including quality, with the bigger (more often encountered) "arm" of the graph essen-

tially displaying a usual response and convergence curve and the smaller arm repeating the initial convergence curve from the first epoch. Epochs where the second convergence path is performed correspond to the population of the OERAPGA collapsing to only one or two individuals shortly after the epoch changes. Since the current population size of OERAPGA is not directly influenced by information from the dynamic optimization problem but the likelihood of offspring solutions outperforming their parents, the question why an epoch change can cause an increase of selection pressure and thereby a collapse of the population while in most other cases and other algorithms it usually leads to an increase in diversity, might be result of the offspring selection nature of OERAPGA where solutions compere with their parents rather than their siblings, but remains an open research question.

– Lastly, the achieved quality depends on the choice of algorithms even on those relatively simple problem instances, with ALPS and OERAPGA performing a bit worse than their less complex competitors. GA and RGA achieve similar results at the end of the epoch with GA reaching better results a little bit earlier than its restarting counterpart.

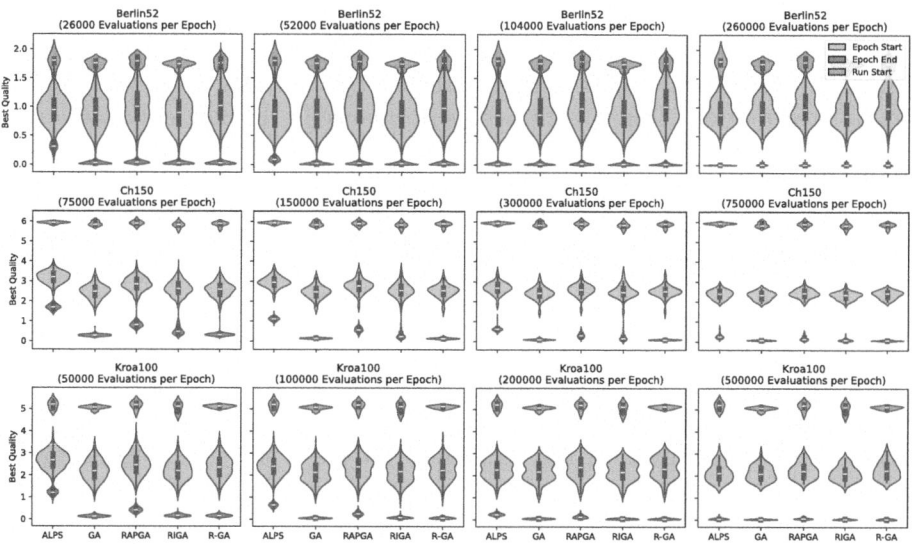

**Fig. 2.** Algorithm performance

In Fig. 2 the performance of the different algorithms on all problem instances is summarized as violin plots. For each combination of problem geometry, epoch length and algorithm three violins are shown: The best quality at the end of an epoch in green, the best quality after the population had to be reevaluated at the beginning of an epoch in blue and the median quality at the start of the run (which are fixed along epoch lengths) as a comparison in orange.

Most notably when comparing the performance of ALPS it can be seen that this algorithm very heavily improves with longer epoch lengths, while ALPS decidedly performs worst for problem instances with faster epoch switches, it matches or outperforms its contemporaries when enough time is given.

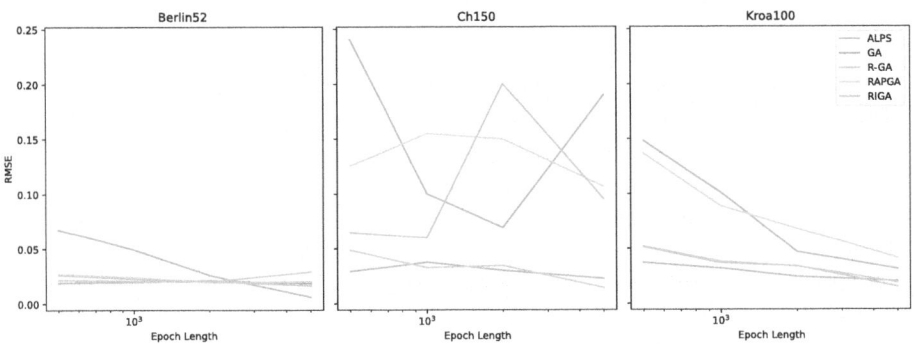

**Fig. 3.** Algorithm performance

A naturally resulting question from the results of the performed diversity analysis is, whether the information obtained by analyzing a previous epoch may be used to predict the algorithms' performance in the next epoch. Figure 3 shows the *root mean squared error* (RMSE) of random forest models pertaining to each combination of algorithm and problem instance. The random forest regression uses the median and final diversity and quality measures as input features to predict the final quality of the next epoch. Generally, it has to be noted that problems easier to solve are easier to predict. Additionally, algorithms that perform poorly compared to their peers are more difficult to predict.

## 4    Conclusions and Outlook

In this paper, an analysis of five different strategies for genetic algorithms to manage genetic diversity in dynamic optimization scenarios was performed using dynamizised versions of the traveling salesman problem. The results show that the diversity pattern in dynamic optimization is non-trivial and multiple effects can simultaneously affect an optimizer. New genetic diversity can arise as a delayed response to dynamic changes and different types of selection schemes behave notably different when faced with this "response". The prediction of an algorithm's future performance based on past experiences seems to be possible, though the models and features can certainly be extended upon, also the presented dynamic problems are assumed to be fairly homogeneous over time, with very similar characteristics in every epoch.

A major aspect of future expansion of diversity analysis in dynamic optimization will be a more thorough analysis of the coupling between diversity and performance over different time scales and how this relationship changes depending on the characteristics of the optimization problem.

**Acknowledgments.** This research was funded in part by the Austrian Science Fund (FWF) [I 5315-N]. The financial support by the Austrian Federal Ministry for Digital and Economic Affairs, the National Foundation for Research, Technology and Development and the Christian Doppler Research Association is gratefully acknowledged.

# References

1. Alza, J., Bartlett, M., Ceberio, J., McCall, J.: On the elusivity of dynamic optimisation problems. Swarm Evol. Comput. **78**, 101289 (2023)
2. Chien, C.F., Lan, Y.B.: Agent-based approach integrating deep reinforcement learning and hybrid genetic algorithm for dynamic scheduling for industry 3.5 smart production. Comput. Indust. Eng. **162**, 107782 (2021)
3. Davis, L., et al.: Applying adaptive algorithms to epistatic domains. In: IJCAI, vol. 85, pp. 162–164. Citeseer (1985)
4. Hornby, G.S.: Alps: the age-layered population structure for reducing the problem of premature convergence. In: Proceedings of the 8th Annual Conference on Genetic and Evolutionary Computation, pp. 815–822 (2006)
5. Karder, J., Werth, B., Beham, A., Wagner, S., Affenzeller, M.: Analysis and handling of dynamic problem changes in open-ended optimization. In: International Conference on Computer Aided Systems Theory. pp. 61–68. Springer (2022). https://doi.org/10.1007/978-3-031-25312-6_7
6. Mühlenbein, H., Gorges-Schleuter, M., Krämer, O.: Evolution algorithms in combinatorial optimization. Parallel Comput. **7**(1), 65–85 (1988)
7. Salgotra, R., Gandomi, M., Gandomi, A.H.: Time series analysis and forecast of the covid-19 pandemic in india using genetic programming. Chaos, Solitons Fractals **138**, 109945 (2020)
8. Tinós, R., Whitley, D., Howe, A.: Use of explicit memory in the dynamic traveling salesman problem. In: Proceedings of the 2014 Annual Conference on Genetic and Evolutionary Computation, pp. 999–1006 (2014)
9. Tinós, R., Yang, S.: A self-organizing random immigrants genetic algorithm for dynamic optimization problems. Genet. Program Evolvable Mach. **8**, 255–286 (2007)
10. Whitley, L.D., Starkweather, T., Fuquay, D.: Scheduling problems and traveling salesmen: the genetic edge recombination operator. In: ICGA, vol. 89, pp. 133–40 (1989)
11. Zhang, S., Tang, F., Li, X., Liu, J., Zhang, B.: A hybrid multi-objective approach for real-time flexible production scheduling and rescheduling under dynamic environment in industry 4.0 context. Comput. Operat. Res. **132**, 105267 (2021)

# Tackling the $\alpha$-Domination Problem Heuristically

Enrico Iurlano[✉][ID], Johannes Varga[ID], and Günther R. Raidl[ID]

Algorithms and Complexity Group, TU Wien, Favoritenstraße 9-11/192-01,
1040 Vienna, Austria
{eiurlano,jvarga,raidl}@ac.tuwien.ac.at

**Abstract.** We focus on the $\alpha$-domination problem, which is capable of modeling influence phenomena in social networks. It formally asks for a minimum cardinality subset of vertices of a given graph such that any vertex is either included in this subset or at least a fraction $\alpha$ of its neighbors is $(0 < \alpha \leq 1)$. We address the search for solutions of high quality within a tight margin of computation time by designing, firstly, a Greedy Randomized Adaptive Search Procedure and, secondly, a Configuration Checking metaheuristic. The latter excels in terms of solution quality and speed and is able to outperform an integer programming formulation solved by the commercial solver Gurobi on a majority of tested instances which have thousands of vertices.

**Keywords:** Domination · Influence in social networks · GRASP · Configuration checking

## 1 Introduction

The problem of finding a minimum dominating set of vertices of an undirected simple graph $G = (V, E)$ is one of the best-known and most intensely studied optimization problems on graphs. Dunbar et al. [6] introduced a generalization of this problem called $\alpha$-*domination problem*, in which for a fixed proportionality parameter $0 < \alpha \leq 1$ the goal is to find a minimum cardinality set $S \subseteq V$ such that each vertex $v \in V$ is already contained in $S$ or at least a fraction $\alpha$ of its neighbors is comprised by $S$; in both cases we say that $v$ is $\alpha$-dominated. The $\alpha$-domination problem can be seen as an interpolation between the classical domination problem, for sufficiently small $\alpha > 0$, and the vertex covering problem, for $\alpha = 1$. It is shown in [6] that for any $0 < \alpha \leq 1$, it is NP-hard to find an optimal solution; moreover, upper and lower bounds for optimal solutions on general graphs but also for special graph classes are derived.

This problem is strongly related to the so-called *Minimum Positive Influence Dominating Set* (MPIDS) problem introduced in [13], in which the aim is to maintain sufficient influence in a social network by utilizing the minimum number of influencing actors (here, even actors need to receive influence from their equals). In the age of constantly growing data on social networks and

A. Quesada-Arencibia et al. (Eds.): EUROCAST 2024, LNCS 15172, pp. 148–156, 2025.
https://doi.org/10.1007/978-3-031-82949-9_14

the increasing relevance of disinformation campaigns [3] and viral marketing [13], the $\alpha$-domination problem can be a more suitable model to determine how influence—even before consolidating it—is achievable by using a few simultaneously deployed actors of assumed loyal behavior.

Practical computational methods for the MPIDS problem and other problems with parallels on a conceptual level are recently receiving increased attention [2, 10], such as, e.g., the *Target Set Selection Problem* [9], which studies the influence under a propagation aspect. Still there are only few approaches known to us that (heuristically) address the $\alpha$-domination problem. An important *caveat* should be taken into account: We have encountered some works, e.g., [11], in which the problem name MPIDS actually refers to 0.5-domination. Thus there has to be paid careful attention not to mix this problem up with the stronger constrained one of the original work [13] and its follow-up papers, e.g., [2].

The following notation together with some conventions will be used. We only consider undirected, simple graphs $G = (V, E)$. We denote for a vertex $v \in V$ by $N(v)$ its neighborhood, i.e., set of all adjacent vertices, and by $\deg(v) = |N(v)|$ the cardinality of the latter. Given a binary vector $c \in \{0, 1\}^{|V|}$ associated to a graph $G = (V, E)$, let us call it an $\alpha$-*dominating labeling* if it is the incidence vector of an $\alpha$-dominating subset of vertices $S$, i.e., $c = (\mathbb{1}_S(v))_{v \in V}$ with $\mathbb{1}_S(v') := 1$ if $v' \in S$ and $\mathbb{1}_S(v') := 0$, otherwise. Moreover, assume that $\alpha \in (0, 1]$ is a fixed constant and let us denote by $\alpha$-DOMINATION the problem of finding an $\alpha$-dominating labeling that minimizes the sum of labels (see later also (1)). Henceforth, given the locality of $\alpha$-DOMINATION, we assume that our graph instances consist of a single connected component containing at least three vertices.

## 2   Solution Approaches

The following is an integer linear program (ILP) formulation of $\alpha$-DOMINATION, where $\lceil \cdot \rceil$ denotes the Gaussian ceiling function:

$$
\begin{aligned}
\min \quad & \sum_{v \in V} c_v \\
\text{subject to} \quad & \sum_{w \in N(v)} c_w + c_v \cdot \lceil \alpha \deg(v) \rceil \geq \lceil \alpha \deg(v) \rceil, \quad v \in V \\
& c_v \in \{0, 1\}, \quad\quad\quad\quad\quad\quad\quad\quad\quad\quad\quad\quad\quad\ v \in V
\end{aligned}
\tag{1}
$$

*Remark 1.* For a slightly generalized version of $\alpha$-DOMINATION, Raghavan and Zhang [11] proposed a strengthened formulation based on the idea of placing a dummy vertex on each edge. Within the setting of our computational evaluation (see Sect. 3) we found that this more recent formulation is surpassed in terms of solution quality by (1) and we therefore do not consider this alternative here.

Our first goal is to design a *Greedy Randomized Adaptive Search Procedure* (GRASP) [7], which should undercut the runtime of a state-of-the-art solver applied to (1) and should at the same time have a comparably good (or even better) solution quality. As the main component of this metaheuristic, we propose the following greedy construction heuristic for $\alpha$-DOMINATION; see also

---

**Algorithm 1.** Greedy construction

---

**Input**: Graph $G = (V, E)$;
**Output**: $\alpha$-dominating labeling $c$

1: $c_v \leftarrow 0 \ \forall v \in V$  `// initialize {0,1}-labeling`
2: $d_v \leftarrow 0 \ \forall v \in V$  `// current` $\alpha$`-domination status (in {0,1})`
3: $U_v \leftarrow \deg(v) \ \forall v \in V$  `// number of not` $\alpha$`-dominated neighbors`

4: **while** $\{v \in V : d_v = 0\} \neq \emptyset$ **do**
5:    Let $A_v$, $v \in V$, be the number of neighbors of $v$ which would be newly $\alpha$-dominated if $c_v$ was set to 1.
6:    Let $s \leftarrow \mathrm{argmax}\{(A_v, U_v) : v \in V\}$ (ties are broken uniformly at random)
7:    $c_s \leftarrow 1$
8:    Update $d_s$, $U_s$; $d_{s'}$ for $s' \in N(s)$, $U_{s'}$ for $s' \in N(s)$.
9: **end while**

10: For $v \in V$, set $c_v \leftarrow 0$ whenever $c_v = 1$ and $c$ allows for updating $c_v$ to 0 without violating $\alpha$-domination of any vertex. `// postprocessing step`

---

11: **return** $c$

---

Algorithm 1: Initially all vertices are 0-labeled. Then, iteratively, the label of a 0-labeled vertex is set to 1; the choice of the vertex is here based on the number of *newly* $\alpha$-dominated vertices of $G$ which this update would yield. In the case of ties, the vertex having the highest number of not yet $\alpha$-dominated neighbors is picked in the spirit of providing progress in as many vertices as possible. Note that in particular for graph classes having frequent occurrences of vertices of degree one (leaves), the following preprocessing can be employed: Without any loss of optimality, the labels of leaves can be fixed to 0 whereas the labels of their neighbors are set to 1.

For the GRASP, we randomize this greedy heuristic by always 1-labeling a next vertex that is randomly chosen from the top-$\rho$ percentile of the candidate vertices, where $0\% < \rho \leq 100\%$ is the randomization parameter. Our GRASP follows the standard template from [7] by iteratively applying this randomized greedy heuristic for obtaining diversified starting solutions, and each of them undergoes a local search. Our local search relies on the following move operator DLC called "Decrease label and compensate". Given a feasible solution $c$ for $\alpha$-DOMINATION together with the choice of a 1-labeled vertex $v$, we perform the update $c_v \leftarrow 0$ and compensate all violations of feasibility (now disallowing a change of $c_v$) by greedily solving an arising set multicovering problem: The set to be covered consists of the vertices that lost their $\alpha$-domination status and the set system consists of closed neighborhoods comprising these vertices either as neighbors or directly as "center" of the neighborhood; the multiplicity of coverage for $v$ depends on the number of its 1-labeled neighbors and is addressed in more detail in Algorithm 2, which relies on two auxiliary quantities: Given a labeling

$c$, let us define

$$e_v := \{w \in N(v) : c_w = 1\}, \ v \in V, \tag{2}$$

respectively

$$isr_v := \left\{ w \in N(v) : c_w = 0, \ \sum_{z \in N(w)} c_z = \lceil \alpha \deg(w) \rceil \right\}, \ v \in V, \tag{3}$$

capturing the set of 1-labeled neighbors of $v$, respectively the set of (0-labeled) neighbors of $v$ that are *indispensable support recipients* of $v$, i.e., which would lose their $\alpha$-domination status if we would carry out the update $c_v \leftarrow 0$.

Now having the DLC operator available, for a feasible solution $c$, we call another feasible solutions $c'$ a neighbor of $c$, denoted $c \sim c'$, if there is a vertex $v$ for which $c_v = 1$ and DLC applied to $c$ yields $c'$. Denote by $\mathcal{U}_k(c)$ the DLC-*neighborhood of order at most $k$* of $c$ as the set of all $(s_v)_{v \in V} \in \{0,1\}^{|V|}$ which are $\alpha$-dominating and for which there are pairwise distinct labelings $c^{(1)}$, $c^{(2)}$, ..., $c^{(k)}$ satisfying $c \sim c^{(1)} \sim \cdots \sim c^{(k)} = s$.

For the local search within the GRASP, we fall back on $\mathcal{U}_K(\cdot)$ for some larger value $K$: As long as a quality-improving neighboring solution $c_{\text{next}}$ in $\mathcal{U}_K(\cdot)$ is found, the search is repeated in the solution-neighborhood of $c_{\text{next}}$, and the process iterates until this search for improvement fails. Due to the vast size of this neighborhood, the idea is to find a promising neighbor in $\mathcal{U}_K(\cdot)$ by employing the scoring function subsequently introduced in (4) and yielding a solution in $\mathcal{U}_{j+1}(\cdot)$ starting from one in $\mathcal{U}_j(\cdot)$. Eventually, each solution lying on the so-arising trajectory of solutions is in particular contained in $\mathcal{U}_K(\cdot)$ such that we postulate a sufficient local exploration around our starting solution and eventually consider the best-quality solution on this trajectory as our result of scanning $\mathcal{U}_K(\cdot)$.

Note that incremental updates of the quantities $e_v$ and $isr_v$ introduced above will not only be important for an efficiency gain in the context of several implementations but also allow the computation of the scoring function

$$\mathsf{Score}(v) := \begin{cases} -\infty & \text{if } c_v = 0, \\ |e_v| - \lceil \alpha \deg(v) \rceil - \tau |isr_v| & \text{if } c_v = 1, \end{cases} \tag{4}$$

which expresses the attractiveness of decreasing the label of a vertex: For already 0-labeled vertices $-\infty$ is returned, and for all other vertices, their "saturation" $|e_v| - \alpha \lceil \deg(v) \rceil$ provides a certain reward that is relativized by a penalty arising from a potentially large cardinality $|isr_v|$; $\tau > 0$ is a parameter to be tuned.

Next, we propose an alternative approach based on *Configuration Checking* (CC) introduced in [4]; see Algorithm 3. Given a local search procedure relying on a move operator, the main idea here is to each time save for the part of the solution being subjected to the move operator the current so-called configuration (a snapshot of attributes of its neighboring solution parts). The move operator

**Algorithm 2.** Decrease-Label-and-Compensate
---

**Input:** $G = (V, E)$; labeling $c$; $e$ and $isr$ already meeting (2)–(3);
vertex $i \in V$ with $c_i = 1$
**Output:** *None*, overwrites all input arguments except for $G$ and $i$.

    `// Decrease label and store not anymore α-dominated vertices:`
1: $U \leftarrow isr_i$ `// these vertices will cause (local) infeasibility`
2: $c_i \leftarrow 0$ and update $e, isr$ where affected by this assignment

    `// Compensate all arisen constraint violations:`
3: Build family of restricted sets $\mathcal{S} := \{e_w \cap U : w \in \bigcup_{v \in isr_i} (N(v) \setminus \{i\})\}$
4: Greedily, find a set covering of $U$ given by $e_{v_1} \cap U, \ldots, e_{v_k} \cap U$
5: **for** $\ell = 1, \ldots, k$ **do**
6:     $c_{v_\ell} \leftarrow 1$ and update $e, isr$ where affected by this assignment
7: **end for**
8: **while** $|e_i| < \lceil \alpha \deg(i) \rceil$ **do**
9:     Pick a random 0-labeled vertex $j \in N(i) \setminus e_i$
10:    $c_j \leftarrow 1$ and update $e, isr$ where affected by this assignment
11: **end while**

    `// Eliminate potential redundancies:`
12: **while** $\emptyset \neq I := \{v : c_v = 1 \wedge isr_v = \emptyset \wedge |e_v| \geq \lceil \alpha \deg(v) \rceil\}$ **do**
13:    Randomly draw $v$ from $I$; $c_v \leftarrow 0$; update $e, isr$; re-evaluate $I$
14: **end while**
15: **return**;

---

can afterwards be re-applied on that part only if its now re-encountered circumstance of attributes differs from what is stored in the current snapshot. In the following, we rely on a "practical" [4] version of this metaheuristic requiring just the occurrence of a (potentially ultimately reverted) change of configurations in the history of configuration changes since the last move application. With the intention to avoid excessive cycling in the solution landscape, the technique is successfully applied to the vertex covering problem and to Boolean satisfiability solving [4].

In our setting, we fall back on the operator DLC and interpret each 1-labeled vertex $v$ as a solution part around which we consider its current configuration, namely the tuple capturing the restriction $c|_{N(v)}$.

*Remark 2.* In preliminary experimentation, we found, by analyzing convergence plots for the CC approach, that in exceptional situations a repeating cycle traversing a small set of solutions of equal quality occurred, lasting until the termination of the procedure. Therefore, we add an additional simple prevention strategy which is implemented in Line 11 of Algorithm 3.

---

**Algorithm 3.** Configuration Checking

---
**Input**: Graph $G = (V, E)$; $b \in \mathbb{N}$, $\tau > 0$
**Output**: $\alpha$-dominating labeling of $G$

1: $c \leftarrow$ greedy solution via Algorithm 1
2: $configCh[v] \leftarrow 1 \ \forall v \in V$ // `tracker for changes of configuration`
3: **while** no stopping criterion satisfied **do**
4:     Pick $v^*$ uniformly at random among the vertices which lie within the best $b$ candidates of $\{\mathsf{Score}(v) : v \in V \text{ with } c_v = 1 \text{ and } configCh[v] = 1\}$.

5:     $\mathrm{DLC}(c, e, isr, v^*)$
6:     $configCh[v^*] \leftarrow 0$
7:     $configCh[w] \leftarrow 1 \ \forall w \in N(v^*)$.

8:     **if** $\sum_{v \in V} c_v < \sum_{v \in V} c_v^{\text{best}}$ **then**
9:         $c^{\text{best}} \leftarrow c$
10:    **end if**
11:    **if** objective function value unchanged since at least 32 iterations **then**
12:        In next iteration, in Line 4, pick $v^*$ among the $b$ best elements of $\{\mathsf{Score}(v) : v \in V \text{ with } c_v = 1 \text{ and } configCh[v] = 0\}$   // `see Remark 2.`
13:    **end if**
14: **end while**
15: **return** $c^{\text{best}}$

---

# 3   Computational Results

We fix $\alpha = 0.5$ for $\alpha$-DOMINATION, mainly motivated by the strong relationship to MPIDS and also the so-called *majority thresholds* [1] for the Target Set Selection Problem. All algorithms of Sect. 2 have been implemented in `Julia` 1.10, which also served with the `JuMP` package as an interface to `Gurobi` 10.0.3 [8] for solving the integer linear program (1).

Table 1 contains on the left side information on the graph instances we use for our experimental analysis; the first ten instances are adopted from [5], while the remaining three are taken from [12]. We emphasize that the latter instances constitute graphs from real-world social networks. The table reports the number of vertices, the average degree ("deg avg"), and the standard deviation of the degrees of the vertices ("deg std"). In preliminary tuning experiments suitable values were determined for the parameters of our procedures: The penalty coefficient is chosen as $\tau := 2$ for the DLC operator; the randomization parameter $\rho$ of the greedy construction heuristic as $\rho = 5\%$; the choice of $b := 4$ turned out to be meaningful for both the GRASP and the CC.

Table 1 further shows in Column "ILP" results from the integer linear program: listed are incumbent solution values ("incmb.") and optimality gaps ("gap") $(z^* - z^{DB})/z^*$, where $z^*$ denotes the best solution found and $z^{DB}$ the dual bound. The next column "greedy avg" shows the average solution values over ten runs of the greedy Algorithm 1—experiments for the greedy algorithm have been ran multiple times due to the randomization present in the tie-breaker (see Line 6 of the algorithm). Similarly, columns "GRASP" and "CC" report these quantities for the respective two metaheuristic approaches again averaged over ten runs; in addition objective values of a best run is additionally reported here. As in the experimental evaluation of [2], the time budget for each run of both metaheuristics was set to $|V|/100$ CPU seconds and is therefore magnitudes smaller than the 3600 seconds runtime reserved for Gurobi. All experiments were carried out using a single thread on a cluster endowed with an Intel(R) Xeon(R) E5-2640 v4 CPU with 2.40 GHz and 160 GB RAM running Ubuntu 18.04.6 LTS.

**Table 1.** Results of all proposed approaches. Time budget ILP: 3600 seconds; time budget GRASP and CC: $|V|/100$ seconds.

| Instance | $|V|$ | deg avg. | deg std. | ILP incmb. | gap | greedy avg | GRASP best | avg | CC best | avg |
|---|---|---|---|---|---|---|---|---|---|---|
| Bipartite-350-350-80 | 700 | 280 | 8 | 350 | 19% | 357.0 | 347 | 347.7 | 346 | **346.7** |
| Bipartite-350-350-90 | 700 | 316 | 6 | 350 | 18% | 354.6 | 348 | 348.4 | 348 | **348.0** |
| Net-20-20 | 400 | 7 | 1 | **161** | 6% | 185.3 | 169 | 170.0 | 170 | 174.2 |
| Net-30-20 | 600 | 8 | 1 | **242** | 8% | 279.2 | 256 | 258.5 | 251 | 263.9 |
| Planar-650 | 650 | 86 | 15 | 310 | 24% | 329.5 | 312 | 314.6 | 306 | **308.5** |
| Planar-700 | 700 | 88 | 15 | 334 | 24% | 356.2 | 338 | 340.3 | 332 | **333.0** |
| Random-950-10 | 950 | 95 | 9 | 463 | 26% | 479.1 | 465 | 465.9 | 453 | **456.4** |
| Random-950-20 | 950 | 191 | 12 | 473 | 26% | 480.4 | 471 | 473.2 | 460 | **462.0** |
| Random-1000-10 | $1k$ | 100 | 9 | 488 | 26% | 503.5 | 489 | 491.1 | 477 | **480.3** |
| Random-1000-20 | $1k$ | 200 | 13 | 494 | 25% | 507.0 | 497 | 499.0 | 485 | **486.4** |
| socfb-Amherst41 | $2k$ | 81 | 63 | **740** | 15% | 807.0 | 801 | 804.4 | 769 | 775.5 |
| socfb-Dartmouth6 | $8k$ | 79 | 75 | **2513** | 20% | 2588.9 | 2731 | 2782.8 | 2529 | 2548.7 |
| socfb-Harvard1 | $15k$ | 109 | 112 | 7588 | 92% | 5263.3 | 5733 | 5793.5 | 5116 | **5158.8** |

Inspecting the results of Table 1, we notice generally quite large optimality gaps for the integer programming approach, in particular, for instances with higher average degrees. With one exception, the greedy construction heuristic always yielded solutions of poorer quality than the ILP approach and these greedy solutions are considerably inferior to the ones resulting from the two metaheuristics. However, the greedy heuristic also is very fast, with a maximum runtime of 0.32 seconds for all instances except for socfb-Dartmouth6 respectively socfb-Harvard1 which took 3.05 seconds respectively 20.49 seconds. Due to the evident advantage of CC over GRASP, we conclude that even multiple restarts with randomized greedy solutions do seem to not direct the local search trajectory towards regions of solutions having the quality of those found by the CC approach. The latter, in fact, is able to achieve the best results on several instances. The only instances where this is not the case are the sparser graphs Net-20-20 and Net-30-20 as well as the social networks socfb-Amherst41 and `socfb-Dartmouth6`; note the standard deviation of their degrees in contrast to the other instances. The last instance indicates that (social) networks with more than 10.000 vertices are apparently better addressed heuristically, since here the (meta)heuristics considerably outperform the ILP approach.

## 4  Conclusion

We proposed two metaheuristics that are able to rapidly generate solutions of high quality for α-DOMINATION. Among these, CC turned out to be the more favorable one, which in general surpasses the ILP approach already on medium-sized instances while using just a fraction of the computation time. As experimental results indicate, our proposed move operator seems to be an effective tool to find—in combination with the introduced scoring function—promising parts of the solution landscape. In future work we plan to increase performance specifically on social networks by trying to integrate into our greedy construction strategy, but possibly also in the selection of local moves, additional information such as, e.g., the deviation of the degree of a vertex from the average degree and by identifying alternative metrics that could help to address the desire for earlier—or even a priori—inclusion of suitable vertices into the α-dominating set.

**Acknowledgments.** This research was funded in part by the Austrian Science Fund (FWF) [10.55776/W1260-N35] within the framework of the doctoral program "Vienna Graduate School on Computational Optimization". Moreover, we acknowledge partial support from Austria's Agency for Education and Internationalization (OeAD) under grant BA05/2023.

## References

1. Ackerman, E., Ben-Zwi, O., Wolfovitz, G.: Combinatorial model and bounds for target set selection. Theoret. Comput. Sci. **411**(44–46), 4017–4022 (2010)
2. Akbay, M.A., López Serrano, A., Blum, C.: A self-adaptive variant of CMSA: application to the minimum positive influence dominating set problem. Inter. J. Comput. Intell. Syst. **15**(1), 44 (2022)
3. Bradshaw, S., Bailey, H., Howard, P.N.: Industrialized disinformation: 2020 global inventory of organized social media manipulation. Tech. rep., Computational Propaganda Research Project at the Oxford Internet Institute (2021). https://demtech.oii.ox.ac.uk/wp-content/uploads/sites/12/2021/01/CyberTroop-Report-2020-v.2.pdf, Accessed 15 Nov 2023
4. Cai, S., Su, K., Sattar, A.: Local search with edge weighting and configuration checking heuristics for minimum vertex cover. Artif. Intell. **175**(9–10), 1672–1696 (2011)
5. Currò, V.: The Roman domination problem on grid graphs. Ph.D. thesis, Universitá di Catania (2014). https://hdl.handle.net/20.500.11769/585454
6. Dunbar, J.E., Hoffman, D.G., Laskar, R.C., Markus, L.R.: α-domination. Discret. Math. **211**(1–3), 11–26 (2000)
7. Feo, T.A., Resende, M.G.: Greedy randomized adaptive search procedures. J. Global Optim. **6**, 109–133 (1995)

8.  Gurobi Optimization, LLC: Gurobi optimizer reference manual (2024). https://www.gurobi.com
9.  Kempe, D., Kleinberg, J., Tardos, É.: Maximizing the spread of influence through a social network. In: Proceedings of the ninth ACM SIGKDD International Conference on Knowledge Discovery and Data Mining, pp. 137–146 (2003)
10. Lozano-Osorio, I., Oliva-García, A., Sánchez-Oro, J.: Dynamic path relinking for the target set selection problem. Knowl.-Based Syst. **278**, 110827 (2023)
11. Raghavan, S., Zhang, R.: Rapid influence maximization on social networks: the positive influence dominating set problem. INFORMS J. Comput. **34**(3), 1345–1365 (2022)
12. Rossi, R., Ahmed, N.: The network data repository with interactive graph analytics and visualization. In: Proceedings of the AAAI Conference on Artificial Intelligence, vol. 29 (2015). https://networkrepository.com
13. Wang, F., Camacho, E., Xu, K.: Positive influence dominating set in online social networks. In: Du, D.-Z., Hu, X., Pardalos, P.M. (eds.) COCOA 2009. LNCS, vol. 5573, pp. 313–321. Springer, Heidelberg (2009). https://doi.org/10.1007/978-3-642-02026-1_29

# A Comparison of Recent Algorithms for Symbolic Regression to Genetic Programming

Yousef A. Radwan$^{(\boxtimes)}$, Gabriel Kronberger[ID], and Stephan Winkler[ID]

University of Applied Sciences Upper Austria, Heuristic and Evolutionary Algorithms Laboratory, Softwarepark 11, 4232 Hagenberg, Austria
yo.radwan@nu.edu.eg, {gabriel.kronberger,stephan.winkler}@fh-hagenberg.at

**Abstract.** Symbolic regression is a machine learning method with the goal to produce interpretable results. Unlike other machine learning methods such as, e.g. random forests or neural networks, which are opaque, symbolic regression aims to model and map data in a way that can be understood by scientists. Recent advancements, have attempted to bridge the gap between these two fields; new methodologies attempt to fuse the mapping power of neural networks and deep learning techniques with the explanatory power of symbolic regression. In this paper, we examine these new emerging systems and test the performance of an end-to-end transformer model for symbolic regression versus the reigning traditional methods based on genetic programming that have spearheaded symbolic regression throughout the years. We compare these systems on novel datasets to avoid bias to older methods who were improved on well-known benchmark datasets. Our results show that traditional GP methods as implemented e.g., by Operon still remain superior to two recently published symbolic regression methods.

**Keywords:** Symbolic regression · Machine learning · Genetic Programming · Transformers · Domain Knowledge · Neural Networks

## 1 Motivation

Symbolic regression (SR) [22, 24] is a supervised machine learning task where a functional mapping between one or multiple independent variables and usually one dependent variable has to be identified based on a dataset containing observations of the independent and dependent variables. In contrast to most other regression methods, the goal is to find a mathematical expression or formula for the regression function, whereby both, the expression structure, and fitting parameter values must be found by the algorithm. Thus, symbolic regression provides the potential to find short interpretable expressions based only on a set of observational data [5, 31]. In this context, SR has been called a hypothesis generation method [18, 22].

© The Author(s), under exclusive license to Springer Nature Switzerland AG 2025
A. Quesada-Arencibia et al. (Eds.): EUROCAST 2024, LNCS 15172, pp. 157–171, 2025.
https://doi.org/10.1007/978-3-031-82949-9_15

Our main goal is to gain a better understanding of recently developed symbolic regression (SR) methods, which mainly use approaches based on deep learning of neural networks to produce interpretable models. Even though the results published in papers are often impressive, the authors often do not invest the time to compare with established algorithms using, e.g., SRBench [29], which is a collection of SR problem instances and a well-curated and maintained list of SR implementations that can be used for benchmarking purposes. Since such comparisons are missing, there is a lack of understanding how well these methods work in practice and whether they truly improve upon established approaches. Even if the methods are tested on SRBench, there is the danger of optimizing methods for the benchmark (Goodhart's law [38]) instead of trying to improve methods in general. This can lead to the effect that the benchmark becomes less useful over time.

For our experiments we have therefore selected a list of real-world datasets from different domains of engineering which are so far not widely used in SR publications and most importantly are not yet contained in SRBench. This set of problem instances can be understood as a validation set that allows us to detect if algorithms are overfit on the SRBench problem instances.

## 2   Literature Review

The need to find mathematical models that describe observations and can be used for predictions, exists since the beginning of all scientific endeavors. Since researchers first tackled this with physics and mathematics-inspired methods, to the use of evolutionary algorithms such as genetic programming, to the entry of the newest contender which is machine learning. Although machine learning, and particularly deep learning, has struggled to enter this area in the past due to its black-box nature, recent creative methodologies have leveraged the power of neural networks and newer architectures such as transformers to create interpretable models that can qualify under the symbolic regression (SR) umbrella. Affenzeller et al. [1] compared traditional machine learning methods including neural networks to GP-based symbolic regression and found that GP-based SR can produce more accurate and more interpretable models models.

SR methods are generally split into regression-based methods (linear and non-linear), expression tree-based (genetic programming, reinforcement learning, transformers), physics-inspired (i.e. AI-Feynman), and math-inspired (i.e., symbolic-metamodel) [31].

### 2.1   Genetic Programming Methods

Genetic programming [22] was the main system for symbolic regression for a considerable portion of its history. It is built upon the idea of generating a population of models and then iteratively improving the population using a methodology similar to the idea of natural selection where weak models are pruned out and better models are selected to generate new, adapted models for the new population. It also includes the idea of mutations which add random changes to models during propagation.

In [41], the authors discussed the use of Gene Expression Programming (GEP) and Sequential Threshold Ridge Regression (STRidge) algorithms in symbolic regression. These methods are used to extract hidden physics from sparse observational data. The effectiveness of these algorithms is demonstrated in various applications, including equation discovery and truncation error analysis, showcasing their ability to identify complex physics problems.

Furthermore, the authors of [41] emphasized the significance of feature selection and engineering in model discovery approaches and demonstrate the potential of these techniques in complex physics problems. The most significant difference between GEP and GP is the fixed vs variable length representations used in the algorithms.

**Integration of Domain Knowledge into Genetic Programming.** Conventional GP methods for symbolic regression generally only used prediction error as their guide through the search space. However, with small datasets or when the data samples do not sufficiently cover the input space, prediction error does not serve as high-quality guidance [27]. This leads these methods to generate partly incorrect models that exhibit incorrect steady-state characteristics or local behavior [27,28] or that do not generalize well to points outside of the training set. Multiple papers have tackled the challenge of incorporating domain knowledge to bridge this gap. Some approached this by the addition of discrete data samples on which candidate models are checked, serving as a sort of internal representation of a constraint [27]. Other papers proposed a multi-objective symbolic regression framework [28] that optimizes models with respect to prediction error and also their compliance with desired physical properties. This framework also proposed a method for selecting a single final model out of the pool of candidate output models.

Another approach is shape-constrained symbolic regression. Kronberger et al. [23] investigate an approach by adding constraints that target the function image and its derivatives. This allows the user to enforce the monotonicity of the function over a selected input range. As a side effect domain knowledge can be used to improve extrapolation accuracy.

**Reducing the Size of the Search Space.** Some methods have extended GP with extra steps to reduce the size of the search space by removing algebraically isomorphic expressions and limiting the complexity of expressions. Exhaustive Symbolic Regression [2] and Grammar Enumeration [17] rely on heuristics-guided exhaustive search of the function space to find all possible structures and then evaluation on a specified cost function to find the best fit.

Another example of a SR system which limits the search space is the Interaction-Transformation Evolutionary Algorithm [12] which can represent functions as interactions between predictors and the application of a single transformation function. Other papers have made use of this representation with other systems such as multi-layer neural networks with the weights being adjusted following the Extreme Learning Machine procedure [11]. This improved or maintained performance while reducing computational cost.

## 2.2 Physics-Inspired Symbolic Regression

As a short overview of physics-inspired methods for symbolic regression, many methodologies have been formulated using physics theorems and inspirations. One example is the QLattice system [6] which is inspired by Richard Feynman's path integral formulation. This method explores many potential SR models and formulates them as graphs that can be interpreted as mathematical equations. This gives the user fairly strong control over the models' interpretability, complexity and performance. Unfortunately, the QLattice code has not been published. We therefore cannot use it for our own experiments.

Another SR method which can be characterized as physics-inspired is the AI-Feynman system [40], which is available as Python code. The performance of AI Feynman relative to other SR implementations is already well understood as it is also included within the SRBench project. The enhanced version of AI-Feynman [39] incorporates Pareto-optimality, aiming for the best accuracy relative to complexity. This version shows marked improvement in noise and data robustness, surpassing previous methods in formula discovery. It introduces a technique to identify generalized symmetries using neural network gradients and extends symbolic regression to probability distributions using normalizing flows and statistical hypothesis testing, enhancing the search process's efficiency and robustness.

The Scientist-Machine Equation Detector (SciMED) [18] merges the expertise of scientific disciplines with cutting-edge symbolic regression techniques in a scientist-in-the-loop approach. It combines a genetic programming-based wrapper selection method with automated machine learning and two-tiered symbolic regression strategies. AI-Descartes [8] is another system that allows to integrate physics-based domain knowledge into symbolic regression using mixed integer non-linear programming.

## 2.3 Neural Network-Based and Deep Learning Methods

With the entrance of deep learning methods into the symbolic regression field, there have been numerous contributions and systems that have relied on neural network based architectures [19,35]. The main feature of these architectures is their ability to be trained end-to-end and their better performance in extrapolation and prediction for points outside the training set as seen in [19]. The main drawback that restricted deep learning methods was their natural complexity limiting interpretability but Kim et al. [19] and many other recent papers have proposed solutions to this issue.

Li et al. [30] proposed a novel neural network that could dynamically adjust its structure in real time, allowing for both expansion and contraction. They mainly addressed the issue that the fixed network architecture often gave rise to redundancy in network structure and parameters and sought to remove this restriction. Their use of adaptive neural networks and innovative activation functions such as the PANGU meta-function allowed them to evolve the trained neural network into a usable mathematical expression.

**Sequence-to-Sequence Models and Transformers.** More recent deep learning contributions have made use of the popular transformer architecture or sequence to sequence architectures. With different variations from convolutional models such as [3] to recurrent network-based approaches such as [9,10], the symbolic regression research community has recently been flooded with transformer-based solutions and sequence-to-sequence models.

Their ability to map numerical data to corresponding symbolic equations and their encode-decoder structure make these architectures attractive for the SR task. Early papers used deep learning architectures to generate function structure and then optimize constants as a secondary step, while later papers attempted full function generation in one step [16,43]. They showed impressive extrapolation performance and high versatility. d'Ascoli et al. [9] even proclaimed that their model outperformed Mathematica functions in sequence extrapolation and recurrence prediction and has highlighted the power of transformers in recurrent sequences in particular.

The major drawback is computational cost and training time, which can be on the order of days. To address this, some papers have resorted to large scale pre-training [4,10]. Thereby, the transformer is pretrained for the task of generating a symbolic equation from a set of input-output pairs. Thus, at test time, the model is just queried with a new set of points and the output is used to guide the search for the equation. This approach has shown to improve with the presence of more pretraining data and more compute.

**Deep Generative Networks.** Some papers have approached symbolic regression using generative AI models. Using conditional generative models and large language models such as GPT, they have shown that this approach may also be viable, although not usually in one step and more of a good primer for function search. Deep Generative Symbolic Regression (DGSR) [14] leverages pretrained conditional generative models to encode equation invariances and provides a foundation for subsequent optimization steps. The paper demonstrates that DGSR achieves higher recovery rates of true equations, especially with a larger number of input variables, and is more computationally efficient at inference than state-of-the-art reinforcement learning solutions in symbolic regression. Holt et al. [14] highlight the advantages of DGSR, particularly in terms of scalability with the number of input variables and computational efficiency.

SymbolicGPT [42], a new transformer-based language model for symbolic regression, leverages the strengths of large language models, including high performance and flexibility. Valipour et al. report impressive capabilities in accuracy, speed, and data efficiency, outperforming other models in these areas [42].

## 2.4  Hybrid Methods

Mundhenk et al. [32] describe a hybrid method that combines neural-guided search with genetic programming for symbolic regression and other combinatorial optimization problems. The approach involves using a neural-guided component to generate initial populations for genetic programming, which evolves to yield progressively better starting points. They report, recovering 65% more expressions from benchmark tasks, outperforming Deep Symbolic Regression [35].

In summary, many novel and reportedly powerful methods for symbolic regression have been proposed in the past few years fuel by the increased capabilities of deep learning architectures and models. However, the comparison with genetic programming based methods or classical machine learning methods is often lacking. We found that the code for many of the methods mentioned above is available online. However, with very few exceptions we failed to run the system on our own datasets. In many cases the code is simply dumped with minimal documentation to an online repository for the purpose of the publication and then abandoned. As a consequence we selected only two systems: *end-to-end symbolic regression using transformers (E2E)* [19] and the *Scientist-Machine Equation Detector (SciMED)* [18] for our comparison and used HeuristicLab [45] and Operon [7] as representative implementations of tree-based genetic programming for symbolic regression. SciMED provides different pipelines to generate models. The GA-SR pipeline uses the gplearn Python library[1] for tree-based genetic programming for symbolic regression and the AutoML pipeline uses TPOT [34], which is a Python library that allows to optimize machine learning pipelines using genetic programming. Table 1 lists the software implementations that we have chosen for our experiment and their capabilities.

**Table 1.** Characteristics and features of the software implementations selected for our experiments.

|            | HeuristicLab | Operon | E2E | SciMED AutoML | SciMED GA-SR |
|------------|--------------|--------|-----|---------------|--------------|
| Year       | 2014         | 2020   | 2022 | 2022          | 2022         |
| Gen. prog. | ✓            | ✓      |     |               | ✓            |
| Neural net.|              |        | ✓   |               |              |
| Dom. know. | ✓            |        |     | ✓             | ✓            |

# 3  Benchmarking Experiments

In running our experiments, we sought to equalize the playing field among the models to allow as fair a comparison as possible given the vast differences between

---

[1] https://gplearn.readthedocs.io/en/stable/.

the models at hand. Each model had a different approach which will be detailed in the following. In most instances, if the accompanying paper offered default parameters or a model checkpoint to use, those parameters were used unless they incurred too much runtime as will be detailed more in the following sections.

In the case of E2E and SciMED the experiments were run on a RTX 2060 GPU with 6GB of VRAM. There are a few notable exceptions, which are mentioned in the corresponding segment, which were run on an M3 Pro chip, the performance differences are noted in case they are of interest. The HeuristicLab and Operon experiments where run on an Intel Core i5-10400 CPU.

## 3.1   Description of Datasets

We used datasets from [24] with the same training and test splits as described in the book. The *chemical 1 (tower)* and *chemical 2 (competition)* datasets stem from continuous processes at Dow Chemical [21]. The *tower* dataset was originally described in [44]. The target variable is the propylene concentration measured at the top of a distillation tower and the input variables are process parameters. The *competition* dataset has as target variable expensive but noisy lab data of the chemical composition (output) of the end-product, and 57 input variables with cheap process measurements, such as temperatures, pressures, and flows (inputs). This dataset was used in the symbolic regression competition at EvoStar conference 2010[2].

The *friction* datasets were sponsored by Miba Frictec company and contain as target variable the friction coefficient for different types of friction materials as measured on an industrial friction testbench. The input variables are sliding velocity, pressure and temperature of friction materials. We used two separate datasets from the same set of experiments. In the first dataset, the target variable is the static coefficient of friction, and for the second dataset the target variable is the dynamic coefficient of friction. The dataset was originally described in [26], where the nominal variable for the friction material was included into the symbolic regression models using factor variables. In our experiments, we simply used a one-hot-encoding as this is supported by all tested software systems.

The *flow stress* dataset was sponsored by LKR Light Metals Technologies, Austrian Institute of Technology, and contains measurements from dilatometer experiments using samples of a well-known aluminium alloy (AA6082). The target variable is the flow stress and the input variables are the strain the strain rate and the temperature. The dataset was originally described in [15], but we here only used a subset for constant strain rate of 0.1 to simplify the problem and speed up the experiments.

The *battery* datasets were originally collected and published by the NASA Ames Research Center [37] and are described in [13]. We used two datasets with preprocessed data from [24] where the goal is to predict the remaining duration

---

[2] https://web.archive.org/web/20120628140646/http://casnew.iti.upv.es/index.php/evocompetitions/105-symregcompetition.

of discharge based on cell voltage, discharge current and cell temperature after ten minutes and twenty minutes of discharge under constant conditions.

Finally, the two *Nikuradse* datasets contain measurements for the flow friction in rough pipes [33]. Symbolic regression results for this dataset have been reported recently in [25,36]. We used two versions of the dataset: in the first dataset the target variable is the turbulent friction $\lambda$, and we use two input variables, the Reynolds number and the relative roughness $r/k$. The second dataset represents Prandtl's collapse, where the target is a transformed turbulent friction factor, and the input variable is a nonlinear combination of the relative roughness, and the Reynolds number [36]. The datasets have been extracted directly from the tables in [33]. All of the datasets were also split into training and test in the same manner for all our experiments. These splits can be seen below in Table 2:

**Table 2.** Training and testing ranges for all datasets

| Dataset | Training partition | Testing partition |
|---|---|---|
| Chemical 1 (tower) | 0...3135 | 3136...4998 |
| Chemical 2 (Competition) | 0...710 | 711...1065 |
| Friction (static) | 0...1008 | 1009...2016 |
| Friction (dynamic) | 0...1008 | 1009...2016 |
| Flow stress (phip=0.1) | 0...4199 | 4200...7799 |
| Battery 1 (10min) | 0...503 | 504...634 |
| Battery 2 (20min) | 0...1099 | 1100...1637 |
| Nikuradse 1 | 0...229 | 230...360 |
| Nikuradse 2 | 0...199 | 200...361 |

Models are compared based on their normalized mean of squared errors (NMSE),

$$\text{NMSE}(\hat{y}, y) = \frac{1}{\text{var}(y)} \text{MSE}(\hat{y}, y) = \frac{1}{\text{var}(y)} \sum_{i=1}^{N} (\hat{y}_i - y_i)^2 , \tag{1}$$

where $\text{var}(y)$ is the variance of the vector of target values $y$ and $\hat{y}$ is the vector of predictions from the model. The NMSE is in the range from zero to one and allows comparing regressors over multiple problem instances.

### 3.2  Methods and Parameters

**Operon and HeuristicLab.** Operon [7] is an efficient state-of-the-art software implementation of genetic programming for symbolic regression. We use it here as a representative for symbolic regression systems based on genetic programming. Operon is implemented in modern C++ and relies heavily on thread-based parallelism to speed-up GP on multi-core machines. It stems out of the same research group that developed and maintains *HeuristicLab* (HL) which is a software environment for heuristic and evolutionary algorithms implemented in C# and uses the .NET platform [45]. It contains an implementation of tree-based genetic programming [20] similar to Operon. We use both, Operon and HeuristicLab, with the same parameters to compare their relative performance. The same parameters were used for all datasets (Table 3).

**Table 3.** Parameters used for Operon and HeuristicLab.

| Parameter | Value |
|---|---|
| Population size and generations | 1000, 100 |
| Selection | tournament with group size 5 |
| Mutation probability | 15 % |
| Maximum tree length and depth | 100, 15 |
| Parameter optimization iterations | 10 |
| Function set | $+, \times, \div, \exp, \log, x^2, \sqrt{x}, x^{1/3}$ |
| Loss function | mean of squared errors |

**End-to-End Transformer:** In the case of E2E [16], the authors had provided a web demo which provided easy inference for users based on a pretrained model that was provided. However, since the web server did not always respond and would sometimes give unexpected errors and also since web APIs in general can cause extra response time over what the true inference time would be, the inference was done locally using the pretrained checkpoint in a somewhat manual sense using the provided example Jupyter notebook after some modification.

For each dataset, the model checkpoint was loaded and then fit 20 times consecutively. For each instance, the model was run for inference on the training and test sets and the NMSE, R2 score, and training time were recorded. All runs were done on the RTX 2060 GPU except a few which were run on an M3 Pro chip, these exceptional runs will be highlighted in the results.

**SciMED:** This method combines evolutionary feature selection with GP-based automated machine learning (AutoML) for enriching the data domain and genetic programming for symbolic regression. Alternatively to GP-based symbolic regression SciMED provides computationally more expensive "Las Vegas search SR" for more stable and accurate results. In each phase it is possible to add domain knowledge.

For our experiments, we used the library provided by the authors with default settings, and called the AutoML component (SciMED AutoML) and the GP-based SR component (SciMED GA-SR) separately. We did not use the evolutionary feature selection component or Las Vegas SR. We also did not use or test the capabilities of SciMED to add domain knowledge in each of the phases. It is important to note that the AutoML component simply calls TPOT [34], a GP-based AutoML package for Python. TPOT searches for the best pipeline including data preprocessing, feature selection methods, and regressors available. SciMED configures TPOT to use 5-fold cross-validation internally and refers to this step as the *numerical* phase. For the GA-SR component SciMED basically wraps the gplearn library and calls this the *analytical* phase. Table 4 lists the (default) parameters values for SciMED which we used for the AutoML and the GA-SR configurations. We executed 20 independent runs for each dataset, but found that the GA-SR phase produced the same results for all twenty iterations because the random seed of gplearn is not changed by SciMED. Training time was also recorded for all runs.

**Table 4.** Parameters used for SciMED AutoML and SciMED GA-SR.

| Parameter | SciMED AutoML | SciMED GA-SR |
|---|---|---|
| Run times | 1 | 20 |
| Generations | 50 | 50 |
| Population size | 100 | 100 |
| Parsimony coefficient | - | 0.05 |
| CV folds | 5 | 5 |

## 4   Results

There are a few key points which can be seen across Table 5. On average, Operon and HeuristicLab find the models with best NMSE on the testing partitions. Both implementations produce similar results but Operon is much faster (speedup ≈ 8) even after accounting for the fact that the HeuristicLab runtimes are for a single-threaded configuration while Operon used 12 concurrent threads.

Only SciMED AutoML was able to produce models with comparable NMSE values on the testing partition. For two out of the nine datasets it even found the best models. On all other datasets either Operon or HeuristicLab produced better results. This is remarkable as SciMED AutoML uses TPOT internally which has access to the most important classical machine learning models such as random forests or extreme gradient boosting for trees (XGBoost). This again provides evidence that GP-based SR can produce models with an accuracy similar to more traditional black-box machine learning methods [1,29].

Our results when using end-to-end transformers for symbolic regression (E2E) were much worse than the other methods. In some cases it even produced models with NMSE larger than one which is worse than a model predicting the mean of the target values. Operon had the best runtime on average and HeuristicLab had the worst runtimes. High dimensionality in the Chemical 1

**Table 5.** NMSE values on training and testing sets as well as the runtime as observed in the experiments. The row with best NMSE value on the testing set for each dataset is marked in bold. Median and interquartile range over 30 independent runs are reported for Operon and HeuristicLab. Operon runtime is for 12 concurrent threads. The quality of Operon and HeuristicLab models is similar but Operon is approximately 8 times faster in single-core performance.

| Dataset | Software | NMSE (train) | NMSE (test) (rank) | Runtime [s] |
|---|---|---|---|---|
| Chemical Tower | HeuristicLab | 0.052 | 0.062 (3) | 14487 |
| | Operon | 0.048 | 0.057 (2) | 148 |
| | E2E | 52.34 | 55.99 (5) | 351 |
| | SciMED AutoML | 0.000 | **0.025** (1) | 12415 |
| | SciMED GA-SR | 0.512 | 0.525 (4) | ≈ 600 |
| Chemical Comp. | HeuristicLab | 0.092 | **0.204** (1) | 2975 |
| | Operon | 0.092 | 0.270 (2) | 29 |
| | E2E | 0.774 | 1.229 (5) | 92 |
| | SciMED AutoML | 0.028 | 0.448 (3) | 7560 |
| | SciMED GA-SR | 1.186 | 1.124 (4) | ≈ 600 |
| Flow Stress | HeuristicLab | 0.002 | 0.003 (2) | 5425 |
| | Operon | 0.000 | **0.001** (1) | 114 |
| | E2E[1] | 0.422 | 0.491 (3) | 30 |
| | SciMED AutoML[3] | 1.912 | 2.227 (4.5) | 1198 |
| | SciMED GA-SR | 1.912 | 2.227 (4.5) | ≈ 600 |
| Friction (dyn.) | HeuristicLab | 0.035 | **0.067** (1) | 3784 |
| | Operon | 0.047 | 0.070 (2) | 18 |
| | E2E | 1.087 | 1.087 (4) | 229 |
| | SciMED AutoML | 0.062 | 0.261 (3) | 1269 |
| | SciMED GA-SR | 332.2 | 453.3 (5) | ≈ 600 |
| Friction (stat.) | HeuristicLab | 0.065 | **0.095** (1) | 3366 |
| | Operon | 0.071 | 0.104 (2) | 21 |
| | E2E | 0.997 | 0.996 (4) | 230 |
| | SciMED AutoML | 0.050 | 0.202 (3) | 6697 |
| | SciMED GA-SR | 283.4 | 422.7 (5) | ≈ 1200 |
| Battery 1 | HeuristicLab | 0.001 | **0.017** (1) | 2529 |
| | Operon | 0.000 | 0.024 (2) | 18 |
| | E2E | 0.058 | 0.347 (4) | 79 |
| | SciMED AutoML | 0.003 | 0.051 (3) | 1093 |
| | SciMED GA-SR[4] | N/A | N/A | ≈ 600 |
| Battery 2 | HeuristicLab | 0.001 | 0.152 (4) | 3767 |
| | Operon | 0.001 | 0.100 (2) | 35 |
| | E2E | 0.175 | 0.151 (3) | 171 |
| | SciMED AutoML | 0.003 | **0.035** (1) | 1004 |
| | SciMED GA-SR | 0.575 | 0.684 (5) | ≈ 600 |
| Nikuradse 1 | HeuristicLab | 0.001 | 0.056 (2) | 578 |
| | Operon | 0.001 | **0.054** (1) | 5 |
| | E2E | 0.304 | 0.905 (4) | 35 |
| | SciMED AutoML | 0.001 | 0.734 (3) | 716 |
| | SciMED GA-SR | 1.000 | 1.005 (5) | ≈ 600 |
| Nikuradse 2 | HeuristicLab | 0.023 | **0.019** (1) | 282 |
| | Operon | 0.021 | 0.021 (3) | 6 |
| | E2E | 0.196 | 0.129 (4) | 50 |
| | SciMED AutoML | 0.023 | 0.020 (2) | 1778 |
| | SciMED GA-SR | 1.486 | 1.429 (5) | ≈ 600[5] |

This was done using the web demo (1 run)
M3 Pro runtime average
Unanimous result across all 20 runs
Would not run
All SciMED GA-SR runs took about the same amount of time of around 10 min

and Chemical 2 datasets, and presence of categorical variables in the Friction (dyn.) and Friction (stat.) datasets influence model performance. The statistical analysis in Table 6(a) and Table 6(b) shows that on average HeuristicLab and Operon perform best over all datasets. Based on a Wilcoxon signed rank test, Operon and HeuristicLab are significantly better than E2E and SciMED GA-SR ($\alpha = 0.05$). SciMED AutoML had medium performance.

**Table 6.** Statistical analysis of experiment results.

(a) Average ranks across datasets

| Software | Average rank |
|---|---|
| HeuristicLab (HL) | 1.8 |
| Operon (Op) | 1.9 |
| SciMED AutoML (ScML) | 2.6 |
| End-to-end Transformer (E2E) | 4.0 |
| SciMED GA+SR (ScSR) | 4.7 |

(b) Pairwise p-values

| | Op | ScML | E2E | ScSR |
|---|---|---|---|---|
| HL | 0.91 | 0.25 | **0.004** | **0.012** |
| Op | | 0.30 | **0.008** | **0.012** |
| ScML | | | 0.055 | 0.096 |
| E2E | | | | 0.570 |

## 5   Discussion and Conclusion

In our experiments Operon remains the best all-around performer showing best to second best test errors and best to second best runtimes. Even though we found many recent publications proposing new SR approaches based on deep learning in the literature review, in many cases no code was published or we did not succeed running the code. As an example AI Descartes [8] requires a commercial solver (BARON) with yearly license costs of several hundred dollars even for a single seat academic license. Often code is published as academic abandonware together with a paper which does not run with up-to-date library versions. As a consequence, we only used the end-to-end transformer [19] and the Scientist-Machine Equation Detector [18] in our comparisons. However, the results of both systems do not reach the quality of results of tree-based genetic programming for symbolic regression as implemented in HeuristicLab or Operon.

**Acknowledgements.** G.K. is supported by the Austrian Federal Ministry for Climate Action, Environment, Energy, Mobility, Innovation and Technology, the Federal Ministry for Labour and Economy, and the regional government of Upper Austria within the COMET project ProMetHeus (904919) supported by the Austrian Research Promotion Agency (FFG).

**Author contributions.** Y.R.: literature review, writing, running all experiments (except for Operon and HeuristicLab), data analysis. G.K.: conceptualization, preparation of datasets and running experiments for Operon and HeuristicLab. S.W.: conceptualization and oral presentation at the conference.

# References

1. Affenzeller, M., et al.: White box vs. black box modeling: on the performance of deep learning, random forests, and symbolic regression in solving regression problems. In: Moreno-Díaz, R., Pichler, F., Quesada-Arencibia, A. (eds.) EUROCAST 2019. LNCS, vol. 12013, pp. 288–295. Springer, Cham (2020). https://doi.org/10.1007/978-3-030-45093-9_35

2. Bartlett, D.J., Desmond, H., Ferreira, P.G.: Exhaustive symbolic regression. IEEE Trans. Evol. Comput., 1–1 (2023). https://doi.org/10.1109/tevc.2023.3280250

3. Biggio, L., Bendinelli, T., Lucchi, A., Parascandolo, G.: A Seq2Seq approach to symbolic regression. In: Learning Meets Combinatorial Algorithms at NeurIPS2020 (2020)

4. Biggio, L., Bendinelli, T., Neitz, A., Lucchi, A., Parascandolo, G.: Neural symbolic regression that scales. In: International Conference on Machine Learning, pp. 936–945. PMLR (2021)

5. Bomarito, G., Townsend, T., Stewart, K., Esham, K., Emery, J., Hochhalter, J.: Development of interpretable, data-driven plasticity models with symbolic regression. Comput. Struct. **252**, 106557 (2021). https://doi.org/10.1016/j.compstruc.2021.106557

6. Brøløs, K.R., et al.: An approach to symbolic regression using FEYN (2021)

7. Burlacu, B., Kronberger, G., Kommenda, M.: Operon C++: an efficient genetic programming framework for symbolic regression. In: Proceedings of the 2020 Genetic and Evolutionary Computation Conference Companion, pp. 1562–1570. GECCO 2020, ACM (2020). https://doi.org/10.1145/3377929.3398099

8. Cornelio, C., et al.: Combining data and theory for derivable scientific discovery with AI-descartes. Nat. Commun. **14**(1), 1777 (2023). https://doi.org/10.1038/s41467-023-37236-y

9. d'Ascoli, S., Kamienny, P.A., Lample, G., Charton, F.: Deep symbolic regression for recurrent sequences. arXiv preprint arXiv:2201.04600 (2022)

10. d'Ascoli, S., Becker, S., Mathis, A., Schwaller, P., Kilbertus, N.: ODEFormer: symbolic regression of dynamical systems with transformers. arXiv:2310.05573 (2023)

11. de Franca, F.O., de Lima, M.Z.: Interaction-transformation symbolic regression with extreme learning machine. Neurocomputing **423**, 609–619 (2021). https://doi.org/10.1016/j.neucom.2020.10.062

12. de Franca, F.O., Aldeia, G.S.I.: Interaction-transformation evolutionary algorithm for symbolic regression. Evol. Comput. **29**(3), 367–390 (2021). https://doi.org/10.1162/evco_a_00285

13. Goebel, K., Saha, B., Saxena, A., Celaya, J.R., Christophersen, J.P.: Prognostics in battery health management. IEEE Instrum. Meas. Mag. **11**(4), 33–40 (2008). https://doi.org/10.1109/MIM.2008.4579269

14. Holt, S., Qian, Z., van der Schaar, M.: Deep generative symbolic regression. arXiv:2401.00282 (2023)

15. Kabliman, E., Kolody, A.H., Kronsteiner, J., Kommenda, M., Kronberger, G.: Application of symbolic regression for constitutive modeling of plastic deformation. Appl. Eng. Sci. **6**, 100052 (2021). https://doi.org/10.1016/j.apples.2021.100052

16. Kamienny, P.A., d'Ascoli, S., Lample, G., Charton, F.: End-to-end symbolic regression with transformers. arXiv preprint 2204.10532 (2022)

17. Kammerer, L., Kronberger, G., Burlacu, B., Winkler, S.M., Kommenda, M., Affenzeller, M.: Symbolic regression by exhaustive search: Reducing the search space using syntactical constraints and efficient semantic structure deduplication. In:

Genetic Programming Theory and Practice XVII, pp. 79–99. Springer International Publishing (2020). https://doi.org/10.1007/978-3-030-39958-0_5

18. Keren, L.S., Liberzon, A., Lazebnik, T.: A computational framework for physics-informed symbolic regression with straightforward integration of domain knowledge. Sci. Rep. **13**(1), 1249 (2023)

19. Kim, S., et al.: Integration of neural network-based symbolic regression in deep learning for scientific discovery. IEEE Trans. Neural Netw. Learn. Syst. **32**(9), 4166–4177 (2021). https://doi.org/10.1109/tnnls.2020.3017010

20. Kommenda, M., Kronberger, G., Wagner, S., Winkler, S., Affenzeller, M.: On the architecture and implementation of tree-based genetic programming in heuristiclab. In: Proceedings of the 14th Annual Conference Companion on Genetic and Evolutionary Computation. p. 101–108. GECCO 2012, Association for Computing Machinery, New York, NY, USA (2012). https://doi.org/10.1145/2330784.2330801

21. Kordon, A.: Evolutionary computation in the chemical industry. In: Yu, T., Davis, L., Baydar, C., Roy, R. (eds.) Evolutionary Computation in Practice, pp. 245–262. Springer Berlin Heidelberg (2008).https://doi.org/10.1007/978-3-540-75771-9_11

22. Koza, J.R.: Genetic Programming: On the Programming of Computers by Means of Natural Selection. MIT Press (1992)

23. Kronberger, G., de Franca, F.O., Burlacu, B., Haider, C., Kommenda, M.: Shape-constrained symbolic regression-improving extrapolation with prior knowledge. Evol. Comput. **30**(1), 75–98 (2022). https://doi.org/10.1162/evco_a_00294

24. Kronberger, G., Burlacu, B., Kommenda, M., Winkler, S.M., Affenzeller, M.: Symbolic Regression. CRC Press / Taylor Francis (2024)

25. Kronberger, G., de Franca, F.O., Desmond, H., Bartlett, D.J., Kammerer, L.: The inefficiency of genetic programming for symbolic regression. arxiv preprint 2404.17292 (2024)

26. Kronberger, G., Kommenda, M., Promberger, A., Nickel, F.: Predicting friction system performance with symbolic regression and genetic programming with factor variables. In: Proceedings of the Genetic and Evolutionary Computation Conference. ACM (2018). https://doi.org/10.1145/3205455.3205522

27. Kubalík, J., Derner, E., Babuška, R.: Symbolic regression driven by training data and prior knowledge. In: Proceedings of the 2020 Genetic and Evolutionary Computation Conference. GECCO 2020, ACM (2020). https://doi.org/10.1145/3377930.3390152

28. Kubalík, J., Derner, E., Babuška, R.: Multi-objective symbolic regression for physics-aware dynamic modeling. Expert Syst. Appl. **182**, 115210 (2021). https://doi.org/10.1016/j.eswa.2021.115210

29. La Cava, W., et al.: Contemporary symbolic regression methods and their relative performance. arXiv:2107.14351 (2021)

30. Li, Y., et al.: MetaSymNet: a dynamic symbolic regression network capable of evolving into arbitrary formulations. arXiv preprint arXiv:2311.07326 (2023)

31. Makke, N., Chawla, S.: Interpretable scientific discovery with symbolic regression: a review. Artif. Intell. Rev. **57**(1), 2 (2024). https://doi.org/10.1007/s10462-023-10622-0

32. Mundhenk, T.N., Landajuela, M., Glatt, R., Santiago, C.P., Faissol, D.M., Petersen, B.K.: Symbolic regression via neural-guided genetic programming population seeding. arXiv:2111.00053 (2021)

33. Nikuradse, J.: Laws of flow in rough pipes. Tech. rep., National Advisory Committee for Aeronautics Washington, NACA TM 1292 - Translation of "Strömungsgesetze in rauhen Rohren" VDI-Forschungsheft 361. Beilage zu

"Forschung auf dem Gebiete des Ingenieurwesens" Ausgabe B Band 4, July/August 1933. (1950)

34. Olson, R.S., Bartley, N., Urbanowicz, R.J., Moore, J.H.: Evaluation of a tree-based pipeline optimization tool for automating data science. In: Proceedings of the Genetic and Evolutionary Computation Conference 2016, pp. 485–492. GECCO 2016, ACM, New York, NY, USA (2016). https://doi.org/10.1145/2908812.2908918

35. Petersen, B.K., Landajuela, M., Mundhenk, T.N., Santiago, C.P., Kim, S.K., Kim, J.T.: Deep symbolic regression: recovering mathematical expressions from data via risk-seeking policy gradients (2021)

36. Reichardt, I., Pallarès, J., Sales-Pardo, M., Guimerà, R.: Bayesian machine scientist to compare data collapses for the Nikuradse dataset. Phys. Rev. Lett. **124**(8) (2020).https://doi.org/10.1103/physrevlett.124.084503

37. Saha, B., Goebel, K.: Battery data set. Tech. rep., NASA Prognostics Data Repository, NASA Ames Research Center, Moffett Field, CA (2007). https://phm-datasets.s3.amazonaws.com/NASA/5.+Battery+Data+Set.zip,    https://www.nasa.gov/content/prognostics-center-of-excellence-data-set-repository

38. Strathern, M.: 'improving ratings': audit in the British university system. European Review **5**(3), 305–321 (1997). https://doi.org/10.1002/(sici)1234-981x(199707)5:3⟨305::aid-euro184⟩3.0.co;2-4

39. Udrescu, S.M., Tan, A., Feng, J., Neto, O., Wu, T., Tegmark, M.: AI Feynman 2.0: pareto-optimal symbolic regression exploiting graph modularity (2020)

40. Udrescu, S.M., Tegmark, M.: AI Feynman: a physics-inspired method for symbolic regression (2020)

41. Vaddireddy, H., Rasheed, A., Staples, A.E., San, O.: Feature engineering and symbolic regression methods for detecting hidden physics from sparse sensor observation data. Phys. Fluids **32**(1) (2020). https://doi.org/10.1063/1.5136351

42. Valipour, M., You, B., Panju, M., Ghodsi, A.: SymbolicGPT: a generative transformer model for symbolic regression. arXiv:2106.14131 (2021)

43. Vastl, M., Kulhánek, J., Kubalík, J., Derner, E., Babuška, R.: SymFormer: end-to-end symbolic regression using transformer-based architecture. arXiv:2205.15764 (2022)

44. Vladislavleva, E.J., Smits, G.F., den Hertog, D.: Order of nonlinearity as a complexity measure for models generated by symbolic regression via Pareto genetic programming. IEEE Trans. Evol. Comput. **13**(2), 333–349 (2009). https://doi.org/10.1109/TEVC.2008.926486

45. Wagner, S., et al.: Architecture and design of the HeuristicLab optimization environment. In: Klempous, R., Nikodem, J., Jacak, W., Chaczko, Z. (eds.) Advanced Methods and Applications in Computational Intelligence, Topics in Intelligent Engineering and Informatics, vol. 6, pp. 197–261. Springer (2014). https://doi.org/10.1007/978-3-319-01436-4_10

# Composable Evolutionary Computation

Jan Zenisek[1,2]([⊠]), Florian Bachinger[1], Florian Holzinger[1], Erik Pitzer[1],
Stefan Wagner[1], and Michael Affenzeller[1,2]

[1] University of Applied Sciences Upper Austria, Softwarepark 11, 4232 Hagenberg,
Austria
[2] Institute for Symbolic Artificial Intelligence, Johannes Kepler University Linz,
Altenberger Straße 69, 4040 Linz, Austria
jan.zenisek@fh-hagenberg.at

**Abstract.** Distributed algorithm design and execution has been a central aspect of evolutionary computation research ever since. Be it to spread and balance workload over many computational nodes to improve runtime performance, or to facilitate new algorithmic strategies, such as co-evolutionary approaches, for instance, to optimize convergence behavior. Although many software-research projects support distributed evolutionary computation, we see potential to further improve the usability of respective algorithm design. In this paper, we present a containerized software system, incorporating a domain specific design language, to address this issue. The performed experiments prove the developed system's applicability and support further research leads.

**Keywords:** Evolutionary Computation · Algorithm Design · Disbributed Computing · Open Source Software · Containerization

## 1  Introduction

Evolutionary Computation (EC) based studies and applications regularly require long runtimes. High dimensional problems (e. g., vehicle routing), domain-specific target functions (e. g., simulation-based), complex operators (e. g., gradient descent), or large data sets (e. g., sensor time series) are just some reasons to aim for faster EC algorithms using distributed computing for load balancing. However, distributed EC is not only faster, but also enables to pursue other algorithmic aspects, e. g., co-evolution strategies, to avoid premature convergence and hence, achieve better results [3].

Well established software frameworks such as *ECJ* [6] or *HeuristicLab* [7] provide large selections of EC algorithms, parallelization engines to execute them and rich dashboards to analyze their performance. For instance, ECJ supports the execution of asynchronous island models over TCP/IP and master/slave fitness evaluation utilizing multiple processors. Similarly, HeuristicLab enables parallel execution of any implemented population-based algorithm via multi-threading and external fitness evaluation via TCP/IP. The most powerful tool

A. Quesada-Arencibia et al. (Eds.): EUROCAST 2024, LNCS 15172, pp. 172–180, 2025.
https://doi.org/10.1007/978-3-031-82949-9_16

for algorithm distribution associated with HeuristicLab is *Hive*, which is designed as a stateless job execution platform, mainly to conduct grid searches for hyper-parameter tuning.

However, in terms of technical implementation, we aim to employ a more modern software stack using containerization technologies like *Docker* or *Kubernetes* and message oriented middleware (MOM) like *Apache Kafka* or *MQTT* for data exchange between containers. To this end, the authors of [5] presented a first containerized EC approach using Docker, which they detailed later in [4]. They implemented a genetic algorithm, split into one master and multiple fitness evaluation containers. The genetic algorithm presented in [2] implements the island model using stateless cloud services and Kafka for data exchange. Further on, the approach of [1] employs Kubernetes for workload distribution and Kafka for data exchange to implement a serverless, island genetic algorithm with a dynamic number of containerized populations.

As the stated examples confirm, there already has been valuable conceptual and engineering work done for distributed EC with modern technologies. However, without profound programming skills and deeper system knowledge, it can be quite cumbersome to go beyond the mere use of available algorithms in these software tools and frameworks. In particular, we see a lack of support in the development of *custom* distributed EC algorithms, which we want to address in this work. To summarize and precise, we aim to improve distributed EC algorithm design, by using a modern, container- and MOM-based technology stack. The results of the herein presented work have been published to our public *GitHub* repositories[1],[2] where anyone can follow our ongoing development progress. With respect to *Docker Compose*, a well-known container management tool, we have therefore named our work *Composable Evolutionary Computation*.

The rest of this paper is structured as follows: In Sect. 2, we detail design, technical implementation and use of the system that we have developed, taking into account the separation of concerns of EC stakeholders. To show the applicability of the system, Sect. 3 documents and analyzes conducted runtime measurements for an *external fitness evaluation* experiment. Finally, we provide a result summary and a brief outlook regarding planned extensions in Sect. 4.

## 2    Composable Evolutionary Computation

In this paper, we present an evolutionary computation system prototype, which incorporates (a) a library of EC paradigm implementations, (b) a development and execution runtime, which supports the algorithm design process and manages their distributed execution, and (c) a description language with corresponding frontend to design new algorithms as operator graph.

We provide a comprehensive overview of the system in Fig. 1 and detail its major components in the following subsections.

---

[1] https://github.com/janzenisek/eurocast2024.
[2] https://github.com/prescriptiveanalytics/.

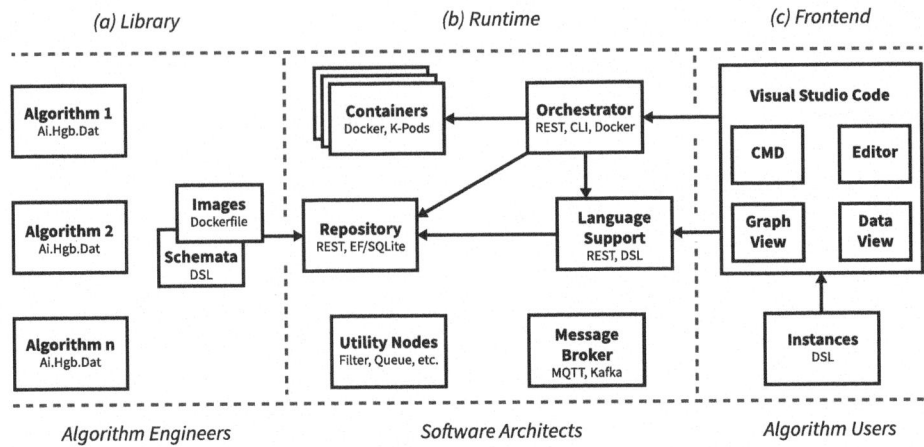

**Fig. 1.** Software architecture of the developed environment for evolutionary computation: On the left-hand side, the algorithm library, which ships with a small set of implemented EC paradigms, using the messaging client *Ai.Hgb.Dat*, is depicted. To extend the library, algorithm engineers have to set up or generate a scheme file and a corresponding docker image for their developments and register them in our central repository (via REST interface, EntityFramework and a SQLite database). On the right-hand side, the algorithm user frontend, which is based on a Visual Studio Code (VSC) extension, is outlined. To ensure optimal user experience, the extension communicates with the *Repository* via the *Language Support*, which responses with real-time code suggestions, such as currently available algorithm types, error checking, syntax highlighting etc. The functionality of this system part is further detailed in Subsect. 2.3 and the corresponding Fig. 2. In the middle, the runtime, developed by this work's authors, is displayed. Each of the visualized blocks is run as an individual software container. The *Orchestrator* represents the centerpiece of this system. By utilizing *Language Support*, it reads and interprets the texts, formulated with the DSL *Seidl* and sent from the algorithm user frontend. According to the therein written statements, the *Orchestrator* fires up and wires algorithm instances as *Containers* – currently using Docker. For data exchange between containers, the *Message Broker* – configurable, MQTT or Apache Kafka – is used. To filter or queue messages between algorithm *Containers*, we provide a set of utility software nodes.

## 2.1   Library

In the algorithm library (a), we offer implementations for popular EC paradigms, such as Genetic Algorithm (GA), Genetic Programming (GP), Evolution Strategy (ES), etc., as basic algorithm building blocks with several standard hyperparameters to tune. The algorithms are made pluggable, so that parallel and distributed concepts, such as island GA, cellular EA, or age layered population structures are easy to design, as indicated in Fig. 2.

## 2.2   Runtime

The components of the developed runtime (b) are visualized in the center part of Fig. 1 and described in the figure's caption. This system part is naturally the most complex and has been the most development-intensive, as it links the other two (cf. library and frontend) and enables the eventual execution of distributed ECs. Its core task is to parse algorithm descriptions and to provision and orchestrate the necessary environment accordingly.

Each node in the designed algorithm operator graph is run as an individual, distributable container. Each graph edge, i. e., the communication between nodes, is implemented using some messaging technology. In our presented runtime architecture, this can be accomplished via the *Message Broker* container. However, in order to make use of this messaging middleware, algorithm engineers have to handle the connection to the broker and apply to its messaging protocol. In order to support algorithm engineers to this end, we suggest using our custom message client[3], first presented in [8]. It incorporates multiple options for data transport protocols, message serialization and de-serialization, and messaging paradigms, for all of which it provides a uniform interface. Moreover, the library ships with a feature to generate the messaging scheme, using code reflection, which saves time for algorithm engineers.

## 2.3   Frontend

Concerning algorithm design (c), we adopt the operator-graph-algorithm concept of *HeuristicLab* [7] using the *Structured Entity Interaction Description Language (Seidl)*[4] [9], and extend the corresponding Visual Studio Code extension for our purpose. As a result to this end, we refer to Fig. 2, where the design and execution of an island genetic algorithm with an evolution strategy, integrated as local search, is demonstrated. In Listing 1.1 a closer look on the *Seidl*-based description from the editor in Fig. 2 is displayed.

---

[3] https://github.com/prescriptiveanalytics/Ai.Hgb.Dat.
[4] https://github.com/prescriptiveanalytics/Ai.Hgb.Seidl.

```
1  ai.hgb.packages.ceal.eurocast2024.experiment:v1
2  import ai.hgb.packages.ceal.eurocast2024:latest
3
4  node PGA ga1 (popSize=1000, generations=1000, mutRate=0.2, migRate=0.10, ...)
5  node PGA ga2 (popSize=5000, generations=1000, mutRate=0.1, migRate=0.05, ...)
6  node PES es (mu=1, lambda=1)
7  node Aggregator agg (popSize=100)
8
9  ga1.mig  ==>            ga2.mig # request migrants from ga2 to ga1
10 ga2.mig  =: fit < 0.05 =>  ga1.mig # request migrants from ga1 if fit < 0.05
11 ga1.imp  -: queue ->   es # publish individuals to a job queue
12 ga1, ga2 -->           agg # publish and collect resulting individuals
13
14 # for i in [1..10]: node PGA ga$i ...
```

**Listing 1.1.** A distributed evolutionary computation experiment. 1: naming and tagging this experiment description; 2: importing the latest package version of composable evolutionary algorithms; 4-5: instantiating plugable genetic algorihms (PGA) with migration operators; 6: instantiating a plugable evolution strategy (PES); 7: instantiating a result aggregation node; 9-10: forming a simple island GA including a migration condition; 11: connecting a GA and a ES for depth search on individuals; 12: result collection; 14: planned syntax to enable hyperparameter grid search.

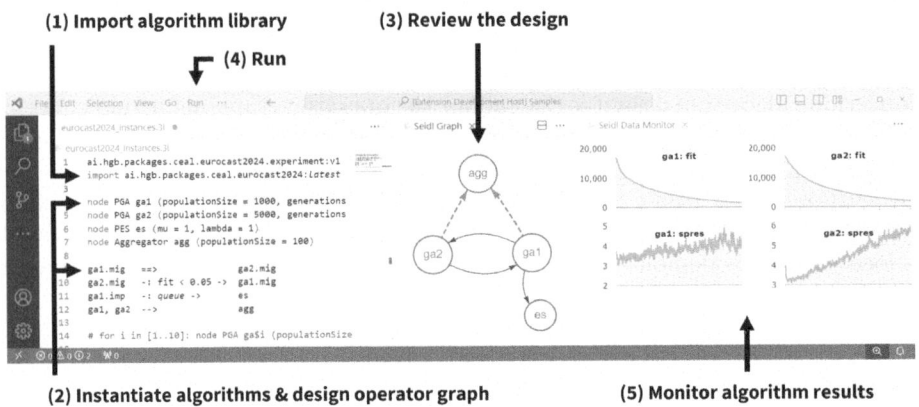

**Fig. 2.** Design, execution and monitoring of a custom composed EC algorithm in a custom Visual Studio Code (VSC) extension: Left-hand side, the language editor with the textual description for a custom algorithm is depicted: After importing the algorithm library (1), the user can instantiate algorithms and design their interaction (2). The editor supports syntax highlighting, code linting (i. a., error detection), code suggestions, etc. A closer look on the herein presented code, is taken in Listing 1.1. In the middle, a synchronized view of the resulting algorithm graph is shown (3). The *Orchestrator* to execute the designed algorithm is accessible via an included command line interface in VSC (4). On the right-hand side, real-time information regarding best fit, selection pressure, etc. of the currently executed algorithms is displayed (5).

# 3    Runtime Experiments

In order to test the applicability of the developed distributed EC system, we designed and conducted a series of experiments with runtime measurements. Therefore, we started with defining a minimalistic, but meaningful use case for our system: We expect the major bottleneck during execution of a distributed, containerized EC algorithm is the data exchange. Hence, for our experiment, we set up a simple genetic algorithm with populations, holding 1 up to $10^5$ individuals in one node and a service for their external fitness evaluation in another node. Both are executed as containers with our system, and we only measure data exchange times with different options available in our included messaging library. We compared the following options:

- Data transport protocols: MQTT via the containerized message broker (executed on localhost for the sake of a fair comparison) – *versus* – a custom shared memory (SM) transport protocol using non-persistent memory mapped files and system-wide named semaphores.
- Messaging paradigms: Publish-Subscribe (pub/sub), which is native to many modern streaming data protocols like MQTT – *versus* – Request-Response (req/res), which, in this case, is a custom implementation based on Publish-Subscribe and response topics.
- Message de-/serialization format: JSON, herein from .NET System.Text – *versus* – MemoryPack[5], which is supposedly very fast, but only available for C# .NET.

For more technical details, the reader is referred to [8].

In Fig. 3 we present the collected results and identify three key findings: First, apart from a short burn-in phase at low exchange counts when using the pub/sub messaging paradigm, the shared memory (SM) protocol is faster than MQTT for data exchange. Second, in each of the tested combinations the pub/sub paradigm outperforms req/res, for which the reason is probably the overhead (i. a., response topic de-/registration per call) of the custom-built routine. Third, MemoryPack is slower than the JSON de-/serialization format at low exchange counts, however getting faster with higher counts and superior from ca. $10^4$. Overall, it can be assumed that the fastest variant with 21.51 ms for 1000 data cycles – transport protocol: Shared Memory, messaging paradigm: Publish-Subscribe, message de-/serialization: MemoryPack, – (cf. Fig. 3d) represents a manageable bottleneck.

# 4    Conclusion and Outlook

With the presented system, we developed an open source software for distributed evolutionary computation (EC), based on a modern technology stack. When designing the system architecture, particular emphasis was placed on separating

---

[5] https://github.com/Cysharp/MemoryPack.

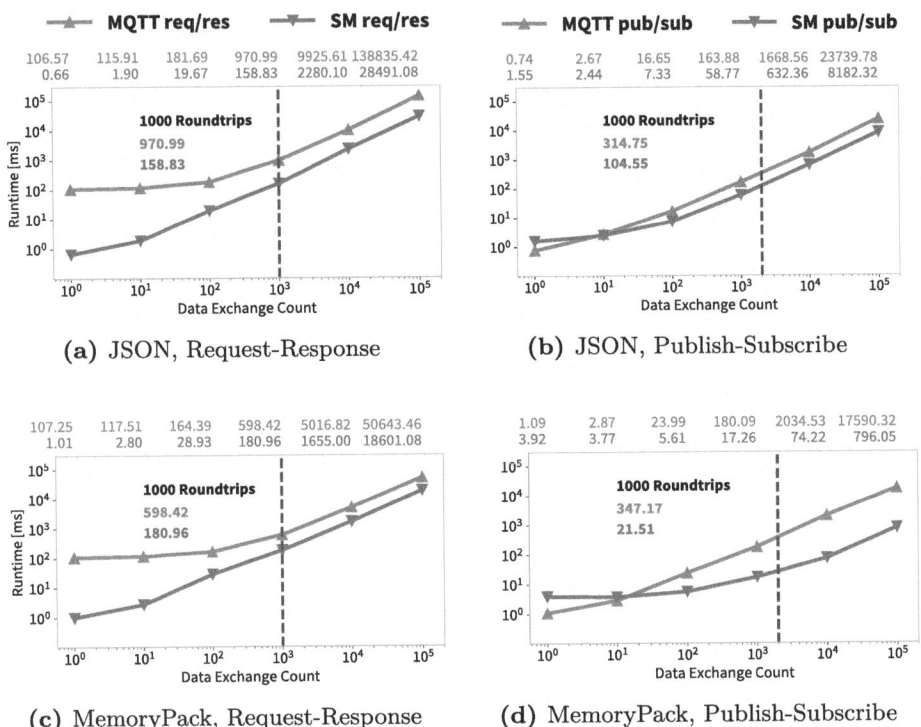

**(a)** JSON, Request-Response

**(b)** JSON, Publish-Subscribe

**(c)** MemoryPack, Request-Response

**(d)** MemoryPack, Publish-Subscribe

**Fig. 3.** Results of the performed runtime experiments: Each plot shows the increasing count of tested data exchanges on the logarithmic x-axis. Correspondingly, on the logarithmic y-axis the averaged runtime for 10 individually measured runs per data exchange count is displayed. In each plot, the runtimes of two data transfer protocols are compared: MQTT vs. our custom Shared Memory (SM) based protocol. The left-hand side plots 3a and 3c show measured runtimes for the request-response exchange pattern. The right-hand side plots 3b and 3d show measured runtimes for the publish-subscribe exchange pattern. The experiment results for using the JSON data de-/serialization format are shown in the upper two plots 3a and 3b. The experiment results for using the MemoryPack data de-/serialization format are shown in the lower two plots 3c and 3d. To achieve a fair comparison between the request-response and the publish-subscribe data exchange pattern, we define the additional metric "roundtrip" as runtime, which is needed for the exchange of a data package from sender to receiver and back to the sender. Thus, in case of the request-response pattern 1000 roundtrips are performed by 1000 data exchanges, while in case of the publish-subscribe pattern, 2000 data exchanges have to be performed. In each plot, the sample benchmark of 1000 roundtrips is displayed by a vertical dashed line. In terms of evolutionary computation, this demonstrates the runtime needed to transfer the individuals of a genetic algorithm's population with size 1000 on one node, to another node for external fitness evaluation and back.

the concerns of EC stakeholders: The system is split into an extendible algorithm library (cf. algorithm engineers), a user-friendly algorithm design frontend (cf. algorithm users) and a fully containerized runtime (cf. software architects). We show the applicability of this system by sketching sample use cases and providing quantitative results of conducted runtime experiments, covering different data exchange options for distributed EC algorithms.

As indicated in a commented line in Listing 1.1, we are currently extending the system's functionality by adding control structures (i. e., loops and conditions) to the DSL in order to ease algorithm hyperparameter grid searches. One further lead to this end is the full automation of this process by integrating an AutoML based approach. Another open issue is problem data access, which currently has to be handled for each algorithm individually, e. g., using docker volume mapping. Thereto, a central, containerized *data provider* service, using a database and a network-based interface, might be a valuable extension. Concerning the set-up technology stack, a further lead is to integrate Kubernetes to our infrastructure, in order to enable container-host shifts and thus, improve online load balancing.

Ultimately, we want to emphasize again that the presented system is in applicable but still prototypic state. Since this work is part of a larger, long-running research project, we expect more updates concerning functionality and use cases to come and thus, want to conclude by promoting our open source repositories[1,2].

**Acknowledgements.** The presented work was done within the project "Secure Prescriptive Analytics", funded by the state of Upper Austria as part of the program "#upperVISION2030".

# References

1. Dziurzanski, P., Zhao, S., Przewozniczek, M., Komarnicki, M., Indrusiak, L.S.: Scalable distributed evolutionary algorithm orchestration using docker containers. J. Comput. Sci. **40**, 101069 (2020). https://doi.org/10.1016/j.jocs.2019.101069
2. García-Valdez, J.M., Merelo-Guervós, J.J.: A modern, event-based architecture for distributed evolutionary algorithms. In: Proceedings of the Genetic and Evolutionary Computation Conference Companion, pp. 233–234 (2018). https://doi.org/10.1145/3205651.3205719
3. Harada, T., Alba, E.: Parallel genetic algorithms: a useful survey. ACM Comput. Surv. (CSUR) **53**(4), 1–39 (2020). https://doi.org/10.1145/3400031
4. Salza, P., Ferrucci, F.: Speed up genetic algorithms in the cloud using software containers. Future Gener. Comput. Syst. **92**, 276–289 (2019). https://doi.org/10.1016/j.future.2018.09.066
5. Salza, P., Ferrucci, F., Sarro, F.: Develop, deploy and execute parallel genetic algorithms in the cloud. In: Proceedings of the 2016 on Genetic and Evolutionary Computation Conference Companion, pp. 121–122 (2016). https://doi.org/10.1145/2908961.2909024
6. Scott, E.O., Luke, S.: Ecj at 20: toward a general metaheuristics toolkit. In: Proceedings of the Genetic and Evolutionary Computation Conference Companion, pp. 1391–1398 (2019). https://doi.org/10.1145/3319619.3326865

7. Wagner, S., et al.: Architecture and design of the heuristiclab optimization environment. In: Advanced Methods and Applications in Computational Intelligence, pp. 197–261. Springer, Heidelberg (2014). https://doi.org/10.1007/978-3-319-01436-4_10

8. Zenisek, J., et al.: A messaging library for distributed modeling. Procedia Comput. Sci. **232**, 606–615 (2024). https://doi.org/10.1016/j.procs.2024.01.060

9. Zenisek, J., et al.: A domain specific language for distributed modeling. In: 35th European Modeling and Simulation Symposium, EMSS 2023 (2023). https://doi.org/10.46354/i3m.2023.emss.015

# Solving the Manhattan Metric Straddle Carrier Routing Problem with Buffer Areas Using a Hybrid Metaheuristic Method

Ahmet Cürebal[1]([⊠]) [iD], Nina Radojičić[1,2]([⊠]) [iD], Leonard Heilig[1]([⊠]) [iD],
and Stefan Voß[1,3]([⊠]) [iD]

[1] Institute of Information Systems, University of Hamburg,
Von-Melle-Park 5, 20146 Hamburg, Germany
{ahmet.cuerebal,leonard.heilig}@uni-hamburg.de
[2] University of Belgrade, Faculty of Mathematics, Belgrade, Serbia
nina@matf.bg.ac.rs
[3] Escuela de Ingenieria Industrial, Pontificia Universidad Catolica de Valparaiso,
Valparaiso, Chile
stefan.voss@pucv.cl

**Abstract.** In recent years, hybrid optimization approaches have been increasingly proposed to solve complex optimization problems across various domains, aiming to combine the advantages of each algorithm. In this paper, we introduce a hybrid metaheuristic to address an optimization problem related to the routing of straddle carriers (SCs) in port operations. The main objective is to ensure the efficient movement of containers between the quay and storage yard by SCs, thereby achieving short turnaround times for vessels while adhering to loading and unloading sequences at quay cranes (QCs). Besides the sequence enforced by precedence relations between containers, the problem also takes into account the limited buffer areas placed within the operational range of QCs. The problem is of particular importance, as the operational efficiency of SC-based terminals is significantly influenced by the routing of SCs. The hybridization includes the incorporation of Variable Neighborhood Descent (VND) into the Greedy Randomized Adaptive Search Procedure (GRASP). The numerical experiments demonstrate the superior performance of the proposed algorithm compared to the exact solver and the results obtained from employing GRASP by itself.

**Keywords:** Hybrid metaheuristic · VND · GRASP · port logistics · container terminals · straddle carrier routing problem

## 1 Introduction

Container terminals are crucial to international trade and the economy, with the volume of containers having increased for decades and expected to continue

ⓒ The Author(s), under exclusive license to Springer Nature Switzerland AG 2025
A. Quesada-Arencibia et al. (Eds.): EUROCAST 2024, LNCS 15172, pp. 181–192, 2025.
https://doi.org/10.1007/978-3-031-82949-9_17

rising in the future. This requires terminals to meet the growing demand by efficiently utilizing their resources to remain competitive. As container terminals are systems comprising various interconnected components, such as berths with QCs, horizontal transport means, stacking areas and other essential sites and equipment, it is crucial for these elements to operate in a coordinated and efficient manner to enhance the overall productivity of terminals.

In general, the productivity of a container terminal is closely related to the flow of containers within the terminal. The flow of containers can be categorized into three main types of movements. The inbound container flow involves containers arriving by vessels and subsequently being transported to the stacking area, where they are stacked before being transported to their next mode of transportation, such as a truck, train or another vessel. The outbound container flow represents the movement of containers in the reverse direction, from the stacking area to the quayside, where they are then loaded onto a vessel by a QC. Additionally, container movement within the stacking area may occur to access a container located beneath another or to relocate a container to a designated position.

Container terminals differ from one another based on their layout and the equipment they utilize. One of the key components that distinguishes terminals is the type of horizontal transport means employed to handle the flow of containers within the terminals. Different types of horizontal transport means are used throughout terminals. They generally differ based on their capabilities in handling lifting, dropping, and stacking operations of containers, as well as whether they operate autonomously or manually. Horizontal transport means that lack the ability to lift or drop containers, such as Automated Guided Vehicles (AGVs) and yard trucks, require loading and unloading by QCs at the quayside or yard cranes at the stacking area. Conversely, horizontal transport means such as SCs and Reach Stackers (RSs) can lift, drop, and stack containers.

In this paper, we address the Manhattan Metric Straddle Carrier Routing Problem with Buffer Areas (MSCRB), as introduced and discussed by Kress et al. (2019). The problem arises in container terminals where SCs serve as the primary mode of horizontal transport. They are responsible for stacking containers in designated areas and transporting containers between these stacking areas and the respective buffer areas located under the QCs. The problem is to determine a routing for SCs and sequence the containers assigned to them, with the objective of reducing the idle times of QCs by minimizing the sum of the exact moments they interact with their respective buffer areas to load and unload containers.

We develop a hybrid metaheuristic with two variations to address the problem, specifically utilizing both the basic and cyclic variants of Variable Neighborhood Descent (VND) within the GRASP framework. The framework handles operational constraints such as precedence relations between containers and safety times. The developed variants are compared with GRASP itself and solutions from the exact solver, Gurobi. Given the dynamic environment of container terminals, the relevant operations must be planned within a reasonable time. To address this, both methods and the exact solver are limited to 180 s.

The remainder of this paper is organized as follows. Section 2 provides a review of the related literature. Section 3 presents a definition of the problem. The details of the proposed solution method are discussed in Sect. 4. Results from the computational experiments are provided in Sect. 5. Finally, concluding remarks are given in Sect. 6.

## 2    Related Literature

Key logistics processes and operations in container terminals as well as optimization methods for these processes have been thoroughly described and classified by Steenken et al. (2004). This foundational work was later expanded in a subsequent publication by Stahlbock and Voß (2008b). More recent analyses by Kizilay and Eliiyi (2021) and Weerasinghe et al. (2024) have addressed both landside and quayside operations, with an emphasis on integrated operations in container terminals.

Several survey papers in the existing literature address horizontal transport means within the broader context of terminal operations. Notably, Stahlbock and Voß (2008a) and Carlo et al. (2014) offer detailed discussions on this topic. The review by Stahlbock and Voß (2008a) focuses on horizontal container movements, including the use of AGVs and double rail mounted gantry cranes, outlining the structure and operational intricacies of seaport container terminals. It also highlights key processes such as berth scheduling, QC scheduling, and horizontal transport operations. Conversely, Carlo et al. (2014) provides an overview of transport operations, emphasizing material handling equipment, industry trends, and proposing a new classification system for transport operations and related academic literature.

Our literature review encompasses studies related to the flow of containers within terminals, without being restricted to a specific type of horizontal transport means. Böse et al. (2000) investigate the coordination of container transportation between vessels and yard areas by QCs and SCs. In their framework, QCs have buffer areas beneath them, although these buffer areas do not have capacity restrictions. They explore two pooling strategies for dispatching: one where fixed numbers of SCs are assigned to QCs serving a single vessel, and another where a fixed number of SCs are assigned to all QCs. The main goal is to minimize vessel port time by maximizing the productivity of QCs, which can be achieved through the efficient scheduling and dispatching of SCs. To address this, they utilize evolutionary algorithms, specifically proposing a genetic algorithm. Kim and Kim (1999) conduct a study on SC routing within a port where QCs are dedicated solely to loading operations. In their model, SCs transport containers between designated yard slots and yard-bay endpoints to facilitate transfers to trailers. The primary objective is to minimize the total distance traveled by the SCs. Additionally, they determine both the number of containers each SC picks up at each yard bay and the sequence in which these yard bays are visited. The routing problem is formulated as an integer programming model. To address this, they introduce an optimization algorithm that employs a two-step solution method: first, determining the number of containers to be picked up at each yard bay during a tour, and second, sequencing the yard-bay visits by the SCs. Skaf et al. (2021) tackle the scheduling problem for unloading operations involving one QC and multiple yard trucks at a container port. They model the problem as a mixed-integer linear programming problem, aiming to minimize the total completion time for all containers. To solve this, they employ both a genetic algorithm and exact enumerative algorithms.

In summary, the existing literature on container terminal operations underscores the importance of efficient routing, dispatching, and scheduling of transport vehicles. Various objectives are pursued, such as minimizing the makespan for horizontal transport vehicles and QCs, reducing the overall distance traveled by horizontal transport means, and minimizing the total completion time for all containers. Despite these different objectives, the primary goal remains consistent: enhancing the overall productivity of the terminal. A reduced turnaround time for vessels is widely recognized as a key metric of this productivity (see, e.g., Li et al. (2023)).

## 3    Problem Definition

The problem considered in this paper arises in a setting where SCs are used as the primary means of horizontal transport, meaning that the flow of containers within the terminal is carried out by SCs. Each container in the terminal has two locations: origin and destination. The execution of a container flow involves an SC picking up the container at its origin location, transporting it to its destination, and then placing it at its final location. QCs are responsible for loading containers onto vessels and unloading them from vessels. Each QC has an area within its operational range designated for container exchange. These areas, known as buffer areas, have a limited capacity for containers.

The process pertaining to the transportation of a distinct container, is termed a *job*. The jobs are classified based on both the origin and destination locations of the related containers. Containers located in the stacking areas that need to be transported to a buffer area for loading onto a vessel by a QC are classified as *loading jobs*. *Unloading jobs* correspond to containers that have been unloaded from a vessel and are waiting in a buffer area for an SC to pick them up and transport them to stacking areas for stacking. Additionally, *restacking jobs* occur when a container related to a loading or unloading job is located beneath another container. For an SC to handle the job, the blocking container must be moved within the stacking areas. Such containers are associated with restacking jobs.

Each QC has a predefined, sequenced list of containers for loading or unloading operations, derived from the vessel stowage plan and crane split. To manage the dynamic nature of the setting with frequently updated data, it is assumed that these container sequences are planned for relatively short timeframes, allowing for the consideration of up-to-date information. Consequently, during each planning period, each QC is specialized in either loading or unloading operations, referred to as a loading crane or an unloading crane, respectively.

The problem involves defining a route for each SC by allocating jobs and determining the sequence of jobs for each SC, while adhering to the capacity restrictions in the buffer areas and maintaining all relevant precedence relations. Note that SCs can process containers in an arbitrary order to some extent, provided that the buffer area capacities are not exceeded and the container sequences at the QCs can be maintained. The objective of the resulting allocations and sequences of containers is to minimize the idle time of QCs, thereby enhancing terminal productivity by directly reducing vessel turnaround time, the duration vessels remain docked. Effective coordination between SCs and QCs is crucial, highlighting the significant impact of SC routing on overall terminal productivity.

In addition to the mentioned assumptions, such as predefined container sequences for QCs and known initial and final destinations for each container, the problem assumes that all containers are uniform in size and that all SCs and QCs are homogeneous. At the start of the planning period, SCs can be positioned at any location within the terminal and some SCs and QCs may already be processing containers, preventing them from taking on new tasks immediately. Buffer areas may also be occupied by containers awaiting further actions. These containers, located in a loading crane's buffer area at the beginning, are not the primary focus of the optimization problem, as their allocation to SCs has already been determined. Thus, they are no longer considered jobs and are ready to be loaded onto vessels. However, their presence still affects QC occupancy and must be considered within the scope. All relevant locations in the terminal are represented by integer points on a Cartesian plane. Distances between these points are measured using the Manhattan metric. The time required for an SC to process a container is calculated by considering the durations for lifting and dropping, along with the transportation time from the initial location of the container to its final destination.

## 4   A Hybrid Metaheuristic

Hybrid algorithms integrate two or more algorithms, leveraging their combined strengths to create a synergistic effect. The primary motivation for hybridizing different algorithms is to take advantage of the complementary aspects of various optimization techniques. By integrating multiple approaches, hybrid algorithms can achieve enhanced performance and increased efficiency compared to individual algorithms executing independently. This synergy is expected to result in more robust and effective solutions for complex optimization problems (Ting et al., 2015; Blum et al.,2011). For an in-depth exploration of the topic, refer to Blum and Raidl (2016). Comprehensive reviews that cover a wide range of hybrid algorithms, investigate the motivations behind their development, and present their categorization can be found in Ting et al. (2015) and Blum et al.(2011). In this context, we developed a hybrid metaheuristic by integrating two variants of sequential VND, Basic VND (B-VND) and Cyclic VND (C-VND), into the improvement phase of the GRASP. This integration results in two variants of hybrid metaheuristics.

### 4.1  Initial Solution

The procedure for creating the initial solution is based on a greedy approach, where containers are considered in the same sequence in which they are processed by QCs. As restacking jobs are blocking other loading jobs or the designated final positions of the containers corresponding to unloading jobs, they are prioritized first. After assigning restacking jobs to SCs in a greedy manner, loading and unloading jobs are assigned to SCs per QC, up to the limit of the buffer capacity. The logic behind the sequence in which QCs are considered is based on the operational nature of the terminal. Consequently, loading QCs are prioritized first, followed by containers to be processed by unloading QCs. Given the terminal layout, after SCs process containers related to loading jobs, they are positioned on the quayside, which is relatively close to the QCs tasked with unloading containers from vessels. The process continues until all QCs process their assigned containers.

### 4.2  Variable Neighborhood Descent

VND, a method for refining solutions, is a simplified version of Variable Neighborhood Search (VNS) designed to systematically change neighborhood structures in a deterministic way. The principle behind VND is that local optimality for a solution in one neighborhood does not guarantee its optimality in other neighborhoods, in which it might yield superior results (Hansen et al., 2010). Starting with an initial solution, VND aims to find a locally optimal solution by exploring various neighborhood structures. This involves an iterative two-step process: first, the improvement step, which enhances the solution within the current neighborhood; and second, the neighborhood change step, which shifts the search to a different neighborhood structure. The specific strategy used in the neighborhood change step when an improvement is found determines the variant of VND. The search process continues until no further improvements are detected in any of the neighborhood structures or until the maximum permitted runtime is reached. In terms of neighborhood change strategy, B-VND restarts the process with the first neighborhood structure upon finding an improvement, while C-VND moves the search on to the next neighborhood structure in a sequenced set of the structures ($\mathcal{N}$).

Specific improvement heuristics are used in VND to structure the neighborhoods for exploring potentially superior solutions. Four operators commonly used in vehicle routing problems are employed, defined as follows:

- Intra-route operator (focused on improvements within a single route): 2-opt
- Inter-route operators (focused on improvements between pairs of routes): 2-relocate, 2-exchange, and 2-opt* (2-opt between two routes)

With respect to the way the operators structure neighborhoods to explore and to enhance the solution, the 2-exchange operator selects two container elements assigned to different SCs and swaps their positions. The 2-relocate operator removes a container element from one SC and inserts it into the sequence of another SC. The 2-opt operator improves a SC's route by reversing segments of the container sequence within the same route. The 2-opt* operator exchanges segments between the routes of two different SCs. The best improvement method is employed while exploring the neighborhood, meaning that after evaluating all solutions generated by a specific operator from a given solution, the best one is chosen to advance the search process. The pseudocode for the B-VND is presented in Algorithm 1.

---

**Algorithm 1:** Basic VND

---

**Input**: An initial solution $s$ with the objective function value $f(s)$,
The set of neighborhood structures $\mathcal{N} = \{N_1, N_2, ..., N_{k_{max}}\}$, where each $N_k$ is a neighborhood structure accessible by index $k$
**Output**: The improved solution $s$

1  $s' \leftarrow s$
2  $k \leftarrow 1$
3  **while** $k \leq k_{max}$ **and** *time limit not exceeded* **do**
4  $\quad$ $s \leftarrow BestImprovement(s', N_k)$     /* Move to the best solution in the $k$-th neighborhood structure */
5  $\quad$ **if** $f(s) < f(s')$ **then**
6  $\quad\quad$ $s' \leftarrow s$
7  $\quad\quad$ $k \leftarrow 1$
8  $\quad$ **end**
9  $\quad$ **else**
10 $\quad\quad$ $k \leftarrow k + 1$
11 $\quad$ **end**
12 **end**
13 **return** $s'$        /* Return the improved solution with respect to all neighborhood structures in the list $\mathcal{N}$ */

---

### 4.3  GRASP with VND

GRASP, as introduced by Feo and Resende (1995), is a metaheuristic designed for combinatorial optimization. It employs a multi-start approach, where each iteration is composed of a construction phase and a subsequent improvement phase. The solution construction procedure at each iteration, which combines the greedy approach presented in Subsect. 4.1 with randomization, is called greedy randomization. After constructing the initial solution, the VND procedure is applied to the newly constructed solution in each iteration. This process continues until the time limit is reached, ultimately returning the best-found solution. The construction procedure allows for exploration of a wider area in the solution space, while the solution framework leverages the incorporation of the VND metaheuristic in the improvement phase.

The pseudocode for the hybrid metaheuristic framework is presented in Algorithm 2.

---
**Algorithm 2: GRASP with VND**

---
1  $s \leftarrow Greedy()$
2  $s \leftarrow VND(s, \mathcal{N})$
3  $s' \leftarrow s$
4  **while** *time limit not exceeded* **do**
5      $s \leftarrow GreedyRanzomized()$        `/* Create a solution using greedy randomized procedure */`
6      $s \leftarrow VND(s, \mathcal{N})$        `/* Apply VND over the created solution */`
7      **if** $f(s) < f(s')$        `/* Check if the refined solution is best */`
8      **then**
9          | $s' \leftarrow s$
10     **end**
11 **end**
12 **return** $s'$   `/* Return the best-found solution within the time limit */`

---

## 5  Computational Experiments

In this section, we present the computational results of the proposed methods and compare them with the results from Kress et al. (2019). The computations were performed on a computer with an Intel i5-7300HQ CPU (2.50 GHz), 8 GB of RAM, running Windows 10 Professional. The algorithms were implemented in Python, and Gurobi 10.0.1 was used as the exact solver. A time limit of 180 s was used as the sole stopping criterion for the proposed methods and as the run time limit for the exact solver, consistent with the exact solver (CPLEX) used in Kress et al. (2019).

The test instances were created following the methodology outlined in Kress et al. (2019). Relevant locations within each problem instance were randomly generated within a two-dimensional Cartesian coordinate system, with dimensions adjusted to reflect real-world data as specified in Kress et al. (2019). These instances vary in size, with different numbers of QCs (3, 4, 5, 6), containers per QC (10, 14, 18, 22), and SC-to-QC ratios (3, 4, 5). Each main instance consistently includes these numbers for QCs, containers, and SCs, but has 45 variations due to different buffer area capacities (3, 4, 5) and restacking job rates (0.05, 0.1, 0.15) relative to the total number of loading and unloading jobs. Furthermore, five different seed values were used for random generation, resulting in multiple variations. For this study, we focused on a subset of these instances, specifically selecting those with a buffer-area capacity of four and a restacking job rate of 0.1. Thus, each primary instance now includes five distinct variations, each differentiated by its seed value.

The methods are compared with each other and with the solutions from Gurobi. A specific procedure was used for this comparison. Given a set of all approaches $J$, let $obj(j)$ represent the objective value obtained by a particular approach $j \in J$. To facilitate comparison, these values are normalized against the smallest (i.e., best) objective value among all approaches in $J$. Let $j^*$ be the approach with the smallest objective value, so $obj(j^*)$ represents this best value. The normalization of each approach $j$ is done by calculating $normalized(j) = obj(j)/obj(j^*)$ for each $j$ in $J$ and for each instance. This results in a normalized value where the best approach $j^*$ has a value of 1, and all other approaches have values relative to this best value. Finally, the average values of instances with the same number of QCs, SCs, and containers per crane are included in Table 1. Note that while $n^q$ represents the number of QCs, the number of SCs is denoted as $n^v$ and $CT$ stands for the number of containers per crane. Additionally, in the section where the normalized values for Gurobi are presented, the values in parentheses indicate the percentage of instances for which Gurobi provided feasible solutions.

**Table 1.** Performance Comparison of Metaheuristics and Gurobi

| $n^q$ | CT | Gurobi $\frac{n^v}{n^q}=3$ | $\frac{n^v}{n^q}=4$ | $\frac{n^v}{n^q}=5$ | GRASP $\frac{n^v}{n^q}=3$ | $\frac{n^v}{n^q}=4$ | $\frac{n^v}{n^q}=5$ | Hybrid (C-VND) $\frac{n^v}{n^q}=3$ | $\frac{n^v}{n^q}=4$ | $\frac{n^v}{n^q}=5$ | Hybrid (B-VND) $\frac{n^v}{n^q}=3$ | $\frac{n^v}{n^q}=4$ | $\frac{n^v}{n^q}=5$ |
|---|---|---|---|---|---|---|---|---|---|---|---|---|---|
| 3 | 10 | 1.031 (100) | 1.016 (100) | 1.004 (100) | 1.023 | 1.015 | 1.008 | 1.009 | 1.003 | 1.003 | 1.003 | 1.005 | 1.005 |
|  | 14 | 1.075 (100) | 1.072 (100) | 1.013 (100) | 1.028 | 1.024 | 1.030 | 1.000 | 1.011 | 1.005 | 1.004 | 1.004 | 1.004 |
|  | 18 | 1.141 (20) | 1.254 (100) | 1.089 (80) | 1.025 | 1.016 | 1.025 | 1.002 | 1.001 | 1.006 | 1.013 | 1.006 | 1.004 |
|  | 22 | (0) | (0) | 1.466 (80) | 1.023 | 1.023 | 1.026 | 1.004 | 1.006 | 1.002 | 1.008 | 1.005 | 1.004 |
| 4 | 10 | 1.033 (100) | 1.01 (100) | 1.005 (100) | 1.021 | 1.018 | 1.007 | 1.005 | 1.008 | 1.003 | 1.002 | 1.005 | 1.003 |
|  | 14 | 1.112 (40) | 1.107 (100) | 1.048 (100) | 1.018 | 1.025 | 1.012 | 1.003 | 1.002 | 1.007 | 1.004 | 1.008 | 1.000 |
|  | 18 | (0) | 2.293 (40) | 1.268 (100) | 1.026 | 1.027 | 1.025 | 1.002 | 1.013 | 1.006 | 1.004 | 1.005 | 1.005 |
|  | 22 | (0) | (0) | (0) | 1.020 | 1.021 | 1.021 | 1.012 | 1.000 | 1.003 | 1.010 | 1.016 | 1.009 |
| 5 | 10 | 1.068 (100) | 1.023 (100) | 1 (100) | 1.025 | 1.020 | 1.015 | 1.007 | 1.003 | 1.006 | 1.005 | 1.007 | 1.005 |
|  | 14 | 3.766 (20) | 1.132 (40) | 1.062 (100) | 1.026 | 1.020 | 1.013 | 1.010 | 1.005 | 1.003 | 1.000 | 1.005 | 1.006 |
|  | 18 | (0) | (0) | (0) | 1.025 | 1.022 | 1.020 | 1.002 | 1.001 | 1.002 | 1.010 | 1.007 | 1.005 |
|  | 22 | (0) | (0) | (0) | 1.012 | 1.020 | 1.020 | 1.003 | 1.004 | 1.006 | 1.011 | 1.007 | 1.009 |
| 6 | 10 | 1.098 (100) | 1.032 (100) | 1.005 (100) | 1.023 | 1.016 | 1.008 | 1.005 | 1.003 | 1.005 | 1.003 | 1.010 | 1.004 |
|  | 14 | (0) | 1.325 (20) | 1.228 (80) | 1.034 | 1.024 | 1.016 | 1.002 | 1.004 | 1.003 | 1.017 | 1.010 | 1.004 |
|  | 18 | (0) | (0) | (0) | 1.026 | 1.017 | 1.013 | 1.001 | 1.002 | 1.001 | 1.019 | 1.002 | 1.006 |
|  | 22 | (0) | (0) | (0) | 1.024 | 1.017 | 1.017 | 1.000 | 1.000 | 1.000 | 1.026 | 1.022 | 1.013 |
| Avg. |  | 1.161 (36.25) | 1.144 (50) | 1.099 (65) | 1.024 | 1.020 | 1.017 | **1.004** | **1.004** | **1.004** | 1.009 | 1.008 | 1.005 |

The first observation from the results is that the hybrid approaches outperformed both GRASP and Gurobi. This indicates that incorporating VND into the improvement phase of GRASP can significantly enhance its performance. The algorithm successfully leverages local optima across all neighborhood structures by employing the neighborhood change strategy during VND. It can be inferred that when employing multiple heuristics to improve the solution, it can be beneficial to consider a strategy that effectively integrates them. When comparing the results between different variants of VND, it can be seen that the hybrid approach with C-VND delivered superior results compared to the hybrid integrating B-VND, especially for larger instances. This suggests that the strategy used while exploring the neighborhoods has a key impact on performance.

The comparison of the results from the best-performing approaches and the exact solvers from this study and Kress et al. (2019) is presented in Table 2

**Table 2.** Comparison with the best approach from Kress et al. (2019)

| $\frac{n^v}{n^q}$ | 3 | 4 | 5 |
|---|---|---|---|
| Best approach from Kress et al. (2019) | 1.011 | 1.013 | 1.011 |
| CPLEX from Kress et al. (2019) | 1.046 (29.6) | 1.024 (32.9) | 1.039 (35.8) |
| Hybrid (C-VND) | 1.004 | 1.004 | 1.004 |
| Gurobi | 1.161 (36.25) | 1.144 (50) | 1.099 (65) |

The average best-found computational times are presented in the Table 3. As stated earlier in this section, a time limit of 180 s was used across all approaches. Therefore, the total run times of the algorithms and Gurobi are not included in the table.

**Table 3.** Best Found Times

| $n^q$ | ct | GRASP $\frac{n^v}{n^q}=3$ | $\frac{n^v}{n^q}=4$ | $\frac{n^v}{n^q}=5$ | Hybrid (C-VND) $\frac{n^v}{n^q}=3$ | $\frac{n^v}{n^q}=4$ | $\frac{n^v}{n^q}=5$ | Hybrid (B-VND) $\frac{n^v}{n^q}=3$ | $\frac{n^v}{n^q}=4$ | $\frac{n^v}{n^q}=5$ |
|---|---|---|---|---|---|---|---|---|---|---|
| 3 | 10 | 69.485 | 56.396 | 76.438 | 94.543 | 75.460 | 78.758 | 96.788 | 98.772 | 84.689 |
|   | 14 | 94.168 | 134.557 | 91.521 | 84.133 | 58.990 | 57.331 | 71.658 | 70.416 | 141.781 |
|   | 18 | 125.612 | 125.624 | 58.383 | 79.919 | 123.243 | 51.975 | 127.749 | 85.954 | 68.267 |
|   | 22 | 102.517 | 82.749 | 18.831 | 106.012 | 69.818 | 75.150 | 121.721 | 65.805 | 101.887 |
| 4 | 10 | 80.519 | 111.357 | 80.182 | 37.847 | 93.295 | 74.063 | 84.448 | 74.172 | 106.655 |
|   | 14 | 81.355 | 80.592 | 81.205 | 113.656 | 103.427 | 124.640 | 130.932 | 79.314 | 82.112 |
|   | 18 | 89.701 | 72.327 | 54.962 | 130.932 | 105.080 | 95.106 | 123.890 | 78.080 | 118.495 |
|   | 22 | 93.455 | 70.301 | 42.598 | 115.736 | 161.195 | 119.946 | 138.567 | 162.485 | 144.595 |
| 5 | 10 | 76.745 | 71.997 | 39.561 | 107.532 | 77.132 | 25.551 | 78.119 | 49.491 | 68.233 |
|   | 14 | 114.840 | 90.820 | 58.330 | 100.753 | 109.928 | 107.509 | 124.558 | 93.737 | 119.089 |
|   | 18 | 99.010 | 122.021 | 70.918 | 140.352 | 138.012 | 134.280 | 161.131 | 159.306 | 137.008 |
|   | 22 | 95.852 | 68.025 | 40.258 | 145.532 | 179.614 | 172.367 | 180.020 | 180.017 | 180.007 |
| 6 | 10 | 122.891 | 65.949 | 105.120 | 57.948 | 98.066 | 105.852 | 94.752 | 127.164 | 81.796 |
|   | 14 | 82.195 | 47.835 | 69.365 | 125.627 | 122.096 | 111.701 | 125.410 | 132.927 | 82.934 |
|   | 18 | 81.768 | 33.734 | 79.032 | 170.420 | 156.420 | 172.384 | 180.020 | 180.006 | 180.008 |
|   | 22 | 108.789 | 65.754 | 68.741 | 180.049 | 180.020 | 180.020 | 180.033 | 180.024 | 180.016 |

# 6    Conclusions and Future Work

This paper has presented two variants of hybrid metaheuristics to address the routing of SCs, considering QC operations, buffer area capacities, and precedence relations among containers to ensure efficient flow between stacking areas and the quayside. The hybridization involves integrating VND into the improvement phase of GRASP. Two variants of VND, B-VND and C-VND, are used, resulting in two distinct hybrid metaheuristics. Numerical experiments demonstrate that the hybrid approaches deliver superior results compared to those from GRASP alone and the exact solver. When comparing the variants of the hybrid approach, it can be observed that C-VND outperforms B-VND on average and particularly for larger instances. From a practical perspective, the resulting routing plan for SCs allows the efficient use of QCs, which in turn enables shorter vessel turnaround times, one of the key metrics for the productivity of a container terminal.

In this paper, we assume that all containers, SCs, and QCs are uniform. To better reflect real-world scenarios, future research could introduce heterogeneous elements. Addressing practical operational challenges might involve integrating yard-related operations, such as storage allocation, into the routing component. Considering uncertainties, such as the unexpected unavailability of SCs or QCs, would provide a more accurate depiction of operational complexities. Additionally, incorporating energy consumption as an objective could help mitigate the environmental impact of terminal operations, aligning with the increasing importance of sustainability.

In summary, while this study offers a foundational understanding of the problem, there are many ways to expand it to better reflect the complexities faced in real-world container terminal operations.

**Acknowledgments.** This research was funded by the German Federal Ministry for Digital and Transport (BMDV) with the funding program for Innovative Port Technologies (IHATEC) within the project TwinSim. Ahmet Cürebal was supported by the Study Abroad Postgraduate Education Scholarship (YLSY) awarded by the Republic of Türkiye Ministry of National Education.

# References

Blum, C., Puchinger, J., Raidl, G.R., Roli, A.: Hybrid metaheuristics in combinatorial optimization: a survey. Appl. Soft Comput. **11**(6), 4135–4151 (2011)

Blum, C., Raidl, G.R.: Hybrid metaheuristics: Powerful Tools for Optimization. Springer, Cham (2016)

Böse, J., Reiners, T., Steenken, D., Voß, S.: Vehicle dispatching at seaport container terminals using evolutionary algorithms. In: Proceedings of the 33rd Annual Hawaii International Conference on System Sciences (HICSS), pp. 1–10. IEEE (2000)

Carlo, H.J., Vis, I.F., Roodbergen, K.J.: Transport operations in container terminals: literature overview, trends, research directions and classification scheme. Eur. J. Oper. Res. **236**(1), 1–13 (2014)

Feo, T.A., Resende, M.G.: Greedy randomized adaptive search procedures. J. Global Optim. **6**, 109–133 (1995)

Hansen, P., Mladenović, N., Moreno Perez, J.A.: Variable neighbourhood search: methods and applications. Ann. Oper. Res. **175**, 367–407 (2010)

Kim, K.Y., Kim, K.H.: A routing algorithm for a single straddle carrier to load export containers onto a containership. Int. J. Prod. Econ. **59**(1), 425–433 (1999)

Kizilay, D., Eliiyi, D.T.: A comprehensive review of quay crane scheduling, yard operations and integrations thereof in container terminals. Flex. Serv. Manuf. J. **33**(1), 1–42 (2021)

Kress, D., Meiswinkel, S., Pesch, E.: Straddle carrier routing at seaport container terminals in the presence of short term quay crane buffer areas. Eur. J. Oper. Res. **279**(3), 732–750 (2019)

Li, B., et al.: Berth allocation and scheduling at marine container terminals: a state-of-the-art review of solution approaches and relevant scheduling attributes. J. Comput. Design Eng. **10**(4), 1707–1735 (2023)

Skaf, A., Lamrous, S., Hammoudan, Z., Manier, M.-A.: Integrated quay crane and yard truck scheduling problem at port of Tripoli-Lebanon. Comput. Indust. Eng. **159**, 107448 (2021)

Stahlbock, R., Voβ, S.: Vehicle routing problems and container terminal operations - an update of research. In: Golden, B., Raghavan, S., Wasil, E. (eds.) The Vehicle Routing Problem: Latest Advances and New Challenges, pp. 551–589. Springer, US, Boston, MA (2008a)

Stahlbock, R., Voß, S.: Operations research at container terminals: a literature update. OR Spectrum **30**(1), 1–52 (2008b)

Steenken, D., Voß, S., Stahlbock, R.: Container terminal operation and operations research-a classification and literature review. OR Spectrum **26**(1), 3–49 (2004)

Ting, T.O., Yang, X.-S., Cheng, S., Huang, K.: Hybrid metaheuristic algorithms: Past, present, and future. In: Yang, X.-S. (ed.) Recent Advances in Swarm Intelligence and Evolutionary Computation, pp. 71–83. Springer International Publishing, Cham (2015)

Weerasinghe, B.A., Perera, H.N., Bai, X.: Optimizing container terminal operations: a systematic review of operations research applications. Maritime Econ. Logist. **26**, 307–341 (2024)

# Route Planning for Parcel Logistics Systems with Reusable Packaging

Georg Brandstätter[✉] [ID], Wolfgang Ponweiser [ID], and Matthias Prandtstetter [ID]

AIT Austrian Institute of Technology, Giefinggasse 4, 1210 Wien, Austria
{georg.brandstaetter,wolfgang.ponweiser,matthias.prandtstetter}@ait.ac.at

**Abstract.** Parcels are usually packed in single-use packaging that the recipient discards after delivery. This is not only wasteful from a resource utilization perspective, but also requires the resulting waste to be collected and centrally disposed of (or recycled), generating even more environmental impact. Reusable packaging, on the other hand, introduces additional complexity into the planning of a logistics system, as empty packages must somehow be collected from previous recipients and reintroduced into the system.

We propose a new optimization problem that handles the planning of vehicle delivery routes that also collect empty packaging and deliver it to prospective senders. The goal is to utilize the available transport capacity of these vehicles, as their cargo hold becomes progressively emptier during the day as the parcels that they started with are delivered to their recipients.

We describe a heuristic optimization algorithm, consisting of a construction heuristic and a local search procedure, that can be used to compute such integrated delivery routes.

We evaluate this algorithm on a set of benchmark instances and compare the resulting solutions to a scenario where parcels are still delivered in single-use packaging.

**Keywords:** Vehicle routing · Pickup and delivery · Heuristic optimization

## 1 Introduction

In current parcel logistics systems, individual shipments are usually packed in disposable cardboard packages that are discarded by the recipient after delivery. This generates large amounts of waste paper that must be collected and disposed of (or, preferably, recycled).

In total, packaging already accounts for 50% of all paper that is used in Europe [2] – a number that is expected to increase by a further 19% by 2030. In the European Green Deal, the European Commission has set the goal to reduce the amount of packaging waste by 15% (compared to 2018) until 2040 through increased reuse and recycling of, among other things, the packaging used in e-commerce deliveries [3].

© The Author(s), under exclusive license to Springer Nature Switzerland AG 2025
A. Quesada-Arencibia et al. (Eds.): EUROCAST 2024, LNCS 15172, pp. 193–201, 2025.
https://doi.org/10.1007/978-3-031-82949-9_18

If packaging is to be reused, empty packages must be collected from recipients and returned to prospective senders. In the interest of efficiency, this should not be done by dedicated package collection tours, but instead be combined with corresponding delivery tours.

Over the course of a working day, the cargo hold of delivery vehicles becomes progressively emptier as packages are taken out and delivered to their recipients. This excess capacity can then be used to store collected empty packages.

We therefore propose an algorithm for planning combined package delivery and collection tours in a parcel logistics system that uses reusable packaging.

## 2   Problem Definition

We consider a planning period $P = \{0, \ldots, D-1\}$ consisting of $D \geq 2$ days.

We are given a set of locations $L = \{\ell_0\} \cup R \cup S$ that consists of the depot $\ell_0$, a set of recipients $R$, and a set of prospective senders $S$. Driving from location $i \in L$ to location $j \in L$ costs $c_{ij}$. These costs are usually proportional to the distance between $i$ and $j$, but may also incorporate other factors such as emissions.

Each recipient $r \in R$ expects a delivery of $q_r \in \mathbb{N}$ parcels that should be delivered to them on day $d_r \in P$ in a single shipment from the depot $\ell_0$. These parcels come in standardized, reusable boxes that fit one parcel each. Within a *pickup window* of $T \in \{1, \ldots, D-1\}$ days after delivery, these now empty boxes must then be picked up from their original recipients and delivered to any of the available prospective senders $s \in S$.

To account for parcels that would actually be delivered before the considered planning period but whose pickup window falls within $P$, as well as for parcels delivered during $P$ whose pickup windows extends beyond the end of $P$, we actually consider a *circular* planning period that wraps around. Thus, the effective pickup window of any recipient $r \in R$ is $t_r = \{d_r+1 \mod D, \ldots, d_r+T \mod D\}$.

Within the entire planning period, a total of $q_s \in \mathbb{N}$ empty boxes should be delivered to each prospective sender $s \in S$. Note that we assume that the total demand for empty boxes matches the total number of parcels delivered, i.e., $\sum_{s \in S} q_s = \sum_{r \in R} q_r$.

All transports are carried out by a homogeneous fleet of vehicles with a capacity for $Q$ boxes. Boxes are not collapsible, so full and empty boxes take up the same volume.

Over the entire planning period, each recipient $r \in R$ is visited exactly twice: one on day $d_r$ for delivery (of full boxes), then again within the pickup window $t_r$ for pickup (of empty boxes). In contrast, prospective senders can be visited multiple times, even on the same day by the same vehicle.

Our objective is to carry out all required transports of both full and empty boxes at minimum cost.

**Similar Problems.** The problem we have introduced combines aspects of the Capacitated Vehicle Routing Problem (CVRP) [7], where different goods are delivered to the recipient from a central depot, and a One-Commodity Pickup-and-Delivery Vehicle Routing Problem (1-PDVRP) [6], where different amounts of a commodity are picked up from and delivered to various locations. In contrast to these two problem, where only one such kind of transport is considered at the same time, we allow both types of deliveries – delivery from a central depot (for full boxes) and the direct delivery of commoditized goods between interested parties (for empty ones) – to be done simultaneously by the same vehicle. To the best of our knowledge, this has not yet been considered in the available academic literature.

Alternatively, it can be seen as a variant of the Vehicle Routing Problem with Backhauls (VRPB) [5] with multiple depots where the amount of goods that needs to be delivered to each is fixed (to $q_s$ in our case).

## 2.1   Feasible Solutions

A feasible solution consists of a set of routes for each day that together fulfill all transportation requests. Each route consists of a sequence of stops at locations $i \in L$ where either full or empty boxes are loaded or unloaded. Full boxes are only loaded at the initial stop at the depot and unloaded whenever a recipient is visited for delivery. Conversely, empty boxes are loaded when recipients are visited for pickup and unloaded at prospective senders.

Specifically, it must be ensured that (a) every recipient $r \in R$ is visited once on their delivery day $d_r$ by a vehicle that delivers them their requested parcels (in full boxes), (b) every recipient is again visited within their pickup window $t_r$ by another vehicle that picks up all empty boxes left there from the previous delivery, and that (c) every prospective sender $s \in S$ receives exactly $d_s$ empty boxes over the course of the planning period.

Additionally, it must be ensured that each individual vehicle route is feasible. This means that (a) the total number of (full or empty) boxes inside the vehicle must never exceed its capacity $Q$ ("capacity-feasibility"), and (b) the total number of empty boxes inside the vehicle must never be negative ("non-exhaustion").

## 3   Algorithm

In this section, we describe a heuristic algorithm for solving the aforementioned optimization problem. It consists of a construction heuristic for generating feasible solutions and a local search procedure for improving existing solutions.

### 3.1   Construction Heuristic

The construction heuristic consists of two phases. In the first phase, we generate a set of routes for each day $d \in P$ that only deliver full boxes to their recipients. In the second phase, we then insert pickup and delivery stops for empty boxes into these existing routes.

**Phase 1.** For each day of the planning period, we initialize our solution with routes generated by the Savings algorithm described by Clarke and Wright [1] for the Capacitated Vehicle Routing Problem (CVRP).

This algorithm works by first generating $|R|$ single-recipient routes and then iteratively merging them into longer routes based on the *savings* of the respective merge.

We first compute $s_{ij}$ for each pair of locations $i, j \in L$ as follows:

$$s_{ij} = c_{i\ell_0} + c_{\ell_0 j} - c_{ij}$$

This represents the *savings* of going directly from $i$ to $j$ instead of going via the depot $\ell_0$ (and thus, the savings of merging a route ending at $i$ with one starting at $j$).

We then consider each such location pair $i, j \in L$ in decreasing order of their savings. If two routes A and B exist such that (a) the route A's final stop (before the depot) is at $i$, (b) the route B's first stop (after the depot) is at $j$, and (c) the resulting merged route is capacity-feasible, the two routes are merged into a single one that first delivers to the recipients of route A and then to the ones on route B in their respective given order.

The algorithm proceeds until no more such merges are possible.

Before moving on the phase 2, we try to improve the resulting solution with the local search procedure described below in Sect. 3.2.

**Phase 2.** In phase 2, we iteratively insert pickup and delivery stops for empty boxes into the routes that were computed in phase 1.

For each recipient $r \in R$, we consider all *candidate routes* within $r$'s pickup window $t_r$. For each such route, we consider all possible positions (in increasing order of insertion cost) along the route where a pickup stop at $r$ could be inserted. Each such insertion position yields a new *partial* route that contains the candidate route's previous stops and the newly inserted pickup, but no corresponding delivery stop yet.

We then try to extend this partial route into a complete one by considering all possible positions after the pickup where corresponding delivery stops at prospective senders could be inserted (again, in increasing order of insertion cost). Once we have found a feasible extension (w.r.t. vehicle capacity and non-exhaustion), we replace the original route with the new one and proceed to the next recipient. If no insertion into a given route is possible, the pickup and delivery stops are added into a new route.

In case the most preferred (i.e., closest) sender does not have sufficient remaining demand to take all the empty boxes we picked up at $r$, we keep inserting delivery stops at other senders until all empty boxes are delivered to some prospective sender.

### 3.2  Local Search

After generating an initial feasible solution with the aforementioned construction heuristic, we try to improve its quality with a local search procedure.

To this end, we use the well-known 2-opt heuristic that was originally pro-posed for the Travelling Salesman Problem (TSP) [4].

The 2-opt algorithm works on individual routes and seeks to improve the order in which stops are visited. It does this by considering all non-consecutive pairs of stops $i$ and $j$ along a route and checking if the route can be improved by reversing the sequence of stops between $i$ and $j$.

We use the *best-improvement* variant of 2-opt where we identify the best sequence of stops to reverse. After each such improvement, we apply 2-opt again to the newly improved solution. Once no more improvements can be found, the local search has found a local optimum and finishes.

In contrast to other optimization problems like the TSP or CVRP where 2-opt is often applied, not all 2-opt moves are necessarily feasible in our case. This is because reversing part of a route can lead to capacity violations or the exhaus-tion of empty boxes, e.g., when the sequence of some pickups and deliveries are reversed. We therefore have to check whether a 2-opt move is actually feasi-ble w.r.t. both vehicle capacity and non-exhaustion before updating an existing route.

# 4    Computational Experiments

We evaluated our optimization algorithm on a set of benchmark instances to investigate its performance, as well as the effects of certain instance parameters on the eventual solution.

## 4.1    Benchmark Instances

The instances we considered during our computational experiments were gen-erated based on real-world data that was provided to us by a parcel logistics company. We received a list of approximately 30k parcels that were delivered to around 14k different locations across 19 work days.

From this, we generated 45 different benchmark instances. The length of the planning period was chosen as 5, 10, or 19 d. For each day, we selected its first 100, 200, 300, 400, or 500 locations as that day's recipients (with $q_r$ set according to how many parcels that were delivered to that location). Finally, we selected pickup windows of 1, 4, or 7 d after initial delivery (limited to $T \leq D - 1$).

We selected the population-weighted centers of gravity of 12 municipalities within the company's delivery area as the locations of prospective senders. Their demands $d_s$ for empty boxes were chosen according to their relative population sizes (i.e., larger cities received a larger share of the available empty boxes). The company's actual distribution center for the delivery area under consideration served as our depot location $\ell_0$. Vehicle capacities were set at $Q = 150$.

## 4.2    Experiments

The algorithm was implemented in Python. All experiments were carried out on a single thread of an Intel i5-8365U CPU.

**Table 1.** Results of our computational experiments, showing the runtime (in seconds), as well as the resulting summed-up route length (in km) for both single-use and reusable packaging scenarios ("1-use" and "reuse", respectively). Additionally, the route length increase (in percent) for the reusable packaging scenario is shown.

| | | | runtime [s] | | distance [km] | | Δ distance [%] |
|---|---|---|---|---|---|---|---|
| $|R|/D$ | $D$ | $T$ | 1-use | reuse | 1-use | reuse | reuse |
| 100 | 5 | 1 | 0.96 | 11.66 | 1222.91 | 1695.88 | 38.68 |
| | | 4 | 0.94 | 8.53 | 1222.91 | 1605.56 | 31.29 |
| | | 7 | 0.91 | 8.58 | 1222.91 | 1605.56 | 31.29 |
| | 10 | 1 | 2.18 | 16.78 | 2421.41 | 3348.42 | 38.28 |
| | | 4 | 1.68 | 20.01 | 2421.41 | 3125.44 | 29.08 |
| | | 7 | 1.91 | 18.84 | 2421.41 | 3393.64 | 40.15 |
| | 19 | 1 | 4.30 | 32.45 | 4660.60 | 6548.09 | 40.50 |
| | | 4 | 3.18 | 35.04 | 4660.60 | 5949.45 | 27.65 |
| | | 7 | 3.60 | 47.23 | 4660.60 | 6082.30 | 30.50 |
| 200 | 5 | 1 | 2.39 | 22.86 | 1620.57 | 2536.87 | 56.54 |
| | | 4 | 2.52 | 28.15 | 1620.57 | 2651.65 | 63.62 |
| | | 7 | 2.72 | 29.75 | 1620.57 | 2651.65 | 63.62 |
| | 10 | 1 | 4.59 | 46.65 | 3275.80 | 4864.73 | 48.51 |
| | | 4 | 4.35 | 49.75 | 3275.80 | 4717.35 | 44.01 |
| | | 7 | 5.05 | 69.67 | 3275.80 | 5064.43 | 54.60 |
| | 19 | 1 | 9.72 | 113.26 | 6202.58 | 9171.36 | 47.86 |
| | | 4 | 8.60 | 101.82 | 6202.58 | 8517.53 | 37.32 |
| | | 7 | 9.74 | 97.03 | 6202.58 | 8880.82 | 43.18 |
| 300 | 5 | 1 | 4.01 | 44.57 | 2064.33 | 3149.59 | 52.57 |
| | | 4 | 3.87 | 44.31 | 2064.33 | 4461.70 | 116.13 |
| | | 7 | 3.96 | 44.76 | 2064.33 | 4461.70 | 116.13 |
| | 10 | 1 | 7.80 | 83.62 | 4064.13 | 6635.70 | 63.27 |
| | | 4 | 7.56 | 89.13 | 4064.13 | 6704.16 | 64.96 |
| | | 7 | 7.96 | 103.50 | 4064.13 | 7295.82 | 79.52 |
| | 19 | 1 | 14.70 | 163.71 | 7610.58 | 12166.20 | 59.86 |
| | | 4 | 15.17 | 169.16 | 7610.58 | 11642.40 | 52.98 |
| | | 7 | 15.19 | 184.86 | 7610.58 | 12563.82 | 65.08 |
| 400 | 5 | 1 | 7.08 | 62.17 | 2344.95 | 4101.62 | 74.91 |
| | | 4 | 7.98 | 69.79 | 2344.95 | 4767.90 | 103.33 |
| | | 7 | 7.83 | 70.40 | 2344.95 | 4767.90 | 103.33 |
| | 10 | 1 | 15.64 | 112.19 | 4744.88 | 8183.75 | 72.48 |
| | | 4 | 13.24 | 122.15 | 4744.88 | 8168.24 | 72.15 |
| | | 7 | 13.22 | 161.51 | 4744.88 | 10042.24 | 111.64 |
| | 19 | 1 | 24.72 | 286.90 | 8962.78 | 14868.11 | 65.89 |
| | | 4 | 34.03 | 301.09 | 8962.78 | 14996.41 | 67.32 |
| | | 7 | 29.79 | 331.01 | 8962.78 | 15476.95 | 72.68 |
| 500 | 5 | 1 | 9.57 | 101.35 | 2729.21 | 5058.25 | 85.34 |
| | | 4 | 9.44 | 134.54 | 2729.21 | 6072.79 | 122.51 |
| | | 7 | 11.34 | 140.19 | 2729.21 | 6072.79 | 122.51 |
| | 10 | 1 | 20.27 | 194.80 | 5388.79 | 9682.60 | 79.68 |
| | | 4 | 18.26 | 208.54 | 5388.79 | 10018.97 | 85.92 |
| | | 7 | 18.10 | 272.17 | 5388.79 | 11470.61 | 112.86 |
| | 19 | 1 | 39.61 | 317.41 | 10254.63 | 17338.54 | 69.08 |
| | | 4 | 41.75 | 366.38 | 10254.63 | 17443.38 | 70.10 |
| | | 7 | 35.61 | 432.07 | 10254.63 | 18267.14 | 78.14 |

In our experiments, we compare two different delivery scenarios: one where single-use packaging is used, and one where parcels are packed in reusable boxes. The former corresponds to a set of regular Capacitated Vehicle Routing Problems (CVRP; one for each day), whereas the latter is the scenario we are considering in the optimization problem defined in Sect. 2.

Solutions for the single-use scenario ("1-use") are computed by initializing them with routes computed by the Savings algorithm (see Sect. 3.1 and locally improving them (with 2-opt as described in Sect. 3.2) until no more improvements are possible. Solutions for the scenario with reusable packaging ("reuse") are computed with the full algorithm described in Sect. 3.

The results of these experiments are shown in Table 1.

**Observations.** First, we observe that for instances of similar size, solving our newly introduced problem requires significantly more computational effort than solving the corresponding CVRP instance. Much of this is likely explained by the fact that the feasibility of a route often needs to be explicitly rechecked (by iterating through all stops one by one) after every change to ensure that the resulting new route is still feasible.

In both scenarios, with and without reusable packaging, we unsurprisingly observe that the problem becomes noticeably harder as the respective instance sizes (especially $|R|$ and $D$) increase. This is a common feature among combinatorial optimization problems caused by the associated growth of the search space. Somewhat surprisingly, however, it seems that the relative performance of the two scenarios remains relatively similar, with the variant with reusable packaging requiring around 10 times more runtime than the one without.

The length of the pickup window $T$ seems to only have a minor (and inconsistent) impact on the problem variant with reusable packaging. Note that $T$ is irrelevant for the problem variant with single-use packaging, so any runtime differences are simply caused by performance variations across different runs.

Between the two scenarios, the one using reusable packaging naturally requires an overall greater route length, as vehicles must simply do more work. Since both variants are only solved heuristically, it is unclear how much of these route length differences are can be explained by lower quality solutions in the "reuse"-case and how much is due to the inherent differences between the two optimization problems. However, it seems clear that solution quality disparity does play at least some role here, as our next observation highlights.

Surprisingly, increasing parameter $T$ seems to worsen the resulting solution, despite these instances being less constrained than the ones with lower $T$ whose solutions would obviously still be feasible for the higher-$T$ ones. In many cases, the instance with $T = 4$ yields the overall shortest routes for scenarios with reusable packaging. Such a value also appears to strike a reasonable balance between the logistics provider's desire for flexibility and the recipients desire to not clutter their home with empty boxes for extended periods of time.

# 5   Conclusion

In this article, we introduced a new optimization problem that deals with the optimal routing of vehicles in a parcel logistics system that uses reusable packaging. These vehicles must not only deliver parcels to their recipients, but additionally pick up the empty boxes they came in at a later time and deliver them to prospective senders who are in need of empty boxes themselves.

We described a heuristic optimization algorithm for solving this problem that consists of a two-phase construction heuristic and a local search procedure.

We then evaluated this algorithm on a set of benchmark instances and compared the resulting solutions to ones where parcels are still delivered in single-use packaging.

## 5.1   Future Work

Our experiments have shown that solving our newly introduced optimization problem requires significantly more computational effort than solving a similarly-sized CVRP instance with similar techniques. As noted, much of this is likely caused by frequent expensive feasibility checks. We would therefore like to investigate whether some of these checks can be prevented through the use of, e.g., more advanced data structures.

We also want to design an exact algorithm based on an integer linear programming formulation for this problem to investigate the quality of our heuristic solution to better understand whether the large discrepancies in route length are due to algorithmic limitations of our current approach or inherent characteristics of the problem and/or the considered instances.

Finally, our goal is to eventually solve larger instances than the ones we considered in this article. While our current algorithm would likely be able to find solutions for such large instances, we believe that more advanced metaheuristic algorithms will be necessary to successfully tackle these.

**Acknowledgments.** This work received partially funding from the Austrian Federal Ministry for Climate Action (BMK) under grant number FO999897763 (ReKEP).

**Disclosure of Interests.** The authors have no competing interests to declare that are relevant to the content of this article.

# References

1. Clarke, G., Wright, J.W.: Scheduling of vehicles from a central depot to a number of delivery points. Oper. Res. **12**(4), 568–581 (1964)
2. Coelho, P.M., Corona, B., ten Klooster, R., Worrell, E.: Sustainability of reusable packaging - current situation and trends. Resources, Conservat. Recycling: X **6**, 100037 (2020). https://doi.org/10.1016/j.rcrx.2020.100037
3. European Commission: European Green Deal: putting an end to wasteful packaging, boosting reuse and recycling (2022). https://ec.europa.eu/commission/presscorner/detail/en/ip_22_7155 Accessed 15 Nov 2023

4. Croes, G.A.: A method for solving traveling-salesman problems. Oper. Res. **6**(6), 791–812 (1958)
5. Parragh, S.N., Doerner, K.F., Hartl, R.F.: A survey on pickup and delivery problems: Part I: transportation between customers and depot. Journal für Betriebswirtschaft **58**, 21–51 (2008)
6. Shi, X., Zhao, F., Gong, Y.: Genetic algorithm for the one-commodity pickup-and-delivery vehicle routing problem. In: 2009 IEEE International Conference on Intelligent Computing and Intelligent Systems, vol. 1, pp. 175–179 (2009). https://doi.org/10.1109/ICICISYS.2009.5357913
7. Toth, P., Vigo, D.: Vehicle routing: problems, methods, and applications. SIAM (2014)

# Selecting User Queries in Interactive Job Scheduling

Johannes Varga[1]([✉]), Günther R. Raidl[1], and Tobias Rodemann[2]

[1] Institute of Logic and Computation, TU Wien, Vienna, Austria
{jvarga,raidl}@ac.tuwien.ac.at
[2] Honda Research Institute Europe, Offenbach, Germany
tobias.rodemann@honda-ri.de

**Abstract.** When solving a job scheduling problem that involves humans, the times in which they are available must be taken into account. For practical acceptance of a scheduling tool, it is further crucial that the interaction with the humans is kept simple and to a minimum. Requiring users to fully specify their availability times is typically not reasonable. We consider and extend a scenario from the literature in which initially users only suggest single starting times for their jobs and an optimized schedule shall then be found within a small number of interaction rounds. In each round a small amount of information can be requested by suggesting alternative time intervals, which are accepted or rejected. We extend the scenario by another form of interaction that allows to request users to indicate alternative time intervals for their jobs. To make the best out of these limited interaction possibilities, we propose a stochastic programming approach that utilizes a Markov model to consider the users' availabilities. The approach is experimentally evaluated and compared to the approach from the literature. Results show that the stochastic programming approach performs significantly better than the former method from the literature, especially when being able to request alternative time intervals from users.

## 1 Introduction

We consider the Interactive Job Scheduling Problem (IJSP) [6], in which human users, e.g., the personnel of a company, need to perform jobs on some shared machines and the availabilities of these users as well as the machines is critical. In such situations, it is rarely practical to ask users to fully specify their availability times. Instead, we assume users initially only propose a single starting time for each of their jobs, and a feasible and optimized schedule shall then be found within a small number of interaction rounds. In each such interaction round, our scheduling approach may make a small number of queries to users to find out more about their availabilities. We investigate two different forms of queries. For the first one, the approach proposes alternative time intervals for the users' jobs,

J. Varga acknowledges the financial support from Honda Research Institute Europe.

A. Quesada-Arencibia et al. (Eds.): EUROCAST 2024, LNCS 15172, pp. 202–210, 2025.
https://doi.org/10.1007/978-3-031-82949-9_19

which the users either accept or reject, and for the second, users are asked to provide alternative possible starting times for their jobs restricted to a timeframe. We use a stochastic programming approach to find the queries in each round that have the highest potential to improve the schedule. To formulate expected costs, subject to the selected queries, we use two different stochastic user models. The first one assumes that the users availability in a timestep only depends on their availability in the previous timestep, and the second one assumes that the user is available in up to two intervals each day with normally distributed interval endpoints.

The IJSP has already been considered in the literature by Varga et al. [5,6]. They only use the first, simpler, type of user query and select queries in each round by calculating an acceptance probability for each query, discarding low-probability queries and selecting those that improve the objective value most. This strategy leads to good convergence towards the best achievable schedule. Our contributions extend these works by considering an additional query type and proposing a stochastic programming approach to get more relevant information from the same amount of interaction.

We are not aware of any other work considering the IJSP or a similar setting. Some approaches to solving a scheduling problem similar to our core problem without the interaction aspect include Mixed Integer Linear Programming [1,7], a genetic algorithm [7], as well as a greedy heuristic and local search [1]. Moreover, there is a rich literature on human-machine cooperation ranging from cooperative optimization approaches, see e.g. Jatschka et al. [2], to the measuring of the level of cooperation, as done for instance by Wiebel et al. [8].

The next section defines the problem formally and introduces the notation used throughout the paper. Afterwards, Sect. 3 describes the user models and how they are used to calculate probabilities and to generate samples of user availabilities. Subsequently, Sect. 4 discusses our stochastic programming approach and Sect. 5 presents the results of an experimental evaluation. Finally, Sect. 6 concludes the work and gives an outlook on future work.

## 2    Problem Formulation and Notation

The time planning horizon $T$ of the IJSP consists of multiple days, each with the same number of discrete time steps. We denote with $U$ the set of users. Each user $u \in U$ has multiple jobs $J_u$, $J := \cup_{u \in U} J_u$, and each job $j \in J$ has to be scheduled on one of multiple machines $M$. For the experimental evaluation, we only use instances with a single machine, i.e. $|M| = 1$, but to be consistent with the literature, we formulate our methods for an arbitrary number of machines. Each job $j \in J$ has a duration $d_j \in \mathbb{N}$ in terms of the number of discrete timesteps. Refer to the set of timesteps in which job $j$ would run if started in timestep $t$ with $T_j[t] = \{t, t+1, \dots, t + d_j - 1\}$ and denote with $T_j^{\text{job}} \subseteq T$ the set of candidate starting times of job $j \in J$, restricted due to the fact that a job has to finish until the end of a day and is not allowed to span multiple days. The objective is to minimize time- and machine-dependent costs $c_{it}$ for using machine $i \in M$ in timestep $t \in T$. It is possible to not schedule a job $j \in J$, and this induces a penalty cost $q_j$.

This scheduling problem can be formulated by the following Integer Linear Program ILP($\mathcal{T}$), which is parameterized with a set of allowed starting times $\mathcal{T}_j$ for each job $j \in J$.

$$\min \quad \sum_{j \in J} \sum_{i \in M} \sum_{t \in \mathcal{T}_j} \sum_{t' \in T_j[t]} c_{it'} x_{jit} + \sum_{j \in J} q_j \left(1 - \sum_{i \in M} \sum_{t \in \mathcal{T}_j} x_{jit}\right) \tag{1}$$

$$\text{s.t.} \quad \sum_{i \in M} \sum_{t \in \mathcal{T}_j} x_{jit} \leq 1 \qquad\qquad\qquad j \in J \tag{2}$$

$$\sum_{j \in J} \sum_{t \in \mathcal{T}_j | t' \in T_j[t]} x_{jit} \leq 1 \qquad\qquad i \in M, \; t' \in T \tag{3}$$

$$\sum_{j \in J_u} \sum_{i \in M} \sum_{t \in \mathcal{T}_j | t' \in T_j[t]} x_{jit} \leq 1 \qquad u \in U, \; t' \in T \tag{4}$$

$$x_{jit} \in \{0, 1\} \qquad\qquad\qquad j \in J, \; i \in M, \; t \in \mathcal{T}_j \tag{5}$$

The binary variables $x_{jit}$ indicate with value one that job $j$ starts on machine $i$ at timestep $t$ and constraints (2)–(4) make sure that each job is scheduled at most once, that jobs do not overlap on the same machine and that jobs of the same user do not overlap.

Running times of jobs $J_u$ also have to take into account user $u$'s availabilities, which are only known partially. To improve the schedule, a limited amount of interaction with the users is allowed. Initially, each user specifies a starting time for each of their jobs that would work for them. In each of multiple rounds, the approach determines a set of most meaningful queries and the users reply to those queries, enriching the knowledge about their availabilities. We denote with $T_u^{\text{avail}}$ the set of timesteps for which user $u$ is known to be available at the current stage of interaction. We consider two different types of queries. The first one has already been used in the literature; it consists of a time interval and the user either accepts it, if they are available in the whole interval, or rejects it otherwise. The second and novel query type consists of a larger timeframe and a duration and the user selects a time interval within the timeframe of the given duration in which they are available, or indicates that there is no such interval within the timeframe. The timeframe is chosen from a predefined set $F$ of timeframes. In our experiments it consists of two timeframes for each day, one from 6am to 2pm, the other from 2pm to 10pm.

## 3   User Models

For high quality queries, a user response that increases the knowledge about relevant user availability intervals has to be likely and to assess the probability distribution over user responses, we use and compare different probabilistic models for the users from the literature [6]. To minimize assumptions about users,

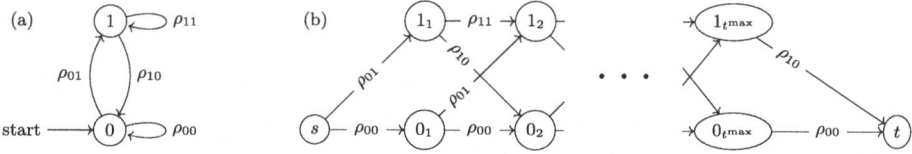

**Fig. 1.** (a) Two-state Markov process and (b) corresponding unrolled state graph. Adapted from [6].

we assume for the first model that the availability of a user in a timestep only depends on the availability of the user in the immediately preceeding timestep. This results in a Markov chain with two states 0 and 1, representing the user being not available and being available, respectively, see also Fig. 1a. Before the first timestep, the user is unavailable and from one timestep to the next the user gets available or stays unavailable with probabilities $\rho_{01}$ and $\rho_{00} = 1 - \rho_{01}$, respectively, if they were unavailable, or the user gets unavailable or stays available with probabilities $\rho_{10}$ and $\rho_{11} = 1 - \rho_{10}$, respectively, if they were available. We will refer to this model with MARKOV. The second model assumes the user to be available in up to two intervals within a day. Both intervals are included independently with a given probability and their starting time and duration follow a normal distribution, rounded to the nearest timestep. If the intervals overlap, we take their union. This model is referred to as ADVANCED and can be formulated as a Markov chain as well, see [6] for details.

The models are used to approximate acceptance probabilities of queries and to generate plausible sets of user availabilities. This is done by unrolling the Markov chain associated with the model by duplicating each state for each timestep and adding a source node $s$ and a target node $t$, see Fig. 1b for the unrolled state graph for the two-state Markov chain. Each state is associated with the user being unavailable or the user being available, and thus each path corresponds to one set of user availabilities and the product of edge weights results in the probability of that outcome. The knowledge about a day, obtained from user replies, is incorporated by manipulating the graph appropriately to rule out incompatible paths. Acceptance probabilities of queries are computed based on the probability $p_{s,v}^{\text{path}}$ to reach node $v$ from the source node $s$ and on the probability $p_{v,t}^{\text{path}}$ to reach the target node $t$ from node $v$, see [6] for more details on the graph construction, the calculation of $p^{\text{path}}$, and the calculation of query acceptance probabilities from $p^{\text{path}}$. To generate sets of availabilities according to the model and considering the knowledge gathered from user replies, we start in the source node $s$ and iteratively select the next node $n$ proportional to the product of the edge weight and $p_{n,t}^{\text{path}}$.

## 4   Solution Approaches

The task in each round is to find most meaningful queries with high potential to improve the current schedule. This task has been solved in the literature by first filtering all queries with an estimated acceptance probability below a threshold $p^{\text{lim}}$ from a set of candidate queries and then selecting, by solving an ILP, those queries that improve the objective the most, assuming the queries are accepted [6]. We refer to this approach as MARKOV($p^{\text{lim}}$) or ADVANCED($p^{\text{lim}}$), depending on the underlying user model.

The drawbacks of the probability threshold approach are that queries with probability above the threshold are treated equally, independent of their calculated probabilities, and that correlations between the replies of different queries are not taken into account. Furthermore, the approach is tailored for yes/no queries and does not work for the newly considered timeframe queries. To overcome these deficiencies, we propose the following two-stage stochastic programming approach that identifies queries that minimize expected costs after user replies. This approach is greedy in the sense that it selects those queries in each round that reduce the expected objective value the most.

$$\min \quad \mathbb{E}_{T^{\text{avail}*}}(\text{ILP}(\mathcal{T}(T^{\text{avail}*}, s^{\text{time}}, s^{\text{frame}}))) \tag{6}$$

$$\text{s.t.} \quad \sum_{j \in J}\left(\sum_{t \in T} s_{jt}^{\text{time}} + \sum_{f \in F} s_{jf}^{\text{frame}}\right) \le b \tag{7}$$

$$s_{jt}^{\text{time}} \in \{0,1\} \qquad\qquad j \in J,\ t \in T \tag{8}$$

$$s_{jf}^{\text{frame}} \in \{0,1\} \qquad\qquad j \in J,\ f \in F \tag{9}$$

The binary variables $s^{\text{time}}$ and $s^{\text{frame}}$ select the yes/no and timeframe queries, respectively, that will be relayed to the users and (7) limits their number to $b$. Objective (6) is to minimize expected costs for the selected queries, subject to user availabilities $T^{\text{avail}*}$ that are assumed to be distributed according to the user model at hand. The term $\mathcal{T}(T^{\text{avail}*}, s^{\text{time}}, s^{\text{frame}})$ denotes the set of timesteps in which jobs are allowed to start. This set is based on the user replies to the selected queries, which are determined based on the users availabilities $T^{\text{avail}*}$.

As the expected costs involve a hard optimization problem, it is challenging if not impossible to model the exact stochastic program by means of an ILP, and therefore, we obtain queries by solving the sample average approximation [3]. To do so, we first sample $n^{\text{samples}}$ possible sets of user availabilities for each user based on the user model and compute the user reply for each sample and possible query. In case of the first form of yes/no queries, this results in the set of starting times $T_j^{\text{pos},(k)} \subseteq T$ for each job $j \in J$, for which the reply would be positive for sample $k$. For timeframe queries, this results in a set of timeframes $F_j^{\text{pos},(k)} \subseteq F$ for each job $j \in J$ in which the reply would be positive and for each of these frames $f \in F_j^{\text{pos},(k)}$ the starting time $t_{jf}^{\text{reply},(k)} \in T$ that the user would choose randomly from their possible starting times within the timeframe.

With that terminology, the ILP for the approximation of the stochastic program can be formulated as $n^{\text{samples}}$ instances of the ILP from [6] of the core scheduling problem without restricting job starting times yet, combining the objectives by taking the mean. This ILP uses variables $x_{jit}^{(k)} \in \{0,1\}, j \in J, i \in$

$M, t \in T$ for each sample $k$ to indicate with value one that job $j$ is scheduled on machine $i$ with starting time $t$. We restrict job starting times according to the selected queries and the corresponding user replies by adding the following constraints for each sample $k$:

$$x_{jit}^{(k)} = 0 \qquad\qquad\qquad j \in J, i \in M, t \in T \setminus T_j^{\mathrm{pos},(k)} \quad (10)$$

$$\sum_{j' \in J_u} \sum_{t' \in T \mid T_j[t] \subseteq T_{j'}[t']} \left( s_{j't'}^{\mathrm{time}} + \sum_{f \in F_{j'}^{\mathrm{pos},(k)} \mid t_{j'f}^{\mathrm{reply},(k)} = t'} s_{j'f}^{\mathrm{frame}} \right) \geq$$

$$\sum_{i \in M} \sum_{j' \in J_u} \sum_{t' \in T \mid T_j[t] \subseteq T_{j'}[t']} x_{j'it'}^{(k)} \qquad u \in U, j \in J_u, t \in T, T_j[t] \not\subseteq T_u^{\mathrm{avail}} \quad (11)$$

Equation (10) prevents starting times that would be rejected by the user. Note that $T_j^{\mathrm{pos},(k)}$ also includes starting times for which we already know that the user would accept them. Inequality (11) only allows a starting time that we are not sure about yet if a query is selected whose time interval covers the jobs' execution time. The sums over $j'$ and $t'$ on the left side account for the fact that, given an accepted query of a longer job, also a shorter job could be scheduled within the time interval of the query, and the sums over $j'$ and $t'$ on the right side strengthen the formulation based on the idea that a disallowed shorter interval also disallows a longer running job when covering the shorter interval. Note that these constraints are slightly more restrictive than they need to be to make the formulation easier and more practical. For instance, if the time intervals of two selected queries overlap, jobs could be scheduled in the union of those intervals and this is not covered by the formulation above.

## 5    Experimental Results

To test our approach, we use the smallest instances[1] of [6] with one machine, six users and 24 jobs since the sample average approximation of the stochastic program does not scale to larger instances when using a reasonably large number of samples. The time horizon of those instances consists of five days, each day starting at 6am and ending at 10pm with four discrete timesteps per hour. Users are simulated and their availability times, which are not (completely) known to the scheduler, are generated according to the ADVANCED model for which we use the following values. The probability of including an interval is 90% and the normal distributions have a standard deviation of one hour. The mean starting times of the intervals are 9am and 1pm, respectively, and their mean durations are four and five hours, respectively. Based on their generated availability times, the users select one possible starting time for each of their jobs uniformly at random and the hypothetical running times of those jobs form the initial knowledge about the user availabilities.

---

[1]  https://www.ac.tuwien.ac.at/research/problem-instances/#ijsp.

We implemented the approaches in Julia 1.10 and used the solver Gurobi 11.0 to solve the ILPs. Each experiment was performed on a single thread of an Intel Xeon E5-2640 v4 with a timelimit of 120 min for each ILP. For the sample average approximation of the stochastic program, we use $n^{\text{samples}} = 50$ samples. The optimality gaps of all solutions found by Gurobi are below 45% and their median is 4.3%.

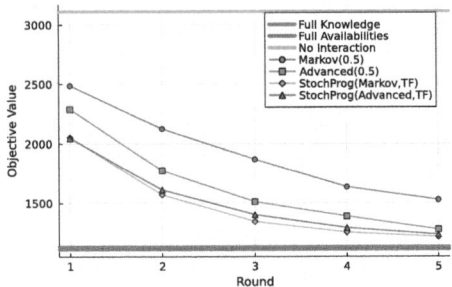

**Fig. 2.** Convergence comparison of the threshold approach with the stochastic programming approach.

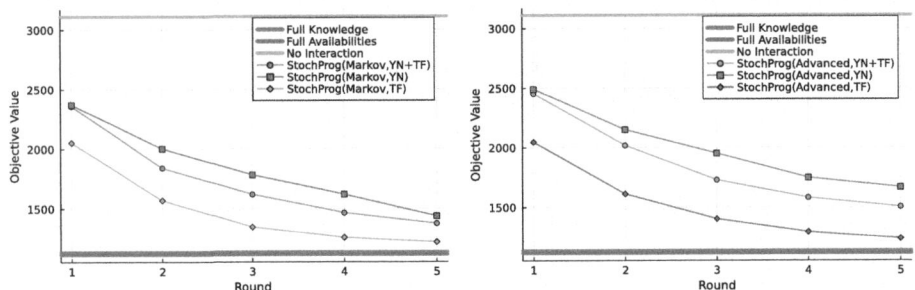

**Fig. 3.** Convergence comparison for the stochastic programming approach when allowing different types of queries for the Markov user model (left) and the advanced user model (right).

Figures 2 and 3 compare the performance of the different approaches with different parameters. They plot the average objective value over 30 instances of the best schedule that is possible with a certain knowledge about user availabilities. The horizontal lines show the objective value with the knowledge that is available before any user interaction ("No Interaction"), assuming full knowledge about user availabilities ("Full Knowledge"), and assuming that all users are—hypothetically—available all the time ("Full Availabilities"). The curves show the average objective values of the best schedule with the knowledge gathered by one of the approaches with one to five interaction rounds.

Figure 2 shows a comparison of the stochastic programming approach STOCH-PROG(MARKOV, TF) and STOCHPROG(ADVANCED, TF) with the probability threshold approach MARKOV(0.5) and ADVANCED(0.5) from [6]. The best configurations of the approaches with $p^{lim} = 0.5$ and only timeframe queries, respectively, were chosen. The stochastic programming approach clearly performs better with a gap to the full knowledge case after five rounds of 7.3% and 9% for the MARKOV and ADVANCED user models, respectively, compared to gaps of 34.7% and 12.7%. Apparently, both user models work almost equally well within the stochastic programming approach, when using only timeframe queries.

Figure 3 compares the stochastic programming approach when allowing only yes/no queries ("YN"), only timeframe queries ("TF") and both ("YN+TF") for the MARKOV model and for the ADVANCED model. The approach with timeframe queries performs with final gaps of 7.3% (MARKOV) and 9% (ADVANCED) significantly better than the one with yes/no queries with final gaps of 26.7% (MARKOV) and 47% (ADVANCED). This is not surprising since the user gives more information with each reply to a query. A bit surprising is the fact that only allowing timeframe queries results in a better performance than allowing both types of queries (final gaps 21.2% and 32.7%) considering the fact that the latter could only select timeframe queries. We explain this with the approximation error related to the limited amount of samples. While the expected objective predicts the actual objective after the users replies quite well for timeframe queries with a mean difference of 1.1%, allowing only yes/no queries results in a mean difference of 17.7%. This indicates that timeframe queries are better compatible with the sample average approximation than yes/no queries. But yes/no queries might still benefit from stochastic programming, either by using more samples for the approximation, or by using a more advanced approach to solve it such as the one described in [4], where the expected objective is estimated by a neural network.

# 6   Conclusion

We investigated the problem of selecting meaningful queries of two different types in an interactive scheduling setting, proposed a stochastic programming approach and compared it with the state-of-the-art. The stochastic programming approach converges significantly faster than the probability threshold approach from the literature. Furthermore, the query type that asks the user to specify alternative running times for their jobs works better than proposing alternative running times to the users.

To solve the stochastic program, we formulated the sample average approximation and solved it with an Integer Linear Programming solver. While this is easy to implement and works reasonably well, it does not scale well to larger instances and has a considerable approximation error. In future work, we plan to overcome these issues by using a more advanced stochastic programming method, such as estimating expected costs via a neural network.

# References

1. Anghinolfi, D., Paolucci, M., Ronco, R.: A bi-objective heuristic approach for green identical parallel machine scheduling. Eur. J. Oper. Res. **289**(2), 416–434 (2021)
2. Jatschka, T., Raidl, G.R., Rodemann, T.: A general cooperative optimization approach for distributing service points in mobility applications. Algorithms **14**(8) (2021)
3. Kleywegt, A.J., Shapiro, A., Homem-de Mello, T.: The sample average approximation method for stochastic discrete optimization. SIAM J. Optim. **12**(2), 479–502 (2002)
4. Kronqvist, J., Li, B., Rolfes, J., Zhao, S.: Alternating mixed-integer programming and neural network training for approximating stochastic two-stage problems. In: Nicosia, G., Ojha, V., La Malfa, E., La Malfa, G., Pardalos, P.M., Umeton, R. (eds.) Machine Learning, Optimization, and Data Science, pp. 124–139. Springer Nature Switzerland, Cham (2024)
5. Varga, J., Raidl, G.R., Rönnberg, E., Rodemann, T.: Interactive job scheduling with partially known personnel availabilities. In: Dorronsoro, B., Chicano, F., Danoy, G., Talbi, E.-G. (eds.) Optimization and Learning: 6th International Conference, OLA 2023, Malaga, Spain, May 3–5, 2023, Proceedings, pp. 236–247. Springer Nature Switzerland, Cham (2023). https://doi.org/10.1007/978-3-031-34020-8_18
6. Varga, J., Raidl, G.R., Rönnberg, E., Rodemann, T.: Scheduling jobs using queries to interactively learn human availability times. Comput. Oper. Res. **167**, 106648 (2024)
7. Wang, S., Wang, X., Yu, J., Ma, S., Liu, M.: Bi-objective identical parallel machine scheduling to minimize total energy consumption and makespan. J. Clean. Prod. **193**, 424–440 (2018)
8. Wollstadt, P., Krüger, M., Wiebel-Herboth, C.B.: Quantifying cooperation between rule-based hanabi agents using information theory. In: Lukowicz, P., Mayer, S., Koch, J., Shawe-Taylor, J., Tiddi, I. (eds.) HHAI 2023: Augmenting Human Intellect: Proceedings of the Second International Conference on Hybrid Human-Artificial Intelligence, Frontiers in Artificial Intelligence and Applications, vol. 368, pp. 422–425. IOS Press (2023)

# Improvements in Large Neighborhood Search for the Electric Autonomous Dial-A-Ride Problem

Maria Bresich[1]([✉]) [iD], Günther R. Raidl[1] [iD], and Steffen Limmer[2] [iD]

[1] Institute of Logic and Computation, TU Wien, Vienna, Austria
{mbresich,raidl}@ac.tuwien.ac.at
[2] Honda Research Institute Europe GmbH, 63073 Offenbach/Main, Germany
steffen.limmer@honda-ri.de

**Abstract.** We consider a practical extension of the classical dial-a-ride problem (DARP) called the electric autonomous DARP where electric and autonomous vehicles provide service for transportation requests with time windows. The planning and scheduling of routes that minimize not only the vehicles' travel cost but also the user excess ride time while considering charging requirements and operational constraints is a challenging optimization problem. In a previous work, we proposed a large neighborhood search (LNS) with a novel route evaluation approach that heuristically inserts charging stops on-the-fly as needed. Here, we go into more detail regarding the preprocessing procedure for reducing the size of instances as well as the tuning of certain LNS parameters. We further investigate this solving approach by evaluating its performance on different configurations of common benchmark instances, illustrating its successful application throughout. An analysis of the performance and impact of different repair operators provides further insights and reveals improvement opportunities.

**Keywords:** Dial-a-ride problem · Electric autonomous vehicles · Large neighborhood search

## 1 Introduction

One consequence of the growth in urban population are rising mobility demands and associated challenges such as traffic congestion and greenhouse gas emissions. This leads to an increasing interest in on-demand transportation and ride-sharing services as a flexible, affordable, and environment-friendlier alternative not only to privately owned cars but also classic public transportation services. In this context, a transportation request of a user or customer consists of a pickup and a drop-off location together with a service time window for either one. Designing minimum cost tours for a fleet of vehicles to serve a set of such requests is the

This project is financially supported by Honda Research Institute Europe GmbH.

A. Quesada-Arencibia et al. (Eds.): EUROCAST 2024, LNCS 15172, pp. 211–220, 2025.
https://doi.org/10.1007/978-3-031-82949-9_20

goal of the dial-a-ride problem (DARP). In the standard DARP [5], the total length of the routes is to be minimized while serving all requests and satisfying operational constraints concerning in particular time windows, route durations, and user ride times. Consideration of different objectives and constraints leads to diverse variants of the DARP as studied in the literature, see e.g., [8,11].

In this work, we consider specifically the *electric autonomous dial-a-ride problem* (E-ADARP) as first introduced by Bongiovanni et al. [2]. The E-ADARP is a challenging but highly practically relevant extension to the DARP, where electric autonomous vehicles (EAVs) are employed. The adoption of autonomous vehicles without human drivers removes the restrictions on route durations and allows for continuous service. In addition to the ride-sharing, electric vehicles (EVs) are another step towards environment-friendlier mobility but their charging requirements have to be taken into account. Route schedules now generally need to include stops at charging stations to (partially) recharge the electric vehicles' batteries and constraints regarding the battery capacity and state of charge (SOC) must be fulfilled. Extending the already NP-hard standard DARP with these and further constraints as well as with the consideration of user inconvenience by including user excess ride times in the objective function further increases the problem's practical solving complexity substantially.

Bongiovanni et al. [2] proposed a mixed integer linear programming (MILP) based approach for the E-ADARP, which they successfully applied to instances with up to five vehicles and 50 customers. As this exact approach has substantial difficulties to scale to larger instances and therefore has only limited practical relevance, Su et al. [15] proposed a deterministic annealing (DA) metaheuristic for solving the E-ADARP. This approach applies an exact route evaluation scheme of linear time complexity based on a forward labeling algorithm. The authors introduce, as a central aspect, the concept of a battery-restricted fragment, which represents a subsequence of pickup and drop-off locations for which the minimum user excess ride time can be independently optimized. Large neighborhood search (LNS) [12] is a metaheuristic that is frequently applied with great success to diverse DARP variants. So did Bongiovanni et al. [1] for the E-ADARP. Moreover, Limmer [9] proposed a bilevel LNS (BI-LNS) variant in which the outer level employs multiple operators to schedule the charging of the EVs first and the inner level greedily inserts customer requests into the routes. This approach is highly scalable, solves instances with up to thousands of requests in reasonable time, and yields on large and very large benchmark instances results that are mostly superior to the earlier approaches.

In a previous work [3], we followed this line of research and developed an LNS for the E-ADARP that combines and significantly extends concepts from the mentioned earlier works. As an alternative to directly dealing with charging stops in the destroy and repair operators of the LNS, we proposed a novel route evaluation procedure that inserts charging stops as needed on-the-fly while also determining respective charging times. As a baseline approach, we formulated the charging station insertion subproblem as a MILP, but we also proposed a computationally more efficient heuristic. The performance of these approaches was studied on two sets of benchmark instances and the heuristic version yielded new state-of-the-art results for most instances.

In this work, we investigate the heuristic approach further and provide more information on our preprocessing of E-ADARP instances and the tuning of important LNS parameters. We consider additional configurations of the benchmark instances for evaluation and the results illustrate the general applicability of our approach as it finds (new) best solutions for almost all instances. The impact of different repair operators is analyzed, allowing for identification of the best performing one as well as of improvement opportunities.

## 2 Electric Autonomous Dial-A-Ride Problem

In the E-ADARP as originally defined in [2], $n$ customer requests have to be served by $n_K$ EAVs, given as set $K = \{1, \ldots, n_K\}$, within a planning horizon of $T^{\mathrm{plan}}$ time units. The problem is modeled on a complete directed graph $G = (V, A)$ where all considered geographic locations constitute the vertex set $V = N \cup O \cup F \cup S$ and the arc set $A$ is defined as $A = \{(i, j) : i, j \in V, i \neq j\}$. Location subset $N = P \cup D$ consists of all customer pickup locations $P = \{1, \ldots, n\}$ and their corresponding drop-off locations $D = \{n + 1, \ldots, 2n\}$ such that the $i$-th request is given by a pair $(i, i+n)$. Each request $i \in P$ is associated with a maximum user ride time $u_i$ that has to be respected. The route of each vehicle $k \in K$ starts at an origin depot $o_k \in O$ and ends at a destination depot $f_k \in F$, with $|O| = |F| = n_K$. Available charging station (CS) locations are denoted by set $S$, and each station $s \in S$ is assigned a charging rate $\alpha_s$, specifying the amount of energy charged per time unit.

Earliest and latest possible service start times $w_i^{\mathrm{start}}$ and $w_i^{\mathrm{end}}$ are given for each vertex $i \in V$ and together they constitute the corresponding time window $[w_i^{\mathrm{start}}, w_i^{\mathrm{end}}]$. The service duration $d_i$ is nonnegative at customer locations $i \in N$ and zero at all other locations. The change in load $l_i$ of a vehicle serving a location $i$ is positive at pickups, negative at drop-offs, and zero otherwise. The maximum load capacity of a vehicle $k \in K$ is denoted by $C_k$, and $Q$ is the homogeneous battery capacity of each vehicle. A vehicle $k$ starts from its origin depot with an initial battery level $B_{k,1}$ and has to arrive at its destination depot with a minimum battery level $\gamma Q$, where $\gamma \in [0, 1]$ is the minimum battery level ratio. Traveling an arc $(i, j) \in A$ consumes $\beta_{i,j}$ battery and takes $t_{i,j}$ time, such that the triangle equality holds for both.

The *route* of a vehicle is a path from its origin to its destination depot, optionally going through pickup, drop-off, and charging station locations, and a corresponding *schedule* assigns a service start time $t_i^{\mathrm{serv}}$ to each node $i$ of the route. The set of $n_K$ vehicle routes together with their schedules constitute an E-ADARP solution, which is called *feasible* if it additionally satisfies the following constraints. The maximum capacity $C_k$ of an EAV cannot be exceed at any time and its battery level has to be within $[0, Q]$ at all times. Besides, each charging station can only be visited by empty EAVs and at most once over all routes.

The goal is to find a feasible solution that minimizes the following weighted sum objective considering the total travel time and total user excess ride time over all routes and requests:

$$\min w^{\text{routing}} \sum_{k \in K} \sum_{(i,j) \in A} t_{i,j} x_{i,j}^k + w^{\text{excess}} \sum_{i \in P} t_i^{\text{excess}} \tag{1}$$

with weight factors $w^{\text{routing}}$ and $w^{\text{excess}}$ and binary decision variables $x_{i,j}^k$ denoting sequential visits of vehicle $k$ to locations $i$ and $j$. The difference between the actual ride time of a user $i \in P$ and their minimum travel time $t_{i,i+n}$ is called the *user excess ride time*; i.e., $t_i^{\text{excess}} = t_{i+n}^{\text{serv}} - t_i^{\text{serv}} - d_i - t_{i,i+n}$.

## 3    Preprocessing

To reduce the complexity of E-ADARP instances, we employ two techniques proposed by Dumas et al. [6] for the pickup and delivery problem (PDP) with time windows and by Cordeau [4] for the DARP: time window tightening and arc elimination. Time window tightening is used to possibly reduce the span of given time windows. We use the extended rules for the E-ADARP given in [15] with the difference that we also take into account potentially already given time windows for charging stations as well as depots when considering these types of locations. We would also like to point out an inaccuracy in one of the rules in [15] for depots $i \in O \cup F$: $w_i^{\text{end}} := \min(w_i^{\text{end}}, \max(w_j^{\text{end}} + d_i + t_{j,i})) \; \forall j \in D$ should be $w_i^{\text{end}} := \min(w_i^{\text{end}}, \max(w_j^{\text{end}} + d_j + t_{j,i})) \; \forall j \in D$.

Arc elimination removes arcs that cannot be part of a feasible solution due to time window, ride time, and other constraints. As a base, we use the rules from [7] for the PDP with time windows and electric vehicles and enhance them by accounting for the existence of multiple origin and destination depots. We also employ a new rule based on vehicle loads that eliminates an arc $(i,j)$ between two pickup nodes $i$ and $j$ if the sum of the demands of requests $i$ and $j$ exceeds the maximum vehicle capacity: $l_i + l_j > \max_{k \in K}(C_k)$. Additional path-based elimination rules from [4,6] enable further arc removals as well as the disclosure of incompatible request pairs, which cannot be part of the same route. This information allows for immediate rejection of certain insertion positions of a request into a route during the LNS repair process and thus a speedup thereof.

## 4    Large Neighborhood Search

In this section, we briefly describe our proposed large neighborhood search based solution approach for solving the E-ADARP but refer to [3] for more details. An initial solution is obtained by first creating for each vehicle a route from its origin to its destination depot and then feasibly inserting as many requests as possible with the time window order based repair operator described below. The resulting solution is feasible except that some requests may still be unserved. In each iteration, random removal [14] is used to pick and delete $\kappa$ served requests from the routes, which are then tried to be reinserted by one of three repair operators. (a) A classic greedy heuristic [14] repeatedly evaluates every possible combination of inserting the pickup and drop-off locations of every unserved request into each route and selects the option with a minimum cost increase each time. (b) A less computationally intensive variant is used in the second operator, where the unserved requests $i \in P$ are sorted and inserted in their cheapest feasible position in non-decreasing order of $w_i^{\text{start}}$. (c) The third operator works in the same way except that a random order is applied to potentially escape local optima. During the repair and when evaluating candidate routes, their costs are increased by a random noise term to promote diversification as also seen in [9, 14].

**On-The-Fly (OTF) Charging Station Insertion.** The employed LNS operators do not deal with the insertion of charging stations (CSs) into the (candidate) routes but instead, this is done on-the-fly as needed during the route evaluation, which also handles the scheduling including the computation of charging times. We refer to [3] for a detailed description including the formulation of the corresponding charging station insertion and evaluation subproblem as a mixed integer linear program and only outline the time-efficient heuristic solving approach in the following. First, all charging stops are removed from the route at hand, before iterating twice over all its stops. This is done once in a forward- and once in a backward-pass during which all necessary information is computed to determine potential time window and battery constraint violations as well as the range of possible CS insertion positions. If a charging stop is needed, all combinations of available CSs and insertion positions are tested for feasibility. If there is at least one option satisfying the battery constraints, the one with the shortest incurred detour is selected, otherwise we pick the one where the vehicle can charge the most energy. After insertion of the respective charging stop into the route, all affected data is updated and the procedure is repeated, thus, further CSs are possibly inserted, until the (in-)feasibility of the route is determined. For details, we refer to [3].

## 5    Experimental Analysis

The proposed approach was implemented in Julia 1.10.0 with Gurobi 10.0.3[1] in single-threaded mode as MILP solver. All tests were run on single cores of 2.4 GHz Intel Xeon E5-2640 v4 processors with a memory limit of 20 GB and a time limit of 300 s. We employ two sets of DARP benchmark instances by Cordeau[2] [4] and Ropke[3] [13], which are enhanced with E-ADARP features and follow the naming scheme "a$n_K$–$n$", where $n_K$ is the number of vehicles and $n$ the number of requests. The weights in the objective function (1) are set

---

[1] https://www.gurobi.com.
[2] https://luts.epfl.ch/wpcontent/uploads/2019/03/e_ADARP_archive.zip.
[3] Available under https://github.com/HRI-EU/e_adarp_material.

**Table 1.** Results on Cordeau and Ropke instances with different values for $\gamma$ and with limited CS visits ($n_s = 1$).

| Instance | $\gamma = 0.1$ | | | | $\gamma = 0.4$ | | | | $\gamma = 0.7$ | | | |
|---|---|---|---|---|---|---|---|---|---|---|---|---|
| | BKS | OTF Heuristic | | | BKS | OTF Heuristic | | | BKS | OTF Heuristic | | |
| | | Obj min | Obj mean | Obj sd | | Obj min | Obj mean | Obj sd | | Obj min | Obj mean | Obj sd |
| Cordeau | | | | | | | | | | | | |
| a2-16 | 237.38 | 237.38 | **237.38** | 0.00 | 237.38 | 237.38 | **237.38** | 0.00 | 240.66 | 240.66 | **240.66** | 0.00 |
| a2-20 | 279.08 | 279.08 | **279.08** | 0.00 | 280.70 | 280.70 | **280.70** | 0.00 | 293.27 | 293.27 | **293.27** | 0.00 |
| a2-24 | 346.21 | 346.21 | **346.21** | 0.00 | 347.04 | 349.20 | 349.20 | 0.00 | 353.18 | 353.18 | **353.18** | 0.00 |
| a3-18 | 236.82 | 236.81* | **236.81** | 0.00 | 236.82 | 236.81* | **236.81** | 0.00 | 240.58 | 240.58 | **240.58** | 0.00 |
| a3-24 | 274.80 | 274.80 | **274.80** | 0.00 | 274.80 | 274.80 | **274.80** | 0.00 | 275.97 | 275.97 | **275.97** | 0.00 |
| a3-30 | 413.27 | 413.27 | **413.27** | 0.00 | 413.34 | 413.37 | 413.37 | 0.00 | 424.93 | 424.93 | 426.12 | 1.59 |
| a3-36 | 481.17 | 481.17 | 482.18 | 1.37 | 483.06 | 483.06 | 485.92 | 2.78 | 494.04 | 494.04 | 497.18 | 2.61 |
| a4-16 | 222.49 | 222.49 | **222.49** | 0.00 | 222.49 | 222.49 | **222.49** | 0.00 | 223.13 | 223.13 | **223.13** | 0.00 |
| a4-24 | 310.84 | 310.84 | **310.84** | 0.00 | 311.03 | 311.03 | **311.03** | 0.00 | 316.65 | 316.65 | **316.65** | 0.00 |
| a4-32 | 393.96 | 393.95* | **393.95** | 0.00 | 394.26 | 394.26 | **394.26** | 0.00 | 397.87 | 397.87 | **397.87** | 0.00 |
| a4-40 | 453.84 | 453.84 | 454.46 | 1.95 | 453.84 | 453.84 | 454.84 | 1.87 | 467.72 | 467.72 | 474.47 | 6.23 |
| a4-48 | 554.54 | 554.54 | 555.38 | 0.73 | 554.60 | 554.60 | 556.98 | 1.49 | 575.35 | 575.62 | 579.63 | 2.40 |
| a5-40 | 414.51 | 414.50* | 414.99 | 0.91 | 414.51 | 414.50* | 415.12 | 1.05 | 418.75 | 418.75 | 421.16 | 3.25 |
| a5-50 | 559.17 | 559.17 | 562.18 | 2.40 | 560.41 | 559.51* | 564.41 | 3.44 | 589.61 | 589.61 | 596.09 | 3.87 |
| Ropke | | | | | | | | | | | | |
| a5-60 | 691.83 | 683.87* | 687.42 | 2.50 | 688.16 | 685.51* | 690.63 | 2.94 | NA | NA | NA | NA |
| a6-48 | 506.72 | 506.45* | 506.77 | 0.21 | 506.85 | 506.45* | 506.84 | 0.30 | 517.12 | 517.12 | 521.62 | 2.95 |
| a6-60 | 692.00 | 690.29* | 693.54 | 2.14 | 692.69 | 690.29* | 693.16 | 2.31 | 714.16 | 714.16 | 731.45 | 10.02 |
| a6-72 | 777.44 | 762.16* | 770.69 | 3.77 | 771.97 | 765.64* | 776.00 | 4.47 | NA | NA | NA | NA |
| a7-56 | 613.10 | 612.53* | 614.70 | 2.30 | 613.66 | 612.78* | 615.27 | 2.51 | 636.56 | 636.56 | 649.37 | 10.43 |
| a7-70 | 760.90 | 756.27* | 761.16 | 3.23 | 761.62 | 756.46* | 760.21 | 2.03 | 816.64 | 816.64 | 840.59 | 16.29 |
| a7-84 | 889.38 | 874.57* | 883.45 | 4.79 | 886.19 | 878.99* | 890.18 | 7.23 | NA | NA | NA | NA |
| a8-64 | 641.99 | 632.21* | 637.93 | 3.89 | 637.95 | 632.95* | 639.02 | 3.05 | 639.06 | 639.06 | 651.33 | 6.63 |
| a8-80 | 803.52 | 793.64* | 802.86 | 4.42 | 793.17 | 794.04 | 800.85 | 5.13 | 837.79 | 837.79 | 862.75 | 15.14 |
| a8-96 | 1053.11 | 1032.76* | 1041.59 | 4.74 | 1048.72 | 1036.22* | 1047.47 | 5.62 | NA | NA | NA | NA |

to $w^{\mathrm{routing}} = 0.75$ and $w^{\mathrm{excess}} = 0.25$ as in [2,9,15]. We consider three different minimum final battery level ratios $\gamma \in \{0.1, 0.4, 0.7\}$ and a restriction to one visit per CS, $n_s = 1$, as stated in the original problem definition. For each instance, our LNS is run 30 times for each configuration.

**LNS Parameter Tuning.** Identifying suitable and robust parameter settings is crucial for the performance of the proposed LNS-based approach, so we use a selection of ten representative instances from the Cordeau and Ropke sets and the open source tool SMAC3[4] [10] for automated tuning. Here, we consider the degree of destruction $\kappa$ that specifies the number of elements selected in the destroy operator and the noise rate $\eta$, which controls how much noise is used for the route evaluation in the repair operators as the noise is randomly sampled from $[-\eta t^{\mathrm{max}}, \eta t^{\mathrm{max}}]$ with $t^{\mathrm{max}} = \max_{i,j \in V} t_{i,j}$. Both parameters are

---

[4] https://github.com/automl/SMAC3.

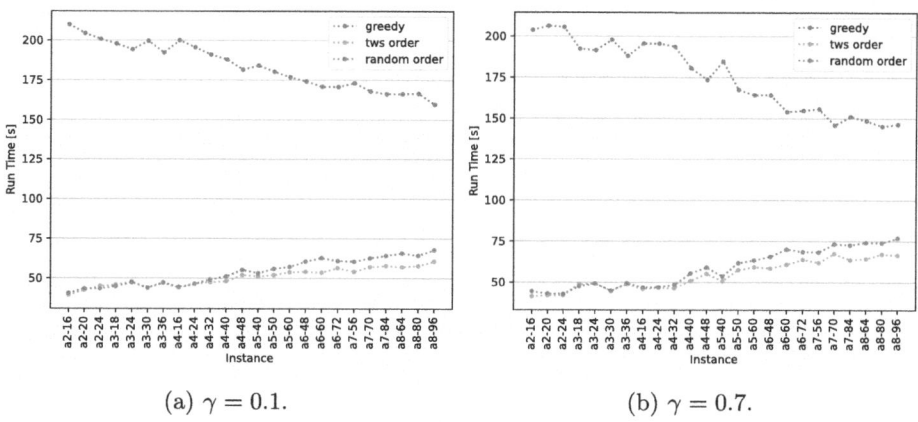

(a) $\gamma = 0.1$.    (b) $\gamma = 0.7$.

**Fig. 1.** Average run time in seconds of the different LNS repair operators over 30 runs for each instance with limited CS visits ($n_s = 1$).

simultaneously tuned by running 10000 trials of our LNS algorithm with possible value ranges of $[3, 96]$ for $\kappa$ and $[0.00, 0.05]$ for $\eta$, leading to a final configuration of $\kappa = 15$ and $\eta = 0.014$.

**Results.** An overview of the performance of our LNS with the on-the-fly (OTF) insertion heuristic regarding the different minimum battery level ratios is given in Table 1. Columns "BKS" show the best known solution values considering results reported in [2,3,9,15]. For our approach, we list minimum and average objective values as well as the standard deviations (sd) over all feasible runs. Results with an asterisk (*) indicate newly found best objective values and bold numbers highlight cases, where the mean objective value coincides with the (new) best known objective value, i.e., where the OTF heuristic yielded the best solution every time. The latter is the case for at least half of the Cordeau instances irrespective of the employed $\gamma$-value, although an instance generally becomes harder to solve with increasing values for $\gamma$ resulting in higher objective values. This illustrates the applicability of our approach over different instance configurations. The results further show that the OTF heuristic is able to find the best solutions for almost all instances and configurations and how it excels especially on the Ropke instances. The impact of the different minimum battery level ratios on the objective values and the solvability is also higher on these larger instances. For the largest tested value of $\gamma = 0.7$, none of the considered approaches, including ours, could solve four of the instances in any trial, as denoted by values "NA", whereas our OTF heuristic solved all other instances in every trial. This strongly suggests that the respective four instances are infeasible.

Besides, we also investigate the performance of the LNS and the contribution of the different repair operators in terms of the mean run time as well as the average number of improvements over all runs for an instance, where an improvement denotes a new best solution during the search process. As the

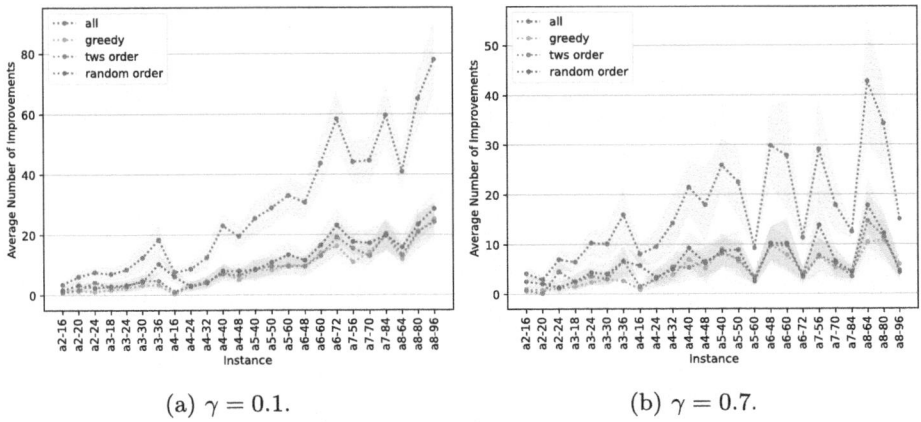

(a) $\gamma = 0.1$.                    (b) $\gamma = 0.7$.

**Fig. 2.** Average number of improvements of the different LNS repair operators over 30 runs for each instance with limited CS visits ($n_s = 1$).

**Table 2.** Performance of LNS repair operators over all instances and runs with a feasible initial solution for different values for $\gamma$.

| Operator | $\gamma = 0.1$ | | | | | | $\gamma = 0.7$ | | | | | |
|---|---|---|---|---|---|---|---|---|---|---|---|---|
| | Runs | Applications | Improvements | Avg. obj gain | Avg. obj gain / impr | Time [s] | Runs | Applications | Improvements | Avg. obj gain | Avg. obj gain / impr | Time [s] |
| greedy | 659 | 216576.59 | 8.90 | −0.000169 | −3.21 | 182.72 | 172 | 269917.33 | 2.87 | −0.000047 | −3.61 | 193.76 |
| tws order | 659 | 216592.04 | 9.58 | −0.000166 | −2.75 | 50.98 | 172 | 269907.62 | 3.36 | −0.000059 | −3.86 | 46.83 |
| random order | 659 | 216554.78 | 11.27 | −0.000178 | −2.57 | 54.52 | 172 | 269891.45 | 4.63 | −0.000060 | −2.96 | 48.05 |

repair method is selected uniformly at random in each iteration, all operators are applied about equally often. The results for the smallest and largest tested $\gamma$-values are illustrated in Figs. 1 and 2 for the run time and the improvements respectively, where "tws order" stands for the time window start based operator. From Figs. 1a and 1b, we conclude that the value of $\gamma$ does not substantially influence the time spent in each operator. As expected, the greedy operator is consistently the computationally most expensive one whereas the other two have similarly low run times. Figure 2 shows that all operators exhibit a similar performance regarding the mean number of improvements with the random order based one being slightly more successful in most cases. Thus, investing more time in the greedy operator does not seem to pay off. We also observe a difference in the pattern of the overall performance for the different instance configurations. In both subfigures, the mean number of improvements is lower for smaller instances, which is due to these instance generally being solved in less iterations. For larger instances, there is an increase in improvements with the number of vehicles and requests respectively in Fig. 2a which indicates consistent improvements during the LNS. In Fig. 2b with the larger $\gamma$ however, the number of improvements drops regarding a steady number of vehicles while increasing the amount of requests. As pairing this $\gamma$-configuration with more requests results in harder instances and considering that the overall number of LNS iterations does not decline compared to the easier configuration, the observations here suggest that our operators might get stuck in local optima earlier, leaving room for further improvement in this regard.

To gain more insights, we employ further performance metrics for the repair operators such as the average objective gains per application and per improvement. These and the previous metrics are reported in Table 2 over all instances and runs where the construction heuristic yields a feasible initial solution. We consider this restriction to avoid bias in our data towards operators finding the first feasible solution, which represents a disproportional large objective gain in our approach. The results show that the mean objective gain per application is in general quite low, which is due to a high number of performed LNS iterations compared to relatively few achieved improvements. Regarding this metric, the random order based operator performs the best, which is in contrast to its performance in terms of average gain per improvement where it achieves the lowest value of all operators. For the greedy operator, we observe again that it finds on average less improvements but when it does, the gain is often higher and especially so for $\gamma = 0.1$. Considering the larger $\gamma$-value, the time window order based operator yields the highest mean gain per improvement despite consuming the least time.

## 6   Conclusions and Future Work

In this work, we considered the electric autonomous dial-a-ride problem and further investigated our LNS-based solving approach with an on-the-fly charging station insertion heuristic. We detailed our preprocessing procedure for reducing E-ADARP instance sizes by adapting and extending reduction rules from the literature. For the performance evaluation, we considered various configurations of minimum battery level ratios, which influence the hardness and solvability of instances. The new results confirm our previous findings on the general success of the OTF heuristic and especially so on larger instances with up to 96 requests and eight EAVs. We observed that the repair operator which considers requests for insertion in a random order performs best in terms of the average number of improvements but yields the lowest objective gain per improvement. Regarding the latter metric, the greedy and time window order based operators achieve the best results depending on the employed $\gamma$-value.

In the future, we want to further improve the scalability of our approach to tackle huge instances with possibly thousands of requests, e.g., by sparsifying the underlying graph, restricting the neighborhoods, or employing more advanced methods for selecting the destroy sets. Utilization of machine learning techniques could be a promising research direction for this.

**Disclosure of Interests.** The authors have no competing interests to declare that are relevant to the content of this article.

# References

1. Bongiovanni, C., Kaspi, M., Cordeau, J.F., Geroliminis, N.: A machine learning-driven two-phase metaheuristic for autonomous ridesharing operations. Trans. Res. Part E Logistics Trans. Rev. **165**, 102835 (2022). https://doi.org/10.1016/j.tre.2022.102835
2. Bongiovanni, C., Kaspi, M., Geroliminis, N.: The electric autonomous dial-a-ride problem. Transp. Res. Part B Methodological **122**, 436–456 (2019). https://doi.org/10.1016/j.trb.2019.03.004
3. Bresich, M., Raidl, G.R., Limmer, S.: Letting a large neighborhood search for an electric dial-a-ride problem fly: on-the-fly charging station insertion. In: Genetic and Evolutionary Computation Conference (GECCO '24) (2024). https://doi.org/10.1145/3638529.3654057
4. Cordeau, J.F.: A branch-and-cut algorithm for the dial-a-ride problem. Oper. Res. **54**(3), 573–586 (2006). https://doi.org/10.1287/opre.1060.0283
5. Cordeau, J.F., Laporte, G.: A tabu search heuristic for the static multi-vehicle dial-a-ride problem. Transp. Res. Part B Methodol. **37**(6), 579–594 (2003). https://doi.org/10.1016/S0191-2615(02)00045-0
6. Dumas, Y., Desrosiers, J., Soumis, F.: The pickup and delivery problem with time windows. Eur. J. Oper. Res. **54**(1), 7–22 (1991). https://doi.org/10.1016/0377-2217(91)90319-Q
7. Goeke, D.: Granular tabu search for the pickup and delivery problem with time windows and electric vehicles. Eur. J. Oper. Res. **278**(3), 821–836 (2019). https://doi.org/10.1016/j.ejor.2019.05.010
8. Ho, S.C., Szeto, W.Y., Kuo, Y.H., Leung, J.M.Y., Petering, M., Tou, T.W.H.: A survey of dial-a-ride problems: literature review and recent developments. Transp. Res. Part B Methodological **111**, 395–421 (2018). https://doi.org/10.1016/j.trb.2018.02.001
9. Limmer, S.: Bilevel large neighborhood search for the electric autonomous dial-a-ride problem. Transp. Res. Interdisc. Perspect. **21**, 100876 (2023). https://doi.org/10.1016/j.trip.2023.100876
10. Lindauer, M., et al.: SMAC3: a versatile Bayesian optimization package for hyperparameter optimization. J. Mach. Learn. Res. **23**(54), 1–9 (2022). http://jmlr.org/papers/v23/21-0888.html
11. Molenbruch, Y., Braekers, K., Caris, A.: Typology and literature review for dial-a-ride problems. Ann. Oper. Res. **259**(1–2), 295–325 (2017). https://doi.org/10.1007/s10479-017-2525-0
12. Pisinger, D., Ropke, S.: Large Neighborhood Search. In: Gendreau, M., Potvin, J.Y. (eds.) Handbook of Metaheuristics, pp. 399–419. Springer US, Boston, MA (2010). https://doi.org/10.1007/978-1-4419-1665-5_13
13. Ropke, S., Cordeau, J.F., Laporte, G.: Models and branch-and-cut algorithms for pickup and delivery problems with time windows. Networks **49**(4), 258–272 (2007). https://doi.org/10.1002/net.20177
14. Ropke, S., Pisinger, D.: An adaptive large neighborhood search heuristic for the pickup and delivery problem with time windows. Transp. Sci. **40**(4), 455–472 (2006). https://doi.org/10.1287/trsc.1050.0135
15. Su, Y., Dupin, N., Puchinger, J.: A deterministic annealing local search for the electric autonomous dial-a-ride problem. Eur. J. Oper. Res. **309**(3), 1091–1111 (2023). https://doi.org/10.1016/j.ejor.2023.02.012

# A Hybrid Metaheuristic for a Tourist Route Recommender

Cristina González-Navasa[1]([✉])[ID], José Andrés Moreno Pérez[2][ID],
and Julio Brito[2][ID]

[1] I3MA, San Cristóbal de La Laguna, Spain
alu0100457599@ull.edu.es
[2] Universidad de La Laguna, IUDR and DIIS, San Cristóbal de La Laguna, Spain
{jamoreno,jbrito}@ull.edu.es

**Abstract.** This work presents a hybrid algorithm for designing tourist routes at destinations that combines two metaheuristics: Greedy Randomised Search Procedure (GRASP) and Variable Neighbourhood Search (VNS). The search for high-quality solutions maximises the sum of the scores (preferences) of the visited points of interest, considering the service characteristics and time limitations. This approach is particularly suitable for tourists planning optimal routes to visit attractions. Users can easily add or remove visits, adjust preference scores, and consider other restrictions. The goal is not to compete with state-of-the-art algorithms for standard tourist trip design problems (TTDP) using classical benchmarks. However, preliminary experiments with these benchmarks show acceptable results. The research aims to develop a component for tourist route recommendation systems that efficiently search for high-quality routes.

**Keywords:** Route design · Metaheuristics · Tourism

## 1 Introduction

An abundance of information about tourist destinations exists that allows tourists to organise their trips in advance. However, sometimes the immense amount of information is unmanageable, and planning a trip becomes the complicated task of selecting activities and points of interest and organising the route based on available time and other limitations. It must be taken into account that nowadays the tourist's experience is related to their personal satisfaction, which is why increasingly attempts are made to offer tools that help tourists and propose personalised itineraries based on their interests.

Tourist Trip Design Problems (TTDP) have been a significant challenge in planning optimal tourist routes, considering various factors such as visitor satisfaction, travel time, and time constraints. These problems have been modelled in the literature using several variants of the Orienteering Problem (OP). At the heart of this research lies the intricate design of tourist itineraries, cast within

© The Author(s), under exclusive license to Springer Nature Switzerland AG 2025
A. Quesada-Arencibia et al. (Eds.): EUROCAST 2024, LNCS 15172, pp. 221–235, 2025.
https://doi.org/10.1007/978-3-031-82949-9_21

the framework of the TTDP and formulated as a Team Orienteering Problem with Time Windows (TOPTW). There exist different versions of the OP and Team Orienteering Problems (TOP) according to their characteristics and limitations, such as the TOPTW, which considers the opening window of each point of interest (POI) and the temporal variability while travelling between POIs.

The developed model addresses not only the inherent complexity of personalised itinerary design, but also the study of different metaheuristic algorithms to find optimal solutions to these complex problems. We are going to use hybrid metaheuristics based on constructive procedures and local searches.

In parallel with our efforts to optimise route planning, we are developing a personalised tourist route recommendation system. This system aims to enrich metaheuristic algorithms to provide tourists with personalised and enjoyable routes based on their preferences and not only on their limitations.

This research contributes to the growing set of knowledge on the applications of the hybrid metaheuristics for TOPTW, shedding light on the potential of these metaheuristics to solve the TOPTW. Furthermore, the development of a personalised tourist route recommendation system expands the practical implications of our work, offering a user-centred approach to improve the overall tourist experience. The tool under development selects a personalised set of points of interest based on tourists' preferences.

A mathematical optimisation model is used to formalise the description, associated constraints, and the object to be optimised. Optimisation techniques are used to obtain a high-quality solution with reasonable computational effort. In this context, metaheuristics are optimal tools and intelligent strategies that facilitate the creation of efficient and adaptable heuristic optimisation algorithms.

To evaluate the performance of the proposed algorithm, we will use classic instances of the specialised literature for TOPTW. However, the goal of our research is not to design and tune a procedure that can compete with state-of-the-art algorithms for classical instances used in the literature. Following the principles of explainable Artificial Intelligence, we intend to design simple algorithms with interpretable rules that have acceptable performance in the instances that the recommender system can encounter in a tourist destination. Future work will expand our exploration of hybrid metaheuristics, incorporating other techniques such as machine learning and simulation procedures, and delve into the implementation and evaluation of the route recommendation system.

The rest of the paper is organised as follows. After the general introduction, Sect. 2 summarises a review of the related literature. Section 3 presents a formal mathematical formulation of the optimisation problem as a TOPTW and describes the proposed metaheuristic algorithm. In Sect. 4, the experiments to analyse the performance of the proposal and the results are described. Finally, Sect. 5 contains the conclusions and directions for future work.

## 2  Literature Review

Route optimisation presents significant challenges across various sectors, including business logistics and the planning of tourist itineraries. TTDP is an optimisation problem that aims to design the best possible travel route for tourists [33].

Some authors use the classical models for obtaining routes, the Travelling Salesman Problem (TSP) or Vehicle Routing Problem (VRP). The difference between both models lies in the requirement to obtain either a single route or several routes. The goal is to find the most efficient route or routes based on distance criteria or the shortest duration through a set of nodes. This is known as an NP-hard problem for its computational complexity, and is relevant in practical applications, mainly in logistics.

Numerous variations and extensions of the TTDP have been developed, which respond to different aspects of the problem. Thus, it is common to find models that incorporate the scheduling of tourist routes considering time restrictions at attractions that operate within specific hours, known as time window constraints (OPTW or TOPTW) [14,19,28]. With respect to time, many references to time-dependent problems (TDTOP) can also be found in the literature [25,26,50], along with other variations. Some investigations [11,12] explore the choice of transportation modes within the TTDP and can be related to urban transport problems [52], considering variants associated with travel duration, traffic congestion and, specifically, reduction of $CO_2$ emissions [40,51].

Models often incorporate multiple restrictions, increasing their complexity. Such models are referred to in the literature as multi-constraint TTDP (MCTTDP or MCTOP) and cater to individual preferences [27,41]. In specific practical scenarios, a variant of the TTDP that includes hotel selection (TTDPHS) is interesting [5,44,52]. These models appear when a tourist plans to visit multiple attractions but does not have enough time to visit them all in one day. Consequently, it is necessary to create a set of itineraries with different time limits and choose overnight accommodation options to continue the journey from these locations the following day. TTDPHS has similarities with the vacation planning problem (VPP), introduced in [13] as an optimisation problem that provides personalised daily routes for tourists travelling in large areas.

In the field of planning tourist routes, metaheuristics serve as the most suitable methods and help develop flexible and effective heuristic optimisation algorithms [35]. Consequently, they are present in practical applications, and the application of metaheuristic algorithms to address TTDPs is widely used, particularly in recommendation systems and in optimising tourist routes [3,43,53]. Essential sources on metaheuristics can be found in the *Handbook of Metaheuristics* [15]. Other interesting hybrid methods integrate machine learning [24,42] or simulation techniques [18,22] with metaheuristics.

The most widely used metaheuristic for TTDP is ILS, and one of the most recent references is [23]. We describe in detail the application to these problems of VNS [20] and GRASP [10], which are the two metaheuristics combined in our hybrid proposal.

Among the first applications of VNS to TOP is from 2007 [1]. Skewed versions of VNS were applied in [47] the basic version of TOP and in [48] for the main extensions the OP for the TTDP: TOP, OPTW, and TOPTW. A TTDP as a multiobjective orientation problem where there are several categories for the POI exists and each POI provides different benefits for each category was solved by designing and applying a multiobjective VNS (MOVNS) in [37]. A Basic VNS where the shaking consisting of removing and inserting several POIS from the routes was used to solve the multi-period orienteering problem with multiple time windows (MuPOPTW) in [45]. Another skewed VNS was applied for the OP with hotel selection (OPHS) in [5]. A General VNS, with several known operators for the shake procedure and for the improvement phase, was applied in [7] for an extension of the TOP that is not inspired by TTDP and has components that can be considered in tourism applications. A VNS that iteratively improves the incumbent solution using a set of local search operators was developed by [30]

TTDP with Hotel Selection was approaching in [52] by combining a Genetic Algorithm (GA) with VNS and by a Differential Evolution Algorithm (DEA). Their TTDP, in spite of TW, consider a series of set of constraints to handle with several extensions of the TOPTW, like compulsory POIs, possible repetitions of visits to the same POI, and others. The set orientation problem that generalises OP by considering POIs to be divided into mutually exclusive clusters was also solved with VNS by [8]. The score associated with each cluster is collected by visiting at least one of the POIs belonging to this cluster. The problem requires determining the closed route that maximises the profit collected without violating a given maximum route duration. They used the VNS version developed by [30]. Finally, among the applications of VNS for TTDP, [34] which use a GRASP-VND algorithm to solve multi-objective fuzzy and sustainable TTDP for groups where VND is in charge of the GRASP optimisation phase.

In addition to this paper, which used VNS and GRASP for the TTDP, other works that applied GRASP for TTDP are the following. Among the first applications of GRASP for TTDP is found in [41] that consider multi-constraint TOPTW (MCTOPTW). A fuzzy GRASP algorithm was applied in [4] to solve a TTDP and in [9] to solve the TTDP with clustered points of interest (POIs). The OP with Hotel Selection (OPHS) is solved with GRASP in [39]. A GRASP is also used in [36] to deal with a 3-objective TTDP that considers the occupancy levels of POIs. The time-dependent extension of the TOPTW (TD-TOTW) that takes into account the temporal variability of the travel time between POIs dependent on both traffic conditions and available means of transport has been achieved using a VNS in [29]. Finally, in [17] we consider the application of a GRASP to the TTDP in the context of a tourist recommendation system and using time-dependent travel times. Table 1 includes the chronologically ordered references of the use of VNS and GRASP for variants of TTDP.

# 3    Problem Formulation, Mathematical Model and Metaheuristic

## 3.1    Mathematical Model

The formal description of the TTDP modelled as a Team-Orienteering Problem with Time Windows for a given set of POIs is detailed below. The goal is to

**Table 1.** TTDP variants solved with VNS and GRASP metaheuristic methods

| Reference | Model | Heuristic | Other |
|---|---|---|---|
| [1] 2007 | TOP | Basic VNS | |
| [47] 2009 | TOP | Skewed VNS | |
| [37] 2009 | MO-OP | MO-VNS | Several POI categories |
| [48] 2009 | TOPTW | Skewed VNS | |
| [5] 2013 | OPHS | Skewed VNS | OP with hotel selection |
| [41] 2013 | MCTOPTW | GRASP | multi-constraint TOPTW |
| [6] 2014 | OPHSTW | GA/VNS | OP with hotel selection and TW |
| [4] 2017 | TOP | Fuzzy GRASP | |
| [9] 2019 | TOP-CP | GRASP | Fuzzy GRASP, TOP with clustered POIs |
| [39] 2020 | OPHS | GRASP | Orienteering Problem with Hotel Selection |
| [21] 2021 | OPTW | SA-VNS,GA-VND | OP with count-dependent scores |
| [34] 2022 | TOPTW | GRASP-VND | Fuzzy MO-TTDP with several features |
| [36] 2022 | MO-TOPTW | GRASP | 3-objective TOPTW with occupancy levels |
| [29] 2022 | TD-TOPTW | GVNS | Time Dependent TOPTW |
| [8] 2023 | S-OP | Basic VNS | Set OP with clusters of POIs |
| [17] 2023 | TOP | GRASP | Change of transport mode |
| [16] 2023 | TOP | GA-VND | TOP with count-dependent scores |
| **This work** | TOPTW | VNS/GRASP | GRASP inside VNS hybrid |

determine a set of paths from the starting point, limited in duration or length by a value, that visits some of the POIs to maximise the total collected score. We provide a mathematical formulation of the TOPTW. An excellent review of OP and its applications and variants, including the team orienteering problem (TOP), the OP with time windows (OPTW), and the TOPTW, is given in [49].

The components of the TOPTW model are as follows:

Parameters:

$i, j$ are indices that represent the POIs $i = 0, 1, ..., n$, $j = 0, 1, ..., n$ and include the point from which each route starts and ends, denoted by 0 (usually the tourist accommodation)

$k$ is an index that represents a route; $k = 1, 2, ..., m$, where $m$ is the number of routes.

$s_i$ is the score or preferences associated with the visit of the POIs $i$; $i = 1, 2, ..., n$.

$r_i$ is the visited time of points $i$; $i = 1, 2, ..., n$.

$t_{ij}$ is the travel time between points $i$ and $j$; $i, j = 0, 1, ..., n$.

$T_k$ is the maximum duration time for each route $k$ including travel, visit times and waiting times.

$e_i, l_i$ represent the opening and closing times of a visited point $i$, respectively; $i = 1, 2, ..., n$.

Decision variables:

$x_{ij}^k$ is a binary variable that is set equal to 1 if route $k$ goes from point $i$ to $j$, and $x_{ij}^k = 0$ otherwise.

$y_i^k$ is a binary variable set equal to 1 if point $i$ is visited by the route $k$, and $Y_i^k = 0$ otherwise.

$z_i^k$ is a real variable that represents the start time of the visit at point $i$

The Team Orienteering Problem with Time Windows (TOPTW) constraints is formulated as follows:

Maximise:

$$\sum_{k=1}^{m}\sum_{i=1}^{n} s_i y_i^k \qquad (1)$$

Subject to:

$$\sum_{k=1}^{m}\sum_{j=1}^{n} x_{0j}^k = \sum_{k=1}^{m}\sum_{i=1}^{n} x_{i0}^k = m \qquad (2)$$

$$\sum_{k=1}^{m} y_i^k \leq 1 \quad i = 1, 2, ..., n \qquad (3)$$

$$\sum_{j=0}^{n} x_{ji}^k = \sum_{j=0}^{n} x_{ij}^k = y_i^k \quad k = 1, ..., m, \ i = 1, 2, ..., n \qquad (4)$$

$$z_i^k + r_i + t_{ij} - z_j^k \leq M(1 - x_{ji}^k) \quad k = 1, ..., m, \ i, j = 0, 1, ..., n \qquad (5)$$

$$z_i^k + t_{i0} \leq T_k \quad k = 1, ..., m, \ i = 1, 2, ..., n \qquad (6)$$

$$z_i^k \geq e_i \quad k = 1, ..., m, \ i = 1, 2, ..., n \qquad (7)$$

$$z_i^k \leq l_i \quad k = 1, ..., m, \ i = 1, 2, ..., n \qquad (8)$$

$$x_{ij}^k \in \{0, 1\} \quad k = 1, ..., m, \ i, j = 0, 1, ..., n \qquad (9)$$

$$y_i^k \in \{0, 1\} \quad k = 1, ..., m, \ i = 1, 2, ..., n \qquad (10)$$

$$z_i^k \geq 0 \quad k = 1, ..., m, \ i = 1, 2, ..., n \qquad (11)$$

The mathematical expression (1) represents the objective function of the problem: maximise the total score collected. Secondly, constraints (2) specify that each route starts and ends at the accommodation or starting point 0. Constraints (3) establish that every point is visited at most once. The set of constraints (4) and (5) establish the connectivity and timeline of each route by the flow conservation rule and the elimination of the subtour, and $M$ is a large constant in the Big M method. Constraints (6) guarantee the limit duration for each route. The time windows constraints are specified by the constraints (7) and (8). Finally, the constraints (9), (10), and (11) define the variables domains.

## 3.2    Metaheuristic Algorithm: GRASP-VNS

Optimisation techniques allow for the task of finding a high-quality solution to the problem with appropriate computational effort. Therefore, approximate procedures that find nearly optimal solutions are the only reasonable way to approach these problems. Metaheuristics are the most suitable intelligent tools for this purpose. Specifically, we propose a hybrid metaheuristic that combines GRASP with VNS, not only using VNS in the GRASP improvement phase, but also including GRASP inside VNS.

The pseudocode shown in Algorithm 1 illustrates the main phases of a GRASP-VNS procedure, where LocalSearch is replaced by the VNS algorithm and $N_{iter}$ is the maximum number of iterations. Each iteration is independent, and the best solution found is saved and returned as a result.

---

**Algorithm 1.** GRASP-VNS

---

**function** GRASP-VNS($N_{iter}$):

    readInput()
    initiate *BestSolution*;
    **for** $k = 1, ..., N_{iter}$ **do**
        (a) *ConstructedSolution* = GRASPConstructPhase();
        (b) *ImprovedSolution* = VNS(*ConstructedSolution*);
        (c) UpdateSolution(*ImprovedSolution, BestSolution*);
    **return** *BestSolution*;

**end** GRASP-VNS

---

GRASP is a two-phase multi-start metaheuristic for combinatorial optimisation proposed by Feo and Resende [10] and widely used to find high-quality routes [32]. It is a metaheuristic algorithm that iteratively constructs solutions by combining greedy construction with randomised improvement. It starts by generating a feasible solution using a greedy algorithm and then applies an optimisation procedure to improve it. GRASP iterates this process for a set number of iterations or until a termination condition is met, selecting the best solution found throughout the iterations as the final result. In the framework for designing tourist routes, GRASP can efficiently explore the solution space to discover high-quality itineraries that meet user preferences and limitations criteria.

GRASP functions in a step-by-step manner, progressively constructing potential solutions by combining greedy selection and randomisation. During each step, the algorithm picks a potential solution (candidate) using a greedy strategy that steers the selection process towards favourable choices. However, GRASP introduces randomness by utilising an RCL to prevent early convergence and encourage research in the exploration process.

The RCL plays a vital role in the GRASP approach. Rather than directly choosing the best candidate solution at each stage, GRASP generates a list of potential candidates by evaluating a subset of the most favourable choices according to specific criteria or quality measures. This subset, defined by the RCL, aims to strike a balance between using the best known solutions and investigating other potential options. The selection among the candidates in the RCL is done in a random manner, adding diversity to the search process and enabling the exploration of various areas within the solution space.

During the construction phase (Algorithm 2), the procedure iteratively selects destinations for the route, considering the preferences of the users and the distance between destinations. The randomised component introduces diversification, preventing the algorithm from getting stuck in local optima.

---

**Algorithm 2.** GRASP Construction Phase
___
**function** GRASPConstructPhase():

    Take an initial empty partial solution *PartSol*
    **while** there are candidate POIs to add to *PartSol*:
        (a) construct RCL with the best candidates to add to *PartSol*
        (b) choose at random a candidate POI from RCL
        (c) update the *PartSol* by adding to it the selected POI
    **return** *PartSol*

**end** GRASPConstructPhase.

---

After the construction phase, an improvement phase is applied to improve the generated route. Normally, this is a local search that may involve swapping nearby destinations to reduce the total distance or including additional destinations if possible within temporal and geographical constraints; delete some nodes from the current route and insert some inaccessible nodes; randomly replace the nodes, to improve the target value; and balance the service time between access

---

**Algorithm 3.** Destructive-Constructive VNS
___
**function** VNS(*Sol*):

    Take solution *Sol* as current solution
    $CurSol = Sol\ k = 1$
    **while** $k < k_{max}$:
        **repeat** a number *rep* of times:
            **Shake**: remove $k$ random POIs from *CurSol*
            **Improve**: *NewSol* = GRASPConstructPhase(*CurSol*)
            **if** *NewSol* is better than *CurSol*:
                **then**
                    $CurSol = NewSol$
                    $k = 1$
                    break
                **else**:
                    $k = k + 1$
    **return** *CurSol*

**end** VNS.

nodes to allocate the available time budget to more profitable nodes. In our proposal, a destructive-constructive VNS is used, as shown in Algorithm 3. Note that also VNS use the construction phase algorithm of GRASP.

We propose a destructive-constructive VNS algorithm to improve the initial route given by the GRASP constructive phase. The main idea is to remove random POIs in the destructive phase of shaking and then apply the constructive GRASP phase as an improvement. The destructive-constructive strategy, also known as the destroy and repair operator, has been applied within some parameters, mainly within the Large Neighbourhood Search (LNS) metaheuristic [2,31,38]. Our VNS starts with a given value for the shake parameter $k_{max}$, which represents the maximum number of POIs to be removed. The algorithm randomly removes a point from the route and attempts to find a new optimal solution using the GRASP procedure. After obtaining the result, it is checked if the current route score has improved. In case of a tie, the route with the least time spent is chosen. If a better solution is found, the search resumes from the beginning with $k$ set to 1. The process ends when the maximum value of parameter $k$ is reached without any improvements.

## 4    Experimentation

To evaluate the performance of the hybrid algorithm, an objective function is used, considering the score, total route time, and other relevant factors to assess the quality of the generated route [46]. An experiment was carried out to test the designed hybrid algorithm.

Various instances were used to assess their performance against the benchmark instances [19], which originate from Solomon's vehicle routing problems with time windows data sets (r203, r104 and rc104 were chosen). These data sets contain the coordinates of different locations, each assigned a specific score, which can be visited. We opted for these data sets because they include uniformly distributed data sets (r203 and r104) and a combination of random and clustered data sets based on the geographical location of POIs (rc104). Additionally, the instances feature wide time windows, which is similar to POIs in a tourist context. It is illustrated in Fig. 1.

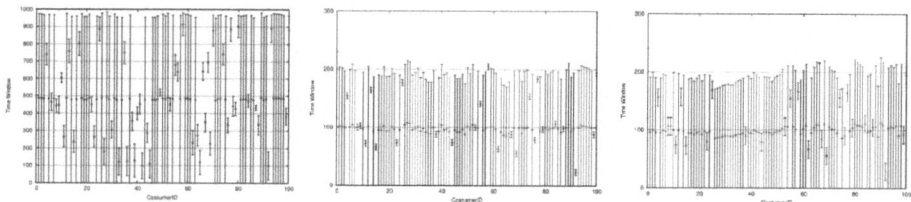

**Fig. 1.** Time Windows for datasets. r203.txt, r104.txt and rc104.txt

**Table 2.** Scores for data sets: r203, r104 and rc104, Num. POIs: 100

| rcl_size | k_max | rep | r203 m=1 (Optimal score: 1028) | | r104 m=2 (Optimal score: 1418) | | r104 m=3 (Optimal score: 835) | | r104 m=4 (Optimal score: 1065) | | rc104 m=3 (Optimal score: 778) | | rc104 m=4 (Optimal score: 975) | |
|---|---|---|---|---|---|---|---|---|---|---|---|---|---|---|
| | | | GRASP | Hybrid | GRASP | Hybrid | GRASP | Hybrid | GRASP | Hybrid | GRASP | Hybrid | GRASP | Hybrid |
| 5 | 5 | 10 | 667.0 | 883.0 | 1224.0 | 1288.0 | 484 | 676 | 770 | 943 | 503 | 708 | 591 | 885 |
| 5 | 5 | 15 | 804.0 | 953.0 | 1190.0 | 1296.0 | 463 | 773 | 779 | 939 | 503 | 666 | 591 | 851 |
| 5 | 5 | 20 | 715.0 | 919.0 | 1186.0 | 1339.0 | 485 | 739 | 663 | 910 | 503 | 691 | 591 | 853 |
| 5 | 7 | 10 | 704.0 | 887.0 | 1197.0 | 1292.0 | 630 | 712 | 660 | 916 | 503 | 708 | 591 | 885 |
| 5 | 7 | 15 | 768.0 | 930.0 | 1179.0 | 1309.0 | 525 | 712 | 567 | 879 | 503 | 696 | 591 | 851 |
| 5 | 7 | 20 | 667.0 | 937.0 | 1156.0 | 1346.0 | 449 | 748 | 657 | 990 | 503 | 691 | 591 | 853 |
| 5 | 10 | 10 | 754.0 | 880.0 | 1168.0 | 1298.0 | 459 | 739 | 669 | 981 | 503 | 708 | 591 | 885 |
| 5 | 10 | 15 | 672.0 | 894.0 | 1195.0 | 1339.0 | 542 | 709 | 665 | 921 | 503 | 696 | 591 | 863 |
| 5 | 10 | 20 | 761.0 | 952.0 | 1141.0 | 1326.0 | 512 | 726 | 616 | 923 | 503 | 691 | 591 | 894 |
| 7 | 5 | 10 | 710.0 | 897.0 | 1156.0 | 1281.0 | 472 | 638 | 598 | 934 | 467 | 635 | 618 | 866 |
| 7 | 5 | 15 | 763.0 | 921.0 | 1179.0 | 1286.0 | 535 | 709 | 698 | 936 | 467 | 695 | 618 | 859 |
| 7 | 5 | 20 | 754.0 | 924.0 | 1157.0 | 1311.0 | 478 | 754 | 790 | 924 | 467 | 684 | 618 | 826 |
| 7 | 7 | 10 | 669.0 | 936.0 | 1125.0 | 1328.0 | 534 | 735 | 689 | 935 | 467 | 635 | 618 | 866 |
| 7 | 7 | 15 | 662.0 | 914.0 | 1131.0 | 1339.0 | 518 | 743 | 596 | 958 | 467 | 722 | 618 | 882 |
| 7 | 7 | 20 | 717.0 | 908.0 | 1152.0 | 1281.0 | 476 | 749 | 608 | 914 | 467 | 684 | 618 | 826 |
| 7 | 10 | 10 | 723.0 | 928.0 | 1134.0 | 1295.0 | 503 | 683 | 610 | 969 | 467 | 635 | 618 | 866 |
| 7 | 10 | 15 | 734.0 | 925.0 | 1151.0 | 1345.0 | 622 | 790 | 666 | 939 | 467 | 722 | 618 | 892 |
| 7 | 10 | 20 | 693.0 | 950.0 | 1179.0 | 1332.0 | 358 | 698 | 709 | 997 | 467 | 684 | 618 | 882 |
| 10 | 5 | 10 | 623.0 | 945.0 | 1160.0 | 1206.0 | 475 | 731 | 521 | 937 | 541 | 667 | 650 | 774 |
| 10 | 5 | 15 | 685.0 | 853.0 | 1165.0 | 1279.0 | 508 | 714 | 573 | 915 | 541 | 688 | 650 | 817 |
| 10 | 5 | 20 | 663.0 | 829.0 | 1121.0 | 1254.0 | 497 | 686 | 556 | 1014 | 541 | 712 | 650 | 782 |
| 10 | 7 | 10 | 651.0 | 912.0 | 1145.0 | 1290.0 | 509 | 739 | 734 | 952 | 541 | 667 | 650 | 774 |
| 10 | 7 | 15 | 678.0 | 936.0 | 1140.0 | 1351.0 | 479 | 716 | 779 | 981 | 541 | 688 | 650 | 817 |
| 10 | 7 | 20 | 697.0 | 921.0 | 1114.0 | 1309.0 | 490 | 707 | 675 | 886 | 541 | 712 | 650 | 856 |
| 10 | 10 | 10 | 636.0 | 924.0 | 1122.0 | 1317.0 | 558 | 742 | 601 | 934 | 541 | 667 | 650 | 806 |
| 10 | 10 | 15 | 739.0 | 908.0 | 1130 | 1310.0 | 573 | 792 | 636 | 972 | 541 | 688 | 650 | 817 |
| 10 | 10 | 20 | 677.0 | 926.0 | 1121 | 1324.0 | 448 | 724 | 619 | 926 | 541 | 712 | 650 | 856 |
| **Optimal score** | | | 68.40% | 88.96% | 81.54% | 92.13% | 60.96% | 86.87% | 61.57% | 88.42% | 64.74% | 88.32% | 63.56% | 86.93% |

It is important to note that tourist problems differ from Benchmark's problems, hence, the same level of solution quality cannot be attained. In this experiment, traditional instances are utilised to evaluate the performance of the proposed hybrid metaheuristic in solving route design problems, rather than aiming for the highest effectiveness. We assessed GRASP-VNS using Gunawan et al. optimal solutions to verify that the optimal solution can be reached by removing a sequence of points.

The Table 2 shown below illustrates the performance of GRASP and the GRASP-VNS hybrid. The parameters considered are the following:

$m$: total number of routes. The outcomes are presented for a single route and two routes on the r203 dataset, and for three and four routes on the r104 and rc104 datasets.

$rcl_{size}$: Size of the restricted candidate list for the GRASP construction phase

$k_{max}$: number of POIs to remove in the VNS shake phase

$rep$: maximum times the process is repeated without any improvements.

In every case, the proposed hybrid metaheuristic yields superior results, suggesting routes with higher scores within the given time frame. It is evident that even with the initial parameter values, the results are quite good. However, due to the destructive-constructive nature of GRASP-VNS, the results can occasionally be slightly worse than in previous instances. Enhancements are observed when the number of candidates in the RCL is increased and when more iterations of the destructive-constructive process are allowed ($rep$). Increasing the number of points removed during the destructive phase of VNS ($k_{max}$) does not necessarily lead to better solutions, as the initial solution is good enough.

## 5  Conclusions

This work shows a simple and clear algorithm that generates high-quality tourist routes necessary for a tourist route recommendation system. The hybrid metaheuristic algorithm combines the well-known GRASP (Greedy-Randomised Adaptive Search Procedure) and VNS (Variable Neighbourhood Search). Unlike traditional hybrid algorithms, our approach integrates the GRASP construction process within the VNS and incorporates destructive-constructive strategies similar to those in LNS (Large Neighbourhood Search).

The goal is to incorporate this algorithm as a component of the tourist route recommendation system. No parameter adjustments or computational enhancements were made, so competing with the best performing algorithms for standard tourist route design models such as TOPTW is unfeasible. Instead, it focusses on subjective valuations of points of interest, ensuring that the results are not overly sensitive to changes.

However, the proposed methodology can be easily adapted to the circumstances that will inevitably arise in practical circumstances. For example, when the user decides, a priori or a posteriori, to forcefully include or explicitly exclude points originally considered. Or also when unforeseen events arise during the route that prevents continuing with what was planned, frequently due to delays in transfers from one point to another. The possibility of starting from a partial solution or modifying the consideration of candidate points of interest during the development of the visits will allow for an online rethinking of the problem data, providing a dynamic solution for the recommender.

Future work will consider additional constraints such as time, clustered POIs, budget, and hotel selection. In addition, integration with other methods, such as machine learning, simulation, or agile optimisation, will enhance dynamic replanning capabilities.

# References

1. Archetti, C., Hertz, A., Speranza, M.G.: Metaheuristics for the team orienteering problem. J. Heuristics **13**, 49–76 (2007). https://doi.org/10.1007/s10732-006-9004-0
2. Aringhieri, R., Cordone, R., Guastalla, A., Grosso, A.: Constructive and destructive methods in Heuristic search, pp. 65–91. Springer International Publishing, Cham (2023). https://doi.org/10.1007/978-3-031-38310-6_4
3. Borràs, J., Moreno, A., Valls, A.: Intelligent tourism recommender systems: a survey. Expert Syst. Appl. **41**(16), 7370–7389 (2014). https://doi.org/10.1016/j.eswa.2014.06.007
4. Brito, J., Expiosito-Marquez, A., Moreno, J.A.: A fuzzy GRASP algorithm for solving a tourist trip design problem. In: 2017 IEEE International Conference on Fuzzy Systems (FUZZ-IEEE). IEEE (2017). https://doi.org/10.1109/fuzz-ieee.2017.8015656
5. Divsalar, A., Vansteenwegen, P., Cattrysse, D.: A variable neighborhood search method for the orienteering problem with hotel selection. Int. J. Prod. Econ. **145**(1), 150–160 (2013). https://doi.org/10.1016/j.ijpe.2013.01.010
6. Divsalar, A., Vansteenwegen, P., Sörensen, K., Cattrysse, D.: A memetic algorithm for the orienteering problem with hotel selection. Eur. J. Oper. Res. **237**(1), 29–49 (2014). https://doi.org/10.1016/j.ejor.2014.01.001
7. Dolinskaya, I., Shi, Z.E., Smilowitz, K.: Adaptive orienteering problem with stochastic travel times. Transp. Res. Part E Logistics Transp. Rev. **109**, 1–19 (2018). https://doi.org/10.1016/j.tre.2017.10.013
8. Dontas, M., Sideris, G., Manousakis, E.G., Zachariadis, E.E.: An adaptive memory matheuristic for the set orienteering problem. Eur. J. Oper. Res. **309**(3), 1010–1023 (2023). https://doi.org/10.1016/j.ejor.2023.02.008
9. Expósito, A., Mancini, S., Brito, J., Moreno, J.A.: A fuzzy GRASP for the tourist trip design with clustered POIs. Expert Syst. Appl. **127**, 210–227 (2019). https://doi.org/10.1016/j.eswa.2019.03.004
10. Feo, T.A., Resende, M.G.C.: Greedy randomized adaptive search procedures. J. Global Optim. **6**(2), 109–133 (1995). https://doi.org/10.1007/BF01096763
11. Garcia, A., Arbelaitz, O., Vansteenwegen, P., Souffriau, W., Linaza, M.T.: Hybrid approach for the public transportation time dependent orienteering problem with time windows. In: Corchado, E., Graña Romay, M., Manhaes Savio, A. (eds.) Hybrid Artificial Intelligence Systems, pp. 151–158. Lecture Notes in Computer Science, Springer, Berlin, Heidelberg (2010). https://doi.org/10.1007/978-3-642-13803-4_19

12. Garcia, A., Vansteenwegen, P., Arbelaitz, O., Souffriau, W., Linaza, M.T.: Integrating public transportation in personalised electronic tourist guides. Comput. Oper. Res. **40**(3), 758–774 (2013). https://doi.org/10.1016/j.cor.2011.03.020
13. Gavalas, D., Konstantopoulos, C., Mastakas, K., Pantziou, G.: Efficient cluster-based heuristics for the team orienteering problem with time windows. Asia-Pacific J. Oper. Res. **36**(01), 1950001 (2019). https://doi.org/10.1142/s0217595919500015
14. Gavalas, D., Konstantopoulos, C., Mastakas, K., Pantziou, G., Vathis, N.: Efficient heuristics for the time dependent team orienteering problem with time windows. In: Applied Algorithms, pp. 152–163. Springer International Publishing (2014). https://doi.org/10.1007/978-3-319-04126-1_13
15. Gendreau, M., Potvin, J.Y.: Tabu Search, pp. 37–55. Springer International Publishing (2019). https://doi.org/10.1007/978-3-319-91086-4_2
16. Ghobadi, F., Divsalar, A., Jandaghi, H., Nozari, R.B.: An integrated recommender system for multi-day tourist itinerary. Appl. Soft Comput. **149**, 110942 (2023). https://doi.org/10.1016/j.asoc.2023.110942
17. González-Navasa, C., Moreno-Pérez, J.A., Brito-Santana, J., Alonso-Afonso, H.: Recommendation of tourist itineraries with dependence on transport time. Transp. Res. Proc. **71**, 77–84 (2023). https://doi.org/10.1016/j.trpro.2023.11.060
18. Guimarans, D., Dominguez, O., Panadero, J., Juan, A.A.: A simheuristic approach for the two-dimensional vehicle routing problem with stochastic travel times. Simul. Model. Pract. Theory **89**, 1–14 (2018). https://doi.org/10.1016/j.simpat.2018.09.004
19. Gunawan, A., Lau, H.C., Vansteenwegen, P., Lu, K.: Well-tuned algorithms for the team orienteering problem with time windows. J. Oper. Res. Soc. **68**(8), 861–876 (2017). https://doi.org/10.1057/s41274-017-0244-1
20. Hansen, P., Mladenović, N., Brimberg, J., Moreno Pérez, J.A.: Variable Neighborhood Search, pp. 57–97. Springer International Publishing (2019). https://doi.org/10.1007/978-3-319-91086-4_3
21. Jandaghi, H., Divsalar, A., Emami, S.: The categorized orienteering problem with count-dependent profits. Appl. Soft Comput. **113**, 107962 (2021). https://doi.org/10.1016/j.asoc.2021.107962
22. Juan, A.A., Faulin, J., Grasman, S.E., Rabe, M., Figueira, G.: A review of simheuristics: extending metaheuristics to deal with stochastic combinatorial optimization problems. Oper. Res. Perspect. **2**, 62–72 (2015). https://doi.org/10.1016/j.orp.2015.03.001
23. Jung, H.B., Kim, H.I., Lee, D.H.: Team orienteering with possible multiple visits: mathematical model and solution algorithms. Comput. Ind. Eng. **190**, 110097 (2024). https://doi.org/10.1016/j.cie.2024.110097
24. Karimi-Mamaghan, M., Mohammadi, M., Meyer, P., Karimi-Mamaghan, A.M., Talbi, E.G.: Machine learning at the service of meta-heuristics for solving combinatorial optimization problems: a state-of-the-art. Eur. J. Oper. Res. **296**(2), 393–422 (2022). https://doi.org/10.1016/j.ejor.2021.04.032
25. Khodadadian, M., Divsalar, A., Verbeeck, C., Gunawan, A., Vansteenwegen, P.: Time dependent orienteering problem with time windows and service time dependent profits. Comput. Oper. Res. **143**, 105794 (2022). https://doi.org/10.1016/j.cor.2022.105794
26. Liao, Z., Zheng, W.: Using a heuristic algorithm to design a personalized day tour route in a time-dependent stochastic environment. Tour. Manage. **68**, 284–300 (2018). https://doi.org/10.1016/j.tourman.2018.03.012

27. Lin, S.W., Yu, V.F.: A simulated annealing heuristic for the multiconstraint team orienteering problem with multiple time windows. Appl. Soft Comput. **37**, 632–642 (2015). https://doi.org/10.1016/j.asoc.2015.08.058

28. Lin, S.W., Yu, V.F.: Solving the team orienteering problem with time windows and mandatory visits by multi-start simulated annealing. Comput. Ind. Eng. **114**, 195–205 (2017). https://doi.org/10.1016/j.cie.2017.10.020

29. Moreno-Pérez, J., Moya-Antón, B.: Analysis of the basic VNS for TD-TOPTW. In: Quesada-Arencibia, A., et al. (eds.) 18th International Conference on Computer Aided Systems Theory, pp. 30–31. IUCTC Universidad de Las Palmas de Gran Canaria (2022)

30. Pěnička, R., Faigl, J., Saska, M.: Variable neighborhood search for the set orienteering problem and its application to other orienteering problem variants. Eur. J. Oper. Res. **276**(3), 816–825 (2019). https://doi.org/10.1016/j.ejor.2019.01.047

31. Pisinger, D., Ropke, S.: Large Neighborhood Search, pp. 99–127. Springer International Publishing (2019). https://doi.org/10.1007/978-3-319-91086-4_4

32. Resende, M.G.C., Ribeiro, C.C.: Greedy Randomized Adaptive Search Procedures: Advances and Extensions, pp. 169–220. Springer International Publishing (2019). https://doi.org/10.1007/978-3-319-91086-4_6

33. Rodríguez, B., Molina, J., Pérez, F., Caballero, R.: Interactive design of personalised tourism routes. Tour. Manage. **33**(4), 926–940 (2012). https://doi.org/10.1016/j.tourman.2011.09.014

34. Ruiz-Meza, J., Brito, J., Montoya-Torres, J.R.: A GRASP-VND algorithm to solve the multi-objective fuzzy and sustainable tourist trip design problem for groups. Appl. Soft Comput. **131**, 109–716 (2022). https://doi.org/10.1016/j.asoc.2022.109716

35. Salhi, S., Thompson, J.: An Overview of Heuristics and Metaheuristics, pp. 353–403. Springer International Publishing (2022). https://doi.org/10.1007/978-3-030-96935-6_11

36. Santos-Peñate, D.R., Moreno-Pérez, J., Rodríguez, C.C., Suárez-Vega, R.: A mathematical model and GRASP for a tourist trip design problem. In: Computer Aided Systems Theory – EUROCAST 2022, pp. 112–120. Springer Nature Switzerland (2022). https://doi.org/10.1007/978-3-031-25312-6_13

37. Schilde, M., Doerner, K.F., Hartl, R.F., Kiechle, G.: Metaheuristics for the bi-objective orienteering problem. Swarm Intell. **3**(3), 179–201 (2009). https://doi.org/10.1007/s11721-009-0029-5

38. Shaw, P.: Using constraint programming and local search methods to solve vehicle routing problems. In: Maher, M., Puget, J.F. (eds.) Principles and Practice of Constraint Programming — CP98, pp. 417–431. Springer Berlin Heidelberg, Berlin, Heidelberg (1998). https://doi.org/10.1007/3-540-49481-2_30

39. Sohrabi, S., Ziarati, K., Keshtkaran, M.: A greedy randomized adaptive search procedure for the orienteering problem with hotel selection. Eur. J. Oper. Res. **283**(2), 426–440 (2020). https://doi.org/10.1016/j.ejor.2019.11.010

40. Souffiau, W., Maervoet, J., Vansteenwegen, P., Vanden Berghe, G., Van Oudheusden, D.: A mobile tourist decision support system for small footprint devices. In: Cabestany, J., Sandoval, F., Prieto, A., Corchado, J.M. (eds.) Bio-Inspired Systems: Computational and Ambient Intelligence, pp. 1248–1255. Lecture Notes in Computer Science, Springer (2009). https://doi.org/10.1007/978-3-642-02478-8_156

41. Souffriau, W., Vansteenwegen, P., Berghe, G.V., Oudheusden, D.V.: The multiconstraint team orienteering problem with multiple time windows. Transp. Sci. **47**(1), 53–63 (2013). https://doi.org/10.1287/trsc.1110.0377

42. Talbi, E.G.: Machine Learning into Metaheuristics: a survey and Taxonomy. ACM Comput. Surv. **54**(6), 129:1–129:32 (2021). https://doi.org/10.1145/3459664
43. Tenemaza, M., Lujan-Mora, S., De Antonio, A., Ramirez, J.: Improving itinerary recommendations for tourists through metaheuristic algorithms: an optimization proposal. IEEE Access **8**, 79003–79023 (2020). https://doi.org/10.1109/ACCESS.2020.2990348
44. Toledo, A., Riff, M.C., Neveu, B.: A hyper-heuristic for the orienteering problem with hotel selection. IEEE Access **8**, 1303–1313 (2020). https://doi.org/10.1109/ACCESS.2019.2960492
45. Tricoire, F., Romauch, M., Doerner, K.F., Hartl, R.F.: Heuristics for the multi-period orienteering problem with multiple time windows. Comput. Oper. Res. **37**(2), 351–367 (2010). https://doi.org/10.1016/j.cor.2009.05.012
46. Vansteenwegen, P., Gunawan, A.: Orienteering problems: models and algorithms for vehicle routing problems with profits. Springer (2019). https://doi.org/10.1007/978-3-030-29746-6
47. Vansteenwegen, P., Souffriau, W., Berghe, G.V., Oudheusden, D.V.: Metaheuristics for tourist trip planning. In: Lecture Notes in Economics and Mathematical Systems, pp. 15–31. Springer Berlin Heidelberg (2009). https://doi.org/10.1007/978-3-642-00939-6_2
48. Vansteenwegen, P., Souffriau, W., Oudheusden, D.V.: A detailed analysis of two metaheuristics for the team orienteering problem. In: Engineering Stochastic Local Search Algorithms. Designing, Implementing and Analyzing Effective Heuristics, pp. 110–114. Springer Berlin Heidelberg (2009). https://doi.org/10.1007/978-3-642-03751-1_9
49. Vansteenwegen, P., Souffriau, W., Oudheusden, D.V.: The orienteering problem: a survey. Eur. J. Oper. Res. **209**(1), 1–10 (2011). https://doi.org/10.1016/j.ejor.2010.03.045
50. Verbeeck, C., Vansteenwegen, P., Aghezzaf, E.H.: Solving the stochastic time-dependent orienteering problem with time windows. Eur. J. Oper. Res. **255**(3), 699–718 (2016). https://doi.org/10.1016/j.ejor.2016.05.031
51. Wu, L., Gu, T., Chen, Z., Zeng, P., Liao, Z.: Personalized day tour design for urban tourists with consideration to $CO_2$ emissions. Chin. J. Popul. Resour. Environ. **20**(3), 237–244 (2022). https://doi.org/10.1016/j.cjpre.2022.09.004
52. Zheng, W., Ji, H., Lin, C., Wang, W., Yu, B.: Using a heuristic approach to design personalized urban tourism itineraries with hotel selection. Tour. Manage. **76**, 103956 (2020). https://doi.org/10.1016/j.tourman.2019.103956
53. Zheng, W., Liao, Z., Qin, J.: Using a four-step heuristic algorithm to design personalized day tour route within a tourist attraction. Tour. Manage. **62**, 335–349 (2017). https://doi.org/10.1016/j.tourman.2017.05.006

# Learning to Select Promising Initial Solutions for Large Neighborhood Search-Based Multi-Agent Path Finding

Marc Huber[1]([✉]) [iD], Günther R. Raidl[1] [iD], and Christian Blum[2] [iD]

[1] Institute of Logic and Computation, TU Wien, Vienna, Austria
{mhuber,raidl}@ac.tuwien.ac.at
[2] Artificial Intelligence Research Institute (IIIA-CSIC), Campus of UAB, Spain
christian.blum@iiia.csic.es

**Abstract.** Anytime Multi-Agent Path Finding (MAPF) is a promising paradigm for finding fast and (near-)optimal solutions to large-scale multi-agent systems within a fixed time budget. The currently leading approach builds on Large Neighborhood Search (LNS), which iteratively optimizes a quickly generated initial solution by repeatedly selecting and replanning paths of subsets of agents using randomized destroy heuristics and Prioritized Planning (PP). In this study, we examine the impact of initial solutions on the quality of final solutions in a state-of-the-art LNS-based anytime MAPF algorithm. Our findings demonstrate that its effectiveness is significantly influenced by the choice of the initial solution. Building on this insight, we propose to run PP many times to create a larger pool of potential initial solutions, from which we then select by means of an offline-trained Machine Learning (ML) model a most promising solution to run the LNS on. Empirical results on well-established MAPF benchmark instances show that the ML model successfully selects a most promising solution from the pool of potential initial solutions. This leads to improved performance of the state-of-the-art LNS-based anytime MAPF method in terms of both the final solution quality and the Area Under the Curve when initiated from the selected solution.

**Keywords:** Anytime Multi-Agent Path Finding · Machine Learning · Large Neighborhood Search

## 1 Introduction

Finding a set of collision-free paths for a group of agents in a shared environment has many important contemporary real-world applications, including automated warehouses [17], robotics, and autonomous vehicles [16]. In computer science, this

This project is partially funded by the Doctoral Program "Vienna Graduate School on Computational Optimization", Austrian Science Foundation (FWF), grant W1260-N35.

A. Quesada-Arencibia et al. (Eds.): EUROCAST 2024, LNCS 15172, pp. 236–250, 2025.
https://doi.org/10.1007/978-3-031-82949-9_22

problem is known as the Multi-Agent Path Finding (MAPF) problem [14]. Desirable solutions to the MAPF problem are those which are conflict-free, but also minimize some objective function. However, finding optimal solutions under various objective functions, such as the sum of costs, has proven to be NP-hard [18], as the state-space grows exponentially with the number of agents. In practice, attempts to solve MAPF instances with a few hundred or more agents using exact or reasonably bounded suboptimal MAPF algorithms typically requires far too much time or memory. In contrast, fast constructive heuristics usually only find low-quality solutions or no feasible solutions in tightly constrained scenarios at all. To address these issues, researchers have explored anytime MAPF approaches [3,6,7] which combine the strengths of both worlds. Anytime algorithms aim to find feasible solutions quickly and then continuously work on improving them as long as time remains, possibly converging to optimality if time allows.

In the context of anytime MAPF algorithms, Large Neighborhood Search (LNS)-based MAPF is a promising approach that relatively quickly finds solutions to the MAPF instances and iteratively improves them to near-optimality by repeatedly selecting and replanning paths of subsets of agents using destroy and repair heuristics [7]. The subset of agent paths selected for replanning is referred to as a neighborhood. If the newly found solution is superior to the incumbent solution, the incumbent solution is replaced by the new solution. This iterative process continues until an allocated time budget is exhausted.

MAPF-LNS [7] is the currently leading LNS-based approach for anytime suboptimal MAPF solving. It first produces an initial solution quickly using an efficient MAPF construction heuristic. Then, MAPF-LNS repeatedly applies randomized destroy heuristics and replans paths of subsets of agents using Prioritized Planning (PP) [12] with random priorities to further improve the solution until the allotted time is exhausted.

While MAPF-LNS has been empirically demonstrated to scale up to large instances with several hundreds of agents, we observed that the quality of the final solution is significantly influenced by the initial solution, even though the quality of the initial solution is not correlated much with the quality of the final solution.

This article proposes ISS-MAPF-LNS, the Initial-Solution-Selecting-MAPF-LNS, which aims to enhance MAPF-LNS's ability to find high-quality solutions by initiating the LNS from a more promising initial solution that is selected from a larger pool. The novel aspect of ISS-MAPF-LNS is an offline-trained machine learning (ML) model that selects from a pool of initial solutions generated by PP a most promising solution to run the LNS on. In more detail, a LambdaMART [2] model is trained to compute *scores* for the pool of PP-produced initial solutions and we select the most promising solution based on these scores. Thus, the learned scoring function reflects how promising each initial solution candidate is to ultimately get a final solution of highest quality when applying the LNS on it.

To assess the performance of ISS-MAPF-LNS, we conduct a series of experiments on five well-established MAPF benchmark instances. The results demonstrate that the trained ML model indeed selects a solution being among the most promising ones from the pool of potentially initial solutions, such that the subsequent LNS leads to a lower-cost final solution than MAPF-LNS applied to an average solution. Moreover, the ML model trained on a specific map with 50 agents scales well to the same map and also to unseen maps with hundreds of agents, leading to improved performance over MAPF-LNS on many instances.

The remainder of this article is organized as follows: Sect. 2 formally introduces the MAPF problem, and Sect. 3 reviews related work. Section 4 empirically analyzes the impact of initial solutions on the quality of final solutions in MAPF-LNS and presents our ISS-MAPF-LNS. Results of computational experiments are discussed in Sect. 5. Finally, in Sect. 6, we conclude and outline promising avenues for future research.

## 2   Problem Definition

Multi-Agent Path Finding (MAPF) encompasses a wide variety of variants, as outlined in [14]. In this study, we focus on the simplest and most studied variant that considers three key elements: (1) vertex and swapping conflicts, (2) the "stay at target" assumption, and (3) the sum of costs objective function. Time and space are discretized. The input to the MAPF problem is a connected, undirected, unweighted graph $G = (V, E)$, along with a set of $m$ agents $A = \{a_1, \ldots, a_m\}$. Each agent $a_i \in A$ has associated a start vertex $s_i \in V$ and a goal vertex $g_i \in V$ (which may coincide). It is assumed that each start vertex is distinct from all other agents' start vertices and also each goal vertex is distinct from all others. At each discrete time step $t$, every agent is located at one of the graph vertices and can either move to a neighboring vertex or wait at its current vertex. A path $p_i = (p_{i,0}, \ldots, p_{i,l(p_i)})$ for agent $a_i$ is a sequence of neighboring vertices, where $l(p_i)$ is the length of the path $p_i$. An edge $(p_{i,t}, p_{i,t+1}) \in E$ indicates a move action, while a vertex $p_{i,t} = p_{i,t+1} \in V$ indicates a wait action. The start vertex is $p_{i,0} = s_i$, while the goal vertex is $p_{i,l(p_i)} = g_i$. It is assumed that an agent remaining at its goal vertex is considered as a wait action if and only if it will subsequently move away from its goal vertex in a subsequent time step before finally returning later. The distance between two vertices, $d(x,y)$, is defined as the length of the shortest path from $x$ to $y$. The delay of path $p_i$ is $\text{delay}(p_i) = l(p_i) - d(s_i, g_i)$. A solution is a set of paths, one for each agent, such that the agents can follow these paths simultaneously without colliding with each other. The objective is to find a solution $P = \{p_i \mid a_i \in A\}$ that minimizes its sum of costs, denoted as $\text{SOC} = \sum_{p_i \in P} l(p_i)$, or, alternatively, its sum of delays, denoted as $\text{SOD} = \sum_{p_i \in P} \text{delay}(p_i)$.

## 3   Related Work

A fast constructive approach to MAPF is Prioritized Planning (PP) [12], which generates a solution by sorting the agents according to some priority function and subsequently planning a shortest path for each agent iteratively such that agents with lower priority avoid collisions with the already planned paths of higher-priority agents. While being fast, PP often produces low-quality solutions or does not find any feasible solution in tightly constrained scenarios.

Research on anytime MAPF has enjoyed an increasing interest in recent years, due to its practical relevance in finding (near-)optimal solutions within a reasonable time budget. This family of algorithms is particularly advantageous in dynamic and large-scale environments where computational efficiency is crucial [15].

In its early stages, several A*-based algorithms have been proposed. These approaches achieve the anytime behavior either by repeatedly calling A* for increasing subproblems [13,15] or by iteratively tightening the bounds of focal search [9], as suggested by Cohen et al. [3]. However, these approaches are primarily effective for instances that are not congested, as the complexity and number of potential conflicts increase significantly in densely populated environments, leading to excessive computational overhead.

In a recent publication, Li et al. [7] proposed MAPF-LNS, which effectively scales to large instances with hundreds of agents and represents the current leading anytime MAPF approach to date. Given a MAPF instance, the algorithm first invokes an efficient suboptimal MAPF algorithm to quickly find an initial solution $P$. Subsequently, in each iteration, it selects paths of a subset of agents $A_s \in A$ using a randomized destroy heuristic, deletes their paths $P_s^- = \{p_i \in P \mid a_i \in A_s\}$ from $P$, and calls PP with random priorities to find a set of collision-free paths $P_s^+$ that also do not collide with paths still in $P$. If the paths in $P_s^+$ have smaller sum of cost than the paths in $P_s^-$, MAPF-LNS adds paths $P_s^+$ to $P$ and $P_s^-$ otherwise. This procedure is repeated until the allocated time budget is exhausted.

Building on the popularity of MAPF-LNS, researchers have proposed several extensions to the original model. Li et al. [8] suggested MAPF-LNS2, which begins with an infeasible solution and repeatedly replans paths of subsets of agents in order to find paths with fewer conflicts. This process is repeated until all paths are conflict-free or the allotted time has elapsed. Huang et al. [4] proposed MAPF-ML-LNS, which learns a ranking function for a collection of paths, $\mathcal{P} = \{P_1^-, P_2^-, \ldots, P_n^-\}$, generated by the destroy heuristics in MAPF-LNS, such that replanning increases the solution quality more. Specifically, given an incumbent solution, MAPF-ML-LNS generates a collection of paths $\mathcal{P}$, using two randomized destroy heuristics. Then, it applies an offline-trained ranking function to $\mathcal{P}$ and replans the paths in descending order of the predicted scores. If a solution with smaller sum of costs is found, it discards $\mathcal{P}$ and continues to the next iteration. In contrast, Lam et al. [6] incorporated MAPF-LNS as primal heuristic in branch-and-cut-and-price. This approach combines the strengths of LNS with branch-and-cut-and-price techniques and allows for more efficient resolution of large-scale MAPF problems while still retaining optimality guarantees. Phan et al. [10] proposed BALANCE, a bi-level multi-armed bandit scheme that dynamically adapts the selection of destroy heuristics and neighborhoods during the search process. This method aims to avoid expensive prior efforts such as

**Table 1.** Variance and correlation results obtained by MAPF-LNS across various scenarios and maps.

| Scenario | random-32-32-20 | | | empty-32-32 | | | ost003d | | |
| | $m = 150, N = 16$ | | | $m = 400, N = 8$ | | | $m = 300, N = 8$ | | |
| | $\sigma$ | $\mu_\sigma$ | $r$ | $\sigma$ | $\mu_\sigma$ | $r$ | $\sigma$ | $\mu_\sigma$ | $r$ |
|---|---|---|---|---|---|---|---|---|---|
| 1 | 10.23 | 14.68 | 0.21 | 81.63 | 70.01 | 0.39 | 156.49 | 133.41 | 0.05 |
| 2 | 5.99 | 11.98 | 0.24 | 60.04 | 71.11 | 0.05 | 135.85 | 157.30 | 0.62 |
| 3 | 6.83 | 12.06 | 0.13 | 71.68 | 85.46 | 0.01 | 58.74 | 96.42 | −0.14 |
| 4 | 8.96 | 13.35 | −0.02 | 49.08 | 59.00 | 0.43 | 66.23 | 93.40 | 0.16 |
| 5 | 11.21 | 16.58 | 0.15 | 93.45 | 77.15 | 0.51 | 62.13 | 122.33 | 0.04 |
| 6 | 7.94 | 13.91 | −0.47 | 83.26 | 67.35 | 0.32 | 139.85 | 133.44 | 0.15 |
| 7 | 12.35 | 21.03 | 0.06 | 69.39 | 79.00 | 0.20 | 108.35 | 154.04 | 0.27 |
| 8 | 9.89 | 20.08 | −0.16 | 111.42 | 96.67 | 0.67 | 149.77 | 139.49 | 0.24 |
| 9 | 12.05 | 18.28 | 0.08 | 74.31 | 73.12 | −0.01 | 112.73 | 141.86 | 0.07 |
| 10 | 7.32 | 13.35 | −0.45 | 52.35 | 66.10 | 0.11 | 152.15 | 165.48 | -0.05 |
| 11 | 7.63 | 15.08 | −0.21 | 81.09 | 76.11 | 0.07 | 107.96 | 151.27 | 0.16 |
| 12 | 7.23 | 16.47 | −0.19 | 94.79 | 81.45 | 0.46 | 23.00 | 50.97 | 0.23 |
| 13 | 5.42 | 10.88 | 0.02 | 46.37 | 68.30 | 0.32 | 112.97 | 134.84 | -0.22 |
| 14 | 9.71 | 15.38 | −0.07 | 66.96 | 73.13 | 0.20 | 104.65 | 140.33 | 0.31 |
| 15 | 11.12 | 19.49 | 0.10 | 43.33 | 66.08 | -0.12 | 94.41 | 112.23 | 0.01 |
| 16 | 9.87 | 17.81 | 0.12 | 76.37 | 66.28 | 0.49 | 83.29 | 109.03 | 0.11 |
| 17 | 11.24 | 18.22 | −0.14 | 61.80 | 65.84 | 0.32 | 114.85 | 157.16 | 0.22 |
| 18 | 6.13 | 12.99 | −0.04 | 59.82 | 66.97 | −0.00 | 79.40 | 115.59 | 0.14 |
| 19 | 6.23 | 12.46 | −0.25 | 50.33 | 75.82 | 0.39 | 44.46 | 61.49 | 0.05 |
| 20 | 8.21 | 12.57 | −0.18 | 69.73 | 69.43 | 0.13 | 128.85 | 156.66 | 0.54 |
| 21 | 6.34 | 9.40 | 0.16 | 56.05 | 68.82 | 0.41 | 98.22 | 120.50 | 0.22 |
| 22 | 7.66 | 16.65 | 0.19 | 56.08 | 76.58 | 0.30 | 184.45 | 175.21 | 0.51 |
| 23 | 8.63 | 17.79 | −0.19 | 52.39 | 66.71 | 0.54 | 81.83 | 128.74 | 0.08 |
| 24 | 6.57 | 14.47 | −0.05 | 87.53 | 87.22 | 0.19 | 75.14 | 116.55 | −0.08 |
| 25 | 11.83 | 15.98 | 0.39 | 82.12 | 85.12 | 0.08 | 65.23 | 72.32 | 0.44 |

data acquisition, model training, and feature engineering by adjusting strategies on the fly based on real-time performance feedback.

Concerning specifically the impact of initial solutions in LNS on the final solution quality, we are unaware of any specific approach in the literature that utilizes ML to learn how to select promising initial solutions for LNS.

## 4    Initial-Solution-Selecting LNS for MAPF

Large Neighborhood Search (LNS) proposed by Shaw [11] is a popular metaheuristic widely used to find near-optimal solutions to hard combinatorial optimization problems within a fixed time budget. It has gained prominence for its ability to escape local optima and explore vast regions of the solution space for a huge number of applications. LNS achieves this by using more appropriate and effective algorithms to find better solutions in a larger neighborhood instead of iterating through all the neighbors.

In contrast to traditional optimization heuristics that often depend heavily on the quality of the initial solution, LNS can exhibit unexpected behavior where poor initial solutions occasionally lead to superior final outcomes compared to starting with high-quality solutions. This phenomenon, akin to the sensitivity to initial conditions observed in chaotic dynamical systems, suggests that the trajectory of the search process in LNS is profoundly influenced by its starting point.

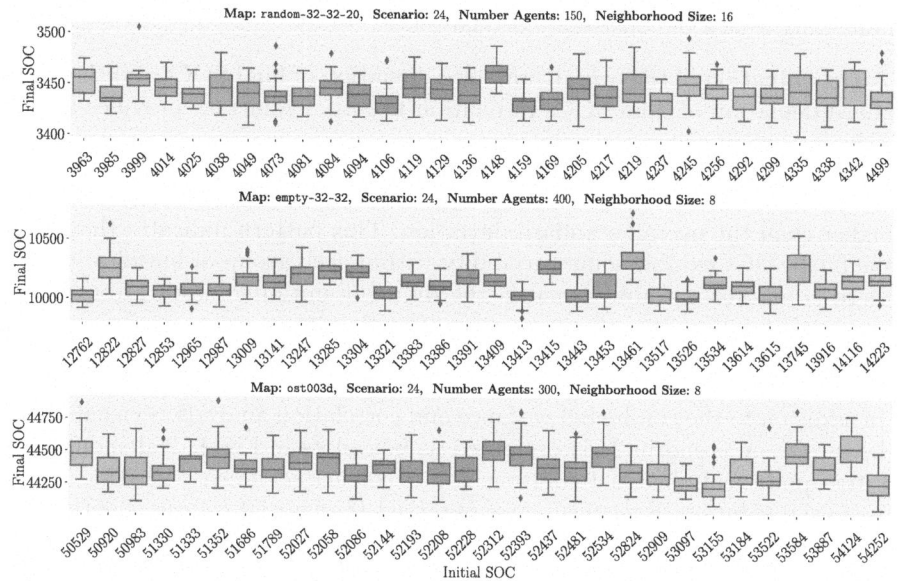

**Fig. 1.** Impact of initial solutions on the quality of final solutions in MAPF-LNS.

To examine this behavior in the context of anytime LNS-based MAPF, we conduct a series of experiments on the following three grid maps from the MAPF benchmark set [14] with the predefined 25 random scenarios, specifically: random-32-32-20 with $m = 150$ agents, neighborhood size $N = 16$, empty-32-32 with $m = 400$ agents, $N = 8$, and ost003d with $m = 300$ agents, $N = 8$. For each instance, we generate 30 initial solutions using PP with random priorities. Each initial solution is then subjected to 30 MAPF-LNS runs, with a time limit of 60 s and $N = \{8, 16\}$.

Table 1 presents the results of these experiments. They show the overall standard deviation ($\sigma$) of final SOCs, the mean of the standard deviations ($\mu_\sigma$) of final SOCs in relation to the initial solutions, and the correlation coefficient ($r$) between final SOCs and initial SOCs across the aforementioned three maps and 25 different scenarios.

The correlation coefficient between the initial and final SOCs varies across the different scenarios and maps, with values ranging from as low as $-0.47$ to as high as $0.67$. This wide range of correlation coefficients, often close to zero or even negative, indicates that the quality of the initial solution does not have a strong linear relationship with the quality of the final solution. Specifically:

- For `random-32-32-20`, the correlation coefficients range from $-0.47$ to $0.39$, with many scenarios showing near-zero or negative correlations.
- For `empty-32-32`, the correlation coefficients range from $-0.12$ to $0.67$, also displaying a wide range with several values close to zero.
- For `ost003d`, the correlation coefficients range from $-0.22$ to $0.62$, again indicating a lack of consistent correlation.

An examination of the overall standard deviation of final SOCs and the mean standard deviation of final SOCs in relation to initial solutions provides insight into the impact of the initial solutions:

- Across all maps and scenarios, the mean of the standard deviations is generally higher than the overall standard deviation. This pattern indicates that while the final SOCs exhibit some variability within each group of initial solutions, there is greater variability across the different initial solution groups. This higher variability between groups signifies that the initial solution plays a significant role in determining the range of possible final SOCs.

In addition to the conducted variance and correlation analysis, a visualization of the results on scenario 24 is presented as box plots in Fig. 1. It demonstrates that the quality of the final solution is not correlated much with the quality of the initial solution. Specifically, we observed that initial solutions with lower SOC do not necessarily lead to higher final SOC. These results suggest that there are more intricate relationships between initial solutions and the final solution quality of the LNS, and there is potential to improve the final solution quality of MAPF-LNS by starting the LNS from a more cleverly selected initial solution.

Building on this insight, we use data-driven methods to learn a ranking model for selecting promising initial solutions generated by PP on which to run the LNS on. The key idea is that by warm-starting MAPF-LNS from a more promising initial solution, it can more efficiently and effectively explore the search space, leading to solutions of higher quality. Consequently, we refer to our approach as Initial-Solution-Selecting-MAPF-LNS (ISS-MAPF-LNS).

Algorithm 1 shows a pseudocode for the training of the ranking model for ISS-MAPF-LNS. The input is a set of training instances $\mathcal{I}$, each consisting of a fixed grid map and a scenario generated by randomly selecting $m$ start and goal vertices on the grid map. For each instance $I \in \mathcal{I}$, the training algorithm generates $T$ initial solutions $(P_I^t)_{t=1,\ldots,T}$ using PP with a random priorities.

---

**Algorithm 1.** Training Algorithm

---

1: **Input:** Training instance set $\mathcal{I}$, nr. of initial solutions $T$, nr. of final solutions $K$
2: **Output:** trained ranking model $\pi_\theta$, nDCG
3: $\pi_\theta \leftarrow$ ranking model
4: $D, D_{\text{train}}, D_{\text{test}} \leftarrow \emptyset$
5: **for** $I \in \mathcal{I}$ **do**
6:     **for** $t = 1$ to $T$ **do**
7:         $S \leftarrow \emptyset$
8:         $P_I^t \leftarrow$ runPP($I$)  // generate initial solution
9:         **for** $k = 1$ to $K$ **do**
10:             $S \leftarrow S \cup$ runLNS($I, P_I^t$)   // generate final solution quality
11:         **end for**
12:         $D \leftarrow D \cup (\phi(I, P_I^t), \text{Median}(S))$  // store features and median of solutions
13:     **end for**
14: **end for**
15: $D_{\text{train}}, D_{\text{test}} \leftarrow$ Split($D$)
16: $\pi_\theta \leftarrow$ HyperparameterTuning($\pi_\theta, D_{\text{train}}$)
17: nDCG $\leftarrow$ Validate($\pi_\theta, D_{\text{test}}$)
18: **return** $\pi_\theta$, nDCG

---

From each initial solution $P_I^t$, MAPF-LNS is invoked $K$ times to produce a set of final solutions $S$. Subsequently, a feature function $\phi : (I, P_I^t) \rightarrow [0,1]^p$ is applied to derive a $p$-dimensional feature vector representing meaningful information for $P_I^t$. This feature vector, along with the median of the objective values of the solutions in $S$, are stored as training data set $D$.

Once the training data collection is complete, $D$ is divided into a training set $D_{\text{train}}$ and a test set $D_{\text{test}}$. Hyperparameter tuning is then performed on $D_{\text{train}}$ using an automated hyperparameter tuning framework that adjusts the parameters $\theta$ of the ranking model $\pi_\theta$. Finally, the model is validated on $D_{\text{test}}$, and the performance, measured by the normalized discounted cumulative gain (nDCG), is recorded.

The feature function $\phi : (I, P_I^t)$ is computed in accordance with Huang et al. [4], where for each agent $a_i \in A$ a set of 16 agent features is considered as listed in Table 2. Subsequently, the minimum, maximum, sum, and average of each feature value across all agents are also determined, resulting in $4 \times 16 = 64$ features in total. Finally, all 64 feature values are normalized to the range of $[0, 1]$ by applying min-max-normalization.

With regard to the ranking model, LambdaMART [2] is a state-of-the-art learning-to-rank approach that has proven to be highly successful in solving diverse real-world ranking problems. While our primary objective is to accurately predict the most promising initial solution, which also alignment with the objectives of simpler binary classification approaches, we encountered significant challenges when training a binary classifier due to issues related to imbalanced data. These challenges persist even when the problem is relaxed to predicting the top three most promising initial solutions. LambdaMART, however, excels in this context by focusing on the ranking order, thereby mitigating the impact of data imbalance. It emphasizes the correct placement of top solutions, ensuring that the most relevant items are identified and ranked appropriately. This ranking-centric approach enables LambdaMART to overcome the limitations of traditional binary classifiers, providing more accurate and reliable predictions, rendering it suitable for the task at hand.

LambdaMART takes as input a feature matrix, relevance scores, and query IDs, where the query IDs group instances that belong to the same query. To transform our data into this format, we assign each feature vector of an instance $I \in \mathcal{I}$ a unique query ID and convert the solution qualities within each instance to relevance scores ranging from one to $T$.

**Table 2.** Features of agent $a_i \in A$ with respect to instance $I$ and solution $P_I$.

| Features | Count |
|---|---|
| Distance $d(s_i, g_i)$ between the start vertex $s_i$ and the goal vertex $g_i$ of agent $a_i$. | 1 |
| Row and column numbers of the start vertex $s_i$ and goal vertex $g_i$ of agent $a_i$. | 4 |
| Degree of the goal vertex $g_i$ of agent $a_i$. | 1 |
| Delay delay$(p_i)$ of the agent $a_i$. | 1 |
| Ratio delay$(p_i)/d(s_i, g_i)$ between the delay of agent $a_i$ and the distance between $a_i$'s start and goal vertices. | 1 |
| The minimum, maximum, sum, and average of the heat values of the vertices along agent $a_i$'s path $p_i$. The heat value of a vertex $v \in V$ is the number of time steps that $v$ is occupied by an agent. If agent $a_i$ revisits a vertex multiple times before reaching its goal, the heat value of that vertex is counted multiple times in both the sum and the average. | 4 |
| The number of time steps that agent $a_i$ spends on a vertex with degree $j$ $(1 \le j \le 4)$ before reaching its goal vertex. | 4 |

# 5    Experimental Evaluation

This section presents a comparative evaluation of the performance of ISS-MAPF-LNS and MAPF-LNS. It begins with a detailed account of the experimental setup, followed by a description of the performed model training. Finally, the obtained results are presented and discussed.

## 5.1   Experimental Setup

We implemented ISS-MAPF-LNS[1] in C++ as an extension of the existing MAPF-LNS2 framework[2]. The gradient boosting framework LightGBM [5] was employed for training LambdaMART [2] models. The evaluation was performed on five representative grid-based maps from the MAPF benchmark suite [14], specifically: `empty-8-8` ($8 \times 8$), `empty-32-32` ($32 \times 32$), `random-32-32-20` (denoted as `random`, $32 \times 32$), `warehouse-10-20-10-2-1` (denoted as `warehouse`, $161 \times 63$), and `ost003d` ($194 \times 194$). For each map and number of agents, the corresponding 25 predefined random scenarios from the MAPF benchmark suite were utilized to determine the start and goal vertices of the agents. Unless otherwise specified, PP with random priorities was employed for generating initial solutions, and a total runtime limit of 60 s along with neighborhood sizes comparable to those used by Li et al. [7] were applied. All experiments were conducted in single-threaded mode on a machine equipped with an AMD EPYC 7402 processor running at 2.80 GHz, with a memory limit of 8 GB.

## 5.2   Model Training

One of three LambdaMART models was trained on map `random` with $m = 50$, and $N = 16$ by applying Algorithm 1 with $|\mathcal{I}| = 1000$, and parameters $T = 30$, and $K = 41$. In this process, the dataset $\mathcal{D}$ was randomly split w.r.t. the query IDs into $|\mathcal{D}_{\text{train}}| = 90\%$ training data and $|\mathcal{D}_{\text{test}}| = 10\%$ test data. This ensured that samples with the same query IDs were contained in the same dataset. Hyperparameter tuning for LambdaMART was conducted on the training dataset $\mathcal{D}_{\text{train}}$ using Optuna [1] with the objective of maximizing the nDCG@3 metric and GroupKFold (k = 5) cross-validation with groups corresponding to the query IDs. The training procedure was performed in an analogous manner on the map `warehouse` with $m = 150$ and $N = 16$, as well as on the map `random` with $m = 50$ and $N = 8$, resulting in a total of three trained models: $M_{\text{r}_{16}}$, $M_{\text{w}_{16}}$, and $M_{\text{r}_8}$.

## 5.3   Testing Procedure

During the testing phase, PP was executed 30 times in ISS-MAPF-LNS to produce a pool of initial solutions, while it was applied only once in MAPF-LNS. The total time required for the generation of initial solutions and the time required for the prediction of scores were subtracted from the total runtime limit of 60 s, with the remaining time allocated for running the LNS from the selected initial solution. The following questions were addressed through experimentation:

1. Can we train a ranking model that performs well on the same grid map with the same and different numbers of agents?

---

[1] https://github.com/isomorphist/ISS-MAPF-LNS.
[2] https://github.com/Jiaoyang-Li/MAPF-LNS2.

2. Can we train a ranking model that generalizes to unseen grid maps with different numbers of agents?

To evaluate these questions, we employed the model $M_{r_{16}}$ in ISS-MAPF-LNS to select promising initial solutions for the maps `random` and `empty-8-8`, the model $M_{w_{16}}$ for the map `warehouse`, and the model $M_{r_8}$ for the maps `ost003d` and `empty-32-32`. For each map and number of agents, 60 ISS-MAPF-LNS runs and 60 MAPF-LNS runs were performed, resulting in a total of $60 \times 25$ evaluations for each approach on each map and number of agents.

### 5.4   Results

Table 3 presents the mean values of the results obtained in our experimental evaluation of ISS-MAPF-LNS (abbreviated as ISS) and MAPF-LNS (abbreviated as LNS), focusing on the following four key metrics:

- **Initial SOD:** Initial Sum of Delays (SOD) of the selected initial solution.
- **Final SOD:** Final SOD after optimization.
- **AUC:** Area Under the Curve (AUC), defined as the integral of the SOD Graph, starting from the time the initial solution is selected until the specified time limit is reached.
- $t_{\text{init}}[s]$: Runtime required to generate initial solutions.

The results demonstrate that for the map `empty-8-8` with 16, 24, and 32 agents, ISS tends to favor initial solutions with lower initial SODs compared to LNS. The values for 16 and 24 agents are 10.560 vs. 10.722, respectively,

**Table 3.** MAPF-Benchmark results obtained by ISS and LNS.

| Map | $m$ | $N$ | Initial SOD | | Final SOD | | AUC | | $t_{\text{init}}[s]$ | |
|---|---|---|---|---|---|---|---|---|---|---|
| | | | ISS | LNS | ISS | LNS | ISS | LNS | ISS | LNS |
| empty-8-8 | 16 | 16 | **10.560** | 10.722 | 2.520 | 2.520 | 151.257 | 151.262 | 0.007 | 0.000 |
| | 24 | 16 | **34.280** | 35.057 | **10.427** | 10.430 | 629.894 | **629.600** | 0.018 | 0.001 |
| | 32 | 16 | 93.760 | **82.563** | 25.133 | 25.185 | **1545.085** | 1548.529 | 0.088 | 0.003 |
| empty-32-32 | 300 | 8 | 2372.84 | **2371.52** | 440.09 | 442.37 | **33518.82** | 33632.40 | 2.69 | 0.09 |
| | 350 | 8 | 3231.12 | **3230.97** | 939.54 | 942.58 | **70978.30** | 71157.98 | 5.42 | 0.18 |
| | 400 | 8 | 4363.44 | **4354.11** | 1805.67 | **1791.05** | 132203.40 | **130981.41** | 11.61 | 0.37 |
| | 450 | 8 | 6170.04 | **6045.67** | 3134.15 | **3101.54** | 219306.41 | **216669.17** | 29.69 | 0.98 |
| ost003d | 100 | 8 | 1441.40 | **1242.43** | 43.67 | **41.27** | 4021.85 | **3698.54** | 3.46 | 0.10 |
| | 200 | 8 | **3902.96** | 4000.67 | **217.78** | 220.86 | **30693.53** | 31512.05 | 11.43 | 0.35 |
| | 300 | 8 | **7970.24** | 7985.14 | **932.51** | 968.17 | **120037.50** | 123283.20 | 22.36 | 0.74 |
| | 400 | 8 | **13055.96** | 13118.59 | 3212.46 | **2931.14** | 312943.46 | **303192.39** | 41.12 | 1.35 |
| random | 50 | 16 | **106.84** | 119.77 | 24.24 | 24.24 | **1466.29** | 1466.62 | 0.12 | 0.00 |
| | 100 | 16 | 467.74 | **462.95** | 125.76 | 125.83 | **7809.09** | 7813.90 | 0.45 | 0.01 |
| | 150 | 16 | 1048.85 | **1026.20** | **342.63** | 342.75 | 22113.44 | **22106.02** | 1.37 | 0.05 |
| | 200 | 16 | 1959.77 | **1958.99** | **815.28** | 818.59 | **54776.02** | 55069.65 | 4.31 | 0.15 |
| | 250 | 16 | **3496.92** | 3515.45 | **1667.38** | 1669.86 | 116124.45 | **115630.32** | 17.71 | 0.61 |
| warehouse | 150 | 16 | **1844.67** | 1853.64 | **115.86** | 116.32 | 8481.24 | **8370.05** | 3.32 | 0.10 |
| | 200 | 16 | 3131.47 | **3024.86** | 258.14 | **257.94** | 19925.99 | **19661.84** | 6.68 | 0.21 |
| | 250 | 16 | **4494.93** | 4534.01 | 464.60 | **462.98** | **38343.22** | 38725.28 | 12.20 | 0.43 |
| | 300 | 16 | 6228.19 | **6044.16** | **751.20** | 756.10 | **66391.85** | 66866.06 | 19.59 | 0.67 |
| | 350 | 16 | 7914.13 | **7696.34** | **1200.63** | 1203.22 | **110245.29** | 110509.65 | 30.02 | 1.07 |

and 34.280 vs. 35.057 for 32 agents. However, for 32 agents, the initial SOD for LNS is 82.563, while that of ISS is 93.760. With regard to the final SOD, both algorithms achieve identical final SODs for 16 agents. However, the final SOD for ISS is marginally superior for 24 agents and slightly better for 32 agents, with values of 25.133 compared to 25.185 for LNS. Regarding the AUC values, ISS outperforms LNS in two out of three cases. It shows superior performance for 32 agents and slightly better performance for 16 agents compared to LNS.

On the map `empty-32-32` with 300, 350, 400, and 450 agents, LNS yields lower initial SODs across all number of agents compared to ISS. However, ISS outperforms LNS slightly in terms of final SOD values for 300 and 350 agents. For instance, the final SOD for 300 agents is 440.09 for ISS compared to 442.37 for LNS. However, LNS achieves significantly superior final SOD values for 400 and 450 agents. With regard to the AUC values, ISS yields significantly lower values for 300 and 350 agents than LNS, whereas LNS achieves significantly lower values for 400 and 450 agents.

For the map `ost003d` with 100, 200, 300, and 400 agents, ISS favors lower initial SODs for 200, 300, and 400 agents compared to LNS. With regard to the final SODs, ISS achieved significantly lower values for 200, and 300 agents, with particularly notable performance for 300 agents. The final SOD for 300 agents was 932.51 for ISS, in contrast to 968.17 for LNS. Moreover, ISS achieves significantly lower AUC values for 200 and 300 agents than LNS, whereas LNS yields significantly lower AUC values for 100 and 400 agents.

On the map `random` with 50, 100, 150, 200, and 250 agents, ISS achieves superior final SODs across all scenarios despite having higher initial SODs in four out of five cases. This indicates that the final solution quality is indeed dependent on the initial solution. For instance, the final SOD for 150 agents was 342.63 for ISS and 342.75 for LNS, but ISS has a significantly higher initial SOD of 1048.85 compared to 1026.20 for LNS. The AUC values for ISS are lower in three out of five cases, which highlights the benefit of initiating the optimization process from a promising initial solution.

For the map `warehouse` with 150, 200, 250, 300, and 350 agents, LNS achieves lower initial SODs in three out of five cases, while ISS outperforms LNS in three out of five cases in terms of final SOD. In particular, ISS exhibits significantly superior results for higher numbers of agents. For example, the final SOD for 350 agents is 1200.63 for ISS compared to 1203.22 for LNS. Regarding the AUC values, ISS achieves significantly superior solutions in three out of five cases lower than LNS, while LNS yields superior solutions for 150 and 200 agents.

With regard to $t_{init}[s]$, for all maps and number of agents, the initialization times are approximately 30 times higher for ISS compared to LNS. This reflects the additional effort required to generate multiple initial solutions.

*Key Insights:*

- **Initial Solution Quality:** In many cases, the initial solutions generated by ISS exhibit lower quality. However, the final solutions achieved by ISS are of a higher quality, particularly in constrained environments such as on maps `warehouse` and `random`.

- **Final Solution Quality and AUC:** In 13 out of 21 cases, the final SODs found by ISS were lower than those of LNS. Moreover, the AUC values obtained by ISS were in 12 out of 21 cases lower than those of LNS. This demonstrates the effectiveness of using LambdaMART to select promising initial solutions.
- **Computational Overhead:** The primary trade-off for the superior performance of ISS is the increased time required to generate initial solutions. This overhead is particularly evident in larger and more complex maps.
- **Seen maps:** (1) `random`: ISS performs particularly well, achieving lower final SODs in four out of five scenarios compared to LNS. This indicates the efficacy of the learned model in handling familiar environments. (2) `warehouse`: ISS shows robust performance, with lower final SODs in three out of five groups compared to LNS. Despite the longer initial solution generation time, ISS effectively optimized the solutions.
- **Unseen Maps:** ISS remains competitive with LNS on unseen maps like `empty-32-32` and `ost003d`, which highlights the generalization capability of the trained models.

The results indicate that the quality of the final solution in LNS is strongly correlated with its initial solution. ISS leverages its ability to select a promising solution from a diverse pool of generated initial solutions, which, although time-consuming, results in better overall optimization. The extended initial solution time for ISS is a trade-off that pays off in terms of final solution quality, particularly in complex and large maps like `warehouse`.

The strength of ISS lies in its ability to learn from training data and apply this learning to both seen and unseen scenarios, providing a robust solution even when starting late in the LNS process. This demonstrates the potential of integrating ML techniques with traditional optimization methods in MAPF problems.

## 6   Conclusion and Future Work

In this work, we addressed the significant dependency of the final solution quality of MAPF-LNS on its initial solution. Despite the fact that the initial solution quality is not strongly correlated with the final solution quality, the choice of an initial solution has a substantial impact on the performance of MAPF-LNS. We proposed ISS-MAPF-LNS, a novel extension of MAPF-LNS. This approach involves executing PP with random priorities multiple times to generate a large pool of potential initial solutions. From this pool, the most promising initial solution is selected using LambdaMART, a state-of-the-art learning-to-rank algorithm, to run the LNS on.

LambdaMART was trained offline on two well-known maps, and the experimental results demonstrate that the trained model generalizes well to different numbers of agents on both seen and unseen grid maps. This indicates that our approach can effectively leverage ML to enhance the performance of MAPF-LNS.

In order to improve the robustness and generalization capability of ISS-MAPF-LNS, future research should focus on creating a more diverse set of training data. By including a wider variety of maps and scenarios during the training phase, we may reduce the model's dependence on specific map features and enhance its ability to generalize to different environments. This broader training dataset may help the model to better understand the diverse characteristics of various maps, leading to more reliable performance in new scenarios.

One of the primary challenges identified is the computational overhead associated with generating multiple initial solutions. An alternative or additional ML-based approach is to employ machine learning techniques to directly predict promising destroy sets, which are crucial components of the LNS optimization process.

# References

1. Akiba, T., Sano, S., Yanase, T., Ohta, T., Koyama, M.: Optuna: A next-generation hyperparameter optimization framework. In: Proceedings of the 25th ACM SIGKDD International Conference on Knowledge Discovery and Data Mining (2019)
2. Burges, C.J.C.: From RankNet to LambdaRank to LambdaMART: An Overview. Tech. rep, Microsoft Research (2010)
3. Cohen, L., et al.: Anytime focal search with applications. In: Proceedings of the 27th International Joint Conference on Artificial Intelligence (IJCAI), pp. 1434–1441 (2018)
4. Huang, T., Li, J., Koenig, S., Dilkina, B.: Anytime multi-agent path finding via machine learning-guided large neighborhood search. In: Proceedings of the 36th AAAI Conf. on Artificial Intelligence (AAAI), pp. 9368–9376 (2024)
5. Ke, G., et al.: Lightgbm: a highly efficient gradient boosting decision tree. Adv. Neural. Inf. Process. Syst. **30**, 3146–3154 (2017)
6. Lam, E., Harabor, D.D., Stuckey, P.J., Li, J.: Exact anytime multi-agent path finding using branch-and-cut-and-price and large neighborhood search. In: Proceedings of the 33th International Conference on Automation Planning and Sched. (ICAPS), pp. 254–258 (2023)
7. Li, J., Chen, Z., Harabor, D., Stuckey, P.J., Koenig, S.: Anytime Multi-agent path finding via large neighborhood search. In: Proceedings of the 30th International Joint Conference on Artificial Intelligence (IJCAI), pp. 4127–4135 (2021)
8. Li, J., Chen, Z., Harabor, D., Stuckey, P.J., Koenig, S.: MAPF-LNS2: fast repairing for multi-agent path finding via large neighborhood search. In: Proceedings of the 36th AAAI Conference on Artificial Intelligence (AAAI), pp. 10256–10265 (2022)
9. Pearl, J., Kim, J.H.: Studies in semi-admissible heuristics. IEEE Trans. Pattern Anal. Mach. Intell. **PAMI-4**, 392–399 (1982)
10. Phan, T., Huang, T., Dilkina, B., Koenig, S.: Adaptive anytime multi-agent path finding using bandit-based large neighborhood search. In: Proceedings of the 38th AAAI Conference on Artificial Intelligence (AAAI), pp. 17514–17522 (2024)
11. Shaw, P.: Using constraint programming and local search methods to solve vehicle routing problems. In: Maher, M., Puget, J.F. (eds.) Principles and Practice of Constraint Programming — CP98. LNCS, vol. 1520, pp. 417–431. Springer (1998)

12. Silver, D.: Cooperative Pathfinding. In: Proceedings of the First AAAI Conference on Artificial Intelligence and Interactive Digital Entertainment (AAAI), pp. 117–122 (2005)
13. Standley, T., Korf, R.: Complete algorithms for cooperative pathfinding problems. In: Proceedings of the 22th International Joint Conference on AI (IJCAI), pp. 668–673 (2011)
14. Stern, R., et al.: Multi-agent pathfinding: definitions, variants, and benchmarks. In: Proceedings of the 12th International Symposium on Combinatorial Search (SoCS), pp. 151–159 (2019)
15. Vedder, K., Biswas, J.: X*: anytime multi-agent path finding for sparse domains using window-based iterative repairs. Artif. Intell. **291**, 103417 (2021)
16. Veloso, M., Biswas, J., Coltin, B., Rosenthal, S.: CoBots: robust symbiotic autonomous mobile service robots. In: Proceedings of the 24th International Joint Conference on Artificial Intelligence (IJCAI), pp. 4423–4429 (2015)
17. Wurman, P.R., D'Andrea, R., Mountz, M.: Coordinating hundreds of cooperative, autonomous vehicles in warehouses. AI Mag. **29**(1), 9 (2008)
18. Yu, J., LaValle, S.M.: Structure and intractability of optimal multi-robot path planning on graphs. In: Proceedings of the 27th AAAI Conference on Artificial Intelligence (AAAI), pp. 1443–1449 (2013)

# A Learning Twolevel Optimization Approach for the Demand Maximizing Battery Swapping Station Location Problem

Laurenz Tomandl[1]($\boxtimes$), Thomas Jatschka[1], Günther Raidl[1],
and Tobias Rodemann[2]

[1] Institute of Logic and Computation, TU Wien, Austria
{ltomandl,jatschka,raidl}@ac.tuwien.ac.at
[2] Honda Research Institute Europe, Offenbach, Germany
tobias.rodemann@honda-ri.de

**Abstract.** The multilevel optimization approach, a strategy for solving large combinatorial optimization problems, involves a process of coarsening a large problem instance into a smaller, more manageable version, solving this simplified instance, and then projecting the solution back to the original problem instance. We propose a two level version of MLO enhanced by integrating machine learning techniques to improve the coarsening process. We demonstrate the efficacy of this approach in addressing a large location allocation problem: the demand maximizing battery swapping station location problem. Our results illustrate that leveraging machine learning to enhance coarsening can improve solution quality by up to 5% and can also reduce computational time, particularly for very large problem instances.

**Keywords:** Multi Level Optimization · Machine Learning · Combinatorial Optimization

## 1 Introduction

Developing effective strategies to scale solution approaches for very large combinatorial optimization problems poses significant challenges. Conventional approaches like Mixed Integer Linear Programming (MILP) perform very well on moderate instance sizes but tend to break if the problem size becomes too large. Therefore the need arises for specialized approaches that can scale with larger problem instances. One such approach is Multilevel Optimization (MLO) [12] which has already been successfully applied to problems such as the traveling salesperson problem [11], bike sharing station planning [4], and vehicle routing [7]. This approach uses three main steps. Firstly, multiple coarsening steps are

This project was financially supported by Honda Research Institute Europe.

applied until the problem is reasonably small in size. Secondly, in a solving step a solution to the coarsest problem instance is produced. Thirdly, repeated projection steps iteratively derive solutions to all larger problem instances until a solution to the original instance is obtained. We adapt this approach to a learning twolevel optimization (LTLO) approach. Our LTLO reduces the multiple coarsening steps into a single step in which multiple elements of the problem are coarsened at once. We do this by employing clustering algorithms such as $k$-medoids, agglomarative clustering or minimum spanning tree clustering. Additionaly, instead of a heuristic to guide the similarity between to be coarsened elements we use a machine learning model that predicts similarities between elements.

In this study, we demonstrate the efficacy of our approach by addressing a large location allocation problem, the Demand Maximizing Battery Swapping Station Location Problem (DMBSSLP). This problem, derived from the Multi Period Battery Swapping Station Location Problem (MBSSLP) introduced by Jatschka et al. [2], focuses on strategically placing battery swapping stations for small-scale electric vehicles within an urban context. Our objective is to optimize the distribution of these stations across a network of potential areas to maximize customer demand fulfillment while adhering to budgetary constraints. Customer demand is represented by the expected number of users traveling between origin-destination pairs (O/D-pairs). We assume that customers select their origin and destination, allowing for specific station assignments. An assigned station might not be on or close to the shortest path, which is why we assume an exponential loss of customers depending on the detour length from the shortest path. Battery swapping stations are subject to capacity constraints, with each station capable of accommodating a limited number of battery recharge slots. Each battery swapping station incurs a setup cost as well as additional expenses associated with each battery slot.

In [8] a Large Neighborhood Search (LNS) is proposed to heuristically solve instances of MBSSLP with up to 2000 areas and 8000 $\Omega$/D-pairs. This approach is later adapted in [3] to a MLO that is able to reasonably address instances with 10000 areas and 100000 $\Omega$/D-pairs on which our implementation is based. The master thesis of Tomandl [9] showed that using a machine learning model combined with an MLO approach is a feasible strategy in the context of DMBSSLP. We experimentally compare our LTLO approach to the version of Jatschka et al. adapted to the DMBSSLP.

Although our LTLO falls short in comparison to a MILP approach, primarily because the specific problem chosen appears to be exceptionally well-suited to be solved by a MILP solver, it outperforms a similar MLO by [3]. To show this we perform an experimental evaluation of our approach, similar to the methodology outlined in [1], using randomly generated artificial benchmark instances containing up to 25600 areas and O/D-pairs. Our findings demonstrate that LTLO enhances solution quality for almost all instances and requires similar computation times for very large instances compared to the MLO from [3]. Furthermore, LTLO outperforms a Two-level Optimization (TLO) approach employing a manually constructed heuristic instead of the learned similarity model in terms of solution quality.

## 2 Demand Maximizing Battery Swapping Station Location Problem

The Demand Maximizing Battery Swapping Station Location Problem (DMBSSLP) is a variation of the Multiperiod Battery Swapping Station Location Problem (MBSSLP) introduced by Jatschka et al. [1]. While the MBSSLP aims to minimize budget expenditure while fulfilling a minimum demand threshold, the DMBSSLP focuses on maximizing demand fulfillment within a fixed budget constraint. To streamline the problem, we eliminate the time dimension and concentrate solely on peak demand times. This simplification allows us to showcase the effectiveness of our LTLO approach more easily. Additionally, we generalize the problem by considering areas for battery swapping stations instead of specific locations, enhancing the interpretability of our LTLO approach which will produce compound locations or areas in the coarse network.

The DMBSSLP is modeled on an undirected bipartite graph $G(Q, L, E)$ with two vertex sets $Q$ and $L$ and an edge set $E$. The set $Q$ represents the O/D-pairs and the set $L$ represents possible areas where battery swapping stations can be built. There are $|Q| = m$ and $|L| = n$ different nodes in each set. The features of an O/D-pair node $q \in Q$ are the number of customers we expect on this O/D-pair called the demand $d_q$, and the set of areas connected to an O/D-pair $q$ is called $N(q) \subseteq L$. The features of an area node $l \in L$ are the maximum number $r_l$ of stations that can be built in that area, the maximum number $s_l$ of battery charging slots each station in that area can hold, the cost for building a station at an area is given by $c_l$, the set of O/D-pairs which are connected to an area $l$ is called $N(l) \subseteq Q$. An edge connecting an area to an O/D-pair signals that at least some partial demand of that O/D-pair can be satisfied at that area. This means the factor $g_{ql}$ represents the percentage of customers who are not lost due to the detour being greater than 0 along this edge. The cost of building a battery slot $b$ is constant for all stations. We can also derive some useful compound features. The total demand that could theoretically be satisfied at an area is $\bar{d}_l = \min(sr_l, \sum_{q \in N(l)} g_{ql} d_q)$. The demand that can flow from an O/D-pair to an area with respect to battery slots built at an area is $\hat{d}_{ql} = \min(\frac{\bar{d}_l}{g_{ql}}, d_q)$.

Concerning these variables, we can describe a MILP formulation for the DMBSSLP. The concrete formulation can be found in the appendix and [9]. Important variables to consider are the $a_{ql}$ and $\bar{a}_{ql}$ values. They are the demand assigned from O/D-pair $q$ to area $l$ and the demand that arrives at area $l$ after the loss is considered respectively.

# 3  Learning Twolevel Optimization for the MBSSLP

## 3.1  Coarsening and Projection

Before diving into the learning aspect of the LTLO, we provide a brief overview of the coarsening and projection processes. A comprehensive description can be found in the appendix and in [9], but is summarized here. Coarsening occurs in two stages. Initially, we coarsen the nodes within the $L$ set, followed by coarsening of the $Q$ set in a subsequent step.

To begin, we establish a partitioning of the nodes. Nodes within each partition are condensed into a singular new node. These partitions are generated using the following clustering algorithms

- $k$-**medoids**, where clusters are formed around a medoid node based on node similarity [5].
- **mst-clustering**, which starts from a minimum spanning tree (mst) and iteratively deletes edges until desired cluster numbers and sizes are attained [13].
- **agglomerative clustering**, where each node begins as its own cluster and merges with other clusters based on similarity, employing different linkage variants to determine cluster similarity. Linkage methods include maximum-linkage, minimum-linkage, average-linkage, and dominant-linking, with the latter prioritizing nodes with higher similarity metrics ($\bar{d}_l$ for area nodes or $d_q$ for O/D-pair nodes) [6]
- **Greedy Heavy Edge Matching** an MLO specific method, which necessitates multiple partitioning steps rather than a single one [10]

Following partitioning, we proceed to coarsen and solve the resulting smaller problem instance. This solution is then projected back to the original problem instance using two separate (MI)LP formulations for the $Q$ and $L$ coarsenings, as detailed in the appendix and in [9].

## 3.2  Learning

Previous approaches such as the one by Jatschka et al. [3] used the Jaccard similarity as a heuristic, which counts the number of common neighbors over the number of total neighbors $J(v_1, v_2) = \frac{|N(v_1) \cap N(v_2)|}{|N(v_1) \cup N(v_2)|}$ as a similarity measure. In contrast, our method utilizes a Neural Network trained to predict the loss of demand when merging two nodes, thus providing a similarity estimation. We developed two separate NNs: one for assessing similarities among the O/D-pair nodes and another for the area nodes.

Training is done in a supervised and offline fashion. Obtaining reasonable training data for the $Q$-NN proves challenging due to the sequence of operations, where coarsening of the O/D-pair nodes occurs subsequent to the coarsening of the area nodes. Consequently, we can only acquire training data for the O/D-pair nodes contingent upon an already established $L$-NN and partitioning method.

Multiple representative instances are created according to the methodology outlined in [1]. To generate training data for the $L$-NN, from a single instance of DMBSSLP, we randomly group nodes into pairs $(l_1, l_2)$. These pairs undergo coarsening, resulting in a coarse node denoted as $l_3$. We derive a dependent variable $z_{l_1 l_2}$ by comparing the loss in demand incurred by coarsening these two specific nodes: $z_{l_1 l_2} = \bar{a}_{ql_3} - \bar{a}_{ql_2} - \bar{a}_{ql_1}$. Here, $\bar{a}_{ql_3}$ signifies the demand satisfied by node $l_3$ in the coarse instance, while $\bar{a}_{ql_1}$ and $\bar{a}_{ql_2}$ represent the satisfied demand of $l_1$ and $l_2$ respectively after the projection. Generally, the satisfied demand in a coarse instance is higher due to a higher connectednes in the coarse problem instance. Our $L$-NN learns to predict this loss of demand, utilizing the following 22 features:

- $r_{l_i}$, $\bar{d}_{l_i}$, $c_{l_i}$ $\hfill i \in 1, 2, 3$
- $\sum_{q \in N(l_1) \cap N(l_2)} d_q$, $\sum_{q \in N(l_1) \triangle N(l_2)} d_q$, $\frac{\sum_{q \in N(l_1) \cap N(l_2)} d_q}{\sum_{q \in N(l_1) \cup N(l_2)} d_q}$
- $\min \left( \sum_{q \in N(l_i)} \hat{d}_{ql_i} g_{ql_i}, \bar{d}_{l_i} \right)$ $\hfill i \in 1, 2, 3$
- $\frac{\sum_{q \in N(l_i)} \hat{d}_{ql_i} g_{ql_i}}{\sum_{q \in N(l_i)} \hat{d}_{ql_i}}$ $\hfill i \in 1, 2, 3$
- $s_{l_3}$, b
- $|N(l_1) \cap N(l_2)|$, $\frac{|N(l_1) \cap N(l_2)|}{|N(l_1) \cup N(l_2)|}$

To train the $Q$-NN effectively, we rely on an $L$-NN and a partitioning method. Coarsening the area nodes is a necessary step before gathering data for the O/D-pair nodes, as skipping this process would render the data non-representative. The data collection process for O/D-pair nodes mirrors that of the area nodes. Initially, we randomly partition O/D-pair nodes as pairs $(q_1, q_2)$ with their corresponding coarse node $q_3$. These pairs undergo coarsening, followed by projecting the solutions back and recording the differences between the coarse and projected solutions, denoted as $z_{q_1 q_2} = \bar{a}_{q_3 l} - \bar{a}_{q_2 l} - \bar{a}_{q_1 l}$. The 20 features recorded for the $Q$-NN are outlined below:

- $d_{q_i}$ $\hfill i \in 1, 2, 3$
- $\sum_{l \in N(q_1) \cap N(q_2)} \bar{d}_l$, $\sum_{l \in N(q_1) \triangle N(q_2)} \bar{d}_l$, $\frac{\sum_{l \in N(q_1) \cap N(q_2)} \bar{d}_l}{\sum_{l \in N(q_1) \cup N(q_2)} \bar{d}_l}$
- $\sum_{l \in N(q_1) \cap N(q_2)} r_l$, $\sum_{l \in N(q_1) \triangle N(q_2)} r_l$, $\frac{\sum_{l \in N(q_1) \cap N(q_2)} r_l}{\sum_{l \in N(q_1) \cup N(q_2)} r_l}$
- $\sum_{l \in N(q_1) \cap N(q_2)} c_l$, $\sum_{l \in N(q_1) \triangle N(q_2)} c_l$, $\frac{\sum_{l \in N(q_1) \cap N(q_2)} c_l}{\sum_{l \in N(q_1) \cup N(q_2)} c_l}$
- $\min \left( \sum_{l \in N(q_i)} \hat{d}_{q_i l}, d_{q_i} \right)$ $\hfill i \in 1, 2, 3$
- $\frac{\sum_{l \in N(q_i)} \hat{d}_{q_i l} g_{q_i l}}{\sum_{l \in N(q_i)} \hat{d}_{q_i l}}$ $\hfill i \in 1, 2, 3$
- $|N(q_1) \cap N(q_2)|$, $\frac{|N(q_1) \cap N(q_2)|}{|N(q_1) \cup N(q_2)|}$

## 4 Experimental Results

All experiments are done on artificial instances created as described in [1]. All computations are done on an AMD EPYC 7402, 2.80GHz 24-core CPU with

**Table 1.** Area node clustering.

| size | ML | | | | | | | Jaccard | | | | | | |
|---|---|---|---|---|---|---|---|---|---|---|---|---|---|---|
| | agglomarative | | | | MLO | $k$-med | mst | agglomarative | | | | MLO | $k$-med | mst |
| | max | min | dom | avg | | | | max | min | dom | avg | | | |
| 100 | 93.4 | 93.5 | 93.3 | 93.4 | 89.4 | 93.0 | 93.2 | 93.4 | 94.2 | 94.3 | **94.6** | 88.7 | 94.2 | 94.4 |
| 200 | 92.6 | 92.6 | 92.6 | 92.6 | 88.6 | **93.0** | 92.7 | 91.4 | 92.3 | 91.9 | 92.6 | 86.9 | 91.5 | 92.3 |
| 400 | 90.1 | 90.5 | 90.7 | 90.3 | 87.0 | **91.0** | 90.5 | 87.5 | 88.0 | 88.2 | 87.3 | 85.8 | 88.1 | 87.7 |
| 800 | 88.9 | 89.0 | 88.6 | 88.5 | 86.9 | **89.3** | 88.9 | 85.2 | 86.1 | 86.3 | 85.9 | 84.9 | 85.8 | 85.8 |
| 1600 | 89.4 | 89.2 | 89.3 | 89.0 | 85.7 | **89.8** | 89.6 | 87.7 | 86.1 | 87.0 | 86.2 | 84.0 | 85.8 | 86.3 |
| 3200 | 89.2 | **89.9** | 89.6 | 89.0 | 85.2 | 89.2 | 89.6 | 85.9 | 86.8 | 86.1 | 86.6 | 83.0 | 86.3 | 86.8 |
| 6400 | 88.6 | **89.3** | 88.4 | 88.2 | 85.0 | 88.9 | 88.9 | 84.6 | 84.7 | 84.2 | 85.1 | 82.4 | 84.7 | 84.5 |
| 12800 | 87.8 | **89.0** | 88.6 | 88.2 | 85.7 | **89.0** | 88.4 | 83.9 | 85.1 | 84.8 | 84.8 | 82.0 | 85.0 | 84.9 |
| 25600 | 86.9 | 87.7 | 87.1 | 86.7 | 84.4 | 88.4 | **88.8** | 84.4 | 85.1 | 85.1 | 85.5 | 81.8 | 85.1 | 84.8 |

up to 50GB Memory. Consistency of problem instances is maintained across experiments and training procedures, employing only instances with identical numbers of areas and O/D-pairs denoted as $n = m$. The NNs are trained on a total of 9000 instances, with 3000 instances each of sizes 1600, 3200, and 6400.

Each instance is used once in the training process, yielding about 1.6 Million datapoints for the $Q$-NN and 170.000 datapoints for the $L$-NN in total. Disparities in the number of generated data points stem from the selective recording criteria; a data point is logged for area nodes only if at least one station is constructed there, and for O/D-pair nodes only if partial demand is satisfied. Consequently, O/D-pair nodes are more likely to be relevant to the solution due to the fulfillment of most demands, while fewer areas actually host built stations.

The architectures of the NNs are varied, incorporating different widths, lengths, and regularization techniques, alongside reduced datasets. Early stopping is used during training. As activation function ReLU is applied in all hidden layers, with Mean Squared Error (MSE) loss utilized for training. The target variables are scaled using symlog transformation. Generalizability tests entail evaluations on 30 independent instances across varied sizes ranging from 100 to 25600.

The manually tuned models for L-nodes yielded the following parametrization for the best found network architecture as 2 hidden layers of 80 nodes each, trained using only 1% of the training data and a batch size of 256. When using larger samples of 20% or 80% of the training data we observed immediate overfitting in the first epoch. To counteract this we explored regularization procedures but what proved to be most effective was to just reduce the number of samples used in training. Results are presented in Table 1, showcasing the average solution quality as a percentage of fulfilled demand over 30 instances. The columns of the table represent different applied partitioning methods on the area nodes using either the learned similarity, shown on the left side, or the Jaccard similarity, on the right side. The rows represent the results concerning the different instance sizes. Notably, for instances of size 25600, not all instances could be solved within the 24-hour time limit. Results demonstrate the learned models robust generalization to both larger and smaller problem instances, with the exception of the smallest instances (size 100), where the ML-model is slightly outperformed by the Jaccard similarity. Additionally, consistency across different partitioning methods is evident, albeit with the MLO method exhibiting slightly inferior performance. The utilization of ML-similarity yields improvements ranging from 1% to 4% across the varying scenarios.

**Table 2.** O/D-pair node clustering.

| size | ML agglomarative | | | | MLO | k-med | mst | Jaccard agglomarative | | | | MLO | k-med | mst |
| --- | --- | --- | --- | --- | --- | --- | --- | --- | --- | --- | --- | --- | --- | --- |
| | max | min | dom | avg | | | | max | min | dom | avg | | | |
| 100 | 93.6 | 92.9 | 89.6 | 93.5 | 93.1 | 93.6 | **93.8** | 93.1 | 93.7 | 90.2 | 93.2 | 93.1 | 93.3 | 93.2 |
| 200 | 92.4 | 92.5 | 88.1 | **92.7** | 91.8 | 92.5 | 92.6 | 92.6 | 92.4 | 88.7 | 92.5 | 92.4 | 92.6 | **92.7** |
| 400 | 89.6 | 90.0 | 87.2 | 90.1 | 89.6 | 90.2 | 90.5 | 90.2 | 89.8 | 87.6 | 90.0 | 90.3 | 90.2 | **90.7** |
| 800 | 89.4 | 88.4 | 85.8 | 89.5 | 88.3 | 89.5 | **90.0** | 89.0 | 89.0 | 87.1 | 89.0 | 89.5 | 89.5 | 89.4 |
| 1600 | 89.3 | 89.2 | 84.7 | 89.8 | 88.7 | 90.2 | **90.2** | 89.5 | 88.9 | 86.0 | 89.9 | 89.4 | 89.2 | 89.4 |
| 3200 | 89.2 | 88.8 | 84.1 | 89.9 | 89.0 | **90.2** | 90.1 | 89.2 | 88.7 | 85.1 | 89.0 | 89.0 | 89.1 | 89.5 |
| 6400 | 89.1 | 88.3 | 83.5 | 89.7 | 88.5 | 89.8 | **89.9** | 88.4 | 88.3 | 85.1 | 88.5 | 88.4 | 88.5 | 88.5 |
| 12800 | 88.8 | 88.2 | 82.2 | 89.4 | 88.2 | 89.7 | **89.8** | 88.2 | 87.8 | 84.5 | 88.1 | 88.0 | 88.3 | 88.3 |
| 25600 | 89.4 | 89.1 | 79.8 | 89.8 | 88.2 | 90.2 | **90.4** | 88.8 | 89.0 | 82.8 | 88.2 | 88.8 | 88.6 | 89.3 |

In Table 2, we present the average solution quality obtained by employing the $L$-NN for the area node partitioning, utilizing mst-clustering along with either Jaccard similarity based partitioning for the O/D-pair nodes, shown on the right side, or partitioning based on our tuned $Q$-NN with 120 nodes in the first hidden layer, followed by a dropout layer of 30% and a final hidden layer of 80 nodes, shown on the left side. The columns again represent different clustering strategies used for partitioning while the rows represent the different instance sizes. The learned similarity in the second step still yields improvements, albeit less pronounced compared to the initial learned $L$-NN similarity, typically ranging from 0.2% to 1%. This suggests that achieving a proficient partitioning of the area nodes holds more significance for solution quality than optimizing the partitioning of the O/D-pair nodes. Moreover, it is observed that mst-clustering consistently outperforms other partitioning methods or performs at least equally as well, except in a single instance where the $k$-medoids method yields superior partitioning. This could potentially be attributed to the initial clustering also being an mst-clustering, although further testing is necessary for confirmation. We also observe that agglomerative clustering using dominant linkage works well considering the $L$-NN but fails for the $Q$-NN as the results are much worse.

Regarding computation time, we found that the MLO method exhibited the slowest performance. Conversely, all other partitioning methods demonstrated similar computation times. An intriguing observation was that for nearly all instance sizes, the Jaccard similarity exhibited faster computation times compared to the ML-similarity. However, for the largest problem instances, the Jaccard similarity was slower in the context of area node clustering, yet took approximately the same time for the O/D-pair node clustering setting. A small extract can be seen in Table 3.

**Table 3.** Area node LTLO computation time in seconds.

| size | ML | | | | | | | Jaccard | | | | | | |
|---|---|---|---|---|---|---|---|---|---|---|---|---|---|---|
| | agglomarative | | | | MLO | k-med | mst | agglomarative | | | | MLO | k-med | mst |
| | max | min | dom | avg | | | | max | min | dom | avg | | | |
| 100 | 1.41 | 1.42 | 1.32 | 1.40 | 1.48 | 1.37 | 1.30 | 1.24 | 1.20 | 1.17 | 1.18 | 0.95 | 1.19 | 1.19 |
| 200 | 2.28 | 2.36 | 2.38 | 2.33 | 3.20 | 2.17 | 1.98 | 1.90 | 1.88 | 1.85 | 1.78 | 2.10 | 1.51 | 1.55 |
| 400 | 4.50 | 4.50 | 4.54 | 4.58 | 7.33 | 3.77 | 3.47 | 3.05 | 3.23 | 3.16 | 3.18 | 3.78 | 2.43 | 2.41 |
| 800 | 12.6 | 12.9 | 12.7 | 12.7 | 19.7 | 10.7 | 10.1 | 9.45 | 9.81 | 10.1 | 10.4 | 13.5 | 6.41 | 6.51 |
| 1600 | 35.7 | 36.5 | 37.0 | 36.0 | 58.5 | 29.3 | 29.3 | 16.0 | 16.5 | 16.6 | 17.0 | 23.7 | 12.6 | 12.6 |
| 3200 | 76.2 | 77.0 | 86.8 | 73.2 | 118.4 | 64.7 | 72.2 | 73.0 | 76.2 | 72.7 | 70.5 | 101.3 | 65.5 | 64.1 |
| 6400 | 310 | 297 | 314 | 318 | 508 | 282 | 290 | 271 | 270 | 243 | 244 | 341 | 278 | 231 |
| 12800 | 1210 | 1150 | 1260 | 1240 | 1600 | 1140 | 1080 | 1020 | 1160 | 1060 | 1100 | 1420 | 1040 | 1060 |
| 25600 | 6530 | 6480 | 6210 | 6710 | 6980 | 5960 | 4640 | 7250 | 7960 | 7330 | 8120 | 9730 | 8640 | 7370 |

## 5    Conclusion and Future Research

We introduced a novel two-level optimization approach for enhancing results in the DMBSSLP, surpassing former multi-level methods reliant on basic heuristics. We trained two networks one for area node similarity and another for O/D-pair node similarity. Experimental results demonstrate significant enhancements: the learned area node similarity yielded improvements of up to 4% compared to Jaccard similarity, while the learned O/D-pair node similarity showed enhancements of up to 1%. When combined, these improvements reached up to 5%.

However, our learning approach's effectiveness was somewhat diminished when implemented in the context of the DMBSSLP, as it was surpassed by a MILP approach which achieved solution qualities of over 94% for the largest instance and was 20 times faster than the other approaches. This is due to both scalability issues resulting from the resource-intensive and slow clustering methods used for partitioning, as well as DMBSSLP being exceptionally well suited to be solved by MILP. Addressing this limitation could involve employing more efficient clustering techniques such as power iteration clustering or implementing direct clustering using machine learning algorithms as well as experimentation on a different set of optimization problems. Another potential improvement could involve modifying the training process to incorporate data from merged clusters rather than merged node pairs using reinforcement learning approaches as a suitable training scheme. Additionally, exploring the integration of Graph Neural Networks instead of densely connected multi-layer perceptrons holds promise, given the problem's inherent graph structure, which aligns well with such an approach.

## Appendix

In this appendix, we provide an overview of the (MI)LP formulations employed to solve DMBSSLP as well as the coarsening procedure to create a coarse instance from a partitioning. The MILP formulation of DMBSSLP is as described in formulas (1)-(8):

The objective (1) is to find the solutions that maximize the fulfilled demand. With the inequality (2) we link the $x$ and $y$ variables and ensure that slots are only opened if a sufficient number of stations are opened in the area. Constraint (3) enforces that the total amount of demand assigned from an OD-pair to an area does not exceed the given demand of the OD-pair. Inequality (4) ensures that the total amount of demand assigned to an area is smaller than the number of slots at the location. With constraint (5) we assert that the total cost of all stations and slots stays within the bounds of the available budget. Lastly, the domain of the $x_l$, $y_l$, and $a_{ql}$ variables are given in (6)-(8).

$$\max \& \sum_{q \in Q} \sum_{l \in N(q)} a_{ql} g_{ql} \tag{1}$$

$$s x_l \geq y_l \qquad\qquad l \in L \tag{2}$$

$$\sum_{l \in N(q)} a_{ql} \leq d_q \qquad\qquad q \in Q \tag{3}$$

$$\sum_{q \in N(l)} a_{ql} \leq y_l \qquad\qquad l \in L \tag{4}$$

$$\sum_{l \in L} (c_l x_l + b_l y_l) \leq B \tag{5}$$

$$x_l \in \{0, \ldots, r_l\} \qquad\qquad l \in L \tag{6}$$

$$y_l \in \{0, \ldots, \lceil \bar{d}_l \rceil\} \qquad\qquad l \in L \tag{7}$$

$$0 \leq a_{ql} \leq \hat{d}_{ql} \qquad\qquad q \in Q, \ l \in N(q) \tag{8}$$

The coarsening of the nodes can be described as follows. The partitioned nodes are collapsed and form a new node which is described in terms of its features and neighbors. We call the set of nodes that is collapsed $L'$ and $Q'$ into a new node $l'$ and $q'$, respectively. The features are then calculated as follows. $N_{l'} = \bigcup_{l \in L'} N(l)$ nodes are neighbored if they are neighbored to at least one collapsed node. The demand assigned along an edge is bound by the demand of that O/D-pair and by the demand along the edges of the collapsed nodes $\hat{d}_{ql'} = \min\left(\sum_{l\in L'} \hat{d}_{q,l}, \, d_q\right)$. The customers not lost can be updated as $g_{ql'} = \frac{\sum_{l\in L'} \hat{d}_{ql} g_{ql}}{\sum_{l\in L'} \hat{d}_{ql}}$. The maximum demand at a station is derived from the previous maximum demands and the new maximum demand flows $\bar{d}'_l = \min\left(\sum_{l\in L'} \bar{d}_l, \, \sum_{q\in N(l')} g_{ql'}\hat{d}_{ql'}\right)$. The setup cost of a station is the weighted average over the maximum demands $c_{l'} = \frac{\sum_{l\in L'} \bar{d}_l c_l}{\sum_{l\in L'} \bar{d}_l}$ and lastly the number of stations allowed to be built at an area is $r_{l'} = \left\lceil \frac{\bar{d}'_l}{s} \right\rceil$. With this information we can obtain a partially coarsened graph where the $L'$ nodes are collapsed. To collapse the $Q'$ we use the following formulas. We consider nodes neighbored if at least one other node is neighbored in the original graph $N_{q'} = \bigcup_{q\in Q'} N(q)$. We update the $g$-factor using the following formula $g_{q'l'} = \frac{\sum_{q\in Q'} \hat{d}_{ql'} \cdot g_{ql'}}{\sum_{q\in Q'} \hat{d}_{ql'}}$. The demand along the edges is updated as $\hat{d}_{q'l'} = \min\left(\sum_{q\in Q'} \hat{d}_{ql'}, \, \frac{\bar{d}'_l}{g_{q'l'}}\right)$ Finally the demands are updated as $d_{q'} = \min\left(\sum_{q\in Q'} d_q, \sum_{l\in N(q')} \hat{d}_{q'l}\right)$.

For projection we follow the reverse coarsening order and first project the O/D-pair nodes projecting the node $q'$ back to the set $Q'$ of original nodes. This is done via a set of independant Linear Programs for each node $q'$.

$$\max \& \sum_{q\in Q'} \sum_{l'\in N^i(q)} \tilde{a}_{ql'} g_{ql'} \tag{9}$$

$$\sum_{l\in N(q)} \tilde{a}_{ql} \le d_q \qquad\qquad q\in Q' \tag{10}$$

$$\sum_{q\in N(l')\cap Q'} g_{ql'}\tilde{a}_{ql'} \le g_{q'l'} a_{q'l'} \qquad\qquad l' \in N(q') \tag{11}$$

$$0 \le \tilde{a}_{ql'} \le \hat{d}_{ql'} \qquad\qquad q\in Q', \, l'\in N(q') \tag{12}$$

The LP maximizes the satisfied demand $\tilde{a}_{ql'}$ (9). Constraint (10) ensures that the allocated demand does not exceed the available demand. With (11) the allocated demand from the coarse solution is not exceeded. Constraint (12) gives the domain for $\tilde{a}_{ql'}$.

To project the node $l'$ back to $L'$ we use the following MILP model

$$\max \& \sum_{l \in L'} \sum_{q \in N(l)} a_{ql} g_{ql} \tag{13}$$

$$sx_l \geq y_l \qquad\qquad l \in L' \quad (14)$$

$$\sum_{l \in L' \cap N(q)} a_{ql} \leq \delta_q \qquad\qquad q \in N(l') \quad (15)$$

$$\sum_{q \in N(l)} a_{ql} \leq y_l \qquad\qquad l \in L' \quad (16)$$

$$\sum_{l \in L'} (c_l x_l + b y_l) \leq c_{l'} x_{l'} + b_{l'} y_{l'} \tag{17}$$

$$x_l \in \{0, \ldots, r_l\} \qquad\qquad l \in L' \quad (18)$$

$$y_l \in \{0, \ldots, \lceil \bar{d}_l \rceil\} \qquad\qquad l \in L' \quad (19)$$

$$0 \leq a_{ql} \leq \hat{d}_{ql} \qquad\qquad l \in L', \ q \in N(l) \quad (20)$$

The model maximizes satisfied demand in the variable $a_{ql}$ in (13). We link the $x$ and $y$ variables (14). The right hand side of constraint (15) represents the demand that is still unsatisfied considering the node $q$. We calculate it as $\delta_q = d_q + \tilde{a}_{ql'} - \sum_{l \in N(q) \setminus S} \tilde{a}_{ql} - \sum_{l \in S'} a_{ql}$ where $S$ is the set of already projected coarse $l'$ nodes and $S'$ is the set of respective projected $l$ nodes. Because of this the MILP problems are no longer independent and are solved in order of the highest satisfied demand to cost ratio as preliminary experiments have shown that this order yields the highest overall satisfied demand. Following this we have constraint (16) which bounds the demand with the number of built slots. Followed by inequality (17) which restricts the budget for the projected nodes with the budget of the coarse node. Constraint (18)-(20) give the domain for the variables.

# References

1. Jatschka, T., Oberweger, F.F., Rodemann, T., Raidl, G.R.: Distributing battery swapping stations for electric scooters in an urban area. In: Olenev, N., Evtushenko, Y., Khachay, M., Malkova, V. (eds.) Optimization and Applications: 11th International Conference, OPTIMA 2020, Moscow, Russia, September 28 – October 2, 2020, Proceedings, pp. 150–165. Springer International Publishing, Cham (2020). https://doi.org/10.1007/978-3-030-62867-3_12
2. Jatschka, T., Rauscher, M., Kreutzer, B., Okamoto, Y., Kataoka, H., Rodemann, T., Raidl, G.R.: A large neighborhood search for battery swapping station location planning for electric scooters. In: Moreno-Díaz, R., Pichler, F., Quesada-Arencibia, A. (eds.) Computer Aided Systems Theory – EUROCAST 2022: 18th International Conference, Las Palmas de Gran Canaria, Spain, February 20–25, 2022, Revised Selected Papers, pp. 121–129. Springer Nature Switzerland, Cham (2022). https://doi.org/10.1007/978-3-031-25312-6_14

3. Jatschka, T., Rodemann, T., Raidl, G.R.: A multilevel optimization approach for large scale battery exchange station location planning. In: Pérez Cáceres, L., Stützle, T. (eds.) Evolutionary Computation in Combinatorial Optimization: 23rd European Conference, EvoCOP 2023, Held as Part of EvoStar 2023, Brno, Czech Republic, April 12–14, 2023, Proceedings, pp. 50–65. Springer Nature Switzerland, Cham (2023). https://doi.org/10.1007/978-3-031-30035-6_4

4. Kloimüllner, C., Raidl, G.R.: Hierarchical clustering and multilevel refinement for the bike-sharing station planning problem. In: Battiti, R., Kvasov, D.E., Sergeyev, Y.D. (eds.) Learning and Intelligent Optimization, pp. 150–165. Springer International Publishing, Cham (2017). https://doi.org/10.1007/978-3-319-69404-7_11

5. Van der Laan, M., Pollard, K., Bryan, J.: A new partitioning around medoids algorithm. J. Stat. Comput. Simul. **73**(8), 575–584 (2003)

6. Murtagh, F., Contreras, P.: Algorithms for hierarchical clustering: an overview. Wiley Interdisc. Rev. Data Min. Knowl. Discov. **2**(1), 86–97 (2012)

7. Pirkwieser, S., Raidl, G.R.: Multilevel variable neighborhood search for periodic routing problems. In: Cowling, P., Merz, P. (eds.) Evolutionary Computation in Combinatorial Optimization, pp. 226–238. Springer Berlin Heidelberg, Berlin, Heidelberg (2010). https://doi.org/10.1007/978-3-642-12139-5_20

8. Rodemann, T., Kataoka, H., Jatschka, T., Raidl, G.R., Limmer, S., Hiromu, M.: Optimizing the positions of battery swapping stations. In: Proceedings to the 6th International Electric Vehicle Technology Conference. JSAE (2023)

9. Tomandl, L.: A learning multilevel optimization approach for a large location allocation problem. Master Thesis, TU Wien, Austria (2023)

10. Valejo, A., Ferreira, V., Fabbri, R., Oliveira, M.C.F.d., Lopes, A.d.A.: A critical survey of the multilevel method in complex networks. ACM Comput. Surv. (CSUR) **53**(2), 1–35 (2020)

11. Walshaw, C.: A multilevel approach to the travelling salesman problem. Oper. Res. **50**(5), 862–877 (2004)

12. Walshaw, C.: Multilevel refinement for combinatorial optimisation problems. Ann. Oper. Res. **131**(1), 325–372 (2004)

13. Xu, Y., Olman, V., Xu, D.: Clustering gene expression data using a graph-theoretic approach: an application of minimum spanning trees. Bioinformatics **18**(4), 536–545 (2002)

# Learning Value Functions for Same-Day Delivery Problems in the Tardiness Regime

Nikolaus Frohner$^{(\boxtimes)}$ and Günther R. Raidl

Institute of Logic and Computation, TU Wien, Vienna, Austria
{nfrohner,raidl}@ac.tuwien.ac.at

**Abstract.** Same-day delivery problems are a class of stochastic decision making problems concerned with delivering orders placed dynamically by stochastic customers on the same day given a fleet of vehicles. We consider a variant where all orders have to be served with the objective to minimize a tardiness penalty function and where their spatiotemporal distribution is known. A well-known baseline approach to increase performance compared to myopic optimization is by sampling and optimizing scenarios in the short-horizon and deriving a consensus solution from the resulting plans. Its drawback is the computational effort required, which may not make it suitable for near real-time decision making. Extending recent methodology from the literature, we replace this online sampling by an offline training of a short-horizon value function using a neural network, which is then used in the online point-in-time optimization, combining current reward plus estimated future value of a solution candidate. In a first computational study on a single-vehicle instance class with unavoidable tardiness, we show that this leads to comparable performance as the sampling approach, while greatly reducing the online decision time.

**Keywords:** Same-Day Delivery · Dynamic Vehicle Routing with Stochastic Customers · Surrogate Function Optimization · Value Function Approximation

## 1 Introduction

In the recent years, same-day delivery problems [9] have gained much attention due to the exploding demand in the fast delivery of goods sparked by the COVID-19 pandemic. They are dynamic vehicle routing problem variants with stochastic customers and have the goal to satisfy customer demand subject to short deadlines efficiently. The orders are mostly unknown in advance and are dealt with upon their availability, hence the route plans change frequently throughout the day, as opposed to static problem variants. Stochastic information is available

---

Postponed publication of the EUROCAST 2022.

as spatiotemporal distribution of those orders, often based on prediction models derived from historical data.

In this work, we consider a problem variant where orders arrive in a delivery area throughout the day and are due within one or two hours upon arrival. As opposed to some other variants in the literature [8,9], every order has to be served and cannot be rejected or delegated to a third party. This is compensated by allowing deadline violations—tardiness—and imposing a penalty upon them. The goal of our problem variant is to minimize a given expected tardiness-dependent penalty function, which is a parameter to the problem. We therefore call it the *Same-Day Delivery Problem with Tardiness Penalty* (SDDPTP). It is a modified variant of [3] focusing on the tardiness aspect, which we formulate as route-based Markov decision process in Sect. 2.

For many different dynamic and stochastic vehicle routing problems [6] a decrease in costs/increase in service level is observed when properly including information about future orders over using solely myopic optimization. A general method to deal with those is based on sampling multiple scenarios consisting of real and sampled orders, solving them, and deriving a consensus solution from the different scenario solutions [1,9]. A drawback of this online method is the high computational demand and resulting runtime at each decision epoch.

For faster decision making, the computational effort is moved to an offline learning phase, where helpful functions are trained to guide the online optimization. For a recent review on methodology for stochastic vehicle routing see Soeffker et al. [7]. In a previous work by Bracher et al. [2] upon which we build, the scenario sampling is only used in an offline phase to train a faster surrogate function to be used in the point-in-time optimization estimating the future mean travel time of routes that can still be delayed. We propose a similar approach in Sect. 3, with the main difference of estimating the tardiness penalty that will accrue in the short-horizon when a specific route is started by a driver.

Section 4 contains our computational study, where we describe the generation of the SDDPTP instances, how we derive the training and test data for the training and evaluation of our machine learning model, and subsequent performance evaluation on unseen full-day test instances. We restrict ourselves to the single vehicle case with a constant load pattern and compare our value function approach with myopic optimization and state-of-the-art scenario sampling. We observe a new promising routing strategy emerging that prefers shorter routes and early depot returns. It leads to substantially reduced tardiness on both training and unseen test data when compared with myopic optimization and comes close to the computationally much more expensive scenario sampling approach.

## 2   Problem Formalization

In this section, we describe the SDDPTP in detail and model it as Markov decision process following the route-based modeling of Ulmer et al. [8] and Voccia et al. [9], where we make suitable adaptions for our problem variant.

## 2.1   Route-Based Markov Decision Process

We are given vehicles $u \in U$, $|U| = m$ with the respective drivers' shift start times $q_u^{\text{start}}$ and respective end times $q_u^{\text{end}}$. Customers are identified as points in a service area $\mathcal{A}$, within which also the depot $\mathcal{D}$ is located. The gross travel time between two orders $C_1, C_2$ (or one order $C_1$ and the depot $\mathcal{D}$) is denoted as $d(C_1, C_2)$. The stop time at a customer is denoted as $\zeta^{\text{c}}$, the loading time at the depot when starting a route as $\zeta^{\text{d}}$, the manipulation time when returning to the depot $\zeta^{\text{r}}$. All those times are assumed to be constant and included in the travel time function $d$.

Orders arrive at times $t^{\text{arr}}(C_i)$ within a planning horizon $[0, H]$ and become immediately available for loading. The deadlines are either one hour or two hour after arrival following a binomial process, given the probability of a one hour order $p_1$ and for two hour orders $p_2 = 1 - p_1$. No orders are known in advance, all orders have to be delivered by performing multiple unalterable tours, where starting a trip after the assigned drivers shift end time $q_u^{\text{end}}$ is not allowed, but finishing is. If after the final return of the last vehicle there are still orders left, the solution is not feasible. All tours start and end at the depot.

The decision epochs $k \in \{0, \dots, K\}$ are triggered by either the vehicles' returns to the depot at times $t(k)$ or when they are ready again after having decided to wait in the depot. The process consists of pre-decision states $S_k$, post-decision states $S_k^x$, and transitions from the latter to the earlier. By definition of our decision epochs, we know that at least one vehicle is in the depot. The set of known orders ready for delivery is denoted by $\mathcal{C}_k$. Each order is included in exactly one driver's feasible tour, which are of the form:

$$\theta_{u,k} = (\mathcal{D}, C_{y_u(1)}, \dots, C_{y_u(l_{u,1})}, \mathcal{D}, C_{y_u(l_{u,1}+1)}, \dots, C_{y_u(l_{u,1}+l_{u,2})}, \mathcal{D}, \dots, \mathcal{D}), \quad (1)$$

with possible multiple returns to the depot. The assignments of the orders to vehicles are denoted by $y_u(o)$ where $o$ is the position in the planned feasible tour and the $l_{u,j}$ is the number of orders of the $j$-th route, its length. The drivers' return times to the depot are denoted by $\boldsymbol{\rho}_k = (\rho_{k,u})_{u \in U}$. The pre-decision state is hence a tuple $S_k = (t(k), \boldsymbol{\theta}_k, \boldsymbol{\rho}_k, \mathcal{C}_k)$, where $\boldsymbol{\theta}_k$ contains the orders from $k - 1$.

Each pre-decision state contains all relevant information to determine further routing plans and induces a set of possible decisions $x \in \mathcal{X}(S_k)$. A decision deals with planning feasible routes for remaining order $\mathcal{C}_k$ and deciding, whether to start the first one of the planned routes now or wait for a time $\Delta$ in the depot, where they could make a short break. Let $\tau(\boldsymbol{\theta}_k)$ be the *raw* tardiness related to the planned routes, which is used in the tardiness penalty function supplied as a parameter to the problem. For each order $C_i$, $a_i(\boldsymbol{\theta}_k)$ denotes the completion of the delivery (assumed to occur after half the stop time) when the plans $\boldsymbol{\theta}_k$ would be executed as-is starting from the current time $t(k)$ or from the earliest depot return time $\rho_{k,u} > t(k)$. This incurs a raw tardiness $\tau_i(\boldsymbol{\theta}_k) = \max(0, a_i(\boldsymbol{\theta}_k) - t_i^{\text{due}})$ per order. We consider the linear tardiness penalty function $\xi^{\text{linear}} = \sum_{i \in \boldsymbol{\theta}_k} \tau_i(\boldsymbol{\theta}_k)$, where with slight abuse of notation $i \in \boldsymbol{\theta}_k$ denote the orders by their indices in the route plan.

We set the (in our case to be minimized) reward $R(S_k, x)$ to the difference in overall tardiness penalty between the plans, i.e., the increase of tardiness:

$$R(S_k, x) = \sum_{i \in \theta_k^x} \xi_i(\boldsymbol{\theta}_k) - \sum_{i \in \theta_k} \xi_i(\boldsymbol{\theta}_k^x). \tag{2}$$

The post-decision state is then $S_k^x = (t(k), \boldsymbol{\theta}_k^x, \boldsymbol{\rho}_k^x, \tilde{\mathcal{C}}_k)$, where $\boldsymbol{\rho}_k^x$ are the drivers' return times at the depot and $\tilde{\mathcal{C}}_k$ the remaining—planned, but not yet started to be served—customers. Two principal actions per vehicle in depot are possible: In case we decide to start a driver's first route with customers $\mathcal{C}_{u,k}^1$, they are excluded from $\tilde{\mathcal{C}}_k = \mathcal{C}_k \setminus \mathcal{C}_{u,k}^1$, while $\rho_{k,u}^x$ is set to $t(k) + \bar{d}(\theta_{u,k}^1)$, with $\bar{d}(\theta_{u,k}^1)$ being the duration of the first route in driver $u$'s plan. If we decide to let the vehicle wait in the depot, then $\rho_{k,u}$ is set to $t(k) + \Delta$. Note the action space explosion, since we have to select from the set of ordered subsets of all the remaining customers and assign to the drivers.

From post-decision to pre-decision state a stochastic transition is performed, in terms of realized orders $\mathcal{C}_r(k+1)$ becoming available between $t(k)$ and $t(k+1)$. This updates the set of remaining orders from the previous post-decision state $\mathcal{C}(k+1) = \tilde{\mathcal{C}}(k) \cup \mathcal{C}_r(k+1)$. Furthermore, the return times $\boldsymbol{\rho}$ and the route plans $\boldsymbol{\theta}_k^x$ are carried over excluding the started routes. The initial state $S_0$ is:

$$(\min_{u \in U} q_u^{\text{start}}, ((\mathcal{D}, \mathcal{D})_1, \dots, (\mathcal{D}, \mathcal{D})_m), q^{\text{start}}, \mathcal{C}_0), \tag{3}$$

where we have an empty routes for each vehicle and the orders $\mathcal{C}_0$ that have already arrived, before the first vehicle has started its shift. The final state $S_K$ is either at $q_u^{\text{end}}$ of the last vehicle or at the last depot return of a vehicle after that, without a route plan and the customers left (ideally none), assuming that there is always one driver shift end after $H$.

The goal is to find an optimal policy $\pi^* \in \Pi$ so that the expected reward starting from the initial state is minimized:

$$\pi^* = \arg\min_{\pi \in \Pi} \mathbb{E}\left[\sum_{k=0}^{K} R(S_k, X_k^\pi(S_k)) | S_0\right], \tag{4}$$

where $X_k^\pi(S_k)$ is the decision rule, selecting a decision when in state $S_k$ according to policy $\pi$. The related Bellman equation for the values of states under an optimal policy is given by

$$V(S_k) = \min_{x \in \mathcal{X}(S_k)} \{R(S_k, x) + V(S_k^x)\}. \tag{5}$$

With the state and action space explosion, there is no hope to solve this equation in practice exactly by backward induction known from exact dynamic programming and we have to make use of approximate/heuristic methods.

# 3 Short-Horizon Value Function Approximation

Due to the infamous "curse of dimensionality", the Bellman equation needs to be solved approximately using forward passes and approximating the state's value function, which represents the expected sum of rewards following a given policy:

$$\hat{V}(S_k) = \min_{x \in \mathcal{X}(S_k)} \{R(S_k, x) + \hat{V}(S_k^x)\} \tag{6}$$

Ulmer et al. [8] employ an approximate value iteration scheme with state space aggregation, where the states are mapped to a different, coarse-grained state space representation. Approximate values $\hat{V}$ are stored in a lookup table, which is randomly initialized for all the proxy states and then used to solve (6) when playing out a randomly sampled episode. Joe and Lau [4] employ a reinforcement learning approach, using temporal difference learning with a neural network instead for the value function approximation to train the $\hat{V}$ offline.

We take a surrogate function approach and follow up on a previous work from Bracher et al. [2] training a value function using supervised learning. We do not seek to estimate the $\hat{V}$ until the end of the day but instead restrict ourselves to the value accumulated in the near future denoted as $\hat{V}(S_k^x)|_{t(k)+\delta}$, where $\delta$ is the duration of the corresponding short horizon. As with scenario sampling approaches, the main assumption is that decisions have the most impact on the near feature, which is deemed sufficient to consider for a substantial improvement.

To generate the training data, we run simulations of full-day instances following our Markov decision process. At every epoch, different decisions are sampled from the decision space and evaluated by sampling and solving a set of scenarios within $[t(k), t(k) + \delta]$ and calculating the average tardiness. These are solved as offline problems with perfect knowledge in the short-horizon and therefore in general resulting in an underestimation of the costs of any policy. We use them as labels to train a surrogate model $\tilde{V}(S_k^x; \boldsymbol{w}) \approx \hat{V}(S_k^x)|_{t(k)+\delta} + \sum_{i \in \boldsymbol{\theta}_{k+1}} \xi_i(\boldsymbol{\theta}_{k+1})$ with parameters $\boldsymbol{w}$, where the second term is the tardiness of the remaining orders, which are part of the offline problem. Features are derived from the post-decision state and the instance, like the number of expected orders until $t(k) + \delta$ or the tardiness in the remaining orders' route plan. In this offline phase, the actual decision selected is with probability $\epsilon$ the best-ranked decision or one at random ($\epsilon$-greedy exploration).

Since shorter routes lead to more available shift time in the short-horizon for the offline problem, we expect that their costs are even more underestimated when compared with longer routes. To mitigate this, we multiply the surrogate model with a correction function $\Gamma(S_k^x, \boldsymbol{w}^{\Gamma})$. It is not trained by supervised learning, but tuned on the full-day training instances in a second phase. A new online strategy is created by heuristically searching at each epoch for the decision $x \in \mathcal{X}(S_k)$ that minimizes $R(S_k, x) + \Gamma(S_k^x; \boldsymbol{w}^{\Gamma}) \cdot \tilde{V}(S_k^x; \boldsymbol{w}) - \sum_{i \in \boldsymbol{\theta}_{k+1}} \xi_i(\boldsymbol{\theta}_{k+1})$, where we need to subtract once the known tardiness of the remaining orders, since they are both considered in $R$ and $\tilde{V}$.

## 4    Computational Study

We implemented the Markov decision process simulator and an adapative large neighborhood search (ALNS) routing heuristic in Python 3.9. The details of the latter are described in more detail in [3]. For the neural network training we used Tensorflow Keras 2.8.[1] All training and test runs were performed on a machine with 2×Intel Xeon Gold 6126 with 12 cores each and 2×Nvidia Tesla P100-PCIE-16GB GPUs using the Grid'5000 testbed.[2]

We consider an instance class with $\omega = 4$ hourly orders to arrive following a Poissonian distribution for a time frame of eight hours, starting from relative time 0 to $8 \cdot 3600$ seconds, with one-hour order frequency of $p = 0.6$, two-hour order frequency of 0.4. The depot is central and the orders' positions follow a uniform distribution on the unit disc, where drivers move with constant pace of 15 minutes per unit on an Euklidean geometry. Constant times are $\zeta^d = 3$ mins, $\zeta^c = 3$ mins, and $\zeta^r = 2$ mins. We restrict ourselves to one driver with shift start at relative time 1h, i.e., $t(k) = 3600$, and ending it at 15h, so that there is enough time to deliver the orders. The instances are designed in a way that tardiness is unavoidable in almost all routes, the eponymous tardiness regime. Hence, starting routes early seems more attractive than delaying, since we are most of the time behind schedule. Therefore we fix the route starting strategy to *earliest*, i.e., if a route is assigned to a driver it is immediately started, otherwise (e.g., when no orders are available or another driver serves the orders) the driver waits for $\Delta = 5$ minutes.

We estimate the performance of decisions $x$ by the sum of the current reward $R(S_k^x)$ and its value in the short horizon $\hat{V}(S_k^x)|_{t(k)+\delta}$ at $t(k) + \delta$, $\delta = 2$ h. Given the recursive nature of the problem, the value is estimated by sampling 30 scenarios until $t(k)+\delta$ and solving the corresponding offline problems, minimizing tardiness as primary and travel time as secondary objective using the ALNS with 100 iterations—see Sect. 3 for more details.

**Table 1.** Performance evaluation neural network on training and validation data with a feature ablation.

| features | RMSE-train | RMSE-val | $R^2$-train | $R^2$-val |
|---|---|---|---|---|
| $\omega', \xi'$ | 88.3 | 81.6 | 0.805 | 0.822 |
| $\rho', \omega', \xi'$ | 32.7 | 32.8 | 0.973 | 0.971 |
| $d', \rho', \omega', \xi'$ | 25.4 | 25.8 | 0.983 | 0.982 |

We create training data by sampling, evaluating, and logging decisions for each encountered epoch on 100 full-day training instances and split training and

---

[1] https://www.tensorflow.org.
[2] Supported by a scientific interest group hosted by Inria and including CNRS, RENATER, several Universities and other organizations (see https://www.grid5000.fr).

validation data by 70/30. The myopic and scenario sampling decisions are always included in the sampled decisions, while three additional (more likely worse) decision are created by perturbing the myopic solution by randomly moving a (not necessarily contiguous) subsequence of orders to the second route and optimizing both routes with a local search with exchange neighborhood. With 80% probability the scenario sampling decisions is used, with 20% the decision is randomly sampled to diversify the state space traversal. This results in a total of 3351 post-decision state/estimated value pairs for training and validation together. The creation takes a couple of hours using multithreading for scenario sampling to evaluate decisions and dominates the offline phase runtime. The training runtime of the neural network is negligible within a minute.

We consider four different features from the post-decision state, the earliest relative arrival time of the driver $\rho'$, the expected arriving orders within the sampling horizon $\omega'$, and the travel time $d'$ and the tardiness $\xi'$ of the known remaining (= not yet started) orders within the route plan. As machine learning model, we use a fully connected feed forward neural network with two hidden layers with 32 nodes each, trained with Adam optimizer [5] on the mean squared error, 200 epochs at most. To combat overfitting, a weight decay of 0.01 is applied, together with early stopping (patience of 50 epochs with a delta of 10) monitoring the validation loss. Overfitting is not observed comparing the training and validation root mean squared error and the $R^2$ in Table 1 for different feature combinations, and finally select all four features explaining the most variance.

**Table 2.** Performance evaluation of different strategies on training and test data, $N = 100$ each.

| strategy | data | $\overline{\xi^{\text{linear}}}$ [min] | $\sigma_{\xi^{\text{linear}}}$ ['] | $\overline{t^{\text{dec}}}$ [s] | $\overline{K}$ | $\overline{\phi}$ [min] | $\overline{l}$ | $\sigma_l$ |
|---|---|---|---|---|---|---|---|---|
| myopic | train | 18.9 | 14.0 | 0.3 | 7.3 | 84.7 | 5.2 | 1.9 |
| consensus | train | 15.3 | 11.3 | 37.7 | 9.6 | 64.2 | 4.0 | 1.3 |
| value-function | train | 18.0 | 11.7 | 6.0 | 12.7 | 44.1 | 2.7 | 0.8 |
| value-function-corr | train | 15.4 | 11.0 | 6.1 | 10.2 | 56.1 | 3.5 | 1.0 |
| myopic | test | 19.4 | 16.0 | 0.3 | 7.9 | 83.5 | 5.1 | 2.1 |
| consensus | test | 16.6 | 13.3 | 36.4 | 10.7 | 65.7 | 4.0 | 1.5 |
| value-function | test | 19.0 | 13.4 | 5.7 | 13.3 | 43.7 | 2.6 | 0.8 |
| value-function-corr | test | 16.6 | 13.1 | 5.3 | 10.6 | 56.2 | 3.4 | 1.1 |

In Table 2, we compare the different tardiness penalties and statistics for the decisions and routes of the two baseline strategies myopic and consensus with the value function approach on training and test data, both consisting of 100 full-day simulations. Without a correction function, we observe that the value function selects substantially shorter routes close to three orders per route, resulting in shorter average route durations in minutes $\bar{\phi}$, the expected bias towards shorter routes. For the training and test data, this leads only to a slightly reduced linear tardiness as compared to the myopic strategy and reduced standard deviation.

As correction function $\Gamma$ we propose a step function, where a factor scales up the surrogate model $\tilde{V}$ when the duration of the first route is less than a given threshold, otherwise it is kept unchanged. We tune by selecting the best combination of thresholds from $\{1800, 2700, 3600, 4500, 5400, 6300\}$ seconds and factors from $\{1.1, 1.15, 1.2, 1.25, 1.3\}$ regarding the mean performance on the training data, resulting in 2700 seconds threshold and a factor of 1.3. The results are shown in Table 2 as strategy value-function-corr and lead to longer routes as desired with reduced and less varying tardiness close to the consensus method. A Wilcoxon signed rank sum test on $\xi^{\mathrm{linear}}$ reveals that for training and test data the corrected value function strategy is now significantly better with a significance level of 1% than the myopic strategy.

Using the neural network, the time per decision $\overline{t^{\mathrm{dec}}}$ is increased to about 5 s, whereas the consensus approach takes over half a minute for a decision. Note that this is a single-threaded comparison—both calculations could be sped up, the neural network by batch evaluation, the sampling by multithreading.

## 5  Conclusions and Future Work

We have formulated a same-day delivery problem with tardiness as a route-based Markov decision process and proposed a supervised learning approach to estimate the value of routing decisions in the short-horizon using a neural network. For a first toy instance class with a single vehicle and constant load pattern, we observed a new promising routing strategy emerging preferring shorter routes and early depot returns. It leads to substantially reduced tardiness on both training and unseen test data when compared with myopic optimization and close to the computationally much more expensive scenario sampling approach. To evaluate its practicability for real-world scenario settings, future research is concerned with the application on a broad set of instance classes with multiple vehicles, varying and larger load patterns, and different delivery area geometries.

**Acknowledgements.** This project is partially funded by the Doctoral Program "Vienna Graduate School on Computational Optimization", Austrian Science Foundation (FWF) Project No. W1260-N35.

## References

1. Bent, R.W., Van Hentenryck, P.: Scenario-based planning for partially dynamic vehicle routing with stochastic customers. Oper. Res. **52**(6), 977–987 (2004)
2. Bracher, A., Frohner, N., Raidl, G.R.: Learning surrogate functions for the short-horizon planning in same-day delivery problems. In: Stuckey, P.J. (ed.) 17th International Conference on Integration of Constraint Programming, Artificial Intelligence, and Operations Research (CPAIOR'21). LNCS, vol. 12735, pp. 283–298. Springer, Vienna, Austria (2021)
3. Frohner, N., Raidl, G.R.: A double-horizon approach to a purely dynamic and stochastic vehicle routing problem with delivery deadlines and shift flexibility. In: Causmaecker, P.D., et al. (eds.) Proceedings of the 13th International Conference

on the Practice and Theory of Automated Timetabling - PATAT 2021: Volume I. Bruges, Belgium (2020)

4. Joe, W., Lau, H.C.: Deep reinforcement learning approach to solve dynamic vehicle routing problem with stochastic customers. In: Proceedings of the International Conference on Automated Planning and Scheduling, vol. 30, pp. 394–402 (2020)

5. Kingma, D.P., Ba, J.: Adam: A method for stochastic optimization. arXiv preprint arXiv:1412.6980 (2014)

6. Ritzinger, U., Puchinger, J., Hartl, R.F.: A survey on dynamic and stochastic vehicle routing problems. Int. J. Prod. Res. **54**(1), 215–231 (2016)

7. Soeffker, N., Ulmer, M.W., Mattfeld, D.C.: Stochastic dynamic vehicle routing in the light of prescriptive analytics: a review. Eur. J. Oper. Res. **298**(3), 801–820 (2022)

8. Ulmer, M.W., Thomas, B.W., Mattfeld, D.C.: Preemptive depot returns for dynamic same-day delivery. EURO J. Transp. Logistics **8**(4), 327–361 (2019)

9. Voccia, S.A., Campbell, A.M., Thomas, B.W.: The same-day delivery problem for online purchases. Transp. Sci. **53**(1), 167–184 (2019)

# Vectorial Genetic Programming—Optimizing Segments for Feature Extraction

Philipp Fleck[1,2]([⊠]) [iD], Stephan Winkler[1,2] [iD], Michael Kommenda[1,3] [iD], and Michael Affenzeller[1,2] [iD]

[1] Heuristic and Evolutionary Algorithms Laboratory (HEAL), University of Applied Sciences Upper Austria, Softwarepark 11, 4232 Hagenberg, Austria
[2] Institute for Symbolic Artificial Intelligence, Johannes Kepler University, Altenberger Straße 69, 4040 Linz, Austria
philipp.fleck@fh-hagenberg.at
[3] Josef Ressel Center for Symbolic Regression, University of Applied Sciences Upper Austria, Softwarepark 11, 4232 Hagenberg, Austria

**Abstract.** Vectorial Genetic Programming (Vec-GP) extends GP by allowing vectors as input features along regular, scalar features, using them by applying arithmetic operations component-wise or aggregating vectors into scalars by some aggregation function. Vec-GP also allows aggregating vectors only over a limited segment of the vector instead of the whole vector, which offers great potential but also introduces new parameters that GP has to optimize. This paper formalizes an optimization problem to analyze different strategies for optimizing a window for aggregation functions. Different strategies are presented, included random and guided sampling, where the latter leverages information from an approximated gradient. Those strategies can be applied as a simple optimization algorithm, which itself ca be applied inside a specialized mutation operator within GP. The presented results indicate, that the different random sampling strategies do not impact the overall algorithm performance significantly, and that the guided strategies suffer from becoming stuck in local optima. However, results also indicate, that there is still potential in discovering more efficient algorithms that could outperform the presented strategies.

**Keywords:** Genetic Programming · Vectorial · Optimization · Gradient

## 1 Introduction

Vectorial Genetic Programming (Vec-GP) for Symbolic Regression (SR) is a extension of GP, where the space of input features is extended to vectors alongside regular scalars [1]. This allows vectorial GP to directly handle higher dimensional data, such as time series, without the need of prior feature engineering to

A. Quesada-Arencibia et al. (Eds.): EUROCAST 2024, LNCS 15172, pp. 272–279, 2025.
https://doi.org/10.1007/978-3-031-82949-9_25

extract scalar features. Instead, vectorial GP models themselves extracts scalar values from the vectors by applying aggregation functions, such as the arithmetic mean. Compared to traditional feature engineering, where scalar features are usually only extracted from the raw vector features, vectorial GP can also extract features from interacting vectors by performing arithmetic operations on vectors before aggregation takes place. Figure 1 shows an example, where the vector variable for temperature and pressure are divided prior to calculating the arithmetic mean to obtain a scalar. The literature already indicates, that vectorial GP outperforms regular GP with feature engineering in various benchmarks [2].

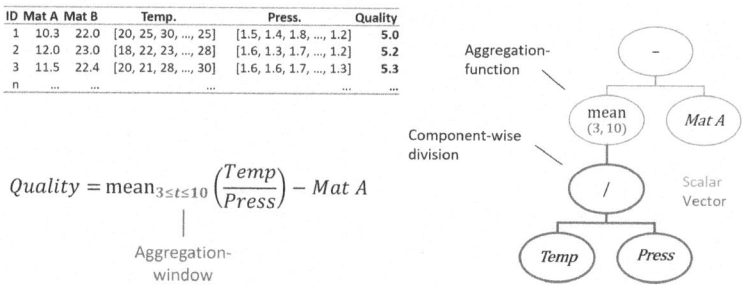

**Fig. 1.** An example dataset containing both scalar and vector input features to predict a scalar target value (the quality). It also shows a GP model that uses a windowed-aggregation function to aggregate a vector into a scalar.

In case of a vector representing a time series, it might be beneficial to aggregate only over a certain time frame. In this sense, vectorial GP can be further extended by adding the ability to aggregate not only over a whole vector, but over a sub-segment of the vector, where GP is also in charge of optimizing the segment bounds. For instance, as also shown in Fig. 1, aggregation might only be done on a specific time frame, for example, between $3 \leq t \leq 10$.

## 2   Problem Description

When using an aggregation function with an aggregation window, GP is now required to optimize two additional parameters for each windowed aggregation function within a GP model. While GP could handle this by allowing the indices to change via mutation, random mutation is not particularly well suited for this task, especially for longer vectors. Instead of relying on mutation as GP's only way of optimizing aggregation windows, this paper is a first step towards identifying other strategies that are more tailored towards optimizing aggregation windows, similar to applying efficient gradient-based algorithms for optimizing continuous, numerical parameters of a fixed GP model [4].

To focus on the problem of optimizing the aggregation window, we use a simplified optimization problem that omits any GP related aspect, only keeping the core problem of optimizing an aggregation window over some fixed data. This Segment Optimization Problem (SOP) is an integer problem, optimizing the parameters $\hat{a}, \hat{b} \in \{i \in \mathbb{N} \mid i < N\}$ representing the start and end index with, minimizing

$$\underset{\hat{a},\hat{b}}{\arg\min} \sum_{i=0}^{M} \Big( \underbrace{\mathrm{f}_{\mathrm{agg}}\big(\boldsymbol{v}_i[\hat{a} : \hat{b}]\big)}_{\text{optimized bounds}} - \underbrace{\mathrm{f}_{\mathrm{agg}}\big(\boldsymbol{v}_i[a : b]\big)}_{\text{known bounds}} \Big)^2 , \tag{1}$$

where $\mathrm{f}_{\mathrm{agg}}$ is a fixed aggregation function, $\boldsymbol{v}_i \in \mathbb{R}^{M \times N}$ are the $M$ samples of vectors with length $N$, $a$ and $b$ representing the known aggregation indices and $\boldsymbol{v}_i[a : b]$ being the sub-vector of a selected vector $\boldsymbol{v}_i$. In essence, the goal of the SOP is to find the minimum deviation when aggregating using the free indices $\hat{a}$ and $\hat{b}$ compared to aggregating using the known indices $a$ and $b$.

## 3  Method

Instead of relying on GPs mutation to identify good aggregation windows, our goal is to define a specialized mutation operator for GP that is tailored towards optimizing the start and end indices of an aggregation window efficiently. Start and end indices can either be optimized simultaneously, i.e. as a multi-dimensional optimization problem, or only a single dimension at a time, i.e. as a single-dimensional optimization problem. We will later analyze which form yields better results.

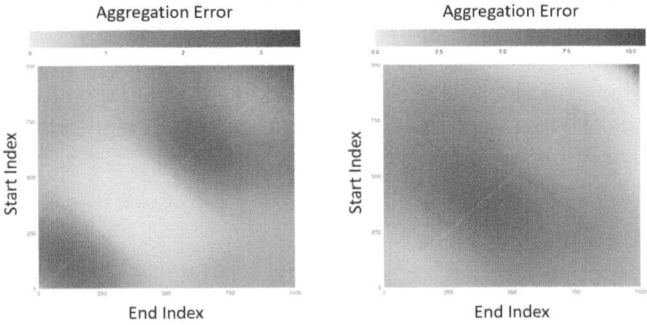

**Fig. 2.** The fitness landscape of two benchmark instances (x3 and x6) with lower (brighter) values indicating better regions in the search space.

Looking at the fitness landscape of some of the benchmark instances in Fig. 2, we can clearly observe, that there is gradient information that could be leveraged for efficient optimization. Therefore, we first approximate the gradient by using a five-point stencil [5] on the neighboring indices ($h = 1$) and then use it to guide the search. The proposed optimization method in this paper is an iterative algorithm with two steps: First, the gradient is calculated and used to guide search towards promising regions. Second, potential solutions are sampled from that promising region, evaluated and the best one is selected for the next iteration. This procedure is continued until a predefined number of total solution evaluations is exceeded.

The firsts guiding step in the optimization procedure is responsible for selecting a promising region, from which samples can be drawn in the second step afterwards. We define three different guiding strategies, shown in Fig. 3: *Full* represents no strategy at all, where the whole solution space is utilized. This strategy serves will serve as a baseline. *Direction* uses the approximate gradient only to guide whether an index should be increased or decreased and does not take the magnitude of the gradient into account. *Range* uses the approximate gradient information to define a promising region by a defined range, where the magnitude of the gradient also influences the distance from the current index.

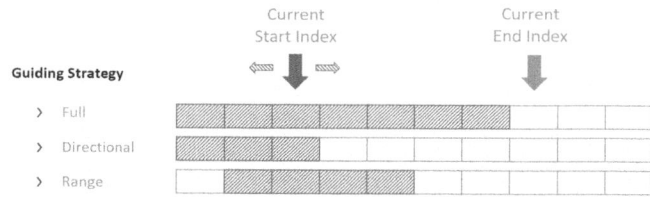

**Fig. 3.** Three different guiding strategies for defining the search space, given a free start index and a fixed end index.

While the random direction simply looks at the direction of gradient, the guided range mimics a traditional gradient descent algorithm with two modifications, shown in Fig. 4. First, we round the gradient step towards the nearest integer, to ensure that the next index will also be valid index. Additionally, we introduce a new parameter, the search-range, that defines how many samples around the next index are considered promising and are thus eligible for being sampled afterwards.

After defining the search space, the second step is responsible of drawing the samples from this search space. For this paper, we have considered three sampling mechanisms, shown in Fig. 5: *Exhaustive* draws all samples from the solution space. This is typically not feasible for a multi-dimensional search space, due to a potentially high number of possible solutions. However, it could be a viable option for a single dimensional space. *Random* draws samples completely at random (without repetition), where the number of samples are defined by an additional sample-size parameter. *Orthogonal* selects the samples equally spaced along each dimension, by first selecting a predefined number of equally spaced points on a continuous line of the search space and then rounding towards the nearest indices and removing any duplicates.

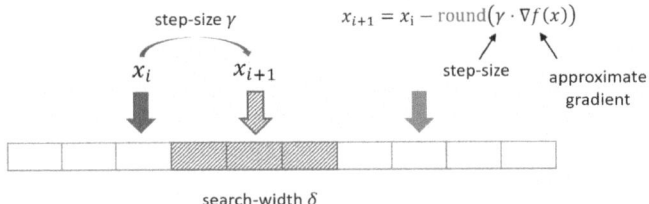

**Fig. 4.** Adoption of a gradient descent step to integer indices, with an additional search-range parameter.

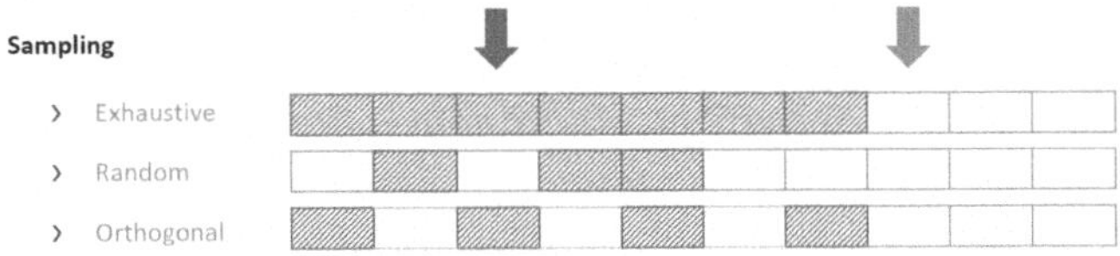

**Sampling**

> Exhaustive

> Random

> Orthogonal

**Fig. 5.** Different sampling strategies for a given search space.

## 4    Experiment Setup

To identify good parameters of the search strategies defined in the previous section, we performed a grid search of the parameters over multiple benchmark instances. However, certain combinations were skipped due to infeasible run-times, e.g. exhaustive search on multi-dimensional search spaces. Each parameter combination was repeated 20 times, and each execution of the optimization algorithm was allowed a total of 100,000 sample evaluations, meaning the total number of iterations varied, depending on the sample-size, for instance.

The generated benchmark instances have different characteristics to represent different challenges and difficulties. For instance, shown in Fig. 6, the second instance shows an overall increasing behavior where the noise stays constant. The most right benchmark, however, does not only have more varying slopes, but also the noise is increasing over time. The benchmark instances were created in multiple steps by creating randomized control values first, that are then used as arguments for other distributions that are finally used to create the vectors. For instance, the most right benchmark is based on the control values $m = \mathcal{U}(2,5) + \mathcal{U}(0.2,4)/80 \cdot t$ and $s = \mathcal{U}(0,0.001) + \mathcal{U}(0.002,0.01) \cdot t$ where $\mathcal{U}$ denotes a uniform random variable and $t$ denotes the time or index. The final vector is then created using a normal distribution $\mathcal{N}(m,s^2)$ with the prior defined control values. Thus, for this benchmark instance, the mean value and also the noise increases with higher $t$. Since the parameters of the distributions change with $t$, the distributions from which a sample is drawn are created for each $t$ independently. The full list and definition of the benchmark instances can found in the additional materials online at https://dev.heuristiclab.com/wiki/ AdditionalMaterial. For the presented results, we used vectors of length 1,000.

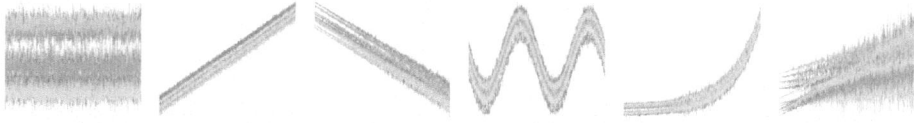

**Fig. 6.** Some exemplary benchmark instances, where each line represent one row in the dataset.

## 5   Result

To compare different optimization strategies, we analyze the run-length distributions, as defined in the black-box optimization benchmarking (BBOB) [3]. This allows an evaluation of not only an algorithms ability of finding a good solution, but also shows how fast an algorithm converges. This is crucial, since a good optimization strategy for the segment optimization problem would be used inside a mutation operator within GP, thus, long runtimes would multiply in the context of GP.

In addition to the presented results, we also analyzed additional parameters, such as the effect of random versus orthogonal sampling, however they showed no significant differences, thus are not discussed further in this paper. We will first look at whether approaching the optimization problem as single- or multi-dimensional performs better, shown in Fig. 7. Overall, the results suggest, that optimizing all dimensions simultaneously performs slightly better, however, for some problem instances, such as x1, using a single dimension yielded better results. This behavior was suspected, since it shows, that some of the benchmark are easy enough to be separable and optimized dimension by dimension.

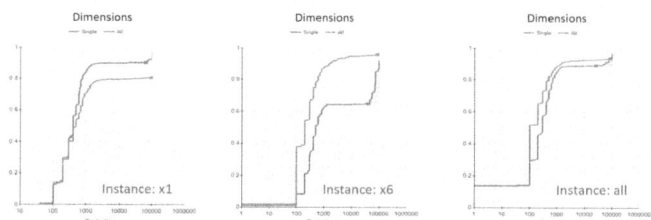

**Fig. 7.** Influence of single- versus multi-dimension on algorithm performance.

Next, we analyze directional search space reduction, where we compare limiting the search space towards a direction randomly versus using the gradient to guide the direction, shown in Fig. 8. The result suggests, that the benefits depend on the problem instance. While for problem instance x5 using a guided direction seems to slow down convergence, overall, the benefits are not conclusive. We suspect, that by using the gradient always to move towards the best option, it forces the algorithm towards local optima without any way of escaping.

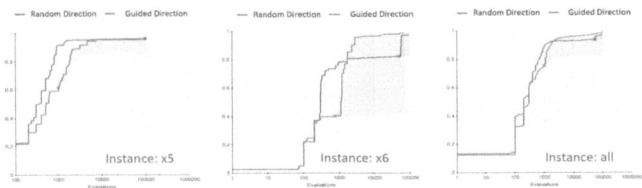

**Fig. 8.** Performance of random versus guided direction.

Next, we analyze limiting the search space within a specific range. Because the range strategy has two additional parameter, the step-size and search-width, we will compare the random version to different settings of the parameters, both shown in Fig. 9. Since the step-size controls the jumping distance from the current index, having low values are expected to yield bad results, since jumping too little makes the search inefficient or halt completely due to the rounding in the gradient step. The effect of the step-size on instance x3 suggest that this assumption holds, since lower step-sizes do not perform well, as shown in Fig. 9a On the other hand, higher step-sizes tend to perform better for instance x3 and might even outperform the random range strategy in finding the best solutions quicker, however, this is not the case for all instances. Along the step-size, the search-width defines how far the search space extends around the next index. The results in Fig. 9b suggests, that having a lower search-width generally causes the algorithm to converge slower. This is especially true for combinations with a low step-size, since the search-range is the only mechanism of changing an index when the gradient step is rounded to zero. Similar to the guided direction, where we suspect that random direction outperforms the guided direction because the algorithm becomes stuck at a local optimum, the same could also be true for guided range to a certain degree. Having a large search-width could help breaking out of the local optimum, but still, the result suggest that a random range would be the better option in most cases.

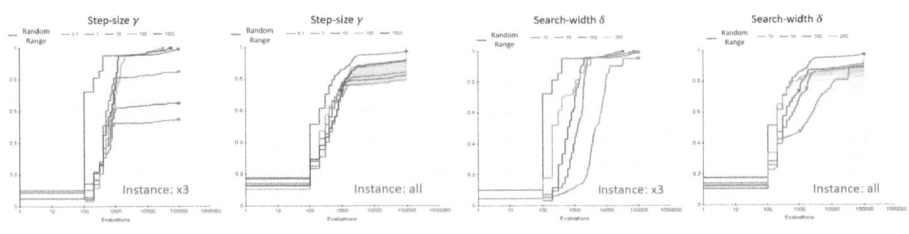

(a) Influence of the step-size.          (b) Influence of the search-width.

**Fig. 9.** Performance of random versus guided search range reduction.

# 6   Conclusion

The results presented in the previous section suggests, that simple random sampling is generally better than using a guided strategy such as guided direction or guided range. We believe that this is mainly caused by the guided strategies tend to work similar to greedy algorithms, and can quickly become stuck in local optima. However, when applying the presented methods in the context of GP, preliminary results suggests, that the guided strategies tend to outperform their random counterparts. We suspect that GP can easily break free of local optima by regular crossover and mutation operations, thus becoming stuck in a local optima is not as critical.

Despite the current result suggesting that the gradient-based strategies do not work well, we still believe that the information of the approximate gradient is extremely useful, because most fitness landscapes of the benchmark instances clearly indicate that there is a gradient that could be exploited for fast optimization. Therefore, we will continue working on leveraging the gradient for a fast optimization algorithm for the segment optimization problem.

**Acknowledgments.** This work was carried out within the Dissertationsprogramm der Fachhochschule OÖ #875441 *Vektor-basierte Genetische Programmierung für Symbolische Regression und Klassifikation mit Zeitreihen (SymRegZeit)*, funded by the Austrian Research Promotion Agency FFG. The authors also gratefully acknowledge support by the Christian Doppler Research Association and the Federal Ministry of Digital and Economic Affairs within the *Josef Ressel Centre for Symbolic Regression*.

# References

1. Azzali, I., Vanneschi, L., Silva, S., Bakurov, I., Giacobini, M.: A vectorial approach to genetic programming. In: EuroGP, pp. 213–227 (2019)
2. Fleck, P., Winkler, S., Kommenda, M., Affenzeller, M.: Grammar-based vectorial genetic programming for symbolic regression. In: Banzhaf, W., Trujillo, L., Winkler, S., Worzel, B. (eds.) Genetic Programming Theory and Practice XVIII. Springer Nature Singapore Pte Ltd. (2021)
3. Hansen, N., Auger, A., Ros, R., Finck, S., Pošík, P.: Comparing results of 31 algorithms from the black-box optimization benchmarking bbob-2009. In: Proceedings of the 12th Annual Conference Companion On Genetic And Evolutionary Computation, pp. 1689–1696 (2010)
4. Kommenda, M., Burlacu, B., Kronberger, G., Affenzeller, M.: Parameter identification for symbolic regression using nonlinear least squares. Genet. Program Evolvable Mach. **21**(3), 471–501 (2020)
5. Sauer, T.: Numerical solution of stochastic differential equations in finance. In: Duan, J.-C., Härdle, W.K., Gentle, J.E. (eds.) Handbook of Computational Finance, pp. 529–550. Springer Berlin Heidelberg, Berlin, Heidelberg (2012). https://doi.org/10.1007/978-3-642-17254-0_19

# Mechatronic Product Development

# Enhancing Manufacturing Efficiency Through Integration of MBSE and Capella in the Digital Thread

Michael Burgstaller[2] , Thomas Schichl[2] , and Mario Jungwirth[1]([⊠]) 

[1] Research Group Smart Mechatronics Engineering,
University of Applied Sciences Upper Austria, Wels Campus, Wels, Austria
`mario.jungwirth@fh-wels.at`
[2] University of Applied Sciences Upper Austria, Wels Campus, Wels, Austria

**Abstract.** The advancement of digitalization in manufacturing has brought about a significant transformation in the industry. The digital thread, a key component this for transformation is defined as the use of digital tools and representations for design, evaluation, and life cycle management. This paper presents a project focused on enhancing the digital thread of a manufacturing line by integrating Model-Based Systems Engineering (MBSE) and Capella. It automates part identification, handling, and transportation in a small-scale manufacturing line, utilizing data from programs like Siemens NX in Capella to generate assembly code for manufacturing. The integration of various software tools like Capella, Siemens NX, and Mechatronics Concept Designer (MCD), along with hardware components like robots and Automated Guided Vehicles (AGVs), is crucial for optimizing manufacturing processes. The physical key components include cameras, sensors, and the UR10 robotic arm, demonstrating a use case of a flexible transport system (FTS) with a gripper and conveyor belt for pick-and-place tasks. The anticipated outcome is improved communication in the digital thread and increased production efficiency through automated processes, reduced manual intervention, and a more agile response to design changes.

**Keywords:** Digital Thread · MBSE · Siemens NX · Mechatronic Concept Designer · Arcadia method · Capella · PLMXML

## 1 General Setting

This work integrates digital tools to enhance manufacturing processes. It leverages software tools as Capella, Siemens NX and others to automate and optimize manufacturing workflows, highlighting the need for efficient data exchange and system integration [1]. The focus of this project is to define a methodology and implement the requirements in the MBSE environment using various software that interact with each other. The MBSE System Capella, based on the ACRDIA Method, is the backbone which is used for creating models. These Models describe the architecture, behavior, requirements, etc. of the system. Through universal datatypes and communication interfaces a bidirectional data exchange will be implemented between Capella a different engineering tools like Siemens NX, Siemens Mechatronics Designer, RoboDK or Unity3D.

© The Author(s), under exclusive license to Springer Nature Switzerland AG 2025
A. Quesada-Arencibia et al. (Eds.): EUROCAST 2024, LNCS 15172, pp. 283–293, 2025.
https://doi.org/10.1007/978-3-031-82949-9_26

Key components like cameras, sensors, grippers, and the UR10 robotic arm are used for demonstrating the use case in a small-scale manufacturing line. This line is part of the Center for Smart Manufacturing (CSM) laboratory at the University of applied sciences upper Austria, Wels Campus.

The result of this project is the implementation of a method to implement a digital thread based on Capella and different engineering tools and the validation and verification of its usage at the CSM laboratory (Fig. 1).

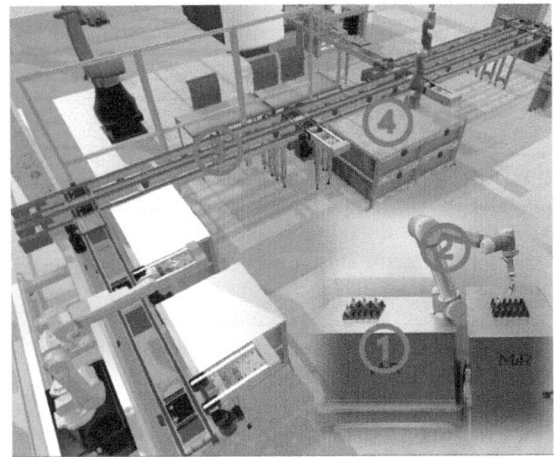

① Mobile industrial Robot MiR100

② Universal robot UR10

③ Conveyor belts

④ Processing station

**Fig. 1.** A model of the setup in the CSM-laboratory as well as the automated guided vehicle system and robotic arm.

## Model-Based Systems Engineering (MBSE)

MBSE is defined by the International Council of Systems Engineering (INCOSE) as "the formalized application of modeling to support system requirements, design, analysis, verification and validation activities beginning in the conceptual design phase and continuing throughout development and later life cycle phases" [3]. It takes a holistic system approach to manage the system information and data relationships, treating all information as a model and therefore adding value to technical processes and project processes. MBSE is a move from a document-centric approach to a model-centric approach. All or part of the textual documents are replaced by models. In MBSE, a model represents a system and its environment. Models are usually created from meta-models (or conceptual models), which are sets of concepts within a system and the relationships among those concepts [4]. Different diagrams allow representing different points of view of the same model.

The MBSE approach supports systems engineering and the complexity resulting from interdisciplinarity. MBSE not only ensures that the language/tool/approach chosen will allow the system to be 'represented', but also ensures that the information can be properly used to support systems engineering. MBSE provides a representation of information in different ways that show specific analysis capabilities for different types of users that have different interests. It also allows refining a system and a system model into subsystem models [5].

A model can be captured via a mathematical equation, a graph, a formal expression, or a drawing. MBSE ensures consistency across all views by using one model at its core from which all the views are derived. Views can express different points of view, for example, the structure of a system, its behavior, and its interaction with its operational context [4]. These views can be represented with different modeling languages and tools following various methodologies, according to the domains involved in the system, the level of detail, the system aspects to be modeled, etc. The model-driven approach is organized around languages (SysML, DSL, UML, etc.), methods (OOSEM, ARCADIA, SPES, etc.), and tools (CAPELLA, CORE, Cameo Systems Modeler, Cameo Enterprise Architecture, Papyrus, etc.) [5].

**The ARCADIA Method**

The Architecture Analysis and Design Integrated Approach (ARCADIA) is an MBSE method developed by the Thales group in 2000, when it evolved from a simple supplier of equipment to a supplier of integrated systems [6]. In 2001, the group carried out a study of the current MBSE standards, methods, and tools, which concluded that the methods covered too limited a part of Thales' activities and were too far from the company's practices. Moreover, the use of UML as a modeling language, in addition to being somewhat complex for use, did not seem to be appropriate for system design. At the same time, a survey was conducted within the company to gather feedback and ideas for improving practices. Despite the diversity of answers, several major general pathways for improvement emerged [7]:

• Understand the customer/user needs;
• Define and share the solution among stakeholders;
• Secure system/software/hardware engineering and prepare subcontracting;
• Evaluate and justify architectural design early;
• Prepare and master verification and validation.

Therefore, in 2006, a first version of the ARCADIA method was released with structured recommendations of a top-down approach where the activities were clearly defined and followed one another in a fixed order [2], in conformance with the ISO/IEC 15288 standard [8].

**The Capella Tool**

The main interest of Capella is that it maintains consistency and coherency between the modeling levels: the constituent elements of each level are linked to each other via traceability links and justification.

As presented in [6], the purpose of Capella is to support system architecture, a key stage in system development. According to the ARCADIA method, Capella starts from the elicitation of the stakeholders' needs, and it guides the design process until the exploration of the different technological and architectural possibilities of the solution domain is realized. Through the method at different levels, it allows a graphical, organized, and simplified understanding of the design stage.

Capella proposes a metamodel that can be used in different ways. Among them, the most common consists of following the classical top-down ARCADIA process (see chapter Method) from the operational analysis to the physical architeture when designing a new system. Capella also allows performing a bottom-up method for retro-engineering (see Chapter Method) when the system development is based on an already existing system or on its parts. Finally, the tool can be used to solve a specific problem by analyzing only one level (for example, an interface problem can be analyzed at the logical architecture level).

**Open product lifecycle data sharing using XML**

Efforts to achieve interoperability among software applications used in the conception, development, engineering, manufacturing and maintenance of products, cost the global manufacturing industry billions of dollars annually. In order to achieve significant cost savings and an important time to market advantage, the global market is now demanding unprecedented levels of interoperability among PLM software applications to help accelerate the execution of product development process threads. Initiatives to improve interoperability in heterogeneous application environments are therefore of vital importance.

PLM XML is a format created by UGS for facilitating product lifecycle interoperability using XML. It is open, published and is compliant with the World Wide Web Consortium (W3C) XML schema recommendation.

Representing a variety of product data both explicitly and via references, PLM XML provides a lightweight, flexible mechanism for transporting high-content product data over the internet. PLM XML schemas are the basis of a rich interoperability pipeline connecting UGS products and third party adopter applications. PLM XML is complementary to existing and emerging XML-based standards, it supports work flows requiring application integration, interoperability and data sharing by improving collaboration efficiency throughout the product lifecycle [9].

**The Digital Thread**

Digital Thread is defined as 'a data-driven architecture that links together information generated across the product and service lifecycle and is envisioned to be the primary or authoritative data and communication platform for a company's products and services at any instance of time.'

It provides seamless views for action of information throughout a product's lifecycle. At its core, it is a 'digital backbone' that closes the loop between the digital and physical worlds to form the foundation of the Digital Twin.

It serves as a single source of truth for all product data across every facet, from concept to design specifications, engineering and build processes, usage history, and service routines through disposal. The information captured and stored digitally enables manufacturers to optimize products, improve ergonomics, usability experience, and quality to seamlessly integrate with operating ecosystems, and better serve consumers (people) throughout a product's lifecycle.

The term digital thread is also used to describe the traceability of the digital twin back to the concept, requirements, parts, components, and control systems that constitute the physical product or asset.

## 2 Concept Development

The entire product lifecycle includes four main phases: product development, product maintenance, product repair, and product recycling. While each phase is important, this paper will focus on the product development phase. Product development involves several key steps: requirements engineering, the concept phase, and the design phase. These steps are crucial for making sure the final product meets all necessary specifications and works as intended. As shown in the accompanying graphic, these steps are key parts of the product development process. Each phase and each part of the phase of the product lifecycle should be connected through an MBSE and PLM backbone to ensure smooth integration, data flow and data availability. This connected approach allows for a more efficient process where information can be easily shared and accessed (Fig. 2).

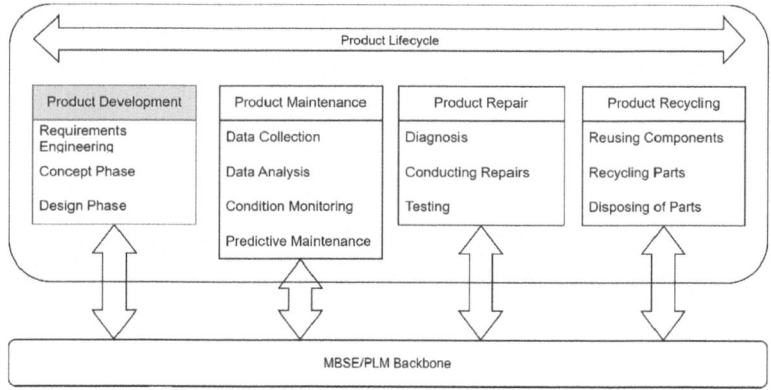

**Fig. 2.** A model of the Product Lifecyle and the connection to the MBSE/PLM Backbone

Having outlined the key phases of the product lifecycle, with a particular emphasis on product development, the focus now shifts to a comprehensive analysis of MBSE software tools and their integration into manufacturing processes. This transition from a broad overview to a specific analysis is essential for understanding product development through effective data integration and communication (Fig. 3).

1. First the requirements for integration and data exchange must be analyzed. The requirements for all other steps should be considered as well. This process considers the specific needs of the various systems and programs involved in the manufacturing process. This analysis helps identify and overcome potential challenges and obstacles in integration, ensuring seamless and efficient data communication.
2. Then, a comprehensive analysis of potential MBSE software tools is conducted to define the requirements for integrating the digital thread into the manufacturing processes. This analysis evaluates the functionalities these software tools offer as well as their compatibility. Specifically, it determines how well these tools can generate, process, and transmit the necessary data as well as their availability and ease of use. This analysis forms the foundation for selecting the most suitable MBSE software that can meet the specific needs.

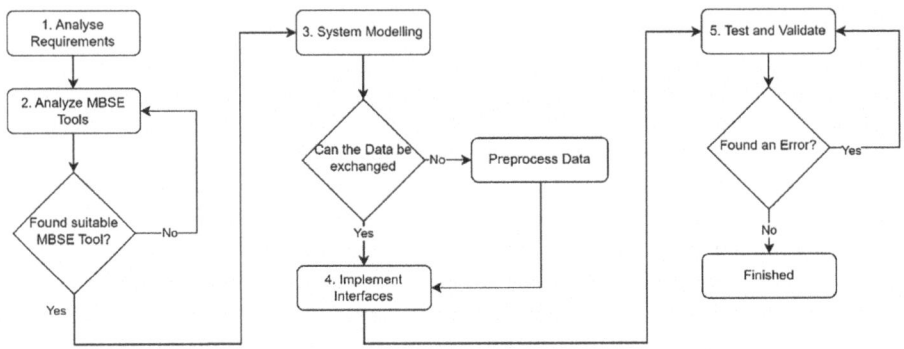

**Fig. 3.** A Flowchart of the method used for the concept development

3. After finding an appropriate MBSE-Tool, a concept for implementing the digital thread is developed. Here, the Arcadia method plays a central role in system modeling. The Arcadia method provides a structured and systematic approach to modeling complex systems by considering various perspectives and levels of system architecture. This model also serves as the basis for defining the data structures that need to be exchanged. It is important to note that not all data and information can be directly exchanged, necessitating the development of alternative methods for data processing and transmission to ensure all relevant information is available.

4. The implementation phase involves developing and implementing the necessary interfaces that enable bidirectional communication between the backbone and other software tools like Siemens NX for example. These interfaces are designed to efficiently and reliably transmit data in both directions.

5. After implementing the interfaces, it is crucial to conduct extensive testing to ensure data continuity and consistency. These tests cover scenarios and use cases to ensure the system functions correctly. Validating the system helps identify potential errors and weaknesses before the system is deployed, so they can be corrected.

## 3   Proof of Concept

This concept is focusing on Capella as a backbone and Siemens NX, Mechatronics Concept Designer, and RoboDK as engineering tools during the product development phase. These tools help to create detailed models, simulations, and designs. The data from these tools are then integrated with Capella using the PLMXML format to ensure compatibility across the system. As described in Sect. 2, Concept Development, this method is now being implemented (Fig. 4).

1. First, the needed requirements must be analyzed. The goal was to establish bidirectional communication where data from a MBSE/PLM Backbone could be transferred to the used programs. Therefore, ensuring data consistency and integrity is crucial, meaning the data should stay accurate and reliable as it moves between systems.

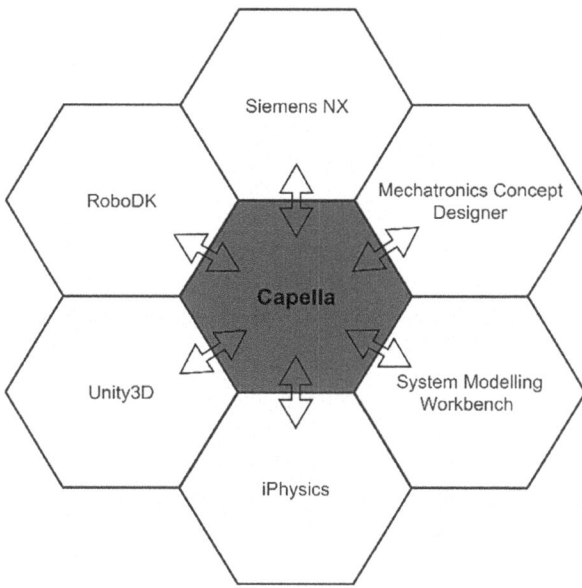

**Fig. 4.** Graph of the Communication between Programs

2. Then, various SYSML and PLM tools, such as Capella, Enterprise Architect, Team-center, and Windchill, were researched. Each tool was evaluated based on several criteria: whether it is open source, its capability for document generation, the pro-grams it can be integrated with, and its availability for use at the university. Following this detailed research, Capella emerged as the most suitable tool.
3. The system modeling phase heavily involves creating a suitable Capella file which can then be used as the basis for the data structures that need to be exchanged. The following section will provide an overview of Capella, its applications, and the specific models that were developed for this project.

**Operational Analysis**

The Operational Analysis describes the users, their needs, and their activities within the chosen context. It focuses on what the user of the system needs to accomplish.

In the Operational Analysis, the fundamental capabilities of the systems are depicted. Here, the conveyor belt must be able to move objects, the server must be able to communicate, and the general flow of the chain is outlined (Fig. 5).

**System Analysis**

The System Analysis describes the missions and functions of the system and its environment. It focuses on what the system needs to accomplish for the user.

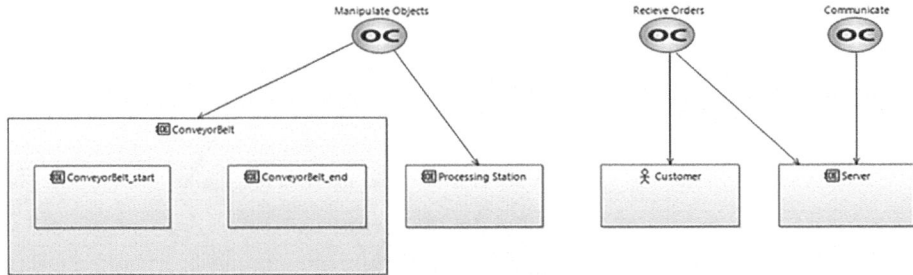

**Fig. 5.** Capella: Operational Analysis

Here, the conveyor belt supplies material, the robotic arm grabs the material, the system moves the material into position, the processing station processes the material, and the conveyor belt picks up the finished material again (Fig. 6).

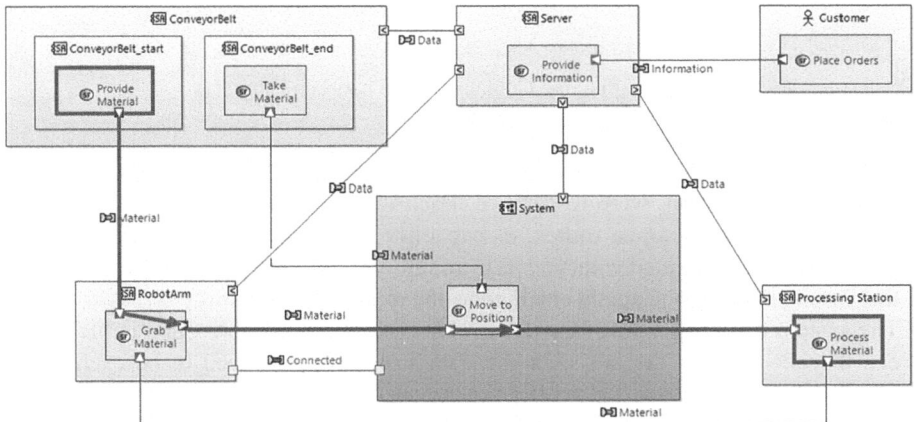

**Fig. 6.** Capella: System Analysis

## Logical Architecture

The Logical Architecture describes the logical system structure, focusing on how the system will work to fulfill expectations. It outlines the logical components and their interactions, detailing how the system's functions are realized to meet the defined requirements and user needs.

In the Logical Architecture, what is depicted in the System Analysis is modeled in more detail. It is now clear that the system is an AGV (an automated guided vehicle). Additionally, the robotic arm now includes a gripper and a sensor. The functional chain, although, in this case, the material flow from the conveyor belt to the processing station, remains the same (Fig. 7).

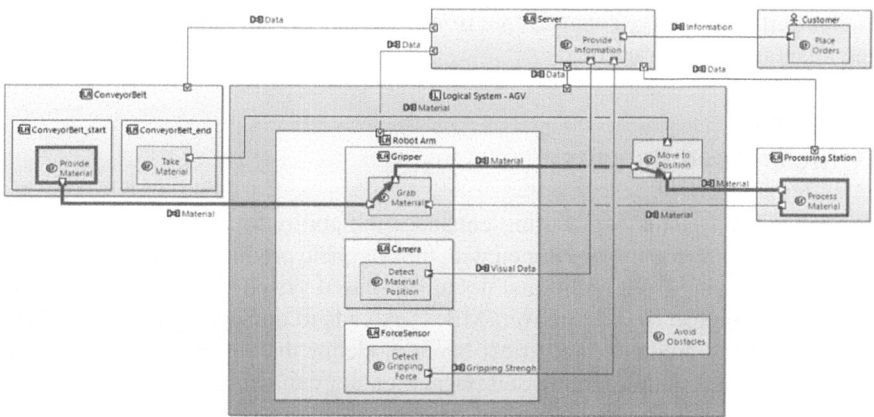

**Fig. 7.** Capella: Logical Archtecture

## Physical Architecture

The lowest layer, the Physical Architecture involves the assignment of functions to behavioral components and actors. In addition to the assignment of functions, the exchange between components and physical connections can also be described.

In the Physical Architecture, the modeling includes the pose of individual components. This includes the position and rotation of the AGV, robotic arm, and gripper. The detailed layout of these components is essential for understanding their interactions and ensuring accurate implementation (Fig. 8).

1. The implementation phase involved developing and configuring the necessary interfaces to enable bidirectional communication. Specifically, custom scripts and APIs were created to facilitate data exchange between Capella and Siemens NX, allowing data to be imported and exported into Capella's system model. For this task PLMXML was also used for standardization purposes. This setup ensured that all relevant information was available for both design and operational phases, enhancing overall efficiency and integration within the manufacturing process.
2. In the final phase, the model underwent detailed testing to verify the accuracy and integrity of the transmitted data. This process was conducted to ensure that all data

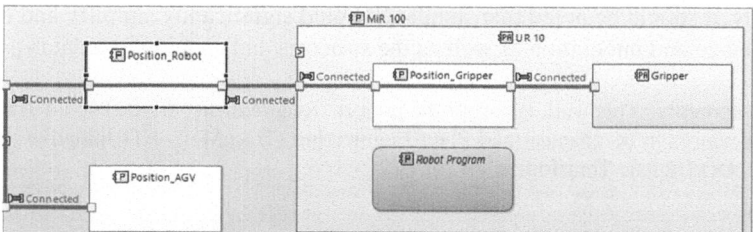

**Fig. 8.** Capella: Physikal Archtecture

exchanged between systems was free from errors, so the reliability and robustness of the integration was confirmed.

## 4  Outcome and Benefits

As model-based systems engineering enhances the ability to capture, analyze, share, and manage the information associated with the complete product life cycle, many organizations are moving from traditional document-based systems engineering to model-based systems engineering. Moreover, MBSE extends to domains beyond engineering to support complex predictive and affect-based modeling that includes the integration of engineering models with scientific and phenomenology models; social, economic, and political models; and human behavioral models [46]. We can see the development of several operational usages and the deep democratization of the MBSE for a wide variety of business areas and companies.

However, to achieve the holistic integration of MBSE systems across the product life cycle, several obstacles still need to be eliminated and solutions found. The multitude of different interfaces, the lack of openness of systems, file formats and data types, as well as the lack of standards are just a few.

If you consider the enormous number of available interfaces through which data can be exchanged throughout the product life cycle, it is difficult to develop holistic, consistent platforms that provide this range of interfaces. Therefore, MBSE systems must be open and extensible through APIs, plug-ins, SDK, or similar.

This openness is not only necessary for an MBSE system. The tools used throughout the product life cycle must be open and expandable.

In addition to these requirements, it is necessary to develop standardized file formats and data types that are not limited to one product or phase.

Capella as an MBSE system is very easy to expand thanks to its API and can therefore interact with any other software tool. In this case, Project PLMXML is chosen as the common file format. This means that Siemens NX and other Siemens tools can be connected without much effort. If tools such as RoboDK as an offline programming system or Unity3D as a system for virtual commissioning are to be integrated, then PLMXML interfaces must first be developed and the models that describe the parameters and behavior of the functions must also be created in Capella. Above all, developing the interfaces is very complex. However, this is only a one-time process.

Finally, it should be noted that standards would significantly simplify and optimize data exchange and integration as well as the structure and creation of a database.

**Acknowledgments.** This work is part of the project "Requirements-driven Digital Transformation Competences in Mechanical and Plant Engineering (TraceMe)". FTI Initiative: UpperVISION2030 OÖ Digitale Transformation 2021/22.

# References

1. Sinnwell, C.: Methode zur Produktionssystemkonzipierung auf Basis früher Produktinformationen – Ein Beitrag zur Integration von Produktionssystemplanung und Produktentwicklung unter Einsatz des MBSE (Dissertation, ISBN 978–3–95974–127–9). (2019)
2. System modeling workbench for teamcenter: https://www.obeo.fr/images/products/misc/Siemens-PLM-System-Modeling-Workbench-for-Teamcenter-fs-5244-A8.pdf. (accessed: 13.11.2023)
3. Friedenthal, S., Griego, R., Sampson, M.: INCOSE model based systems engineering (MBSE) initiative. In: Proceedings of the INCOSE 2007 Symposium, San Diego, CA, USA, p. 11 (2007)
4. Cloutier, R.: SEBoK: Guide to the Systems Engineering. (2019). Available online: https://sebokwiki.org/wiki/Guide_to_the_Systems_Engineering_Body_of_Knowledge_(SEBoK) (accessed on 3 August 2023)
5. Baron, C., Grenier, L., Ostapenko, V., Xue, R.: Using the ARCADIA/Capella Systems Engineering Method and Tool to Design Manufacturing Systems—Case Study and Industrial Feedback. Systems **11**, 429 (2023). https://doi.org/10.3390/systems11080429(accessedon05.06.2024)
6. Voirin, J.L.: Conception Architecturale des Systèmes Basée sur les Modèles Avec la Méthode Arcadia. ISTE Group, London, UK (2018)
7. Bonnet, S.: The Spirit of Arcadia and Capella in 7 Minutes. Available online: https://www.youtube.com/watch?v=BtzhlZUaWA8&feature=youtu.be (accessed on 14 April 2021)
8. ISO/IEC/IEEE 15288:2015: Systems and Software Engineering—System Life Cycle Processes. ISO/IEC JTC 1/SC 7; ISO: Geneva, Switzerland, 2015
9. Open product lifecycle data sharing using XML: https://www.plm.automation.siemens.com/ko_kr/Images/Siemens-PLM-Open-Product-Lifecycle-Data-Sharing-Using-XML-wp_tcm72-11521.pdf (accessed 05.06.2024)

# Leveraging Learning Factories for Mechatronic Systems Development: A Collaborative Approach

Pavel Kopylov[1], Jule Wegen[1], Thomas Schlechter[2(✉)], Karen Manfredi[3],
Letizia Nicoletti[3], Antonio Padovano[4], Martina Cardamone[4],
and Emmanuel Francalanza[5]

[1] EIT Manufacturing CLC North, Gothenburg, Sweden
`{pavel.kopylov,jule.wegen}@eitmanufacturing.eu`
[2] University of Applied Sciences Upper Austria, 4600 Wels, Austria
`thomas.schlechter@ieee.org`
[3] CAL-TEK S.r.l., 87036 Rende, CS, Italy
`{k.manfredi,l.nicoletti}@cal-tek.eu`
[4] Department of Mechanical, Energy and Mechanical Engineering (DIMEG), Arcavacata Di
Rende (CS), University of Calabria, 87036 Rende, Italy
`{antonio.padovano,martina.cardamone}@unical.it`
[5] Department of Industrial and Manufacturing Engineering, University of Malta, Msida 2080,
MSD, Malta
`emmanuel.francalanza@um.edu.mt`

**Abstract.** This article explores the transformative potential of learning factories in mechatronic systems development through the LEONARDO project. By fostering collaboration between universities, commercial companies, and industry associations, the project bridges the gap between theory and practice, supporting digital transformation in higher education. The LEONARDO project introduces innovative teaching methods and develops the Learning and Experimenting open-Access Factory, later in the document referred to as LEAF, to teach Industry 5.0 concepts. This hands-on approach enhances student engagement, creativity, and collaboration, preparing them for real-world challenges. The article discusses the implementation of the mentioned approach, its benefits for students, universities, and industry, and addresses skills gaps.

**Keywords:** Industrial Engineering · Learning Network · Training Collaboration

## 1  Learning Factories in Mechatronic Systems Development

### 1.1  What is a Learning Factory?

This article explores the transformative potential of learning factories in mechatronic systems development. Learning factories offer a dynamic, collaborative environment that bridges the gap between academia and industry, creating a mutually beneficial ecosystem

A. Quesada-Arencibia et al. (Eds.): EUROCAST 2024, LNCS 15172, pp. 294–303, 2025.
https://doi.org/10.1007/978-3-031-82949-9_27

[1]. The case study presented within the context of the LEONARDO project - which is the starting point for the discussion in this paper - underscores the power of international cooperation, the sharing of knowledge, and the collective drive to advance mechatronic education and innovation [2].

In the realm of mechatronics, an intricate fusion of mechanical engineering, electronics, and computer science, the education of future engineers demands an environment that reflects the dynamism of the field. Traditionally, learning factories found their primary home in universities. In the LEONARDO project, we intend to involve not only universities but also commercial companies and industry associations, bridging between theory and practice, offering a vibrant, immersive setting where students learn by doing. The LEONARDO project aims to support the digital transformation plans of higher education institutions (HEIs) by introducing innovative teaching methods and increasing the capacity and readiness of these institutions to manage an effective shift towards digital education [3]. Specifically, LEONARDO focuses on developing a pedagogical approach and curriculum design guidelines that support the teaching of Industry 5.0 content via a combination of digital technologies, such as e-learning, as well as a Learning and Experimenting open-Access Factory (LEAF). The LEAF toolkit and other materials will be developed to support professors and instructors in teaching Industry 5.0 concepts and human-centric factories, effectively"training the trainers". The concept of learning factories is not new, and it has taken various forms over the years. Within the framework of EIT Manufacturing, multiple projects have explored learning factories in the context of manufacturing and Industry 4.0. Initiatives like TFKnownet [4], Lift Europe [5], and Mach4.0 [6] have demonstrated the potential of learning factories in enhancing students' practical knowledge, preparing them for the industry's challenges. However, the competence of learning factories can be shared more effectively. To enhance Europe's competitive position, access to learning factories and resources must be made available to a broader community. EIT Manufacturing is actively constructing a platform for sharing training resources across Europe. Websites like skills.move, an online course offering training in various manufacturing areas, are integral to this effort. The LEONARDO project plays a significant role in this initiative, driven by the belief that the experience gained should be shared with the broader community. Collaboration and knowledge sharing are the keystones to advancing mechatronics. Collaboration fosters a strong, interconnected learning ecosystem that advances mechatronic education. Collective sharing strengthens our knowledge and benefits the entire community. This approach transcends individual institutions and aims to enhance education and innovation on a broader scale. As we journey forward, the LEONARDO project partners are happy to extend an open invitation to institutions and organizations to join us.

## 1.2  LEAF as a Learning Factory

Students have changed and the university needs to adapt to encourage and motivate them. The learning factory concept increases students' interest, boosts soft skills, improves comprehension, and helps them retain knowledge [7]. The term learning factory indicates a learning concept based on a mix of knowledge transfer and practical experience related to the implementation of acquired knowledge. Unlike teaching, the term 'learning' emphasizes the importance of training through experience. A learning factory is defined by [8], as can as well be seen in Fig. 1:

- processes that are authentic, include multiple stations, and comprise technical as well as organizational aspects,
- a setting that is changeable and resembles a real value chain,
- a physical product being manufactured, and
- a didactical concept that comprises formal, informal and non-formal learning, enabled by own actions of the trainees in an on-site learning approach.

A learning factory can have different applications and purposes [1]: teaching, training, or research. Consequently, the learning outcomes may be competence development and/or innovation. In a teaching setting, a realistic replication of certain aspects of a factory helps students to remove the burden of risk by involving them in actively receiving explicit and tacit knowledge and gaining experience in different fields [9].

The LEONARDO project seeks to transform Industrial Engineering and Management (IEM) education by establishing innovative teaching methods, materials, and tools with a human-centric approach in the context of the Industry 5.0 paradigm. Practically, the project will leverage an Industry 5.0 replica of a brewing system as a hands-on learning environment for IEM students. The brewing system, named LEAF, will facilitate innovative learning approaches and new teaching methods. As a learning factory, it adheres to the previously explained definition (Fig. 1).

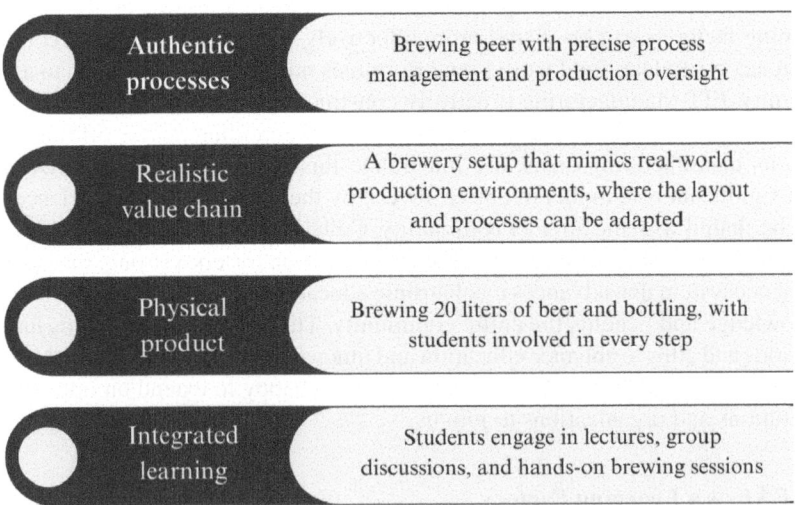

**Authentic processes** — Brewing beer with precise process management and production oversight

**Realistic value chain** — A brewery setup that mimics real-world production environments, where the layout and processes can be adapted

**Physical product** — Brewing 20 liters of beer and bottling, with students involved in every step

**Integrated learning** — Students engage in lectures, group discussions, and hands-on brewing sessions

**Fig. 1.** Adaptation of the Learning Factory definition to the LEONARDO project LEAF

The LEAF brewing system is designed to replicate a real brewery's processes on a smaller scale. This setup includes multiple stations such as mashing, boiling, fermenting, and bottling, providing students with a comprehensive understanding of the brewing process. The system is adaptable, allowing for adjustments to produce different types of beer, reflecting real-world supply chain dynamics and market conditions. Students participating in the LEAF project are involved in every step of the brewing process, from initiating production to bottling the final product. This hands-on experience is complemented by formal lectures on human-centricity, informal group discussions, and practical brewing sessions. This integrated learning approach ensures that students gain both explicit and tacit knowledge, preparing them for future careers in the industry.

Human-centricity is integrated into every aspect of the learning experience in the LEAF. The small-scale replica of a brewing system is not just a technical setup; it is designed to enhance student engagement, creativity, and collaboration. The LEAF setup encourages active participation and hands-on learning. Students are not passive recipients of information; they are active contributors to the brewing process. This engagement fosters a deeper connection to the material and encourages critical thinking and problem-solving. The brewing system is designed to facilitate teamwork. Students work in groups to manage different stages of the brewing process, mirroring real-world collaborative environments. This experience helps them develop essential soft skills such as communication, teamwork, and leadership. The concept has also been proven within the context of the 2024 SGI Smart Green Island Makeathon, the results presented in [10].

The LEONARDO project, with its emphasis on human-centricity, offers a unique and engaging educational experience that prepares students for the challenges of Industry 5.0. By placing students at the center of the learning process, the LEAF project not only enhances technical skills but also fosters creativity, collaboration, and well-being. This holistic approach ensures that students are well-equipped to thrive in the modern industrial landscape.

## 2    Human-Centric Industry 5.0 and LEAF

Within the LEONARDO Project, the main aspect of human-centricity lies in fostering a highly resilient and adaptable workforce. This workforce is essential for thriving in today's rapidly evolving and uncertain business landscape, where employees must cope with challenges, bounce back from setbacks, adapt quickly to changes, and contribute to innovation and growth. Achieving this high resiliency requires a focus on human empowerment and inclusivity, empathetic and social interaction, as well as ethical and responsible technology engineering. Figure 2 illustrates this setup graphically for more clarity. The following sections will describe the individual fields in more detail.

### 2.1    Human Empowerment and Inclusivity

Human empowerment and inclusivity are crucial for building a resilient workforce. Empowering individuals means enabling them, with or without the aid of technology, to make informed decisions and develop the skills and confidence necessary to pursue their goals. It is essential that all individuals, regardless of their background, identity, or abilities, have equal access to opportunities, resources, and participation within the industrial setting. This inclusivity ensures that a diverse range of perspectives and talents can contribute to the success and innovation of the industry.

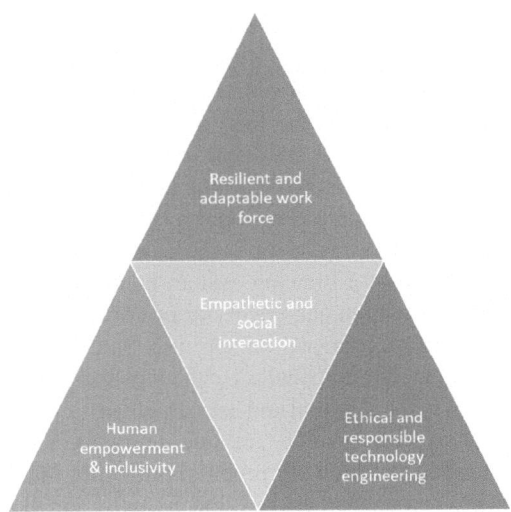

**Fig. 2.** Human-centricity in the context of the LEONARDO project LEAF

## 2.2 Empathetic and Social Interaction

Creating a supportive work environment where employees feel valued, understood, and connected is fundamental for resilience. As humans work alongside machines and AI systems in future factories, promoting social and empathetic interactions - whether human-to-human (H2H), human-to-machine (H2M), or machine-to-machine (M2M) - becomes vital for effective collaboration, mutual learning, and understanding. These interactions foster a sense of community and cooperation, which is essential for navigating the complexities of modern industrial environments.

## 2.3 Ethical and Responsible Technology Engineering

For a resilient workforce, it is imperative that technology engineers commit to upholding fundamental human rights, values, and the dignity of users and stakeholders. They must prioritize transparency and accountability while considering the broader societal implications of technological innovations, including sustainability and environmental impacts. Ethical and responsible technology engineering ensures that technological advancements enhance rather than undermine the well-being of individuals and society as a whole.

Integrating these three factors - human empowerment and inclusivity, empathetic and social interaction, and ethical and responsible technology engineering - supports the development of a resilient workforce. This workforce is well-equipped to meet the demands of the rapidly changing industrial landscape, driving both innovation and growth within human-centric factories.

## 2.4 The Importance of Human Centricity for Industry 5.0

The LEONARDO project, a collaborative initiative between universities and industry, is intentionally designed to meet the evolving needs of both academic institutions and students while keeping the real and relevant needs of the industry in focus. This approach enables a dynamic adaptation to changing circumstances. The project aims to produce hands-on guidelines for universities on training students using the LEAF methodology, tailored to meet the workforce requirements of organizations within the Industry 5.0 paradigm. Moreover, it emphasizes the mutual learning process where industrial organizations also learn how to teach and learn from their staff. Rather than offering a complete training methodology, LEONARDO aims to highlight the process of learning in a didactic and action-based environment. This environment fosters continuous learning, requiring students to work in teams, collaborate with industry, meet commercial demands, balance needs with available technology, and engage in planning and forecasting. Engineers from the industry gain insights into how quickly employees can adapt to new requirements and technology, identify effective strategies for introducing technological changes, and experiment with various technological aspects of the industrial process.

In Industry 5.0, the synergistic collaboration between humans and autonomous systems is critical, leading to the emergence of new skill sets and professional profiles. This transition necessitates a workforce proficient in advanced technical skills and cognitive abilities. Key skills include proficiency in artificial intelligence (AI) and machine learning, as these technologies underpin the automation and smart systems defining Industry 5.0. Additionally, expertise in data analytics is crucial for interpreting and leveraging the vast amounts of data generated by interconnected devices and systems. Technical skills in robotics, cyber-physical systems, and human-machine interfaces are also essential, ensuring employees can effectively collaborate with autonomous systems and optimize their integration into production processes. [11].

Beyond technical competencies, Industry 5.0 demands robust cognitive skills such as complex problem-solving, critical thinking, and creativity. These skills enable workers to innovate and adapt to rapidly changing technological landscapes. Profiles that combine technical expertise with strong interpersonal skills are particularly valuable, facilitating effective teamwork and communication between humans and machines. Moreover, the level of skills required varies across different job roles. For instance, a machine operator does not need to build machine learning models but must understand how AI suggests different actions, the factors involved, and why specific recommendations are given by AI. This nuanced understanding allows operators to effectively interact with AI systems and make informed decisions. By fostering these skill sets through collaborative learning environments like learning factories, organizations can prepare their workforce for the demands of Industry 5.0, driving innovation and maintaining a competitive advantage in the evolving industrial landscape.

In the rapidly evolving landscape of Industry 5.0, critical skills for employees are subject to frequent change, making it essential for universities and educational providers to collaborate closely with the industry. This collaboration ensures that educational programs are continuously updated to reflect the latest technological advancements and industry needs. By working directly with companies, educational institutions can tailor their curricula to include the most relevant and in-demand skills, preparing students effectively for the workforce. Moreover, this partnership allows industries to have a clear overview of the teaching processes and the skill sets of their future employees, facilitating a smoother transition from education to employment.

The LEONARDO Project, which employs the teaching factory methodology for brewing, exemplifies the benefits of such collaborations. This project integrates real-world industrial tasks into educational settings, enabling students to gain hands-on experience with current technologies and practices. Utilizing a didactic factory allows for experimentation and learning without the high costs and risks associated with industrial production. This method enhances the practical skills of students and ensures they are well-versed in addressing contemporary industrial challenges. In the context of Industry 5.0, where technology and skills evolve rapidly, such collaborative initiatives are crucial for fostering a workforce capable of continuous learning and adaptation, driving innovation, and maintaining competitive advantage.

## 3  Collaborative Approach at LEONARDO

The LEONARDO project exemplifies a robust collaborative approach, integrating the efforts of universities, commercial companies, and the broader industry to effectively utilize the LEAF methodology. This collaboration is facilitated through a variety of interactive and practical initiatives, including meetings, workshops, hackathons, and webinars. For instance, webinars on human-centric industrial engineering bring perspectives from industrial companies, universities, and student associations. Practical brewing workshops with students, makeathons during events like SGI Smart Green Island Makeathon, and numerous presentations highlight the active, hands-on nature of the collaboration [10].

In the LEONARDO project, each partner plays a critical role in ensuring the success of the collaborative approach. Universities are pivotal in defining the curriculum and formulating the didactical approach, ensuring that educational content remains current and relevant to Industry 5.0 needs. They provide academic oversight and ensure the pedagogical soundness of the training methodologies. Industry partners contribute technical expertise and define the technical parameters of the actual LEAF. They co-design the learning factory, ensuring it meets the practical needs of the industry and can be used jointly with universities. These partners offer insights into real-world applications and industry standards, ensuring students gain relevant and applicable skills.

Dissemination of findings and methodologies is a joint effort, targeting both academic circles and the general community. Academic dissemination focuses on university teachers and students, sharing best practices and innovations. Broader dissemination aims to engage industries and other interested actors, showcasing the benefits of the teaching factory (TF) approach and encouraging its adoption across various sectors. International cooperation is emphasized, leveraging the diverse perspectives and expertise of partners from several European countries. This international consortium ensures that the project's outcomes are relevant and beneficial to a wide range of stakeholders, transcending national boundaries. While the project is centered on the brewing industry, its communication and dissemination strategies are designed to engage actors across different industries. The brewing process, with its clear and relatable end-product, serves as an effective demonstration of the collaborative approach, making the learning outcomes tangible and easily understood. This not only attracts new students to mechatronic education but also inspires them through a practical, hands-on approach.

The LEONARDO project directly addresses several challenges of manufacturing industry highlighted in the Future of Jobs Report by the World Economic Forum [12], particularly those related to the rapid evolution of required skills and the growing demand for engineers. The World Economic Forum's "Future of Jobs" report emphasizes that the fastest-growing roles are driven by technology, digitalization, and sustainability. These roles necessitate a workforce proficient in both advanced technical skills and cognitive abilities. Skills such as analytical and creative thinking are identified as paramount, with an anticipated disruption of 44% of workers' skills within the next five years. The report underscores the need for continuous upskilling and reskilling, which aligns perfectly with the objectives of the LEONARDO project.

The LEONARDO project, through its collaborative framework, ensures that training programs are continuously updated to reflect the latest technological advancements and industry needs. By working directly with companies, educational institutions can tailor their curricula to include the most relevant and in-demand skills, preparing students effectively for the workforce. This partnership also allows industries to have a clear overview of the teaching processes and the skill sets of their future employees, facilitating a smoother transition from education to employment. The international nature of the LEONARDO project allows for the sharing of best practices and innovations across borders, enhancing the quality and applicability of mechatronic education globally.

Moreover, the project promotes the development of a workforce capable of continuous learning and adaptation. This is achieved through the integration of real-world industrial tasks into educational settings, enabling students to gain hands-on experience with current technologies and practices. Utilizing a didactic factory allows for experimentation and learning without the high costs and risks associated with industrial production. This method enhances the practical skills of students and ensures they are well-versed in addressing contemporary industrial challenges. By fostering these skill sets through collaborative learning environments like learning factories, the LEONARDO project helps bridge the skills gap highlighted in the World Manufacturing Forum's report, driving innovation, and maintaining a competitive advantage in the evolving industrial landscape.

## 4  Conclusion

The LEAF approach is indispensable in the context of Industry 5.0, where the integration of advanced technologies with human-centric processes is paramount. This approach necessitates experimentation, interaction, and the fostering of creativity. It emphasizes decision-making within teams and encourages collaboration across various sectors. By adopting the TF methodology, educational institutions can ensure that their training programs remain relevant and effective, preparing students to meet the dynamic demands of modern industries.

The LEONARDO project provides a practical example of how to implement the TF approach. It underscores the importance of fostering collaboration with industry partners, ensuring that project tasks are not divided but performed together. This collective effort allows for the co-creation of knowledge and skills, aligning educational outcomes with industry needs. Through such collaboration, universities and companies can jointly design and utilize learning factories, providing students with hands-on experience and exposure to real-world industrial challenges.

The expected outcomes of implementing the TF approach through the LEONARDO project are significant for HEIs, students, and companies. For HEIs, it leads to the development of the LEAF teaching methodology and approach, which enhances the academic curriculum and keeps it aligned with industry standards. For students, it offers a more engaging and practical learning experience, fostering a deeper understanding of engineering concepts and their applications. For companies, it ensures a steady pipeline of well-trained graduates who are ready to contribute to innovation and growth. Additionally, the project helps in popularizing engineering education, making it more appealing to prospective students and ensuring that the future workforce is well-equipped to handle the challenges of Industry 5.0.

**Acknowledgments.** This work is supported by the LEONARDO project, funded by the European Commission under [Funded by the European Union] the Erasmus + program KA-220 Cooperation Partnerships for Higher Education - No. 2023–1-IT02-KA220-HED-000164699. The views expressed belong to the author(s) alone and do not necessarily reflect the views of the European Union or the Erasmus + National Agency -INDIRE. Neither the European Union nor the granting administration can be held responsible for them.

**Disclosure of Interests.** The authors have no competing interests to declare that are relevant to the content of this article.

# References

1. Abele, E., et al.: Learning factories for future oriented research and education in manufacturing. CIRP Ann. **66**(2), 803–826 (2017)
2. Darun, M., Palm, D., Athinarayanan, R., Hummel, V., von Leipzig, K.: The learning factory – a new stimulus to enhance international collaboration. Procedia Manufacturing 31, 290–295 (2019), research. Experience. Education. 9th Conference on Learning Factories 2019 (CLF 2019), Braunschweig, Germany
3. Hulla, M., Hammer, M., Karre, H., Ramsauer, C.: A case study based digitalization training for learning factories. Procedia Manufacturing 31, 169–174 (2019), research. Experience. Education. 9th Conference on Learning Factories 2019 (CLF 2019), Braunschweig, Germany
4. EIT Manufacturing: Teaching Factory Knowledge Sharing Network
5. https://www.tfknownet.com/
6. EIT Manufacturing: LIFT European Network of Learning Factories. https://www.eitmanufacturing.eu/news-events/activities/lift-european-network-of- learning-factories/
7. EIT Manufacturing: Learning Factory to Implement Industry 4.0 in Machining. https://www.eitmanufacturing.eu/news-events/activities/learning-factory- to-implement-industry-4–0-in-machining/

8. Maarof, M., Bohari, M.: Students Experience Using Learning Factory at the Faculty of Industrial Management. Journal of Governance and Integrity (2023). https://doi.org/10.15282/jgi.6.2.2023.9652

9. Abele, E.: Learning Factory. In: Laperrière, L., Reinhart, G. (eds) CIRP Encyclopedia of Production Engineering. The International Academy for Production, Springer, Berlin, Heidelberg (2016). https://doi.org/10.1007/978-3-642-35950-7_16828-1

10. Kemeny, Z., et al.: Complementary research and education opportunities - a comparison of Learning Factory facilities and methodologies at TU Wien and MTA SZTAKI. Procedia CIRP **54**, 47–52 (2016)

11. Schlechter, T., Zarev, L., Kuchroo, T., Topa e Ferreira, F.M., Parameswaran Ramachandran, S., Hallemann, E. R-M.: Student Centric Feedback Based Case Study on Modern Educational Methodologies in Engineering Subjects - can we Fill the Industrial and Educational MINT Gap?, EDULEARN24 Proceedings. Palma de Mallorca, Spain. (2024). https://doi.org/10.21125/edulearn.2024

12. Rikala, P., Braun, G., Järvinen, M., Stahre, J., Hämäläinen, R.: Understanding and measuring skill gaps in Industry 4.0 - A review. Technological Forecasting and Social Change, 201 (2024). https://doi.org/10.1016/j.techfore.2024.123206

13. World Economic Forum: The Future of Jobs Report 2023, available at https://www.weforum.org/publications/the-future-of-jobs-report-2023/

# CNN Based Radar Kick Sensor Gesture Recognition Prototype

Shadman Mahmud[1], Thomas Schlechter[1(✉)], and Andreas Loeffler[2]

[1] University of Applied Sciences Upper Austria, 4600 Wels, Austria
shadman.mahmud@students.fh-wels.at, thomas.schlechter@ieee.org
[2] Continental Business Area Autonomous Mobility, 88131 Lindau, Germany
andreas.3.loeffler@continental-corporation.com
https://www.fh-ooe.at/en/, https://www.continental.com/de/

**Abstract.** The concept of kick sensors is aiding users to open or close vehicle doors applying a simple kick gesture using the foot. These sensors have usually been implemented using ultrasound, capacitive sensing, computer vision, and **24GHz** Continuous Wave (CW) radar. This paper discusses the algorithm development and implementation of a kick sensor on a **60GHz** frequency modulated CW radar platform using deep learning. The goal is to develop a robust yet cost-effective solution for real-time kick gesture recognition. This has been achieved using one transmitting and one receiving antenna, an efficient data compression approach, and a convolutional neural network with a low memory requirement that is capable of achieving **97%** accuracy on test data. The final prototype can detect kicks and send control signals to open or close a vehicle's tailgate at an accuracy level of **88%**. Future improvements are discussed as well.

**Keywords:** Gesture Recognition · FMCW Radar · CNN · Radar Kick Sensor

## 1 Introduction

Capacitive, ultrasonic, and vision-based sensors provide cheap solutions for kick sensing, but their performance is affected by variations in the physical environment around them [11]. Such variations have less of an effect on radar sensors. A Frequency Modulated Continuous Wave (FMCW) radar sensor can perform kick-sensing operations while providing range and velocity information. This makes FMCW kick sensing worth exploring because of the versatility it provides over other technologies. It is a more expensive solution comparatively, but it provides the scope for integrating multiple functions besides the kick-sensing function.

Reference designs posted by Texas Instruments [6,7] show that capacitive and ultrasonic solutions for kick sensors have been explored. Two vision-based approaches have been presented in [12,16] that use the rear fish-eye camera found in most modern vehicles for kick sensing. The former uses computer-vision algorithms like edge detection, whereas the latter uses a deep learning

A. Quesada-Arencibia et al. (Eds.): EUROCAST 2024, LNCS 15172, pp. 304–315, 2025.
https://doi.org/10.1007/978-3-031-82949-9_28

model. The former approach is less adaptable to varying environments, giving the deep learning method an advantage. The deep learning approach is able to achieve a kick detection accuracy of 93% and uses an Artificial Intelligent (AI) accelerator during real-time operation. A 24 GHz CW radar is used for kick sensing by [4,14]. The classifier model in [14] achieves 99% accuracy while occupying 248 kB of space in the memory. More radar-based approaches have been explored, while the fields of application are different, including fall detection [8], human activity classification [9,10], and hand gesture recognition [2]. To the best of our knowledge, kick sensing using a 60 GHz FMCW radar with deep learning is yet to be explored, which this document deals with.

The structure of this document is as follows. Section 2 introduces the technical background and methodology of implementation of the kick sensor prototype. Results are presented in Sect. 3, while Sect. 4 summarizes the findings and provides an outlook for future extensions.

## 2  Methodology

Radar development boards come equipped with a radar chip for transmitting and receiving radar signals and a baseboard for providing power and handling data processing. In the development and implementation of the kick sensor prototype, two different baseboards sharing a common radar chip, as shown in Fig. 1, are used. Test measurements taken with the left hardware combination are used for the development of the data processing and classification algorithm. After algorithm's performance is validated, it is implemented on the hardware combination on the right. The end result is a kick sensor prototype, and this methodology section portrays the steps taken to reach it.

### 2.1  Kick Sensor Environment Definition and Radar Settings

A kick sensor suitable for placement in most vehicles of low and high height shall detect kicks while having a 20 cm to 40 cm ground clearance. As has been explored in practical trials, a fast-paced kick results in a radial velocity of around 31 cm/s with the foot lifting by approximately 8.4 cm above the ground. Translation of these requirements to radar settings [13] indicates a chirp sweep bandwidth of 3.75 GHz, periodic chirps with a duration of 2.57 ms, including delays, 42 samples per chirp, and 32 chirps per frame. This enables a range resolution of 4 cm, a maximum detectable range of 64 cm, and a maximum detectable velocity of roughly 48 cm/s. The Analog to Digital Converter (ADC) sampling frequency is set to 2 MHz, while one Tx and one Rx antennae are enabled. These specifications are implemented on an Infineon BGT60TR13C FMCW radar sensor with an Atmel baseboard, shown in Fig. 2.

### 2.2  Radar ADC Data Processing Chain

In this section, the workflow for processing radar ADC data is described in detail. After the radar settings have been defined, the ADC data processing pipeline

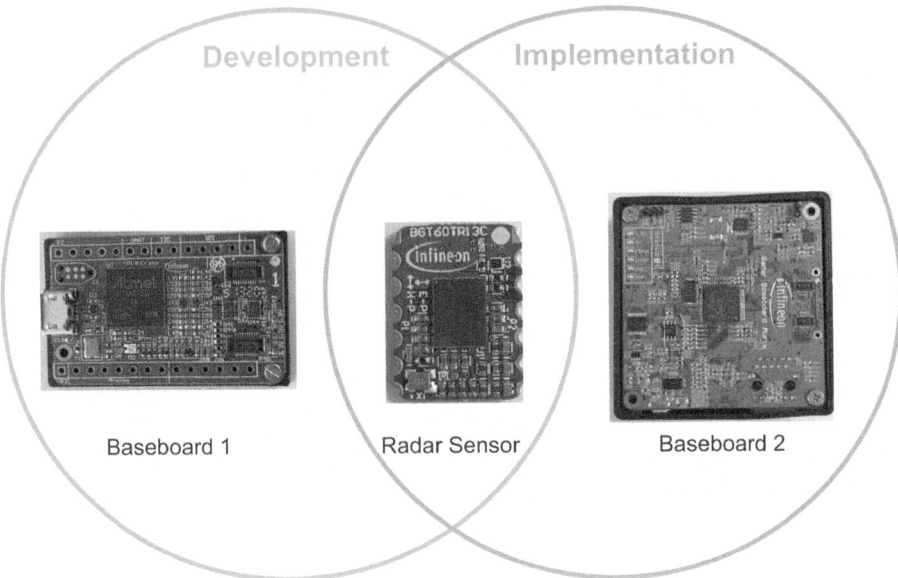

**Fig. 1.** Hardware Used for Development and Implementation.

shown in Fig. 3 is used. Measurements of the oscillatory motion of a pendulum are taken, and the raw ADC data is input into this pipeline. During processing, a Fast Fourier Transform (FFT) implementation is used to extract range and velocity information from the received radar signals or chirps [3,18]. This requires a 2D-FFT, which is an FFT applied along two dimensions of the received signal. The use of a Chebyshev window function accompanies this signal processing task to reduce spectral leakage [5]. Figure 4 shows the usage of the window function on a received chirp in both the time and frequency domain. The green bounding box indicates the peak corresponding to the distance of the pendulum's bob. The peak in the red bounding box occurs due to the radar sensor's self-reflection.

The 2D-FFT delivers a radar frame with Doppler values along the columns, referred to as Doppler bins. This frame is first compressed by taking the maximum along each Doppler bin and then transposed. This procedure is repeated for all the available frames, which are then sequentially merged and scaled to uint8 values. Figure 5 shows the resulting sinusoid wave pattern, whose time period is the same as the time period of the oscillation of the pendulum.

This confirms that the radar settings and data processing is performed correctly. To remove the frequency components from self-reflection in Fig. 4, a finite impulse response [1] constrained-band equiripple bandpass filter [2] is applied on every chirp before performing the FFT. The filter is of order ten and heuristically designed to pass frequency components corresponding to the 20cm to 40cm range. Since the filter has a linear phase [15], it preserves the phase relationships within the radar signal. Due to its tap delay, the first ten samples of every chirp

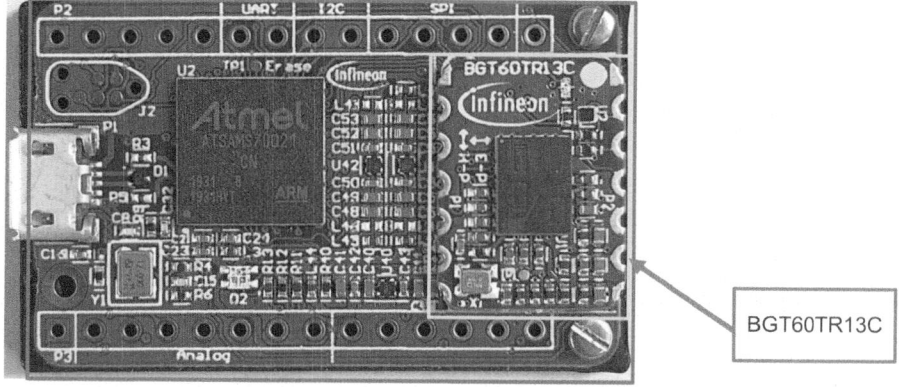

**Fig. 2.** Development Setup using BGT60TR13C with Atmel Baseboard.

are removed after filtering, effectively making every chirp contain 32 samples. Figure 6 demonstrates the effectiveness of this filter. This filter also helps to reduce the intensity of the white lines along the middle of the pattern in Fig. 5. The white line appears due to high values caused by the radar's self-reflection, and the filter attenuates these values. This is evident in the patterns shown in Fig. 7, which indicate valid and invalid kick gestures.

### 2.3    CNN Setup

Several single-channel PNG images of dimensions 32x32 are obtained. These contain valid and invalid kick gestures that result from processing ADC data. To collect this ADC data, the radar sensor was made to face toward the ground at a distance of 38cm and triggered. Measurements are taken of valid gestures that include slow and fast-paced kicks, invalid ones that include a static ground surface, people walking around the sensor, and objects rolling in its view. The objective is the simulation of scenarios that are plausible when the kick sensor is equipped on a car. These images are transformed into a suitable data-set for training a Convolutional Neural Network (CNN). The data-set contains the two classes 'kick' and 'no-kick'.

The CNN sketched in Fig. 8 is used for classifying the detections from the data sets. Following the CNNs in [2,19], this CNN is designed with the goal of attaining high classification accuracy while using a low number of parameters and Multiply Accumulate Operations (MAC) [17]. It consists of three convolutional layers and one fully connected layer, being fed with 2050 trainable parameters, and executing 246926 MAC operations. When compiled, its size in memory is 50kB. Despite requiring less memory, it achieves an accuracy of 97% on the validation set during training. During inference, it provides two predictions corresponding to the 'kick' and 'no-kick' classes.

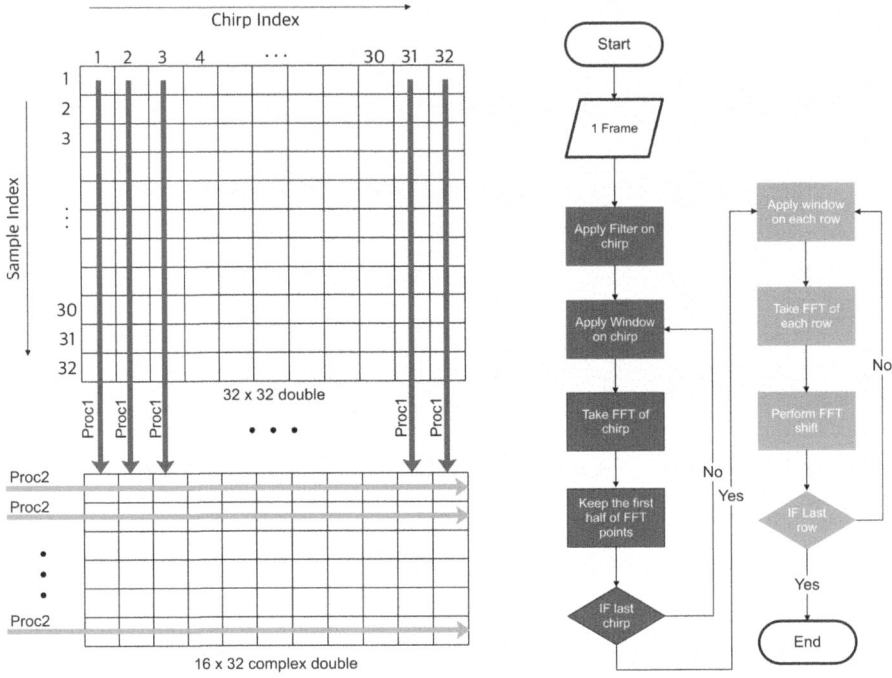

**Fig. 3.** ADC Data Processing Pipeline.

## 2.4    Implementation

The described ADC processing and the CNN combined makes the kick sensor algorithm. This algorithm, implemented using Matlab and Pytorch, is converted to C code for embedded implementation. The platform used for this task is the BGT60TR13C on an Infineon Aurix TriCore TC356TA baseboard. This serves as the hardware for implementation of the kick sensor prototype, shown in Fig. 9. The TC356TA microcontroller unit on the baseboard has three Central Processing Unit (CPU) cores, two of which are used for the kick sensor application. One CPU core interfaces with the BGT60TR13C. It receives radar frames in real-time, which are stored in a buffer. When it is filled up, it stops receiving new frames and passes all the frames it contains to the kick sensor algorithm, which is located on the second CPU core. Here the radar ADC frames are processed into gestures, which are then classified by the CNN.

Since the CNN classifies all the gestures sent from the buffer at once, an integer threshold value is assigned. If the number of kicks registered as per the CNN exceeds this threshold value, it is then decided that the user made a kick. This is a simple but effective way of controlling the robustness of the performance of the kick sensor. By simply increasing or decreasing the threshold, CNNs with high or low accuracies can be used. The threshold can be set high if the CNN used has high accuracy. Due to the high threshold, it can be ensured that the CNN

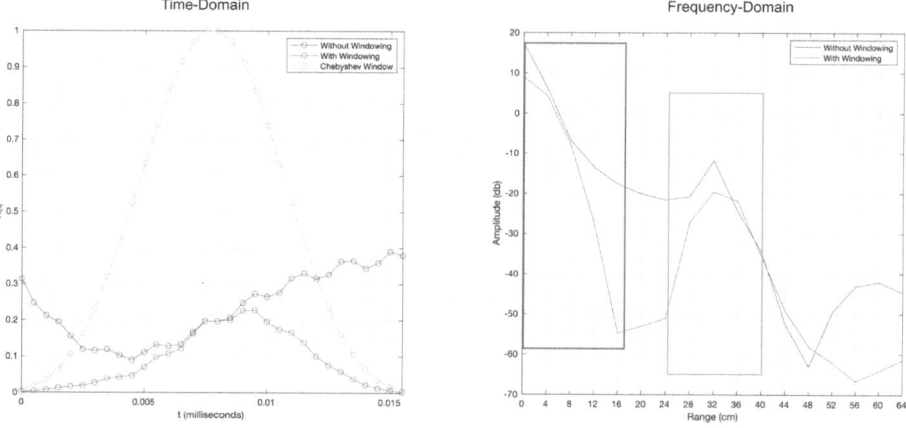

**Fig. 4.** Usage of the Chebyshev Window Function. (Color figure online)

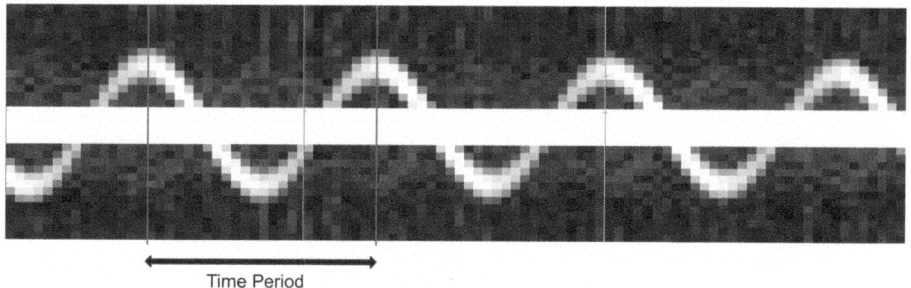

Time Period

**Fig. 5.** Resulting Sinusoid Wave Pattern.

is confident that a kick has been executed. On the other hand, if the accuracy is low, the threshold can be lowered, thus allowing a CNN of low accuracy to make mistakes in classifying and still provide correct results in the end.

In either case, if the threshold value is exceeded, a control pulse is sent to one of its pins to actuate the tailgate of a car. The width of this control pulse is variable from 50ms all the way up to 5s. After all the frames have been processed, the DSP algorithm stops, and the buffer starts to get filled up again. The process repeats as a deterministic loop. It takes 5s for the buffer to fill up with 64 frames and 300ms for them to be processed by the DSP algorithm. This timing can be changed by just changing the buffer size. If decreased, the buffer will be filled up faster, and the DSP algorithm will take even less time to process as there will be less frames. Even then, this loop will still be real-time.

To know the status of this loop when the board is running, three unique light indicator sequences are used. When the loop is in buffering phase, a blinking orange LED is lit on the status LED of the radar baseboard. During the DSP phase, the status LED turns static red, and if a kick is detected, then for the

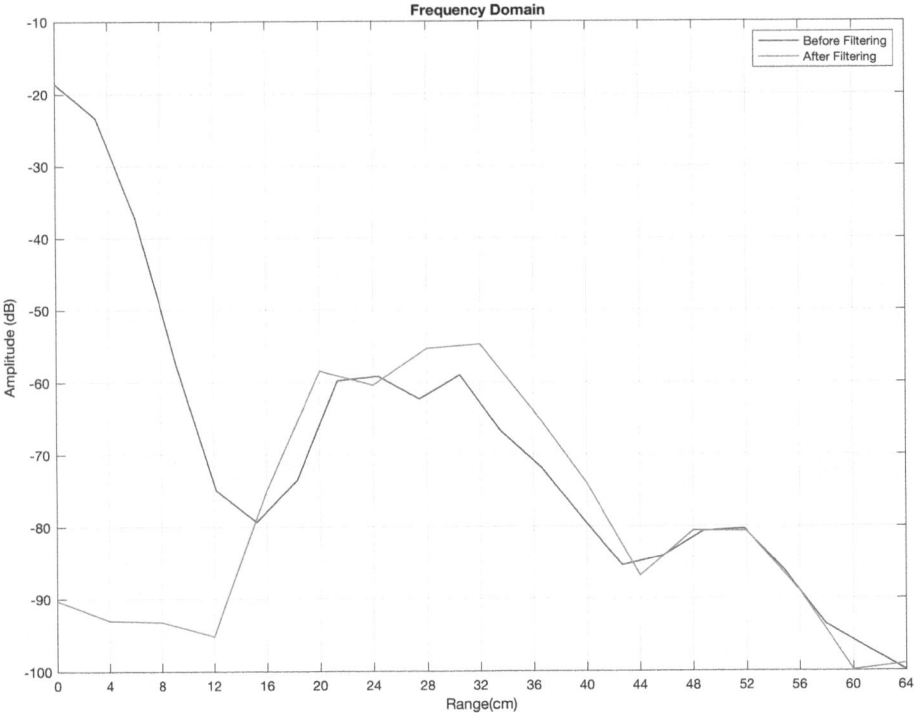

**Fig. 6.** Demonstration of the Effectiveness of the used Filter.

next buffering duration, the LED lits greenish yellow. If no kick is detected, the LED shows the usual blinking orange. Figure 10 shows the kick sensor prototype in its three states during operation.

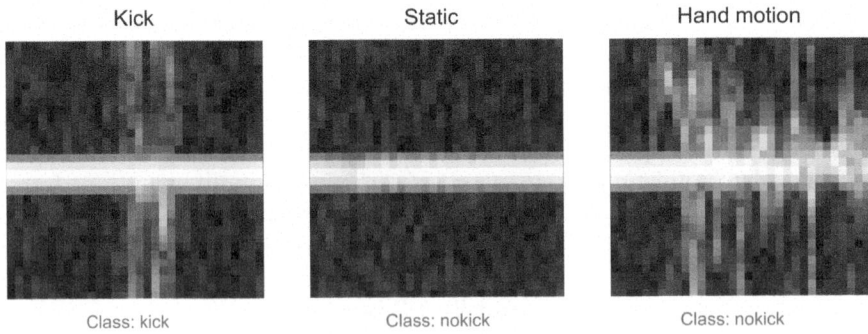

**Fig. 7.** Pattern Illustration.

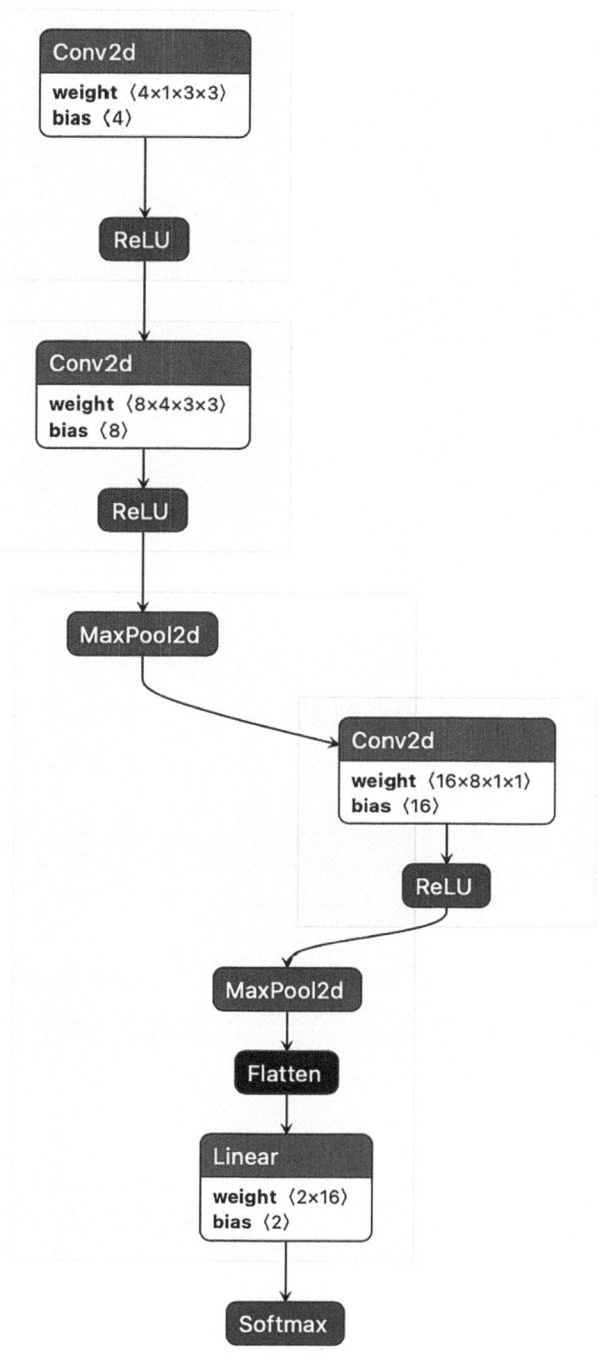

**Fig. 8.** CNN used for Classification.

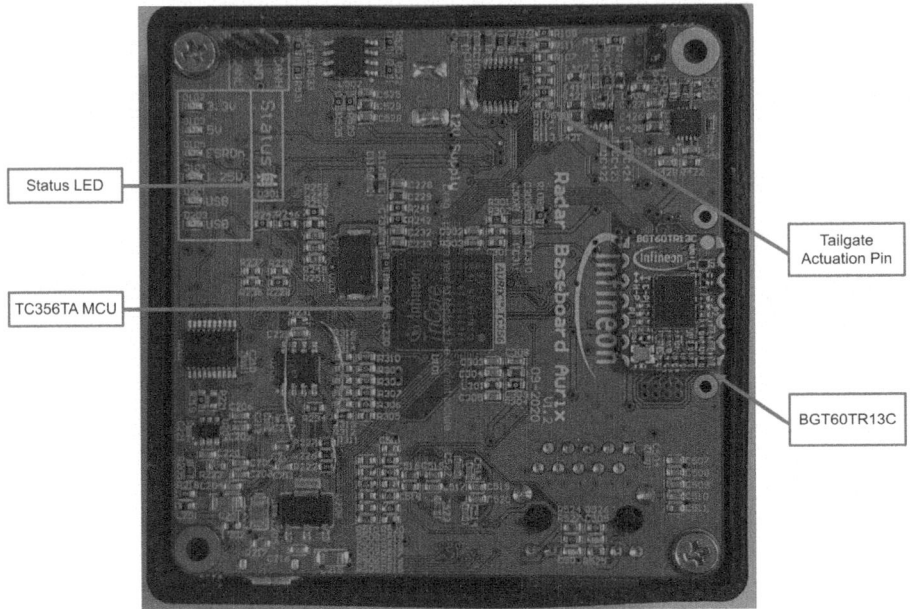

**Fig. 9.** Implementation Setup using BGT60Tr13C with Infineon Aurix TriCore TC356TA baseboard.

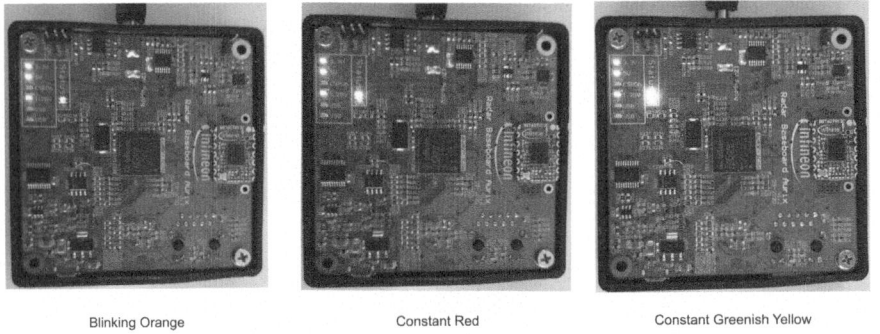

**Fig. 10.** Kick Sensor Prototype.

## 3    Results

The kick sensor prototype is finally tested on a vehicle placed at a height of 40cm from a concrete floor, shown in Fig. 11. These conditions differ from when measurements were taken to create the initial data-set. Hence, new measurements are taken in the new environment, and the ADC data is subsequently processed. A new data-set is developed using six kinds of kicks in the 'kick' class. These are slow and fast kicks in the straight, left, and right diagonal directions, as illustrated in Fig. 11 c. The 'no-kick' class contains the same activities as before but in a new environment. The CNN is trained with this new data-set for a limited time and achieves an accuracy of 88%. With the CNN being of slightly lower accuracy now, the threshold value is reduced to 4. Having made these changes, the kick sensor has not failed to recognize the six kinds of valid kick gestures. It also does not make false detections when looking at the static ground or when objects are rolled below it. However, walking close to the kick sensor makes it believe a kick is performed. The reason for this is the limitation of the data-set used to train the CNN. When creating this data-set, walking at a 30cm distance from the kick sensor has been included in the 'no-kick' class, which the kick sensor does not falsely detect as a kick. Still, walking close to the sensor is missed, making the CNN in the kick sensor believe that the person walking close by is making a kick gesture.

There is also the opportunity to implement the DSP loop used here in a slightly different way. Instead of the buffer being filled up with 64 frames every time, it can be filled up with 32 frames once at a time. These 32 frames are passed to the DSP. Due to data compression, these 32 frames are converted into a single 32x32 gesture that is immediately classified by the CNN. Subsequently, when the next buffering phase arrives, the buffer is filled with one new frame. This new frame is immediately passed to the DSP algorithm, which processes and appends it to the the previous gesture. The first column in that gesture is removed, and the CNN now classifies this modified gesture. This way, the old gesture is modified with new gestures over time. This approach enables faster performance. The concrete implementation, which we will call sliding window kick detection, will be part of a follow-up study.

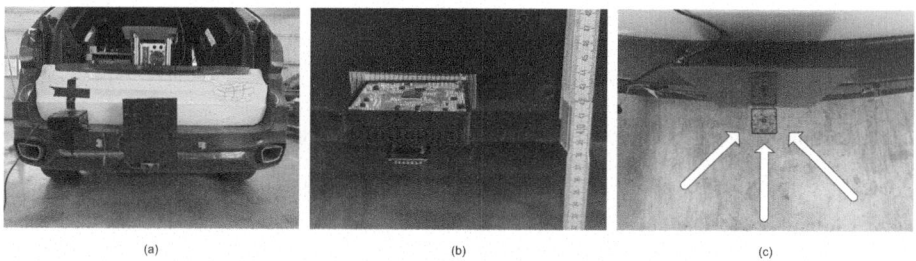

(a)                      (b)                      (c)

**Fig. 11.** Kick Sensor Test Environment.

## 4   Conclusion

We have demonstrated that a highly reliable 'kick' detection can be guaranteed using the approach presented in this paper. The used combination of the proposed DSP chain along with a CNN has already exhibited that it can perform well, reaching 97% accuracy on the initial data-set while delivering 88% considering the modified real-world data-set. Future work on this kick sensor can include training the CNN thoroughly while covering multiple scenarios. It is noteworthy that the Aurix baseboard incorporates a DSP chip for providing hardware acceleration when performing FFT. This has not been used in this study. Using the chip can improve performance such that every frame is processed as soon as it is available without depending on a buffer.

**Acknowledgments.** We like to thank our fellow colleagues from Infineon for their continuous support during the development of this project and publication.

**Disclosure of Interests.** The authors have no competing interests to declare that are relevant to the content of this article.

# References

1. Banerjee, S., Sinha, A.: Performance analysis of different DSP algorithms on advanced microcontroller and FPGA. In: 2009 International Conference on Advances in Computational Tools for Engineering Applications. IEEE (jul 2009). https://doi.org/10.1109/actea.2009.5227848
2. Ehrnsperger, M.G., Brenner, T., Hoese, H.L., Siart, U., Eibert, T.F.: Real-time gesture detection based on machine learning classification of continuous wave radar signals. IEEE Sensors J. **21**(6), 8310–8322 (mar 2021). https://doi.org/10.1109/jsen.2020.3045616
3. Gamba, J.: Radar signal processing for autonomous driving. Springer Singapore (2020). https://doi.org/10.1007/978-981-13-9193-4
4. Innosent Gmbh: 24ghz cw radar kick sensor. Online (Mar 2023). https://www.innosent.de/en/automotive/kick-sensor/
5. Harris, F.: On the use of windows for harmonic analysis with the discrete fourier transform. Proc. IEEE **66**(1), 51–83 (1978). https://doi.org/10.1109/proc.1978.10837
6. Texas Instruments: Reference design for capacitive kick sensor. Online (Mar 2023). https://www.ti.com/tool/TIDA-01409
7. Texas Instruments: Reference design for ultrasonic kick sensor. Online (Mar 2023). https://www.ti.com/tool/TIDA-01424
8. Jokanovic, B., Amin, M.: Fall detection using deep learning in range-doppler radars. IEEE Trans. Aerosp. Electron. Syst. **54**(1), 180–189 (Feb 2018). https://doi.org/10.1109/taes.2017.2740098
9. Kim, Y., Alnujaim, I., Oh, D.: Human activity classification based on point clouds measured by millimeter wave MIMO radar with deep recurrent neural networks. IEEE Sensors J. **21**(12), 13522–13529 (jun 2021). https://doi.org/10.1109/jsen.2021.3068388
10. Kim, Y., Moon, T.: Human detection and activity classification based on micro-doppler signatures using deep convolutional neural networks. IEEE Geosci. Remote Sens. Lett. **13**(1), 8–12 (Jan 2016). https://doi.org/10.1109/lgrs.2015.2491329
11. Kinnaird, C.: Comparing capacitive and ultrasonic kick to open sensing. Online (Sep 2017). https://e2e.ti.com/blogs_/b/behind_the_wheel/posts/comparing-capacitive-and-ultrasonic-kick-to-open-sensing

12. Liu, J., et al.: Vision-based feet detection power liftgate with deep learning on embedded device. J. Phys.: Conf. Series **2302**(1), 012010 (Jul 2022). https://doi.org/10.1088/1742-6596/2302/1/012010

13. Mauro, G., Chmurski, M., Servadei, L., Pegalajar-Cuellar, M., Morales-Santos, D.P.: Few-shot user-definable radar-based hand gesture recognition at the edge. IEEE Access **10**, 29741–29759 (2022). https://doi.org/10.1109/access.2022.3155124

14. Shankar, Y., Santra, A.: Valid kick recognition in smart trunks based on hidden markov model using doppler radar. In: 2019 International Radar Conference (RADAR). IEEE (Sep 2019). https://doi.org/10.1109/radar41533.2019.171245

15. Smith, S.W.: Digital signal processing. Newnes (2003)

16. Su, C.L., Lu, M.C.: Vision-based automatic trunk opener for automotive electronics. In: 2018 IEEE International Conference of Safety Produce Informatization (IICSPI). IEEE (Dec 2018). https://doi.org/10.1109/iicspi.2018.8690515

17. Taghavi, M., Shoaran, M.: Hardware complexity analysis of deep neural networks and decision tree ensembles for real-time neural data classification. In: 2019 9th International IEEE/EMBS Conference on Neural Engineering (NER). IEEE (Mar 2019). https://doi.org/10.1109/ner.2019.8716983

18. Tong, Z.T.Z., Reuter, R., Fujimoto, M.: Fast chirp FMCW radar in automotive applications. In: IET International Radar Conference 2015. Institution of Engineering and Technology (2015). https://doi.org/10.1049/cp.2015.1362

19. Truong, T.D., Nguyen, V.T., Tran, M.T.: Lightweight deep convolutional network for tiny object recognition. In: Proceedings of the 7th International Conference on Pattern Recognition Applications and Methods. SCITEPRESS - Science and Technology Publications (2018). https://doi.org/10.5220/0006752006750682

# Comparison of Different Battery-Powered Tag Positions for Lower Limb Gesture Detection

Christina Hofer[1]([✉]), Julia Mayer[1], Valentin Sturm[1], Klaus Pendl[1], Erwin Schimbäck[1], Christian Kastl[1], and Frederick Runte[2]

[1] Linz Center of Mechatronics GmbH, 4040 Linz, Austria
`christina.hofer@lcm.at`
[2] HANNING ELEKTRO-WERKE GmbH & Co. KG, 33813 Oerlinghausen, Germany
`frederick.runte@hanning-hew.com`
`https://www.hanning-hew.com/`

**Abstract.** Gesture recognition is certainly gaining popularity across various domains. In scenarios where dexterity with hands or feet is challenging, such recognition methods proves particularly advantageous. The objective of this study is to compare the efficacy and suitability of an existing control scheme employing battery powered tags on lower limbs on different new positions for controlling a medical treatment bed. Following an evaluation of the new options, the best-resulting position is examined more closely and then compared with the previous published version. Thereby the preexisting neural network of the previous version is used to achieve findings of the model accuracy. The system takes gyroscope and acceleration data as input variables transmitted by a wireless tag. By comparing the positioning of the tag at the ankle with the placement in the trouser pocket, an accuracy of 97.6% which constitutes a significant improvement of the previous model with an overall accuracy of 89.1%. Given the highly favorable initial results, the potential exists to improve the performance by recording larger amounts of data, giving a greater variety of information.

**Keywords:** Gesture Recognition · Human-Machine-Interaction · Neural Network · Machine Learning · Wearable Device

## 1 Introduction

Gesture recognition constitutes a pivotal field within computer science and language technology. Its core objective lies in accurately identifying and interpreting human gestures through mathematical algorithms. Gestures, such as hand signals or facial expressions, can be inferred from certain movement or physical state. Emotion recognition from facial expressions and hand gestures is also part of this field [1]. Upper-Limb Gesture Recognition involves detecting and interpreting hand and arm movements to understand user intentions. Researchers have developed wearable gesture recognition algorithms to improve reliability and robustness. These algorithms process data from multiple sensors to recognize gestures more accurately [2]. Combining data from different sensors (e.g., Inertial Measurement Units (IMUs) and Electromyography Sensors (EMGs)) enhances gesture recognition performance, in contrast to evaluating the sources individually. Fusion techniques integrate information to create a more comprehensive understanding of user movements [3,4]. The integration of lower limb gestures alongside manual hand gestures is gaining prominence. Researchers recognize the growing importance of incorporating feet-based gestures into human-computer interaction systems [5]. In robotics, lower limb gestures can enhance robot control and navigation. For instance, a robot could follow a user's foot gestures to assist with tasks [6]. Individuals with upper limb disabilities can benefit from lower limb gestures. Controlling devices (e.g., smartphones, smart home systems) hands-free improves accessibility [7]. This article presents different positions of a contactless lower-limb worn tag to control a medical treatment bed. This document is structured as follows: Sect. 2 states the main problem. Section 3 points out the different tag positions and the final selection. Section 4 points out how the preprocessing and the data acquisition was implemented by using the selected tag. Results and conclusion are described in Sect. 5 and 6 respectively.

## 2   Problem Statement

A significant challenge of currently available medical treatment beds is the inability to operate them hands-free. Thus, in scenarios where such an operational mode is advantageous or even necessary, the integration of wearable wireless sensors for control provides valuable assistance to operators. This work presents an updated solution for the height adjustment of a medical treatment bed by means of predefined gestures of the lower limbs with the aim of facilitating a hand-free operational mode. The predecessing model was discussed in [5], and already focused on a position in which the tag was in the trouser pocket. This provided solid results, nevertheless certain critical elements still needed to be examined more closely. Due to the tag's consistent slippage within its previous position in the trouser pocket, compounded by variations in pocket placement across different pants, it occasionally yielded weak signals. As part of our research, we have made the strategic decision to assess a new tag position and directly compare it with the previously examined location. Our primary objective is to mitigate and reduce errors arising from tag positioning while simultaneously optimizing the response time of the medical treatment bed. Furthermore, the gesture chosen as a termination condition in the last model, namely a tapping movement, was excluded, given its propensity to induce misdetections. This comprehensive evaluation aims to enhance the overall performance of our system.

## 3    Tag Comparision and Selection

The position of the wireless tag was optimized by comparing different placements. Since one of the main criteria is to wear the tag on the leg, a number of different configurations were analyzed. As shown in Fig. 1, three new positions were considered. Participants in Fig. 1 wear the tags while sitting and standing. To minimize the risk of slipping and to ensure a constant hold, the tags are attached with a velcro strap.

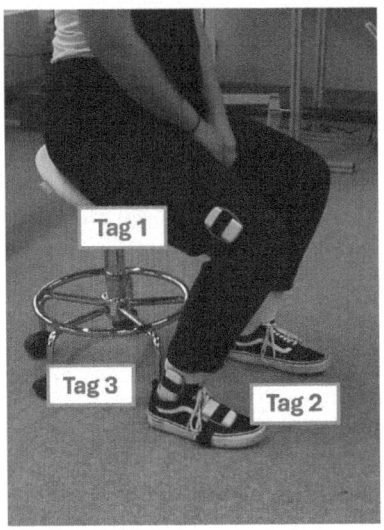 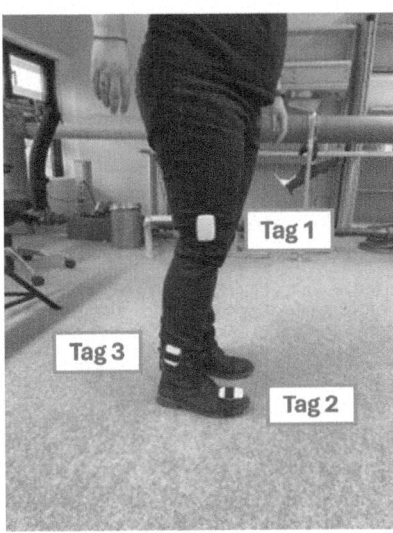

**Fig. 1.** New tag placements to compare: above the knee (Tag 1), instep of the foot (Tag 2), ankle (Tag 3)

### 3.1    Measurement Data Evaluation

Measurement recordings were conducted to assess the impact of three new tag positions. In this initial phase, two test participants were recorded, with simultaneous data collection from the tags. As already shown in Fig. 1, the tags were fixed to the leg performing the gestures on the three positions. In addition to the measurements, the trials were recorded on video to provide more information for later analysis. In contrast to the old measurements, where each gesture was recorded separately, this time a sequence of gestures was specified, which the subjects had to perform during the recordings. The gestures selected are shown in Table 1. Furthermore, the tapping gesture, introduced in [5], was omitted, since the old version contained errors which we attributed to said gesture. In order to be able to evaluate the recordings more effectively, additional criteria were created to provide a better decision in terms of the tag. These criterias are:

**Table 1.** Gestures and Classes included in predefined measurement sequence

| Class | Gesture | Gesture Number |
|---|---|---|
| Class 0 - C0 | Standing still, Walking, Massage | G0, G1, G2 |
| Class 1 - C1 | Pump up/down | G3 |
| Class 2 - C2 | Pump sideways | G4 |

1. Tag Placement
2. Comfort of Wearing
3. Signal Intensity
4. Distinguishability of Gestures

During the experimental sessions, it was observed that not all tags were consistently recorded due to the displacement of Tag 1 (positioned above the knee). The occurrence of slippage and unintended opening of the velcro fastening led to discomfort for the test subjects. Consequently, the decision was made to exclude Tag 1 from further detailed examination, given that it did not meet the predefined criteria during the initial evaluation. Following the recording of data from both test subjects, the initial analysis focused on the raw data from the remaining two tags. Raw data from Tag 2 and Tag 3 provided strong signals, i.e. the gestures which were recorded were easily distinguishable, upon a visual inspection. In pursuit of further insights, the raw data underwent transmission through the existing 1D Convolutional Neural Network (CNN) augmented with an orientation filter. This process aimed to provide an initial estimation of the accuracy associated with various tag positions. In the context of human activity recognition, it is common to work within the one-dimensional domain, as opposed to the more typical two-dimensional domain encountered in CNNs. Specifically, human activity data often involves sequential or time-series information, such as sensor readings over time, which aligns with the one-dimensional nature of the data [8]. Figure 2 shows the first evaluation of the model, describing the accuracy and loss of the model. The result of placement at the ankle gives an accuracy of 68.5% and at the instep of the foot an accuracy of 58.3%. The estimated accuracy quantifies the proportion of correctly classified samples in classification tasks. For this comparison, a limited dataset was used for training in the initial model estimation. This procedure was carried out in order to be able to perform further evaluations.

## 3.2 Tag Evaluation and Selection

After thorough analysis of several measurements, including an evaluation of the four criteria mentioned in Sect. 3.1, we decided for a single tag position for further evaluation. By attaching the tag with a velcro fastener, the movement is significantly reduced in comparison to the previous version in the trouser pocket. The improved fastening minimizes various errors that could be caused by the orientation filter, as repeated changes in orientation, paired with an inherent

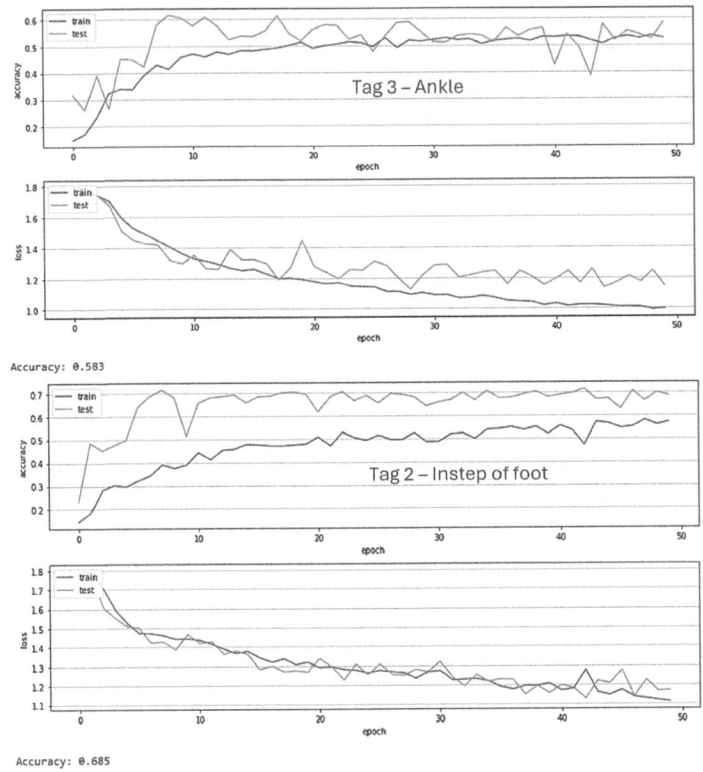

**Fig. 2.** Comparison of Tag 2 and Tag 3 after using CNN model defined in [5]

lag of correction of said filter, may increase various error. Furthermore, the signal intensity is strengthened by the fixation and clearer signals are obtained in acceleration and gyroscope axes, which can provide better prediction accuracy in terms of faster activation and deactivation of the treatment bed movement. Based on feedback from the participants, the ankle tag was reported to be highly comfortable during gesture performance. Subsequent measurements and data recordings were conducted using Tag 3, positioned on the ankle.

## 4    Data Recording and Pre-processing

The following measurements and descriptions focus on the placement of the tag at the ankle. The same sensor, that was used for the previous measurements with placement in the trouser pockets, was also used for the measurements on the ankle. A significant advancement that highlights the sensor used in the past and present is the wirelessly connected, battery-powered tag. This tag discerns performed gestures through motion data and subsequently relays relevant commands to the treatment bed's control system. The result is a seamless, contactless control mechanism [5]. The frequency rate recorded was 59.5 Hz. Eight

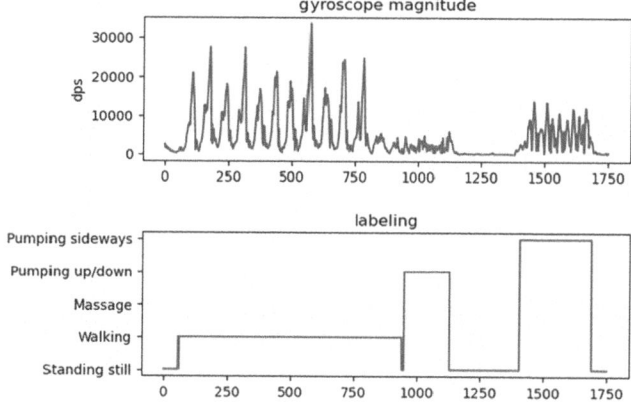

**Fig. 3.** Representation of raw data and labeled data after using the video software

participants had to perform a predefined test sequence, with raw data being saved for further analysis. Thereby the tag was placed on the ankle of the foot being performed. Two measurements were made in standing position and two measurements while sitting, with all gestures (Table 1) present in the sequence. In addition to the sensor data, video recordings were ancillary captured. These recordings served as valuable documentation for the study. To streamline the labeling process of individual gestures, specialized software was used. This software enables the correlation between unprocessed signal data and the corresponding video footage, enhancing the accuracy of gesture annotations (Fig. 3). As various gestures were performed in a test recording, the data had to be subsequently labeled in order to be usable for training the neural network. The newly labeled data, comprising both raw sensor data and associated annotations, undergoes processing through the existing orientation filter. In order to mitigate the impact of orientation changes during usage, the previously established orientation filter is used. Leveraging the acquired motion data, this filter estimates the direction of gravity with respect to the coordinate frame associated with the tag [5]. This processed data is now prepared for utilization in training or fine-tuning neural network models.

## 5   Results

In order to get comparable results to the old model, the same CNN was used. Since we are provided with sequential data, i.e. acceleration and gyroscope data, the 1-D CNN is still essential. The focus of the first evaluations and calculations of the accuracy of the network was on the categorical classifier, which corresponds to the categories according to the Table 1, where C0, C1 C2 represent the categories move up (C1), move down (C2) or no movement (C0). Eight participants were included in the study to compare the performance of the new model with the previous version. The dataset collected from these participants

322    C. Hofer et al.

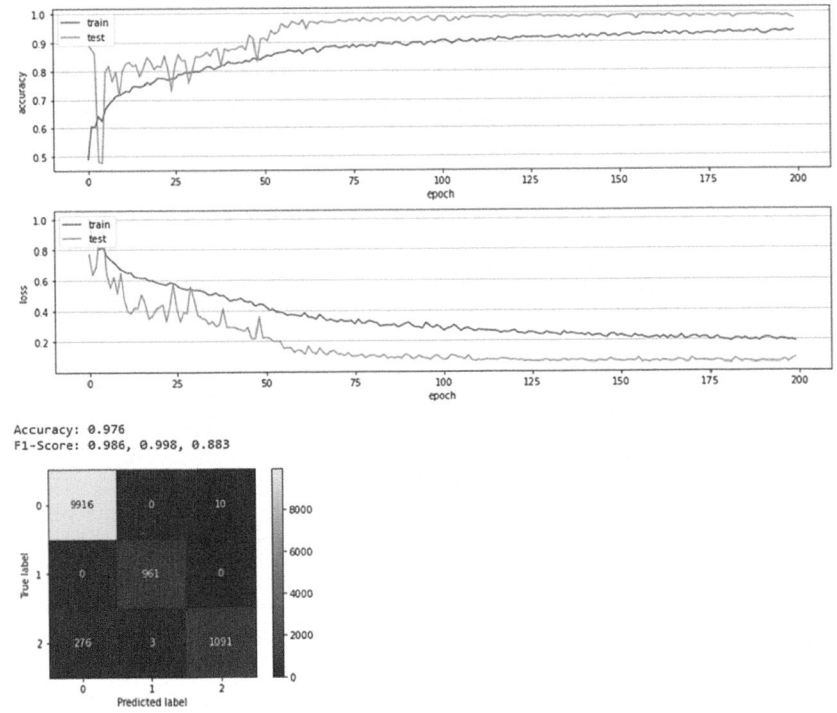

**Fig. 4.** Depiction of the training process with respect to training and test error, loss and final confusion matrix with accuracy and F1-Score.

was utilized for training the neural network. After running 200 epochs, the categorical classifier achieved an impressive overall accuracy of 97.6%, which is shown in Fig. 4. In contrast, the previous model achieved only 89.1% accuracy using the same categorical classifier in the CNN. The accuracy measures the proportion of correctly classified samples. It's particularly relevant for classification tasks. For a categorical classifier, it's the ratio of correct predictions to the total number of samples. In Fig. 4, one can observe the training process, the behavior of the epochs, and the overall accuracy. In the first subplot of Fig. 4, the accuracy of the test and training process of 200 epochs is shown and below the loss over the time. The F1 scores of the three classes provide valuable insights into a classification model's ability to correctly identify relevant instances. The confusion matrix in Fig. 4 shows how well the gestures are predicted by comparing it to the actual class labels (Table 1). To evaluate the model's performance, a novel dataset was collected, and this raw data was subsequently fed into the model. The raw data is visually represented in the first two subplots of the accompanying Fig. 5, with the annotated gesture clearly marked. The third subplot displays the model's predictions, which align seamlessly with the observed gestures (Table 1). Notably, the model rapidly discerned between upward, downward, and no movement. Furthermore, practical testing on the medical treatment bed confirmed that the model accurately responded to the gestures.

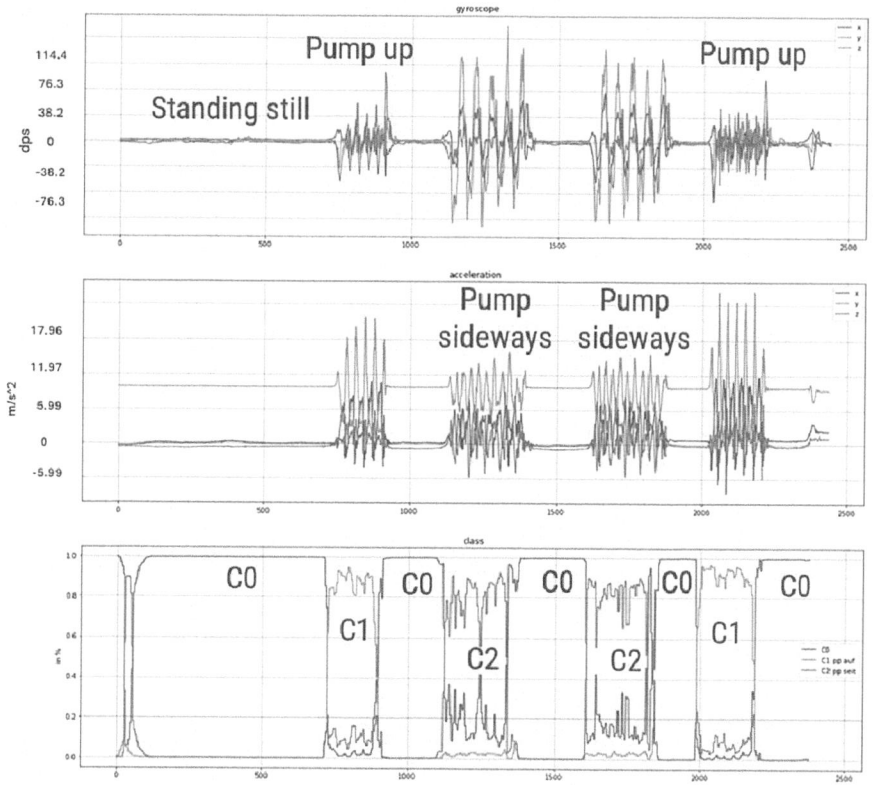

**Fig. 5.** Results after using CNN Model by predefined gesture sequence - Gyroscope Data, Acceleration Data and Modeloutput

## 6   Conclusion

To improve the application of wearable sensor devices for controlling a medical treatment bed, three new tag positions were considered and evaluated. This evaluation included the wearing comfort, the quality of the data and first results on the prediction of the gestures. In order to achieve a suitable comparison between the old position and the new one, a closer look was taken at one of the three new tag positions after evaluation. The position at the ankle proved to be promising, as the stable fixation at the ankle with a velcro fastener reduced the gesture mismatch. Furthermore, a better accuracy of the CNN model was achieved, which is associated with a faster recognition of the gestures. The gestures were tested sitting and standing and the system responded faster when switching on and off. Exactly the same number of people were recorded for training purposes in order to achieve a suitable comparison with the old position. With the new model, the control of the therapy table is already very efficient, although recording more test and training subjects would provide even more information for the neural network, which might lead to better analysis.

**Acknowledgements.** This work has been supported by the COMET-K2 Center of the Linz Center of Mechatronics (LCM) funded by the Austrian federal government and the federal state of Upper Austria.

# References

1. Zhang, J., Yin, Z., Chen, P., Nichele, S.: Emotion recognition using multi-modal data and machine learning techniques: a tutorial and review **59**, 103–126 (2020). https://doi.org/10.1016/j.inffus.2020.01.011
2. Putz, V., Mayer, J., Fenzl, H., Schmidt, R., Pichler-Scheder, M., Kastl, C.: Cyber-physical mobile arm gesture recognition using ultrasound and motion data. In: IEEE Conference on Industrial Cyberphysical Systems (ICPS), pp. 203–208 (2020). https://doi.org/10.1109/ICPS48405.2020.9274795.
3. Bustoni, I.A., Hidayatulloh, I., Ningtyas, A., Purwaningsih, A., Azhari, S.: Classification methods performance on human activity recognition. In: Journal of Physics: Conference Series, vol. 1456, pp. 012027 (2020). https://doi.org/10.1088/1742-6596/1456/1/012027
4. Bloomfield, R.A., Teeter, M.G., McIsaac, K.A.: A convolutional neural network approach to classifying activities using knee instrumented wearable sensors. IEEE Sens. J. **20**(24), 14975–14983 (2020). https://doi.org/10.1109/JSEN.2020.3011417
5. Tischler, C., Pendl, K., Schimbäck, E., Putz, V., Kastl, C., Schlechter, T.: Lower Limbs Gesture Recognition Approach to Control a Medical Treatment Bed. Eurocast (2022)
6. Yue, L., Zongxing, L., Hui, D., Chao, J., Ziqiang, L., Zhoujie, L.: How to achieve human-machine interaction by foot gesture recognition: a review. IEEE Sens. J. **23**(15), 16515–16528 (2023). https://doi.org/10.1109/JSEN.2023.3285214
7. Mehr, J.K., Akbari, M., Faridi, P., Xing, H., Mushahwar, V.K., Tavakoli, M.: Artificial-intelligence-powered lower limb assistive devices: future of home care technologies. Adv. Intell. Syst. **5**(6) (2023). https://doi.org/10.1002/aisy.202200361.
8. O'shea, K., Nash, R.: An introduction to convolutional neural networks (2015). arXiv preprint arXiv:1511.08458

# Model-Based System Design, Verification and Simulation

# Comparison of Physiological Data Acquisition for Modeling of Drivers in Autonomous Vehicles

Raul Fernandez-Matellan[1]([✉]) [iD], David Puertas-Ramirez[2] [iD],
David Martín Gómez[1] [iD], and Jesus G. Boticario[2] [iD]

[1] Intelligent System Lab, Universidad Carlos III de Madrid,
Av. de la Universidad 30, Leganés, Spain
`raulfern@pa.uc3m.es`
[2] Adaptive Dynamic Online Educational Systems Based on User Modelling,
Universidad Nacional de Educación a Distancia,
Calle de Bravo Murillo 38, Madrid, Spain

**Abstract.** Humans can undergo rapid emotional changes and these changes can significantly affect their ability to perform tasks. Consequently, when we develop Human-Centred Symbiotic Artificial Intelligence (HCSAI) systems to support the interaction between autonomous systems and drivers, the intelligent system controlling the vehicle must adapt to the state of the user. This symbiotic relationship highlights the importance of collaboration and cooperation between humans and agents of artificial intelligence (AI). In the field of Autonomous Vehicles (AV), measurements must be made using non-invasive devices that do not interfere with the driving task. We have therefore used wristbands to measure physiological signals. This comparison is used to select the right equipment for setting up user modelling in different levels of autonomous vehicles. We compared the accuracy, precision and ease of use of three different wristbands: Fitbit Sense2, Empatica E4 and Emotibit. We tested the performance of the bands in two different driving scenarios: SAE Level 4 environment using autonomous golf carts (iCab), and a real-world SAE Level 2 driving environment in Scotland using a Toyota Prius equipped with Comma OpenPilot technology. The Fitbit Sense2 does not allow researchers to access raw data. The Emotibit and the Empatica E4 are designed for research, so they provide access to raw data, while the Empatica E4 is easier to use than the Emotibit. The comparison calls for the development of open source codes that will facilitate integration with different operating systems and other devices, as well as an easy way to use the devices in real time.

**Keywords:** Physiological signals · Human-centric symbiotic artificial intelligence · Autonomous driving

This work was supported by the Spanish Government under Grants TED2021-129485B-C41 and TED2021-129485B-C44.

# 1    Introduction

Research into autonomous vehicles has increased significantly in recent years, motivated by the goal of eliminating human error on the road, thereby reducing fatalities [29] and allowing passengers/drivers to engage in Non-Driving Related Tasks (NDRT) such as reading, using smartphones, or even sleeping. The ultimate goal is to achieve SAE Level 5 autonomy, as defined by SAE International [26], where the vehicle can perform all driving tasks in any Operational Design Domain (ODD) without the need for human intervention.

ALVINN [23], a pioneering example, had achieved SAE Level 2 autonomy by controlling both lateral and longitudinal movement in a controlled environment under human supervision. However, despite over 30 years of progress, the global autonomous fleet is currently dominated by SAE Level 0 (fully manual) and SAE Level 1 (speed control only) vehicles. In fact, we confidently argue that the reason for the lack of full deployment of autonomous vehicles is the oversight of the human element in research and development efforts.

The inclusion of human-in-the-loop approaches has led to the development of Human-Centred Symbiotic Artificial Intelligence [21]. HCSAI prioritise collaboration, cooperation, and mutual enhancement between humans and AI agents. They strive to create an environment where humans and AI agents work seamlessly together, leveraging each other's strengths and compensating for each other's weaknesses. Rather than focusing on replacing human capabilities, AI systems should be designed to enhance them. This symbiotic relationship underscores the importance of collaboration and cooperation between humans and AI agents. Consequently, when we develop HCSAI systems to support the interaction between autonomous systems and drivers, the intelligent system controlling the vehicle must adapt to the emotional state of the user. This area of research falls under the umbrella of affective computing [22]. Recognising that everyone possesses unique characteristics and abilities, we argue that the next frontier in artificial intelligence (AI) lies in creating human-centred models that enhance natural human abilities. Emotional states can be measured in a variety of ways, including analysis of posture, spontaneous movements, gestures, facial expressions, blink frequency, gaze tracking, voice tone, or physiological signals. We choose to use physiological signals because they are directly linked to the autonomous nervous system and are not affected by low light conditions for cameras or obstructions for facial recognition (e.g. sunglasses, masks).

In our autonomous vehicle research, measurement of physiological signals is critical, so we tested, analysed and compared three different wristbands: Fitbit Sense 2, Empatica E4, and Emotibit. Building on our previous work [25], where we highlighted the importance of considering the user's state to enhance the autonomy of Autonomous Vehicles. This paper presents a comparison of the ability of these wristbands to measure physiological signals to predict a driver's state in a SAE Level 3 of autonomy, where vehicles have "environmental sensing" capabilities and can make informed decisions on their own, such as accelerating past a slow moving vehicle. But they still need human intervention. The article is divided into several sections, starting with a review of the relevant literature, followed by a detailed examination of the specifications of each wristband. The comparison is then presented in the context of autonomous vehicles. Finally, the paper concludes with conclusions and future work.

## 2   Related Work

As automation increases and fewer tasks are required of the user, it becomes easier to get distracted, making it much harder to remain aware of the situation [2]. This has been identified as a significant problem in conditional autonomous vehicles [4,16,19], where the user still needs to be in a"Fallback Ready State" (FRS) [25]. A solution to this problem is to model the user's state and provide feedback to help maintain this FRS while driving. Different approaches look to model attention [3], drowsiness [12], or distraction [30]. While other authors also seek to model the user's interaction with autonomous vehicles, focusing on aspects such as acceptance [31] and trust [10,11,15].

Regardless of the user's state of interest, the choice of specific sensors remains a topic of debate, with options that include physiological, visual, or combination of both [14,20]. With a multimodal approach giving the best results given the complexity and individual variations among users [4,24]. The selection of suitable physiological sensors is especially difficult, given the variety of types of signal and applications [13]. For lab-based simulation experiments, researchers often choose invasive sensors because they provide more reliable readings [1,7]. However, these sensors are typically unsuitable for real-world conditions and impractical for use in moving vehicles. Therefore, in real-world scenarios, researchers prefer non-intrusive wireless devices, such as wristbands [24,28], which measure Heart Rate Variability and Electrodermal Activity. These wristbands offer the most reliable data under real-world conditions [13]. However, while some overviews of the sensors are available [13,20], we discovered a lack of real use case reviews comparing the usability of the most popular sensors. More concerning, we found that some manufacturers do not provide adequate developer tools, limiting the types and frequency at which some signals can be extracted or even making it impossible in some cases. These circumstances prompted us to undertake this review to provide our honest feedback on some of the most popular wristbands.

## 3   Devices Specifications

### 3.1   Presentation

We decided to conduct a market analysis to explore potential devices that would fit our research approach. The decision not to design and build our own device is due to the fact that it is outside the scope of the main objective of the project. In our comparative study, we included the Fitbit Sense2 to represent the broader category of smartwatches available from different manufacturers. Emotibit was included to represent the open source community and Empatica E4 was selected for its established reputation in the field of physiological signal monitoring.

**Fitbit Sense 1 and 2.** We examined two different versions of the Fitbit devices: Fitbit Sense1 and Fitbit Sense2. These devices are designed for activity tracking purposes, targeting the general consumer demographic, and therefore have a user-friendly interface and provide comprehensive processed data such as step counts or sleep statistics. The main difference between the two generations is the introduction of continuous EDA functionality in the second generation, which enables continuous monitoring of electrodermal activity [8]. This device offers a good interface with a tactile screen, which allows the user to feel more comfortable while wearing the wristband. It has a button on the side, but its functionality is not related to the recording of physiological signals. Figure 1 shows the main location of the different sensors.

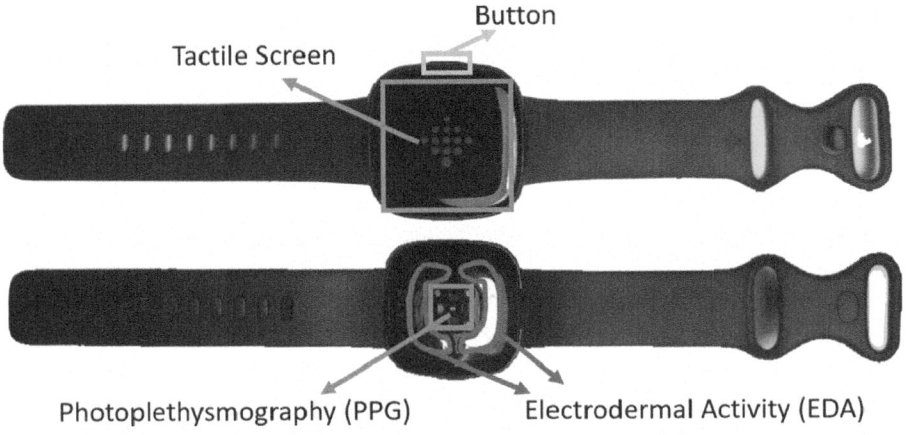

**Fig. 1.** Location of the main sensors in Fitbit Sense 2: the touch screen, the side button, the PPG and the EDA sensor

**Emotibit.** Emotibit is a prototype based on the ESP32 microcontroller device platform. Known as the open-source physiological wristband, it stands out for its transparency and accessibility, with all codes openly available on GitHub [18]. Figure 2 shows the location of the different sensors.

**EmbracePlus and Empatica E4.** Empatica has been a mainstay in research for many years, facilitating the integration of physiological data into the analysis process. While the comparison focuses primarily on the Empatica E4 device, we also sought to include the newer generation, known as EmbracePlus , which has a shorter history in research applications [6]. Figure 3 shows the location of the different sensors in Empatica E4.

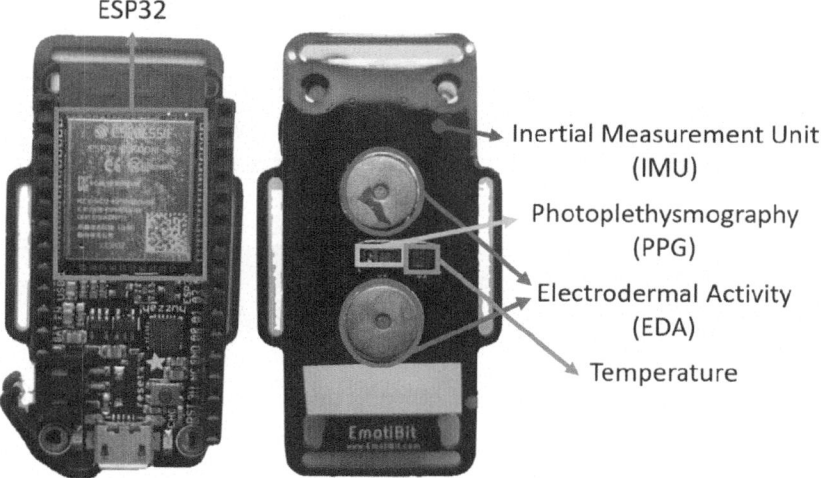

**Fig. 2.** Location of Emotibit's main sensors: EDA sensors, temperature sensor, PPG sensor, IMU and the location of the ESP32 microcontroller

## 3.2   Hardware Comparison

This section presents a hardware comparison of each device. Table 1 illustrates the different sensors mounted on each wristband. It is evident that Fitbit Sense incorporates a greater number of sensors, including an altimeter, GPS, and microphone, which can be utilized for the purpose of tracking sporting activities or answering phone calls. Nevertheless, these sensors are not the most crucial for the recognition of the user's state within an autonomous vehicle. Conversely, EmbracePlus, the latest iteration of Empatica, incorporates gyroscope data. In this comparison, we are interested in the sample frequency that each wristband offers. We exclude Fitbit from consideration as it does not provide the raw signal. Emotibit provides a sample frequency of 25 Hz for motion data (accelerometer, gyroscope and magnetometer), while Empatica has a sample frequency of 32 Hz only for the accelerometer. With regard to the PPG signal, Emotibit offers a 25 Hz signal, while Empatica provides a 64 Hz signal. In the case of temperature, Emotibit provides a 7.5 Hz signal, while Empatica provides a 4 Hz signal. Finally, in the case of EDA, Emotibit provides a 15 Hz signal, while Empatica provides a 4 Hz signal. Both sample frequencies are sufficient for our application, and the decision of choosing one device or another should be made on the basis of usability.

## 3.3   Mode of Use

This section will examine the usability of the different wristbands, with particular emphasis on the connection mode, the recording mode and the access to raw data files.

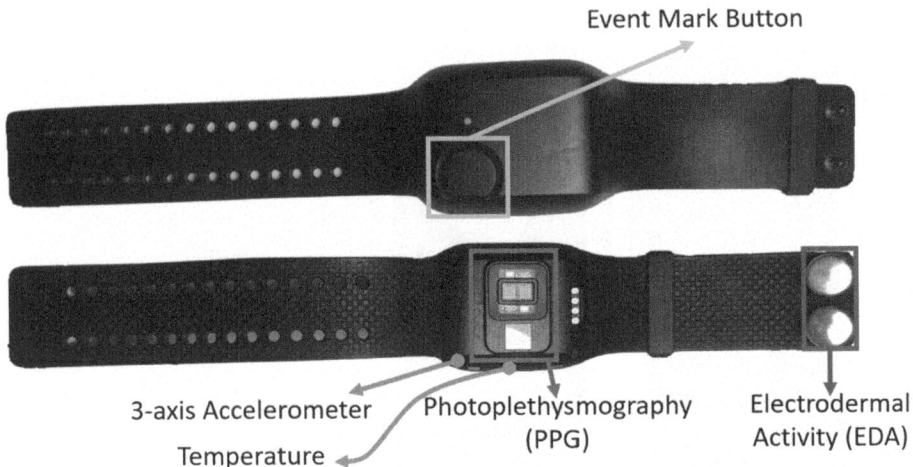

**Fig. 3.** Location of Empatica E4's main sensors: EDA sensors, event marker button, PPG sensor, accelerometer and temperature sensor

**Table 1.** Comparison of hardware among wristbands

| Sensor | Empatica E4 | Emotibit | Fitbit Sense2 |
|---|---|---|---|
| EDA | Yes | Yes | Yes |
| PPG | Yes | Yes | Yes |
| SpO2 | No | No | Yes |
| Temperature | Yes | Yes | Yes |
| Gyroscope | No | Yes | Yes |
| Accelerometer | Yes | Yes | Yes |
| Altimeter | No | No | Yes |
| GPS | No | No | Yes |
| Microphone | No | No | Yes |

### 3.4   Empatica E4

Empatica is a device designed for research purposes, providing direct access to raw data. The method used thus far involves connecting the wristband to the smartphone via Bluetooth, where the Empatica app is installed. This then uploads the recording session to the app's private cloud, which offers an interactive panel displaying the basic signals, including heart rate, blood volume pulse, accelerometer and temperature. The raw data can then be downloaded as a single .csv file for each signal. Figure 4 illustrates the diagram of the explained connectivity architecture. Occasionally, multiple attempts have been observed to be required to synchronize the wristbands with the host device through Bluetooth. While the device itself is comfortable, the belt is challenging to fasten correctly. Its optimal location for wear is the width of one finger between the wristband bones. However, if it is not sufficiently tightened, it may move from its ideal position.

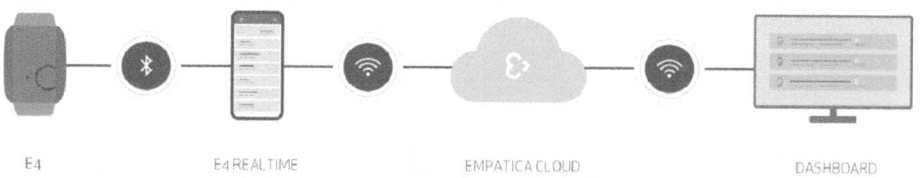

E4                    E4 REALTIME                    EMPATICA CLOUD                    DASHBOARD

**Fig. 4.** Empatica E4 operation mode [6]

**EmbracePlus.** EmbracePlus represents the latest iteration of Empatica E4, which was recently launched. We had the opportunity to test the device and found that its operational mode differs significantly from Empatica's. Although the sensors are similar to those found in Empatica, the design and comfortability have been enhanced. They have incorporated a screen that makes the wristband more user-friendly. However, this device is clearly designed for long-term health monitoring problems and offers easy-to-access information related to healthcare care. With respect to the raw signal, they are also available in .AVRO files. The wristband is connected to the app via Bluetooth, after which the data is uploaded to a cloud. This information can then be downloaded and treated.

### 3.5   Emotibit

The Emotibit operational mode is different. The connectivity of the device can be observed in Fig. 5, which illustrates the integration of the Emotibit oscillo-scope, which is necessary for the device to begin recording. This connection is established through a custom LAN network. The information is continuously stored on an SD card that is located on the device. Connecting the SD card to a PC allows the recorded files to be converted to .csv files that contain the raw signals. The device is based on an ESP32 microcontroller, which results in reduced comfort compared to other devices. Additionally, the device has been observed to lose some recordings when it is not properly attached to the body skin and when the fastening methods are not correctly applied.

### 3.6   Fitbit Sense

The Fitbit device is designed for commercial purposes and therefore offers an intuitive and straightforward user experience. Its interface and belt design are both highly comfortable. Figure 4 illustrates the Empatica E4 schema, which is the operational mode used with the Fitbit device. The device is first connected

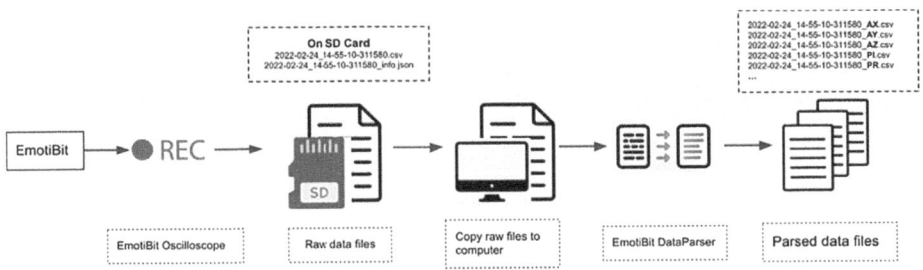

**Fig. 5.** Emotibit operation mode [18]

to the host via Bluetooth, after which the information is uploaded to the Fitbit cloud. This information is then processed using the device's private algorithms. The primary distinction between Fitbit and other devices is that it does not allow the download of real-time data from the signals. While it is possible to download information such as the number of steps, calories, and other process data, the raw signal data at the time of this study was not accessible.

## 4    Testing on Autonomous Driving Environment

### 4.1    Driving Scenarios

Two distinct user-vehicle experiences were designed, encapsulating various driving scenarios to formulate a comprehensive methodology. This methodology aims to capture the essential characteristics and requirements across the spectrum of vehicle automation. The scenarios, hosted at the University of the West of Scotland (UWS) and University Carlos III of Madrid (UC3M), feature varying automation levels, with the intent to thoroughly investigate user-vehicle interaction rather than solving specific, isolated issues. The setups incorporate advanced software and hardware, including OpenPilot and ROS2, providing real and immersive autonomous driving experiences, and emphasizing user-centric data collection for model enhancement.

The first scenario has been configured and tested at the UWS with a Toyota Prius PHEV. Here, autonomous functionality is performed by OpenPilot software [5] which overrides the vehicle's original CAN messages and sends its custom CAN messages through the vehicle's CAN bus to determine the exact behaviour of the actuators (i.e., steering wheel, brake, throttle, etc.). The second scenario is also an outdoor real scenario at UC3M, where an autonomous vehicle prototype with level 4 automation has been used and configured to create real experiences in the university campus area. This second vehicle is denominated iCab (Intelligent Campus AutomoBile) [17] and is a prototype of an autonomous vehicle based on an electric golf cart, where the direction wheel has been removed, so the user has the real feeling of an autonomous vehicle of level 5 of automation (fully autonomous). The user can only activate the brake in case of panic during the trajectory in fully autonomous mode. The brake system has been incorporated using a linear motor actuator to push the on-wheel mechanism and create the corresponding friction to decelerate the autonomous vehicle. The software to manage the fully autonomous mode is based on ROS2 (Robot Operating System 2) [27] for ensuring the connection between packages in real-time and guaranteeing temporal synchronization among sensors. Therefore, as a summary, the proposed driving scenarios (UWS & UC3M) deal with to model of the user inside of two real autonomous vehicles. Figure 6 demonstrate the different wristbands tested on each driver environment.

In our area of research, there are two main objectives in modelling the driver of the vehicle. The first is to work with offline data, for example to understand which variables have more influence in the different states of the driver. The second is to create a dynamic interaction between the driver and the car, in which case working with real-time data is mandatory.

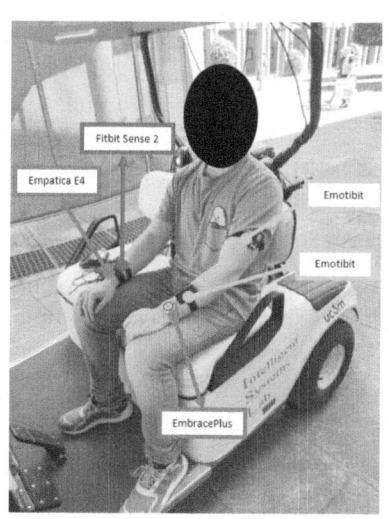

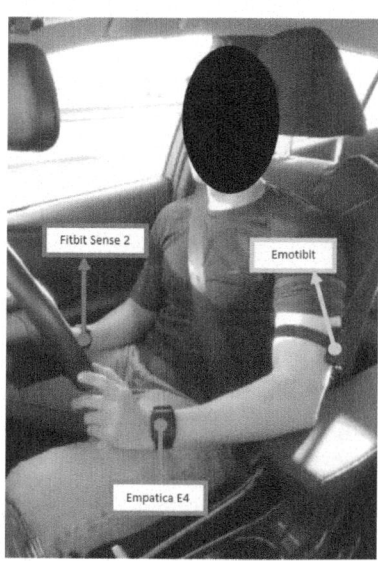

(a) SAE Level 4 AV                    (b) SAE Level 2 AV

**Fig. 6.** Tested wristband on two different driving environments

## 4.2   Recording for Offline Modelling

The Empatica E4, EmbracePlus and Emotibit devices are used for offline data collection and modelling. This is useful for detecting how physiological signals change with each level of attention experienced by the user of the autonomous vehicle. The user's attention has been modelled based on four levels, with data from the Empatica E4 device being used because it has been used for the longest period of time and has recorded the most hours in an SAE Level 2 of autonomy and in real driving conditions. A significant number of recordings have been made with the Empatica E4 to make the most of the device, given that it will cease to be functional from August 2024 onwards. This will allow for the introduction of the EmbracePlus product line, which has been found to be compatible with the existing working scheme, although it will require adaptation to the new form of data structure. The following illustrative model is presented as an example to justify the power of physiological signals in user modelling.

**Multimodal Approach for User Modelling in AV.** To demonstrate the importance of user modelling in AV, we developed a model to detect four levels of driver awareness within an autonomous vehicle scenario. Our model uses a pretrained feature extraction network and Principal Component Analysis (PCA) to reduce data dimensionality before training a feedforward network. Training data, generated from real driving experiences and converted into images, facilitates network processing. Four datasets were generated, each from a different male driver (three between 20–30 years old, one between 40-50 years old). All drivers gave informed consent for their data to be treated and manipulated anonymously for the purposes of this research project, and were given permission to operate an SAE Level 2 autonomous vehicle in a real-world driving environment. The data set was divided into 70% training, 15% validation and 15% testing. We identified four distinct states of user awareness based on the recordings:

- **Low-Low (LL)**: Minimal awareness, maximum relaxation, driver not attentive or able to regain control promptly.
- **Low (L)**: Relaxed single-task driving state on a familiar, low-traffic route.
- **High (H)**: OpenPilot controls the vehicle, requiring the driver to monitor both the vehicle and the surroundings, increasing attention.
- **High-High (HH)**: Involves lane changes and unexpected events, increasing uncertainty, and driver stress.

The proposed model utilizes seven images generated from signals captured by the Empatica device, employing the Recurrent Plot technique. These signals include acceleration in the x, y, and z axes, blood volume pulse (BVP), skin conductance (EDA), heart rate (HR), and skin temperature (TEMP). Implemented using PyTorch, the model leverages transfer learning with ResNet50 [9] for feature extraction. PCA is then applied to reduce the dimensionality of the data. During feature extraction, ResNet50 operates without training parameters to resize the images into vectors, which are subsequently concatenated. PCA, initially fed with unlabelled data, produces a vector of 100 features. The classifier, with trainable parameters, distinguishes between the four states (LL, L, H, HH) and offers flexibility in its configuration. Figure 7 illustrates the schematic of the proposed ResNet model. The model's accuracy, defined as the percentage of correct labels predicted, was evaluated and showed performances of 70.3% for user 1, 78.9% for user 2, 78.4% for user 3, and 77.9% for user 4. These results demonstrate a significant correlation between the states of consciousness and the recorded physiological signals. Notably, more than 80% of the values classified as low-low were accurately labelled, demonstrating the model's ability to identify cases of user inattention with high reliability. This method highlights the network's capability to detect different levels of user attention in a complex scenario.

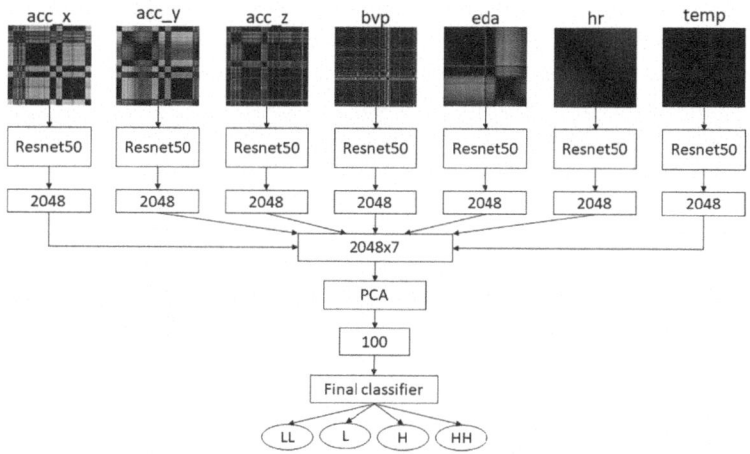

**Fig. 7.** Architecture of the proposed ResNet model

### 4.3   Online Interaction

The next step in the research is to obtain a reading of the data that allows real-time data processing. If possible, this data should be integrated with the control software of the autonomous vehicle (ROS) so that it can make decisions based on the user's state. Fitbit's architecture does not allow for this type of real-time interaction. In the case of Empatica, they have a streaming server for Windows, but unfortunately, from August 2024 onwards, all of these products will no longer be available to service the new EmbracePlus device. Currently, the new device does not have the capacity for real-time monitoring. The final option to consider is Emotibit. It has been suggested that this is a viable option, although it would be the responsibility of the researchers to implement it. Therefore, as a prospective avenue for future research, the Emotibit device can be modified to facilitate real-time interaction, which is crucial for improving human-vehicle communication.

## 5   Discussion

Given the new found problem of user modeling in Autonomous Vehicles [4,16,19,25], the selection process of physiological sensors has been a topic of discussion [13, 20]. However, an overview of sensors and theoretical characteristics doesn't provide the full information on the practicality and usability of those sensors. Especially when using sensors in a Real World context instead of a more controlled simulation environment [1, 7].

Technical characteristics could indicate that the Fitbit Sense2 [8] is the best-equipped wristband in terms of the variety and number of sensors it has. However, it lacks the ability to access raw data, limiting its usability in experiments. In contrast, Emotibit [18] and Empatica E4 [6] are two devices primarily designed to study physiological responses, with similar sensor capabilities. Emotibit has a higher sampling frequency and additional features, such as a gyroscope and magnetometer. Emotibit also offers versatility in placement on the human body, including the wrist, finger, arm, and leg. Empatica, on the other hand, specifies the optimal positioning in its documentation, mainly recommending the wrist, while emphasising higher accuracy and stability of readings. The devices also differ in the complexity of the processed signals they provide. For example, Emotibit's electrodermal activity comprises five different signals, while Empatica provides a single signal for this measure.

A drawback of the Emotibit is its prototype-like appearance, with a board-like form factor that may compromise aesthetics and wearer comfort. In addition, the Emotibit's lack of buttons limits the interaction between the user and the device, potentially hindering usability. Its higher profile design also contributes to a higher susceptibility to movement during experiments, affecting data accuracy. In contrast, Empatica has addressed these shortcomings in its newer development, EmbracePlus, by incorporating a user-friendly screen interface that improves the overall usability and user experience.

The most important consideration when selecting a wristband is its data collection architecture. The Fitbit Sense 2 is excluded from consideration because it does not provide access to raw, unprocessed data, limiting its utility to research applications that do not require physiological signal processing, but rather rely on processed data such as step counts, calorie expenditure or sleep metrics. Empatica's default mode is to upload data to its proprietary cloud platform for later download. Conversely, Emotibit stores data internally on an SD card in the wristband, without relying on cloud storage. Empatica uses a Bluetooth connection to facilitate the transfer of data to its server, which, once initiated, tends to remain stable, albeit with occasional start-up errors. Emotibit, on the other hand, requires the oscilloscope program to run concurrently on the same local area network (LAN) as the wristband. Currently, corporate networks cannot support this functionality, so a LAN must be created using external equipment, a workaround achieved by creating a LAN with a smartphone as the host. The data must then be parsed through an intermediary application (data parser) to extract .csv files containing the sensor readings.

Another topic of discussion is the Real-Time integration of physiological signals. As a first step, an off-line computation can be performed to understand the meaning of physiological signals or detect certain states [1, 7]. This initial phase is crucial for considering the human factor in the vehicle and analysing the impact of certain variables [14,20]. However, when the acquisition methodology is integrated into the vehicle's decision-making process, real-time functionality becomes essential. By default, none of the three wristbands are capable of real-time platforms across different operating systems. In our application, one of our vehicles runs autonomously on ROS 1 and ROS 2. Integration with ROS is facilitated by the use of Linux software, which is not provided directly by the manufacturers. Empatica E4 provides a Windows server that enables real-time functionality, while Emotibit, as an open source platform, makes its ESP32 code available for adaptation by anyone interested. However, for both cases, the integration process is not straightforward as there is no official documentation, published papers, or discussion threads dedicated to this specific issue. Although feasible, there is no external support available to effectively navigate this integration process. Furthermore, Empatica's new EmbracePlus wristband removes the real-time server, focusing on more long-term offline experiments.

## 6    Conclusions and Future Work

The final choice between devices depends on the specific requirements of the project. Based on our experiments, analysis, and extensive review, commercial devices such as the Fitbit Sense1 and Fitbit Sense2 are unsuitable for physiological signal recording due to the lack of access to raw data but are proving to be highly effective for alternative research endeavours. Emotibit stands out as an open source platform built on the ESP32 architecture, providing access to its drivers and facilitating integration into different recording architectures. In contrast, Empatica E4 stands out as the ideal solution for quickly initiating recording activities, bypassing the need for complex LAN configurations and multiple application installations. However, data upload and processing are handled exclusively by proprietary algorithms within its private cloud infrastructure.

Each of the three wristbands comes with its own set of advantages and disadvantages. Emotibit is notable for its customizable standard code, while Empatica E4 excels with its simplified setup procedures. Fitbit Sense2 is recognized for its user-friendly interface, making it ideal for various project types. Although developing real-time integration code is beyond the scope of this comparison, it presents a promising direction for future research and development.

**Acknowledgements.** This work was supported by the Spanish Government under Grants TED2021-129485B-C41 and TED2021-129485B-C44.).

## References

1. Arakawa, T., Hibi, R., Fujishiro, T.a.: Psychophysical assessment of a driver's mental state in autonomous vehicles. Transport. Res. Part A: Policy Pract. **124**(May 2018), 587–610 (2019). https://doi.org/10.1016/j.tra.2018.05.003
2. Bainbridge, L.: Ironies of automation. In: Analysis, design and evaluation of man–machine systems, pp. 129–135. Elsevier (1983)

3. Bonyani, M., Rahmanian, M., Jahangard, S., Rezaei, M.: Dipnet: Driver intention prediction for a safe takeover transition in automated vehicles. SSRN Electron. J. (April) (12 2021). https://doi.org/10.2139/ssrn.3982515

4. Collet, C., Musicant, O.: Associating vehicles automation with drivers functional state assessment systems: a challenge for road safety in the future. Front. Human Neurosci. **13**, 408476 (2 2019). https://doi.org/10.3389/FNHUM.2019.00131/BIBTEX

5. Comma.ai: openpilot - open source advanced driver assistance system (2024). https://comma.ai/openpilot

6. Empatica Inc.: Empatica E4 (2024). https://www.empatica.com/en-eu/

7. Giorgi, A., et al.: Neurophysiological mental fatigue assessment for developing user-centered Artificial Intelligence as a solution for autonomous driving. Front. Neurorobot. **17** (2023). https://doi.org/10.3389/FNBOT.2023.1240933

8. Google Fitbit: Fitbit (2024). https://www.fitbit.com/

9. He, K., Zhang, X., Ren, S., Sun, J.: Deep residual learning for image recognition. In: 2016 IEEE Conference on Computer Vision and Pattern Recognition (CVPR), vol. 2016-Decem, pp. 770–778. IEEE, Las Vegas, NV, USA (6 2016). https://doi.org/10.1109/CVPR.2016.90

10. Huang, C., Wen, X., He, D., Jian, S.: Sharing the road: how human drivers interact with autonomous vehicles on highways. In: Proceedings of the Human Factors and Ergonomics Society Annual Meeting, vol. 66(1), 1437–1441 (2022). https://doi.org/10.1177/1071181322661165

11. Hunter, J.G., et al.: The interaction gap: a step toward understanding trust in autonomous vehicles between encounters. In: Proceedings of the Human Factors and Ergonomics Society Annual Meeting, vol. 66(1), 147–151 (9 2022). https://doi.org/10.1177/1071181322661311

12. Kim, W., Jeon, E., Kim, G., Yeo, D., Kim, S.: Take-over requests after waking in autonomous vehicles. Appl. Sci. **12**(3), 1438 (1 2022). https://doi.org/10.3390/app12031438

13. Lohani, M., Payne, B.R., Strayer, D.L.: A review of psychophysiological measures to assess cognitive states in real-world driving. Front. Human Neurosci. **13**(March), 1–27 (3 2019). https://doi.org/10.3389/fnhum.2019.00057

14. Lopez-Aguilar, A.A., Navarro-Tuch, S.A., Camacho-Bustamante, L.M., Bustamante-Bello, M.R.: An analysis of monitoring technologies for the objective evaluation of user experience on autonomous vehicles. In: 2023 International Symposium on Electromobility, ISEM 2023, pp. 1–6. IEEE (10 2023). https://doi.org/10.1109/ISEM59023.2023.10334750

15. Lu, J., et al.: Modeling driver's real-time confidence in autonomous vehicles. Appl. Sci. **13**(7), 4099 (3 2023). https://doi.org/10.3390/app13074099

16. Ma, J., Wu, Y., Rong, J., Zhao, X.: A systematic review on the influence factors, measurement, and effect of driver workload. Accident Anal. Prevent. **192**, 107289 (11 2023). https://doi.org/10.1016/J.AAP.2023.107289

17. Marin-Plaza, P., Hussein, A., Martin, D., de la Escalera, A.: iCab use case for ROS-based architecture. Robot. Auton. Syst. **118**, 251–262 (2019). https://doi.org/10.1016/J.ROBOT.2019.04.008

18. Montgomery, S.M., Nair, N., Chen, P., Dikker, S.: Introducing emotibit, an open-source multi-modal sensor for measuring research-grade physiological signals. Science Talks **6**, 100181 (2023)

19. Morales-Alvarez, W., Sipele, O., Léberon, R., Tadjine, H.H., Olaverri-Monreal, C.: Automated driving: a literature review of the take over request in condi-

tional automation. Electronics (Switzerland) **9**(12), 1–34 (2020). https://doi.org/10.3390/electronics9122087

20. Nacpil, E.J.C., Wang, Z., Nakano, K.: Application of physiological sensors for personalization in semi-autonomous driving: a review. IEEE Sensors J. **21**(18), 19662–19674 (9 2021). https://doi.org/10.1109/JSEN.2021.3100038

21. O'Neill, T.A., Flathmann, C., McNeese, N.J., Salas, E.: Human-autonomy teaming: Need for a guiding team-based framework? Comput. Human Behav. **146**, 107762 (9 2023). https://doi.org/10.1016/J.CHB.2023.107762

22. Picard, R.W.: Affective computing. MIT press (2000)

23. Pomerleau, D.A.: Alvinn: an autonomous land vehicle in a neural network. In: Advances in Neural Information Processing Systems, vol. 1 (1988)

24. Puertas-Ramirez, D., Fernandez-Matellan, R., Martin-Gomez, D., G. Boticario, J., Tena-Gago, D.: Improving autonomous vehicle automation through human-system interaction. In: The 37th annual European Simulation and Modelling Conference, pp. 294–300. Toulouse, France (2023). http://e-spacio.uned.es/fez/view/bibliuned:92-Ponencias-Dpuertas-0001

25. Puertas-Ramirez, D., Serrano-Mamolar, A., Martin Gomez, D., Boticario, J.G.: Should conditional self-driving cars consider the state of the human inside the vehicle? In: Adjunct Proceedings of the 29th ACM Conference on User Modeling, Adaptation and Personalization, pp. 137–141. ACM, New York, NY, USA (6 2021). https://doi.org/10.1145/3450614.3462243

26. SAE International: Taxonomy and Definitions for Terms Related to Driving Automation Systems for On-Road Motor Vehicles. Tech. rep., SAE International (2021). https://doi.org/10.4271/J3016_202104

27. Stanford Artificial Intelligence Laboratory et al.: Robotic Operating System (2024). https://www.ros.org

28. Tavakoli, A., Kumar, S., Guo, X., Balali, V., Boukhechba, M., Heydarian, A.: HARMONY: a human-centered multimodal driving study in the wild. IEEE Access **9**, 23956–23978 (2021). https://doi.org/10.1109/ACCESS.2021.3056007

29. WHO: Global status report on road safety 2023. Tech. rep., World Health Organization, Geneva (2023). https://www.who.int/teams/social-determinants-of-health/safety-and-mobility/global-status-report-on-road-safety-2023

30. Yang, S., Kuo, J., Lenné, M.G.: Patterns of sequential off-road glances indicate levels of distraction in automated driving. In: Proceedings of the Human Factors and Ergonomics Society Annual Meeting vol. 63(1), 2056–2060 (2019). https://doi.org/10.1177/1071181319631204

31. Zhang, Q., Zhang, T., Ma, L.: Human acceptance of autonomous vehicles: Research status and prospects. Int. J. Ind. Ergon. **95**, 103458 (2023). https://doi.org/10.1016/j.ergon.2023.103458

# Automated Control of Robots via 5G Communication from Multi-accesss Edge Computing

Akira Sasaki[1], Nobuo Kobayashi[1], Yoshiro Takanashi[1], Naoya Yamamoto[1], and Atsushi Ito[2]([✉]) [iD]

[1] GClue, Inc., 134-3 Ikkimachi Turuga, Aizu-wakamatsu-shi, 965-0006 Fukushima, Japan
akira@gclue.jp
[2] Faculty of Economics, Chuo University, 742-1 Higashi Nakano, Hachioji-shi, 192-0351 Tokyo, Japan
atc.00s@g.chuo-u.ac.jp

**Abstract.** This paper describes the results of developing a PST5G-enabled robot driving and working function with automatic and remote control. This system is unique because it is mainly configured to use the cloud. All the processes for automatic robot control were reallocated to the cloud side, leaving only the minimum configuration on the edge side to build a system that can run automatically. In order to automatically control a robot in a 5G environment, we organized the necessary elements, investigated the limitations of the elements, measured the delay of each element, and summarized the results. In order to identify the limitations of the 5G environment and Multi-Accesss Edge Computing (MEC), we constructed multiple test environments, investigated the limitations, and measured the delay of each element.

**Keywords:** 5G · Post 5G · ROS2 · MEC · Delay of video · Delay of telemetory

## 1 Introduction

Various surveys were conducted to gather information necessary for essential robot control in a 5G environment. Automated robots are generally equipped with frameworks for object recognition and automatic running based on deep learning, and a laptop computer with a high-end GPU and CPU is indispensable. In the 5G environment, we conducted a survey to migrate these functions to the cloud and organized and measured the delay of various elements.

## 2 Elements Required for Automatic Robot Control

### 2.1 Robot Middleware

Robot middleware is indispensable for robot automation. Robot middleware, including basic components and visualization tools, is publicly available in the

© The Author(s), under exclusive license to Springer Nature Switzerland AG 2025
A. Quesada-Arencibia et al. (Eds.): EUROCAST 2024, LNCS 15172, pp. 342–353, 2025.
https://doi.org/10.1007/978-3-031-82949-9_31

form of OSS, and these components can be used to build the basic parts necessary for robot control. This allows developers and researchers to concentrate on application development and provides an ecosystem that enables efficient robot development without reinventing the wheel. Currently, the mainstream robot middleware includes ROS, ROS2, Ignition, Isaac, and OpenRTM. The features and functions of the various robot OSs are described in the literature [1]. Among them, ROS2 is a middleware that has been redesigned based on the experience with ROS and is provided by solving many problems. ROS2 has been widely used in industrial equipment and has begun to be incorporated into many products. Typical products that incorporate ROS2 include Autoware [2], a platform for self-driving cars, and VIPER [3], NASA's rover for Mars. In the current robot middleware market, there are currently no options other than ROS2 (Table 1), and this project also adopted ROS2 as its robot framework and conducted various surveys.

**Table 1.** Comparison of robot middlware ptoducts

| Frameworks | for product development | for research |
|---|---|---|
| ROS | Difficult | Possible |
| ROS2 | Possible | Possible |
| Ignition | Difficult | Possible |
| Isaac | Possible | Possible |
| OpenRTM | Difficult | Possible |

### 2.2 Middleware for Self-driving

Regarding robot automation, middleware for automated driving is as essential as robot middleware. Let's explore some of the automatic driving frameworks that are currently supporting ROS2. Autoware [2] is a popular choice for LiDAR-based automatic driving vehicles. Nav2 [4] is specifically designed for UVG. Isaac Autonomous Mobile Robots (ARM) [5] is developed by NVIDIA. Moveit [13] is a widely used framework for controlling robot arms. Lastly, we have ArduRover [6], a framework that operates on GPS.

Robot automation consists of three stages: 1. recognition, 2. decision-making, and 3. operation/running. In 1. recognition, the robot estimates its surroundings and its position from camera and sensor information. In the judgment and operation/running stages, the system determines a route based on the information obtained in the first stage and issues operation commands. The processing of 2 and 3 requires a GPU-equipped PC for the server, which is problematic due to the high cost of the system, increased power consumption, and occupied space. As a reference, the recommended specifications of the Autoware startup machine for the 3rd Automated AI Challenge (2021 simulation) [7] are as follows (Table 3).

**Table 2.** Comparison of middlewares for self-driving

| framework | ROS2 capability |
|---|---|
| Autoware | support |
| Nav2 | support |
| Isaac AMR | partial support |
| ArduRover | partial support |

**Table 3.** Requirements for Autoware

| Items | REquirements |
|---|---|
| OS | Linux(Ubuntu18.04) |
| CPU | Intel Corei7(8 cores) |
| Memory | 16GB (min) |
| Strage | SSD 30GB (min) |
| GPU NVIDIA | Geforce GTX 1080 (min) |

### 2.3  Video Transmission Middleware

Currently, GStreamer [8] is a mainstream video transmission middleware and widely adopted in various products. GStreamer is a free multimedia framework, optimized for NVIDIA's CUDA library for GPUs and capable of processing streaming video in GPU space. There is also SurroRTG SDK [9] by Surrogate and intdash by aptpod.

### 2.4  Communication Middleware for ROS2

ROS2 requires an environment where broadcast and multicast are available, and middleware is required for communication with ROS2 in Wide Area Network (WAN) where multicast is not allowed. Fastdds [10], a DDS used in ROS2, provides a means to realize ROS2 communication in a WAN environment through Fastdds Integration Service. In addition, the intdash ROS2 Connector enables ROS2 communication in a WAN environment.

## 3  MEC

### 3.1  MEC

MEC stands for Multi-Accesses Edge Computing, In Japan, DoCoMo's dOIC and KDDI's AWS Wavelength are available as data centres for MEC.

## 3.2  dOIC

When connecting dOIC to a device, a dedicated access point (mobile.d-oic.com) is used to connect. By subscribing to the dOIC Cloud Direct line, it is possible to connect to the dOIC and a fixed IP address is allocated. The connection between the device and the server is made via a closed network.

## 3.3  AWS Wavelength

AWS Wavelength is a service that enables connection to MEC servers on AWS using 5G lines contracted with KDDI. It is possible to set up an instance allocated a fixed IP in the MEC Zone of AWS Wavelength.

## 3.4  Comparison of dOIC and AWS Wavelength MEC

A comparison of dOIC and AWS Wavelength is summarised below (Table 4). In dOIC, a fixed IP is allocated to the device side and communication with the server is possible in a closed network. In Wavelength, no fixed IP is allocated to the device side, and the server side is allocated a fixed IP in the general network and can communicate with the server. Wavelength enables low latency communication at specific base stations.

**Table 4.** MEC Comparison

| MEC | device-side IP | server-side IP | low-latency base stations |
|---|---|---|---|
| dOIC | Fixed IP | Closed Network Fixed IP | Not specified |
| Wavelegth | No Fixed IP | General Network Fixed IP | Specified |

## 3.5  Ristrictions of Using MEC

One of the major limitations of running ROS2 on MEC is the restriction on the use of broadcast and multicast. In an MEC environment, this limitation imposes many restrictions (Table 5). Wavelength can avoid this limitation by using the multicast function of the AWS Transit Gateway [11]. In dOIC, it is necessary to build a mechanism to circumvent the broadcast-multicast restriction.

**Table 5.** Restrictions on use of broadcast and multicast

| MEC | Multicast | ROS2 | Solution |
|---|---|---|---|
| dOIC | Ristricted | Not work | Introduce middleware |
| Wavelegth | Ristricted | Not work | Transit Gateway |

# 4   Performance Measurements

## 4.1   Measurement Items

To design a robot in a 5G environment, we first carried out various measurements. The measurements were divided into three categories: line speed measurement, telemetry delay measurement, and video transmission delay measurement. Each environment was constructed and implemented.

## 4.2   Circuit Speed Measurement

Speed measurements were carried out by building a speed test server that can be accessed using the HTTP protocol. The speed test server is speedtest.net [12], which was developed by Ookla and is installed in more than 4000 locations worldwide, was installed in dOIC (Fig. 1), and measurements were carried out. The machine used for the measurements is in Table 6.

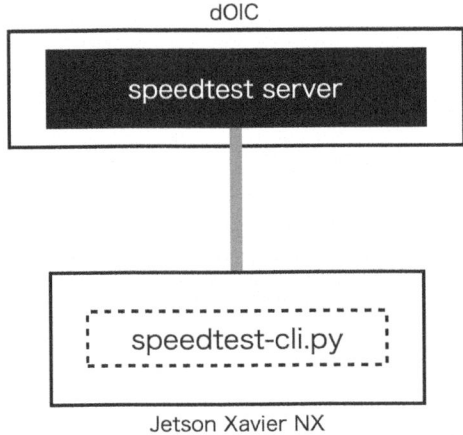

**Fig. 1.** Location of servers for Speedtest

**Table 6.** Devides for Speedtest

| Device | Specification | Location |
|---|---|---|
| Speedtest server | 1CPU instance | dOIC |
| Measurement device | Jetson Xavier NX | Edge |

The measurements were carried out with a Python program that can connect to the speedtest server provided by Oakla.

### 4.3   Telemetry Delay Measurement

The telemetry delay measurements were conducted with utmost thoroughness between ROS2 Nodes. The ROS2 version used was Foxy. The sending ROS2 node added Timestamp to the data, and the receiving ROS2 node created a program to call back the received data directly to the sending ROS2 node, ensuring the validity of our experiment. The following three environments were meticulously constructed and implemented. In the local network measurement (Fig. 2), we measured the ROS2 Node-to-ROS2 Node communication delay. In the cloud-direct P2P measurement (Fig. 3), since communication between ROS2 Nodes is not possible due to the broadcast/multicast usage limitations, the Fastdds Integration Service was built, and tcp-tunneling was used for the ROS2 Node-to-ROS2 Node communication. In the measurement with cloud-direct P2P (Fig. 3), communication between ROS2 Nodes is not possible due to the limitation of broadcast/multicast usage, so we used aptbot's intdash to perform communication between ROS2 Nodes.

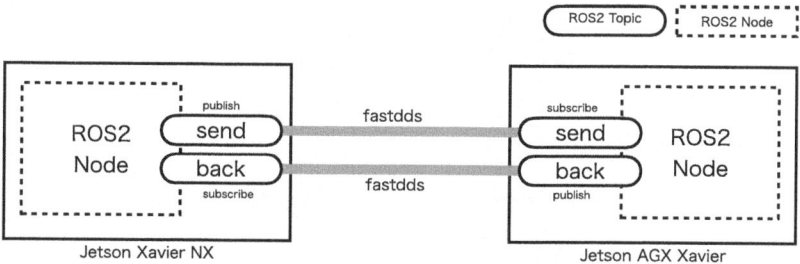

**Fig. 2.** Measurement in Local network

### 4.4   Network Environment for Video Transmission

The video transmission delay was measured in a total of four patterns: local network (Fig. 2), cloud direct P2P (Fig. 3) with a CIS camera and a USB camera.For the video transmission, a pipeline was constructed using GStreamer, and various codecs were transmitted using UDP/RTP protocols. The delay was measured by taking a picture of a stopwatch displayed in 1/100ms increments with a camera on the transmitting device, displaying the result on the receiving display, and taking a picture of both of them simultaneously with a camera.

The machines used for video transmission were Jetson series for both sender and receiver (Table 7).

### 4.5   Telemetry Delay

Delay measurements of DSS, the communication protocol of ROS2, have been made by the literature [14]. According to this, data transfers of 32KB or less within a single PC have a delayed result of 1 ms or less.

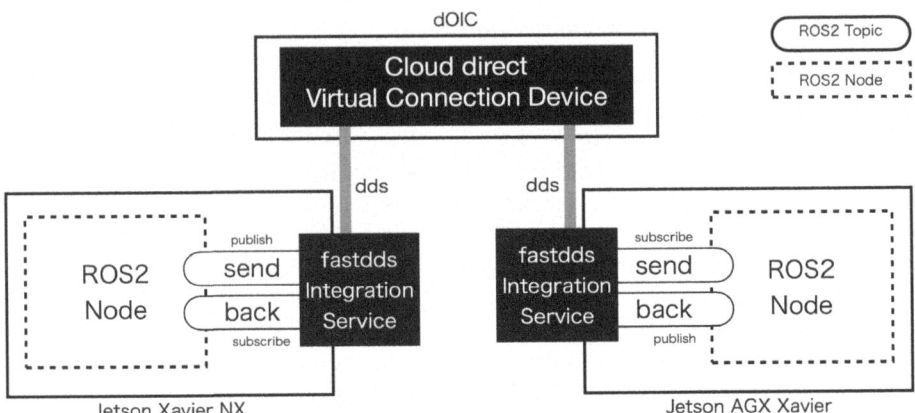

**Fig. 3.** Measurement by cloud direct P2P

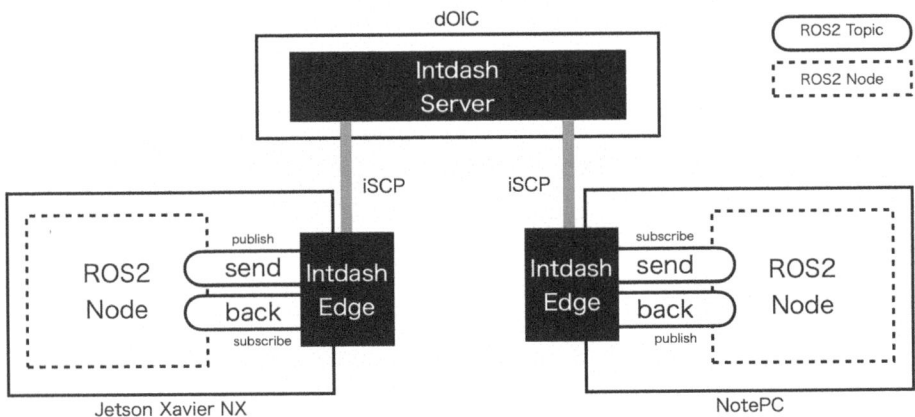

**Fig. 4.** Measurement in MEC environment

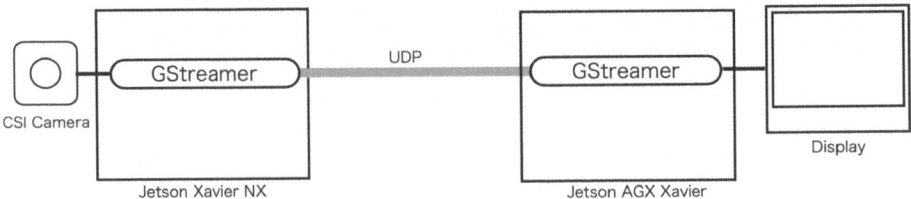

**Fig. 5.** Measurements in the local network (CSI cameras)

**Table 7.** Specification of devices

| Device | Specification |
|---|---|
| Sender | Jetson Xavier NX |
| Receiver | RTX3070 + Note PC |

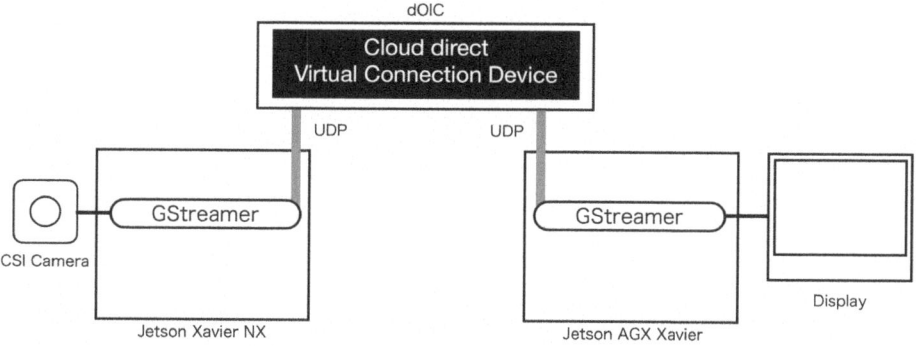

**Fig. 6.** Measurements in cloud direct P2P (CSI cameras)

## 4.6 Video Delay

The document [16] states that it takes about a 100ms delay for 1080p video to be displayed on the display after capturing the video from the camera. Regarding video transmission delay measurements, the document [15] states that the acceptable delay for a vehicle traveling remotely at 10km/h is about 600ms.

# 5 Measurement

## 5.1 Line Speed Measurement

Measurements were made in 5G and 4G+ environments using the Unix ping command (Table 8). The 5G environment resulted in a response time of 12ms faster than the 4G+ environment.

**Table 8.** ping

| Circuit | Location | ping (average of 50 measurements) |
| --- | --- | --- |
| 4G+ | Ueno | 40.2538 ms |
| 5G | Akihabara | 28.463 ms |

Next, the line speed was measured using the speed test server in the 5G and 4G+ environments (Table 9). The 5G environment resulted in an uplink speed of about 35mbps higher than the 4G+ environment.

## 5.2 Telemetry Delay Measurement

Telemetry delay measurements between ROS2 Nodes were performed (Table 10). By including timestamps in the data and comparing the sending and receiving

**Table 9.** Speed measurements (average of 5 measurements)

| Circuit | Location | Upload | Download | Web PING |
|---------|----------|--------|----------|----------|
| 4G+ | Ueno | 12.95 Mbps | 90.11 Mbps | 48.32 ms |
| 5G | Akihabara | 48.78 Mbps | 276.05 Mbps | 32.85 ms |

times, the round-trip delay time is measured, and the value is halved and summarised as the telemetry delay in one direction. The data size was measured with a data size of about 10 bytes. The telemetry can be transmitted locally with a very low latency of 2ms, but the latency is about 20–30 times higher when the telemetry is transmitted via a 5G line and middleware.

**Table 10.** Telemetry delay

| Environment | Delay |
|-------------|-------|
| LAN | 2 ms |
| Cloud direct P2P | 50 ms |
| dOIC + Intdash | 60 ms |

### 5.3 Delay of Video Transmission

Video-related delay measurements were carried out (Table 11, Table 12, Table 13). For video latency, the H264, jpeg, and NV12 formats resulted in the lowest transfer time latency for both the local and cloud-direct P2P environments. As for the NV12 format, there was no problem with transmission in the local environment, but transmission in the 5G environment was unsuccessful due to network noise.

**Table 11.** Delay in video transmission of CSI cameras (LAN)

| Resolution | FPS | H264 | H265 | MJPEG | VP9 | NV12 |
|------------|-----|------|------|-------|-----|------|
| 1280x720 | 30 fps | 100 ms | 200 ms | 100 ms | 150 ms | 100 ms |
| 640x360 | 30 fps | 100 ms | 200 ms | 100 ms | 150 ms | 90 ms |
| 320x180 | 30 fps | 100 ms | 200 ms | 100 ms | 100 ms | 90 ms |

**Table 12.** Delay in video transmission of USB cameras (LAN)

| Resolution | FPS | H264 | MJPEG |
|---|---|---|---|
| 1280x720 | 30 fps | 140 ms | 100 ms |
| 640x360 | 30 fps | 140 ms | 100 ms |
| 320x180 | 30 fps | 140 ms | 100 ms |

**Table 13.** Delay in video transmission of CSI cameras (Cloud direct P2P)

| Resolution | FPS | H264 | H265 | MJPEG | VP9 | NV12 |
|---|---|---|---|---|---|---|
| 1280x720 | 30 fps | 150 ms | 250 ms | Fail | 300 ms | Fail |
| 640x360 | 30 fps | 150 ms | 250 ms | 150 ms | 200 ms | Fail |
| 320x160 | 30 fps | 150 ms | 250 ms | 150 ms | 150 ms | Fail |

**Table 14.** Delay in video transmission of CSI cameras + object detection (LAN)

| Resolution | FPS | H264 | H265 | MJPEG | VP9 | NV12 |
|---|---|---|---|---|---|---|
| 1280x720 | 30 fps | 350 ms | 200 ms | 150 ms | 140 ms | Fail |
| 640x360 | 30 fps | 350 ms | 200 ms | 150 ms | 120 ms | 100 ms |
| 320x160 | 30 fps | 350 ms | 200 ms | 150 ms | 120 ms | 100 ms |

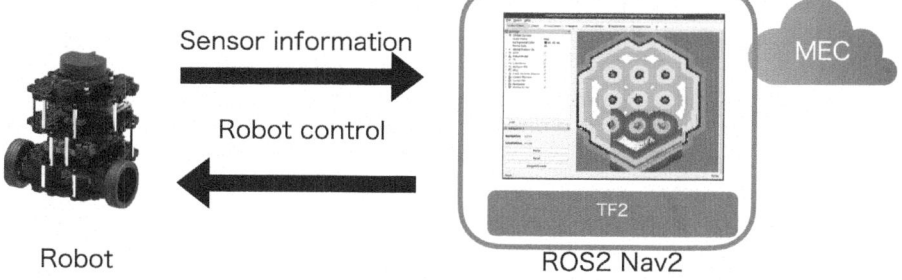

**Fig. 7.** Final configuration

The results of the inference of object detection and the video transmission are also included as reference data (Table 14).

Robot(ROS2 Nav2)

MEC
Multi-access Edge Computing

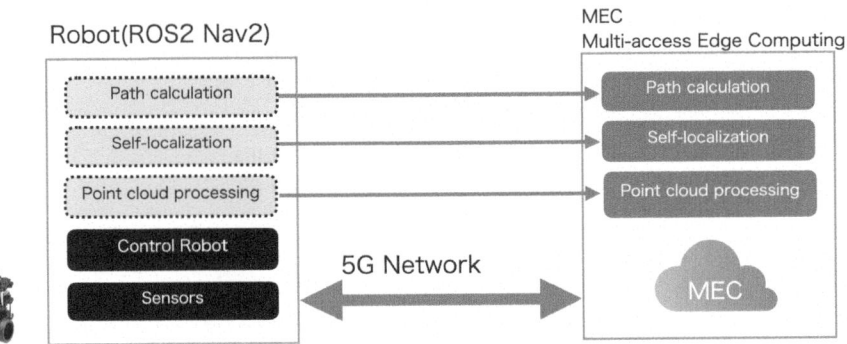

**Fig. 8.** Funtion sharing between a robot and network

## 6   Conclusions

The measurement results confirmed that the line speed is sufficient to control the robot with 5G. The ping speed was also confirmed to be about 10ms faster than that of 4G+, and values enabling lower latency control than the current system were measured. In terms of video transmission, it was confirmed that under favorable conditions, it is necessary to design the robot on the assumption of a delay of 150 ms to 200 ms in a 5G environment.

We finally developed an autonomous driving-related process of ROS2 Nav2 to the MEC side and adjusted TF2, and we successfully achieved autonomous driving from the MEC (Fig. 7). In this configuration, Path calculation, self-localization, and point cloud processing are performed by ROS2 Nav2 on the MEC (Fig. 8).

**Acknowldegment.** These results were obtained as a result of a project commissioned by the New Energy and Industrial Technology Development Organisation (NEDO) under the Post-5G Information and Communications Systems Infrastructure Enhancement Research and Development Project (JPNP20017).

## References

1. Hara, Y., Irie, K., Yoshida, T., Tomono, M.: Functional comparison and communication evaluation of robotics middleware ROS, ROS2, Ignition and Isaac, 25th Robotics Symposia (Mar 2020)
2. Autoware Foundation: Autoware. https://gitlab.com/autowarefoundation/autoware.ai
3. VIPER: Nasa. https://www.nasa.gov/viper/lunar-operations
4. Nav2: Nav2. https://navigation.ros.org/
5. Isaac AMR: NVIDIA. https://www.nvidia.com/en-us/deep-learning-ai/industries/robotics/
6. ArduRover: ArduPilot. https://ardupilot.org/rover/

7. 3rd Selfdriving AI charrange: JSAE. https://prtimes.jp/main/html/rd/p/000000042.000041897.html
8. GStreamer: GStreamer. https://gstreamer.freedesktop.org/
9. SurrogateRTG, surrogate. https://docs-beta.surrogate.tv/
10. Fastdds: ePromise. https://fast-dds.docs.eprosima.com/en/latest/
11. AWS Transit-Gateway: AWS. https://aws.amazon.com/jp/transit-gateway/
12. speedtest.net: Oaaka. https://www.speedtest.net/
13. moveit: moveit. https://moveit.ros.org/
14. Morita, R., Matsubara, K.: Mechanism of Dynamic Binding a Proper DDS Implementation for Optimizing Inter-node Communication in ROS2 (ETNET2018) (March 2018)
15. Mizushima, T., Kamikura, K., Omae, M.: Evaluation of influence of delay of image information on steering maneuver in remotely controllable automated driving system. Trans. Soc. Automotive Eng. Japan **50**(3), 970–976 (2019). https://doi.org/10.11351/jsaeronbun.50.970
16. TOkusa, Y., Matsuya, T., Kuga, Y., Murai, J.: Improving the naturalness of internet video conversation using a low-latency pipeline. In: DICOMO 2013, pp. 911–917 (July 2013)

# Automatic Classification of Cow's Behavior During Grazing

Atsushi Ito[1,2(✉)] ⓘ, Kota Nagakura[1], Lily Unume[1], Yuko Hiramatsu[1],
Tomoko Nakano[1], Yoshikazu Nagao[3], Rika Fukumori[4], Hirosugu Yamamoto[2],
Yukitoshi Otani[2], Shiro Suyama[2], Masaki Yasugi[5], and Yasutoshi Yoshiura[5]

[1] Faculty of Economics, Chuo University, 742-1 Higashi Nakano, Hachioji-shi,
192-0351 Tokyo, Japan
atc.00s@g.chuo-u.ac.jp
[2] Faculty of Engineering, Utsunomiya Universiry, 7-1-2 Yoto, Utsunomiya-shi,
321-0904 Tochigi, Japan
[3] Faculty of Agriculture, Utsunomiya University, 443 Shimokomoriya, Moka-shi,
321-4415 Tochigi, Japan
[4] Food and Environment Sciences, Rakunou Gakuen University, 582 Midori-cho,
Ebetsu-shi, 069-0836 Bunkyodai, Hokkaido, Japan
[5] Faculty of Marine Science and Technology, Fukui Prefectural University,
Eiheiji-cho, Yoshida-gun, 910-1142 Matsuokakanesadajima, Fukui, Japan

**Abstract.** The situation surrounding dairy farmers is changing at a
dizzying pace, with soaring feed costs, declining demand for dairy products, and an increasing number of farmers being forced to leave their
farms. To solve this situation and to improve Japan's food self-sufficiency
ratio, there is a need for high-value-added dairy products. However, there
are many problems around farming, such as breeding methods, increased
production costs, reproductive performance, and health management of
dairy cows. Grazing is one way to solve these problems, but it has yet to
be widely used because it requires pasture management according to the
foraging conditions. In this paper, we describe the intermediate results
of our study on a technology for automatic classification of cow behavior
during grazing, which is one of the challenges.

**Keywords:** dairy farming · grazing · animal welfare · value-added
dairy products · deep learning · sensor network · IoT

## 1 Introduction

### 1.1 Current Situation in Dairy Farming

Distorted supply chains due to the situation in Ukraine also affected the dairy
industry. In particular, the price of concentrate feed, which is mainly made from
cereals, has increased by more than 50% [1] due to the weak yen, among other
factors. Due to these effects, more and more dairy farmers are forced to run their
farms at a loss, and the number of farmers leaving the dairy industry has been
increasing in recent years [2]. Dairy farmers need a stable, self-sufficient management system independent of foreign feed imports yet ensuring profitability.

A. Quesada-Arencibia et al. (Eds.): EUROCAST 2024, LNCS 15172, pp. 354–364, 2025.
https://doi.org/10.1007/978-3-031-82949-9_32

## 1.2  Instability of Dairy Farm Management

Due to the nature of seasonal changes in milking volume, it is not easy to adjust the supply-demand balance in milk sales, and in general, centralized collection and multiple sales are conducted through designated milk producers' associations [3]. In such a structured sales system, the workflow of milk production is as follows.

- (1) to collect milk from dairy farmers
- (2) to bring it to designated organizations
- (3) to pack it at milk manufacturers.

Thus, it is difficult for dairy farmers to benefit from price transfers, and it is difficult for them to turn around their performance by simply raising prices in response to rising costs like other producers, as described in Fig. 1.

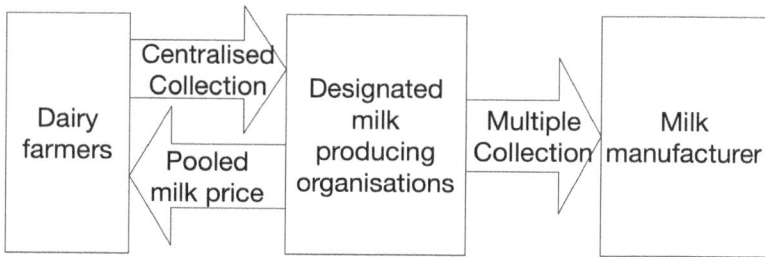

**Fig. 1.** Supply chain of milk production

In other words, dairy farm operators cannot stabilize their business through price adjustments. Therefore, they would like to have a more sustainable and stable management system than other producers. In terms of government policy, while the Livestock Production Cluster Project was implemented in 2015 to provide generous subsidies to compensate for the shortage of butter, the recent Milk Production Control Plan, which aims to retire 40 000 dairy cows in two years by 2022, is being implemented, and incentives of 150 000 yen per retired dairy cow are being offered. This policy has been reversed, with a subsidy of 150,000 yen per retired dairy cow [4,5]. Given the rapid changes in the environment in which dairy cows are kept, the need for a stable management system is not just a desire, but a pressing necessity. It's a call to action that we cannot afford to ignore.

## 1.3  Environment of Grazing in Japan

In the commonly practiced house rearing, restricting the behavior of cows not only brings stress, falls due to underdeveloped legs and feet, and the risk of lower milking output but also makes it easy to neglect proper management and maintenance of excreta disposal, which can easily have a negative impact on cow health and milk quality (Fig. 2). In contrast, pastoral rearing not only reduces stress by not restricting behavior but also promotes the growth of the legs and feet and even reduces the risk of accidents at night [6]. Grazing is also ideal from the point of view of reduced feed costs and animal welfare. Ranching on roughage is not only expected to reduce feed costs but also to ensure stable rearing in the future. As mentioned above, a rearing system that relies on foreign imports could be severely compromised if the supply chain becomes distorted, as has happened this time. On the other hand, roughage contains high levels of vitamin A, it is said to improve milk quality, and a shift to a rearing system based on roughage is considered to have sufficient merit [7]. In addition, from the perspective of 'animal welfare' in the SDGs, which have been promoted in recent years, it can be said that pasturage, where animals are reared in a form similar to that of the wild, is more ideal than shack rearing, where animals are kept in a small space to provide food for humans. Japan has received an E rating out of A-G ratings in the Animal Protection Index (API) published by the World Animal Protection Council (WAP) [8], and in the current situation where the promotion of exports of livestock products is required in the future due to declining domestic demand, this is an issue that should be addressed to gain global trust [9,10] a shift to pasture-raised cattle would make the management system of dairy farming more stable.

### 1.4    Theme of This Research

This paper describes a technology that uses IoT to understand cattle grazing behavior. This information is necessary for feed and health management in grazing. In Japan, pastureland is not so large, and due to the climate, it is challenging to grow the grass that cattle prefer. For this reason, filling cattle with grass alone is challenging, and additional feed is usually given in the cattle shed. However, if too much of this additional material is given, the cattle suffer from indigestion and become ill. Therefore, it is necessary to estimate the amount of grass eaten by the cattle while grazing and supplement any shortfall. Therefore, this study aims to measure the body movements of grazing cows and use this information to estimate their behavior, particularly the time of foraging and, from this, the amount of grass they have eaten. Section 2 describes related research; Sect. 3 presents the apparatus we have built to measure the behavior of grazing cattle; Sect. 4 describes the experimental results; and Sect. 5 provides a summary and future work.

## 2    Related Works

### 2.1    Research Outside Japan

Several studies on rearing methods have been conducted outside Japan. For example, in a study by Jessica Werner, University of Hohenheim, Germany [11],

In cattle barn rearing (problem)

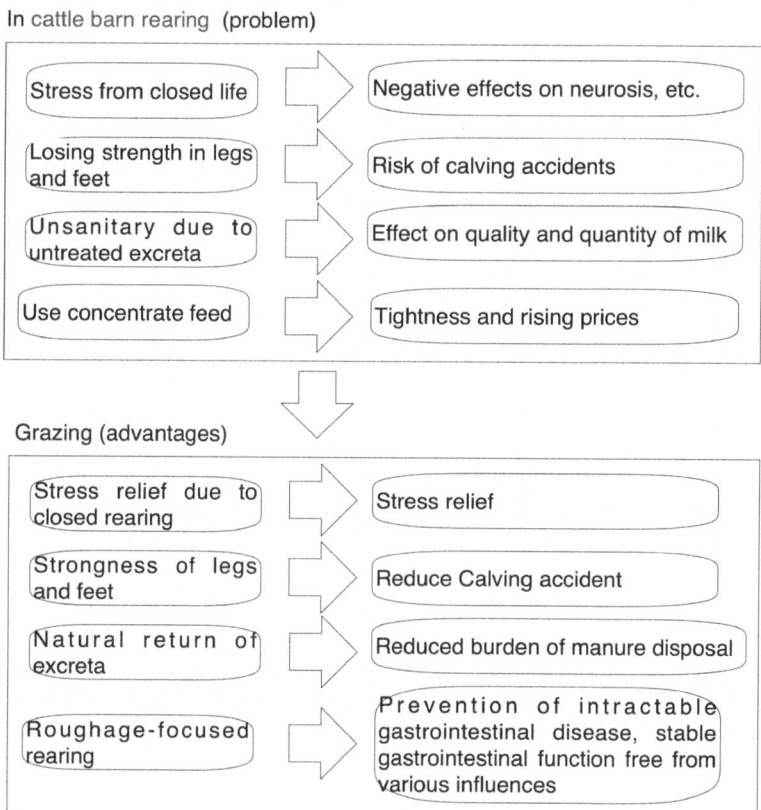

Grazing (advantages)

**Fig. 2.** Advantages of grazing

cattle behavior was measured using RumiWatch and MooMonitor+, which are said to have a higher accuracy than visual observation. In considering cattle behavior as an essential indicator of forage quantity and animal performance, health, and welfare, methods to automate this are being explored, as appropriate forage allocation is essential for maximum pasture utilization. Specifically, research is being conducted on methods to compare the behavioral characteristics of cows allocated sufficient grass with those allocated restricted grass and to automatically adjust grass allocations accordingly. Research in Germany, which accounts for about 20% of EU milk production and is derided as a dairy power-house, will benefit the Japanese dairy industry, even considering the differences in the natural environment. In order to deepen inter-industry exchange and gain overseas know-how, we believe that efforts should be made to encourage animal welfare and promote exports of livestock products.

## 2.2  Our Previous Work

We have been researching and developing a sensor network system using LoRa to automatically observe the behavior of cows grazing on a vast pasture since FY 2019 [12]. LoRa is a wireless communication method that is one of the LPWA (Low Power Wide Area). This communication technology enables communication over long distances with low power consumption. An outline of our sensor work for a cow is described in Fig. 2. Based on this system, we experimented with collecting cow behavior and tried to analyze behavior using AI.

# 3  Behavioural Classification

The following section describes the methodology for this study's behavioral analysis of grazing cattle. The general flow is shown in Fig. 3. First, before going out to pasture, the cattle are fitted with devices to log their acceleration and angular velocity. Then, the cattle are followed closely during grazing, and their behavior is videotaped. Currently, smartphones are used. After grazing, the video is watched and labeled on a second-by-second basis. The data is used to build a machine-learning model and evaluate its accuracy. Last year, we used a method whereby the observer used a device to send the behavior pattern to the sensor and record it simultaneously. However, this time, we decided to extract the behavior from the video because, in that case, delays, wrong presses, and forgotten presses of buttons inevitably occurred. The accuracy of the data itself did not improve.

## 3.1  Types of Cattle Behaviour

In this experiment, labelling was done according to the following classification

- Walking
- Stationary
- Foraging
- Chewing
- Body licking
- Licking other cattle
- Rubbing body against tree

## 3.2  Data Collection Methods

Cattle behavior was acquired using a 6-axis accelerometer. The M5 Stack Core2 was used. That device has a 6-axis accelerometer and operates at 30 Hz. This sensor data was recorded on microSD along with the RTC time. The recorded data format is as follows.

*Date, Month, Day, Hour, Minutes, Seconds*

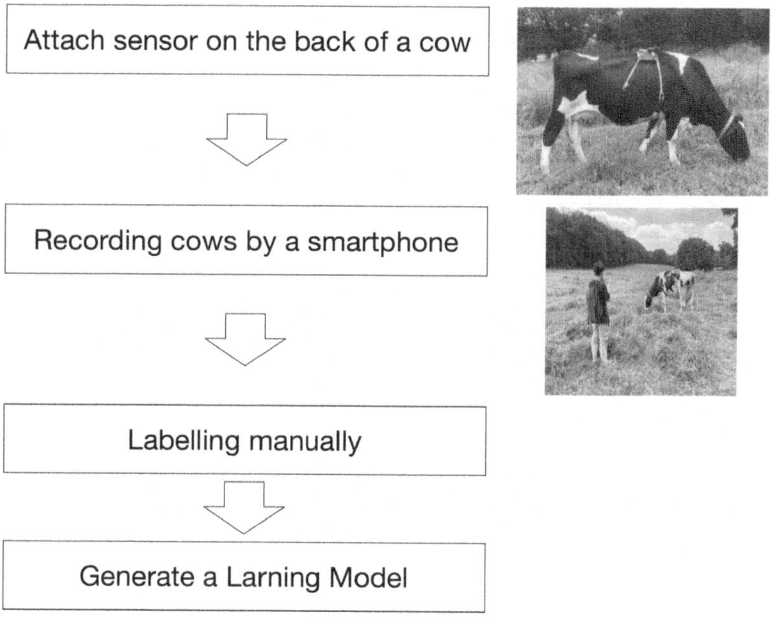

**Fig. 3.** Flow of experiment

2023,09,30,09,15,29,3,

$Accelerometer(xyz - axis)$
$0.198730, 0.272705, 1.011963$

$Gyrosensors(roll, pitch, yaw)$
$0.479628, 0.307987, -8.725753$

$flags(CowID)$
$07, 07$

### 3.3   Learning Model

We reused the learning model that was used in last year's experiment [12]. Last year, we used 1D CNN to speed up the computation. The details of the Neural Network was as follows.

$model = keras.Sequential([$
$Conv1D(filters = channel\_size, kernel\_size = kernel\_size, strides = 1,$
$padding = "same", activation = "relu", input\_shape = (windowsize, 1)),$
$Conv1D(filters = 1, kernel\_size = 8, padding =' same', activation =' tanh'),$
$GlobalMaxPooling1D(),$
$keras.layers.Dense(378, activation =' relu'), keras.layers.Dropout(0.2),$

$keras.layers.Dense(378, activation =' relu'), keras.layers$
$keras.layers.Dropout(0.2), keras.layers$
$keras.layers.Dense(3, activation =' softmax')$
$])$

The execution environment was Google Colaboratory [13]. In machine learning, it was also decided to learn three behaviors with relatively large amounts of data, namely walking, standing still, and foraging, as learning only proceeds for behaviors with small amounts of data.

# 4   Experimental Results

## 4.1   Data Pre-Processing

Behaviors were tagged in 1-second from the video by hand. The IDs of each behavior are as follows.

- walking = 1
- standing still = 2
- foraging = 3

An example of output data was as follows.

$(start)Hour, Minutes, Seconds, (end)Hour, Minutes, Seconds, behavior flag$
$9, 48, 33, 9, 49, 17, 1$

The rightmost data shows the behavior. The first three data from the left are the times the behavior starts, and the next three are the times at which the behavior ends. Sometimes, it takes only a few seconds, and sometimes, as in foraging, it continues for several minutes. This information was matched with the information recorded on the SD card, and the output values of the accelerometer and gyro sensor during a specific time interval were extracted and filed for each behavior pattern. Next, to apply FFT to this data, the XYZ-axis data from the accelerometer and the roll, pitch, and yaw values from the gyro sensor were separated and extracted, respectively. A short-time Fourier transform (STFT) was then applied to these six data series and transformed every 128 data samples; as the 30 Hz sensor, approximately 4 s was used as a single interval. An overlap of 50% was also applied. Note that a HAMMING window was applied in this experiment. Figure 4 shows an example of the FFT results. Finally, the values resulting from applying the FFT to the XYZ-axis of the accelerometer and the roll, pitch, and yaw values of the gyro sensor for a specific time interval were grouped and converted into a vector, which was used as one data set for machine learning. A label file was also created.

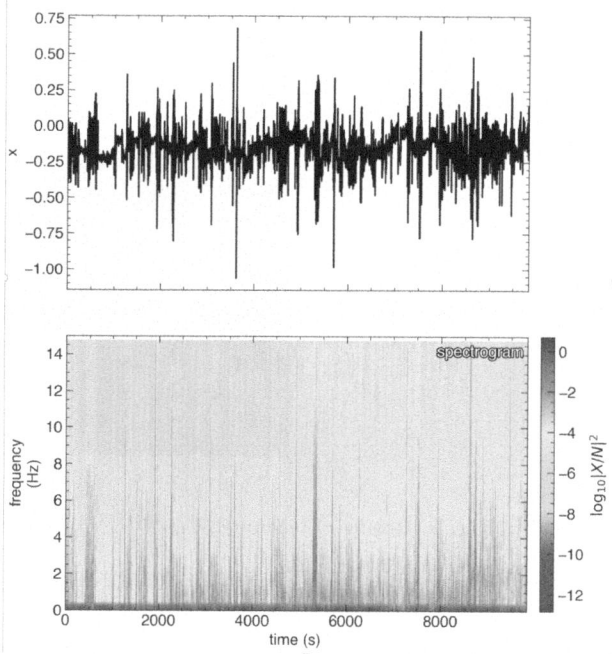

**Fig. 4.** Sensor output and Result of FFT

## 4.2   Machine Learning

The data used in this experiment were recorded on 30 September 2023 for two cows. We will refer to the data for these two cows as A and B. The following machine-learning experiments were conducted using these data.

- Test1: Learning data A (acceleration, gyro), test data B (acceleration, gyro)
- Test2: Training data B (acceleration, gyro), test data A (acceleration, gyro)
- Test3: Learning data A (acceleration), test data B (acceleration)
- Test4: Learning data B (acceleration), test data A (acceleration)
- Test5: Learning data A (gyro), test data B (gyro)
- Test6: Learning data B (gyro), test data A (gyro)

Figures 5 and 6 show the results of the machine learning experiments. The blue line in the figures shows the accuracy during training, and the orange line shows the accuracy during testing. In Fig. 5, it can be seen that the test accuracy could be a lot higher. In Fig. 6, the accuracy during testing fluctuates significantly, and the results are unstable. The Confusion Matrix also shows that Test 1 cannot recognize stationary states. The situation was similar in other combinations of experiments. In fact, the sensor output values appear to differ depending on the behavior pattern to a certain extent. So, in the future, we would like to construct a useful learning model for behavior identification by adjusting the parameters during training, diversifying the way data are combined, and adjusting the length of the STFT interval. Also, as we currently only have data from two cows, we would like to conduct experiments with more data in the next year.

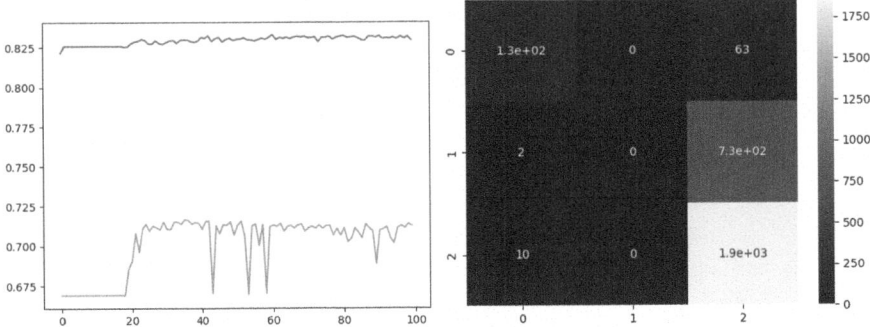

**Fig. 5.** Result of learning (Test1)

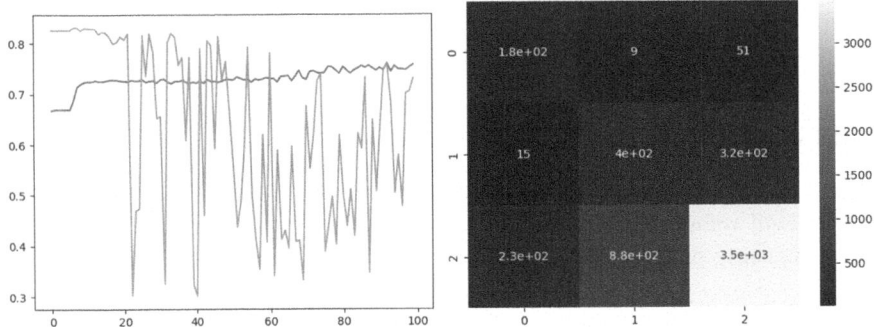

**Fig. 6.** Result of learning (Test3)

## 5    Conclusion

### 5.1    Findings from This Experiment

This experiment involved constructing a flow to extract behavior data from two cows during grazing for analysis, which yielded significant findings. The unique sensor output characteristics for each behavior pose intriguing questions for future research. Importantly, the optimization of various parameters and the method of data integration could revolutionize the field of animal behavior and data analysis.

## 5.2  Application of Experimental Result

In promoting grazing, we consider it necessary to establish higher productivity and sustainability. Starting grazing costs a certain amount of money, including land and the introduction of electric fences. If grazing can be made profitable enough to disregard such costs, this rearing method will expand. Therefore, research into appropriate grazing methods is needed to improve profitability. With the analysis of cattle behavior using accelerometers, it is possible not only to compare data on one behavior with data on another behavior but also to compare data on one behavior under certain conditions with data on the same behavior under different conditions. For example, data may differ between walking on warmer days and walking when the temperature is cooler. There was a noticeable difference in the condition of cattle when grazed in August and in September when the weather was relatively cooler, including fatigue due to the heat. Suppose we can understand the differences in behavior under different temperatures by comparing such data. In that case, we will be one step closer to devising ways to prevent a decline in milking yield. For example, it would be possible to devise appropriate grazing times and rearing methods by estimating the number of hours after grazing when fatigue appears based on differences in acceleration during walking or by comparing the degree of drinking water and estimating the optimum intake.

**Acknowldegement.** We thank Mr Asano and Mr Uda of the Farm attached to the Faculty of Agriculture, Utsunomiya University, for their cooperation in data collection. This research was performed as part of "Demonstrative research and development for solving regional problems through data linkage and utilization (2nd)" from 2019-2020 (Project number: 21402). This research is also supported by JSPS KAKENHI Grant Number 17H02249, 18K111849, 20H01278, 20H05702, 22K12598, 23H03649, 23K28338.

# References

1. Ministry of Agriculture, Forestry and Fisheries : The situation regarding livestock and dairy farming. https://www.maff.go.jp/j/chikusan/kikaku/lin/l_hosin/attach/pdf/index-233.pdf (in Japanese), Accessed 26 May 2024
2. Central Dairy Council :Survey on the State of Dairy Farm Management in Japan. https://www.dairy.co.jp/20230317.pdf(in Japanese), Accessed 26 May 2024
3. J-Milk : Milk Supply Chain. https://www.j-milk.jp/news/h4ogb4000000alqh-att/JapanSupplyChain2022.pdf (in Japanese), Accessed 26 May 2024
4. Ministry of Agriculture, Forestry and Fisheries : Examples of livestock cluster initiatives. https://www.maff.go.jp/j/chikusan/kikaku/tikusan_sogo/l_cluster_jirei.html(in Japanese), Accessed 26 May 2024
5. Ministry of Agriculture, Forestry and Fisheries : Emergency Support Project for Dairy Farm Management Improvement. https://www.maff.go.jp/j/chikusan/gyunyu/rakunou_keieikaizen.html(in Japanese), Accessed 26 May 2024
6. Ministry of Agriculture, Forestry and Fisheries : Grazing Room. https://www.maff.go.jp/j/chikusan/sinko/shiryo/houboku/houboku.html(in Japanese) Accessed 26 May 2024

 7. Feed Division, Livestock Production Bureau, Ministry of Agriculture, Forestry and Fisheries : The situation regarding feed. https://www.maff.go.jp/j/chikusan/sinko/lin/l_siryo/attach/pdf/index-970.pdf(in Japanese), Accessed 26 May 2024
 8. World Animal Protection : Animal Protection Index. https://api.worldanimalprotection.org/, Accessed 26 May 2024
 9. Ministry of Agriculture, Forestry and Fisheries : Export of Livestock Products (2023). https://www.maff.go.jp/j/chikusan/shokuniku/attach/pdf/tikusan_butuno_yusyutu-11.pdf (in Japanese), Accessed 26 May 2024
10. Animal Quarantine Service, Ministry of Agriculture, Forestry and Fisheries : Export of even-toed ungulates. https://www.maff.go.jp/aqs/hou/exguuteirui2.html(in Japanese), Accessed 26 May 2024
11. Werner, J., Umstatter, C., Leso, L., et al.: Evaluation and application potential of an accelerometer-based collar device for measuring grazing behavior of dairy cows. Animal **13**(9), 2070–2079 (2019). https://doi.org/10.1017/S1751731118003658
12. Hara, K., Ito, A., Ashibe, S., Nagao, Y., Sasaki, A.: Classification of cow's behavior during grasing by AI. In: 13th IEEE International Conference on Cognitive Infocommunications (CogInfoCom2022), Budapest, Hungary, pp. 65-70 (2022). https://doi.org/10.1109/CogInfoCom55841.2022.10081627
13. Google Colaboratory. https://colab.research.google.com/notebooks/intro.ipynb#scrollTo=rz9AvcZBaA1z, Accessed 26 May 2024

# Programming Learning Through the Use of ChatGPT

Ami Otsuka[1], Akira Sasaki[2], and Atsushi Ito[1]([✉]) [iD]

[1] Faculty of Economics, Chuo University, 742-1 Higashi Nakano, Hachioji-shi 192-0351, Tokyo, Japan
atc.00s@g.chuo-u.ac.jp
[2] GClue, Inc, 134-3 Ikkimachi Turuga, Aizu-wakamatsu-shi, Fukushima 965-0006, Japan
akira@gclue.jp

**Abstract.** Programming skills are increasingly required in a variety of professions, but learning programming is generally challenging. Yet, as the field of application expands, software engineers are in short supply. This paper describes a study we conducted to build a means to help beginning programmers learn coding and related theory systematically by using ChatGPT as a new approach, thereby enabling many people to acquire programming skills. This trend can be called a shift from codingcentered to documentation-centered learning. The purpose of this study is to improve individual skills, not to contribute to group programming projects.

**Keywords:** Programming education · ChatGPT · Software engineering · Generative AI · Interactive AI

## 1 Introduction

### 1.1 The Aim of This Research

Technology has become an integral part of our daily lives, and software is at the heart of this. For this reason, programming skills are increasingly required in many professions, and basic knowledge and background in programming are also necessary to understand the future of society. However, for many people, learning programming is a challenging task. Particularly for first-time learners, the tendency to emphasize only knowledge of how to write code without a sufficient understanding of the overall structure and design of the program may inhibit learning programming. Therefore, this paper proposes a new approach to programming learning. Specifically, it is a learning method centred on the creation of requirements definitions using OpenAI's interactive AI, ChatGPT. They enable learners to gain a deep understanding of the design and structure of the entire program and aim to learn through the experience of creating and publishing their software. To this end, the current status and problems of programming learning are clarified, and new learning methods are proposed and evaluated. Furthermore, based on these, a vision of the future is developed. It then provides insights into how programming education should evolve and how advanced technologies such as interactive AI should be used.

A. Quesada-Arencibia et al. (Eds.): EUROCAST 2024, LNCS 15172, pp. 365–375, 2025.
https://doi.org/10.1007/978-3-031-82949-9_33

A new educational method of programming learning is proposed based on the current situation. It uses interactive AI, which enables students to learn not only coding but also upstream process skills, such as requirement definition and design, at the same time. The three key points are as follows.

- 1. Shift in the focus of learning: The focus of programming learning has shifted from creating programs to creating requirements definitions.
- 2. Development of interactive AI-based learning materials: providing programming learning materials based on using interactive AI
- 3. Supporting requirements definition learning: providing requirements definition learning materials that are easier and simpler, with an awareness of upstream process creation.

Based on our previous research, we believe that learning with interactive AI enables students to think and create their programs with the assistance of the AI and to deepen their understanding by making improvements as necessary. As a result, they will feel more interested in programming, increasing their learning effectiveness. Furthermore, such an active learning attitude is expected to contribute to embedding programming skills in long-term memory, enabling learning results to be utilized at will. In addition, programs created with the assistance of interactive AI are easier to read, and it is easier to understand why clean code should be written. By receiving assistance from interactive AI, the participants can gain experience in creating relatively large deliverables and understand the significance of dividing the code into functions for each function. Such experience helps create programs that are easy to maintain and extend. It is essential to provide suitable learning examples using interactive AI and demonstrate its effectiveness, such as using games like Othello as the subject matter. The structure of this paper is as follows: Sect. 2 describes related research; Sect. 3 describes interactive AI and its application to software development; Sect. 4 describes practical examples of software education using interactive AI; and Sect. 5 summarises and discusses future visions and challenges Sect. 5.4.

## 2 Related Works

In recent years, research on the application of interactive AI, as represented by ChatGPT, to education has been progressing. Reference [1] evaluates the impact of ChatGPT on university education, focusing mainly on computer securityoriented specializations. It could be used as an assistant to discuss problems encountered when solving assignments or to speed up the learning process. Finally, the paper discusses how higher education in computer science should adapt to tools such as ChatGPT. According to reference [2], artificial intelligence (AI) has the power to revolutionize the education sector by enhancing the teaching and learning experience, improving student learning outcomes, and streamlining administrative tasks, and the perceived usefulness of ChatGPT has a positive impact on ChatGPT usage and student satisfaction It is believed to have a positive impact on the use of ChatGPT and student satisfaction.

# 3   Application of Interactive AI to Software Development

As shown in Table 1, interactive AI is being developed by various companies and has different definitions, but for this paper, it is defined as an agent that can naturally converse with its users using natural language as an interface. Attempts are underway to apply such AI to software development. Reference [7] provides a comparison of the accuracy of using CPT-4, text-davinci-003 (the base model of ChatGPT), Codex (code-davinci-002) and CODEGEN-16B [8] for software development. In addition, HumanEval [9] is used as an example. The results presented here show that the accuracy of GPT-4 was 82%, whereas the accuracy of text-DaVinci-003, Codex (code-DaVinci-002), and CODEGEN16B was 65%, 39%, and 30%, respectively. These studies suggest that GPT-4 for coding is highly useful.

**Table 1.** Definition of Interactive AI

| Developer | Definition |
|---|---|
| IBM | Interactive Artificial Intelligence (AI) refers to technologies like chatbots and virtual agents that can interact with users. These technologies can mimic human communication by using large amounts of data, machine learning, and natural language processing to recognize speech and text input and translate and interpret between multiple languages. [3] |
| Google | Interactive AI is a type of AI that can simulate human conversation. It is possible through Natural Language Processing (NLP), a field of AI that enables computers to understand and process human language, and Google's underlying models that enhance new generative AI capabilities. [4] |
| Open AI | There is no official version, but the website states the following [5]. We are rolling out custom versions of ChatGPT that we can create for a specific purpose: GPT. GPT is a new way for anyone to create a tailored version of ChatGPT to be more helpful in their daily life, at specific tasks, at work, or home—and then share that creation with others. GPTs can help us learn the rules of any board game, help teach kids math, or design stickers |
| Microsoft | Intelligent agents that can handle human language play a growing role in personalized, ubiquitous computing and the everyday use of devices. Agents need to be able to communicate and collaborate with humans in ways that are seamless and natural, and to be able to learn new behaviors, concepts, and relationships as first-class operations. In other words, our devices need to be able to converse with us [6] |

Interactive artificial intelligence (AI) refers to technologies such as chatbots and virtual agents that can interact with users. These technologies can mimic human communication by using large amounts of data, machine learning, and natural language processing to recognize speech and text input and translate and interpret between multiple languages.

# 4 Experiments in Software Development Using Interactive AI

## 4.1 Developing Othello

The impetus for this study came from the author Otsuka's creation of Othello in the Google Collaboratory environment in May 2023, during a Python lecture in the Introductory ICT Exercise at Chuo University. Creating an Othello program is suitable for learning in the following ways.

- 1. Everyone knows the rules of Othello, and the game is intuitive and easy to understand
- 2. Many topics can be learnt, such as 8-way search and recursion, which are frequently used in game creation.

It was considered to be scalable and could be made into a good piece of work by devising a design, improving operability, creating opponents, and so on. The creation of the Othello program can be broadly divided into the following four steps.

- 1. Designing the fundamentals: creating the underlying code, such as the definition of the two-dimensional array that stores the Othello stones and the program for turning over the stones
- 2. Extending the functionality: as Othello can only be played in standalone mode and it is boring to play two roles per player, an AI is introduced to fight against it. Start with a simple AI that randomly places stones in the available locations.
- 3. Design: In the initial stage, Othello's stones were represented by the letter '●,' which was visually difficult to understand, so the design was improved to be represented as a graphic using matplotlib.
- 4. Creation of a menu screen: It is unnatural for the game to start just by executing the program, so a menu screen should be created. This screen should explain how the game works and be visually easy to understand.

The relationship between the learner and the interactive AI in this Othello development is shown in Fig. 1. The learner gives instructions to the interactive AI in the form of prompts, and the interactive AI generates and presents not only the generated code but also a detailed description. This kind of interaction took place during the construction of the Othello game application. In this kind of work, it is essential that no human coding is required or only minimal coding and fine-tuning is required to complete an app with several hundred lines, which is an advantage of using an interactive AI. Through the creation of Othello, the following points became clear.

- 1. If the interactive AI can be mastered, code input can be kept to a minimum, i.e. anyone can code
- 2. The accuracy of the instructions to the interactive AI, i.e. the prompts, determines the quality of the software
- 3. The prompts are the software specification itself

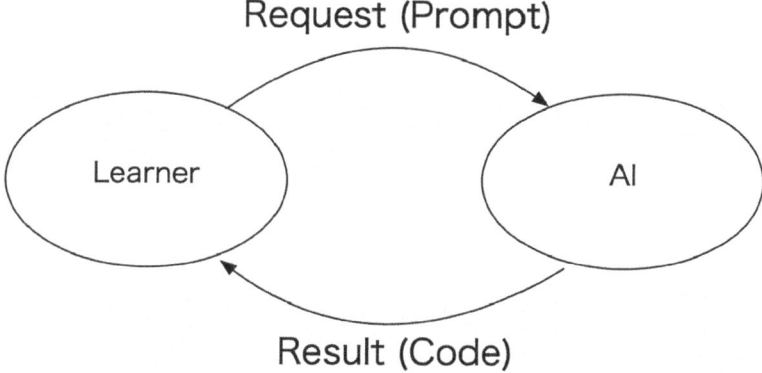

**Fig. 1.** Relation between learner and AI

### 4.2 Building a Game Development Platform

In the second semester of FY2023, Otsuka continued to build games using interactive AI based on its experience in developing Othello, and on 28 October, started a 100-day continuous app development project. The idea is to develop an app for 100 days without a single day's rest, and at the time of writing (19 December), 53 days have passed. The project aims to develop many apps with interactive AI to check their effectiveness and to put together a platform for developing game apps. Ultimately, the aim is to use the platform as a base for programming learning materials. Expressly, in addition to importing pygame, game-specific additional functions are classified into six classes: game loop, sprites (composite display of characters), UI, events, state machine (state management), and object management (number of innovators appearing, etc.) to a programming environment.

We mainly use game loops and state machines when creating an Othello application. If we want to create a shooting game, we should do the following:

- Move the fighter plane → Game loop.
- Turn the fighter and rotate the image → Sprite
- Prepare lots of enemy characters
- Determines collision, fires bullets → Management class
- React to collision → Event listener
- Start/game over screen → State machine
- Varying stages per level → State machine

On Day 1 of the 100-day project, an Othello game took about 30 h, including preliminary preparations. However, on Day 50, the abovementioned modules were in place and could be built in six hours. If it is simple, it can be completed in one or two hours. Table 2 shows the interaction (prompts and answers to them) to optimize the Othello program.

**Table 2.** Example of converstion between learner and AI to generate othero game

| Acter | Conversation |
|-------|--------------|
| User | Pointing out areas for improvement in this programme. (The rest is omitted) |
| ChatGPT | IThis Othello game program is very well organised and covers the basic gameplay logic well. However, there are some areas for improvement: reduction of code redundancy, etc. (The rest is omitted) |
| User | I want to run this Othello game in pygame. Modify the program and output. The state transitions as follows. (The rest is omitted) |
| ChatGPT | To implement the Othello game in Pygame, some modifications and additions are required. The basic structure is provided here, but to make it work in practice, you need to define state classes such as State1, State2 and State3 and implement the necessary logic in those classes |
| User | When neither of these can be hit, the system should properly transition to state3. Currently, the system stops when neither player is able to hit |
| ChatGPT | In order to ensure proper state transitions when neither player can hit anymore, the game state needs to be checked within the update method of the State2 class and a transition to State3 triggered if necessary. Make the following change (abbreviated) With this change, the game state is evaluated in the update method of State2 and a transition to State3 is triggered when neither player has any more moves to play. This logic accurately reflects the game's end condition based on the Othello game rules |

### 4.3   How to Use Interactive AI in Programming

There are various waterfall models, v-models [10] and X-models [11] for software development. Here, we consider the relationship between the v-model and software development using interactive AI. The V-model is shown in Fig. 2. The waterfall model folded back after coding and is characterized by a clear relationship between the various design and testing phases. As shown in Fig. 3, the V-model is rewritten using the relationship between the learner and the AI shown in Fig. 1. Here, the requirements analysis (what kind of game application is desired) and acceptance testing (is the generated game as intended?) are handled by humans. However, the interactive AI supports the rest of the process.

The Relation between a learner and AI is described in Table 3. The generative AI assists in requirements definition, basic design, detailed design, unit testing, comprehensive testing, and system testing, while the coding part is left to the generative AI. This situation allows learners to learn the essence of software engineering as they consult with the interactive AI to elaborate on items such as requirement analysis and requirement definition, which have not been emphasized much in software learning in the past but are, in fact, very important in software development.

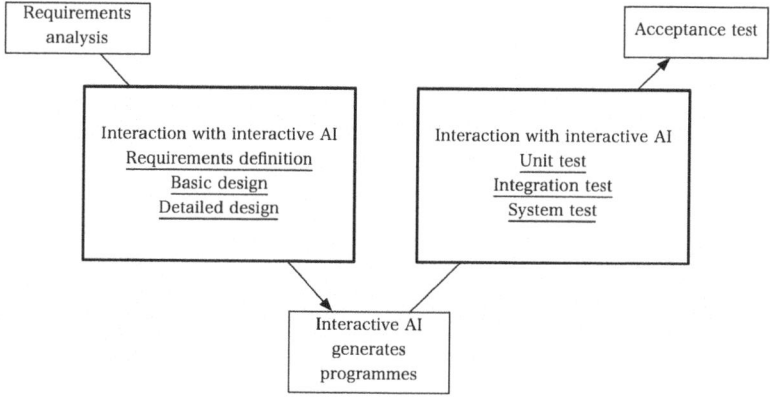

**Fig. 2.** V-model

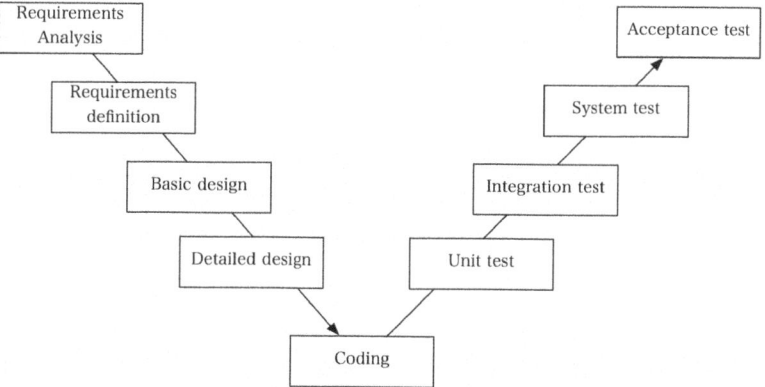

**Fig. 3.** Relation between learner and AI on V-model

### 4.4 Considerations in the Use of Interactive AI

The use of AI technologies, such as interactive AI, has the potential to help alleviate some of the challenges of traditional programming learning. However, even when using them, it is necessary to understand the characteristics of interactive AI as follows.

**Optimal Question Structure.** How should you structure your questions to get the answers you are looking for? It requires an understanding of the following. Simply asking a question specifying the language and purpose of the language you want to use will likely result in a program that works differently than expected. This case is a significant barrier, especially in the early stages of learning programming.

**Constraints on Output Due to Character Limits.** This constraint becomes more pronounced when attempting to create long programs, and output from the AI is often cut off in the middle.

**Table 3.** The Relation between a learner and AI

| Phase | Performed by | Role of AI |
| --- | --- | --- |
| Requirements Analysis | Learner | NA |
| Requirements Definition | Learner | Support |
| Basic design | Learner | Support |
| Detailed design | Learner | Support |
| Coding | AI | Code generation |
| Unit test | Learner | Generate test case |
| Integration test | Learner | Fixing error |
| System test | Learner | Generate test case and Fixing error |
| Acceptance test | Learner | NA |

While generating a programme using an interactive AI is relatively easy in itself, understanding how it works and using it appropriately requires a good deal of understanding and effort. Having the AI generate the programs that make up a single part many times, checking their operation, and selecting the ones that are easy to read and work appropriately requires a certain amount of time and effort. Interactive AIs also are quick to adopt advanced programming techniques, such as using classes out of the blue, which may be difficult for novice users to understand. Another problem is that not all interactive AIs can write all programs perfectly. Mistakes are often made, especially when attempting to generate long programs, and significant differences in the quality of the generated programs appear. It is the users' responsibility to accurately communicate the purpose and requirements of the program, which is an essential factor for AI to function well. In addition, if a generated program does not work as expected, although it is possible to find out the cause of the error in more detail by asking the interactive AI about the short and unfriendly error messages displayed in the development environment, even if these are sent to the AI, it is not always possible to output a program that does not generate the relevant error However, even if this is sent to the AI, it is not always possible to output a program that does not generate the error in question, and trial and error will continue.

Even with AI's assistance, it is essential that humans have a deep understanding of the program in order to extend and maintain it; although AI is a great tool to assist users, users' own skills need to be developed and deeply understood in order to properly evaluate, understand, and utilize its results. Furthermore, interactive AI has character limits for input and output. This limit sometimes prevents the interactive AI from continuing to output the "continue" question, making it often difficult to understand what the AI is indicating. Thus, while interactive AI can certainly help alleviate some of the challenges of traditional programming learning, various obstacles exist to its use. Users are expected to understand and use interactive AI while developing their own programming skills.

# 5  Conclusions

## 5.1  Application of Interactive AI to Programming Education

Programming education with interactive AI can be defined as Self-Directed Learning in which AI is a powerful partner. Self-directed learning is characterized by the learner taking control of his or her learning process, setting goals, selecting strategies, and making assessments. This form of learning is not only more self-paced than traditional teacher-led education but also has the advantage of increasing learner autonomy and confidence.

In conventional programming education, students generally follow the instructions and problems given by the teacher or books, which may not be responsive to the learner's needs and pace, making it difficult to maximise the effectiveness of learning. Learners may also face problems such as monotony of learning progression, time and cost burdens, and learning helplessness, where they lose motivation to challenge themselves. On the other hand, learning with interactive AI allows learners to progress at their own pace and deepen their learning according to their needs. In other words, it enables learners to explore specific issues in depth and learn the entire flow of software development by their self-assigned learning goals, thereby improving the self-determination and self-management skills required to promote self-managed learning.

Furthermore, interactive AI can check the learner's level of understanding and provide feedback, which has the advantage of enabling the learner to monitor their own learning outcomes as part of their self-assessment, thus fostering selfefficacy and confidence. Furthermore, in classes with teachers, the output of the interactive AI can be used as an additional resource for in-class discussion and problem-solving. In this way, interactive AI and teacher-led learning can complement each other to support more profound understanding and knowledge retention. Thus, the new learning method proposed in this paper, which utilizes interactive AI, can be a tool for learners to promote self-directed learning, compared to traditional learning methods. Not only will learners be able to enjoy the benefits of self-managed learning, such as fostering self-efficacy and confidence, responding to individual needs, and promoting deeper understanding and long-term memory, but also synergistic effects with classroom teaching, which indicates a promising path for programming education using interactive AI as a new educational method It can be said that.

## 5.2  Vision for the Future

The realization of our proposal will significantly advance programming learning. In particular, as described in Sect. 5, we focus on'games' as a teaching tool for interactive AI programming techniques. For most students, games are the most familiar software, and they often have sufficient knowledge of how they work and how to play them. Only some students are interested in game development. Another advantage is that games have fixed rules, and the definition of requirements is relatively simple.

Until now, game development has required advanced programming skills and a wealth of practical experience, but if students and programming beginners can easily tackle the task with the support of interactive AI, it can be expected to be extremely useful as a teaching tool and the following benefits will be generated.

- Shifting the focus of programming learning from programming to creating requirements definitions allows students to learn how to give shape to their own ideas. By giving specific definitions of requirements to interactive AI, it will be possible to create programs based on them, and many students will be able to develop their own games and publish them. Evaluations from friends and teachers can be motivating.
- Interactive AI-based learning can train students in upstream problem solving, as prompts as specifications are essential. AI is expected to help students gain a deeper understanding of software development and experience firsthand that the program's quality will also improve.
- By making it easier to develop games, it is possible for individuals or small groups of people to create games and upload them to Google Play, for Example. Students develop their creativity and programming skills and support entrepreneurship by making the games industry a market for programming learners.

This vision of the future is made possible by the nature of games and the powerful learning support of interactive AI. Games are accepted if they are attractive, even if there are problems with their behavior, and the culture of enjoying bugs allows students to learn through free trial and error. In addition, the use of interactive AI provides a place where programming learning can be more practical, focusing not only on learning theory, but also on creating concrete programmes.

### 5.3 Additional Requirements

It is necessary to acquire the expertise to understand and solve these challenges, and support from classes and mentors in related specialized fields is important. So, the use of interactive AI requires the following points to be considered.

- If users do not structure their questions correctly, they will not get the answers they seek. This situation can be a major obstacle, especially in the early stages of programming learning.
- Understanding and appropriate use of the answers provided by AI and the code it generates requires a certain amount of understanding and effort; even with AI, not all programs can be written perfectly. A deep understanding of the learner is still required to resolve errors and to extend and maintain programs.
- A good understanding of security risks is required, including precautions in handling personal and confidential information such as company secrets.

### 5.4 Future Development

In the future, to utilize interactive AI as a programming education tool, we plan to create content for teaching materials with games in mind and conduct demonstration experiments using them to confirm their usefulness.

**Acknowledgments.** This research his research is supported by JSPS KAKENHI Grant Number 20H01278, 20H05702, 22K12598, 23H03649, 23K28338.

# References

1. Malinka, K., Perešíni, M., Firc, A., Hujnák, O., Januš, F.: On the educational impact of Chat-GPT: Is Artificial Intelligence ready to obtain a university degree? arXiv 2023, arXiv:2303.11146 (2022)
2. Boubker, O.: From chatting to self-educating: Can AI tools boost student learning outcomes? Expert Syst. Appl. **238**(3), 121820 (2023)
3. What is conversational AI? https://www.ibm.com/topics/conversational-ai
4. Conversational AI https://cloud.google.com/conversational-ai?hl=en
5. OpenAI https://openai.com/blog/introducing-gpts
6. Conversational Intelligence: https://www.microsoft.com/enus/research/project/conversational-intelligence/
7. Bubeck, S., et al.: Sparks of Artificial General Intelligence: Early experiments with GPT-4. arXiv preprint arXiv:2303.12712v5 (2023)
8. CODEGEN-16B: https://huggingface.co/Salesforce/codegen-16B-mono
9. Human Eval: https://github.com/openai/human-eval
10. Rossman, B.: Application Lifecycle Management-Activities, Methodologies, Disciplines, Tools, Benefits, ALM Tools and Products. Emereo Pty Ltd, (2010)
11. Pradeep, T., Nasib Singh, G.: New Algorithm for Component Selection to Develop Component-Based Software with X Model, Lecture Notes on Software Engineering, Vol. 1, No. 3, August 2013

# ChatGPT Language Model as Support for Teaching and Self-learning in the Field of Engineering and Technical Sciences

Anna Czemplik and Iwona Karcz-Duleba(✉)

Department of Control Systems and Mechatronics, Faculty of Information and Communication Technology Wroclaw University of Science and Technology, Wrocław, Poland
{anna.czemplik,iwona.karcz-duleba}@pwr.edu.pl

**Abstract.** Widespread availability of ChatGPT has posed new challenges for teaching and learning. The paper examines whether and how the chat can be used to support teaching and self-learning in engineering and technical sciences domains. ChatGPT (version 3.5) was tested and assessed in a similar way as our students were. Different types of exams (exclusion tests, multiple choice tests, open questions) were carried out in two areas: control theory and metaheuristics. On average, the chat received quite good marks. However, it had a problem with questions that required detailed information and understanding of the subject. A number of conclusions have been drawn from the research. In general, AI can be helpful to teachers and students if used wisely. However, it must be emphasized that the use of the chat can not be uncritical, and almost all information should be carefully checked and validated, especially in engineering and technical sciences where precision and unambiguity are important.

**Keywords:** ChatGPT · Teaching Support · Engineering · Technical Sciences

## 1 Introduction

Artificial Intelligence (AI) based systems have recently sparked many heated discussions about their potential opportunities and threats. The subject of our analysis is not to assess the capabilities of artificial intelligence in general, but only the AI interface, which is ChatGPT (version 3.5), and its usefulness for knowledge acquisition and verification in an engineering education process. We tested ChatGPT-3.5 because it is commonly available to everyone free of charge (so it is widely used by students); it is already being used in many areas, and it is extensively advertised and discussed.

With the release of ChatGPT by OpenAI [1], many ideas for the use of AI by ordinary users, including students, appear in the public domain. The key feature of ChatGPT is the use of a large language model (LLM) and ability to

A. Quesada-Arencibia et al. (Eds.): EUROCAST 2024, LNCS 15172, pp. 376–387, 2025.
https://doi.org/10.1007/978-3-031-82949-9_34

converse in a natural language - asking questions, generating text on a given topic. It is known that ChatGPT is good at writing essays (much to the chagrin of teachers), for proofreading texts, writing simple computer programs. It is also able to pass medical exams [2,3]. In addition, in academic teaching the chat can help to create more engaging and up-to-date teaching materials, provide learning aids, speed-up lesson planning, develop tests and define assessment criteria. The chat itself adds that it can also help in adaptation of teaching materials to specific topics and objectives, clarifying students' questions, supporting language learning with explanations and exercises, evaluating students' work and providing constructive feedback, providing virtual tutoring and guidance on inclusive classroom practices, supporting teachers' special needs, and planning strategies for effective classroom management.

The global availability of ChatGPT also raises many concerns among an academic staff about losing their position and status as a privileged source of knowledge, and even worse – losing their jobs. Another important issue is cheating by students and distortion of reality by providing false information generated by AI. On the other hand, it is also known that ChatGPT often 'confabulates' or 'hallucinates' and makes up plausible stories, so expert knowledge is needed to evaluate correctness of answers.

Therefore, we want to find out if ChatGPT is suitable for supporting learning in engineering and technical sciences, which require more rigorous and precise language and where uncertain information can even lead to life and health threatening situations. Therefore, the main research questions are:

– How to use ChatGPT for knowledge acquisition and verification in an engineering education process?
– How to prepare students to effectively use this technology?
– How to guide students to use the technology responsibly and wisely?
– How to ask questions to the chat and how to check accuracy of answers?

In Sect. 2, the general characteristics of the object of interest is presented. Section 3 contains a description of the sources related to the topic. In Sect. 4 the chat research methodology is discussed. Results of the research on the chat exams and writing simple program codes, are provided in Sect. 5. The evaluation of chat responses by students attending the control theory course is also presented there. In Sect. 6 the obtained results are discussed and some comments are made on the context of interaction with the chat. Section 7 summarizes the paper.

## 2   Characteristics of the Research Subject

Based on available sources, after listening to many lectures and discussions on the Internet and gathered from our own experience, it is possible to enumerate main characteristics of ChatGPT from the user's point of view:

– it is a language model not a knowledge model,

- it does not quote, but constructs a response - LLM predicts a next word (called a token) based on the text observed so far,
- it is not designed to answer questions precisely, but to generate data in an appropriate form,
- it does not provide sources of information (because it is expensive and slow to label any piece of information, not to mention about unauthorized use),
- it does not determine probability of word collocations,
- it does not evaluate information,
- it may have limited domain knowledge,
- it always gives an answer, whether it is correct or not,
- it has been trained mainly on English sources (other languages are poorly represented),
- it does not have access to the Internet,
- it has been trained on texts available until 2022,
- it has a tendency to 'hallucinate' or 'confabulate' factual information,
- it does not analyze images, diagrams or patterns,
- it is very good at mechanical (repetitive) tasks.

An inspiring example in education, where the chat is really helpful, is a language teaching, especially foreign languages. AI can help a language teacher to create different exercises for a lesson, suggest the most effective techniques to use when teaching certain vocabulary or grammar structures. In the academic teaching of foreign languages (technical, business, medical, etc.), the chat can simplify difficult technical short texts - or vice versa (from easy to more advanced), give simple definitions of some technical terms and create materials for special purposes, to name but a few. From a self-learning point of view, ChatGPT can suggest a virtual, more personalized tutor for language learning. Academic teachers of English as a foreign language have shared with us some of their experiences of using the chat:

- teacher needs to be very precise in defining requests,
- teacher must keep full control over all material received from chat,
- the chat can not be asked for too much at once, as it often does not output what the teacher expects,
- if the final effect is not satisfactory, the chat can reformulate it in a different form,
- teaching materials can be better tailored to student's' special needs,
- the chat can help a language teacher understand specialized technical topics and present them to students in a foreign language.

In conclusion, the chat can save a teacher a lot of time in preparing a lesson, but the final decision about what to use and how to use it should always be made by the teacher.

In engineering and technical education many of the characteristics presented (such as the lack of precision or confabulation) are serious barriers in using ChatGPT. In addition, the use of the chat can be limited by the quality of data the chat is trained on. The source of data is the internet, which collects both reliable and (intentionally or not) unreliable data. In the past, content on the internet was mainly created by specialists, but now it can be created by anyone, so it contains a significant percentage of emotionally charged topics and information that is not necessarily "true", but the most popular, intriguing, falsifying common opinions, sensational, attracting attention. You can always find completely different opinions on the same subject, e.g. medicines, diets, economics. Therefore, from a scientific point of view, confidence in the credibility of the chat must be limited.

## 3   Related Works

ChatGPT model is the subject of numerous studies and tests, but many results and conclusions have recently been published mainly on various forums dedicated to AI technologies. The number of scientific publications is also growing, but at a much slower rate, arguably due to a longer publication cycle. Another difficulty lies in the lack of definition of objective evaluation indicators that make it possible to compare different studies. This methodology is still under development.

In [4], ChatGPT model was tested on various natural language processing (NLP) tasks using 25 public NLP datasets. In total, about 38000 questions were asked. Authors concluded that, among other things, ChatGPT can factually justify its answers, is poor at recognizing emotions, is not neutral, tends to evaluate content superficially, is susceptible to manipulation and has a tendency to find negative connotations in the text. Authors noticed that it can be used mainly for writing and proofreading texts, for searching information, in education as an organizational support (virtual assistant).

Some of the first studies on ChatGPT assistance in academic teaching were reported in [5]. ChatGPT's abilities to solve assignments of various levels was examined in the field of computer security. Different types of exams were carry out: 1) written exams with open questions and multiple choice, 2) term essays, 3) programming tasks as predefined code completion, small project, term project, interactive project. There were at least 50 types of tasks for each category of examination method in the Czech language. ChatGPT was used in three different modes: copy and paste, interpretation of the answer by the user and assistant when the user interacts with AI by asking additional questions before obtaining the final satisfactory result. Responses obtained from AI were graded in the same way as for regular students and compared with their results. ChatGPT answers to open-ended written exam questions were similar to those of students, while test answers were not always correct. The AI performed worse than students writing therm essays, but did better on simple programming tasks. In general, ChatGPT would pass all exams.

The use of ChatGPT to improve academic performance in economic and financial research was presented in [6]. In this area, ChatGPT can be used for: generating of simulations and scenarios for economic and financial models, analyzing of large data sets (including data interpretation, identification of trends and patterns that may not be immediately apparent to humans), generating reports and summaries of economic and financial data, making forecasts and predictions based on historical data, generating code that can be used in various economic and financial applications. The author noticed potential benefits of using the chat in improving efficiency, accuracy, flexibility, objectivity, speed and consistency of research processes. He also identified limitations such as: dependence on data quality, limited domain knowledge, generation of unrelated or generic responses and some ethical considerations.

## 4   Methodology

The subject under consideration is the use of ChatGPT in the process of education and self-study in engineering fields. The research has been carried out in two areas: a classical control theory and metaheuristic optimization methods. While the first field is well established, with over 150 years long history, the other, much younger, is constantly evolving. The long development of the control theory field may lead to an insufficient representation of some fundamental subjects in the chat training sets, since they are mainly found in academic textbooks and these are relatively scarce on the internet. In the field of metaheuristics, the number of research papers is constantly growing, and so they are available sources for AI. However, this has also some drawbacks, such as a not entirely consistent terminology or knowledge of the latest ideas based on too few sources.

Instructions (prompts) for ChatGPT were given in English (as most of the LLM sources are in this language). The tasks of concern consolidated knowledge that was definitely known by 2022 and did not include formulas, derivations, diagrams, standards, etc. Different types of tasks were given to ChatGPT (formulating questions):

- exclusion tests (E), where only one answer is correct; in the metaheuristic exam two types of tests were distinguished – with four answer options (E1) and with true/false answer (E2),
- multiple response test (M), where more than one answer can be correct,
- open questions (O).

Exemplary tasks are collected in Table 1. Questions were repeated ten times in different sessions. The tasks were performed in the form of a written test and evaluated on the basis of answer selection (tests) and elaboration (open questions). ChatGPT was not informed about the evaluation of the answer given. In the field of control theory, tasks were also performed in the mode of oral exam, where follow-up questions were asked if the chat answer was not satisfactory. The context of the questions was always given, by beginning them with the prompt "In the context of control theory/metaheuristic $\cdots$". As an additional task, ChatGPT was asked to write some code in Matlab on specific topics in both areas.

The problem is how to verify and evaluate the usefulness of ChatGPT so that it is not user's opinion (impression). In the literature, for example, the perceived usefulness and satisfaction of students has been studied [7]. However, such an evaluation, does not measure the effectiveness of learning (e.g. exam pass rate). Typically, students perceive their knowledge as adequate because they are unaware of what they should know and are unable to distinguish between what is important and what is not. Therefore, ChatGPT was assessed in the same way as a student in an exam and grades were given by specialists in a given field. Additionally, students completing the course in the control theory were asked to assess answers of AI to the exam.

**Table 1.** Examples of test questions given to ChatGPT: a) from the control theory; b) from metaheuristics

a)

| Type | Questions |
|------|-----------|
| E | The stability of a linear object does not depend on a size of a disturbance: |
|   | a) always, b) never, c) sometimes, d) most often |
| M | What can be tested based on static characteristics? |
|   | a) linearity, b) stability, |
|   | c) transition time from one state to another, |
|   | d) equilibrium state with constant excitations, |
|   | e) equilibrium state under any excitations |
| O | What it is stability? |
|   | What is process variable and control variable? |

b)

| Type | Questions |
|------|-----------|
| E1 | In the elite selection method, the best individual is selected: |
|    | a) always, b) never, c) sometimes, d) most of the time |
| E2 | In Particle Swarm Optimization a mutation operator is most important: |
|    | a) true, b) false |
| M | A mutation, depending on its range, may cause: |
|   | a) small deviations from the parents' characteristics, b) random walk, |
|   | c) reducing diversity, d) using only available possibilities (features), |
|   | e) large jumps to areas "in between" the parents' characteristics |
| O | Enumerate differences between algorithms of swarm intelligence |
|   | and evolutionary algorithms |
|   | Present, in steps, a general scheme of evolutionary algorithms operation |

# 5    Results

## 5.1    Exams

**Control Theory.** The percentage of correct answers in the control theory exam and the number of follow-up questions are shown in Fig. 1. The best results were obtained for open questions (O) (on average, 96% of correct answers). The worst results were obtained for the exclusion test (E) (on average 38% of correct answers) - only one question was always answered correctly, while two were never answered correctly. In six cases, the chat changed the choice to a good one after 4–8 sessions. The chat answered the multiple choice test (M) at a medium level (on average 61% of good answers).

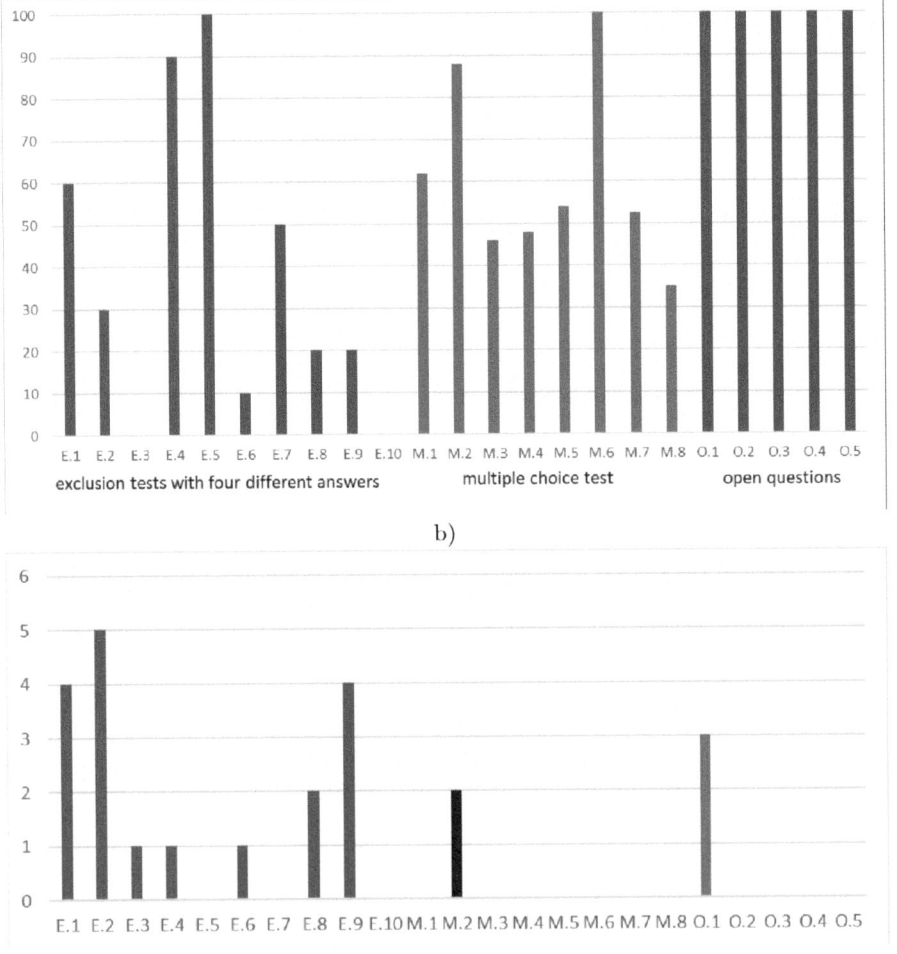

**Fig. 1.** a) Percentage of correct answers in control theory; b) The number of follow-up questions.

In the oral mode, in most cases of the exclusion test follow-up questions were needed, e.g. "Are you sure?", "That's not true", "What... do you mean?", "Why...?". These led to the correct answer in all but three cases. In the multiple-response test, follow-up questions improved performance in one case. The entire exam would be passed at a medium level (on average 65%), but ChatGPT would not pass the exclusion test.

**Metaheuristics.** The percentage of correct answers in the metaheuristics is visualized in Fig. 2. The best results were obtained for tests with true/false tests (E2) (on average 97% of correct answers). Wrong answers were obtained only in a few cases. The worst results were obtained in the exclusion test with four different answers (E1) (on average 35% of correct answers). Two questions were rarely answered correctly and others to a moderate level. If only these questions were taken into account, the chat would fail the test, and if you treated every chat session as a student, only half of them would pass the test. ChatGPT passed the multiple choice test and answered open questions quite well (on average about 80% of correct answers), although there were some inaccuracies in the answers to open questions. The entire exam would be passed at a good level (on average 72%).

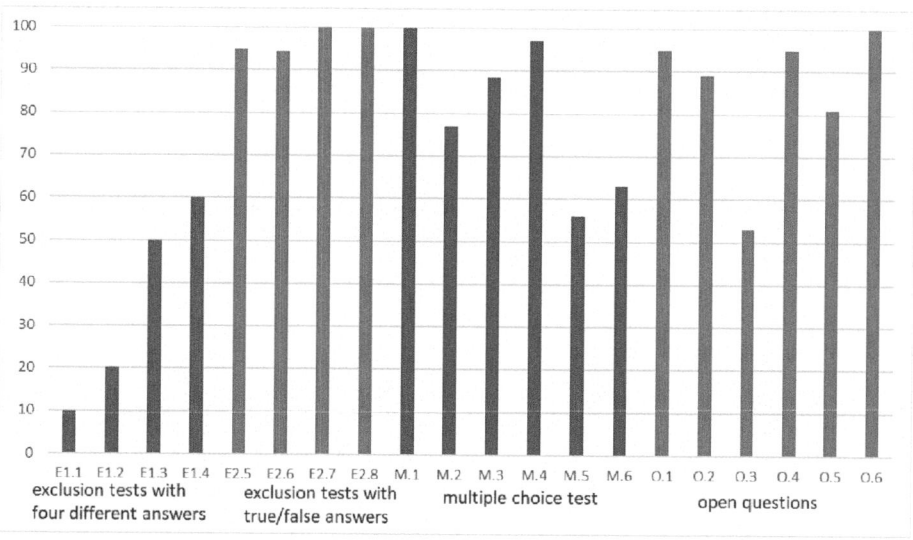

**Fig. 2.** Percentage of correct answers in metaheuristics

**Results According to the Type of Question.** A comparison of the percentage of correct answers for different types of questions is provided in Fig. 3. Based on the results, it can be concluded that the percentage of correct answers depends less on the type of question than on the domain. However, in both exams, the exclusion tests with four different answers performed the worst. Overall, the chat gave the best answers to open questions, as it is better prepared for such tasks. It is also easier to obtain a positive evaluation of such an elaboration (just as when evaluating a student's answer). ChatGPT may have problems with questions that require understanding of the topic and more detailed knowledge, as in the case of exclusion tests with multiple answers. The efficiency of ChatGPT is comparable for exclusion tests in both domains, while multiple choice tests were passed better in metaheuristics. Open questions were undeniably better answered in the control theory section.

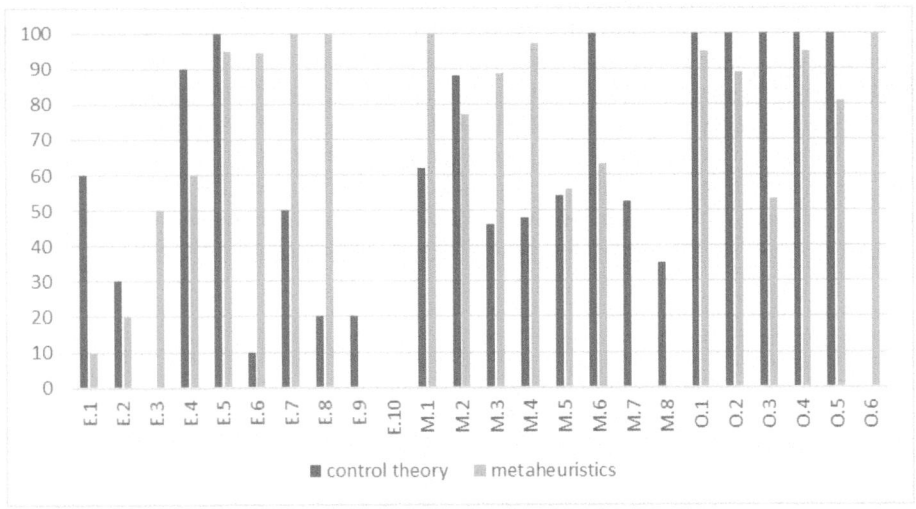

**Fig. 3.** Percentage of correct answers in both domains. Comparison of different types of questions

## 5.2  Writing Simple Codes

As a machine learning model, ChatGPT has been trained on a dataset including code examples, so it can generate code in many programming languages. Thus, ChatGPT was asked to write a simple code in Matlab, such as designing PI controller settings and writing a program for binary/real coded Simple Genetic Algorithm. In practice, much of the software did not work because, for example, the AI chose the wrong function parameters or programmed the wrong loops. ChatGPT was not able to debug the code either, even when the number of lines with detected errors was given.

The chat encountered serious problems with control theory tasks. However, the codes obtained could also be inspiring, for example by showing a quite different approach to a problem. The better results in metaheuristics could be due to the broader availability of codes in the database from which the chat could choose. Unfortunately, some of the working codes turned out to be wrong in the principles of the tasks/algorithms.

## 5.3 ChatGPT 3.5 Assessed by Students

Finally, students attending classes on the control theory were asked to rate the exams written by ChatGPT, to find out their personal attitudes concerning AI answers. Students gave the chat rather quite high marks of 90–100% (in contrast to teachers), but noticed that the answers were rather general. Why such high marks? Probably because students do not know the subject as deeply as experts. In addition, they are more familiar and experienced with modern technologies and are more likely to believe them more. So the question can be asked: would a student be able to prepare a good answer to an exam question using only ChatGPT, based on such a high level of confidence? There is a high probability that students will uncritically believe in information provided by the chat.

# 6 Discussion

## 6.1 General Positive Observations

ChatGPT generates nice texts and quite simple sentences. Longer answers are given in points. The structure of a chat answer is clear: a short answer, a justification, a summary. ChatGPT always justifies answers, even test ones. The chat can summarize the topic in a few points or, conversely, expand on the points given. The AI recognizes a command (*select, rate, ...*), a question (even without a question mark at the end) and a disclaimer (*are you sure?, that's not true.*). This type of response can make the learning process more effective and allow students to understand the topic better.

## 6.2 General Negative Observations

ChatGPT does not notice all the keywords for a question, or it does not recognize that the word is a keyword. It was easy to confuse the AI – in several cases, when the same question was asked again by mistake, the chat gave the wrong answer this time, considering the previous one to be wrong. Such contradictory answers can be a source of confusion for a student who is learning. It happens that ChatGPT does not recognize the content level of the conversation based on the questions – sometimes it will explain a general topic in great detail, focusing on one aspect, or vice versa. It is harder to get an unambiguous answer – the chat "softens" answers. Without context, the chat may give an inaccurate answer, as the database may contain definitions for a given term from different fields (for example *linearity*). It may be unstable in the sense that it gives different (even contradictory) answers to the same question. This situation can lead to the spread of misinformation, especially among students just acquiring knowledge, who may accept incorrect answers as a general truth. When asked for the source of information the answer is based on, the chat sometimes gave references to non-existing methods, books, articles so the user needs to checked them carefully. Working codes generated by the AI may turn out to be wrong in principle, which a student, just learning the subject may not realize. What's more, a student relying on such software may not gain the experience needed to code effectively.

### 6.3   Self Learning

Students not actively participating in classes may think that they will learn on their own using only ChatGPT, but this assumption may be wrong. Usually a teacher introduces the material gradually – first principles and general rules, then exceptions. The teacher also knows the level of students' knowledge and adjusts the level of topics discussed. The chat may give exceptions to a topic right away in the short answer, and a student may not recognize them. In addition, the chat may also use knowledge not yet available to the student (for example, advanced areas of mathematics). Obviously, the student can be inspired by the chat, e.g. having no idea about the topic, the chat can guide her/him or show the topic from a different perspective. But, if a student wants to acquire reliable knowledge and understand some topics, other sources are still better – especially textbooks, but also online sources such as Wikipedia.

### 6.4   Context Is Important

Currently, artificial intelligence does not have the ability of contextual understanding. When using ChatGPT, it is very important to provide it with the right context. In the classroom, a context is defined not only by the subject matter but also by the level of the audience - a different level of detail is used to explain the subject to beginners than to advanced students. The lecturer uses specific terminology, which may vary, e.g. from country to country, so the chat may not recognize/localize the topic in a field. ChatGPT often has problems recognizing context learned from many sources, which may define concepts differently. An imprecise question from a teacher may be understood by a student in the context of the current course, but rarely by the chat. If a student using the chat does not provide a context, he may get an incorrect answer recognizing it. ChatGPT responds the best to questions where the answer is "it depends" and often uses this form.

## 7   Conclusions

There is no doubt that AI, used wisely, can help teachers and students to improve and accelerate learning and self-learning processes. ChatGPT's ability to carry on a human-like conversation can be useful in learning new things. The availability of the chat at virtually any time and place can be invaluable to a student (especially when preparing for an exam).

ChatGPT can also be helpful in engineering and technical education, but with some caveats - its use should be cautious and critical. In many cases the chat does not recognize nuances and subtleties. Problems with the precision and interpretation of concepts can be significant in some fields, both established (such as control theory) and developing (such as metaheuristics). Engineering often involves drawings, diagrams, which ChatGPT 3.5 cannot handle. But it can now provide formulas.

The availability of ChatGPT undoubtedly enables or even encourages students to cheat during a university learning process. This poses a challenge for teachers assessing student progress. For example, to create tasks that cannot be solved directly via chat (or copied directly, such as diagrams) and to switch from accessing finished work (projects, codes, etc.) to assessing the critical thinking involved in the process. In general, however, teachers would rather have no problem distinguishing between a student's independent response and a chat-assisted response.

Unfortunately, chat can make students lazy, and a lack of intellectual training can lead to helplessness when it comes to bigger challenges in the future. Misuse of AI can also lead to a reduction in the level of education and grades achieved.

We believe that this analysis will help to find the right way to use AI to support teaching in engineering and technical sciences for the benefit of students and teachers as well. The academics staff should not be afraid of new technologies but take up the challenge. The quality of these tools are increasing over time, and, in turn, their error rate will decrease, thus we are going to continue our studies on ChatGPT version 4.

# References

1. OpenAI Homepage. https://platform.openai.com/. Accessed May 2024
2. Kung, T., Cheatham, M., Medenilla, A., et al.: Performance of ChatGPT on USMLE: potential for AI-assisted medical education using large language models. medRxiv (2022). https://doi.org/10.1101/2022.12.19.22283643
3. Gilson, A., Safranek, C., Huang, T., Socrates, V., Chi, L., et al.:: How does ChatGPT perform on the medical licensing exams? The implications of large language models for medical education and knowledge assessment. medRxiv (2023). https://doi.org/10.1101/2022.12.23.22283901
4. Kocoń, J., Cichecki, I., Kaszyca, O., Kochanek, M., Szydło, D., et al.: ChatGPT: Jack of all trades, master of none. Inf. Fusion **66**(5), 101861 (2023). https://arxiv.org/pdf/2302.10724.pdf
5. Malinka, K., Perešíni, M., Firc, A., Hujnák, O., Januš, F.: On the educational impact of ChatGPT: is artificial intelligence ready to obtain a university degree? In: Proceedings of the 2023 Conference on Innovation and Technology in Computer Science Education, vol. 1, pp. 47–53 (2023). arXiv:2303.11146
6. Muneer, A.: Exploring the role of artificial intelligence in enhancing academic performance: a case study of ChatGPT (2022). https://doi.org/10.2139/ssrn.4312358
7. Boubker, O.: From chatting to self-educating: can AI tools boost student learning out-comes? Expert Syst. Appl. **238**(3), 121820 (2023)

# Analytical Conversion of the Strejc Model to the First Order with Time Delay (FOTD) Model

Anna Czemplik[✉][iD]

Department of Control Systems and Mechatronics, Faculty of Information and
Communication Technology, Wrocław University of Science and Technology,
Wrocław, Poland
anna.czemplik@pwr.edu.pl

**Abstract.** Several variants of analytical conversion of the Strejc model
to the First-Order Time Delay (FOTD) model have been proposed. This
conversion extends the applicability of control system design methods
that are based on FOTD models. An example of applying the Ziegler-
Nichols method to a control system with the Strejc model is presented.
Additionally, the reverse operation - converting the FOTD model to the
Strejc model - is also feasible and can be employed as a method for
identifying the Strejc model.

**Keywords:** Strejc Model · First Order Time Delay Model

## 1 Introductions

### 1.1 Design of Control Systems

Design of control systems usually involves using one of a number of tuning methods. Typically, we focus on the fact that the design method defines specific formulas for calculating controller parameters based on a simple process model.
However, this aspect alone is insufficient. A full definition of method should
encompass both the model identification method and the anticipated quality
indicators of the designed control system. In practice, it is the type of the model
and the quality indicators that determine the choice of method, and the formulas
are the way to attain these objective (see Fig. 1).

Each design method assumes the optimization of chosen quality indicators,
such as control time, overshoot, integral indicators, stability margin. The application of the selected method ensures that these indicators are achieved in the
control system on the model (CSM). However, the final purpose of the project
is to achieve the assumed indicators in the control system on the plant (CSP).
Discrepancies between the indicator values for the CSM and CSP arise due to
the inherent inaccuracies of the model (see Fig. 2).

© The Author(s), under exclusive license to Springer Nature Switzerland AG 2025
A. Quesada-Arencibia et al. (Eds.): EUROCAST 2024, LNCS 15172, pp. 388–401, 2025.
https://doi.org/10.1007/978-3-031-82949-9_35

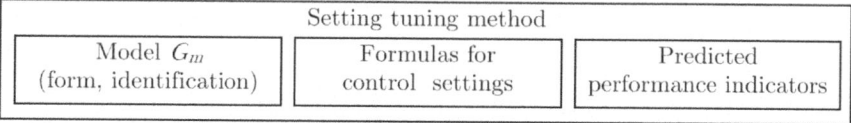

**Fig. 1.** Definition of tuning method.

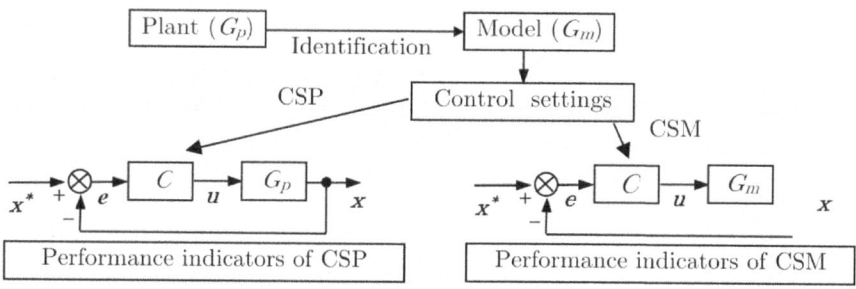

**Fig. 2.** Control System on the Plant (CSP) and on the Model (CSM).

## 1.2  Type of Models and Identification Methods

The review of design methods compiled by O'Dwyer [1] is widely known. The review encompasses 1731 methods, primarily categorized by the underlying model type utilized in the design process. Among these methods, 649 employ a first-order with time-delay (FOTD) model

$$G_m(s) = \frac{k}{T_m s + 1} e^{sT_0} \left( or \ G_m(s) = k\frac{T_z s + 1}{T_m s + 1} e^{sT_0} \right) \qquad (1)$$

Besides, a second-order with time delay (SOTD) model is often used, as well as higher order models, pure delay models, models with integration, and unstable object models (Table 1).

**Table 1.** Models used in the design of control systems. [1]

| Model type | FOTD | SOTD | Other stable model | Non specific | Model with an integrator | Unstable model | Sum |
|---|---|---|---|---|---|---|---|
| Number of methods | 649 | 291 | 103 | 169 | 339 | 182 | 1731 |

Another popular model of Strejc also contains only three parameters

$$G_m(s) = \frac{k}{(Ts+1)^n}. \tag{2}$$

However, only a few described design methods use the Strejc model. There are not many such methods of control design, but, for example, there is the well-known Preuss method [2].

The widespread acceptance of the FOTD model is due to its simplicity and efficiency - it contains only three parameters ($k$ - gain, $T_m$ - time constant, $T_0$ - transport delay), which can be determined from the simple step response of the plant $h(t)$. This kind of model can be identified in various ways but identification method affects the values of time parameters of model. And this, in turn, affects the control parameters calculated from the tuning rules and, finally it affects the parameters of the control system. The tuning method should be associated with the identification method. However, many design methods operate under the assumption that the model is known, neglecting the need to specify an identification method [1].

The most commonly used method involves determining a straight tangent at the inflection point of the process curve $h(t)$. The time constant $T_m$ and transport delay $T_0$ are directly obtained from this graphical construction (see Fig. 3).

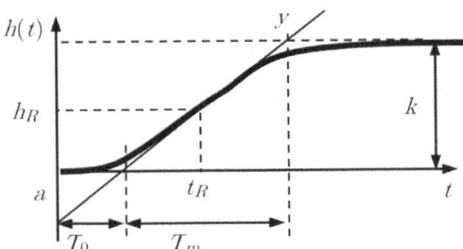

**Fig. 3.** Identification using the straight tangent method.

It's a graphical method, thus susceptible to errors. Nevertheless, it can also be implemented numerically based on measurement data obtained during experimentation or simulation.

### 1.3    Conversion the Strejc Model to FOTD

Can the parameters of the FOTD model be determined analytically? In this study it is assumed that the starting point for analysis is a plant (model) described by an $n$th-order transmittance (2). This model (see Fig. 4) may stem from theoretical assumptions (a) or from previous identification (b). The following solutions are available: a) when we have the theoretical Strejc model, the step response (1) can be generated and then FOTD model identification methods (3) can be applied, b) if the Strejc model arises from identification (2) and the process curve is available, the identification of the FOTD model (3) can also be performed.

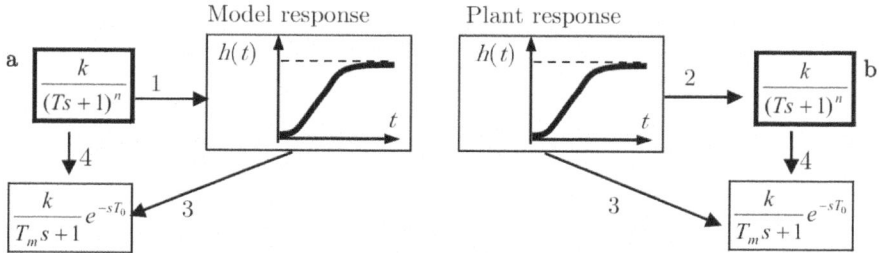

**Fig. 4.** The Strejc model and FOTD.

The purpose of this research is to determine the parameters $T_m$ and $T_0$ directly from the parameters $T$ and $n$ (4) and one reason is to enable the application of design methods with FOTD models to Strejc models.

## 2    Accurate Conversion of the Strejc Model to FOTD

### 2.1    Properties of the Strejc Model [3]

What we know about the Strejc model? First of all, the analytical form of the step response $h(t)$ and the impulse response $g(t)$ is known

$$h(t) = k \left( 1 - \sum_{i=1}^{n} \frac{1}{(i-1)!T^{i-1}} t^{i-1} e^{-t/T} \right),$$ (3)

$$g(t) = \dot{h}(t) = \frac{k}{(n-1)!T^n} t^{n-1} e^{-\sigma t}.$$ (4)

The key point, however, is that the inflection point of the function $h(t)$ is possible to determine (see Fig. 3) time $t_R$ and value of function $h(t_R)$

$$t_R = (n-1)T,$$ (5)

$$h_R = h(t_R) = k(1 - \frac{1}{e^{(n-1)}} \sum_{i=1}^{n} \frac{(n-1)^{i-1}}{(i-1)!}.$$ (6)

The formula for the straight tangent at the point of inflection has the form

$$y = R \cdot t - a$$ (7)

where the slope $R$ is the value of the derivative function at time $t_R$, that is

$$R = g(t_R) = k \frac{(n-1)^{n-1}}{(n-1)!e^{n-1}T}$$ (8)

## 2.2   Accurate Solution

The slope $R$ also results from the following geometric relationships

$$R = \frac{k}{T_m} = \frac{a}{T_0} = \frac{h_R}{t_R - T_0}.$$ (9)

On this base we can accurately calculate the time parameters $T_m$ and $T_0$

$$T_m = \frac{k}{R} = k_{Tm}T, \quad k_{Tm} = \frac{(n-1)!e^{n-1}}{(n-1)^{n-1}},$$ (10)

$$T_0 = t_R - \frac{h_R}{R} = k_{T0}T, \quad k_{T0} = \frac{(n-1)^n - (n-1)!e^{n-1} + (n-1)!S_{n-1}}{(n-1)^{n-1}}.$$ (11)

So there are formulas for conversion Strejc model to FOTD. Both $T_m$ and $T_0$ are proportional to the time constant $T$ of the Strejc model, but the proportionality coefficients ($k_{Tm}$, $k_{T0}$) are complex functions of $n$th order, in particular (11) where $S_{n-1}$ means

$$S_{n-1} = \sum_{i=1}^{n} \frac{(n-1)^{i-1}}{(i-1)!}.$$ (12)

Functions (10) and (11) can be drawn (see Fig. 5)

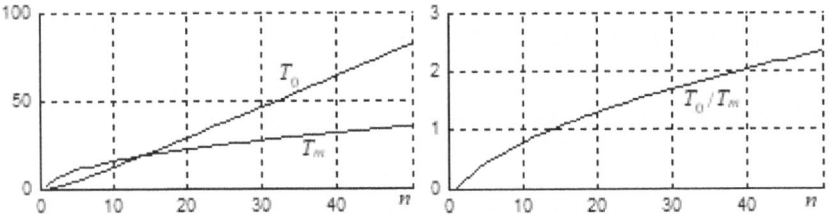

**Fig. 5.** Parameters $T_m$ and $T_0$ as a function of $n$ order.

All functions of the variable $n$ are of practical interest for discrete values of $n$, but for readability reasons graphs are represented by continuous lines.

## 3   Approximate Conversion of the Strejc Model to FOTD

### 3.1   Methods

Formulas (10) and (11) are accurate, but difficult to apply - we need to calculate the strong and sum of $n$ elements ($S_{n-1}$). The goal of the research is to simplify the formulas, with the assumption that the target formulas should be quite accurate primarily for small values of $n$, because this are typical for real plants (let's assume $n$ less than 10 or even $n$ less than 6). Various methods of simplification were examined.

1. **(F)** - use analytical formulas that simplify expressions, for example the Stirling formula $(n! = \sqrt{2\pi n} \cdot n^n / e^n)$,
2. **(S)** - searching and optimization with simple functions (trial-and-error optimization),
3. **(I)** - classical interpolation of functions in an assumed range of $n$ values which is easy to implementation:
   - selection of interpolation nodes $(n_0, n_1, ..., n_k)$ and the base of functions $\mathbf{B}(n_i) = [F_0(n_i), F_1(n_i), ..., F_k(n_i)]$,
   - calculation of a vector of exact function values $\mathbf{f} = [f(n_0), f(n_1), ..., f(n_k)]$ on the base formulas (10) and (11),
   - the interpolating polynomial for any node $n_i$ is of the form: $W(n_i) = a_0 F_0(n_i) + a_1 F_1(n_i) + ... + a_k F_k(n_i) = \mathbf{B}(n_i)\mathbf{A}$ (where $i = 0 \div k$)
   - the vector of coefficients $\mathbf{A} = [a_0, a_1, ..., a_k]^T$ is calculated from the system of $n$ equations

$$\mathbf{VA} = \mathbf{f} \ \rightarrow \ \mathbf{A} = \mathbf{V}^{-1}\mathbf{f} \tag{13}$$

4. **(A)** - approximation in an assumed range of $n$ values
   - nodes of approximation $(n_0, n_1, ..., n_k)$ and the base of functions $\mathbf{B}(n_i) = [F_0(n_i), F_1(n_i), ..., F_k(n_i)]$ were selected,
   - vector of exact function values $\mathbf{f}$ was calculated,
   - the Levenberg-Marquardt algorithm (LMA) was applied (function in Mathematica).

The quality of interpolation and approximation depends largely on the choice of the basis of the function $\mathbf{B}(n_i)$ and the choice of interpolation/approximation nodes. Various functions based on the shape of the graph have been tried. Two nodal points were used during interpolations: $n = [2, 6]$ or $n = [2, 10]$ (better results were obtained for $n = [2, 6]$). For approximations, a set of nodes in the range of $n = 2 \div 10$ was used (see Fig. 6).

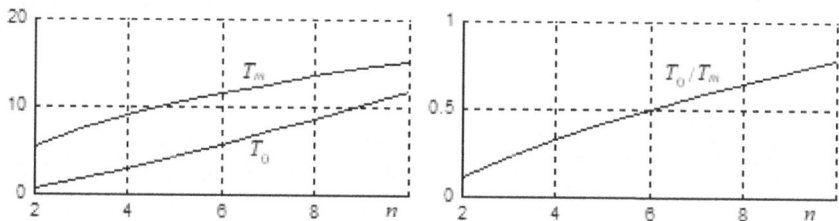

**Fig. 6.** Parameters $T_m$ and $T_0$ in range of conversion.

Various variants of functions and nodes were examined. In the end, three sets of formulas were selected, which were referred to as:

- *sim* - simulation solutions (accurate formulas),
- *easy* - solutions obtained in the simplest way (it can be said that is a substitution of analytical formulas),
- *use* - solutions proposed for use in design methods,
- *best* - solutions with a wider range of application.

## 3.2    Simplified Formulas for Calculating the Time Constant $T_m$

The general formula for the time constant (10) includes a coefficient $k_{Tm}$, which can be determined either exactly or approximately (Table 2).

**Table 2.** Simplified formulas for $T_m$.

| Symbol | Formula | Methods of simplify |
|---|---|---|
| 1) | $k_{Tm} = \dfrac{(n-1)!\,e^{n-1}}{(n-1)^{n-1}}$ | (10) |
| 2) *easy* | $k_{Tm} = \sqrt{2\pi(n-1)}$ | (F) Stirling formula |
| 3a) | $k_{Tm} = k_a\sqrt{2\pi(n-1)}$ | (S) $k_a = 1.01 \cdot (1 + e^{-n}/\sqrt{2\pi})$ |
| 3b) | $k_{Tm} = k_a\sqrt{2\pi(n-1)}$ | (S) $k_a = 1.01 \cdot (1 + e^{-n}/e$ |
| 4a) *use* | $k_{Tm} = (a_0 + a_1 e^{-n})\sqrt{2\pi(n-1)}$ | (I) $a_0 \approx 1.016, a_1 \approx 0.509$ |
| 4b) | $k_{Tm} = (a_0 + a_1/n)\sqrt{2\pi(n-1)}$ | (I) $a_0 \approx 0.983, a_1 \approx 0.203$ |
| 5) | $k_{Tm} = a_0 + a_1\sqrt{n-1}$ | (I) $a_0 \approx 0.307, a_1 \approx 2.412$ |
| 6) | $k_{Tm} = a_0 + a_1\sqrt{n-1}$ | (A) $a_0 \approx 0.249, a_1 \approx 2.442$ |

Charts for all formulas (see Fig. 7) show values $T_m$ calculated relative to accurate values. Of particular note are the formulas marked as *easy* and *use*.

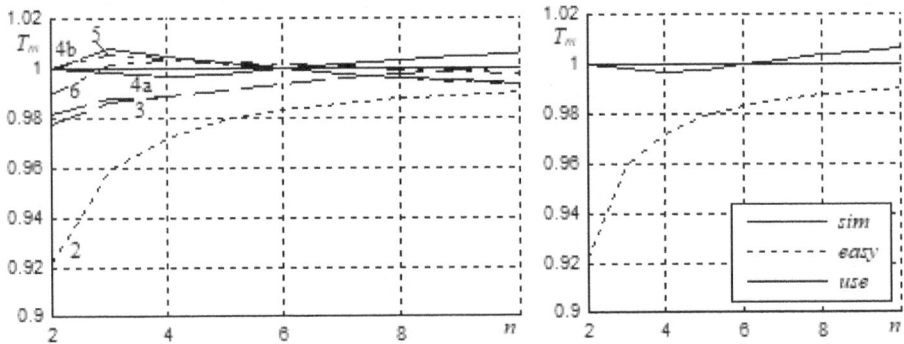

**Fig. 7.** Functions $T_m(n)$ relative to accurate values (in particular *easy* and *use*).

## 3.3    Simplified Formulas for Calculating the Transport Delay $T_0$

In the case of the delay $T_0$ the simplification of formula (11) is more complex due to the sum of $n$ elements ($S_{n-1}$). The basis of the simplification is the expansion of the exponential function into Maclaurin series

$$e^x = \frac{f(0)}{0!}x^0 + \frac{f'(0)}{1!}x^1 + \frac{f^{(2)}(0)}{2!}x^2 + \dots + \frac{f^{(m)}(0)}{m!}x^m + R_{m+1}. \qquad (14)$$

We restrict the expansion of function $e^x$ to $m + 1$ elements, apply the Lagrange rest, substitute $x = m = n - 1$ and finally get the following

$$e^{n-1} = \sum_{i=1}^{n} \frac{(n-1)^{i-1}}{(i-1)!} + R_n = S_{n-1} + R_n, R_n = e^c \frac{(n-1)^n}{n!} = k_n \frac{(n-1)^n}{n!}. \quad (15)$$

The accuracy of the expansion depends on the parameter $c$ (the correction factor $k_n$), which can depend on the value of $x$ (i.e. $n-1$). The sum can be transformed into the expression $S_{n-1} \approx e^{n-1} - k_n R_n$ and used to simplify the formula (11)

$$T_0 = k_{T0}T = \frac{(n-1)(n-k_n)}{n}T. \quad (16)$$

The coefficient $k_{T0}$ can be determined either exactly or approximately (Table 3). Charts for all formulas (see Fig. 8) show values $T_0$ relative to accurate values.

Table 3. Simplified formulas for $T_0$.

| Symbol | Formula | Methods of simplify |
|---|---|---|
| 1) | $k_{T0} = \frac{(n-1)^n - (n-1)!e^{n-1} + (n-1)!S_{n-1}}{(n-1)^{n-1}}$ | $S_{n-1} = \sum_{i=1}^{n} \frac{(n-1)^{i-1}}{(i-1)!}$ (11,12) |
| 2 ÷ 4 | $k_{T0} = \frac{(n-1)(n-k_n)}{n}$ | general form of $k_{T0}$ |
| 2) | $k_n = 1.25 \cdot (1 + e^{-n})\sqrt{n-1}$ | (S) |
| 3a) | $k_n = a_0 + a_1\sqrt{n-1}$ | (I) $a_0 \approx 0.474, a_1 \approx 0.963$ |
| 3b) use | $k_n = a_0 + a_1\sqrt{n}$ | (I) $a_0 \approx -0.189, a_1 \approx 1.149$ |
| 4a) | $k_n = a_0 + a_1\sqrt{n-1}$ | (A) $a_0 \approx 0.345, a_1 \approx 1.032$ |
| 4b) | $k_n = a_0 + a_1\sqrt{n}$ | (A) $a_0 \approx -0.236, a_1 \approx 1.172$ |
| 5a) easy | $k_{T0} = a_0 n + a_1\sqrt{(n)}$ | (I) $a_0 \approx 0.916, a_1 \approx -1.096$ |
| 5b) | $k_{T0} = a_0(n-1) + a_1\sqrt{n-1}$ | (I) $a_0 \approx 0.789, a_1 \approx -0.507$ |
| 6) | $k_{T0} = a_0 n + a_1\sqrt{n}$ | (A) $a_0 \approx 0.968, a_1 \approx -1.213$ |

### 3.4  Simplified Formulas for Calculating the Ratio $T_0/T_m$

An approximation of the relationship between $T_0$ and $T_m$ calculated from exact formulas (10, 11) has also been proposed. General form for the ratio is

$$k_{T0m} = T_0/T_m \quad (17)$$

Table 4 contains the solutions tested. The accurate and simplified values of $k_{T0m}$ shows Fig. 9 (all values $k_{T0m}$ calculated relative to accurate values). Because of the applications, the formula marked *best* is of particular importance.

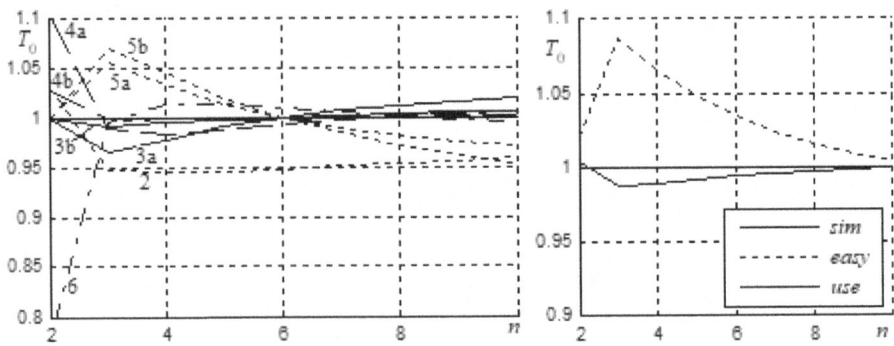

**Fig. 8.** Functions $T_0(n)$ relative to accurate values (in particular *easy* and *use*).

**Table 4.** Simplified formulas for $k_{T0m}$.

| Symbol | Formula | Methods of simplify |
|---|---|---|
| 1) | $k_{T0m} = T_0/T_m$, where $T_0$ (11), $T_m$ (10) | |
| 2a) | $k_{T0m} = a_0 + a_1 n$ | (I) $a_0 \approx -0.091, a_1 \approx 0.097$ |
| 2b) | $k_{T0m} = a_0 + a_1\sqrt{n-1}$ | (I) $a_0 \approx -0.212, a_1 \approx 0.315$ |
| 2c) | $k_{T0m} = a_0 + a_1\sqrt{n}$ | (I) $a_0 \approx -0.429, a_1 \approx 0.376$ |
| 3) | $k_{T0m} = a_0 + a_1\sqrt{n}$ | (A) $a_0 \approx -0.447, a_1 \approx 0.385$ |
| 4) *best* | $k_{T0m} = a_0 + a_1\sqrt{n}$ | (I) $a_0 \approx -0.428, a_1 \approx 0.377$ |
| 5) | $k_{T0m} = a_0 + a_1\sqrt{n}$ | (A) $a_0 \approx -0.44, a_1 \approx 0.38$ |

## 3.5    Analytical Conversion of Strejc Model to FOTD (summary)

Based on the conducted research, four methods of analytical conversion of the
Strejc model into the FOTD model are proposed (Table 5). The reference point
is the exact formulas (*sim*). Set *easy* are the simplest formulas but not very
accurate. Formulas refered as *use* are much more accurate. However, the set *best*
s a combination of a very simple formula (*best*) for approximating the coefficient $k_{T0m}$ and good formula (*use*) for the $k_{Tm}$ coefficient. We can see, that all
formulas are quite good but especially formulas *use* and *best*.

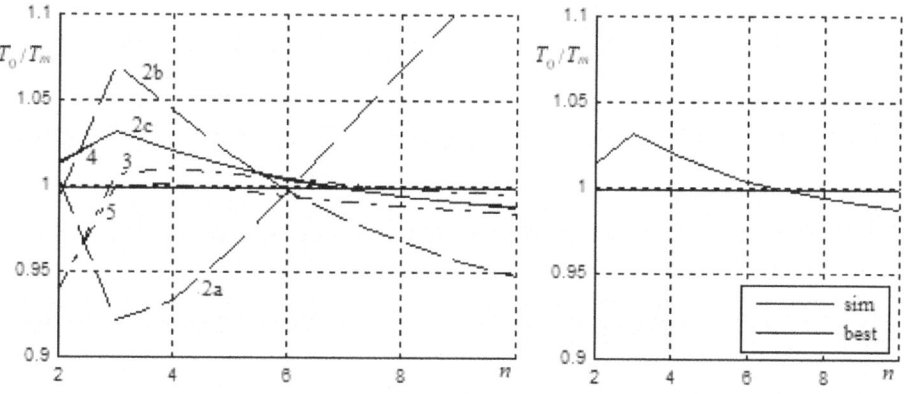

**Fig. 9.** Functions $k_{T0m}(n)$ relative to accurate values (in particular *best*).

**Table 5.** Simplified formulas for $T_m$ and $T_0$.

| Symbol | $T_m = k_{Tm}T$ | $T_0 = k_{T0}T$ or $T_0 = k_{T0m}T_m$ |
|---|---|---|
| sim | $k_{Tm} = \frac{(n-1)!e^{n-1}}{(n-1)^{n-1}}$ | $k_{T0} = \frac{(n-1)^n - (n-1)!e^{n-1} + (n-1)!S_{n-1}}{(n-1)^{n-1}}$ |
| easy | $k_{Tm} = \sqrt{2\pi(n-1)}$ | $k_{T0} = a_0 n + a_1\sqrt{n}$<br>$a_0 \approx 0.916, a_1 \approx -1.096$ |
| use | $k_{Tm} = (a_0 + a_1 e^{-n})\sqrt{2\pi(n-1)}$<br>$a_0 \approx 1.016, a_1 \approx 0.509$ | $k_{T0} = \frac{(n-1)(n-k_n)}{n}, \ k_n = a_0 + a_1\sqrt{n}$<br>$a_0 \approx -0.189, a_1 \approx 1.149$ |
| best | $k_{Tm} = (a_0 + a_1 e^{-n})\sqrt{2\pi(n-1)}$<br>$a_0 \approx 1.016, a_1 \approx 0.509$ | $k_{T0m} = a_0 + a_1\sqrt{n}$<br>$a_0 \approx -0.428, a_1 \approx 0.377$ |

In Fig. 10 we can see how accurate this conversion is.

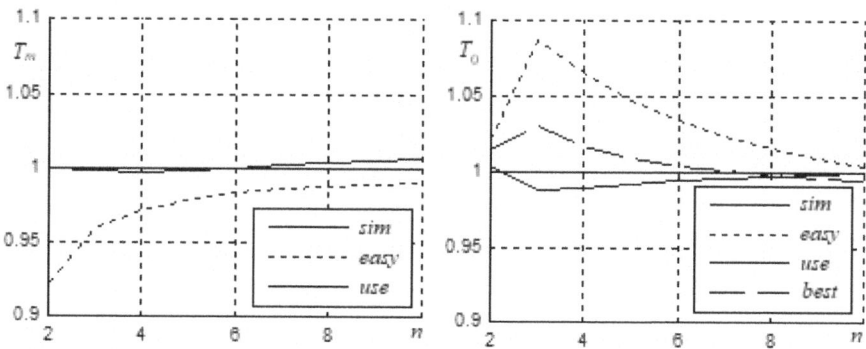

**Fig. 10.** Values $T_m$ i $T_0$ calculated against accurate values.

## 4    Application of Conversion

### 4.1    PID Tunning

First example is a control project with the Ziegler-Nichols tuning method [4]. This method is based on the FOTD model and uses the tangent method for identification. The Ziegler-Nichols method defines the formulas for PI controller ($K_p = 0.9T_m/(k \cdot T_0)$, $T_i = 3.33T_0$) and assumes Quarter-Decay Ratio (QDR) as a quality indicator.

It was assumed that the Strejc model acts as the plant $G_p$ (see Fig. 11). Analytical conversion to determine parameters of FOTD model was carried out in four ways (Table 5). Four variants of values $T_m$ and $T_0$ were obtained and four variants of PI parameters ($K_p$, $T_i$) were calculated.

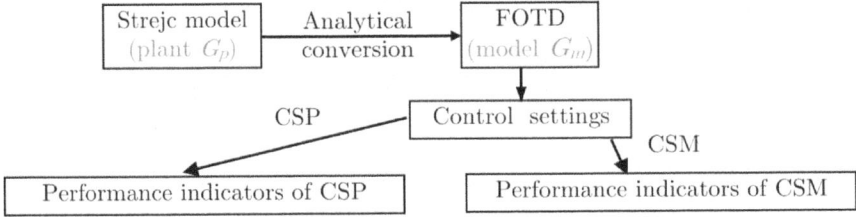

**Fig. 11.** Application of conversion the Strejc model to FOTD.

Such research was carried out for $n$ equal in term $2 \div 10$. On the Fig. 12 are presented only step response for $n$ equal 2 and 10. Each response of control systems (CSP, CSM) were made for four controller settings - the differences are minimal.

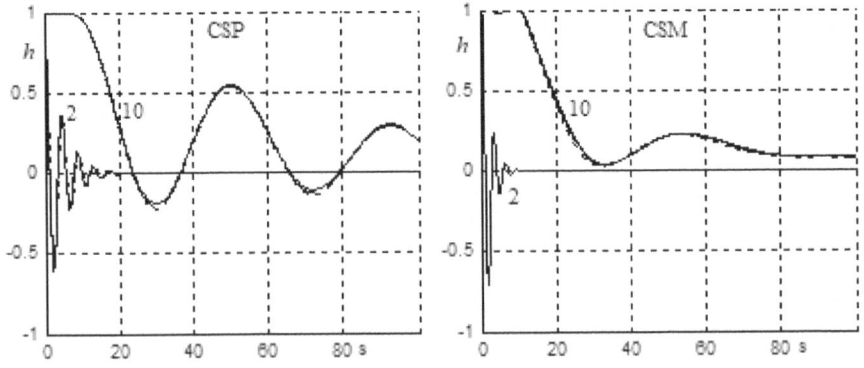

**Fig. 12.** Step responses of control system on the plant (CSP) and on the model (CSM).

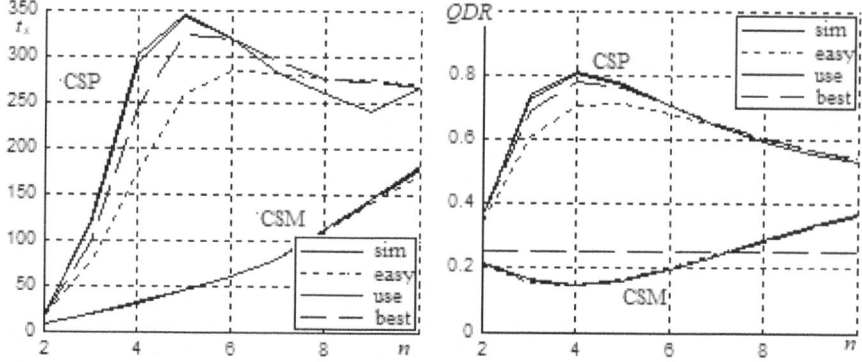

**Fig. 13.** Settling time $t_s$ and $QDR$ depending of $n$ and conversion method.

Differences are more apparent in the charts of indicators - settling time $t_s$ and $QDR$ (see Fig. 13).

Indicators determined for CSM depend on the order $n$ and practically do not depend on conversion variants because the controller determined for a given FOTD model and run on the same model works according to the assumptions of the design method. Whereas the same design settings used in the CSP give worse indicators than for the CSM (it is a normal phenomenon). Interestingly, the largest differences are for $n$ equal to 5. Research using simplified formulas gives similar results, especially when formulas referred to as *use* are used.

The similar research was carried out for the Chain-Horsens-Reswick design method [4] as well as for the pidtune function from Matlab. The change in quality resulting from the transfer of regulation from the model (CSM) to the process (CSP) was different than for the Ziegler-Nichols method, but the use of approximate formulas in the tests did not change the observations. This means that the simplified conversion of the Strejc model was sufficiently accurate.

### 4.2   Identification of Strejc Model

Another example of the application of simplified formulas is the identification of the Strejc model. There are two primary methods for identifying the Strejc model, both of which are based on the tangent at the inflection point (see Fig. 3). The first method uses measurements $T_0$, $T_m$, $t_R$ and Table 6. The following rows in the table are based on exact formulas: $k_{T0m}$ (11) and (12), $t_R/T$ (5), $h_R$ (6). First, the ratio $k_{T0m} = T_0/T_m$ is calculated and located in the table. The corresponding column simultaneously specifies the order of the model ($n$) and the ratio $t_R/T$, which allows the calculation of the time constant $T$ [3]. However, using the table is not very practical.

The second method (Id2) base on measurements $t_R$ and slope $R$, and following formulas

$$n = 1 + \frac{2\pi R^2 t_R^2}{k^2}, T = \frac{t_R}{n-1}. \tag{18}$$

**Table 6.** Table for identification the Strejc model.

| $n$ | 2 | 3 | 4 | 5 | 6 | 7 | 8 | 9 | 10 |
|---|---|---|---|---|---|---|---|---|---|
| $k_{T0m}$ | 0.104 | 0.218 | 0.319 | 0.410 | 0.493 | 0.470 | 0.642 | 0.709 | 0.773 |
| $t_R$ | 1 | 2 | 3 | 4 | 5 | 6 | 7 | 8 | 9 |
| $h_R$ | 0.264 | 0.323 | 0.353 | 0.371 | 0.384 | 0.394 | 0.401 | 0.407 | 0.413 |

These formulas follow from formulas (5), (8) and the Stirling formula $((n-1)! = \sqrt{2\pi(n-1)} \cdot (n-1)n^{n-1}/e^{n-1})$ which gives good approximations for large $n$.

The proposed method (Id3) is based on measurement $T_0$ and $T_m$ and set of formulas which was referred to *best* (Table 5). First, the ratio $k_{T0m} = T_0/T_m$ is calculated and then following formulas were used

$$n = \left(\frac{k_{T0m} - c_0}{c_1}\right)^2 = \left(\frac{T_0 - c_0 T_m}{c_1 T_m}\right)^2, \quad T = \frac{T_m}{(a_0 - a_1 e^{-n})\sqrt{2\pi(n-1)}} \quad (19)$$

where $c_0 = 0.428$, $c_1 = 0.377$, $a_0 = 1.016$, $a_1 = 0.509$.

Figure 14 shows the results of identifying two example transfer function: $G_1 = 4/((40s+1)(15s+1)(2s+1))$ and $G_2 = (4s+1)G_1$ (3th-order without zeros and 3th-order with one zero).

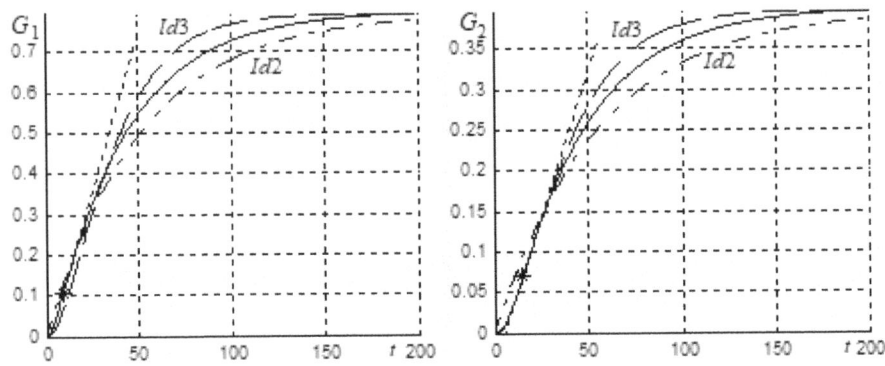

**Fig. 14.** Examples of identification.

The results are promising, but require further research for different types of objects (different sets of poles and zeros). The main difficulty in the planned research is the lack of analytical formulas to calculate the parameters of the inflection point of the step response for transfer function with different poles. We expect that the Id3 method will be more accurate than Id2 for small values of $n$.

# 5    Conclusions

Research have shown that the proposed simplified conversion of the Strejc model is sufficiently accurate. However, the mere conversion of the Strejc model to FOTD model is not enough to easily extend the applied design methods based on FOTD because the methods are sensitive to the value of $n$. The issue requires further research and simplified conversion methods may facilitate this.

The simplified formulas called *best* are sufficiently accurate, easy to determine by interpolation and at the same time the most universal (both for design and identification).

**Disclosure of Interests.** The authors have no competing interests to declare that are relevant to the content of this article.

# References

1. O'Dywer, A.: Handbook of PI and PID controller tuning rules. Imperial College Press, London (2009)
2. Preuss H. P.: Prozeßmodellfreier PID-Regler- Entwurf nach dem Betragsoptimum. Automatisierungstechnik, R. Olenbourg Verlag, vol. 39, pp. 15–22 (1991)
3. Strejc V.: Naherungsverfahren für aperiodische Übertragungscharakteristiken. Regelungstechnik 1959/4
4. Åström, K.J., Hagglund, T.: Advanced PID Control. Systems and Automation Society, ISA - The Instrumentation (2006)

# Neural Analysis Parameters Occurring in a Smart Building

Andrzej Stachno$^{(\boxtimes)}$

Department of Control Systems and Mechatronics,
Wroclaw University of Science and Technology, Wroclaw, Poland
andrzej.stachno@pwr.edu.pl

**Abstract.** Building automation systems, such as KNX, enable the acquisition and storage of device parameters, facilitating comprehensive measurement data collection. They combine various sensors, including PIR sensors for presence detection, with newer technologies such as high-frequency sensors, ultrasonic sensors and vision sensors equipped with artificial neural networks to enhance detection capabilities. These systems also use data archiving devices for comprehensive analysis, leading to insights into health, energy consumption and device performance. The analysis of electrical parameters enabled by KNX systems involves measuring the energy consumption of devices and then classifying them using artificial neural networks to optimize computational efficiency and improve identification accuracy.

**Keywords:** Artificial Neuron Networks · Successive Values of a Time Series · Environmental Measurements in an Smart Building

## 1 The Need to Analyze Environmental Activities in a Smart Building

An intelligent building collects many different parameters, such as temperature, humidity, wind speed, energy consumption and gas concentration measurements. Some of these parameters may be influenced by the existing building infrastructure, for example changes in room temperature and humidity, while others are only monitored and analyzed. These parameters, independent of the operation of technical devices, provide valuable information about the building and the people staying in it [1].

Another measurement issue commonly applied in automated buildings is power measurement and analysis of disturbances within it. This measurement allows understanding the characteristics and quality of the supplied electrical power to the building. By analyzing these disturbances, it's possible to identify electrical devices connected to the building's power grid and assess their impact on the power system's stability. Conducted experiments demonstrate high accuracy in such identification, enabling effective management of the electrical grid and optimization of device performance within the building [2].

A. Quesada-Arencibia et al. (Eds.): EUROCAST 2024, LNCS 15172, pp. 402–411, 2025.
https://doi.org/10.1007/978-3-031-82949-9_36

## 2    Measurement Methods and Data Analysis

With this architecture in place, communication devices can be seamlessly connected, even within expansive structures.. This system allows for the integration of over 61,000 sensory and executive devices that perform building automation tasks [3]. The system's topology consists of lines connected to different areas (Fig. 1).

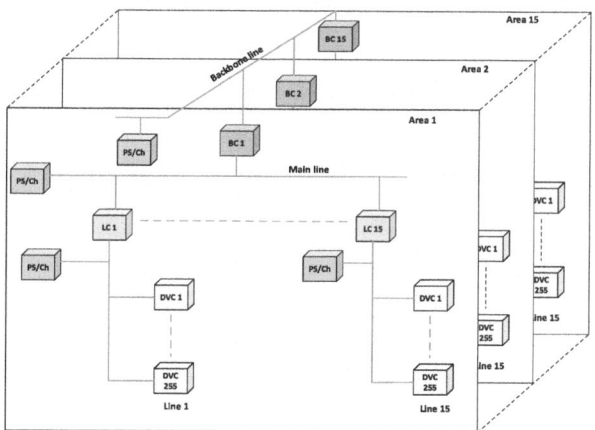

**Fig. 1.** Topology KNX system.

With this architecture, it is possible to connect communication devices even in very large buildings. The devices that are part of the automation system can come from over 500 manufacturers worldwide and are compatible with each other at the communication level. This compatibility is ensured by verification from the supervisory institution known as the KNX Association. For the purposes of the experiment, the system was simplified to a single line, which contained measuring devices and a data archiving element [4]. After appropriate processing, this data was subjected to neural analysis.

For the Experiment, the Following Environmental Parameters Were Measured:

- temperature,
- carbon dioxide concentration,
- volatile organic compounds (VOCs),
- atmospheric pressure,
- relative humidity,

The following devices were used for measurements:

- True Presence Multisensor.
- Presence sensor,
- Air quality sensor.
- PLC controller with data archiving module.

A neural analysis application created in Matlab by MathWorks was used as the analysis tool. All measuring devices and the data archiving system communicate using the KNX protocol.

# 3  Measurement Environment and Experiment Procedure

Experiments for human identification using neural networks were conducted in a research room with an area of 36 m² and a volume of 100 m³. The test room, equipped with sensors, is shown in Fig. 2.

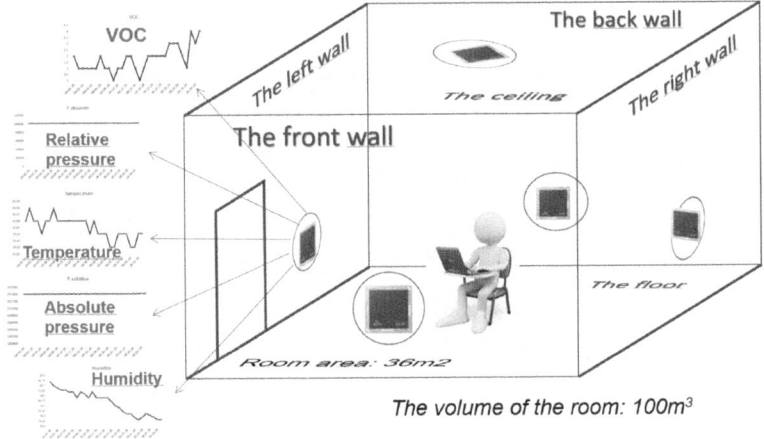

**Fig. 2.**  Test room during a person identification experiment.

Sensors were mounted on the walls and ceiling, connected to a data archiving server via a communication bus. The measurement data reflecting nine different scenarios are illustrated in Fig. 3.

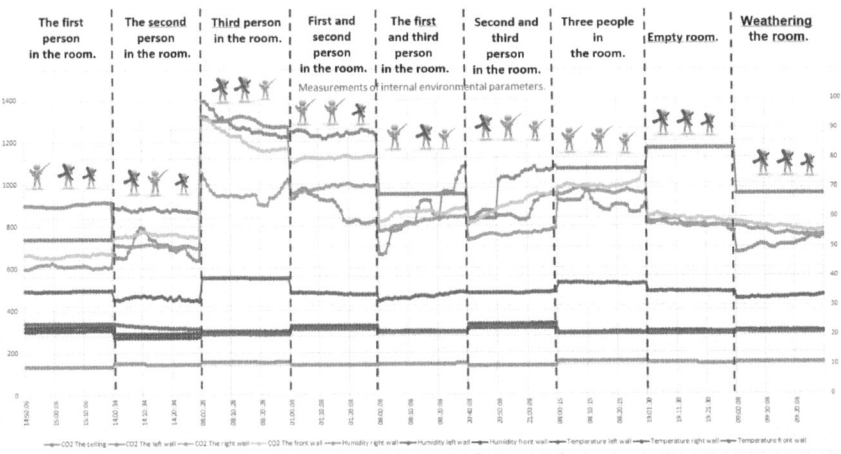

**Fig. 3.**  Measurement data reflecting nine different scenarios of people in the test room.

Measurements were carried out using multisensors operating in the KNX system, analyzing the following parameters:

- 4 measurements of $CO_2$ concentration (on the ceiling, left, right, and front walls),
- 2 measurements of atmospheric pressure (relative and absolute),
- 3 measurements of humidity (on the left, right, and front walls),
- 3 measurements of temperature (on the left, right, and front walls),
- 1 measurement of volatile organic compounds (under the ceiling).

Three individuals participated in the experiment. Each of them, either alone or in combination with others, stayed in the test room. Additionally, measurement data were collected from an empty and ventilated room.

For each scenario, measurement data were collected for 30 min with a measurement interval of 1 min. This resulted in a vector consisting of 13 time series for each scenario. For neural analysis purposes, this vector was divided into two parts: training data (20 samples) and test data (10 samples). The set of measurement vectors is shown in Fig. 4.

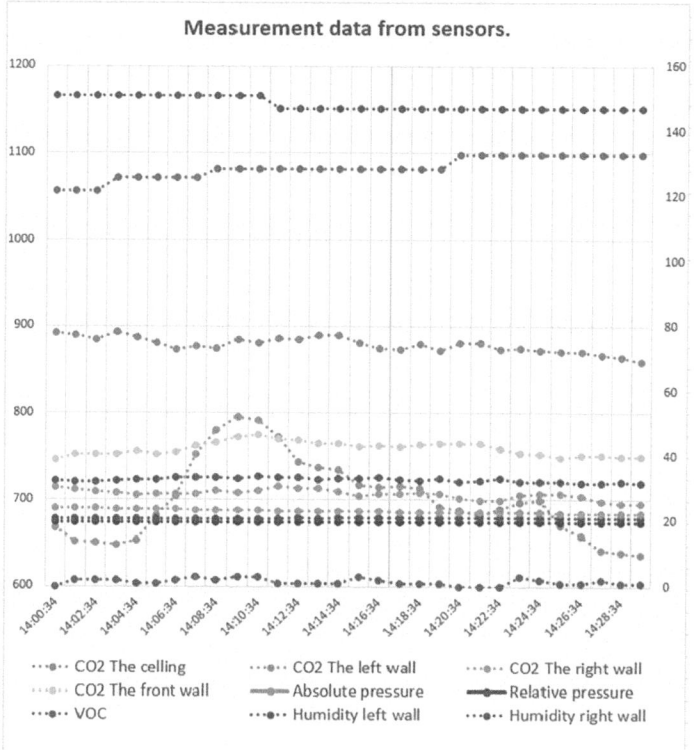

**Fig. 4.** Vector of measurement data presented in the form of a time series.

In the neural analysis, the artificial neural network sequentially presented the test data associated with each scenario, featuring different sets of personal data. The network then identified the given scenario by presenting the test data to its inputs [4].

The subject of the research was the identification of individual people staying in the test room based on environmental parameters obtained from multi-sensor measurements used in building automation and their analysis using artificial neural networks. The task of the proposed neural system was to learn the measurement scheme for all units individually and in groups, creating all possible combinations and additional situations: empty and ventilated rooms. The artificial neural network identified a specific situation based on previously presented measurement patterns.

Out of all 90 research samples, 78 situations (87%) were correctly identified. The most identification errors were observed in the case of the second and third person. An interesting aspect is the fact that these people are related. This issue will be analyzed in subsequent experiments.

## 4    Measurements of Electrical Parameters in a Smart Building

To more accurately reflect the electrical characteristics of a device used in the building without disconnecting it from the power supply, analyzing its energy consumption is helpful. This type of electrical characteristic can be represented using a measurement time series [5]. To increase the amount of measurement information regarding a specific electrical parameter, the time series was supplemented with data from measurements of higher current and/or voltage harmonics. An example of a measurement point—a harmonic vector, including the amplitudes of individual current harmonics from the first to the twenty-first, is presented in Fig. 5.

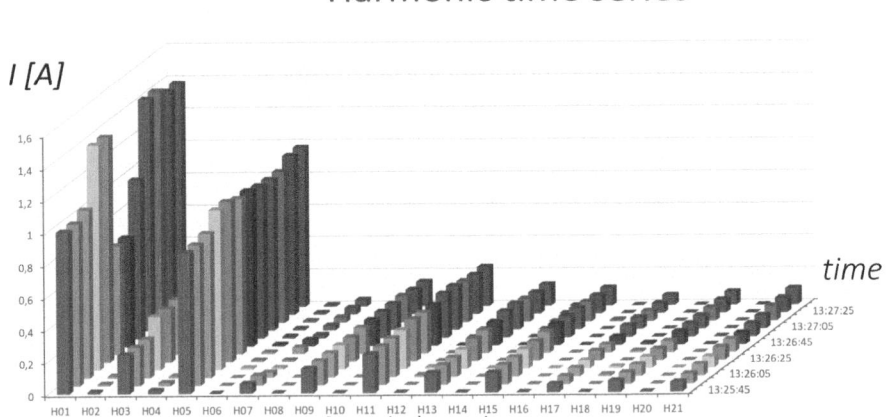

**Fig. 5.**  Electrical harmonic time series.

An extension of this vector concept is the measurement time series, which consist of successive harmonic current vectors at specific time intervals. This forms a Harmonic Time Series (HTS). The results of measurements of the mentioned electrical parameters can be used to identify devices connected to the power network.

## 5  Device Profiling Based on Harmonic Time Series

By analyzing the differences in harmonic time series [3], individual disturbances introduced by electrical devices can be identified. Figures 4a and 4b depict harmonic time
series of two different electrical devices: a toaster and a coffee maker. Despite having
very similar electrical functionalities - heating - there is a distinct difference in the sev-
enth harmonic (Fig. 6). Similar differences in harmonic time series have been observed
for other electrical devices [6]. Based on this, the concept of profiling electrical devices
based on their harmonic time series has been proposed.

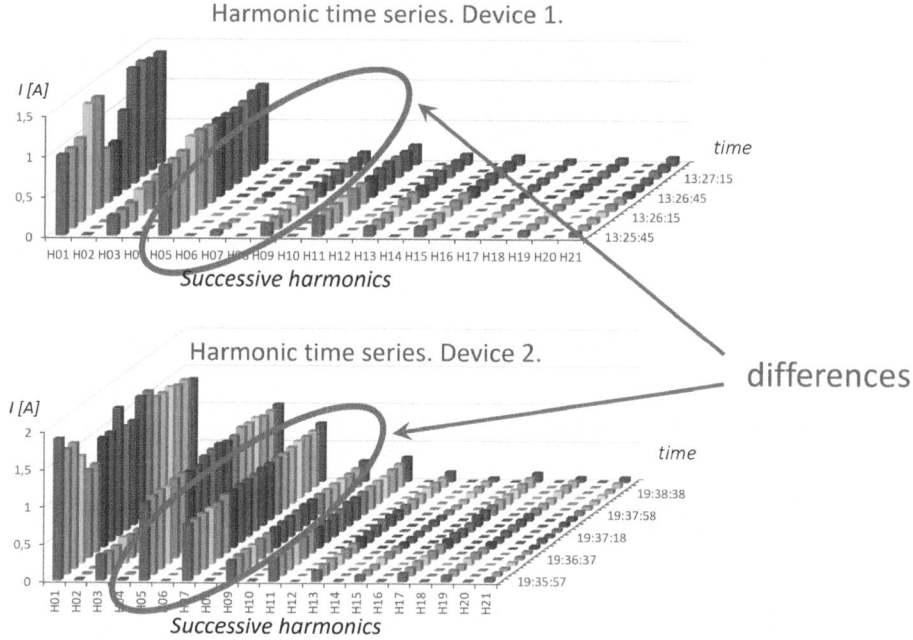

**Fig. 6.** Differences in harmonic time series for two electrical devices.

Since the analysis is based on the identification, data was measured internal environmental parameters of the building such as temperature, humidity, concentration of
$CO_2$ and VOC can conclude that persons of a similar impact on the environment, for
example. Exhaling a similar amount of $CO_2$ will be less recognizable by the neural system identification profile a passenger. Identification at the level of 50%, with the worst
identified situation, however, gives the opportunity to improve the result by increasing
the training data, or by modifying the internal parameters of the artificial neural network.
It should also be remembered that standard sensors for measuring basic environmental
parameters were used for the tests. Their appropriate selection or implementation of
a newer generation of measuring elements (with much greater accuracy and dynamics
of measurement) will significantly improve the precision of the obtained identification
results.

## 6   Study of Electrical Device Identification Based on Their Harmonic Profiles

As part of experiments aimed at demonstrating differences in harmonic time series, a measurement analysis was conducted for the following devices:

- laptop,
- LED light bulb,
- electric motor.

Harmonic time series corresponding to these devices were presented in Fig. 7.

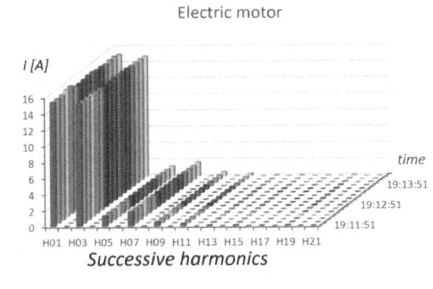

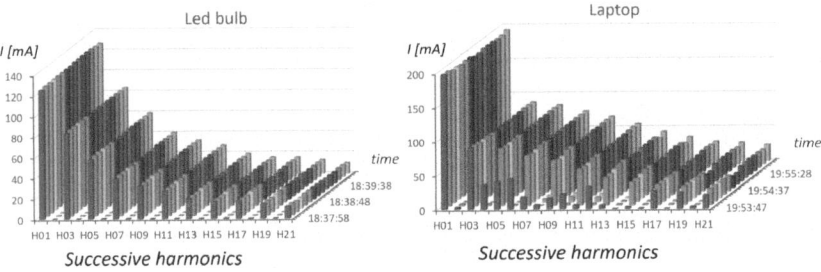

**Fig. 7.** Harmonic time series for an electric motor, an LED bulb and a laptop.

The aim of the analysis was to identify the basic profiles of devices based on their harmonic time series and to extract sets of devices working together along with their basic components from the measurement data. An example of harmonic time series for the simultaneous operation of a laptop and an LED bulb was presented in Fig. 8.

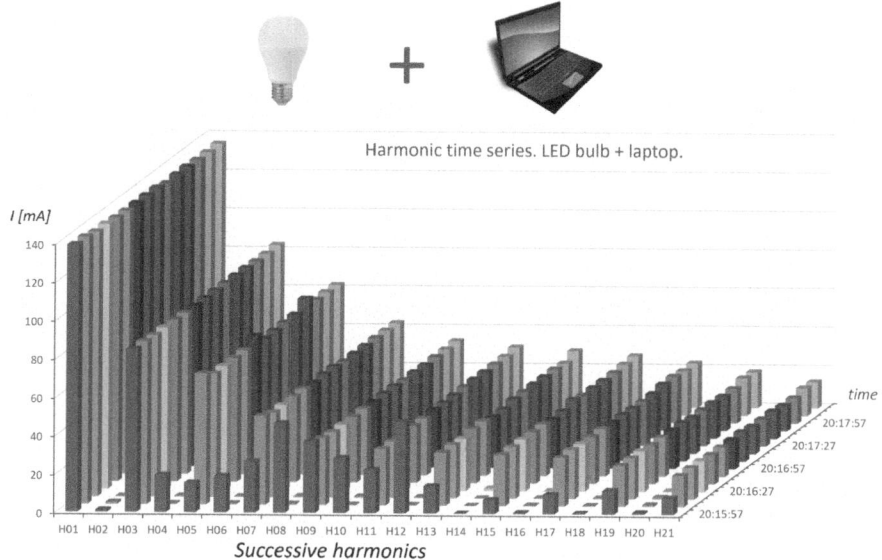

**Fig. 8.** Harmonic time series for an LED bulb and a laptop working simultaneously.

To identify basic electrical devices, an artificial feed-forward neural network with backpropagation was employed. The neural network structure consisted of one layer comprising four neurons to ensure quick device identification [7]. The methodology of analysis and identification included:

- Training of the artificial neural network: presenting individual harmonic profiles to the neural network, with each device operating independently. The neural network input consisted of the harmonic time series corresponding to the device measurement, while the output of the network contained the device identifier. The training data comprised 200 measurement points.
- Testing of the artificial neural network: presenting harmonic time series derived from measurements of multiple devices operating simultaneously.

The neural network determined the identifiers of devices detected in the presented harmonic time series on its outputs. The testing data consisted of 100 measurement points.

The results of device identification are presented in Fig. 9.

The results of neural identification of tested devices in a real electrical installation allow us to determine with high accuracy which devices operate in the power supply network. The best results were achieved when identifying the LED bulb - 100% correct results. The worst for the electric motor - 84% correct identifications.

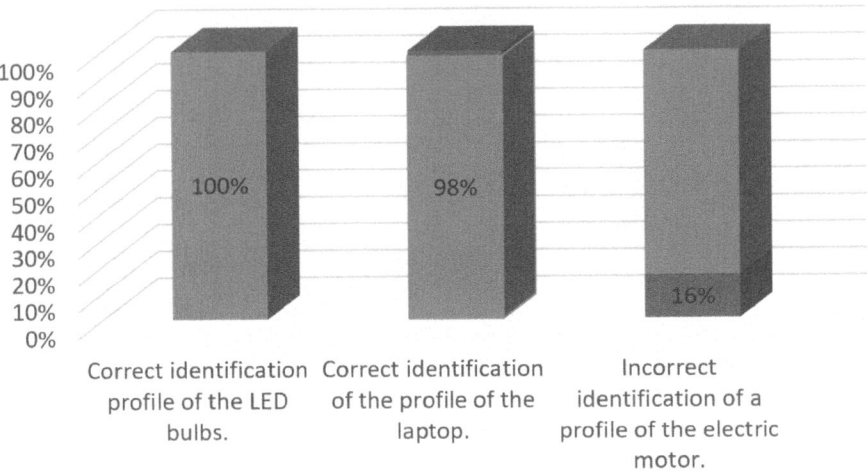

**Fig. 9.** Results of neural identification of tested devices in a real electrical installation.

## 7  Summary and Conclusion

In the data analysis part regarding environmental parameters, the basis of identification relied on the measurement data of internal environmental parameters of the building, such as temperature, humidity, $CO_2$ concentration, and volatile organic compounds (VOCs). From this, it can be concluded that effective identification and recognition of individuals based on their individual profiles using artificial neural networks is possible. It's important to note that standard sensors primarily used for presence detection were utilized in the tests, and their application for measuring basic environmental parameters is only an additional functionality. This approach is driven by the aim to minimize costs associated with installing as few sensors as possible. However, the appropriate selection or implementation of newer generation measuring elements (with significantly greater accuracy and measurement dynamics) will significantly improve the precision of the obtained identification results.

The analysis of the electrical power supply network of the building shows that artificial neural networks, processing measurement data based on harmonic profiles of time series of basic devices, can identify electrical devices connected to the power grid. This enables the analysis of the correctness of complex building automation systems, which consist of basic electrical devices. The extraction of individual devices allows for determining how many and what electrical devices are operational in the building, enabling their monitoring.

# References

1. Stanley, N., Eugene, H.: An Introduction to Econophysics. Correlations and Complexity in Finance, PWN (2001)
2. Peitgen, H.O., Jurgens, H., Saupe, D.: Introduction to Fractals and Chaos, PWN (2002)
3. KNX Association: KNX Advanced Course Documentation – Januar 2019 ISBN-13: 979–8635617861
4. Technical Analysis of the Financial Markets, WIG PRESS, (1999)
5. Jabłoński, A.: Intelligent buildings as distributed information systems. CASYS: International Journal of Computing Anticipatory Systems **21**, 385–394 (2008)
6. Stachno, A., Jabłoński, A.: Hybrid method for forecasting next values of time series for intelligent building control / Andrzej Stachno and Andrzej Jabłonski [i in.]. W: Computer aided systems theory - EUROCAST 2015 : 15th International Conference, Las Palmas de Gran Canaria, Spain, February 8–13, 2015 : revised selected papers. Pt. 1 / Roberto Moreno-Díaz, Franz Pichler, Alexis Quesada-Arencibia (eds.). Berlin; Heidelberg: Springer, cop, pp. 822–829, (Lecture Notes in Computer Science, ISSN 0302–9743; vol. 9520) (2015)
7. Stachno A.: Neural Personal Profile Identyfication Based on Environmental Performance Analysis of Inteligent Building, Computer aided systems theory - EUROCAST 2019: In: 17th International Conference, Las Palmas de Gran Canaria, Spain, February 17–22, 2019: revised selected papers. Pt. 2, Roberto Moreno-Díaz, Franz Pichler, Alexis Quesada-Arencibia (eds.). Berlin; Heidelberg: Springer, cop, .pp. 388–395, (Lecture Notes in Computer Science, ISBN 978–3–030–45095–3) (2020)

# Efficient Manipulation of Control Flow Models in Evolving Software

Tomáš Fiedor[1,2], Jiří Pavela[1,2(✉)], Adam Rogalewicz[1],
and Tomáš Vojnar[1,3]

[1] Faculty of Information Technology, Brno University of Technology, Brno, Czechia
{ifiedortom,ipavela,rogalew}@fit.vutbr.cz
[2] Red Hat Czech, Brno, Czechia
[3] Faculty of Informatics, Masaryk University, Brno, Czechia
vojnar@fi.muni.cz

**Abstract.** When looking for certain kinds of software bugs, successive versions of software are compared. Performance-related bugs are a notable example. Methods used for detecting such bugs are, however, expensive and need to be applied carefully. At the same time, current software development is rapid, with new software versions released everyday. In this paper, we aim at two particular ways how to optimize difference analyses of performance (but possibly other aspects of the software too) of successive software versions. Namely, we propose (1) an efficient layered representation of the program control flow spanning across the program history, and (2) methods for efficient matching of pairs of corresponding functions in different software versions and for selecting those whose differential analysis should be performed. We have implemented our approach and performed experiments on two selected versions of the CPython project. The results indicate that our approach is a promising direction for improving the performance analysis of real world programs.

**Keywords:** Evolving software · Static analysis · Dynamic analysis · Diff analysis · Call graph · Control flow graph · Function Matching

## 1 Introduction

Over the last years, the software development community has seen a massive rise in the popularity of *Continuous Integration and Continuous Delivery (CI/CD)* practices. In particular, CI/CD aims to automate building, testing, and deploying software projects during their entire development lifecycle, naturally leading to *evolving software* that is constantly updated with new features without breaking the build.

As more developers adopted CI/CD in their software projects, numerous success stories have been publicly shared, thus further accelerating interest and demand for CI/CD solutions among software developers. Numerous companies reported impressive results ranging from reducing the development costs by 78%

© The Author(s), under exclusive license to Springer Nature Switzerland AG 2025
A. Quesada-Arencibia et al. (Eds.): EUROCAST 2024, LNCS 15172, pp. 412–428, 2025.
https://doi.org/10.1007/978-3-031-82949-9_37

(HP), to increasing the number of deployments to more than ten per day (Flickr) or 50 million a year (Amazon) [9]. Moreover, an empirical study [8] on open-source projects found out that projects using CI/CD practices, as compared to projects without CI/CD, on average (1) save 1.6 h on integrating pull requests; (2) manage to release twice as often; (3) catch bugs earlier; and (4) help the developers avoid breaking the build.

In their current state, most CI/CD test environments focus on finding functional bugs only, i.e., bugs that lead to software crashes and/or incorrect results. Other types of bugs, such as *performance bugs*, are often overlooked. However, a study of Mozilla Firefox [16] concluded that, compared to any other type of bugs, performance bugs (1) take more time to fix – up to 2.8 times more than even security fixes; (2) require more experienced developers to fix; and (3) the fixes are spanning up to 2.6 times more files. Moreover, if such bugs remain in the software unnoticed for a long time (thus becoming the so-called *dormant* bugs), the time needed to fix them almost doubles [5]. In extreme cases, this can even lead to hundred-million dollar projects being abandoned after several years of intense development [7].

Recently, there have been attempts to integrate performance testing to CI/CD [2,10]. However, these solutions usually provide only basic performance testing support (e.g., regression testing, micro benchmarking, or load testing) and focus on the latest software version only. In our previous work [6], we have introduced *Perun*: a novel tool-suite for performance testing and analysis. Perun supports more complex performance analyses that require precise profiling and can possibly take into account multiple previous versions of the software. Such larger perspective is generally necessary to find root causes of hard-to-detect performance issues, especially in the case of so-called *creeping degradations*: performance degradations of software caused slowly over the time.

In order to integrate more complex performance analyses, e.g., into a CI/CD pipeline, we need them to be efficient. A possible approach is to analyse only those source files that have been changed since the last analysis. This is successfully used in practice, e.g., by Facebook/Meta Infer [1] in the area of static analysis. In our ongoing work on efficient performance analyses, we build on this principle and focus our analysis to, among other, code fragments with control flow changes. However, this poses numerous challenges in terms of efficient representation, versioning, storage, and difference analysis of control flow models, i.e., control flow and call graphs, in evolving software.

In this work, we address the above challenges by proposing (1) an efficient *layered representation* of control flow models; (2) a hierarchical version labeling system – using, among others, hashes of *version control system (VCS)* versions and local repository changes – along with accompanying algorithms for storage, retrieval, and intelligent lazy deletion of individual versions; (3) six new heuristics for function matching adapted specifically for evolving software to improve the matching accuracy; and (4) a generic algorithm for difference analysis of call and control flow graphs that builds on the matching heuristics. We have implemented the proposed solutions in the particular context of the Perun analyser and present a use-case demonstration with experimental results that confirm these solutions can indeed bring significant efficiency and false match rate improvements. Moreover, we believe that the data structures and algorithms that our solution is based on are general enough to be useful in other tools that leverage control flow information, allowing them to be used efficiently in CI/CD.

## 2    Preliminaries

In Perun, we employ, among other, two kinds of program *control flow models (CFM)*: (1) Control Flow Graphs (CFGs) to represent the structure of particular functions, and, (2) Call Graphs (CGs) to represent the calling relation between particular functions. Their usage is quite versatile: we use CFGs to, e.g., match functions that were renamed between two versions, allowing us to omit them from the subsequent analysis if just the name changed, and we can potentially use CGs to, e.g., improve the precision of the results reported to the user by supplying a more precise trace leading to a detected bottleneck.

CFGs consist of nodes and edges where nodes represent *basic blocks* – sequences of instructions without branching; and edges represent direct and indirect jumps between basic blocks.

**Definition 1 (Basic Block).** *A basic block $BB$ is a straight-line sequence of instructions $i_0, i_1, \ldots, i_{n-1}$ with no branches in (apart from the entry point) and no branches out (apart from the exit point). We denote by $len(BB)$ the length of the basic block, i.e., the number of instructions in $BB$.*

In the rest of the paper, we assume dealing with *instructions* from the assembly language of the x86_64 architecture, but the proposed algorithms should be applicable to any other CPU architecture or machine-level instruction set without a loss of generality. The concrete instruction set and architecture are relevant as they determine the set of registers and control flow related instructions, such as jumps or calls.

**Definition 2 (Program Control Flow Graph).** *The* control flow graph *(CFG) of a program $P$ is a directed graph $CFG_P = (\mathcal{B}_P, \mathcal{C}_P, T_P)$ where $\mathcal{B}_P$ is the (finite) set of basic blocks of $P$, $\mathcal{C}_P \subseteq \mathcal{B}_P \times \mathcal{B}_P$ is the control flow relation, and $T_P : \mathcal{C}_P \to \{\text{fallthrough}, \text{jump}\}$ is a mapping of edges to their type.*

Note that we extend the classical definition of a CFG with an additional mapping $T_P$ that assigns each edge its type. When a conditional branching occurs in a CFG (e.g., as a result of a comparison or a jump instruction at the end of some basic block), one or more of the outgoing edges usually represent the control flow to the jump destination (jump edges), while a single edge represents the control flow to the instruction directly succeeding the jump condition (the fallthrough edge), which is taken when the jump condition is not satisfied. This mapping has one practical advantage: it allows us to deterministically traverse two or more CFGs in a lockstep and compare their basic blocks and/or structure.

Manipulation with the CFG of the entire program is usually impractical as many analyses are performed on the function level. Even in the case of inter-procedural analyses (such as those we will introduce in Sect. 4), we often need to limit the control flow to the scope of individual functions.

**Definition 3 (Function Control Flow Graph).** *Let $CFG_P$ be the CFG of a program $P$. The CFG of a function $f$ of $P$ is the subgraph $FCFG_f = (\mathcal{B}_f, \mathcal{C}_f, T_f)$ of $CFG_P$ where $\mathcal{B}_f \subseteq \mathcal{B}_P$ is the finite set of basic blocks of the function $f$, $\mathcal{C}_f \subseteq \mathcal{B}_f \times \mathcal{B}_f \subseteq \mathcal{C}_P$ is the control flow relation of $f$, and $T_f : \mathcal{C}_f \to \{\text{fallthrough}, \text{jump}\}$ such that $T_f \subseteq T_P$.*

Call graphs consist of nodes that represent functions in a program and edges that represent the caller/callee relation between the functions.

**Definition 4 (Call Graph).** *The call graph (CG) of $P$ is a multi-rooted directed graph $CG_P = (\mathcal{F}_P, \mathcal{E}_P, \mathcal{R}_P)$ where $\mathcal{F}_P$ is the set of functions of $P$, $\mathcal{E}_P \subseteq \mathcal{F}_P \times \mathcal{F}_P$ is the call relation (relating callers and callees), and $\mathcal{R}_P \subseteq \mathcal{F}_P$ is the set of $CG_P$ roots.*

Note that contrary to some of the established CG definitions, we require the CG to support multiple root nodes as, in practice, many types of programs, e.g., (shared) libraries, may expose multiple valid entry point functions.

## 3   Control Flow Models Representation

In our experience, a typical workflow of dealing with control flow models in program analysis can be summarized into three steps: (1) (re)construct the models from source or binary files, dynamic run traces, logs, or any other available resources; (2) analyse the models according to the problem domain; and (3) discard the models. If a particular model is required again later on, e.g., as a part of some more complex aggregate analysis, it is simply reconstructed on-demand once more. Although this approach works for simple enough use cases, it is insufficient for scenarios where repeated reconstruction of control flow models or their post-processing is too expensive—as is the case with Perun.

Notably, obtaining precise CGs and CFGs using static analysis on binary executable files is notoriously difficult and expensive, mainly due to *function pointers* or *dynamic dispatch calls* found in many modern programming languages. Moreover, such control flow models are generally unsound and incomplete when constructed using static analysis on binary files only. Similarly, constructing a precise CG using just dynamic analysis is often infeasible in practice as the number of potential execution paths through a program rapidly grows with the size of the codebase. Such control flow models are, however, at least sound but generally still incomplete [14].

A naive solution to this problem might be to simply cache or persistently store all the constructed models so that they can be accessed at a later time. However, such a simple approach is impractical for numerous reasons, e.g., the space requirements for storage of models would be needlessly high as each static and dynamic model would be stored separately, and the lookup for a model tied to a concrete project version would be difficult without a proper versioning scheme. Also, combining the statically and dynamically constructed models into a single more precise model requires further, potentially expensive, post-processing step on each retrieval given those models are stored separately.

That is why we propose an efficient representation of a CG that composes both static and dynamic models obtained by various tools or run configurations, while allowing to manipulate with any individual model or a combination of models. Our representation is based on the definition of CGs in Definition 4.

First, we extend CGs with a set of so-called *layers*. Each node or edge of the CG must then belong to at least one layer but may belong to multiple or even all layers in the graph. (Alternatively, one can view this such that each node and edge is labelled by a set of layer identifiers.) The layers correspond to a single specific model or a combination of some simpler models. Each layer is associated with a tuple (*source, config*) with *source* specifying the type of the model, e.g., static or dynamic, and *config* specifying the analysis tool, the configuration of the tool used, and/or the parameters the given program was run or compiled with. Figure 1 shows an example of the proposed representation with three layers.

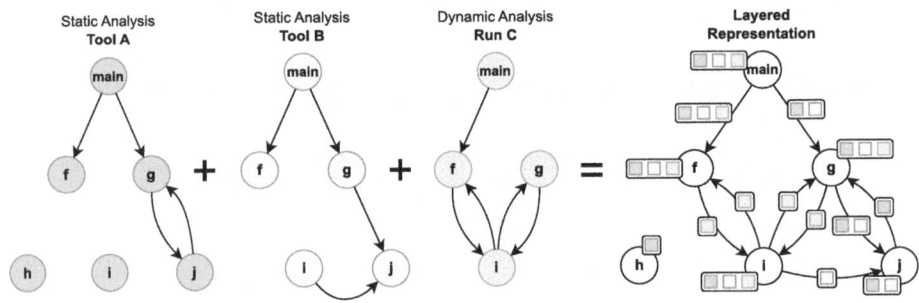

**Fig. 1.** An example of the proposed *layered* call graph representation with three distinct layers. Each color-coded layer corresponds to a concrete source of CG data, e.g., two different static analysis tools *A* and *B*, and one dynamic run *C*. Together the layers form a single, potentially disconnected, graph structure.

Second, the CG nodes maintain a link to the *function control flow graph (FCFG)* corresponding to the function represented by the node. Our implementation in Perun currently supports a single FCFG associated with a function only as in our experience there tends to be generally not so much variation between FCFGs obtained by different disassembly or analysis tools. However, extending the implementation to accommodate for multiple FCFGs or their combinations is straightforward. Figure 2 illustrates the inclusion of the FCFG representation within the CG nodes.

Note that Definition 4 defining CGs does not make any assumption about the connectivity of the graph (in the extreme case, the CG may contain no edges

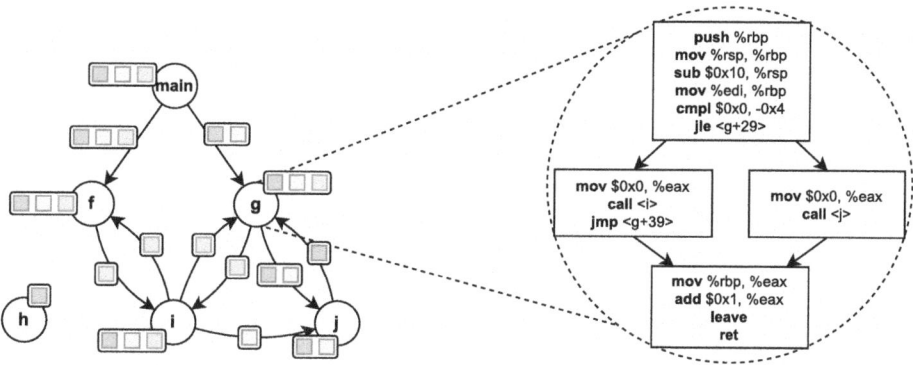

**Fig. 2.** A schematic illustration of the combined representation of a layered CG and a nested FCFG representation stored within the CG nodes.

at all). It is critical to not impose any restrictions on the graph connectivity, at least in the representation itself, as disconnected CGs obtained by static analysis are quite commonly encountered in practice, e.g., as a result of callbacks registered within a third-party library that cannot be properly analysed due to missing source code or debug information. A major benefit of this single-graph layered representation is that by extending the static CG with data from particular dynamic runs may cause previously disconnected parts of the CG to be reconnected as long as the dynamic runs visit the appropriate functions.

Using this representation and the accompanying features (such as the selection operator, versioning, or reuse of dynamic models introduced in the following sections), Perun is able to efficiently store even extensive control flow models combined from multiple sources, hence increasing the models precision. Perun can then leverage those models to quickly identify functions that have been changed in a new project version and focus on the performance of those particular functions, or apply other profiling optimizations that utilize call or control flow graph information.

### 3.1 CFM Layer Selection Operator

To easily manipulate individual layers or their combinations within the layered representation, Perun defines a *layer selection operator* $\sigma$ that allows individual analyses to choose a subset of layers that will form a *frozen view* over the selected layers. Our implementation of a frozen view does not allow direct updates to the view itself to avoid invalidation of iterators and possible inconsistencies, but provides access to the original CFM representation that can be updated. Note that the frozen view can be configured to preserve or exclude the links to the FCFG of individual CG nodes.

Additionally, we establish new auxiliary *convenience layers* to be used with the selection operator that predefine some commonly used combinations of layers, e.g., the *mixed* layer that combines all static and dynamic layers restricted to nodes and edges reachable from the root nodes.

Perun relies on the selection operator to obtain submodels of the entire control flow model restricted by custom user-defined conditions, e.g., a CFM view of concrete dynamic runs that may be reused in newer CFM versions as described in Sect. 4.5. Moreover, the matching and analysis algorithms introduced in Sect. 4 are designed to work on the view objects obtained by the selection operator. Figure 3 presents an example of the selection operator usage.

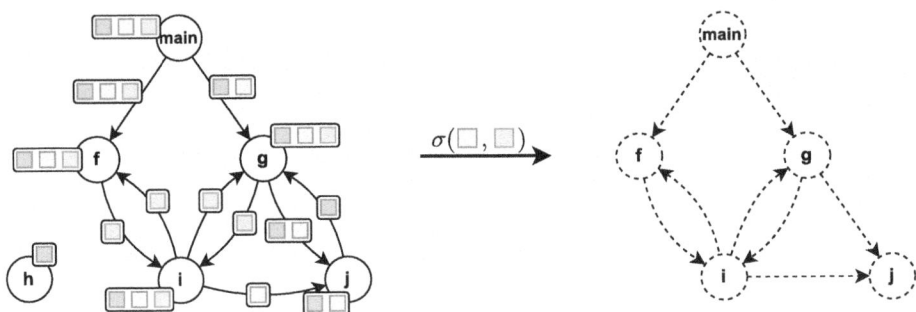

**Fig. 3.** An example of the proposed layer selection operator $\sigma$ used to obtain a combined view of two distinct layers (static, $A$) and (dynamic, $C$).

## 3.2   Call Graph Versioning

As projects evolve over time, new project versions are continuously released and both the CFG and CG may change as the project developers add new features or refactor the existing code. Some tools, such as Perun, need to frequently access some of those versions of the control flow models for comparison or other types of analyses. However, reconstructing precise multi-layered models can be extremely expensive, especially when using multiple static analysis tools and/or executing numerous dynamic runs to obtain control flow data. Therefore, we want to store the once constructed models for possible future use.

Perun already supports storing auxiliary data and models linked to concrete VCS versions, e.g., Git commits. However, versioning the models using the VCS versions only is generally insufficient as certain models might correspond to the so-called *dirty versions*[1], or even a different project setup or configuration. Naturally, we want to support the linkage of models to dirty versions or specific project configurations since we usually repeat the profiling when trying to fix a performance regression introduced in a concrete project version, hence introducing possibly many new dirty versions.

---

[1] A project version is considered *dirty* if it contains *uncommited* changes, i.e., changes that were not yet published in a commit.

To solve the above issue with naive versioning, we propose a compound version identification $version(CFM) = (v, h, s, c, t)$ where $v$ is the VCS version (e.g., a commit hash); $h$ is a CFM version computed in a VCS-specific versioning algorithm (e.g., an SHA hash in Git) from files used for the CFM extraction; $s$ is the repository state, either *clean* or *dirty*; $c$ is a configuration name of the project setup, e.g., `release`, `debug`, `nightly-build`, etc.; and $t$ is the timestamp of the CFM creation.

As the number of stored *dirty models* (i.e., models linked to dirty VCS versions) and their size can become significant over time, especially for large actively maintained projects, we propose a lazy deletion algorithm to counter this issue. When traversing the project VCS history to retrieve a specific CFM version, the deletion algorithm identifies and deletes *obsolete* models, i.e., dirty models of the same project configuration in VCS versions other than the current `HEAD`[2].

# 4    Function Matching and Difference Analysis

Perun mainly focuses on detecting code changes between (recent) project versions. More precisely, Perun aims to automatically identify functions that were changed in a concrete (analysed) project version, as those functions are more likely to manifest new changes in performance as well as are more likely to be fixed by the developers [3–5]. Identifying changed functions naively by source code diff analysis leads to a significant number of false positives as many types of source code changes may have no impact on the behaviour or performance of a function, e.g., renaming variables, changing comments or refactoring code to macro expansions. Hence, the analysis needs to be performed on a finer representation of functions, e.g., on the level of the control flow.

However, any such diff algorithm must first match functions from the new project version to their corresponding functions in the previous version[3]. We search for a bijection $m : \mathcal{F}'_{P_b} \leftrightarrow \mathcal{F}'_{P_t}$ where $\mathcal{F}'_{P_b} \subseteq \mathcal{F}_{P_b}$ and $\mathcal{F}'_{P_t} \subseteq \mathcal{F}_{P_t}$ are the largest possible subsets of functions from the previous (also called *baseline*) and current (called *target*) versions of a program $P$ for which such a bijection $m$ could be constructed w.r.t. some concrete chosen function correspondence criterion. This problem is computationally hard—indeed, even finding an isomorphism between two call graphs is a well-known NP-complete problem [11]. As such, it is in general infeasible to find a perfect solution to this problem. However, we believe we can find a good enough solution applicable to wide range of projects.

---

[2] Using Git terminology, `HEAD` refers to the most current version in a given branch or a specific version if we find ourselves in a `HEAD`-detached state.

[3] Informally, for each function we want to find its origin: a possibly renamed or changed function that is still enough structurally similar to the origin so one could argue that this function is indeed the evolved version of the origin. Whether two function implementations are enough structurally similar is of course highly subjective—one can hardly come up with an exact formal definition in this case.

Our solution to this problem is inspired by existing works in this area [11,13] that are, however, mostly tailored for malware similarity analysis and other security-oriented analyses, and as such cannot rely on the availability of function names in the analysed programs. Hence, we propose a set of three matching heuristics based on *function summaries* inspired by [11], and three matching heuristics based on *function call context* that complement the function summary heuristics with a context-aware approach.

### 4.1   Function Matching Using Function Summaries

Function summaries are key characteristics about a function derived from its control flow data that can be exploited for fast identification of matching candidates. Formally, we define function summaries as follows.

**Definition 5 (Function Summary).** *Let $CFG_f$ be the function control flow graph of a function $f$. A function summary $S$ of $f$ is a tuple $S_f = (\beta, \phi, \epsilon, \iota, \mu)$ where $\beta$ is $|\mathcal{B}_f|$, i.e., the number of basic blocks in $f$; $\phi$ is the number of function call instructions in $CFG_f$; $\epsilon$ is $|\mathcal{C}_f|$, i.e., the number of edges in $CFG_f$; $\iota$ is $\sum_{b \in \mathcal{B}_f} len(b)$, i.e., the total number of instructions in $CFG_f$; and $\mu$ is $max_{b \in \mathcal{B}_f} len(b)$, i.e., the maximum length of a basic block in $CFG_f$. Let $\mathcal{S}_f$ denote the* summary set *of functions that share the same summary as $f$, including $f$.*

However, in our experience, using such summaries for function matching in real-world programs with hundreds of thousands of lines of code, such as CPython[4], can lead to a substantial number of false matching candidates. Large codebases typically contain many tiny functions, possibly consisting of only a single basic block. Consequently these blocks will most likely be matched as identical in terms of their function summaries. To combat this issue, we extended the function summaries with additional metrics to reduce the number of false matches. These extended summaries are then used only in the strictest matching heuristic.

**Definition 6 (Extended Function Summary).** *Let $CFG_f$ be the function control flow graph of a function $f$. An* extended function summary $ES$ *of a function $f$ is a tuple $ES_f = (\nu, \beta, \phi, \epsilon, \iota, \mu)$ where $\nu$ is the name of the function $f$ and the remaining members of the tuple have the same meaning as in $S_f$.*

*Extended Function Summary Exact Matches.* Our first heuristic matches functions from $\mathcal{F}_{P_b}$ and $\mathcal{F}_{P_t}$ that have the same extended summaries. In particular, it matches functions that have identical name in the baseline and target versions, as well as the key characteristics of their FCFG, i.e., the function summaries. The goal is to quickly identify functions that have either not changed at all or changed just enough to not affect their FCFG in the target version.

---

[4] The reference C implementation of Python interpreter: https://github.com/python/cpython.

*Function Summary Unique Renames.* Our second heuristic attempts to match functions that appear to be simply renamed without any substantial change that would alter their FCFG. First, we identify functions whose name appears exclusively in the target or baseline version denoted as $\mathcal{F}_{missing} \subseteq \mathcal{F}_{P_b}$ and $\mathcal{F}_{new} \subseteq \mathcal{F}_{P_t}$, respectively. Next, we match only those functions $f_m \in \mathcal{F}_{missing}$ and $f_n \in \mathcal{F}_{new}$ that have the same unique function summary, meaning no other functions $f'_m \in \mathcal{F}_{missing}, f'_m \neq f_m$ or $f'_n \in \mathcal{F}_{new}, f'_n \neq f_n$ belong to $\mathcal{S}_{(f_m, f_n)}$, i.e., share the same function summary.

*Function Summary Exclusive Renames.* The last heuristic aims to match renamed functions that did not meet the summary uniqueness criteria in the *Function Summary Unique Renames* heuristic and instead satisfy the summary and FCFG *exclusiveness* condition. We consider two functions $f_m \in \mathcal{F}_{missing}$ and $f_n \in \mathcal{F}_{new}$ to have an exclusive summary and FCFG[5] iff their summaries and FCFGs are equal, hence must belong to the same summary set $\mathcal{S}_{(f_m, f_n)}$, and $\nexists f' \in \mathcal{S}_{(f_m, f_n)} \cap (\mathcal{F}_{missing} \cup \mathcal{F}_{new})$ whose $FCFG_{f'}$ is equal to $FCFG_{f_m}$ or $FCFG_{f_n}$. The exclusiveness check is iteratively repeated until no new renames are found as the FCFG equality check result depends on the so-far known renames (see Sect. 4.4). Intuitively, this heuristic relaxes the requirement of summary uniqueness and instead, as a trade-off, introduces a new requirement of FCFG equality. Note that summary equality generally does not imply FCFG equality due to possible changes on the instruction level of individual basic blocks.

## 4.2 Function Matching Using Call Contexts

The next three heuristics are based on the notion of function's immediate neighbourhood in terms of the call relation.

**Definition 7 (Function Call Context).** *The caller context $\overline{C}_f$ of a function $f \in P$ is the set of functions in $P$ that may call $f$, formally: $\overline{C}_f = \{\overline{c} \mid (\overline{c}, f) \in \mathcal{E}_P\} \subseteq \mathcal{F}_P$. The callee context $\underline{C}_f$ of $f$ is the set of functions in $P$ that may be called from $f$, formally: $\underline{C}_f = \{\underline{c} \mid (f, \underline{c}) \in \mathcal{E}_P\} \subseteq \mathcal{F}_P$. The function call context $\overline{\underline{C}}$ of $f$ is then $\overline{\underline{C}}_f = \overline{C}_f \cup \underline{C}_f$.*

Note that in practice when comparing the $\overline{C}$, $\underline{C}$ or the entire $\overline{\underline{C}}$ of two functions, the function names within the sets must be translated according to the already known function renames.

*Unique Function Call Contexts.* The first heuristic matches a function $f_b \in \mathcal{F}_{P_b}$ with $f_t \in \mathcal{F}_{P_t}$ iff they have the the same *unique* $\overline{C}$, $\underline{C}$ and their names are either identical or are candidates for a rename, i.e., $f_b \in \mathcal{F}_{missing} \subseteq \mathcal{F}_{P_b}$ and $f_t \in \mathcal{F}_{new} \subseteq \mathcal{F}_{P_t}$. Intuitively, this approach can match functions that might

---

[5] Note that the FCFG equality check is done using the algorithm introduced in Sect. 4.4.

have different summaries and/or FCFGs as long as the functions $f_b$ and $f_t$ are used in exactly the same call contexts, thus nicely complementing the summaries heuristics.

*Equal Function Call Contexts.* This next heuristic relaxes the uniqueness requirement of the previous heuristic and instead limits the matching only to functions with the same name to reduce the risk of false matches. More concretely, function $f_b \in \mathcal{F}_{P_b}$ and a function $f_t \in \mathcal{F}_{P_t}$ will be matched iff their $\overline{C}$, $\underline{C}$ and names are equal.

*Similar Function Call Contexts.* This last heuristic matches functions $f_b \in \mathcal{F}_{P_b}$ and $f_t \in \mathcal{F}_{P_t}$ with the same name and similar call contexts. We define context similarity in terms of subsets: contexts $\overline{\mathcal{C}}_{f_b}$ and $\overline{\mathcal{C}}_{f_t}$ are similar iff $\overline{\mathcal{C}}_{f_b} \subseteq \overline{\mathcal{C}}_{f_t} \vee \overline{\mathcal{C}}_{f_t} \subseteq \overline{\mathcal{C}}_{f_b}$ and $\underline{\mathcal{C}}_{f_b} \subseteq \underline{\mathcal{C}}_{f_t} \vee \underline{\mathcal{C}}_{f_t} \subseteq \underline{\mathcal{C}}_{f_b}$. The intuition behind this heuristic is that function call contexts may often change between versions and may contain new, or lack some previously present, callee or caller functions. To reduce the number of potential false matches, only functions with the same name are eligible for matching.

### 4.3   Heuristics Application Order

In general, we designed these heuristics to be applied in a sequence such that each subsequent heuristic tries to match the functions that still remain unmatched. Although these heuristics could be applied in an arbitrary order, we propose a specific application order: from the most strict to the most lenient ones. This way we avoid potential mis-matches that would happen if the lenient, low-confidence heuristics were applied first.

The proposed ordering is as follows: 1. *Extended Function Summary Exact Matches*, 2. *Function Summary Unique Renames*, 3. *Unique Function Call Contexts*, 4. *Function Summary Exclusive Renames*, 5. *Equal Function Call Contexts*, and 6. *Similar Function Call Contexts*.

Note that the heuristics are not applied in exactly the same order as they were defined.

The intuition behind this ordering is that the first three heuristics attempt to find the "low-hanging fruit" in terms of function similarity by checking for complete summary or context equality. *Function Summary Exclusive Renames* is used next as it relies on the already known renames from the second and third heuristics, and no subsequent heuristic is designed to identify renames. Also, while the *Unique Function Call Contexts* heuristic could potentially find more matches after the *Function Summary Exclusive Renames* is executed, the subsequent *Equal Function Call Contexts* heuristic will be able to identify those as well, hence no precision is lost by this specific ordering.

The last two heuristics work the best when the known renames mapping is as precise as possible, hence why they are applied only after all the heuristics that can extend the known renames mapping. Naturally, the *Similar Function Call Contexts* heuristic is potentially the least precise one, and as such is left to be applied the last. Any remaining functions not matched by any of the heuristics are either considered a low confidence name-only match if they appear in both baseline and target, or new or deleted if their name counterpart is not found in the other version.

## 4.4    Control Flow Graph Difference Analysis

Once the function bijection $m$ is constructed (or when candidate matches are being evaluated, e.g., in the *Function Summary Exclusive Renames* heuristic), the matched functions may be compared. Our FCFG diff analysis algorithm works by traversing the $FCFG_{f_b}$ and $FCFG_{f_t}$ in lockstep in a deterministic manner and comparing every pair of visited edges and basic blocks according to the equality criterion. Given our use-case for FCFG diff analysis in Perun, the algorithm simply returns whether two functions are equal or not. Moreover, we can implement this check efficiently: upon encountering the first difference we can terminate the analysis early.

The traversal starts at the entry basic block and continues to the subsequent basic block through the next yet unvisited outgoing edge. We chose the next unvisited outgoing edge according to its type: the `fallthrough` edge has the highest priority as there may be at most one such edge; while the remaining `jump` edges are ordered according to the destination address to ensure deterministic traversal of the edges. Whenever the algorithm reaches a basic block that has no remaining unvisited outgoing edge, or the basic block is already present in the current CFG traversal path[6], the traversal backtracks to the previous basic block. We keep the current CFG path in a stack structure.

We compare individual basic blocks on a per-instruction basis: the instructions are iterated from the first to last and for each instruction, its *mnemonic* and operands are compared. However, comparing the individual basic blocks for an absolute equality is generally too strict in practice, as address or register operands might change in subsequent compilations due to a number of reasons not associated with code changes in the analysed function. Hence, we compare individual basic blocks in a generic manner – the algorithm defines several comparison criteria listed from the most to least strict: (1) absolute instructions and operands equality, (2) instructions equality with register bijection (3) instructions equality with register bijection and ignoring addresses or offsets, (4) instructions equality while ignoring the operands, and (6) the number of instructions. Note that when we compare the fully unfolded destinations of call instructions, i.e., we take into account any previously detected renaming.

## 4.5    Reusing Dynamic Models

We will close our approach with a discussion on how to efficiently reuse the dynamic models. We emphasize that obtaining precise dynamic control flow

---

[6] By CFG traversal path, we mean the sequence of basic blocks $BB_0, BB_1, \ldots, BB_i$ where each pair of adjacent basic blocks $(BB_n, BB_{n+1}) \in \mathcal{C}_P$ for $0 \leq n < n + 1 \leq i$.

models is often quite expensive as it typically entails, e.g., running the entire test suite with some form of profiling or tracing enabled. As such, when a control flow model is being constructed for a new project version, we reuse parts of the dynamic models observed in previous versions of the software. This way, we get to reduce the number of dynamic runs that need to be executed in order to improve the accuracy of the static models (and, in extreme cases, possibly even skip the runs altogether if the entire dynamic model can be reused). However, we want the reuse to be conservative to not accidentally include dynamic call relations that may no longer exist in the new versions of the project.

The algorithm for identifying reusable parts of the dynamic models iterates over all matched baseline and target function pairs $(f_b, f_t) \in m$ and evaluates whether the functions satisfy at least one of these two conditions: (1) the difference analysis determined that $f_t$ has not changed compared to $f_b$, or (2) the callee contexts restricted to the static control flow models only, $\mathcal{C}^s_{f_b}$ and $\mathcal{C}^s_{f_t}$, are equal. If at least one condition is satisfied, the entire dynamic callee context $\mathcal{C}^d_{f_b}$ is reused in $f_t$ as its dynamic callee context $\mathcal{C}^d_{f_t}$. The intuition is simple: if the FCFGs or callee contexts obtained by the same static analysis tools are identical, then the dynamic call relations are highly likely[7] to be present in the new project version as well – provided the same dynamic runs are still executable in the new project version.

As the algorithm depends on the function mapping and difference analysis results, it is currently scheduled only after those analyses have finished. However, we plan to explore the possibility of running the algorithm simultaneously with the function matching and diff analysis to improve both their recall and precision.

## 5    CPython Use-Case Demonstration

To demonstrate the capabilities and efficiency of the proposed heuristics and algorithms, we applied them on the CPython project; more precisely on its versions 3.10.4 and 3.11.0a7. We have selected two use-cases that demonstrate our approach.

- **UC1:** Constructing static control flow models of both CPython versions, and observing the efficiency and accuracy of both the function matching heuristics and diff analysis criteria.
- **UC2:** Comparing our matching heuristics with our implementation[8] of the matching algorithm described in [11].

We measured the results for both use-cases on a Linux Fedora 40 machine with 8 cores and 16 threads, AMD Ryzen 7 PRO 5850U 1.9 GHz CPU and 16 GB of RAM. All measurements were repeated 7 times with the first two runs being

---

[7] Nonetheless, this algorithm is generally not sound nor complete. More advanced inter-procedural analyses would likely be needed to enhance the precision of this algorithm.

[8] As far as we know, the authors did not publish a software artifact with their implementation.

discarded as warm-up runs. Our implementation is written in Python 3.10 and we used the *Angr* [15] library for the static CFM construction. The total number of functions discovered in the CPython binary by Angr in 3.10.4 and 3.11.0a7 versions is 5262 and 5486, respectively.

## 5.1   Use-Case 1: Function Matching and Diff Analysis

Table 1 shows the results obtained by running the heuristics in the proposed order on CFMs constructed for CPython 3.10.4 and 3.11.0a7. We list for each heuristic the number of matched functions as $|match|$, the number of identified renames as $|rename|$ and the number of remaining functions to match in each version as $|remain_{3.10}|$ and $|remain_{3.11}|$. Overall, our heuristics successfully matched 95% of the functions in both CPython versions and identified 22 renames out of 150 missing ($\mathcal{F}_{missing}$) and 374 new ($\mathcal{F}_{new}$) names. Functions identified as renames were manually inspected and we confirmed that they indeed represent a simple rename without a significant, that is, control flow model altering change. The remaining 219 *baseline* and 443 *target* unmatched functions represent either actually new and deleted functions, or functions that have structurally changed so much that it is unclear whether they are corresponding to their baseline or target counterpart in any other way than just by their name.

**Table 1.** An overview of the number of matches and renames identified by each individual heuristic. The heuristics were applied exactly in the order defined in Sect. 4.3.

| Function Matching Heuristic | $|match|$ | $|rename|$ | $|remain_{3.10}|$ | $|remain_{3.11}|$ |
|---|---|---|---|---|
| *Ext. Function Summary Exact Matches* | 3945 | 0 | 1317 | 1541 |
| *Function Summary Unique Renames* | 0 | 19 | 1298 | 1522 |
| *Unique Function Call Contexts* | 147 | 0 | 1151 | 1375 |
| *Function Summary Exclusive Renames* | 0 | 3 | 1148 | 1372 |
| *Equal Function Call Contexts* | 103 | 0 | 1045 | 1269 |
| *Similar Function Call Contexts* | **826** | 0 | 219 | 443 |
| **Total** | **5021 (95%)** | **22** | **219** | **443** |
| **Avg. runtime [s]** | 0.1569 | | | |

Table 2 shows the results of our FCFG diff analysis algorithm executed after the function matching step. The Table lists the different equality criteria described in Sect. 4.4 and the number of changed ($|changed|$), resp. unchanged ($|same|$), functions each criterion identified. We plan to build on the proposed difference analysis with these equality criteria, and possibly some more advanced tools such as DiffKemp [12], in our future work on optimised profiling. The optimised profiling relies, among other, on the ability to control the strictness of the function equality comparison within the employed function difference analysis, which is supported by our analysis approach.

**Table 2.** An overview of the number of functions identified as changed, resp. unchanged, using the various diff analysis equality criteria defined in Sect. 4.4.

| FCFG Diff Analysis Equality Criterion | $|changed|$ | $|same|$ | Avg. runtime [s] |
|---|---|---|---|
| *Exact instructions and operands equality* | 4002 | 1019 | 0.3100 |
| *Exact instructions equality, register and op. bijection* | 4001 | 1020 | 0.6173 |
| *Exact instructions equality and register bijection* | **1370** | **3651** | **2.3170** |
| *Exact instructions equality* | 1363 | 3657 | 0.9184 |
| *Instruction count* | 1285 | 3736 | 0.8184 |

### 5.2  Use-Case 2: Comparison

In the second use-case, we compared our three summaries-based and three call context matching heuristics with the existing two-step matching algorithm from [11]. We summarise the obtained results in Table 3; although the algorithm proposed by [11] managed to overall match approximately 3% more functions and identify almost four times more renames, it suffers from 25% false match rate and several orders of magnitude worse run time.

The vast difference in performance and false match rate can be explained by the assumption about the connectivity of the CG made by the authors of [11]. The originally proposed algorithm consists of two steps. First, a summary-based iterative matching is used; in its initial step, it finds exact and unique summary matches, and subsequently traverses and matches the rest of the CGs based on the existing call relations $\mathcal{C}_P$. However, for partially disconnected CGs with a lot of call context changes – e.g., CPython CGs of different major versions constructed by Angr – this approach may fail and lead to many unmatched functions. Second, the computationally expensive[9] and less precise N-gram similarity

**Table 3.** A comparison of identified matches, renames, false positives and runtime overhead of the proposed heuristics (divided into the summary-based and call context-based categories) with the two-step matching algorithm in [11].

| Algorithm | $|match|$ | $|rename|$ | $|false\ matches|$ | Avg. runtime [s] |
|---|---|---|---|---|
| *Proposed function summaries* | 3945 | 22 | 0 | 0.0817 |
| *Call contexts matching* | 1076 | 0 | 0 | 0.0752 |
| **Total** | 5021 | 22 | 0 | 0.1569 |
| *Function summaries in* [11] | 1703 | 9 | 20 | 1.3564 |
| *N-gram similarity matching in* [11] | 3475 | 80 | 1278 | 448.0557 |
| **Total** | 5178 | 89 | **1298** | **449.4121** |

[9] The algorithm needs to compute similarity for every pair of unmatched baseline and target functions. Each such function comparison entails the computation and comparison of N-gram sets for every pair of baseline and target basic blocks within those functions.

matching is used to match all of the remaining functions, resulting in poor performance and high false match rate as no cut-off value for the similarity measure is defined.

## 6   Conclusion

In this work we propose (1) an efficient layered control flow models representation that conservatively reuses parts of dynamic models, (2) a hierarchical versioning system for the storage of said models, (3) six function matching heuristics tailored specifically for evolving software, and (4) a fast control flow difference analysis algorithm.

We have demonstrated our function matching heuristics and diff analysis in an use-case with CPython project that resulted in a 95% functions successfully matched with no detected false positives tied to the function renames discovery. Although our heuristics match about 3% less functions compared to the existing approach in [11], they are faster by several orders of magnitude and work even on partially disconnected CGs.

**Acknowledgments.** The work was supported by the project GA23-06506S of the Czech Science Foundation, FIT-S-23-8151 of the BUT FIT, Brno Ph.D. Talent Programme, Red Hat Inc. and Horizon Europe CHESS 101087529.

**Disclosure of Interest.** Jiří Pavela and Tomáš Fiedor are, or have been in the past, funded by Red Hat, Inc. research scholarships.

## References

1. Infer: Differential workflow. https://fbinfer.com/docs/steps-for-ci/
2. Jenkins CI performance plugin. https://jenkinsci.github.io/performance-plugin/RunTests.html
3. Chen, J., Yu, D., Hu, H., Li, Z., Hu, H.: Analyzing performance-aware code changes in software development process. In: Proceedings of ICPC 2019, pp. 300–310 (2019)
4. Chen, J., Shang, W.: An exploratory study of performance regression introducing code changes. In: Proceedings of ICSME 2017, pp. 341–352 (2017)
5. Chen, T.H., Nagappan, M., Shihab, E., Hassan, A.E.: An empirical study of dormant bugs. In: Proceedings of MSR 2014, p. 82–91 (2014)
6. Fiedor, T., Pavela, J., Rogalewicz, A., Vojnar, T.: Perun: performance version system. In: Proceedings of ICSME 2022, pp. 499–503 (2022)
7. Fukami, C., Mccubbrey, D.: Colorado benefits management system (c): seven years of failure. Commun. Assoc. Inf. Syst. **29**, 97–102 (2011)
8. Hilton, M., Tunnell, T., Huang, K., Marinov, D., Dig, D.: Usage, costs, and benefits of continuous integration in open-source projects. In: Proceeding of ASE 2016, p. 426–437 (2016)
9. Humble, J.: Continuous delivery: evidence and case studies. https://continuousdelivery.com/evidence-case-studies/

10. Javed, O., Dawes, J.H., Han, M., Franzoni, G., Pfeiffer, A., Reger, G., Binder, W.: PERFCI: a toolchain for automated performance testing during continuous integration of python projects. In: Proceedings of ASE 2020, pp. 1344–1348 (2020)

11. Lee, Y.R., Kang, B., Im, E.G.: Function matching-based binary-level software similarity calculation. In: Proceedings of RACS 2013, p. 322–327 (2013)

12. Malík, V., Vojnar, T.: Automatically checking semantic equivalence between versions of large-scale c projects. In: Proceedings of ICST 2021, pp. 329–339 (2021)

13. Nagarajan, V., Gupta, R., Zhang, X., Madou, M., de Sutter, B., de Bosschere, K.: Matching control flow of program versions. In: Proceedings of ICSM 2007, pp. 84–93 (2007)

14. Rimsa, A., Nelson Amaral, J., Pereira, F.M.Q.: Practical dynamic reconstruction of control flow graphs. Softw. Pract. Exp. **51**(2), 353–384 (2021)

15. Shoshitaishvili, Y., et al.: SOK: (State of) The Art of War: offensive techniques in binary analysis. In: Proceedings of SP 2016 (2016)

16. Zaman, S., Adams, B., Hassan, A.E.: Security versus performance bugs: a case study on firefox. In: Proceedings of MSR 2011, p. 93–102 (2011)

# Textile Sensor Surrogate Modeling Using Sparse Identification

Martin Steiger$^{(\boxtimes)}$ , Phillip Petz , and Stephan Schuler

Univeristy of Applied Sciences Upper Austria, Hagenberg, Austria
{martin.steiger,phillip.petz,stephan.schuler}@fh-hagenberg.at

**Abstract.** This paper addresses a possible surrogate model of a textile-based force sensor as introduced by Schuler et al., that is based on capacitance changes of conductive pads on the sensor surface caused by physical deformation. The proposed model is supposed to capture dynamic relationships between capacitance, force, and pull distance using a novel approach based on discrete Preisach hysteresis models in combination with Sparse Identifications of Non-linear Dynamics (SINDy), that is especially suitable for embedded systems applications.

**Keywords:** Soft Sensors · Sparse Identification · Hysteresis Modeling

## 1 Soft Textile Sensor Principle

Schuler et al. [8] conducted a preliminary study to investigate the fabrication and calibration of a textile-based shear force sensor as depicted in Fig. 3. This research provided a heuristic model to approximate sensor performance metrics, whereby the empirical validation revealed a major accuracy issue. Main cause are the hysteretic properties of the sensor material also investigated in [12]. Compensating this error is especially difficult when integrating the sensor in resource-limited embedded systems. Given the difficulties using surrogate models as a predictive tool is advantageous.

We propose a hysteretic approach based on the well-known discrete Preisach models [7] due to its trivial implementation in hardware. Figure 1 and 2 provide a glimpse of the available force sensor measurements of Schuler at al. [8], whereby following visual insights a hysteresis can be spotted regarding pull distance and associated pull force (Fig. 1). However no such correlation is visible comparing the corresponding capacitance changes to the pull force at first glance (Fig. 2), because they essentially follow the pull force and not the pull distance curve. Therefore we follow a technique introduced by Brunton et al. [4], which is capable of both modeling statical and dynamical relations between measurements when set up accordingly called Sparse Identification of non-linear Dynamics. With this technique we hope to find surrogate models that describe the mapping of the capacitance data to the force and furthermore to the pull distance.

A. Quesada-Arencibia et al. (Eds.): EUROCAST 2024, LNCS 15172, pp. 429–442, 2025.
https://doi.org/10.1007/978-3-031-82949-9_38

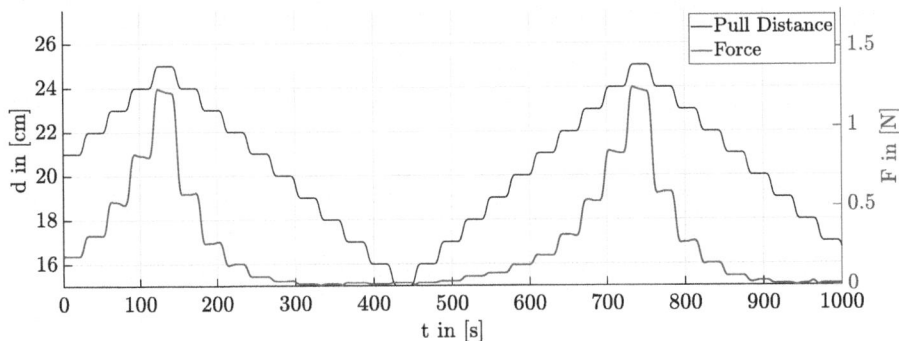

**Fig. 1.** Textile force sensor data: pull distance/force over time (left), pull force over pull distance (right).

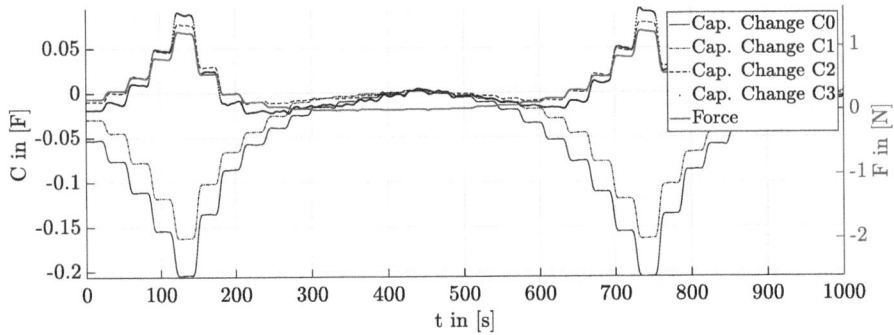

**Fig. 2.** Textile force sensor: capacitance changes ($C0...C3$) over time.

## 2   Sparse Identification of Non-linear Dynamics

There exist various ways to model non-linear dynamical system behaviour from measurement data ranging from simple block-oriented models known from classical digital signal processing (e.g. Hammerstein/Wiener cascades) to sophisticated methods based on neural networks such as neural ordinary differential equations (N-ODEs) [5]. However most of these models are black-box, therefore they are not meant to be interpretable. Recently a method introduced by Brunton et al. [4] has sparked attention for being able to discover governing system equations from possibly noisy measurement data using sparsity-promoting regression algorithms. Although this method is originally designed to identify non-linear ordinary differential equations of the form $d/dt\ u(t) = f(u(t))$, a generalization to $y(t) = f(u(t))$ is straightforward and beneficial for further considerations. Let be given time series measurement data of two signals $u(t) \in \mathbb{R}^m, y(t) \in \mathbb{R}^n$ as $U = (u(t_\ell))_{\ell=0}^{L-1}$ and $Y = (y(t_\ell))_{\ell=0}^{L-1}$ at $L$ collocation points $t_\ell$. Those collocation points are not necessarily equidistant. Furthermore let be given an ansatz function library with $K$ elements as in Definition 1.

**Definition 1 (Ansatz Function Library).** *Let be given* $K$ *non-conjugate maps* $a_k : \mathbb{R}^m \to \mathbb{R}$. *A set of such distinguishable ansatz functions is defined as*

$$\mathcal{A} = \{a_k : \mathbb{R}^m \to \mathbb{R}, k = 1...K \mid a_i \neq a_j \forall i, j \in \{1, 2, ..., K\}\} \tag{1}$$

*and is called an ansatz function library.*

We propose

**Theorem 1.** *Any memoryless* $f : \mathbb{R}^m \to \mathbb{R}^n$ *can be approximated with a weighted sum of appropriate ansatz functions in the library* $\mathcal{A}$ *as* $f(u) \approx \hat{f}(u) = \mathcal{A}(u)\Xi,\ \Xi \in \mathbb{R}^{K \times n}$

Following Theorem 1, we are confronted with a simple linear regression problem to determine the weight coefficients $\Xi$ of the proposed model

$$\hat{\Xi} = \underset{\Xi}{\operatorname{argmin}}(||Y - \mathcal{A}(U)\Xi||_2) = \mathcal{A}(U)^+ Y \tag{2}$$

which can be solved using the Moore-Penrose pseudo inverse $\mathcal{A}(U)^+$, SVD or equivalent algorithms. However, Brunton et al. suggest that $\Xi$ is usually sparse since real dynamical systems typically contain few relevant terms [4]. To promote sparsity, the minimization problem is redefined

$$\hat{\Xi} = \underset{\Xi}{\operatorname{argmin}}(||Y - \mathcal{A}(U)\Xi||_2 + \lambda ||\Xi||_p) \tag{3}$$

by also minimizing the weight coefficient $p$-norms. The selection of $p$ is crucial for the required optimization procedure, as $p = 0$ yields a mixed integer optimization problem and $p = 1$ resembles LASSO regression [10]. As mentioned, Brunton et al. introduced the model in Theorem 1 to determine the governing equations of an ordinary differential equation. For this case $y(t)$ simply resembles the derivative of the system state variable $u(t)$, which may either be measured or numerically calculated using an arbitrary difference operator $D$.

$$Y = \dot{U} = D \cdot U \tag{4}$$

There exist various extensions of this algorithm for noisy measurement data, reconstructing implicit equations and for other different dynamical system forms such as difference equations. As an example, we utilize the methods based on sparse identification of non-linear dynamics (SINDy) [4] to model the force acting on a textile-based sensor developed by Schuler et al. [8]. It is composed of four conductive pads on top of an elastic piece of fabric with a ground plane on the bottom as depicted in Fig. 3. Consequently those pads can act as plate capacitors, whereby their respective capacitance is attached to the pad geometry and consequently to the deformation of the fabric medium. Schuler et al. tested the sensor principle by measuring the capacitance changes when pulling the fabric for fixed distances on a testing rig. As mentioned in Sect. 3, there are dynamical effects present in the time series measurement data, namely the pull force time series includes a hysteresis with regard to the pull distance. This originates from the elastic properties of the fabric medium. However this behaviour seems to affect the capacitance values too. In an attempt to generate an approximate model of the pull force based on the capacitance values, we employ a simple memory-less polynomial model of 3rd order containing up to three unique multiplicative capacitance value combinations per ansatz function, e.g., $C_0, ..., C_3$, $C_0^2, C_0 \cdot C_1, ..., C_3^2, C_0^3, C_0^2 \cdot C_1, ..., C_3^3$. For this purpose, the available data set has been split into a training and test portion to estimate the model quality. We evaluated several possible ansatz function orders, but found as evidenced in Table 1 that increasing the order parameter decreases the training data approximation error, but limits model generalization in general, indicated by an increase in the test data error. Even a simple linear model yields remarkably good results and anything beyond 3rd order is therefore discarded as non-beneficial (Fig. 4).

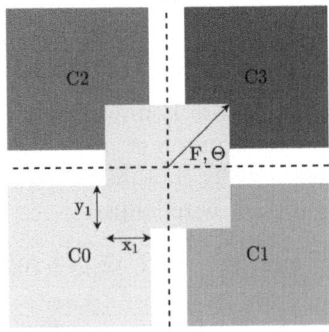

**Fig. 3.** Textile force sensor layout according to Schuler at al. [8].

**Table 1.** NRMSE, $R^2$ errors regarding memory-less SINDy models to approximate the pulling force from capacitances.

| Model | Training Data | | Test Data | |
|---|---|---|---|---|
| | NRMSE | $R^2$ [%] | NRMSE | $R^2$ [%] |
| 1st order | 8.5e−2 | 99.27 | 7.8e−2 | 99.41 |
| 2nd order | 6.6e−2 | 99.56 | 9.6e−2 | 99.16 |
| 3rd order | 5.5e−2 | 99.69 | 12e−2 | 99.08 |
| 4th order | 4.7e−2 | 99.77 | 14e−2 | 98.02 |

Contrary to Sect. 1, even a simple static model can be used to calibrate the force sensor accordingly and accurately reconstruct pull forces based on capacitance readings. However, this paper goes one step beyond: can the pull distance be modeled based on the capacitance values? As displayed in Fig. 1, there

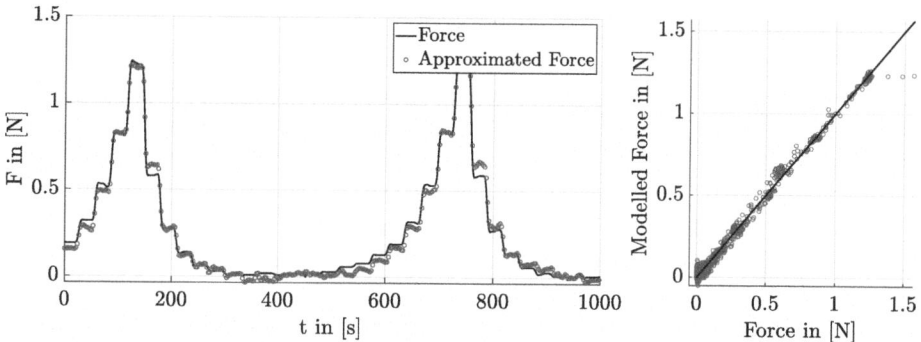

**Fig. 4.** Application of a 3rd order polynomial SINDy model (blue) on the capacitance data $C_0, ..., C_3$ to model the pull force (red). (Color figure online)

is clearly a hysteretic connection between pull distance and pull force, resulting from the fabrics material properties. Such hystereses can only be modeled dynamically, as conducted within the next Section.

## 3    Sparse Hysteretic Models

Ordinary, partial and differential algebraic equations are one way to describe dynamical systems, whose output depends on the history of inputs resp. the system state itself. Hysteresis models provide another approach to describe natural phenomenons in mechanics, physics etc. For the scalar case let $u(t) \in \mathbb{R}$ be a system input and $y(t) \in \mathbb{R}$ be the corresponding system output at time $t \geq 0$. Applying the definition of Willerich [11] inspired by Bertotti [2] and Visintin [9] yields

**Definition 2 (General Hysteresis Operator).** *Let be given maps* $u : [0, t] \rightarrow \mathbb{R}, u \in \mathcal{C}^0([0, t])$ *and* $y$. *Then the mapping* $\mathcal{H} : \mathbb{R} \rightarrow \mathbb{R}$ *is called the general hysteresis operator if the following conditions are met*

1. *rate-independence*
   *Let be given a continuous and monotonous map* $\phi : [0, T] \rightarrow [0, T]$ *with* $\phi(0) = 0$ *and* $\phi(T) = T$. *Then*

$$\mathcal{H}[u \circ \phi] = \mathcal{H}[u] \qquad (5)$$

2. *causality*
   *The value of* $y(t), t \in [0, T]$ *depends on the current input value* $u(t)$ *and past input values* $u(\tau), \tau \in [0, t]$. *For two functions* $u_{1t}$ *and* $u_{2t}$ *of the form*

$$u_t(\tau) = \begin{cases} u(\tau) & 0 \leq \tau \leq t, \\ u(t) & t < \tau \leq T \end{cases} \qquad (6)$$

$u_{1t} = u_{2t}$ *implies that* $y_{1t} = y_{2t}$.

Equation (5) states that the general hysteresis operator $\mathcal{H}$ is invariant of time scale warping if the start and end value are the same. Furthermore Eq. (6) implies that $y$ only depends on an initial value and the evolution of the input value $u$ [11]. There are many approaches to design the hysteresis operator, but in this document reconstructing $\mathcal{H}$ from measurement data shall be the main topic. Let be given a discrete set of scalar time domain measurements $D = \{u(t_i), y(t_i)\}_{i=0}^{N-1}$ on an (equidistant) discrete time grid $(t_i)_{i=0}^{N-1}$, $\{i \in [1, ..., N-1] | t_{i+1} - t_i = \Delta t\}$ of the in- and outputs of an arbitrary non-linear system. We imply that an appropriate model to reconstruct $y$ given $u$ is a hysteresis, which can usually be verified by visual inspection of the measurements.

### 3.1  Discrete Preisach Hysteresis

Scalar Preisach hysteresis operators are well-established models to describe systems as in Definition 2. It consists of the superposition of finitely many so-called relay operators, whereby the most elementary form is called the Preisach relay as depicted in Fig. 5. A mathematical description is provided in Definition 3 according to Willerich [11].

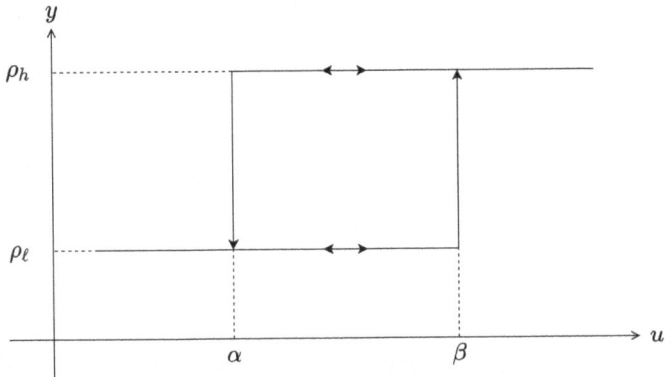

**Fig. 5.** Preisach relay operator.

**Definition 3 (Preisach Relay).** *Let be given two model parameters* $\alpha, \beta \in \mathbb{R}$ *with* $\beta \geq \alpha$ *and an initial relay state* $\rho_0 \in \{\rho_\ell, \rho_h\}$, *whereby* $\rho_h > \rho_\ell$ *then we define a relay map* $\mathcal{R}_{\alpha,\beta}[u, \rho_0](t) : \mathbb{R} \to \mathbb{R}$. *Additionally, we define* $X_u(t) := \{\tau \in (0, t] : u(\tau) = \alpha \text{ or } \beta\}$ *to keep track at which times* $u$ *reaches the* *relay thresholds [1]*

$$\mathcal{R}_{\alpha,\beta}[u,\rho_0](0) = \begin{cases} \rho_h & \text{if } u(0) > \beta, \\ \rho_0 & \text{if } \alpha < u(0) < \beta, \\ \rho_\ell & \text{if } u(0) < \alpha. \end{cases}$$

$$\mathcal{R}_{\alpha,\beta}[u,\rho_0](t) = \begin{cases} \mathcal{R}_{\alpha,\beta}[u,\rho_0](0) & \text{if } X_u(t) = \emptyset, \\ \rho_\ell & \text{if } X_u(t) \neq \emptyset \text{ and } u(\max X_u(t)) = \alpha, \\ \rho_h & \text{if } X_u(t) \neq \emptyset \text{ and } u(\max X_u(t)) = \beta. \end{cases} \quad (7)$$

The first part of Eq. (7) determines the initial state of the Preisach relay operator based on a previously selected $\rho_0$ and the second part evaluates what threshold $\{\alpha, \beta\}$ has been reached last. Furthermore $\rho_\ell$ and $\rho_h$ are usually set to $\pm 1$, but other values may be chosen. As already mentioned the weighted superposition of Preisach relays with different threshold parameters (but the same initial value) forms the Preisach operator $\mathcal{P}[u,\rho_0](t) : \mathcal{C}^0(0,t) \to \mathbb{R}$. Formally there are two ways to describe $\mathcal{P}$, namely a discrete and continuous formulation. Since we have given a set of discrete measurement points $D$ that characterize the desired hysteresis behaviour, the discrete variant is used in the following. For the sake of completeness, the continuous Preisach operator states over a set of thresholds $S := \{(\alpha, \beta) | \alpha, \beta \in \mathbb{R}, \beta \geq \alpha\}$ and an Lebesgue integrable weighting function $w(\alpha, \beta)$ [11].

$$\mathcal{P}_c[u,\rho_0](t) = \int \int_S w(\alpha, \beta) \mathcal{R}_{\alpha,\beta}[u,\rho_0](t) d\alpha d\beta \quad (8)$$

As evident, finding an appropriate weight function $w(\alpha, \beta)$ is a challenging task and the discrete model shall be used instead. Furthermore the discrete variant is advantageous in embedded systems environments.

$$\mathcal{P}_d[u,\rho_0](t) = \sum_{k=1}^{K} w_k \mathcal{R}_{\alpha_k,\beta_k}[u,\rho_0] \quad (9)$$

whereby $K \in \mathbb{Z}$ is a finite number and $(\alpha_k, \beta_k)$ are unique combinations of threshold parameters. When using a Preisach operator of standard measure, the thresholds $\alpha_1, ..., \alpha_K$ and $\beta_1, ..., \beta_K$ are spaced by regular intervals, fulfilling our threshold criterion $\beta_k > \alpha_k$. This can be visualized appropriately by introducing a plane as in the original paper by Preisach [7], also called the Preisach plane. It is a 2D plane, whereby the threshold parameters $(\alpha, \beta)$ represent the axes and in which the state of all relays can be visualized. Left in Fig. 6 the discrete grid of the threshold parameters is displayed. On the right hand side, an exemplary visualization of the relay states is depicted. Blue nodes represent relay operators which currently yield $\rho_\ell$ and red nodes those which yield $\rho_h$. At first, all relay operators emit the initial system state $\rho_0$ (set to $\rho_\ell$ in this scenario). If the system input $u$ rises above a threshold $T_\beta$ all relays with $\beta_k < T_\beta$ switch to $\rho_h$ (upper right corner). Increasing the signal even further causes more relays to display such behaviour. Decreasing $u$ below a threshold $T_\alpha$ causes the relays with $\alpha_k > T_\alpha$ to turn off again (bottom right corner). The dividing line between 'on' and 'off' relays resembles a staircase curve, which in turn contains all information of the Preisach relays. For continuous models, this curve can be evaluated using the Everett function [11].

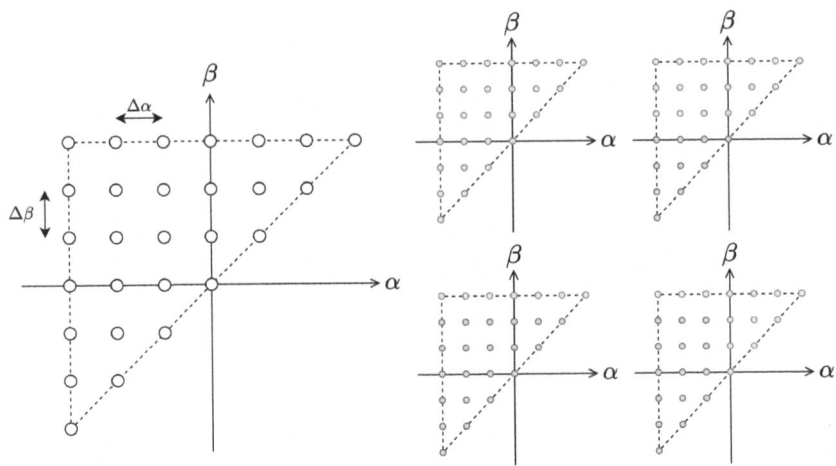

**Fig. 6.** Discrete Preisach plane (left) and Preisach staircase curve (right) for a given $u(t)$. (Color figure online)

In order to create a Preisach model using system measurements $D$, we have to determine the weight coefficients in Eq. (9) given a set of threshold values $\alpha$ and $\beta$. Initially we separate the set of time series into input $U = (u_n)_{n=0}^{N-1}$ and output signals $Y = (y_n)_{n=0}^{N-1}$, whereby $u_n$ respectively $y_n$ represent $u(t_n)$ and $y(t_n)$ within an equidistant time grid. All vector notations are column vectors if not stated otherwise. We approximate

$$Y = \mathcal{H}[U] \approx \mathcal{P}_d[U, \rho_0] = \sum_{k=1}^{K} w_k \mathcal{R}_{\alpha_k, \beta_k}[U, \rho_0] = \mathcal{R}_{\alpha, \beta}[U, \rho_0]W \qquad (10)$$

whereby $W$ represents a $\mathbb{R}^K$ weight column vector and $\mathcal{R}_{\alpha, \beta}$ a $\mathbb{R}^{N \times K}$ of evaluated relay elements with different threshold parameter pairs. A problem of similar form has been introduced by Brunton [4] when first presenting the SINDy method. The only significant difference is that the weight vector $W$ is not assumed sparse. However experiments indicate that $W$ indeed contains few relevantly large elements. Consequently we apply the SINDy method on the following optimization problem

$$\hat{W} = \underset{\xi}{\operatorname{argmin}} \left( ||Y - \mathcal{R}_{\alpha, \beta}[U, \rho_0]W||_2 + \lambda||W||_\epsilon \right) \qquad (11)$$

whereby $\lambda||W||_\epsilon$ is a regularization term to encourage sparsity. As a reminder, SINDy utilizes a large library of potential ansatz functions to select the most relevant elements whose weighted sum approximate an arbitrary non-linearity. We may choose those ansatz functions as we please and are consequently treating the relay operators as pseudo functions. Furthermore the original SINDy paper proposes the sequential thresholded linear least squares algorithm [4], which is also utilized to solve Eq. (11). What remains is the relay threshold parameter selection as depicted in Fig. 6 for discrete models. Minimum (the smallest $\alpha$) and maximum (largest $\beta$) of the thresholds is largely determined by the corresponding dynamic range of the measurement data. As a variable parameter we introduced the number of relays along the edges of the triangle defined in the discrete Preisach plane in Fig. 6. As a test of the proposed method, we have given various measurements of the textile-based force sensor by Schuler et al. [8] being stretched by a fixed distance. Those contain the pull distance, required pull force the capacitances at the four conductive pads and the ambient temperature. Similar to Hookes law of elasticity, there is a hysteresis relationship between the pull distance and required force, which we try to model using a Preisach operator with 1325 relay elements in total ($M = 50$ elements on the triangle sides). The optimization results using the SINDy methods are depicted in Fig. 7.

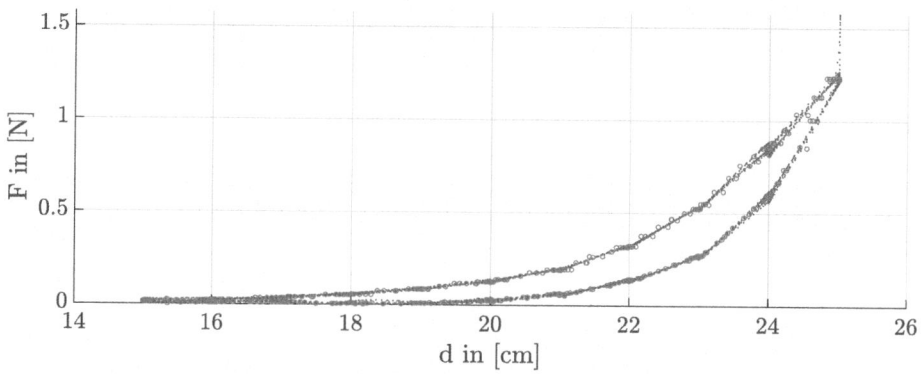

**Fig. 7.** Hysteresis comparison of the original data (red) and the found Preisach model (blue). (Color figure online)

## 3.2   Adaptive Hysteron Grid

An elementary hurdle of the used discrete Preisach model is the selection of Preisach relay (hysteron) parameters $\alpha_k$ and $\beta_k$. In the previous chapter the grid spacing within the Preisach plane is set to be uniform, which automatically involves a trade-off. A close-meshed grid leads to a larger model with potentially high accuracy, but is prone to overfitting and requires elaborate calculations. On the other hand a coarse grid leads to compact models with lower overall accuracy which may be unable to capture essential hysteresis features. To automate this trade-off we propose a non-uniform plane grid that has higher density in regions of interest, similar to the ones used in spline regression. As a reminder, splines are commonly used to approximate smooth non-linear memory-less functions $y(x)$

$$\hat{a} = \underset{a}{\operatorname{argmin}} \left\{ ||Y - \sum_{i=1}^{q+K+1} a_i B_{i,Q,\tau_i}(X)||_2 \right\} \qquad (12)$$

whereby $Q$ is the spline order, $K$ is the number of knots (anchor points) and $B_{i,Q,\tau_i}$ resembles a single B-spline as introduced by De Boor [3]. Without deep-diving into spline theory, those B-splines are parameterized by so-called knots $\tau$ that usually span the (expected) dynamic range of $x$ and have different multiplicities dependig on the desired smoothness. A spline of order $Q$ is a piece-wise polynomial function of order $Q$ such that its derivatives up to order $Q-1$ are continuous at every knot [6]. Consequently we are presented with a similar selection problem as with the hysteron parameters: many knots lead to accurate models but are prone to overfitting and vice versa. In spline theory, there already exist many approaches to automatically choose appropriate non-uniform knot spacings that avoid over- or underfitting the data. The most commonly used method is the penalized spline estimation whereby the coefficients $a_i$ are constrained

$$\hat{a} = \underset{a}{\operatorname{argmin}} \left\{ ||Y - \sum_{i=1}^{Q+K+1} a_i B_{i,Q,\tau_i}(X)||_2 \right\} \text{ s.t. } \sum_{i=1}^{Q+K+1} a_i^2 < C \qquad (13)$$

This basically resembles the optimization problem in Eq. (11), causing some coefficients $a_i$ to vanish and therefore ignoring some knots. Consequently we have implicitly done that already. However this is not computationally efficient, as the underlying model still has to be large since most implementations start with a uniform time grid.

A second method is provided by De Boor [3] and exists as an up-to-date MAT-LAB routine (newknt) translated from a FORTRAN77 subroutine (newnot). This routine attempts to find the best placement of knots that minimizes the error of an existing $Q$-th order spline approximation $F$ with $Q + K + 1 = N$ coefficients. Initially the knots are equidistributed on $(A, B) = (\tau_1, \tau_N)$. Those knots are now re-distributed according to the $K$-th root of the $K$-th derivative of $F$, whereby high absolute values of the derivative lead to more knots in this area. Simplified, this means that there are more knots places in areas with lots of changes, yielding better approximation accuracy and smoothness. A more sophisticated pseudo-code is given in Algorithm 1. We can also apply this method in a hysteresis context. Instead of a non-uniform Preisach plane, we can identify an adaptive hysteron grid as in Fig. 8 that contains more hysterons in areas with rapid changes, increasing the overall discrete Preisach model resolution in the areas of interest and yielding more accurate approximation results.

The comparison of both the penalizing method (which is implicitly performed by SINDy) on its own and combined with the adaptive hysteron method starting from the same uniform Preisach plane grid are depicted in Table 2. It can be observed that the adaptive methods yields higher accuracy, but also a way less sparse weight vector $W$ as in the optimization problem (11) due to overfitting. In comparison to the achieved accuracy improvement, this trade-off has to be considered carefully.

---

**Algorithm 1.** De Boor optimized knot sequence [3], `newnot F77`

---

1: $F$ is an existing spline approximation with $N$ uniform knots in $(A, B) = (\tau_1, \tau_N)$
2: create a piece-wise const. $H_K \propto d^K F$ with break sequence $\tau$ iteratively, $H_0 = (F(\tau_1), ..., F(\tau_N))$, be aware that $\tau$ has a higher multiplicity at the edges (e.g. $\tau = [1, 1, 1, 2, 3, 4, 5, 5, 5])$
3: **for** k = 1 ... $K$ **do**
4:     **for** i = 1 ... $N - 1$ **do**
5:         $H_{k,i} = \frac{|H_{k-1,i}|}{\tau_{i+1}-\tau_{i-1}} + \frac{|H_{k-1,i+1}|}{\tau_{i+2}-\tau_i}$
6:     **end for**
7: **end for**
8: create a piece-wise lin. function by integrating $H_K$, $G(X) = \int_A^X H_K(Y)^{1/K} dY$
9: the new knots $\tilde{\tau}$ are determined iteratively
10: **for** i = 1 ... $N + 1$ **do**
11:     $s = G(B)/N$ (step size)
12:     $\tilde{\tau}_i = A + G^{-1}((i-1)s)$
13: **end for**

---

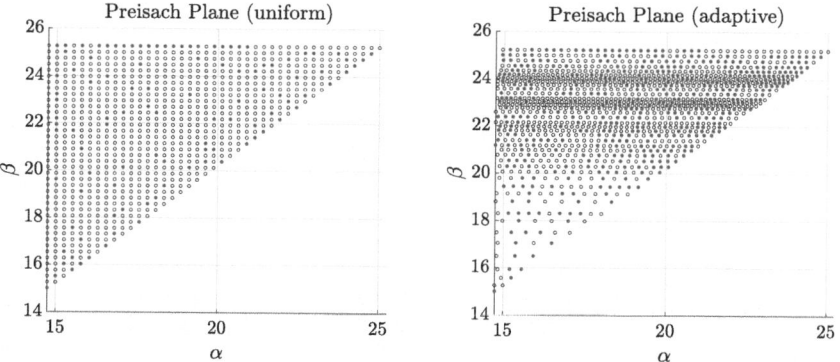

**Fig. 8.** Preisach planes with uniform (left) and adaptive hysteron grid (right). Non-zero weighted hysterons are marked red. (Color figure online)

**Table 2.** NRMSE, $R^2$ and NNZ performance metric for uniform and adaptive hysteron grid.

| Model | Training Data | | Test Data | | |
|---|---|---|---|---|---|
| | NRMSE | $R^2$ [%] | NRMSE | $R^2$ [%] | NNZ |
| Uniform Hysterons | 5.13e-2 | 99.74 | 5.52e-2 | 99.74 | 109 |
| Adaptive Hysterons | 4.39e-2 | 99.81 | 5.12e-2 | 99.78 | 478 |

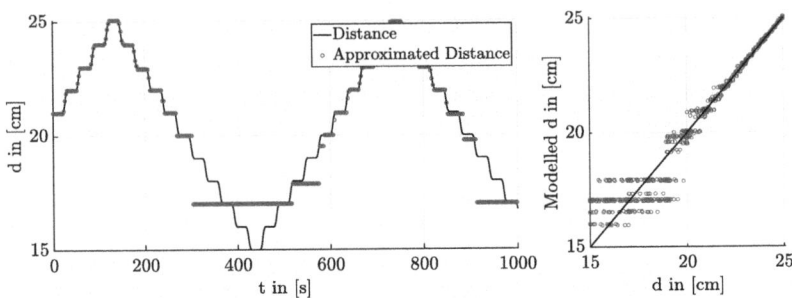

**Fig. 9.** Application of a 3rd order polynomial SINDy model + uniform reverse hysteresis (blue) on the capacitance data $C_0, ..., C_3$ to model the pull distance (red) (Color figure online)

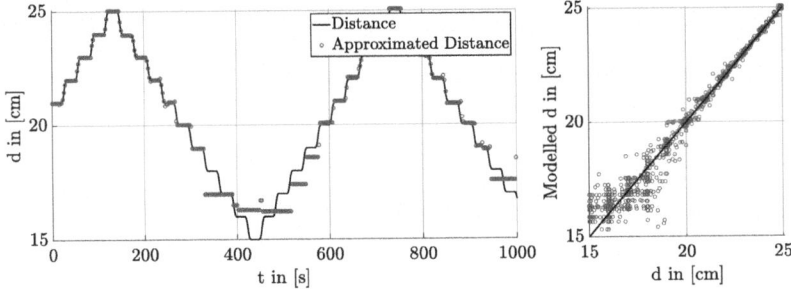

**Fig. 10.** Application of a 3rd order polynomial SINDy model + non-uniform reverse hysteresis (blue) on the capacitance data $C_0, ..., C_3$ to model the pull distance (red) (Color figure online)

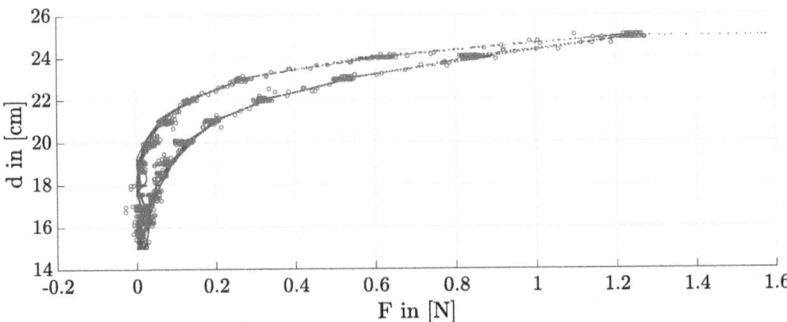

**Fig. 11.** Hysteresis comparison of the distance data (red) and the found Preisach model (blue) (Color figure online)

# 4    Conclusions

In Sect. 3.1 an accurate surrogate model has been provided to calculate the pull force based on the pull distance with a hysteretic mapping. However the research question in Sect. 2 is whether the pull distance can be estimated based on capacitive changes in the textile force sensor pads. Since both a (non)linear static model for estimating the pull force from the pad capacitances and a dynamical model that connects pull distance and force can be provided, finding a surrogate model mapping $C0...C3$ onto the pull distance is trivial. The hysteretic model from Sect. 3.1 simply has to be inverted and we can reuse our static model directly. However, since pull distances below 20 cm do not lead to a significant pull force as evidenced visually in Fig. 1, we expect the resulting model to perform poorly for low pull distances. This is also displayed in Fig. 9 in case of a Preisach model with uniform knots and Fig. 10 for non-uniform knots. For this reverse hysteretic model, the adaptive hysteron grid proves beneficial as low pull distances essentially represent a very steep section in the resulting force-distance hysteresis as displayed in Fig. 11. The comparison of the corresponding accuracies of both the uniform and non-uniform hysteretic surrogate models can be found in Table 3. Concluding the findings in this paper, we can state that valid and accurate surrogate models for both the pull force and pull distance can be generated solely from capacitance data. Using discrete Preisach models of appropriate sparsity furthermore encourages the implementation in hardware by means of a sensor calibration measure.

**Acknowledgment.** This work is part of the project SparseRF, that has been funded by the Austrian Research Promotion Agency (FFG) and the state of Upper Austria under grant 40338 **FFG**

# References

1. Bermúdez, A., Gómez, D., Venegas, P.: Preisach hysteresis model. some applications in electrical engineering. In: Sahu, P.D.R. (ed.) Modern Permanent Magnets, chap. 2. IntechOpen, Rijeka (2021). https://doi.org/10.5772/intechopen.99590
2. Bertotti, G., Mayergoyz, I.D.: Contributors for volume one. In: The Science of Hysteresis, pp. xi–xii. Academic Press, Oxford (2006). https://doi.org/10.1016/B978-012480874-4/50001-4, https://www.sciencedirect.com/science/article/pii/B9780124808744500014
3. de Boor, C.: A Practical Guide to Spline, vol. 27 (1978). https://doi.org/10.2307/2006241
4. Brunton, S.L., Proctor, J.L., Kutz, J.N.: Discovering governing equations from data by sparse identification of nonlinear dynamical systems. Proc. Natl. Acad. Sci. **113**(15), 3932–3937 (2016). https://doi.org/10.1073/pnas.1517384113, https://www.pnas.org/doi/abs/10.1073/pnas.1517384113
5. Chen, T.Q., Rubanova, Y., Bettencourt, J., Duvenaud, D.K.: Neural ordinary differential equations. In: Bengio, S., Wallach, H., Larochelle, H., Grauman, K., Cesa-Bianchi, N., Garnett, R. (eds.) Advances in Neural Information Processing Systems 31, pp. 6571–6583. Curran Associates, Inc. (2018), http://papers.nips.cc/paper/7892-neural-ordinary-differential-equations.pdf

6. Goepp, V., Bouaziz, O., Nuel, G.: Spline regression with automatic knot selection (2018)
7. Preisach, F.: Über die magnetische nachwirkung. Z. Phys. **94**, 277–302 (1935)
8. Schuler, S., Petz, P., Eibensteiner, F., Langer, J.: A textile based capacitive pressure and shear force sensor. In: 2023 IEEE International Conference on Flexible and Printable Sensors and Systems (FLEPS), pp. 1–4. IEEE (2023)
9. Sprekels, J.: Visintin, a.: Differential models of hysteresis. berlin ctc., springer-verlag 1994. xi, 407 pp., 46 figs., dm 94.-. isbn 3-540-54793-2 (applied mathematical sciences 111). ZAMM - J. Appl. Math. Mech. / Zeitschrift für Angewandte Mathematik und Mechanik **76**(3), 144–144 (1996). https://doi.org/10.1002/zamm.19960760304, https://onlinelibrary.wiley.com/doi/abs/10.1002/zamm.19960760304
10. Tibshirani, R.: Regression shrinkage and selection via the lasso. J. R. Stat. Soc. Ser. B Stat Methodol. **58**(1), 267–288 (1996)
11. Willerich, S.: Anwendung vektorieller Hysteresemodelle zur Charakterisierung ferromagnetischer Werkstoffe. Phd thesis, Technical University Munich - TUM (2021). https://mediatum.ub.tum.de/doc/1540406/1540406.pdf
12. Wohlrab, S., Petz, P., Eibensteiner, F., Langer, J.: Influences of coating and spandex compositions of conductive textiles used as strain sensors using an automated test system. In: Arai, K. (eds.) Science and Information Conference, pp. 306–321. Springer (2022). https://doi.org/10.1007/978-3-031-10464-0_20

# Discrimination Criteria for Modeling Association, Aggregation, and Composition in UML Class Diagrams

Miguel Alemán-Flores(✉) 🄳

Centro de Tecnologías de la Imagen (CTIM), Instituto Universitario de Cibernética,
Empresa y Sociedad (IUCES), Universidad de Las Palmas de Gran Canaria Campus
de Tafira, 35017 Las Palmas, Spain
miguel.aleman@ulpgc.es

**Abstract.** A class diagram in the Unified Modeling Language (UML) is a powerful tool to model the structure of a system by means of classes, their attributes and operations, the relationships between them, and some additional elements. In this type of models, associations between classes play a crucial role and are determining in the subsequent stages of the development. UML provides three main types of associations for class diagrams in order to distinguish several scenarios: simple associations, shared aggregations, and composite aggregations. Several interpretations of what these three types of relationships mean and how they reflect usual situations in business or software modeling have been proposed, which causes some misunderstandings and makes it difficult to achieve the common interpretation which would be desirable in a unified language. This work intends to extract the key factors which help us decide what type of relationship best describes the domain we try to model. By means of a set of criteria which characterize them, the main differences and similarities are extracted, not only from a semantic point of view, but also considering the implications they have in the structure of the model, and the constraints which appear when using certain additional elements, such as association classes and self-associations. Furthermore, a series of examples covering a wide range of applications is provided to illustrate the distinction and make it possible to extract analogies.

**Keywords:** Modeling · UML · Class diagrams · Association ·
Aggregation · Composition

## 1 Introduction

A class diagram, either as a conceptual model, a software structure representation, or a design proposal, should contain the entities involved in the system or sub-system and the relationships between them. This allows a precise understanding of the domain as well as a feasible and practical implementation. Associations are simple links between instances of the same or different

© The Author(s), under exclusive license to Springer Nature Switzerland AG 2025
A. Quesada-Arencibia et al. (Eds.): EUROCAST 2024, LNCS 15172, pp. 443–457, 2025.
https://doi.org/10.1007/978-3-031-82949-9_39

classes. There is no hierarchical relationship or whole-part interpretation. They just reflect a connection between objects. Shared aggregations (also referred to simply as aggregations) are a particular type of associations which indicate a whole-part relationship. Some objects are contained into a set, or linked to a hierarchically higher element. The fact that they can be shared restricts the responsibilities of the whole, which does not control the life cycle of the parts. Finally, composite aggregations (also known as compositions) represent strong whole-part relationships in which the parts are controlled (or even owned) by the whole [14]. The distinction between simple associations, shared aggregations, and composite aggregations has led to numerous interpretations with quite *ad-hoc* applicability, since they are not always consistent with other proposals. Although a formal specification is presented in [8], there is still some ambiguity, due to the imprecision of the verbal descriptions and the meanings which are conferred to each type of association. Furthermore, conflicts may arise in many cases between the meaning and function of a certain entity in the real world, and the restricted role it plays in a particular application. For this reason, both the semantics and the subsequent structure must be taken into account when deciding which type of association is selected.

In spite of the reluctance of some authors to include shared aggregations as a different type of associations [11], it may be useful to explicit the distinction between simple associations and aggregations. It is true that, implementation-wise, the differences might be slight. However, since aggregations involve a hierarchical relationship, there are certain types of operations we need to consider, such as adding or removing parts (contained objects), finding parts, dealing with all parts simultaneously (e.g., changing attributes), or traversing the hierarchy recursively. The majority of these operations are not needed or are managed in a different way when dealing with simple associations. Therefore, a guide to decide when a shared aggregation is used can be very helpful.

This work presents a series of criteria for deciding whether a simple association, a shared aggregation, or a composite aggregation can represent the meaning attached to a certain relationship and whether the implications of that link for the structural model correspond to the desired behavior. The relationships between these criteria have also been analyzed to extract a reference for the distinction between the three types of associations. Finally, the application in several scenarios and the implications when combined with other elements are also discussed.

## 2   Related Works

The main issue regarding modeling associations consists in distinguishing shared aggregations from plain associations, and determining the constraints involved in each type of aggregation. According to [11], the distinction between aggregation and association is often a matter of taste, rather than a difference in semantics. In their interpretation, the only real semantics that aggregation adds to association is the constraint that chains of aggregate links may not form cycles, whereas other constraints, such as existence dependency, are specified by the multiplicity, not by the aggregation marker itself. For this reason, the authors claim that we may think of it as a modeling placebo. In [3], the author advises not using aggregations without some form of explanation. Since the interpretation may differ from the modeler to the observer of the model, a meaning for each particular case should be provided. This, in fact, makes it impractical to use them, because UML would no longer be that unified. From the point of view of the implementation, the main differences arise when comparing composite aggregations with the other two types of associations, but it is not always clear whether an association can be considered a shared aggregation or not. In [5], the author claims that there is not much difference in the way both relationships are implemented and, therefore, it would be very difficult to look at the code and determine whether a particular relationship ought to be an aggregation or an association. For this reason, he proposes to ignore the aggregation relationship altogether. In a similar way, the uselessness of this distinction has been proposed in [4].

Nevertheless, some recommendations or guidelines regarding the use of different UML associations have been proposed in previous works. In [10], some design decisions are discussed in order to improve the interaction between classes. The work in [6] focuses on compositions and their identification in Java software. In [7], the author describes how the intentional interpretation improves the expressiveness of the modeling language. The work in [12] discusses a way to present a class diagram in the form of a description logic and how to optimize it. Regarding the proposal of discriminating aspects, a set of dimensions to characterize the different types of associations was presented in [1]. On the other hand, the formalization of whole-part relationships was addressed in [2], whereas the transformations between UML diagrams and ontologies have also been tackled in works like [13].

The main contribution of this work consists in presenting certain criteria which combine semantics and structure in order to identify the best type of association for each case. Furthermore, those criteria can be applied in a wide variety of domains and scenarios and allow finding analogies between them.

## 3    Criteria

In order to illustrate all three situations, three examples are presented in Fig. 1. The first one corresponds to an educational center and represents the link between the teachers and the subjects which are taught by them. The second one corresponds to an application to manage songs to be played and represents playlists with songs contained in them. Finally, the third one corresponds to an application to create presentations, which consist of slides. To distinguish both types of aggregations from simple associations, shared aggregations are depicted with a white diamond at the whole end, whereas composite aggregations are depicted with a black diamond at the whole end.

These three examples, together with other presented to illustrate particular scenarios, will now be analyzed using a set of criteria in which some differences

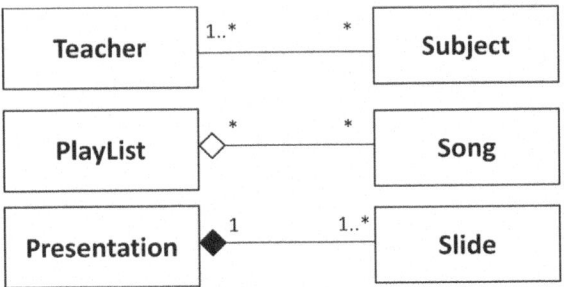

**Fig. 1.** Examples of simple association (top), shared aggregation (middle), and composite aggregation (bottom).

can be found. Some of these criteria have been previously described in [1], where they were denoted as dimensions, although, as explained below, the interpretation given in this paper and the perspective from which they are studied are different. Moreover, some additional criteria have been included to extend the analysis and obtain a robust characterization.

### 3.1  Life Cycle

This aspect determines whether an object is responsible for the creation and deletion of the instances linked to it. Considering the examples in Fig. 1, neither are the instances of Teacher responsible for creating or deleting new instances of Subject nor do subjects control the creation and deletion of new teachers. Similarly, playlists do not create or delete new instances of songs, they just incorporate already existing songs to the list, and obviously, songs do not create or remove new lists. However, the objects of the class Presentation are responsible for adding new slides or removing certain slides they contain. Therefore, the life cycles are independent in associations and shared aggregations, but, in composite aggregations, the whole acts as a controller or owner, whereas the parts are controlled or owned.

### 3.2  Multiplicity

Multiplicity identifies the possible values for the number of instances of a class that are linked to an instance of the class at the other end. An upper and lower bound can be fixed. In the case of associations, there is no constraint for the upper limits at both ends. As far as a number greater than 0 is allowed (although not necessarily required) for the multiplicity at both ends, the link is feasible. Similarly, in shared aggregations, there is no limit for both the whole-end and the part-end. Since the aggregation is shared, the same part can be contained in several containers. Nevertheless, in the case of composite aggregations, there are only two options for the multiplicity at the whole-end, either 1 or 0..1. In particular, the multiplicity can be 0..1 when the existence of an instance of the class at the part-end is possible outside the whole, either independently or as part of a different composite. For example, a point can be part of a polygon, part of a segment, part of a circle, or be an independent element. For this reason, constraints on the links (e.g., a xor constraint) are sometimes necessary to explicit certain restrictions on the multiplicities. At the part-end, any multiplicity which allows a number greater than 0 is possible.

Focusing on the examples above, there is no limit for the number of subjects a teacher can teach or the number of teachers who can teach a subject (although lower and upper limits can be set according to the particular domain, such as a minimum of one teacher for each subject). Similarly, a playlist can contain any number of songs and a song can be included in any number of playlists. However, a presentation can contain any number of slides (in this case, with a minimum of one, although other compositions may include the possibility of no components), but a slide belongs to a single presentation.

### 3.3  Delete Propagation

Delete propagation determines what happens when an instance is deleted. In an association, if an object is deleted, the links are deleted as well, but the associated objects remain, unless multiplicity constraints require it (using the terminology used in [1], we can say that the delete-propagation property has the value Link). Similarly, in a shared aggregation, deleting the whole-end does not imply deleting the part-end and vice versa. However, if the whole-end of a composition is deleted, the components are also deleted (in this case, the value is Cascade). On the other hand, deleting a component only implies deleting the link. For example, deleting an instance of Teacher does not convey the deletion of the instances of Subject associated with it, and vice versa. Deleting a song does not imply the deletion of the playlists in which it is contained, and deleting a playlist does not imply deleting the songs contained in it. However, although deleting a slide does not imply deleting the presentation, when deleting a presentation, the slides contained in it are also deleted. From a logical point of view, the fact that, in a composite aggregation, the deletion of the whole implies the deletion of its parts does not mean that any circumstances in which the deletion of an object implies the deletion of other objects are translated into a composite aggregation.

### 3.4  Linking Capability

Some authors (e.g., [1]) consider the temporal behavior and analyze whether an object can be dynamically connected or disconnected. However, in this work, the linking capability is studied to determine whether an object can or cannot create or delete a link to another object. The fact that the class which adds or removes a link does not always correspond to the actor who performs the operation is an important issue to take into account. For example, if a user includes a contact into a group, it is not the class User that has the method to do it, but the class Group. Therefore, the responsibility represented in behavior diagrams, such as use case diagrams, is different from the structural responsibility represented in class diagrams. Three possibilities for the linking capability are proposed in this work: External (E) if the objects are linked from an external class; Active (A) if an object determines the link; and Passive (P) if it is linked by the other instance, but cannot be linked by itself. For example, the classes PlayList and Presentation should be provided with a method to add links to instances of Song or Slide. Therefore, the classes PlayList and Presentation are active in the creation of the link, whereas Song and Slide are Passive. However, the instances of Teacher and Subject will probably be linked from an external class (associations could be implemented as intermediate classes) or, in case the implementation allocated the linking method in one of the classes with an interface to access it, it could also be at the other end.

## 3.5  Visibility

This feature determines whether an object can only be accessed from its associated instances. In the case of aggregations and associations, the objects may be visible from outside the associated objects, but, in a composition, the instances of the part-end are only visible from or through the whole-end instance. That is, teachers, subjects, songs and playlists can be accessed from other classes, but the slides of a presentation are accessed from the presentation itself, i.e., as part of it.

## 3.6  Transitivity

The whole-part interpretation of shared and composite aggregations leads to a transitive relationship. Parts of a whole can play the role of a whole in a different relationship, and sub-parts of a part of a whole are parts of such whole. In Fig. 2, if a country has provinces and the provinces have cities, the cities belong to the country (composite aggregation). Similarly, if a championship has teams and each team has players, the players are indirectly aggregated into the championship (shared aggregation). However, in a simple association, transitivity is optional. There are situations in which a derived association can be extracted by combining different associations, but this is not mandatory. For instance, if a teacher is linked to a subject and a subject is linked to a room, we could be interested in deriving in what rooms a teacher gives their lectures. Nevertheless, if a person is a friend of another person, who has their own friends, the first and the last individuals do not necessarily have to be friends (although a have-common-friends relationship could be derived, as certain social networks do).

## 3.7  Identity Projection

This criterion indicates whether an object projects its identity onto the associated instances. This happens from the whole-end to the part-end in a composite aggregation. For instance, if building B1 has different rooms, R1, R2..., a room

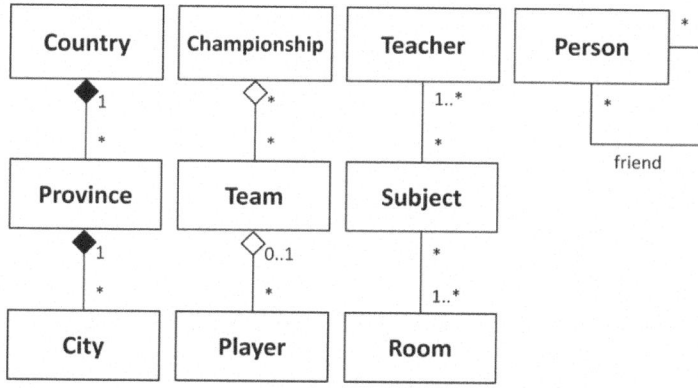

**Fig. 2.** Examples of transitivity in compositions, aggregations and associations: decomposition of countries into provinces and cities; inclusion in championships of teams consisting of players; derived association between teachers and rooms through the subjects they teach; and self-association of people as friends.

R1 is such inside that building, and the building is part of the identification of the room (it is room R1 in building B1, different from room R1 in building B2). However, as shared aggregations are shareable, a part is not identified by means of a whole it is included in, i.e., the identity of the whole is not projected onto its parts. Similarly, identity is not projected onto the opposite end in a simple association. Moreover, the whole is not identified by its parts, either in a shared or a composite aggregation. Therefore, only the identity of the whole-end in a composite aggregation is projected onto the part-end.

## 3.8   Object-Level Reflexivity

Only associations can be reflexive on an object level. The fact that both types of aggregations, shared or composite, convey a whole-part meaning, makes it senseless to make them reflexive. In other words, an object can be associated with itself, but cannot contain itself. This does not prevent a class from having a reflexive association (or self-association), since object-level reflexivity refers to the link between an instance and itself, not between an instance and a different instance of the same class. Therefore, an object of a class can contain (in a shared or composite aggregation) different objects of the same class, but not itself. For instance, a category of products can contain sub-categories, which are also instances of the class Category, and a category can be included in several parent categories. A more complex structure can be represented with the composite pattern, using leaf categories, which only contain products, and compound categories, which may contain products and categories as well. In Fig. 3, an employee can be their own chief, but a category and a task cannot be included into themselves. That is, class-level reflexivity is allowed in all three types of links, but object-level reflexivity is only allowed in simple associations. Since the main interest lies in the discrimination capability of each criterion, object-level reflexivity has been considered in this proposal.

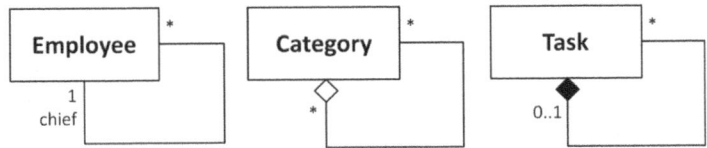

**Fig. 3.** Reflexive association, aggregation and composition.

## 3.9   Comparison of the Criteria

We must take into account that these criteria are not completely independent and not all combinations are possible. Table 1 summarizes the aspects which help identify the three types of links, and the values which these aspects can take for each option.

**Table 1.** Criteria in associations, shared aggregations, and compositions (W stands for whole-end, P for part-end). Life cycle: I (independent), C (controller), c (controlled). Multiplicity: ∀ (any value is possible), 1 (mandatorily 1), 0..1 (optionally 1). Delete propagation: L (link), C (cascade). Linking capability: E (external), A (active), P (passive). Visibility: Y (visible), N (not visible). Transitivity: O (optional), M (mandatory). Identity projection: Y (Projected), N (not projected). Object-level reflexivity: Y (possible), N (not possible).

|  | Association | Shared Aggregation W-P | Composition W-P |
|---|---|---|---|
| Life cycle | I | I - I | C - c |
| Multiplicity | ∀ | ∀ - ∀ | 1 \| 0..1 - ∀ |
| Delete propagation | L | L - L | C - L |
| Linking capability | E | A - P | A - P |
| Visibility | Y | Y - Y | Y - N |
| Transitivity | O | M - M | M - M |
| Identity projection | N | N - N | Y - N |
| Object-level reflexivity | Y | N - N | N - N |

In Table 2, those features which provide similar information are combined in order to extract a common criterion and reduce the set of conditions. Hence, linking capability and transitivity are related to a whole-part relationship and help discriminate both types of aggregations from simple associations. On the contrary, object-level reflexivity is only feasible in simple associations and allows excluding both types of aggregations. Regarding life-cycle dependency, delete propagation, restricted visibility, and identity projection, they are associated with the creation of instances and imply a composite aggregation. Conversely, a multiplicity greater than 1 in the candidate whole-end excludes the possibility of a composite aggregation.

**Table 2.** Main reference criteria for the decision-making process: whole-part relationship; possibility of association between an object and itself; creation of instances in one end from the instances at the other end; possibility of multiplicities greater than 1 at both ends. For each criterion, Y: possible type of relationship.

|                        | Association | Shared Aggregation | Composition |
|------------------------|:-----------:|:------------------:|:-----------:|
| Whole-part             |             | Y                  | Y           |
| Object reflexivity     | Y           |                    |             |
| Creation of instances  |             |                    | Y           |
| Multiplicities > 1     | Y           | Y                  |             |

If we compare the criteria proposed in this work with those used in [1], in this work, life cycle and transitivity have been introduced, as they provide us with some clear and useful information for the discrimination. Furthermore, the temporal behavior has been reformulated and substituted by the linking capability, whereas reflexivity and antisymmetry have been circumscribed to object-level reflexivity.

## 4   Class Structure and Behavior

In this section, the implications of the different types of associations in the structure of the corresponding classes and their behavior regarding certain operations in frequent scenarios are described. In Fig. 4, we can see an example with three different links in a university center. Let us suppose that each course is given by one or more teachers and, in case many students have signed up for a course, they are divided into different groups. While the life-cycle of an instance of the class Course restricts the life-cycles of its groups, each group can add students who already exist and who remain even if the group is canceled. On the other hand, courses and teachers are just linked when the assignment is carried out.

In Fig. 5, a catalog is a set of products which are included from the catalog itself, i.e., the catalog must have a method to add new products. It can also be decomposed into different categories, such as types of products or sections. However, a product which is included into a category is already present in the catalog and, when removed from a category, it remains into the catalog. According to this example, labels are associated to products, but are not considered sets of products (they might be considered as such with a different interpretation of the

**Fig. 4.** Example with three different associations relating courses, teachers, groups, and students in a university degree.

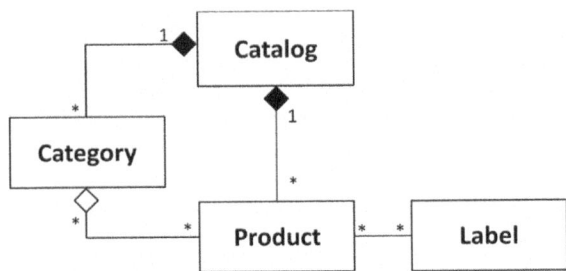

**Fig. 5.** Combination of associations, aggregations, and compositions in a UML diagram for the catalog of a store with products included in categories and tagged with labels.

domain). They are only used to tag products with certain features, such as *new*, *offer*, etc.

A huge range of scenarios are possible, but we usually need certain operations when dealing with shared or composite aggregations, which are not required for simple associations. For example, the class Group should have methods to add or remove students. Additionally, we might desire to find a student inside a group or send a message to all students inside a group. We might also want to change a mark to all students in a group. If groups have subgroups, we might be interested in finding a student inside the subgroups of a course or a group (this could require traversing the hierarchy recursively).

As explained in [14], the three main ways to implement an association are mutual friends, a unidirectional link, and an intermediate object. The use of mutual friends makes the access faster, but duplicates the associations and requires the synchronization of both classes. Implementing the associations in one of the classes may require the implementation of the get method for the opposite class as a query. Finally, an intermediary object could be used as a table to link pairs of instances.

Regarding aggregations, some authors have classified groupings trying to find certain patterns. As examples, we can identify the following cases (adapted from [9] and reformulated according to this proposal):

- Integral Object - Assembled Part (such as Film - Scene)
- Manufactured Object - Material (such as Dish - Ingredient)
- Divisible Object - Portion (such as Cake - Piece)
- Geographical Area - Place (such as State - City)
- Bunch - Individual (such as Forest - Tree)
- Group - Member (such as Team - Player)

Analyzing this classification according to the three types of associations, we can conclude that integral objects, divisible objects, and geographical areas are composites. On the other hand, manufactured objects and groups are shared aggregations (even if a player cannot simultaneously play in several teams, their existence is not determined by that of the team). From their meaning, Bunch-Individual relationships could be composite or shared, depending on the context. However, by combining meaning and structure, we can consider that shared aggregations of this type are in fact Group-Member relationships (e.g., roses are not created as part of a bunch, which is made later). Finding analogies and extracting patterns like those described above can help characterize scenarios which are completely different in the concepts they represent, but extremely similar in their behavior.

## 5   Association Classes

In certain cases, associations require some attributes which cannot be added to one of both ends, since they provide information about the link itself, i.e., they qualify both ends in that particular association. Association classes allow us to represent this type of scenarios by including classes attached to the association (they are depicted with a dashed line connecting the class with the association).

In standard associations, this is relatively common. For instance, we may want to model the amount of money which a certain tax payer has donated to a non-governmental organization (NGO) throughout a year in order to take it into account for their tax revenue. This amount is not a single value for a particular tax payer or a particular NGO, but a single amount (i.e., year total amount) for the association of an instance of the class TaxPayer and an instance of NGO. In a shared aggregation, this phenomenon is also common. Imagine we are interested in recording the date a given contact was included into a group. If a contact can belong to many groups and contacts can be added to a group on different dates, this date refers to a pair Group-Contact and qualifies both in that particular link. The previous two examples are illustrated in Fig. 6. However, there is no point in using association classes with composite aggregations. Due to the fact that a component (part-end) cannot be part of several composites (whole-end), the attributes of that link can be considered as attributes of the component, and there will not be similar attributes for that instance of the component in another composite aggregation.

In Fig. 7, a workout consists of a series of exercises, which can be used in different workouts and which have a number of repetitions within each workout. Moreover, the same exercise may be included in the same workout several times, and the order of the exercises is important. For this reason, the property {sequence} has been included. Due to the fact that the number of repetitions of an exercise can vary depending on the workout where it is included, this attribute must be part of an association class (in this case, the class Reps). In addition, the number of repetitions can even vary when the same exercise is included several times in the same workout. On the other hand, each exercise is related to one or

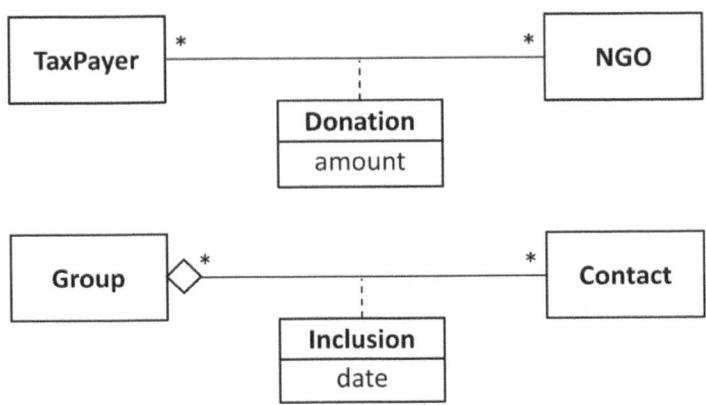

**Fig. 6.** Association classes in simple associations and shared aggregations.

more parts of the body. These parts can be divided into smaller parts (identified in the diagram by the role sub-parts), which, in turn, can also be divided.

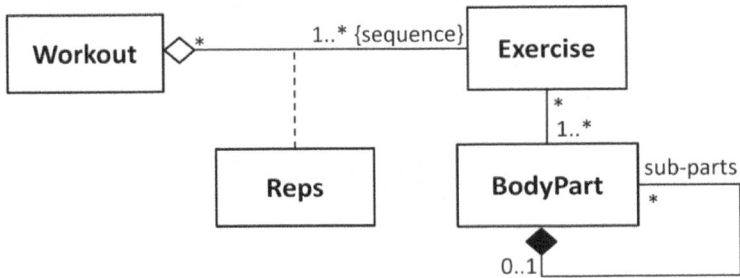

**Fig. 7.** Combination of shared aggregations, association classes, simple associations, and self-associations in the description of physical exercise routines.

# 6    Application of the Criteria

In order to illustrate how the criteria described above match some of the different examples which have been presented in this work, Table 3 indicates which aspects are met in each case, and what type of association is derived from them. As mentioned in Sect. 3.9, some criteria provide similar information. Therefore, only one criterion from each subset has been indicated in this table, although the others could also be used.

Those cases in which a class is related to itself are shown separately in Table 4, since object-level reflexivity must also be considered. This criterion restricts the

**Table 3.** Main reference criteria for the decision-making process in several examples of relationships between different classes: whole-part relationship (W-P); creation of instances at one end from the instances at the other end (Creation); possibility of multiplicities greater than 1 at both ends (M > v1).

|  | W-P | Creation | M >1 | Type |
|---|---|---|---|---|
| Teacher-Subject |  |  | Y | Association |
| TaxPayer-NGO |  |  | Y | Association |
| Exercise-BodyPart |  |  | Y | Association |
| Playlist-Song | Y |  | Y | Aggregation |
| Group-Student | Y |  | Y | Aggregation |
| Workout-Exercise | Y |  | Y | Aggregation |
| Team-Player | Y |  |  | Aggregation |
| Presentation-Slide | Y | Y |  | Composition |
| Country-Province | Y | Y |  | Composition |
| Course-Group | Y | Y |  | Composition |
| Building-Room | Y | Y |  | Composition |

options to simple associations, but is not required in this type of relationships. For instance, the fact that an employee is the chief of their own department eliminates the possibility of a shared or composite aggregation. However, the fact that a person is not a friend of themselves does not eliminate the possibility of a simple association.

**Table 4.** Main reference criteria for the decision-making process in several examples of self-associations: whole-part relationship (W-P); possibility of association between an object and itself (Refl.); creation of instances at one end from the instances at the other end (Creation); possibility of multiplicities greater than 1 at both ends (M >1).

|  | W-P | Refl | Creation | M >1 | Type |
|---|---|---|---|---|---|
| Person-Person (friend) |  |  |  | Y | Assoc. |
| Employee-Employee (chief) |  | Y |  |  | Assoc. |
| Category-Category (subcateg.) | Y |  |  | Y | Aggreg. |
| BodyPart-BodyPart (subpart) | Y |  | Y |  | Compos. |

# 7    Conclusion

The distinction between simple associations, shared aggregations, and composite aggregations is not always clear, and the selection of the right alternative is usually domain-dependent. However, some aspects can be taken into account to identify them. The choice of the right alternative translates into a more precise model, a better understanding of the domain, and a more efficient implementation. By analyzing several scenarios which exemplify each option, and considering the consequences that they have, this paper has proposed some aspects that can guide us in the selection of the right alternative. The different types of associations have been compared according to a set of criteria which involve both the semantics behind the related concepts and the structure under their subsequent implementation. Furthermore, the constraints and implications of these options when combined with association classes have also been considered.

We have seen that certain aspects can act as representatives of the rest of criteria which have been analyzed and, therefore, they summarize the different possible configurations. For instance, the creation of instances at one side of the association from instances on the other side is inextricably related to life-cycle dependency and implies delete propagation. Furthermore, restricted visibility and identity projection are closely related to this aspect. Similarly, a whole-part relationship usually conveys linking capability and transitivity.

In addition, the set of examples which have been presented can be used to extract analogies and set patterns which condense the different aspects which have been analyzed. Some of the criteria which have been considered also show that it is useful to distinguish shared aggregations from simple associations. For instance, transitivity, linking capability, or reflexivity are different for simple associations and shared aggregations, and some operations are usually involved in shared aggregations, but not so often in simple associations. In some cases, the meaning makes the distinction practical; in some other cases, it is the structure and the behavior that recommend this identification. With these criteria in mind, not only can the modeler determine in a more precise way which association is the most suitable, but any viewer can also interpret the model in a safer way, reducing misunderstandings. It is crucial that the Unified Modeling Language be really unified and that different interpretations of the symbols do not lead to failure in further steps of the development.

# References

1. Albert, M., Pelechano, V., Fons, J., Ruiz, M., Pastor, O.: Implementing UML association, aggregation, and composition. a particular interpretation based on a multidimensional framework. In: Eder, J., Missikoff, M. (eds.) CAiSE 2003. LNCS, vol. 2681, pp. 143–158. Springer, Heidelberg (2003). https://doi.org/10.1007/3-540-45017-3_12
2. Barbier, F., Henderson-Sellers, B., Le Parc-Lacayrelle, A., Bruel, J.M.: Formalization of the whole-part relationship in the unified modeling language. IEEE Trans. Software Eng. **29**(5), 459–470 (2003). https://doi.org/10.1109/TSE.2003.1199074
3. Fowler, M.: (2003). https://martinfowler.com/bliki/AggregationAndComposition.html. Accessed Nov 2023
4. Gómez-Fuentes, M.C., Cervantes-Ojeda, J., García-Nájera, A.: Association and aggregation class relationships: is there a difference in terms of implementation? In:

2021 9th International Conference in Software Engineering Research and Innovation (CONISOFT), pp. 44–53 (2021). https://doi.org/10.1109/CONISOFT52520.2021.00018

5. Martin, R.C.: UML for Java Programmers. Prentice Hall, Upper Saddle River, NJ (2002)
6. Milanova, A.: Precise identification of composition relationships for UML class diagrams. In: Redmiles, D.F., Ellman, T., Zisman, A. (eds.) 20th IEEE/ACM International Conference on Automated Software Engineering (ASE 2005), 7-11 November 2005, Long Beach, CA, USA, pp. 76–85. ACM, (2005). https://doi.org/10.1145/1101908.1101922
7. Milicev, D.: On the semantics of associations and association ends in UML. IEEE Trans. Software Eng. **33**(4), 238–251 (2007). https://doi.org/10.1109/TSE.2007.37
8. Object management group (OMG): Meta-Object Facility (MOF) specification, version 2.5.1 (2017). https://www.omg.org/spec/UML/About-UML/. Accessed Nov 2023
9. Odell, J.J.: Six different kinds of composition. J. Object-Orient. Program. **5**(8), 143–158 (1994)
10. Parsons, D.: Objects Working Together: Association, Aggregation and Composition, pp. 141–175. Springer International Publishing, Cham (2020). https://doi.org/10.1007/978-3-030-54518-5_7
11. Rumbaugh, J., Jacobson, I., Booch, G.: The Unified Modeling Language Reference Manual, second edition, chap. 13. Addison-Wesley, Reading, Massachusetts (2004)
12. Sergievskiy, M.: Description logic application for UML class diagrams optimization. Int. J. Adv. Comput. Sci. Appl. **8**, 269–272 (2017)
13. Vo, M.H.L., Hoang, Q.: Transformation of UML class diagram into owl ontology. J. Inf. Telecommun. **4**(1), 1–16 (2020). https://doi.org/10.1080/24751839.2019.1686681
14. Wazlawick, R.S.: Object-Oriented Analysis and Design for Information Systems. Morgan Kaufmann, Elsevier, Waltham, MA, USA (2014)

# Author Index

The manufacturer's authorised representative in the EU is Springer
Nature Customer Service Centre GmbH, Europaplatz 3, 69115 Heidelberg,
Germany. If you have any concerns regarding our products, please
contact ProductSafety@springernature.com

Printed and bound by CPI Group (UK) Ltd, Croydon, CR0 4YY
29/04/2026
02099546-0005